Civil Law & Litigation
for Paralegals

McGraw-Hill Business Careers Paralegal Titles

MCGRAW-HILL PARALEGAL TITLES: WHERE EDUCATIONAL SUPPORT GOES BEYOND EXPECTATIONS.

Building a solid foundation for a successful paralegal career is becoming more challenging as the needs of students and instructors continue to grow. The McGraw-Hill paralegal texts offer the solution to this ever-changing environment. Integrated real-world applications in each chapter teach students the practical skills needed for a thriving career in the field. A common vocabulary among all McGraw-Hill titles ensures consistency in learning. Up-to-date coverage of the available technology used in a legal setting and a purposefully designed set of pedagogical features with shared goals across the list provide the systems needed for students to fully grasp the material and apply it in a paralegal setting. With a thorough set of ancillaries and dedicated publisher support, these texts will facilitate active learning in the classroom and give students the skill sets desired by employers.

Civil Law & Litigation for Paralegals

Neal R. Bevans, J.D.
Western Piedmont Community College

Boston   Burr Ridge, IL   Dubuque, IA   Madison, WI   New York   San Francisco   St. Louis
Bangkok   Bogotá   Caracas   Kuala Lumpur   Lisbon   London   Madrid   Mexico City
Milan   Montreal   New Delhi   Santiago   Seoul   Singapore   Sydney   Taipei   Toronto

The McGraw·Hill Companies

CIVIL LAW & LITIGATION FOR PARALEGALS

Published by McGraw-Hill/Irwin, a business unit of The McGraw-Hill Companies, Inc., 1221 Avenue of the Americas, New York, NY, 10020. Copyright © 2008 by The McGraw-Hill Companies, Inc. All rights reserved. No part of this publication may be reproduced or distributed in any form or by any means, or stored in a database or retrieval system, without the prior written consent of The McGraw-Hill Companies, Inc., including, but not limited to, in any network or other electronic storage or transmission, or broadcast for distance learning.

Some ancillaries, including electronic and print components, may not be available to customers outside the United States.

This book is printed on acid-free paper.

1 2 3 4 5 6 7 8 9 0 VNH/VNH 0 9 8 7

ISBN 978-0-07-352461-0
MHID 0-07-352461-1

Vice president of editorial: *Elizabeth Haefele*
Publisher: *Linda Schreiber*
Associate sponsoring editor: *Natalie J. Ruffatto*
Developmental editor II: *Tammy Higham*
Sr. marketing manager: *Keari Bedford*
Marketing specialist: *Megan Gates*
Lead producer, media technology: *Damian Moshak*
Project manager: *Marlena Pechan*
Lead production supervisor: *Jason Huls*
Lead designer: *Marianna Kinigakis*
Typeface: *10/12 Times New Roman*
Compositor: *Aptara, Inc.*
Printer: *Von Hoffmann Corporation*

Library of Congress Cataloging-in-Publication Data

Bevans, Neal R., 1961-
   Civil law and litigation for paralegals / Neal Bevans.
      p. cm. — (McGraw-Hill business careers paralegal titles)
   Includes index.
   ISBN-13: 978-0-07-352461-0 (alk. paper)
   ISBN-10: 0-07-352461-1 (alk. paper)
   1. Civil procedure—United States. 2. Trial practice—United States.
 3. Legal assistants—United States—Handbooks, manuals, etc. I. Title.
 KF8841.B48 2008
 347.73'5—dc22

                                            2007003647

Dedication

For my wife, Deb, with all my love.

About the Author

Neal R. Bevans, J.D.
Western Piedmont Community College

Neal Bevans is a former Assistant District Attorney and private attorney. A veteran of over 150 trials, Bevans has tried every major felony from rape, murder, and narcotics to armed robbery. One of his cases was televised nationally on Court TV. He has had extensive civil litigation experience while working as an insurance defense attorney. He has a Juris Doctor degree from the University of Georgia (Order of the Barrister) and has been a college instructor for more than 10 years. A multiple-year honoree in *Who's Who Among America's Teachers,* Bevans is the author of numerous textbooks and magazine articles.

Preface

Civil litigation is the lifeblood of private legal practice, as well as an important part of government practice. Paralegal students are far more likely to be involved in civil lawsuits than criminal cases, business disputes, and intellectual property suits combined. Civil litigation courses are part of the core curriculum in every paralegal program in the country. This text was designed to help prepare students for the practical world of divorces, car wreck cases, and medical malpractice claims that they will see every day in civil practice. In addition to discussing theoretical constructs, the text offers extensive ancillary materials and supplemental material.

In *Civil Law & Litigation for Paralegals,* the author provides students with an in-depth analysis of the wide variety of civil cases, laying out the basic foundation of the American legal system, proceeding through the investigation and implementation of a civil case, and following the case through to appeal. The premise of this book is not only to teach the basics of civil litigation but also to give students the chance to build a skill set and create material for a portfolio that they can show to prospective employers.

The text also addresses the specific duties of paralegals in civil practice. Each chapter presents students with examples of the important role that paralegals play in every stage of civil litigation, from client intake to bringing an appeal. The text balances the theoretical underpinnings of the law with the practical examples and hands-on experience that all students need to completely understand the topic.

KEY CHARACTERISTICS OF *CIVIL LAW & LITIGATION FOR PARALEGALS*

Writing Style

The author's clear and coherent writing is one of the best features of the text. The author clearly communicates his enthusiasm for the topic throughout the text.

Chapter Features

Each chapter has a standard format, including:

- Clearly stated chapter objectives.

Each chapter sets out 10 objectives for the student–reader.

- Introductory paragraph.

The major topics in the chapter will be set out in this lead-in paragraph.

- Material presented in a logical way.

The topics discussed in the chapter flow in a logical, common-sense manner.

- Material supplemented by numerous sidebars, charts, diagrams, and so forth.

The text contains numerous charts, diagrams, and other illustrations, as well as sidebars designed to illuminate specific topics throughout the chapter.

- Learning styles taken into consideration.

The topics in the chapters are discussed in a variety of ways to take advantage of different student–reader learning styles.

- Significant cases.

The text also places strong emphasis on seminal or otherwise important cases in specific areas of practice to help demonstrate the importance of case law to civil litigation.

- Terms and legal vocabulary.

All terms and legal vocabulary are defined immediately for the student. The first time a key word or legal term is mentioned in the text, a definition of it appears in the margin. This location helps students grasp the meaning without breaking the flow of their reading by having to turn to the glossary.

- Extensive use of hypotheticals.

The author uses hypothetical questions and other scenarios to illustrate the points under discussion in each chapter. These scenarios also provide an excellent foundation for classroom discussion.

- Case in Point features.

Each chapter contains a significant case designed to expand on the topics discussed in the chapter. There are also questions for students based on the case to assist their understanding of the case and its relevance to the chapter concepts.

- "Real world" flavor.

The text places heavy emphasis on the practical aspects of civil litigation practice. Each chapter presents interview excerpts from paralegals who actually work in the field, including not only an overview of what brought them into the law but also their daily activities, outlined in the "Day in the Life" sections that appear at the conclusion of each chapter.

- Eye on Ethics feature.

Ethics is crucial for any legal professional. Each chapter explores an important ethical question and explains the relevance of ethical systems for the day-to-day practice of civil law.

- Examples of court documents.

The text also presents numerous court documents for the student–reader, including contracts of representation, complaints, answers, discovery requests, motions, and many others. Each of these court documents is annotated with an explanation of the various component parts.

- Real Paralegal Life: Building a Skill Set feature.

Each chapter also contains a practical application designed to help students build a specific skill set. These practical applications include analyzing evidence, creating a personal court directory, billing hours, and basic investigative techniques, among others.

- Creating a portfolio.

Each chapter contains a section that requires students to generate a specific document or other work product that will go into their portfolio. The purpose of the portfolio is to create a body of work that demonstrates the student's competency in this essential area.

Pedagogy

The text has numerous features that take advantage of the varied learning styles students employ. On the basis of the recognition that students who apply their newly acquired knowledge often retain it much better than those who do not, this text requires students to apply the knowledge that they have gained. Each chapter has practical examples of court documents, pleadings, motions, and other real-life exercises that emphasize the material discussed in each chapter.

The text is written in clear language that engages the student, keeps the reader's interest, and presents information in a variety of methods to take advantage of different learning styles. Each new concept is presented in a multilayer fashion, first with the basic concepts and then with greater complexity once the intellectual foundation is laid. Charts and diagrams are provided to illustrate concepts as they are discussed and provide the instructor with additional material for class discussion. Sidebars, tables, and interviews are also presented to supplement the chapter information in a different format for students who may not fully grasp the concepts on initial presentation. Finally, practical, hands-on assignments and discussion questions reiterate and emphasize the concepts, which enables greater comprehension and retention by the student. The author fills the text with a balance of theoretical discussions and practical examples, all presented in a well-written, enjoyable style.

Non–Gender-Specific Language

In recognition of the negative impact of gender-specific language, the author has adopted the convention of employing "he or she" whenever the text demands the use of the third-person singular voice.

INSTRUCTOR'S MANUAL

The author has developed an impressive instructor's manual to accompany the text. Recognizing the needs of instructors for multiple resources, the author provides the following features:

- Suggested syllabi and lesson plans.
- Annotated outlines for each chapter.
- Answers to all end-of-chapter questions.
- Test bank, which includes a variety of question types:
  - Essay questions (5 per chapter).
  - Short answer (10 per chapter).
  - Multiple choice (25 per chapter).
  - True-False (10 per chapter).
- PowerPoint slides for each chapter.

Acknowledgments

The author appreciates the helpful comments from the reviewers of this book:

Laura Bean
MIT College

Sally Bisson
College of Saint Mary

Ernest Davila
San Jacinto College, North Campus

Regina Dowling
Branford Hall Career Institute

Amy Feeney
Wilmington College

Terri Lindfors
Minnesota School of Business

Victoria H. Lopez
Southwestern College

Angela Masciulli
MTI College

Broderick Nichols
University of Memphis

Kathleen Reed
University of Toledo

Barbara A. Ricker
Andover College

David Rosen
Queens College

Linda Silakoski
Lake Erie College

Debbie Vinecour
SUNY-Rockland

Debra Wicks
Pittsburgh Technical Institute

Timothy M. Williams
Baker College

The author also thanks the following people for their assistance in creating this book: Deborah Bevans, Lisa Mazzonetto, Darlene Burgess, Tammy Higham, Peter Vanaria, Natalie Ruffatto, Linda Schreiber, and Beth Baugh.

A Guided Tour

Civil Law & Litigation for Paralegals provides the student with an in-depth analysis of the wide variety of civil cases, laying out the basic foundation of the American legal system, proceeding through the investigation and implementation of a civil case, and following the case through to appeal. It not only teaches the basics of civil litigation but also gives students the chance to build a skill set and create material for a portfolio that can be used for prospective employers. The pedagogy of the book applies three goals:

- Learning outcomes (critical thinking, vocabulary building, skill development, issues analysis, writing practice).

- Relevance of topics without sacrificing theory (ethical challenges, current law practices, technology application).

- Practical application (real-world exercises, portfolio creation, team exercises).

Chapter Objectives introduce the concepts students should understand after reading each chapter as well as provide brief summaries describing the material to be covered.

CHAPTER OBJECTIVES

The student will be able to:

- Explain the differences between civil law and other types of law.
- Describe the burden of proof in a civil case.
- Explain the role of pleadings in civil cases.
- Explain the difference between a finding of liability and a finding of guilt.
- Describe the function of damages in civil cases.
- Define the role of the U.S. Constitution in the American legal system.
- Explain the difference between statutes and case law.

This chapter introduces the U.S. court system and details the important differences between various areas of law.

SURF'S UP!

COMPUTER-AIDED EVIDENTIARY PRESENTATIONS

In the age of the Internet and the widespread availability of computer networked law offices, several companies specialize in providing assistance to attorneys preparing to try a civil case. Visual aids are important for juries, whether it is simply providing the details of the accident site or laying out the complexities of a medical malpractice case. Today, companies offer a broad range of services, from simple aids to computer animation. Examples of companies that provide these services include Insight Legal Graphics and Animation (www.insightlegalgraphics.com) or High Impact Litigation, Inc. (www.highimpactlit.com), both of which specialize in assisting attorneys preparing for trial by generating a wide variety of exhibits, diagrams, graphic designs, computer animation, PowerPoint slides, and nearly every type of trial aid imaginable. Other companies, such as Power Graphics, Inc. (www.power-graphics.com), concentrate on taking the various evidentiary exhibits in a case and presenting them in as dramatic a fashion as possible. For instance, these companies can blow up an important photograph or diagram so that it is truly enormous—making it much easier for the jury to see all of the important details.

Surf's Up! focuses on the increasing use of technology and the Internet, using relevant Web sites and giving students real-world experience with technology.

Eye on Ethics raises legitimate ethical questions and situations attorneys and paralegals often face. Students are asked to reference rules governing these issues and make a decision.

Eye on Ethics

FREELANCE PARALEGALS

The role of the paralegal in the United States has been slowly changing. The traditional arrangement, in which a paralegal works full-time for an attorney, is slowly giving way to independent contractors: freelance paralegals who hire themselves out to attorneys on a case-by-case basis. Freelance paralegals are part of a new movement of paralegals who take greater control of their own destinies.

Although becoming a freelance paralegal has many attractions, there are some downsides. For one thing, there is the issue of the unauthorized practice of law. Freelance paralegals, especially those in more conservative parts of the country, have felt pressure from attorneys who do not like competition.

In some states, such as California, where paralegals are regulated and distinctions are made between document preparers and legal assistants, the rule about unauthorized practice of law remains the same. When it comes to giving legal advice, you just can't.

Legal document assistants are not permitted to practice law. They can help people complete legal forms, but they cannot give legal advice.

SPOT THE ISSUE!

Wally Whistleblower was fired last year by Spurious, Inc. Wally alleges that he was fired when he brought the company's questionable accounting practices to the attention of the shareholders. He has brought a wrongful termination suit against Spurious, Inc. Wally's attorney, Laura Litigator, is questioning a Spurious employee at a deposition. Also present at the deposition is Barry Barrister, representing Spurious, Inc. Laura asks the following question:

Q: At any point in your employment with Spurious, did you ever observe any accounting practices that you thought were questionable, unethical, or illegal?
A: Well, I would have to say—
Mr. Barrister: Objection. This question goes into privileged matter. I direct the witness not to answer this question.

Is this question objectionable? What privilege could Mr. Barrister be asserting in this case? Is this a legitimate objection or could it be subject to a motion for sanctions under the discovery rules?

Spot the Issue! introduces a situation asking students to think critically about identifying or solving the legal issue at hand.

Legal Research Maxim offers students tips for specific research and assistance in researching chapter issues.

LEGAL RESEARCH MAXIM

Whenever there is an issue surrounding discovery, it is always best to begin with the rules of discovery, usually found in the Rules of Civil Procedure. However, you must keep in mind that these rules may be supplemented, enacted, or otherwise modified by statutes. You should review the rules, the statutes, and case law to have a solid understanding of discovery issues.

RESEARCH THIS!

Does your state elect or appoint judges? How does the process work? Research your state statutes and determine exactly how judges are selected to serve in various courts. Locate recent cases from your state's highest appellate courts that clearly define the practice of law and delineate the roles of paralegals and attorneys. Are these rules clear? Do they make clear distinctions between the two roles?

Research This! engages students to research cases in their jurisdiction that relate to chapter material, reinforcing the critical skills of independent research.

Practice Tips offer dos
and don'ts in the practice
of law, as well as
provide helpful hints
and reminders
for paralegals.

PRACTICE TIP

Because more and more paralegals are being named in civil actions by disgruntled former clients, it is vitally important for a paralegal to stay away from any allegation of unauthorized practice of law. There are two methods to avoid an allegation of overstepping professional boundaries. One is to always introduce yourself as a paralegal or legal assistant. In addition to this practice, you should always inform individuals who seek legal advice that you are not authorized to give it. By maintaining these practices, you may avoid becoming involved as a named party in a civil action.

CASE IN POINT

Georgia Community Support & Solutions, Inc.
v.
Berryhill
275 Ga. App. 189, 620 S.E.2d 178 (2005)
PHIPPS, Judge.

Georgia Community Support and Solutions, Inc. (GCSS), a nonprofit organization that assists disabled adults and their families, sued Shirley Berryhill, whose disabled son had used its services, for defamation and tortious interference with business relationships. The verified complaint alleged that Berryhill had maliciously published false information about GCSS and its executive director, Whitney Fuchs, in emails and on an internet website. The trial court dismissed the complaint under Georgia's anti-SLAPP (Strategic Lawsuits Against Public Participation) statute, OCGA § 9-11-11.1, finding that Berryhill's statements were privileged and that GCSS had brought the suit for the improper purpose of chilling her right to speak out on an issue of public concern. GCSS appeals, arguing that substantial evidence supported its claims and that Berryhill's statements were not privileged. Because the undisputed facts do not support the trial court's findings, we reverse.

The undisputed facts are as follows. Berryhill's adult son, Robert, suffers from mental retardation and requires constant supervision and care. In July 2000, GCSS placed him with an independently contracted home caregiver. On July 15, 2002, Berryhill posted a message on an internet website for families of disabled adults complaining about the quality of care her son had received from GCSS. In the message, Berryhill stated that her son had been "dumped" at a house where he slept on a "4-foot settee in a back corner, lost a rapid 35–40 pounds, [and] became afraid to speak to [his family]." She further stated that she could not locate and that she would not know where he was

Constitution, the Department of Human Resources, and other private individuals might be able to investigate the nature of my concerns about my son's treatment and care, and to remedy such concerns, if possible."

After a non-evidentiary hearing, the trial court granted Berryhill's motion to dismiss, finding that GCSS had not met the substantive verification requirements of the anti-SLAPP statute. In particular, the court found that Berryhill's statements were privileged communications and that GCSS had sued her for the improper purpose of preventing her "from bringing the plight of her son under the care of GCSS to the attention of the media, the government and the public at large."

The General Assembly enacted the anti-SLAPP statute to encourage Georgians to participate "in matters of public significance through the exercise of their constitutional rights of freedom of speech and the right to petition government for the redress of grievances." The statute requires, among other things, that a written verification under oath accompany any claim asserted against a person arising from an act "which could reasonably be construed as an act in furtherance of the right of free speech or the right to petition government for a redress of grievances." The statute defines such an act as any written or oral statement, writing, or petition made before or to a legislative, executive, or judicial proceeding, or any other official proceeding authorized by law, or any written or oral statement, writing, or petition made in connection with an issue under consideration or

Case in Point offers a significant
case designed to expand on the
topics discussed in the chapter.
Students are given questions
based on the case to further
assist their understanding of the
case and its relevance to the
chapter materials.

CYBER TRIP

National Federation of Paralegal Associations http://www. paralegals.org/ National Association of Legal Assistants www.nala.org American Association for Paralegal Education www.aafpe.org

Cyber Trip provides a list of links relevant to the chapter topics. Students
can access these links to learn more about the material in the text.

COMMUNICATION TIP

Memoranda to File

Whenever you speak with someone important to a case or discuss an issue that may have any significance to a client, always write up a memorandum about it. You might think that you will remember any significant conversation or discovery in a case, but the human memory is a great deal more fragile than most of us are willing to believe. Whenever you discuss anything of significance with a client, witness, judge's secretary, or anyone else having a bearing on a case, immediately create a memo and put it into the file. Save the digital version of the memo in the client's file on the computer or network, but also make a back-up hard copy. If this sounds like overkill, keep in mind that a short telephone conversation could become the major focus of a legal malpractice action several years from now. Being able to produce a contemporaneously written memo may short-circuit a potential claim and also as-

quick memorandum to the file about any conversation. Consider this example:

Memorandum to File

TO: File

From: Paula Paralegal

RE: TC with John Smith

Date: May 24, 2006

I spoke with client John Smith this morning, and he said that he definitely does not want his Aunt, Myra Smith, called to testify in this case. I explained to him that Ms. Smith has critical information in this case and by not calling her, we put the entire case in jeopardy, but he was adamant. I discussed this decision with Allison Attorney, and she agreed that we would not call the client's aunt to the stand in this case. Ms. Attorney suggested that I send a letter to the

Communication Tips in each chapter help students with one of the most crucial aspects of a professional career—communication. Students will examine all forms of communication and their importance on the job.

A Day in the Life presents interview excerpts from paralegals who actually work in the field, giving an overview of not only what brought them into law but also their daily activities.

A Day in the Life: John Purvis

SCREENING CASES

John Purvis spends a large part of his day screening potential cases. He summarizes his screening duties as follows: "What usually happens is a possible client will call the office and I or one of the other legal assistants will screen the call. There are a multitude of calls that you are going to get. Many people will call up complaining about something that a doctor did. Seventy-five percent of those are things that are not actionable as medical malpractice claims. When we are screening calls, if a case sounds like one with real merit, we then present it to one or all of the partners. We usually have a weekly meeting where we go over all of the pending cases, their status, and any potential statutes of limitations problems. The attorneys then vote on whether or not it's a case that they want to investigate. Then we have the person come in and have a sit-down meeting with them. At the meeting there is at least one attorney and one legal assistant. We listen to what the person has to say about their medical treatment. Then we try to give them an overview of what is involved in bringing a medical malpractice case, what it takes to proceed on a case, and also inform them about the low likelihood of getting a recovery. The statistics show that only a small percentage of the medical malpractice cases that are brought are successful. If the client is willing to proceed and understands that there are risks associated with going forward, and that there will be expenses that they are going to incur in continuing with the action, then we agree to take the matter on an inv

Career Prep suggests questions for students to pose to working paralegals. This exercise sends the student in pursuit of more information about what a career as a paralegal will really be like.

Career Prep

Locate a recent news report of an automobile accident and then prepare a legally sufficient complaint based on the report. Make sure that you not only make correct factual allegations but also allege the jurisdictional basis and satisfy the other required elements of a complaint. Finally, locate your state court rules on notice pleading and include copies of these rules with the final draft of your complaint.

Real Paralegal Life in each chapter offers a practical application designed to help students build a specific skill set, including analyzing evidence, creating a personal court directory, billing hours, and basic investigative techniques.

 Real Paralegal Life: Building a Skill Set

JOHN PURVIS

John Purvis is a senior legal assistant at a firm that specializes in civil litigation. He has worked there for years and spends a great deal of his time concentrating on medical malpractice cases. "When it comes to med/mal," he says, "we handle strictly plaintiff work in medical malpractice cases." When the firm decides to accept a case, Purvis's focus is investigation. According to him, "We have the client list of every physician they have ever seen; we have them execute medical authorization releases. We take that information and immediately send out requests to all medical providers for complete copies of all their records, diagnostics, lab reports, that type of thing. Depending on the type of injury, we may also request actual copies of x-rays, MRIs, CAT-scans, any diagnostic tool that may be useful in the ultimate evaluation and potential review by an expert."

At his firm, they use a team approach to litigation, so "when we take a case to trial, we use two or three attorneys, letting [the opposition] know that we are bringing the full resources of the firm to a case."

Summary

The process of evaluating a potential civil case involves many different elements. A case evaluation must take into account various factors, including the nature of the possible claim, the facts setting out the defendant's liability, the law, the likelihood of recovery, and the extent of the plaintiff's injuries. Rule 11 of the Federal Rules of Civil Procedure—and its analog found in most state court rules—requires that an attorney must investigate a claim before bringing it. This investigation must focus on not only the facts of the case but also a review of the applicable laws. Before a plaintiff can bring an action against a defendant, the plaintiff must have a cause of action. A cause of action is a legally recognized wrong committed against the plaintiff that entitles the plaintiff to recovery in a court of law.

To investigate a claim adequately, the law firm must first meet and consult with the client to gather as much information as possible. The initial client consultation involves obtaining extensive information from the client, including the details of the plaintiff's injury, background on the

Chapter Summary provides a quick review of the key concepts presented in the chapter.

Key Terms used throughout the chapters are defined in the margin and provided as a list at the end of each chapter. A common set of definitions is used consistently across the McGraw-Hill paralegal titles.

Key Terms

Case evaluation, 62	Medical authorization, 67
Rule 11, 64	Statute of limitation, 70
Liability, 65	Witness locator service, 73
Cause of action, 66	Skip tracing, 73
Initial client meeting, 67	

Review Questions

1. What are the terms that refer to the two main parties in a lawsuit?
2. How is a person defined as a "party" to a lawsuit?
3. What is personal jurisdiction?
4. What role does a paralegal have in drafting a complaint?
5. What is a forum, and what relation does it have to a court's jurisdictional power?
6. Compare and contrast obtaining personal jurisdiction through the defendant's presence in the forum and his or her domicile in the forum.
7. Explain how a forum can obtain personal jurisdiction over a defendant through minimum contacts under the *International Shoe* case.

Review and Discussion Questions ask students to apply critical thinking skills to the concepts learned in each chapter. The Review Questions reinforce the objectives of the chapter. The Discussion Questions focus on more specific legal topics and promote dialogue among students. Both sets of questions are found at the end of each chapter.

Exercises at the end of each chapter offer short scenarios to test the students' retention and understanding of the chapter materials.

Exercises: Skill Builders

Locate a fellow student who has been involved in a car accident. Interview this person, using the details provided in this chapter as a guide to the comprehensive nature of your interview. Pretend that this student is a new client. Prepare a complete client questionnaire and prepare as much detail as possible about this incident.

Portfolio Assignment

Portfolio Assignment 5-1: Draft a complaint in the Cherry case. Using the facts set out in Appendix A, draft a complaint in the Cherry case.

Portfolio Assignment 5-2: Draft a letter to a client. Using the facts in the Baker case in Appendix B, draft a letter to Mr. Baker explaining that your firm has decided not to accept Mr. Baker's case and also explaining that the statute of limitations for Mr. Baker's action appears to have run out. Your letter should detail not only the firm's conclusion that the case should not be filed but also the meeting with Mr. Baker and the facts as the firm has come to understand them.

Portfolio Assignments are designed to use the skills mastered in the chapter and convert them into a practical legal document that can be used as samples of work during interviews to fully demonstrate the student's competency in each area.

Crossword puzzles at the end of each chapter utilize the key terms and definitions to help students become more familiar using their legal vocabulary.

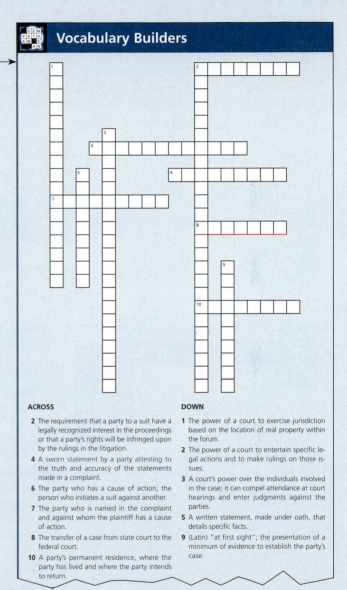

Vocabulary Builders

ACROSS

2 The requirement that a party to a suit have a legally recognized interest in the proceedings or that a party's rights will be infringed upon by the rulings in the litigation.

4 A sworn statement by a party attesting to the truth and accuracy of the statements made in a complaint.

6 The party who has a cause of action; the person who initiates a suit against another.

7 The party who is named in the complaint and against whom the plaintiff has a cause of action.

8 The transfer of a case from state court to the federal court.

10 A party's permanent residence, where the party has lived and where the party intends to return.

DOWN

1 The power of a court to exercise jurisdiction based on the location of real property within the forum.

2 The power of a court to entertain specific legal actions and to make rulings on those issues.

3 A court's power over the individuals involved in the case; it can compel attendance at court hearings and enter judgments against the parties.

5 A written statement, made under oath, that details specific facts.

9 (Latin) "at first sight"; the presentation of a minimum of evidence to establish the party's case.

Supplements

Instructor's Resource CD-ROM An Instructor's Resource CD-ROM (IRCD) will be available for instructors. This CD provides a number of instructional tools, including PowerPoint presentations for each chapter in the text, an instructor's manual, and an electronic test bank. The instructor's manual assists with the creation and implementation of the course by supplying lecture notes, answers to all exercises, page references, additional discussion questions and class activities, a key to using the PowerPoint presentations, detailed lesson plans, instructor support features, and grading rubrics for assignments. A unique feature, an instructor matrix, also is included that links learning objectives with activities, grading rubrics, and classroom equipment needs. The activities consist of individual and group exercises, research projects, and scenarios with forms to fill out. The electronic test bank will offer a variety of multiple choice, fill-in-the-blank, true/false, and essay questions, with varying levels of difficulty and page references.

Online Learning Center The **Online Learning Center (OLC)** is a Web site that follows the text chapter-by-chapter. OLC content is ancillary and supplementary and is germane to the textbook—as students read the book, they can go online to review material or link to relevant Web sites. Students and instructors can access the Web sites for each of the McGraw-Hill paralegal texts from the main page of the Paralegal Super Site. Each OLC has a similar organization. An Information Center features an overview of the text, background on the author, and the Preface and Table of Contents from the book. Instructors can access the instructor's manual and PowerPoint presentations from the IRCD. Students see the Key Terms list from the text as flashcards, as well as additional quizzes and exercises.

The OLC can be delivered multiple ways—professors and students can access the site directly through the textbook Web site, through PageOut, or within a course management system (i.e., WebCT, Blackboard, TopClass, or eCollege).

PageOut: McGraw-Hill's Course Management System PageOut is McGraw-Hill's unique point-and-click course Web site tool, enabling you to create a full-featured, professional-quality course Web site without knowing HTML coding. With PageOut, you can post your syllabus online, assign McGraw-Hill Online Learning Center or eBook content, add links to important offsite resources, and maintain student results in the online grade book. You can send class announcements, copy your course site to share with colleagues, and upload original files. PageOut is free for every McGraw-Hill/Irwin user and, if you're short on time, we even have a team ready to help you create your site! To learn more, please visit http://www.pageout.net.

Create a custom course Website with **PageOut**, free with every McGraw-Hill textbook.

Contact your McGraw-Hill publisher's representative or visit www.mhhe.com/solutions to learn more.

Brief Contents

Table of Contents

Chapter 1

Introduction to the Court System

CHAPTER OBJECTIVES

The student will be able to:

- Explain the differences between civil law and other types of law.
- Describe the burden of proof in a civil case.
- Explain the role of pleadings in civil cases.
- Explain the difference between a finding of liability and a finding of guilt.
- Describe the function of damages in civil cases.
- Define the role of the U.S. Constitution in the American legal system.
- Explain the difference between statutes and case law.

This chapter introduces the U.S. court system and details the important differences between various areas of law.

INTRODUCTION TO THE AMERICAN JUDICIAL SYSTEM

Before we can discuss the many fascinating aspects of civil litigation, we must begin with an examination of the American judicial system. The purpose of this chapter is to introduce you to the important distinctions between civil law and other types of law, as well the sources of judicial authority. Finally, we will examine the major features of both the federal and state court systems. As you will see, there any many different sources of legal authority, and each plays an important role in the overall pattern of civil litigation.

CIVIL LAW

Civil law is a broad category encompassing an enormous variety of cases. Divorce actions, medical malpractice, child custody, and personal injury cases are all types of civil law. Because this is a book about civil litigation and procedure, we will touch on many of these disparate areas of law as we discuss the course of a civil case. Before we examine the details of civil litigation however, we must address a more fundamental question: What is civil law?

What Is Civil Law?

Civil law refers to the large body of cases brought by individuals against other individuals. When a person sues someone for defamation or a corporation seeks to enforce an employment contract

SURF'S UP!

Individuals who are new to the practice of law are often surprised to learn of the technology gap between this profession and nearly every other. Law is a conservative profession and traditionally has been very slow to adopt new technologies. Devices that have found immediate acceptance in accounting and medicine have been slow to find their way into the legal field. Given the vast adoption of personal computers, it is surprising to learn that there is still a significant percentage of attorneys who have not used a laptop or desktop computer. Many still dictate memoranda and other items to secretaries, who transcribe them in much the same way that they did 30 years ago.

However, the predisposition against technology has finally begun to change. Younger lawyers who have used computers and other devices since childhood are at the forefront of this movement, but there are also other reasons for law as a profession to adopt computer software and other labor-saving devices. Throughout this book, we will examine the expanding role of technology in the practice of law and show how you, as a paralegal, can increase your marketability to a firm by demonstrating your understanding of and ability to use various technological innovations.

against an employee, these are both civil cases. What makes civil litigation so interesting is that there are an almost infinite variety of cases that fall under the general heading of civil law. Unlike criminal law or other specialized areas, legal professionals who work in civil litigation must be prepared for a wide assortment of cases. Fortunately, the rules that govern civil cases are uniform and relatively straightforward, even if they do apply to a myriad of case types.

How Does Civil Law Differ from Other Areas of Law?

There are dozens of other branches of law. Administrative law deals with the rules and regulations that govern governmental agencies. Admiralty law governs the law of the sea. Bankruptcy law is concerned with discharging debts through court proceedings. Criminal law focuses on punishing lawbreakers. Domestic law involves divorces, alimony, and child custody issues. Civil law is different than these other areas of law in several important respects. For instance, civil cases differ from the previously mentioned types of cases in all of the following ways:

- Parties
- Pleadings
- Rules
- Burden of proof
- Outcome

The Parties

In civil suits, private parties sue other private parties. Unlike criminal cases, which are brought by the government against an individual, a civil case involves private issues and grievances. Although governmental agencies can bring civil suits against individuals, the point of the litigation is to enforce a right or sue for damages. There are some important terms regarding civil suits that all legal professionals should know. The person who brings a civil suit is referred to as the **plaintiff**. The person who is being sued is the **defendant**. These terms are almost exclusively reserved for civil cases. Other names are used to refer to the parties in non-civil cases. The person or business filing for bankruptcy, for instance, is referred to as a "petitioner." In criminal cases, the government brings an action against an individual or corporation to enforce statutes. The government is not referred to as a plaintiff in such a case. Instead, the government is simply termed the "state," "the people," or "United States" (among other terms).

As you read pleadings in civil cases, you will see that the **style** or **caption** of the case always lists the names of the plaintiffs and defendants. Civil cases are captioned: *Plaintiff A v. Defendant B.* Because the government always brings criminal cases, the government is listed by name, not as a plaintiff. Criminal cases are captioned *Government (or State) v. Defendant.* By examining the caption or style of the case, you can easily decipher if it is a civil or criminal action. Bankruptcy cases are captioned *In re John Doe* (i.e., in the matter of John Doe).

plaintiff
The party initiating legal action.

defendant
The party against whom a lawsuit is brought.

style (caption)
The heading or title used in all legal pleadings.

FIGURE 1.1

2001 Plaintiffs in 75 Largest Counties

Source: Bureau of Justice Statistics Bulletin, "Tort Trials and Verdicts in Large Counties, 2001." U.S. Department of Justice, November 2004.

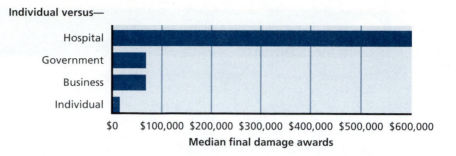

A civil action is usually based on a private wrong suffered by an individual, corporation, or other entity. The plaintiff brings suit when he, she, or it has suffered a financial, emotional, or physical loss. The right to bring a civil suit is not limited to natural persons only. Corporations and businesses may also sue in their own right. There are even provisions that allow government agencies to bring civil suits. See Figure 1.1 for plaintiffs in the 75 largest counties. Civil actions encompass these and many other types of actions. We will address the many ramifications of these actions throughout this text.

The Pleadings

complaint
Document that states the allegations and the legal basis of the plaintiff's claims.

petition
A request made to a governmental entity; often used synonymously with "complaint," though a petition is a more general term.

answer
The defendant's response to the plaintiff's complaint.

Civil actions are also unique in the type of pleadings that are used to initiate lawsuits. In a civil case, the plaintiff files a **complaint**, also known as a **petition**. See Figure 1.10 at the end of the chapter. This complaint sets out the plaintiff's factual allegations against the defendant and asks a court to award monetary damages to the plaintiff as a result of the defendant's actions. The defendant responds with an **answer**, also known as a reply. In the answer, the defendant denies the plaintiff's factual allegations and also denies any responsibility for the plaintiff's injuries. See Figure 1.2 for an example of the heading or caption of a civil case.

The style of any pleading reflects the identities and status of all parties to the suit. The plaintiff is identified by full legal name when he or she is a person and by full title when the plaintiff is a business or government entity. Similarly, the style must correctly identify the defendant. A style that lists the incorrect name of the defendant may be subject to dismissal for failing to correctly identify exactly who is the subject of the action. Beyond identifying the parties, the style also identifies the court in which the action is pending and provides information about the case file number, sometimes called the civil action number. This number is important because it is the docketing number assigned by the court system to that action. Case file numbers are unique to each case and must be included on all documents subsequently filed in the case. Many courts

FIGURE 1.2

Civil Case Caption

STATE OF EDWARDS
COUNTY OF PLACID

SUPERIOR COURT OF PLACID COUNTY

CIVIL ACTION FILE NO.: _____

Elizabeth Louise,   )
)
        Plaintiff,   )
)
        v.   )   **COMPLAINT**
)
)
Wilson Johnson,   )
)
        Defendant.   )
)
_____)

RESEARCH THIS!

Throughout this text, you will find a section in each chapter in which you will be asked to research specific legal topics raised in the chapter. The purpose of this feature is to emphasize specific material from the chapter and assist you in learning additional and important legal topics. For the purposes of this first assignment, research the sources available in your local law library, online sites, or other sources to determine what research assistance you have access to. For instance, do you have access to a law library? Many public libraries contain a legal section. Does your local branch have legal texts? Try an online search through Google, Yahoo!, or another search engine, using the search string "online legal research."

LEGAL RESEARCH MAXIM

Throughout this text, you will also be given specific research tips and maxims to assist you in researching issues raised in the chapter. For instance, in this first chapter, you should be aware that not all online research services are created equal. Some online sources only cover a few years' worth of case decisions. For legal researchers, depth of coverage is always important, and you should seek out sites that provide decades of case analysis, not simply the most recent cases from a state or federal court. For instance, this chapter mentions the famous *International Shoe* case. If you were doing online legal research on a site that only provided coverage for the past ten years or so, your research would never reveal this case. You would be hard pressed to call your research complete if you were unable to locate one of the most important cases on jurisdiction.

also require that in addition to identifying the parties, the court, and the case file number, the parties must also identify the document filed. In Figure 1.2, for example, the parties identify the pleading as a complaint.

It is important to note that the term "pleadings" has different meanings in different jurisdictions. For instance, in some areas, pleadings refers exclusively to the complaint and answer, whereas in others, it is a term that refers broadly to all documents filed in the civil action.

The Rules

As we will see throughout this book, civil actions follow their own set of rules with regard to the filing of pleadings, the various stages of a civil action, and even the enforcement of the ultimate verdict. All states have enacted their own versions of the Rules of Civil Procedure. We will discuss individual states as well as the Federal Rules of Civil Procedure throughout this book. See Figure 1.3 for an example of the Rules of Civil Procedure.

The Burden of Proof

Whenever a party brings an allegation in any type of case, that party must prove those allegations. The standard or **burden of proof** varies depending on the type of case involved. In civil cases, for example, the burden of proof is usually **preponderance of the evidence**. This standard requires the plaintiff to prove that the allegations in the complaint are more likely true than not. Many

burden of proof
Standard for assessing the weight of the evidence.

preponderance of the evidence
The weight or level of persuasion of evidence needed to find the defendant liable as alleged by the plaintiff in a civil matter.

FIGURE 1.3
Federal Rules of Civil Procedure—Rule 8. General Rules of Pleading
Source: FED. R. CIV. P. 8.

(a) Claims for Relief. A pleading which sets forth a claim for relief, whether an original claim, counterclaim, cross-claim, or third-party claim, shall contain (1) a short and plain statement of the grounds upon which the court's jurisdiction depends, unless the court already has jurisdiction and the claim needs no new grounds of jurisdiction to support it, (2) a short and plain statement of the claim showing that the pleader is entitled to relief, and (3) a demand for judgment for the relief the pleader seeks. Relief in the alternative or of several different types may be demanded.

commentators have described it as the plaintiff's burden to tip the scales of proof in the plaintiff's direction. Others have attempted to quantify it by saying that if the plaintiff can establish the facts to 51%, then the plaintiff has satisfied preponderance of the evidence. There are different burdens of proof in different types of actions. For instance, in criminal cases, the burden of proof is beyond a reasonable doubt. If preponderance of the evidence is considered to be a slight tipping of the scale in the plaintiff's favor, proof beyond a reasonable doubt would require the government to swing the scale entirely to its side. Although preponderance of the evidence is the most commonly seen burden of proof, there are situations in which a civil litigant might have to prove his or her case by **clear and convincing evidence**. The standard of "clear and convincing evidence" is higher than preponderance of the evidence and less than proof beyond a reasonable doubt. It falls somewhere between these two burdens. Clear and convincing evidence requires the fact finder to determine with substantial certainty that the party's allegations are true.

clear and convincing evidence
Having a high probability of truthfulness, a higher standard being preponderance of the evidence.

The question often arises: Why would civil cases usually require preponderance of the evidence but then, in rare instances, require a higher degree of proof? Clear and convincing evidence is reserved for instances in which the result for the parties will have a substantial impact on their lives. A court might require clear and convincing evidence in any of the following actions:

- Committing an individual to a mental institution.
- Deciding to withdraw life support from a patient in a persistent vegetative state.
- Parental rights.
- Disbarment of an attorney.
- Fraud.
- Allegation of improper actions in an election.

In each of these examples, the issues involved have such a significant potential impact on the parties that courts routinely require a higher standard of proof before allowing the action. Whether it involves removing life support from a patient or disbarring an attorney, these actions will have such drastic consequences that many states require the standard of clear and convincing evidence before a judge is authorized to make a ruling on them.

beyond a reasonable doubt
The requirement for the level of proof in a criminal matter in order to convict or find the defendant guilty. It is a substantially higher and more-difficult-to-prove criminal matter standard.

The burden of proof in a civil case, whether it is clear and convincing evidence or preponderance of the evidence, is never as high a standard as that required in criminal cases. Prosecutors in a criminal trial must prove that the defendant is guilty **beyond a reasonable doubt**. Although legal commentators and authorities have wrestled for centuries over the exact meaning of this term, most define it as substantial or overwhelming evidence that the defendant committed the crime with which he, she, or it is charged. Proof beyond a reasonable doubt means that the individual jurors in the case are convinced of the evidence against the defendant and have no major objections to the case presented. This higher standard is required in criminal cases for the very simple reason that it should be more difficult to imprison a person than it is to assess monetary damages against him or her.

liability
A jury's determination that one party is responsible for injuries to another party; the basis for an award of damages.

The Outcome

In a civil trial, jurors are asked to determine which side has presented a more believable version of the facts. In a bench trial, the judge must make this determination. See Figure 1.4. Unlike criminal cases, in which jurors are called upon to determine guilt or innocence, the juries in civil cases face a determination of **liability**. Civil juries determine whether or not one party is

FIGURE 1.4
Comparing Bench and Jury Trials in State Courts

Source: Federal Judicial Center, Integrated Data Base (Civil), fiscal years 2002–03.

Type of Jurisdiction	Tort Trials Terminated in U.S. District Courts		
	Number of Tort Trials	Jury Trial	Bench Trial
All tort trials	1,647	71.4%	28.6%
Diversity of citizenship	1,091	87.2	12.8
Federal question	345	61.4	38.6
U.S. defendant	205	4.9	95.1
U.S. plaintiff	6	**	**

Note: Detail may not sum to total because of rounding.
**Too few cases to obtain statistically reliable data.

PRACTICE TIP

One important aspect of working in the legal field is organizing all of the information that you will need on a daily basis. One way to do this is to create your own paralegal resource. You need a resource for a simple reason: time. When you work in the legal field, time is money. The more time you can save on a particular job, the sooner you can move on to the next. Creating a paralegal resource is one of the best ways to save time and effort. The couple of hours that you spend creating one will save you hundreds of hours over your career. In addition, having a resource that contains virtually everything you need, from telephone numbers to notes about how certain judges like their orders submitted, will make you look even better to your firm. In fact, having all of this information at your fingertips will make you seem almost superhuman.

Whether you create your resource in file folders, notebooks, or a computer, a good resource should have all of the following information:

- Telephone numbers, addresses, and email addresses.
- Calendar.
- Where to find certain courthouse records.
- Attorneys' and judges' "peculiarities."
- Forms, forms, and more forms.
- Brief and memo bank.
- Frequently asked questions.
- Computer passwords and log-in information.
- Vendor/supplier information.

If putting together your own paralegal resource sounds unusual, it isn't. Legal professionals have been creating their own handy references for decades. Many attorneys keep important data in manila file folders, word processing files, or digital devices. In the modern world, many paralegals keep all of this information in databases. Whatever method you currently use to hang on to important information, you will need to pull it all together and put it in one place. It might be a large file folder on your desk. It might just as easily be on your laptop, stored in a network folder, or backed up on a disk. However you decide to store it, you should organize your important information, put it in one place, and start using it to make your job easier.

---

guilty
A verdict only available in criminal cases in which the jury determines that the defendant is responsible for committing a crime.

liable to the other party. A civil jury never determines, for instance, that a party is **guilty**. Instead, if the jury believes the plaintiff, the jury finds the defendant liable to the plaintiff. In contrast, if the jury determines that the defendant has the more likely version of the truth, the jury might easily find that the plaintiff is liable to the defendant or that the defendant is not liable to anyone.

damages
Money paid to compensate for loss or injury.

Once a determination of liability has been made, the next step in a civil case is the determination of **damages**. Damages refer to monetary payments made by one party to another that attempt to compensate the party for his or her losses. In situations in which the jury believes that the defendant is not liable, the jury will order that no damages be awarded. However, if the jury sides with the plaintiff, the jury must make a determination about damages, specifically, how much money the defendant should pay to the plaintiff.

SOURCES OF LEGAL AUTHORITY IN THE UNITED STATES

One of the first questions that any legal professional must answer is, "What is the law?" Is the law simply a body of statutes, or is it something more? As we will see throughout this book, there is no easy answer. For instance, one could easily argue that the source of all legal authority in the United States derives from the U.S. Constitution.

U.S. Constitution

The United States Constitution took effect in 1789. It is one of the most influential documents in world history. The Constitution sets out the basic framework for the federal and state governments, creates three separate branches of government, and details the rights allotted to citizens. Constitutional law is a complex subject and not one that we will address in any depth here. All governmental authority flows from the provisions of the U.S. Constitution. In addition to the

FIGURE 1.5
U.S. Constitution,
Article I. Section 3

> Clause 1: The Senate of the United States shall be composed of two Senators from each State, chosen by the Legislature thereof, for six Years; and each Senator shall have one Vote.
>
> Clause 3: No Person shall be a Senator who shall not have attained to the Age of thirty Years, and been nine Years a Citizen of the United States, and who shall not, when elected, be an Inhabitant of that State for which he shall be chosen.

federal Constitution, each state also has its own constitution, setting out the rights, duties, and obligations of state governments. See Figure 1.5 for an excerpt of the Constitution that begins to outline guidelines for the U.S. Senate.

Although the Constitution provides the framework for the government, it does not provide much guidance on issues such as bringing civil actions, prosecuting crimes, or enforcing judgments. For answers to those questions, we must turn to other sources of the law, including statutes, case law, and common law.

Statutes

statute
Written law enacted by the legislative branches of both federal and state governments.

Statutes consist of legislative bills that are voted on by the legislative branch of government and enacted by the executive branch. On the federal level, the U.S. Congress is the legislative branch, and it votes on bills before sending them to the president for signature. If the president signs the legislation, it becomes a binding law. On the state level, the legislature votes on bills and submits them to the governor for signature. In both instances, the laws that are created are referred to as statutes. But this is only one small part of the large body of what American legal scholars consider to be the *law*.

Administrative Rules and Regulations

Once a statute has been created, a governmental agency may create an administrative rule or regulation to put the statute into effect. For instance, the 16th Amendment gives the federal government the power to levy income taxes but provides no details about the process of actually carrying out tax collection (see Figure 1.6). Instead, the Treasury Department, acting through its Internal Revenue Service, creates administrative rules and regulations that govern

 COMMUNICATION TIP

If there is one skill that all legal professionals should have in abundance, it is the ability to communicate clearly and succinctly in writing. Written communication is still the cornerstone of the legal profession, even in this era of email, faxes, and the World Wide Web. We will examine written and other forms of communication throughout this text, but in this chapter, we focus on written communication.

Why are written communication skills so important? For most people, clear writing indicates clear thinking. The ability to communicate an idea or a position effectively in writing is the central core of what an attorney does. We all tend to think of attorneys as individuals who communicate through the spoken word—in closing arguments to juries, motions before a judge, or simply discussing legal implications with clients. But the reality of legal practice is just the opposite of the popular impression. Attorneys spend large portions of every day reading and writing. They read case decisions, statutes, law reviews, and a wealth of other material, and they write letters to clients, briefs to appellate courts, complaints, answers, motions, and a myriad of other materials. If they cannot present themselves well in writing, their legal practice will suffer.

Attorneys expect the same high level of writing skills on the part of their staff. Paralegals and others who work closely with attorneys must have mastered the basics of written communication. That is one reason we devote an entire section to it in every chapter of this book. In future chapters, you can anticipate assignments ranging from questions surrounding basic grammar to the development of motions that would be submitted to a judge.

FIGURE 1.6
Amendment XVI

> The Congress shall have power to lay and collect taxes on incomes, from whatever source derived, without apportionment among the several states, and without regard to any census or enumeration.

how to, when to, and who should pay income taxes. These rules and regulations carry the same force as a statute.

Ordinances

As we have seen, statutes are laws passed by a state or federal government. However, there is an entire class of laws passed by local governments, such as municipalities and towns, that regulate behavior at a local level. These are not referred to as statutes. Instead, they are called **ordinances**. An ordinance has limited application. The ordinance has a strict geographic limit, such as the town limits or the county boundary. Ordinances cannot conflict with statutes. If they do, the ordinance is ruled unconstitutional and the statute takes precedence.

ordinance
A law passed by a local government, such as a town council or city government.

Case Law

case law
Published court opinions of federal and state appellate courts; judge-created law in deciding cases, set forth in court opinions.

In addition to statutory law, there is another, equally important source of law: **case law**. Case law is the huge body of published decisions by appellate courts. Laypersons do not realize the significance of case law. When an appellate court reaches a decision in a case on appeal, the reasons for the decision are encapsulated in a written opinion. In many instances, case law is synonymous with common law, discussed subsequently.

An opinion not only discusses the facts of the particular case on appeal but also the law that applies to the facts. For legal professionals, case law can be one of the most important sources of legal authority in the United States. The importance of case law can be demonstrated by reviewing a decision by the United States Supreme Court.

Case Law and the United States Supreme Court

Suppose that the U.S. Congress passes a bill stating that the punitive damages available to civil litigants are limited to a specific formula. The formula set out by the federal legislation is that punitive damages (monetary payments made above and beyond the monetary damages intended to compensate the plaintiff for his or her injuries) must be limited to twice the amount of proven actual damages. The statute is clear and unambiguous. The most that an injured plaintiff could receive in any case, no matter how egregiously the defendant acted, is a sum that is twice the plaintiff's actual damages. Therefore, if the plaintiff's proven damages are $1,000, the most that the plaintiff could receive is $2,000. However, if a litigant who falls under this statute appeals to the U.S. Supreme Court, that Court is free to rule that the Congress overstepped its bounds by limiting awards in this way. The Court's written opinion in that case would be vitally important case law for anyone else with a pending case involving punitive damages. That case law would be as important as any statute.

The significance of case law is that it both explains and expands on statutes and other sources of law. The true power of appellate courts is their ability to review decisions of lower courts. All courts have the responsibility to interpret the Constitution, statutes, ordinances, and even other case law, but the appellate courts can review the decisions of lower courts and modify those interpretations in accordance with their own views. The appellate court's interpretation of these issues is not only binding on the parties in a particular appeal but also on all others who have similar issues. Once an appellate court, such as the U.S. Supreme Court, adopts a new interpretation of a law or rules that a particular statute is unconstitutional, that interpretation becomes the law of the land and is just as binding as any statute.

There are quite literally hundreds of examples of the impact that appellate decisions have had on civil litigation. A court's ruling on evidence may affect whether a plaintiff is permitted to introduce evidence of the defendant's previous driving record in a personal injury case. Another court's ruling on collateral source payments might well allow the defendant to present evidence to the jury that the plaintiff has already been compensated for some of his or her injuries through insurance.

One might be tempted to think that the only important source of case law in the United States is the U.S. Supreme Court. However, case law comes from every level of the court system. As we will see subsequently in this chapter, both state and federal courts generate case law—and do so at different levels, from trial courts to appellate courts to the U.S. Supreme Court.

Common Law

common law
Judge-made law, the ruling in a judicial opinion.

The final category of sources of legal authority is **common law**, an ancient source of legal authority. Stretching back to our legal roots in England, common law was literally the law of the common people. In an age when most people were illiterate, judges were among the few professionals who could read and write. As a result, there were very few statutes created by the government. Instead of statutory law, judges were forced to create their own rules. A judge might decide, for instance, that if a man was attacked and it took longer than a year for him to die of his injuries, the person who attacked him could not be tried for murder. The so-called "Year and a Day" rule was a common law rule that governed English (and American) jurisdictions for years. The theory behind the law was simple: Given the standards of the medical profession in the Middle Ages, if a victim lingered for at least 12 months, it was quite likely that he died from something other than the injuries he sustained in his attack. As judges continued to reach decisions in cases, they amassed a huge body of legal principles and standards that came to be called "common law."

JURISDICTION

jurisdiction
The power or authority of the court to hear a particular classification of case.

No discussion of judicial authority could be complete without an examination of the topic of jurisdiction. **Jurisdiction** refers to the power of a court to decide issues in the case and impose those decisions on the parties. There are many different types of jurisdiction, including the following two major types:

- Subject matter jurisdiction
- Personal jurisdiction

Subject Matter Jurisdiction

subject matter jurisdiction
A court's authority over the res, the subject of the case.

When a court has **subject matter jurisdiction**, that court is permitted to entertain the issues raised in the suit and make binding rulings on those issues. There are many examples of courts that lack subject matter jurisdiction to consider specific types of cases. Small claims court, for instance, is often listed as a court of limited jurisdiction precisely because it is barred from criminal cases and may consider only litigation concerning civil cases for which a specific amount of money is contested. Many small claims courts are limited to a consideration of cases in which the contested amount is $2,000 or less (though the amount varies considerably from state to state). In addition to small claims courts, many other courts have strict rules about subject matter jurisdiction. If a person or business wishes to file bankruptcy, that filing must occur in the federal bankruptcy courts, simply because these are the only courts authorized to hear these actions.

On the local level, some courts have broad subject matter jurisdiction; in states in which the most powerful local court is referred to as superior court (also known as district court or county Court in some states), this court may have the power to hear a broad range of actions, from felony crimes to divorce cases (see Figure 1.7). In fact, in many states, the superior court was the original court, and other local courts were created out of the vast powers of this court.

FIGURE 1.7
Subject Matter Jurisdiction of Superior Court (Georgia)

Source: GA. Const. art. 6, §4, P I.

The superior courts shall have jurisdiction in all cases, except as otherwise provided in this Constitution. They shall have exclusive jurisdiction over trials in felony cases, except in the case of juvenile offenders as provided by law; in cases respecting title to land; in divorce cases; and in equity cases. The superior courts shall have such appellate jurisdiction, either alone or by circuit or district, as may be provided by law.

General and Limited Jurisdiction

In addition to issues surrounding subject matter jurisdiction, there are other issues that litigants must address. These include the basic powers of the court. Courts of **general jurisdiction** are empowered to hear a broad range of cases, including civil, criminal, probate, divorce, and child custody issues, among many others. A court of general jurisdiction may consider any of these issues and make binding rulings on the issues presented to it. However, there are also many courts in the United States that are classified as courts of **limited jurisdiction**. A limited jurisdiction court may hear only specific types of cases. Small claims court is one example. This court is authorized to consider civil cases in which the parties contest a monetary amount below a specific amount ($5,000 in many states). If the amount in controversy is higher than the threshold amount or if the case involves additional issues outside of the court's authority, the court must transfer the case to another court. On the federal level, the bankruptcy court is an example of a court with limited jurisdiction. It may entertain all issues associated with personal or business bankruptcies but is not empowered to consider other issues, such as criminal charges or wrongful death claims.

Personal Jurisdiction

In addition to subject matter jurisdiction, courts must also have power over the parties, or **personal jurisdiction**. A court may obtain such authority through a variety of means, such as the presence of the parties in the county or other means, which we will discuss in Chapter 5.

Personal jurisdiction is often described as the court's power to adjudicate the issues in a case and reach a decision that affects the parties' legal rights. These jurisdictional issues are concomitant; they must exist together. A court may have subject matter jurisdiction, but if it lacks personal jurisdiction, it is barred from considering the case. The opposite scenario is also true. When both types of jurisdiction exist in a case, the court may proceed to consider the issues. Both subject matter jurisdiction and personal jurisdiction must combine to provide the **forum** with the authority to consider the issues in the case. Here, the forum refers to the actual location where the case must be brought. A court with sufficient personal and subject matter jurisdiction becomes the forum where the action is brought and decided.

A court may acquire personal jurisdiction over a party by any of a number of methods, including:

- Physical presence in the forum.
- Domicile or residence in the forum.
- Property ownership in the forum.
- Consent.
- Minimum contacts.

Physical Presence in the Forum

When a party is present within the geographic limits of the court's power, the party may be served with a service of process, and by the party's mere presence, the court acquires personal jurisdiction in the case. Although there are many extrapolations of this rule, including a prohibition against the use of trickery or deceit to get the party into the forum, we limit our discussion to the fact that presence alone can equate to personal jurisdiction.

Domicile or Residence in the Forum

A court may also acquire personal jurisdiction over a party by the simple fact of the party maintaining a domicile in the county. In many cases, a **domicile** refers to a permanent residence in a particular area. For instance, when a person maintains several different homes in different areas, it may become necessary for the party urging the court to exercise personal jurisdiction to prove that the opposing party's main residence is in the forum.

Property Ownership in the Forum

There are provisions that allow certain types of cases to proceed simply because a party owns property in a particular forum. This is referred to as **in rem jurisdiction**. Although actions based on in rem jurisdiction are generally limited to litigation concerning real estate, such as boundary disputes, tax evaluations, and similar actions, the mere fact that real property is located within the forum may be enough to give the court personal jurisdiction over a party.

---

general jurisdiction
The court is empowered to hear any civil or criminal case.

limited jurisdiction
The court is empowered to hear only specified types of cases.

personal jurisdiction
The court's power over the individuals involved in the case; when a court has personal jurisdiction, it can compel attendance at court hearings and enter judgments against the parties.

forum
The proper legal site or location.

domicile
The place where a person maintains a physical residence with the intent to permanently remain in that place; citizenship; the permanent home of the party.

in rem jurisdiction
A court's authority over claims affecting property.

Consent

A party may always consent to the court's jurisdiction. In its pleadings, for example, a party may decide to forgo a challenge to the court's jurisdiction, consent to personal jurisdiction, and then proceed to a defense of the allegations.

Minimum Contacts

All states have provisions that allow a forum to acquire jurisdiction, especially in business cases, when a party has had sufficient minimum contact with the forum state to justify a finding that the party has submitted to the court's personal jurisdiction. This rule was first announced in the case of *International Shoe Co. v. Washington*, 326 U.S. 310 (1945), in which the U.S. Supreme Court announced a complex test to determine if a specific party has availed itself of sufficient contacts with the forum to have essentially submitted itself to the court's authority. The bane of law students since it was decided, *International Shoe* remains a difficult case to decipher.

FEDERAL AND STATE COURT SYSTEMS

Now that we have discussed the important role played by case law in providing a source of legal authority, we address the issue of how the court systems in the United States are organized. We begin our discussion with the federal court system and then proceed to the various state systems.

The Levels of the Federal Court System

The federal court system is authorized under Article III of the U.S. Constitution, which provides not only the structure for the federal court system but also clearly establishes the judiciary as a separate and equal branch that moderates the power of the executive and legislative branches. Federal judges are appointed by the president and confirmed by the U.S. Senate. Once appointed, federal judges serve for life. They cannot be removed from their positions, unless they commit a crime or violate some other law. Federal judges are thus insulated from the day-to-day world of politics and are free to make unpopular decisions. Over the centuries, federal judges have made many controversial decisions, from forced desegregation to a woman's right to receive an abortion.

Trial Courts: U.S. Federal District Courts

If we think of the federal court system diagrammed as a pyramid, then the U.S. District Courts would be at the bottom of the pyramid. These are the trial courts for the federal system. These courts are empowered to hear both civil and criminal cases. There are a total of 94 federal judicial districts scattered across the United States and Puerto Rico.

Federal district courts empanel juries, consider evidence, hear witness testimony, and reach verdicts. As we will see in Chapter 5, federal courts have limited jurisdiction. They are able to hear only certain types of cases. When a final verdict is reached in a federal district court, the losing party usually has the right to appeal to the U.S. Circuit Court of Appeals.

Appellate Courts: U.S. Circuit Courts of Appeal

Because federal courts cover the entire nation, cases from federal district courts are appealed to specific appellate courts. There are 13 separate judicial circuits. As you can see in Figure 1.8, some judicial circuits cover large swaths of the United States, while some, like the 2nd Judicial District, cover a relatively small geographic area. Population determines the boundaries of judicial circuits. The eastern seaboard of the United States has a denser population, which accounts for the smaller size of the judicial circuits.

United States Supreme Court

The United States Supreme Court is one of the most famous courts in the world. In terms of authority and prestige, it is easily one of the most important. Decisions of the United States Supreme Court can affect everyone in the United States and even have ramifications for other countries. The U.S. Supreme Court is the nation's highest appellate court. Its decisions on federal appellate issues are final. Composed of nine justices, the U.S. Supreme Court begins its term on the first Monday of each October and continues through June or July of the next year. Authorized by Article III of the U.S. Constitution, the U.S. Supreme Court is the final authority on issues related to the interpretation of the Constitution. The Court also has the power to rule federal statutes

FIGURE 1.8   **Geographic Boundaries of United States Courts of Appeal**

Source: www.uscourts.gov.

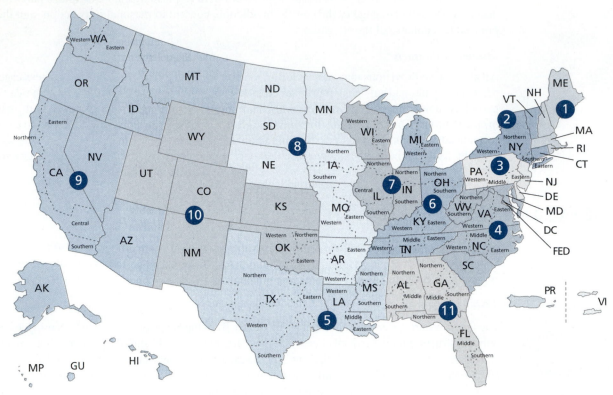

unconstitutional and therefore unenforceable. Although many cases are submitted to the Supreme Court, the vast majority never make it past the hurdle of certiorari.

The United States Supreme Court, like many state supreme courts, is vested with the authority to decide which cases it will hear. If the Court believes that a specific case lacks merit or does not present any significant issue for the justices to review, the Court will deny **certiorari** or cert. A denial of cert means that the Court refuses to hear the appeal, whereas if the Court decides that the case should be heard, it will grant cert. The decision to grant cert does not mean that a party has won on appeal. Instead, it simply means that the Court has agreed to consider the appeal.

certiorari
(Cert) (Latin) "To make sure." An appellate court's authority to decide which cases it will hear on appeal.

The Levels of the State Court System

In many ways, the state court system is a mirror of the federal system. However, state courts are limited to the geographic limits of the state, and therefore, they have far less bureaucracy than the federal system. Just as we did with the federal system, we start our discussion at the bottom of the court pyramid with trial courts.

Trial Courts

Trial courts on the state level fulfill many of the same roles as federal district courts. These are the courts in which witnesses testify, juries consider verdicts, and judges make rulings on evidence. Because there is a great deal of variation among the states, there is no clear consensus when it comes to the names applied to trial courts. Some states might refer to their trial courts as superior court, whereas others refer to them as district or state courts. Many states have different levels of trial courts, with one level empowered to hear only specific types of cases and another empowered to hear others. In any event, just as we saw with federal district courts, losing parties in trial courts on the state level have the right to appeal to an appellate court.

Appellate Courts

All states have appellate courts. In many states, the layers are virtually identical to those found on the federal level, with a trial court, an intermediate court of appeals, and a state supreme court. However,

SPOT THE ISSUE!

In this section, you will review a factual scenario and then discuss the legal implications of the material presented. You should work through the factual presentation and attempt to summarize as many different significant legal issues as possible. This is an excellent way to train yourself as a legal professional in civil practice.

Marie recently opened a craft store and ordered a large amount of merchandise from a single supplier, Crafts 'R Us. When she negotiated the order, which is for more than $10,000, the supplier agreed to provide terms. Marie was authorized to receive the material after paying 10% of the total price, with the balance due within 90 days of the receipt of the material. Marie submitted a check to Crafts 'R Us for $1,000, and the check was cashed. The supplier shipped only half of the total order and is now refusing to ship the rest until Marie pays the balance of $9,000. Marie was counting on being able to sell some of the merchandise as a way to pay for the outstanding balance. Without the merchandise, she will be unable to generate enough income to pay for the rest of the order, and she has very little savings, certainly not enough to pay the balance of the order.

Marie has come to our firm. What legal issues are presented by her situation?

PRACTICE TIP

There are some cases that are an exception to cert. Death penalty cases, for example, may be appealed directly to the State and U.S. Supreme Courts without first applying for cert.

it is important to note that not all states follow this arrangement. Some have only a single layer of appellate courts. In the states with two layers of appellate courts, most refer to the first layer as the state court of appeals, which is the court in which losing parties from the trial court level appeal their cases. These courts have appellate justices who are empowered to review the issues on appeal and issue written opinions about the merits of the case. In most states, the losing party in the state court of appeals has the option to appeal to the state's highest court: the state supreme court.

State Supreme Courts

Just like the U.S. Supreme Court, all states have a court of final authority on appellate issues (see Figure 1.9). Although this court is usually referred to as the state supreme court, it may go by a different name in some states. In New York, for example, the state's highest court is referred to as superior court. State supreme courts share many similarities with the U.S. Supreme Court. For instance, these courts also have cert authority in most of their cases, which gives them the right to decide which cases they will hear and which they will not.

Federal vs. State Law

The final point we must consider in this chapter regarding the legal system in the United States is the different layers of law that may affect the proceedings in any civil case. For instance, the United States is composed of states that have their own statutory and case law binding on cases brought in state courts, but each state is also a member of the union and therefore bound by federal law. These layers often lead to conflict, especially when an action may be filed as either a state or a federal action. Which court has precedence? Where should the plaintiff file a complaint?

FIGURE 1.9
Diagram of Typical State Court System

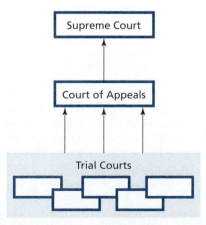

Peters

v.

Alpharetta Spa,
LLC, 915 So.2d 908,
(La. App. 1 Cir. 2005),
CARTER, C. J.

In this appeal, we review whether the trial court correctly found insufficient minimum contacts to support personal jurisdiction in Louisiana courts over the nonresident defendant. For the following reasons, we affirm.

FACTS

Mark H. Peters, M.D. (Dr. Peters) filed a lawsuit in Terrebonne Parish, Louisiana, seeking protection from "collection activity" on the part of defendant, Alpharetta Spa, L.L.C. (Alpharetta), a Georgia limited liability company in which Dr. Peters was a member prior to relocating to Terrebonne Parish. The lawsuit was filed in response to a demand letter that had been mailed by Alpharetta directed to Dr. Peters for an alleged deficiency/penalty pursuant to the terms of an Operating Agreement (the Agreement) between Dr. Peters and Alpharetta. Dr. Peters alleged that the Agreement was "not freely negotiated" and that he had grounds to dissolve the Agreement, thereby voiding any alleged deficiency/penalty amount that Alpharetta was seeking to collect from him.

Alpharetta maintains and operates a medical business used to enhance its members' plastic surgery practice. Alpharetta operates exclusively in the state of Georgia. The Agreement between the parties was negotiated and executed in the state of Georgia. During the entire time that the Agreement was in effect between the parties, Dr. Peters was a resident of the state of Georgia. He later relocated to the state of Louisiana after the Agreement was terminated. Dr. Peters currently resides and practices medicine in Terrebonne Parish.

In response to Dr. Peters' lawsuit, Alpharetta filed a declinatory exception raising the objections of lack of personal jurisdiction and improper venue. Alpharetta maintained that it had absolutely no contact with the state of Louisiana, and that therefore, no Louisiana court could exercise jurisdiction over it. Additionally, Alpharetta argued that the Agreement between the parties contained a valid and enforceable forum selection clause, designating the courts in the state of Georgia as the exclusive forum for "any dispute or matter arising under" the Agreement. After a hearing, the trial court sustained Alpharetta's exception and dismissed Dr. Peters' petition. Dr. Peters appeals, assigning one error: "the trial court erred in interpreting too narrowly the scope of Louisiana courts' specific personal jurisdiction over a party that has committed a wrongful act against a Louisiana citizen in this State." Essentially, Dr. Peters argues that the demand letter mailed by Alpharetta and received by him in the state of Louisiana constituted a "wrongful collection" activity, because it was an "improper and oppressive attempt to harass and collect" pursuant to an invalid contract, causing him an injury in this state.

LAW AND ANALYSIS

We must decide whether a nonresident defendant's mailing of a demand letter to a Louisiana domiciliary is sufficient contact with the state of Louisiana so as to exercise personal jurisdiction over the nonresident defendant. An appellate court conducts a de novo review of the legal issue of personal jurisdiction over a nonresident by a Louisiana court. However, the trial court's factual findings underlying the decision are reviewed under the manifest error standard of review. In determining whether there is personal jurisdiction, we must look to the long-arm statute of Louisiana, which provides that "a court of this state may exercise personal jurisdiction over a nonresident on any basis consistent with the constitution of this state and of the Constitution of the United States." LSA-R.S. 13:3201B. The limits of the Louisiana long-arm statute and of constitutional due process are coextensive; the sole inquiry into jurisdiction over a nonresident is whether it comports with constitutional due process requirements.

For the exercise of personal jurisdiction over a nonresident defendant to comport with constitutional due process requirements, the defendant must have purposefully established certain "minimum contacts" with the forum state such that he could reasonably anticipate being haled into court there, and the exercise of personal jurisdiction must be such that it "does not offend traditional notions of fair play and substantial justice." *International Shoe Co. v. Washington*, 326 U.S. 310, 316, 66 S.Ct. 154, 90 L.Ed. 95 (1945). Minimum contacts are established when the nonresident defendant "purposely avails itself of the privilege of conducting activities within the forum state."

A court's exercise of personal jurisdiction may be "specific" or "general." A court may exercise specific jurisdiction over a defendant when the alleged cause of action arises out of, or is related to the defendant's purposeful contacts with the forum state. A court may exercise general jurisdiction over a defendant when the defendant has engaged in "continuous and systematic contacts" with the forum, but the contacts are not necessarily related to the lawsuit.

The "purposeful availment" requirement ensures that the nonresident defendant will not be haled into a jurisdiction solely as a result of a random, fortuitous, or attenuated contact, or by the unilateral activity of another party or a third person. There has developed a two-part test in personal jurisdiction analysis. First, it must be shown that the defendant has established minimum contacts with the forum state—i.e., it has purposefully directed its activities at the residents of the forum state. Once that is shown, "a presumption arises that jurisdiction is reasonable and the burden of proof and persuasion shifts to the defendant opposing jurisdiction to present 'a compelling case that the presence of some other considerations would render jurisdiction unreasonable.'"

In this case, Dr. Peters does not argue that the trial court has general jurisdiction over Alpharetta. He does not allege any contacts by Alpharetta other than the demand letter sent to him in Louisiana. He does not allege that Alpharetta owns property in Louisiana, that any of its members reside in Louisiana, that any of its members ever traveled to Louisiana, or that it conducts any type of business in Louisiana. Alpharetta is a limited liability company with its principal place of business near Atlanta, Georgia. From the facts alleged, we do not find the level of "continuous and systematic contacts" necessary to justify the exercise of general jurisdiction. Thus, in order to justify the exercise of specific personal jurisdiction, we must consider only whether Alpharetta's purposeful contact of sending a demand letter to Dr. Peters, who was domiciled in Louisiana, gave rise to or relates to Dr. Peters' cause of action.

After a thorough review of the record, we find that Dr. Peters' cause of action against Alpharetta did not arise out of any transaction of business conducted by Alpharetta in the state of Louisiana. Alpharetta is not in the collection business. Alpharetta's medical business is, and always was, conducted solely in the state of Georgia. The demand letter was the result of Alpharetta's attempt to enforce the terms of the Agreement between it and Dr. Peters. Accordingly, the demand letter did not give rise to Dr. Peters' lawsuit. Rather, the basis of this cause of action was to determine the legal effect of the Agreement. Dr. Peters' allegations revolve around the negotiations between the parties prior to the execution of the Agreement, as well as the actual terms and provisions of the Agreement. The Agreement was negotiated and executed in the state of Georgia. Dr. Peters relocated to Louisiana after the Agreement and the relationship he had with Alpharetta were terminated. Alpharetta sent the demand letter to Dr. Peters in Louisiana simply because that is where Dr. Peters resided at the time that Alpharetta sought to enforce a provision in the Agreement. It was merely fortuitous that Dr. Peters relocated to Louisiana. By mailing the letter to Dr. Peters in Louisiana, Alpharetta never anticipated being haled into a Louisiana court to resolve a dispute arising out of the Agreement. To the contrary, both parties specifically anticipated that any dispute or matter involving the Agreement would be litigated in the state of Georgia.

We conclude that Dr. Peters' cause of action did not arise out of the mailing or receiving of the demand letter. It follows that Alpharetta cannot be said to have purposefully availed itself of the privilege of conducting activities within the state of Louisiana, such that it should have reasonably anticipated Louisiana litigation. Therefore, we find that the trial court correctly sustained Alpharetta's declinatory exception raising the objection of lack of personal jurisdiction and properly dismissed Dr. Peters' petition.

CONCLUSION

For the reasons assigned, the trial court judgment dismissing Dr. Peters' petition for lack of personal jurisdiction over the nonresident defendant/appellee, Alpharetta Spa, L.L.C., is affirmed. Costs of this appeal are assessed against plaintiff/appellant, Mark H. Peters, M.D.

AFFIRMED.

Source: From Westlaw. Used with permission of Thomson/West.

Case Questions:

1. According to the ruling in this case, how was Dr. Peters involved with Alpharetta Spa, LLC?

2. What business does Alpharetta Spa, LLC, conduct?

3. Where is Alpharetta Spa, LLC, located?

4. What is the "forum selection clause" contained in the agreement between the parties?

5. According to the court, does the demand letter create a sufficient basis for personal jurisdiction? Why or why not?

6. Did Alpharetta Spa, LLC, have sufficient minimum contacts with the state of Louisiana? Explain your answer.

7. What effect does the court ruling have on Dr. Peters's action against Alpharetta Spa, LLC?

The general rules, first promulgated in Article VI of the U.S. Constitution, establish that when there is a conflict between state and federal laws, federal law will predominate. The Supremacy Clause controls conflicts between federal and state laws, giving preference to federal actions. Throughout the United States, the interplay of federal and state laws could be represented as two systems overlaid, with the federal system on top and the state system below.

 # Eye on Ethics: Introduction to Ethics for Paralegals

Throughout this text, we will address important ethical issues for paralegals. Although attorneys have codes of ethics that paralegals must be familiar with, paralegals have their own code of ethics as well. As we go through the material in this book, we will tackle many ethical issues, from confidentiality to fee splitting. Does your state have a paralegal code of ethics? Locate a copy of it and print it. You will find that ethics is one of the most important aspects of day-to-day legal practice.

FIGURE 1.10
Complaint in a Car
Wreck Case

STATE OF EDWARDS
COUNTY OF PLACID

SUPERIOR COURT OF PLACID COUNTY

CIVIL ACTION FILE NO.: _____

Elizabeth Louise,   )

)

        Plaintiff,   )

)

        v.   )   **COMPLAINT**

)

)

Wilson Johnson,   )

)

        Defendant.   )

)

_____)

COMPLAINT

COMES NOW, the Plaintiff, Elizabeth Louise, and complaining of the Defendant alleges the following:

1. The Plaintiff is a citizen and resident of Placid County, State of Edwards.

2. The Defendant is, upon information and belief, a citizen and resident of Springfield County, Edwards.

3. On or about April 6, 2005, at approximately 12:45 A.M., the Plaintiff, Elizabeth Louise, was operating a 2004 Buick LeSabre automobile, owned by the Plaintiff and Plaintiff's husband, Von Louise, in an easterly direction on Home Street, within the City Limits of the Town of Harrisburg, County of Placid, State of Edwards.

4. At the time and location averred in paragraph number three, the Defendant was operating a 2001 Honda Civic automobile in an easterly direction on the same street as the Plaintiff.

5. It is further alleged upon information and belief that at all times relevant hereto, the Defendant owned the 2001 Honda Civic automobile being driven by the Defendant.

6. At the time and place stated above, the Plaintiff, Elizabeth Louise, had slowed and stopped her 2004 Buick LeSabre automobile in respect and in obedience to a traffic light emitting a signal compelling her to stop.

7. At the time and place stated above, the automobile operated by the Defendant did, without justification, and without warning, drive into and collide with the rear of the vehicle operated by the Plaintiff, while the Plaintiff's automobile was at a complete stop in obedience and in conformity with the traffic signal.

8. The Defendant was negligent in that he:
   a. Failed to keep reasonable and proper control of his vehicle.
   b. Failed to keep a proper lookout in his direction of travel and to operate his automobile in a safe manner.
   c. Drove his vehicle carelessly and in willful and wanton disregard of the rights and safety of others including the Plaintiff, Elizabeth Louise.

9. That as a proximate cause of the Defendant's negligence, the Plaintiff, Elizabeth Louise, suffered severe and permanent injuries in excess of $10,000.00.

WHEREFORE, the Plaintiff prays that the Court as follows:

1. That the Plaintiff, Elizabeth Louise, have and recover a judgment against the Defendant in an amount in excess of $10,000.00 for personal injuries.

2. That the Plaintiff have and recover of the Defendant a sum to be determined at trial, but in any event, no less than $10,000.00 for damage to personal property.

3. That prejudgment interest be awarded as provided by law.

4. That the costs of this action be taxed against the Defendant.

5. That all issues raised be tried before a jury.

6. For such other and further relief as the Court may deem just and proper.

This the _____ day of October, 2005.

Debra Blum
Attorney for Plaintiff
State Bar No. 00-0000

A Day in the Life: Lisa Mazzonetto

Lisa Mazzonetto has worked for a small firm for several years. Although the firm handles a large percentage of divorce and child custody cases, it also takes on other cases, including contract disputes and other claims.

"The thing I like about [our practice] is that I get to go to court a lot," she says." There is a lot of client contact in being a paralegal at a family law practice. You manage a lot of cases, and you get a lot of phone calls from upset clients. There is also a lot of paperwork. The pleadings are extensive, and then you have equitable distribution of the marital estate. That involves a lot of affidavits. Then you've got discovery. I do my best to stay on top of it all.

"I also spend a lot of time making sure that my attorney stays organized. I check the file to make sure that the most recent correspondence is there and any other communications. I also often summarize the opposing side's stand on particular issues, to help [my attorney] stay on top of any new developments.

"Clients are always nervous about going to trial. I help prepare them for trial. Based on the initial meeting, I'll set up an outline of questions that we may ask. I like to go through the questions before they testify. It helps them get a little more comfortable with testifying. People get very nervous about taking the stand. I'll take them to an empty courtroom a few days before the trial so that they can see what it's like. The hardest part for clients when they testify is staying focused on the issues in the hearing. Some of them want to go off on tangents. I find that it helps them focus to have them work on the files with us."

For Lisa Mazzonetto, a typical day involves a lot of client contact:

CLIENTS

"I'll have them go through their inventory lists and organize their files with me. I want them to be involved and not obsess about issues.

"Unfortunately, we're always dealing with domestic violence issues. A lot of our clients take out domestic violence orders to keep their husbands from hurting them.

"Sometimes you get late-night phone calls from clients who have questions about their case or sometimes just want to vent."

PUBLIC RECORDS

"That also means that I'm pulling a lot of criminal files and digging up convictions on opposing parties. I hire a lot of private investigators. They not only investigate the other party, but they sometimes act as civil process servers."

PREPARING FOR TRIAL

"We have a lot of clients who are scared about testifying in court. We work with them a lot to get them comfortable on the stand. People get nervous, and it helps to show them the courtroom and have them work on the file with you. They can review the documents, look at the pleadings; it helps them stay focused."

SPEAKING WITH OTHER ATTORNEYS

"Sometimes, I'll talk directly with opposing attorneys. They'll want to know about specific issues or want to talk over some points. It's not like the old days; there are a good amount of attorneys who will talk with a paralegal. Of course, there are some [who] won't have anything to do with you."

Real Paralegal Life: Building a Skill Set

VISITING THE COURTHOUSE

One of the most important skills you can acquire as a paralegal is the ability to navigate successfully among the various courts in your area. As you embark on your career as a paralegal, you should take time to visit the local courthouse.

The problem with going to the courthouse is that it is an intimidating place. That's why you should read through these ten tips to help you feel more assured when you visit the courthouse for the first time.

1. Realize that everybody had to walk through that door for the first time. Take a moment and realize that everyone in this place once felt anxious when they walked into the courthouse. Every one of them was intimidated by the courthouse, no matter how blasé they act now. This is as true for attorneys as it is for paralegals. Sometimes it's even worse for attorneys, because everyone expects them to know their way around.

2. Don't give in to nervousness. Part of the problem with the courthouse is that is was designed to be an intimidating place. As you pass through the front door, keep this in mind. The architecture was created with the goal of making the average citizen feel respectful and maybe even a little bit afraid. When you walk in, look like you've been there a hundred times before. Get that self-confident, slightly bored look on your face. Sometimes looking like you know what you're doing is half the battle.

3. Ask questions. When in doubt, ask questions. However, having said that, there is a trick to asking questions.
   Many people think that the first rule in asking questions is knowing what to ask. They're wrong. The real first rule in asking questions is knowing the right person to ask. Look around the courthouse. Find someone who looks sympathetic. Skip the obviously busy people. They don't have the time or the inclination to answer questions. Smile. Always smile before you ask a person a question. They will almost always smile back. Get to the point. Don't beat around the bush; fire away. Don't be afraid that it is a stupid question; hit them with both barrels.

4. Get the lay of the land. If you're nervous about where to go or what to do, get there early and see what other people do. Find a place to sit where you can pretend to read the newspaper and see what other people are doing. Then do it yourself.

5. Project confidence. You are a legal professional here to do a job. You may not know exactly where everything is, but you can find it. But you shouldn't be cocky or arrogant. That won't get you anywhere.

6. Be polite. Say "please" and "thank you." You'd be surprised how rarely people in the courthouse hear those magic words. It doesn't help to go marching in and demand things. Being nice pays off. You really do catch more flies with honey than vinegar.

7. Look the part. You should dress professionally if you want to be treated like a professional. It also gives you just a little bit more confidence.

8. Don't think you can learn it all in one hour. You can't. It's impossible. If you could pick up everything that you needed to know about the courthouse in one trip, the courthouse wouldn't be such an intimidating place. Think of your trips to the courthouse as learning sessions. Each time you go, you learn more. There are lawyers who've practiced for 20 years who still learn something new about the courthouse that they didn't know before.

9. Clean up after yourself. Put the books and microfilm and other things back where you got them. If you can't remember where you got something, ask someone. You'll score big points with court personnel if you just put things back where they belong. If the courthouse has rules preventing you from pulling your own files, follow them.

10. Let the Internet work for you. Many courthouse offices now have official Web pages. You can find out a lot of information without having to leave your office. There is plenty of information on the Web these days, and the nice thing is that you can find it 24 hours a day, 7 days a week.

If you follow these tips, you should find that the courthouse isn't as intimidating as you first thought. You might even discover that after a few trips there, you'll start feeling like a veteran. Then you can take pity on someone who has just walked through the metal detector and seems anxious and lost.

Career Prep

Contact a local law firm and interview a paralegal who works there. Ask some basic questions, such as why this person decided to become a paralegal. Then, proceed to other issues, such as the most common misconceptions about the practice of law and what things a new paralegal should know before going to work for a firm. Ask this person what he or she finds appealing about the legal practice. What are some of the things about law that the paralegal likes least, and why? What are some important skills that a paralegal can bring to a practice specializing in civil actions?

Summary

Civil law is a distinct specialty within a much broader field of legal areas. Unlike criminal law, civil law is concerned with a finding of liability and assessing damages against a party. Civil litigants must prove their cases to a preponderance of the evidence.

The authority for the American legal system derives from the U.S. Constitution. This document creates the framework of the federal and state systems and also provides basic rights for citizens. However, the legal system is also built on other forms of legal authority, such as statutes. Statutes are created by legislatures and enacted by the executive branch. Case law, in contrast, consists of the large body of written judicial opinions in cases on appeal. Common law is another form of legal authority. Common law stretches back for centuries and was originally an embodiment of judicial principles that would be applied in routine cases.

The federal court system is organized into three levels. At the bottom are the trial courts, called federal district courts. Appeals from these courts go to the U.S. Circuit Courts of Appeal. There are 13 courts of appeal scattered across the nation. A litigant may appeal from the Circuit Court of Appeals to the United States Supreme Court, which is the final authority on appeal.

Key Terms

Plaintiff, 2	Statute, 7
Defendant, 2	Ordinance, 8
Caption, 2	Case law, 8
Style, 2	Common law, 9
Complaint, 3	Jurisdiction, 9
Petition, 3	Subject matter jurisdiction, 9
Answer, 3	General jurisdiction, 10
Burden of proof, 4	Limited jurisdiction, 10
Preponderance of the evidence, 4	Personal jurisdiction, 10
Clear and convincing evidence, 5	Forum, 10
Beyond a reasonable doubt, 5	Domicile, 10
Liability, 5	In rem jurisdiction, 10
Guilty, 6	Certiorari, 12
Damages, 6	

Review Questions

1. Compare and contrast the different burdens of proof in civil and criminal cases.
2. What is the relationship of the United States Constitution to statutes and case law?
3. What is common law?
4. What is case law?
5. How do statutes compare to ordinances?
6. What is the top court in the United States federal court system?
7. What responsibilities does the top court in the federal system have?
8. Name the trial courts in the federal court system.
9. What duties do federal trial courts have?

10. How many circuit courts of appeal are there in the United States?

11. Create a diagram showing the organization of your state-level court system. How are these courts organized? How do appellate courts factor into your diagram?

12. Describe how civil litigation is different from criminal law.

13. What is jurisdiction?

14. Compare and contrast personal and subject matter jurisdiction.

15. What is certiorari?

16. Why are ethical issues so important for paralegals?

17. Create a chart showing the differences between civil and criminal cases.

18. How are the monetary damages paid to a party in a civil case different than the fine that a criminal defendant must pay as part of his or her sentence? How are they alike?

19. Explain why it is important to understand the organization and function of a courthouse.

20. What is the significance of the *Peters v. Alpharetta Spa, LLC,* case in regard to a discussion of personal jurisdiction?

Discussion Question

1. We have seen that there are several layers of courts on both the state and federal levels. When the country was originally created, there were very few courts. What does the breadth and complexity of the American court system say about our nation? Are we a nation of laws or a nation of lawyers?

Exercises: Skill Builders

For the purposes of this assignment, review the following factual scenario and then determine, on the basis of material in this chapter, whether this is a civil case or a criminal case.

Juan is driving home one day, and while he is proceeding through a green light, a driver from the intersecting lane of traffic runs the red light and plows into Juan's car. Juan is severely injured. When police and emergency workers arrive on the scene, the other driver appears to be driving under the influence of alcohol. Is this potentially a civil case or a criminal case?

Portfolio Assignment

Each chapter of this book contains a portfolio assignment. The reason for these assignments is to help you start building a complete portfolio of information and samples of your work that will help you not only get a job but also perform your day-to-day duties.

Portfolio Assignment 1-1: Prepare a complete list of all of the courts in your area, including federal, state, traffic, small claims, and any other courts with which you might come into contact. List the judges who work in those courts, the names of support personnel, and addresses, including Web sites, if any. Put this information into a file in your portfolio labeled "Important Contacts."

Portfolio Assignment 1-2: Locate your state's statutes that govern the jurisdiction of the various courts. Pinpoint the jurisdictional requirements of each. Which courts have subject matter jurisdiction to hear cases such as divorce, child custody, felony charges, adoption, name changes, cases involving $1,000 or less in controverted amounts, and actions involving claims for $20,000 or more?

Portfolio Assignment 1-3: In a double-spaced, three-page paper, describe the organization of federal and state courts in your state. For this assignment, you must research the structure and function of both state and federal courts in your state and provide an explanation of the function of the courts. You should also discuss how these various courts interact with one another.

Vocabulary Builders

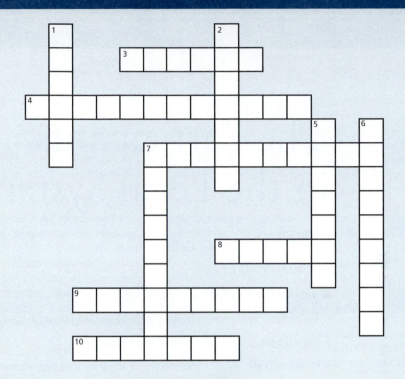

ACROSS

3 A verdict only available in criminal cases where the jury determines that the defendant is responsible for committing a crime.

4 The power of a court to make rulings.

7 The power of an appellate court to decide which cases it will hear.

8 Also known as caption; the heading or title used in all legal pleadings.

9 A law passed by a local government, such as a town council or city government.

10 Also know as style; the heading or title used in all legal pleadings.

DOWN

1 The location of the court; a court that possesses both personal and subject matter jurisdiction over the case.

2 A law that is voted on by the legislature branch of and enacted by the executive branch.

5 Monetary payments assessed against a party who has been deemed liable to another party in a civil case.

6 A jury's determination that one party is responsible for injuries to another party; the basis for an award of damages.

7 Also known as a petition, it is the pleading filed by the plaintiff and served on the defendant that sets out the plaintiff's factual allegations that show the defendant is responsible for the plaintiff's injuries.

Chapter 2

The Participants in the Legal System

CHAPTER OBJECTIVES

The student will be able to:

- Explain the function of judges in civil litigation.

- Describe the day-to-day functions of paralegals who specialize in civil practice.

- Explain how a person becomes an attorney.

- Demonstrate an understanding of how various legal professionals work together.

- Explain the billing procedures used at most law firms.

- Describe the various courthouse personnel and their duties.

In this chapter, we examine the various participants involved in civil litigation, including judges, lawyers, clients, and paralegals. It is important to understand not only the role played by each of these participants but also how they all work together.

JUDGES

judge
Trier of law.

We have all seen **judges** portrayed on television and in movies. Whereas fictional judges often break the rules, real-life judges have vast authority and exercise it in vital ways in our legal system. Judges preside in both civil and criminal cases, but we will focus on the role played by judges in civil cases. At the most basic level, judges are responsible for the orderly administration of justice in our legal system. They are given powers to compel parties and witnesses to act in a reasonable way. Judges also ensure that cases do not get bogged down and move steadily toward resolution.

Judges are required by court rules and their own ethical codes to be neutral and objective in all suits. They are not permitted to influence the jury to vote in a particular way or to control the events in a trial such that one side is guaranteed to win. A judge who engages in such behavior would receive a reprimand from the judicial ethics board and face the prospect of having a ruling overturned by a higher court.

Judges are bound by a strict code of ethical conduct that prohibits them from engaging in many outside activities. They cannot, for instance, own stock in companies that have cases pending before them. They cannot be members of any group that knowingly discriminates against members of society. The judicial code for judges not only prohibits actions that may or may not be illegal but also any activity that has even the appearance of impropriety. Under that strict code of conduct, a judge must avoid any conduct that could cause a potential ethical concern. As a

FIGURE 2.1

Excerpt from Code of Judicial Conduct

Source: Code of Judicial Conduct, Texas.

CANON 2

Avoiding Impropriety and the Appearance of Impropriety in All of the Judge's Activities

A. A judge shall comply with the law and should act at all times in a manner that promotes public confidence in the integrity and impartiality of the judiciary.
B. A judge shall not allow any relationship to influence judicial conduct or judgment. A judge shall not lend the prestige of judicial office to advance the private interests of the judge or others; nor shall a judge convey or permit others to convey the impression that they are in a special position to influence the judge. A judge shall not testify voluntarily as a character witness.
C. A judge shall not knowingly hold membership in any organization that practices discrimination prohibited by law.

result, most judges are vigilant in their personal and financial relationships to uphold the ethical standards of their profession. See Figure 2.1.

A judge is a civil servant. Judges work for and are paid by local, state, or federal governments. In most situations, judges are attorneys. In fact, many work as attorneys for several years before being appointed to a judicial position. However, there are some judicial positions that do not require any legal training and very little higher education. Magistrate and other low-level judicial positions are held by individuals who have a bachelor's degree or less. These individuals are responsible for issuing warrants and hearing small claims. Higher-level judicial positions such as superior court judges are filled by individuals with law degrees.

As you can see in Figure 2.2, judges are usually paid well but not as well as successful attorneys. Given the earnings discrepancy between judges and attorneys, a person would be tempted to ask why an attorney would give up a lucrative practice to become a judge. There are several reasons: Judges often feel a strong commitment to the community and want to contribute. Some attorneys have grown tired of the grind of a legal practice and seek the relative security and predictable work schedule that most judges enjoy. Finally, the position of judge is still widely respected. The respect and service to the community often offset the financial losses associated with taking the position.

Becoming a Judge

In most situations, judges are attorneys before they ever put on a black robe. Most states require that their judicial positions be filled by attorneys licensed to practice in that state. In addition to membership in the state bar, most attorneys who become judges have significant experience practicing law and bring that practical knowledge to bear in their role as judge. States use many different methods to select their judges. For instance, a state may use any of the following methods to choose an individual to fill a vacant judicial position:

- Judicial appointment
- Election
- Judicial selection committee

Judicial Appointments

When a new judicial position is created or a current position is vacated, some states allow the state's governor to appoint an individual to fill it. The governor also may use an executive committee to assist in the judicial selection. In either event, the governor may choose a qualified individual to fill the judicial position.

CYBER TRIP

Concord Law School info.concordlawschool.edu
U.S. Department of Labor—offers an overview of the process of becoming a judge http://www.bls.gov/oco/ocos272.htm
National Association of Legal Assistants—offers an overview of paralegal certification http://www.nala.org/cert.htm
National Association of Legal Professionals http://www.nals.org/certification/professionalparalegal/index.html

FIGURE 2.2

Judicial Pay

Source: Bureau of Labor Statistics, Occupational Outlook Handbook, 2004–2005 edition.

Judges, magistrate judges, and magistrates had median annual earnings of $94,070 in 2002. The middle 50 percent earned between $44,970 and $120,390.

RESEARCH THIS!

Does your state elect or appoint judges? How does the process work? Research your state statutes and determine exactly how judges are selected to serve in various courts. Locate recent cases from your state's highest appellate courts that clearly define the practice of law and delineate the roles of paralegals and attorneys. Are these rules clear? Do they make clear distinctions between the two roles?

LEGAL RESEARCH MAXIM

Whenever you conduct any type of legal research, it is absolutely essential to learn the proper method to cite the cases and statutes you locate. Any good book on legal research will tell you how to go about doing this, but two of the most influential works about citations are *The Bluebook* and the *ALWD Citation Manual.* Both works provide substantial information about the correct ways to cite cases and statutes on both state and federal levels.

A citation is a shorthand method to tell others where to locate the case or statute to which you are referring. In a basic example, suppose that you wish to direct another person to the *Smith v. Jones* case.

Because there may be more than one *Smith v. Jones* case, you must direct your reader to the correct one. Legal citation is the way to do that. For instance, your citation to a particular *Smith* case could look like this:

  Smith v. Jones, 123 Pl. App. 456 (2005).

This citation tells the reader that the *Smith* case can be found in Volume 123 of the Placid State Court of Appeals Reporter, page 456. Of course, there is no state of Placid. Instead, a citation from your state would insert the appropriate abbreviation for your state's appellate courts.

Election

Many states elect judges in the same way that they elect other officials. A person who meets the minimum requirements would file to run for the post of judge, and voters would have the opportunity to choose among several contestants. Some states not only elect local judges but also justices for the court of appeals and state supreme court. In many states, these judicial elections are as partisan, and sometimes as bitterly contested, as any political election.

Judicial Selection Committee

Another method used by some states to choose a new judge is a judicial selection committee. This committee, working directly for either the executive branch or the state supreme court, recommends candidates to fill specific judicial openings. The methods outlined here are not exclusive of one another; some states use all three methods, depending on the judicial position to be filled.

The Role of the Judge

Judges are responsible for the orderly administration of justice. To that end, they control the various phases of a civil lawsuit and can force the parties to abide by the rules of civil procedure.

Judges as Referees

One of the primary duties of a judge essentially is to act as referee between the litigating parties. A judge can enforce rulings, control the behavior of the parties, and even dismiss claims, all to maintain the dignity of the proceedings. A judge's determination about issues in a case remains in effect until the case is finished. A party is usually not permitted to appeal a judge's ruling in the middle of the proceedings but instead may do so only when the case has been resolved. We will discuss appellate issues in general, and the exceptions to this rule in particular, in Chapter 13, Appeals.

FIGURE 2.3
Motions
Source: O.C.G.A. § 9-11-7
(Georgia).

> (1) An application to the court for an order shall be by motion which, unless made during a hearing or trial, shall be made in writing, shall state with particularity the grounds therefor, and shall set forth the relief or order sought. The requirement of writing is fulfilled if the motion is stated in a written notice of the hearing of the motion.

Judicial Rulings

A judge not only controls the proceedings but also makes rulings on the law, motions, and evidence during the lawsuit. A judge interprets the law, and the judge's decision on legal points remains in effect until a higher court changes that decision. In addition to ruling on points of law, the judge is also responsible for ruling on motions and evidence.

Motions

motion
A procedural request or application presented by the attorney in court.

A **motion** is a request by a party for a court to take some action (see Figure 2.3). Motions come in a variety of forms. When a judge grants a motion, he or she agrees to the request. When the judge denies a motion, he or she disagrees with the request. We devote an entire chapter to a discussion of motions (Chapter 9).

Evidence

A judge not only rules on motions but also on evidentiary matters. We will discuss evidence in Chapter 7. If a judge rules that evidence is admissible, it means that the jury will be allowed to see and hear it. A ruling of inadmissibility means that the jury will not be allowed to consider that evidence. Judges must determine not only if evidence is relevant to the proceedings but also if the evidence will cause prejudice to one side.

Judges as Fact Finders

There are times when the judge has additional duties. For instance, when the parties request a bench trial, the judge not only considers the legal issues but also acts as the jury. In a bench trial, there is no jury present, and the judge must act as fact finder. In such a situation, the judge will enter a verdict at the conclusion of the evidence that serves the same function that a jury's verdict would. The verdict is the fact finder's determination about which side has presented the more believable version of the case.

ATTORNEYS

Attorneys are essential to the American legal system. They are responsible for representing clients and safeguarding their interests. Attorneys act not only as advocates but also as counselors, delegates, and guardians. The process of becoming an attorney is demanding, and the profession offers immense challenges and rewards. We begin our discussion of the important role that attorneys play by first addressing the question of how a person becomes an attorney.

Becoming an Attorney

Prior to the 20th century, becoming an attorney was a relatively straightforward proposition. A person, almost always a man, would work as an apprentice for an established attorney. After working with the attorney for several years, the apprentice would qualify for admission into the state bar. In some cases, the members of the bar would question the applicant. In other situations, the fact that a senior attorney vouched for the applicant would be enough to admit the person into the profession. Once admitted, the new attorney would remain a member of the bar for the rest of his life, unless stripped of his license for committing an offense. Stripping a lawyer of his or her license is still referred to as **disbarment**.

disbarment
Temporary suspension or permanent revocation of an individual's license to practice law.

In the early 20th century, many state bars began changing their admittance policies. Law schools, which have existed in the United States for more than two centuries, solidified their hold on the profession by requiring any applicant for the state bar to have graduated from an approved school. In addition to graduation from an approved law school, an applicant must also have

SURF'S UP!

In previous years, one of the few ways to locate information about attorneys was through the Martindate-Hubbell legal directory. This multivolume publication included short biographies of all attorneys who had contributed, listed their office information, and provided details about their specializations. Although Martindale-Hubbell still exists, there are now many more sources for learning information about attorneys, including:

Attorney Locate	www.attorneylocate.com
Attorney Pages	www.attorneypages.com

Lawyers.com	www.lawyers.com
Martindale-Hubble	www.martindale.com

In addition to these sites, many state bars now list members on their main Web pages. These listings include some biographical information as well as the areas of practice for the attorneys. This information is important for not only individuals who are seeking legal advice but also those who are looking for potential employers.

earned a bachelor's degree, had his or her background investigated, and have successfully passed a written examination.

Ethical Codes

Each state bar maintains a strict ethical code for attorneys licensed in that state. These ethical codes are often closely modeled on the American Bar Association's (ABA) Model Rules of Professional Conduct. Although the ABA promulgates rules and makes many suggestions about ethical practices, the enforcement of ethical rules falls to the individual states' bar associations or state courts. The ABA does not have the power or the responsibility to police individual attorneys. Instead, the ABA is a national organization that lobbies for attorney rights, promotes greater respect for the law, and has a role in accrediting paralegal educational programs.

Attorney Ethical Rules are usually found in state statutes and the bylaws for individual state bar associations. The ethics rules govern all aspects of an attorney's professional life, from admittance to the bar to actions that will result in an attorney being suspended or disbarred. Although state bars maintain records about admitted members, most bars do not actually sanction attorneys. They create rules and investigate claims, but the authority to sanction attorneys normally falls to the state's highest court (usually called the state supreme court). When an attorney violates an ethical rule, there are several possible sanctions that can be imposed against him or her. The sanctions run from the lowest form (private reprimand) to the ultimate bar sanction (disbarment):

- Private reprimand
- Public reprimand
- Temporary suspension of license
- Disbarment
- Criminal prosecution

Private Reprimand

private reprimand
The minimum censure for an attorney who commits an ethical violation; the attorney is informed privately about a potential violation, but no official entry is made.

Attorneys who commit minor ethical violations are subject to a **private reprimand**. This sanction, the lowest form of punishment for an ethics violation, is usually imposed when an attorney has neglected some aspect of a case but not to an extent that it seriously injures a client's legal rights. A private reprimand often comes in the form of a letter from the state bar to the offending attorney discussing the violation and strongly urging the attorney to refrain from such activity in the future. Private reprimands are not published, and the only people with knowledge of the reprimand are the offending attorney and the investigating arm of the state bar.

Public Reprimand

public reprimand
A published censure of an attorney for an ethical violation.

A **public reprimand** is a more serious ethical sanction than a private reprimand, and details of the attorney's misdeeds are usually published in the state's appellate reporter. Public reprimands are considered the midpoint between a private reprimand and the much more serious sanction of temporary suspension. They are imposed when an attorney has received a private reprimand yet continues to engage in questionable conduct.

Temporary Suspension

temporary suspension
A punishment for an ethical violation; an attorney is temporarily prohibited from practicing law or representing clients.

An attorney who receives a **temporary suspension** is barred from the practice of law for a specified period. This period could be as short as a few days to several years, depending on the seriousness of the offense. A temporary suspension is authorized when the attorney has committed a serious breach in handling a case for a client, has neglected to pursue a legal claim, or has not been diligent in handling client affairs.

Disbarment

An attorney who has committed a serious ethical violation or been convicted of a major crime can be disbarred. Disbarment strips the attorney of his or her license to practice law. An attorney who is disbarred in one jurisdiction is usually disbarred in all other jurisdictions as well. When an attorney is disbarred, he or she cannot practice law in any form. Disbarment is a form of professional death sentence. A disbarred attorney can sometimes petition to have his or her license reinstated, but many disbarments are permanent. An attorney who has been convicted of a felony, stolen client funds, or abandoned a client in the midst of a legal action is eligible for disbarment.

Criminal Prosecution

An ethical violation can also rise to the level of criminal activity. When an attorney embezzles client funds, for example, it is both an ethical violation and a crime. In such a situation, the offending attorney faces state bar sanctions, as well as a fine or prison sentence if convicted of a crime.

Common Ethical Violations

Although there are many different types of ethical violations, attorneys who commit ethical violations can be classified into one of three very broad categories:

1. The attorney has financial trouble.
2. The attorney has a drug or alcohol problem.
3. The attorney is suffering from a personal or mental health problem. In such a situation, an attorney might easily be tempted to commit one of the most common forms of ethical violation: commingling funds.

Commingling Funds

commingling
A term for mixing a client's funds with the attorney's personal funds without permission; an ethical violation.

When an attorney engages in **commingling** funds, he or she takes money from a client trust account and uses it as the attorney's personal funds. An attorney who transfers proceeds from a client's settlement or trust account into the attorney's personal account, even with the intention of paying the money back, has committed the offense of commingling funds and is liable for disbarment, as well as criminal prosecution. Commingling is a form of embezzlement and one of the most serious ethical violations. The end result of commingling is the loss of the attorney's license to practice law and criminal prosecution for embezzlement.

Lack of Diligence

Some attorneys are sanctioned for their failure to follow through on important client matters. An attorney who agrees to represent a client has the duty of diligence toward that client. The requirement of diligence means that the attorney must follow through on the client's problems and take all legal actions to bring the case to a successful resolution. An attorney is required by state ethics rules to represent the interests of the client zealously, and when the attorney fails to do so, he or she can be cited by the bar for lack of diligence.

Law School Education

These days, all attorneys must graduate from a law school before they will be admitted into the state bar. When a person graduates from law school, he or she receives a *juris doctor* degree. This degree, somewhere between a bachelor's degree and a Ph.D., entitles a person to sit for the state bar examination and practice law. Although there are night law schools around the country, and at least one online program, most law schools follow a format that has remained virtually unchanged for centuries. Law school lasts for three years, on a full-time basis, and is extremely rigorous. Even when the student graduates, the work isn't over. Simply graduating is no longer enough to qualify a person for the practice of law. Now, a graduate must also take and receive a passing score on the state bar examination.

The Bar Examination

bar examination
A test administered to graduates from approved law schools that determines the applicant's knowledge of the law and suitability to practice in the state.

After the hard work that it takes to enter and complete law school, one might think that a **bar examination** would be redundant. However, all states require graduates to take an examination before they will be admitted into the profession. The bar examination consists of multiple choice and essay questions and can last as long as three days. Studying for and taking the bar examination can be an enormously stressful event. After all, if the applicant fails the bar exam, he or she cannot practice law, though the applicant is free to retake the exam in the future. Some very prominent attorneys did not pass the bar examination on their first attempt, yet went on to very successful careers after passing it on the second or even third attempt.

Joining the State Bar

state bar
The organization that licenses and oversees the practice of law and the conduct of attorneys in the state. An attorney must be a member of the state bar before he or she will be allowed to practice in that state.

Once the law student has taken and passed the bar examination, he or she is admitted into the **state bar**. This milestone is a joyous day for individuals who have literally spent years and tens of thousands of dollars to achieve the goal of becoming an attorney. New members are sworn in and receive a printed license to practice law. From that point on, the person is now an attorney, qualified to give legal advice, represent clients in trials, and collect fees for the services provided.

Specialization

In an age in which every profession seems to have specialized, it might seem odd to realize that attorneys do not graduate with specialties in particular areas of law. A new member of the bar is free to practice any type of law that appeals to him or her. Unlike medical doctors, they do not receive any specialized education in civil or criminal law. Instead, they learn their trade as they go. However, once they are licensed, all attorneys have the obligation of continuing their education by attending mandatory continuing legal education courses that cover topics as varied as ethics, litigation, trial practice, law office management, and the proper handling and disposition of client funds.

Many state bars also offer attorneys the chance to receive certification as specialists in certain areas of the law. States such as Ohio and Georgia, for example, offer specialist certificates to attorneys in the areas of personal injury or medical malpractice. An attorney receives such recognition by successfully completing courses in these areas and handling a minimum number of these types of cases. Once certified, an attorney is permitted to add this information to business cards and advertisements.

Civil Attorneys

Even though law school students do not specialize in particular areas of law as they proceed through law school, most graduates have a firm idea of the area of law that appeals to them most. For some, it will be probate or tax law. For others, trial work will have a strong pull. Others may be drawn to education or writing. A law degree opens up many opportunities in both private and government work. Many new attorneys go to work for private law firms and specialize in civil cases.

A civil attorney is an attorney who routinely represents one side or another in a lawsuit. There are an amazing variety of civil suits, from personal injury cases to divorce actions, and an attorney could easily spend his or her entire career handling just one type of case. Personal injury cases, such as suits arising from car wrecks, are some of the most common types of cases in the United States and offer plenty of business for law firms. Most attorneys involved in personal injury cases usually specialize as plaintiffs' or defendants' attorneys.

FIGURE 2.4
Civil Trial Cases and Verdicts in Large Counties, 2001

Source: Bureau of Justice Statistics, United States Department of Justice.

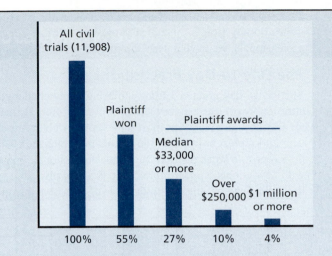

- During 2001, juries decided almost 75% of the 12,000 tort, contract, and real property trials in the nation's 75 largest counties. Judges adjudicated the remaining 24%. Tort cases (93%) were more likely than contract cases (43%) to be disposed of by jury trial.

- The 11,908 civil trials disposed of in 2001 represent a 47% decline from the 22,451 civil trials in these counties in 1992.

- In jury trials, the median award decreased from $65,000 in 1992 to $37,000 in 2001 in these counties.

- Two-thirds of disposed trials in 2001 involved tort claims, and about one-third involved contractual issues.

- Overall, plaintiffs won in 55% of trials. Plaintiffs won more often in bench trials (65%) than in jury trials (53%) and in

- contract trials (65%) more than in tort (52%) or real properly trials (38%).

- An estimated $4 billion in compensatory and punitive damages were awarded to plaintiff winners in civil trials. Juries awarded $3.9 billion to plaintiff winners, while judges awarded $368 million. The median total award for plaintiff winners in tort trials was $27,000 and in contract trials $45,000.

- Punitive damages, estimated at $1.2 billion, were awarded to 6% of plaintiff winners in trials. The median punitive damage award was $50,000.

- Plaintiffs prevailed in about one-fourth (27%) of medical malpractice trials. Half of the 311 plaintiffs who successfully litigated a medical malpractice claim won at least $422,000, and in nearly one-third of these cases, the award was $1 million or more.

PRACTICE TIP

Most law schools have the following minimum requirements:

- Applicant must have a bachelor's degree.

- Applicant must have achieved a specific minimum score on the LSAT (Law School Admission Test).

- Applicant must have a minimum grade point average in his or her undergraduate courses.

- In some cases, the law school may require a sample of the applicant's writing ability and a recommendation from a selection committee.

Plaintiffs' Attorneys

Attorneys who routinely represent individuals who have been injured in personal injury cases are usually referred to as plaintiffs' attorneys, because plaintiff is the name for the party who initiates a suit. As we will see in the next chapter, a classification as a plaintiffs' attorney brings with it special issues. These attorneys are compensated in specific ways and have particular concerns about how they will prove their cases against defendants.

Defendants' Attorneys

On the other side of a civil suit are the defendants' attorneys. These lawyers routinely represent people who have been named in civil actions. They are compensated differently than plaintiffs' attorneys, and their focus in a civil case is also different. Because they represent people who have been sued, they work hard to prove that the plaintiff has failed to prove all allegations against their client.

Legal Ethics

No matter in what area of law an attorney eventually practices, whether as a prosecutor, government representative, plaintiffs' attorney, probate attorney, or any of hundreds of other positions occupied by lawyers, all members of the bar must abide by a code of ethics. This code governs all their professional activities and can be used as the basis to strip the attorney of his or her license if the attorney violates an ethical provision. Because ethics is such an important topic for all legal professionals, we devote a section of every chapter to ethical issues.

The Day-to-Day Practice of Law

The day-to-day practice of law can bring many challenges and also many rewards. Although an attorney's work can be very stressful, it also offers financial rewards. It is certainly not true that all attorneys are rich, but most make comfortable salaries. Some earn millions of dollars each year and represent high-profile clients in publicized cases. However, the vast majority of attorneys report to work just like any other professional. Their daily activities might include meeting with new clients, appearing in court, drafting pleadings, writing letters, and conducting depositions. We examine the day-to-day role of attorneys in civil cases throughout this book.

PARALEGALS

paralegal
A person qualified to assist an attorney, under direct supervision, in all substantive legal matters with the exception of appearing in court and rendering legal advice.

Paralegals play an absolutely vital role in the American legal system. Although their status may not be as clearly defined as that of attorneys, even this shortcoming is gradually being rectified. Many states have begun certifying individuals as paralegals, or legal assistants, and this certification process is helping further define a profession without which the legal system would come to a crashing halt. Paralegals act as assistants to attorneys at every level of the legal system and work for everything from one-person local firms to huge multinational corporations. What is even more surprising than the broad diversity of the roles played by paralegals is that they are actually finally receiving the recognition that they deserve. This certainly was not always the case.

Historical Development of the Paralegal Profession

Attorneys have always had assistants. Whether referring to them as clerks, legal secretaries, or some other name, attorneys have always needed others to help them in their practices. An attorney with no support staff can actually accomplish very little. However, attorneys have always jealously guarded their roles as legal professionals and traditionally been unwilling to recognize the validity of any other class of legal workers as fellow professionals. That mindset has been very slow to change.

In the mid 1970s, those who had always worked as legal assistants, and sometimes as the attorneys' right arms, finally began to organize themselves. Local paralegal associations gave rise to national movements and the formation of groups such as the National Association of Legal Assistants and the National Federation of Paralegal Associations. These groups promoted professional standards and better pay for what had always been a high-stress, intensively trained profession. See Figure 2.5 for statistics about the employment of paralegals.

Daily Activities of Paralegals

It is not an overstatement to say that paralegals are involved in every level of the legal practice. They are the bedrock of the profession, and their day-to-day activities make the practice of law possible. Depending on the type of firm for which they work, they might interview witnesses,

 PRACTICE TIP

Because more and more paralegals are being named in civil actions by disgruntled former clients, it is vitally important for a paralegal to stay away from any allegation of unauthorized practice of law. There are two methods to avoid an allegation of overstepping professional boundaries. One is to always introduce yourself as a paralegal or legal assistant. In addition to this practice, you should always inform individuals who seek legal advice that you are not authorized to give it. By maintaining these practices, you may avoid becoming involved as a named party in a civil action.

FIGURE 2.5
Bureau of Labor Statistics: Paralegals
Source: Bureau of Labor Statistics, Occupational Outlook Handbook, 2004–2005.

Paralegals and legal assistants held about 200,000 jobs in 2002. Private law firms employed 7 out of 10 paralegals and legal assistants; most of the remainder worked for corporate legal departments and various levels of government. Within the federal government, the U.S. Department of Justice is the largest employer, followed by the Social Security Administration and the U.S. Department of Treasury. A small number of paralegals own their own businesses and work as freelance legal assistants, contracting their services to attorneys or corporate legal departments.

Paralegals and legal assistants are projected to grow faster than the average for all occupations through 2012. Some employment growth stems from law firms and other employers with legal staffs increasingly hiring paralegals to lower the cost and increase the availability and efficiency of legal services.

draft legal documents, or meet with clients. Paralegals may also work as trial specialists, helping an attorney try a case. Their daily activities can present constant challenges. They can find themselves interviewing clients, obtaining police reports, drafting motions, and preparing discovery materials, while also fielding telephone calls and making sure that each file is properly documented. In fact, paralegal duties are so extensive that we discuss them at length in every chapter of this text.

Paralegals not only play an important role in private firms but also in government agencies. Prosecution offices across the country now use paralegals to draft indictments, work with witnesses, and track criminal convictions. Government agencies have begun to see the advantages of employing someone who is trained in the law to assist attorneys with cases. As you can see in Figure 2.6, there are many different areas where paralegals are employed.

Licensing and Certifying Paralegals

In recent years, many states have either passed or considered passing legislation that would regulate the paralegal profession in the same way that other professionals are licensed. In the states that have passed these bills, paralegal licensing boards have been created. These boards are responsible for licensing paralegals, creating minimum standards for admission, and setting up educational requirements for new paralegals. Eventually, all states will regulate paralegals in the same way that nurses, dentists, and lawyers are currently monitored.

Paralegals and legal assistants have existed for decades, but it was only in the 1970s that they formally organized themselves under the title of paralegals. National paralegal organizations trace their origins to this period. Of the many national paralegal organizations, two stand out: the National Federation of Paralegal Associations (NFPA) and the National Association of Legal Assistants (NALA). Each group has created its own model rules of ethical conduct for paralegals.

 PRACTICE TIP

What is the difference between a "paralegal" and a "legal assistant?"

There has been a split about what to call the legal professionals who help attorneys almost from the time that the first assistant was hired. Is the person who works hand-in-glove with the attorney, helping draft pleadings, dealing with clients, and performing an essential service, a "paralegal" or a "legal assistant"? Actually, there is no clear answer. Some groups are attracted to the term legal assistant because they feel the name is a more accurate description of what this profession actually does. Others cling to the term paralegal because of its historical antecedents. Some states, such as California, have actually quantified the difference between paralegals and legal assistants, but most have not. Throughout this text, we refer to the profession as paralegals, for the sake of clarity and for the simple reason that the term has existed longer, but this choice does not mean we are ignoring the strong argument that can be made to label these professionals "legal assistants."

COMMUNICATION TIP

One of the most common complaints by attorneys is that their support staff cannot write well. Although it may be true that the American education system does not emphasize written communication skills as much now as it has in the past, it is also true that attorneys expect high standards. For an attorney, reading and writing is a daily practice, and the ability to communicate effectively, and correctly, is an absolutely essential skill. Therefore, anyone contemplating a career in the legal profession must be aware of and use proper grammar and spelling. Some practices that will help you maintain good written communication skills include:

- Always use the grammar and spell check feature on your word processing software.
- Always double-check your writing before submitting it to anyone.
- Never use a word unless you can define it.
- Use a guide for tricky questions.

On the last point, many writers keep a copy of Strunk and White's *The Elements of Style* close at hand. This small book has had a huge impact on American writing since its publication in the early 1900s.

The NFPA has maintained an ethics board since 1995. It posts ethical opinions on its Web site so that other paralegals can obtain guidance on specific issues.

National paralegal associations resemble the ABA in that they have created model ethical rules but cannot actually impose them on a state level. Many states have codified paralegal ethical codes in the same way that they have codified attorney ethical standards. However, there are some important differences in the professional standing of paralegals. One of these important differences revolves around the issue of certification versus licensure.

Licensure is an action by the state or federal government that serves as a prerequisite to practicing a profession. Attorneys are licensed. They operate under state statutes, and their licenses can be revoked by an action of the state bar. Certification, in contrast, usually refers to standards set by a private group.

Although several states are actively considering the licensing of paralegals, most have no plans to do so. Paralegals in these states operate in a gray area: They are not attorneys, but they work closely with them. They engage in legal activities on a daily basis, but they have no state license that clearly states their qualifications. Faced with this dilemma, many paralegals opt for certification from one of the national paralegal associations. The NALA offers a certification program that entitles paralegals to use the credential "Certified Legal Assistant" when they successfully complete the intensive testing.

CLIENTS

Although attorneys and paralegals are absolutely essential to the justice system, without clients, there would be no need for either. When a person hires an attorney, it is often because that person has been unsuccessful in attempting to resolve the problem him- or herself. Most people are reluctant to speak with attorneys and would much prefer to avoid conflict and controversy. However, there are times when hiring an attorney is inevitable. When clients first appear at an

FIGURE 2.6
Median Annual Earnings in the Industries Employing the Largest Numbers of Paralegals in 2002

Source: Bureau of Labor Statistics, Occupational Outlook Handbook, 2004–2005.

Federal government	$53,770
Legal services	36,780
Local government	36,030
State government	34,750

SPOT THE ISSUE!

Carl works as a freelance paralegal in a state that has a statute providing that the unauthorized (or unlicensed) practice of law is a misdemeanor. One day, an individual approaches Carl and asks his advice about how best to proceed in filing for a divorce. Carl informs the man that he is a paralegal, not an attorney, and then proceeds to prepare the complaint for divorce, arranges to have the complaint served on the man's wife, prepares a motion to accompany the complaint, prepares interrogatories to be answered by the man's wife, and tells the man about the possible dispositions of his marital property. However, Carl refuses to sign any of the paperwork. Is Carl practicing law without a license?

attorney's office, they are often confused and anxious. They turn to paralegals not only for information but also for reassurance. Throughout this text, we will draw a distinction between the unauthorized practice of law, such as giving legal advice, and the very real need to help and reassure clients about their cases. Clients need good legal representation. When the case is resolved, the client will be satisfied with the result and be able to move on with his or her life. Clients also pay the bills that make it possible for attorneys and paralegals to work as legal professionals.

COURTHOUSE PERSONNEL

So far, our discussions about the legal field have been tied to the participants. However, there is an entire group of professionals who are indirectly involved in lawsuits and without whom the legal system could not function. These are the agencies and departments responsible for maintaining public records and administering the day-to-day functions of legal professionals. We group all of these professionals together under the slightly misleading name of "courthouse personnel." However, you should keep in mind that not all of these people actually work in the courthouse. Many work at other locations. It is absolutely essential for anyone considering a career as a legal professional to understand what courthouse personnel actually do.

It is important to understand that there is a great deal of variation from state to state in the names used to describe various public offices. There is no standard system in place across the United States to describe the office that houses records of civil and criminal actions, hears probate matters, or keeps records concerning real estate transactions. Because of this variation in names, you must familiarize yourself with your own local system, learning not only what the various departments are called but also what each contains.

Clerk of Court

clerk
A government official responsible for maintaining public records.

Clerks are responsible for storing and maintaining all records of court proceedings. Clerks' offices are open to the public. Clerks and deputy clerks keep track of every case filed in the courthouse and store documents relating to all cases. Their role is central to the orderly administration of justice, because it is the clerks that keep track of the payment of fines, the assessment of sentences, and the organization of the mountain of paperwork generated by even the most routine cases. Deputy clerks are often found in the courtroom during calendar calls and hearings, because they are charged with the duty of keeping a record of the disposition of every case.

The clerk's office maintains records about all civil and criminal cases in the county. Most clerks' offices are computerized, and by simply entering a person's last name, you can find out whether that person has been sued, divorced, or convicted of a crime. The clerk's office is a good place to start if you are investigating anyone or to locate information about other pending or closed cases.

Registrar of Deeds

Also called the registrar's office, or the land office, the deed room is where all records of real estate transactions are stored. Here, you can find out how much a person paid for his or her house and get a complete picture of what real estate this person owns. However, the deed room has a wealth of other information. Uniform Commercial Code (UCC) filings can tell you whether a

Tegman

v.

Accident & Medical Investigations, Inc.
(see 107 Wash.App. 868, 30 P.3d 8
(Wash. App. Div. 1, 2001))
BECKER, A.C.J.

When a paralegal performs legal services with [the] knowledge that there is no supervising attorney responsible for the case, the paralegal will be held to an attorney's standard of care. Attorneys have a duty to keep their clients informed about material developments in their cases. The trial court found that Deloris Mullen, a paralegal, and Lorinda Noble, an attorney, while employed by a non-lawyer who represented accident victims, breached this duty and caused harm to the plaintiffs when they failed to advise them of the risk involved with allowing a non-lawyer to settle their cases. We affirm the judgments.

The trial court's findings of fact present the following account of the events surrounding this dispute. Between 1989 and 1991, plaintiffs Maria Tegman, Linda Leszynski, and Daina Calixto were each injured in separate and unrelated automobile accidents. After their accidents, each plaintiff retained G. Richard McClellan and Accident & Medical Investigations, Inc. (AMI) for legal counsel and assistance in handling their personal injury claims. McClellan and AMI purported to represent each plaintiff in seeking compensation from insurance companies for their injuries. Each plaintiff signed a contingency fee agreement with AMI, believing that McClellan was an attorney and AMI a law firm. McClellan has never been an attorney in any jurisdiction.

McClellan and AMI employed Camille Jescavage and Lorinda Noble, both licensed attorneys. Jescavage and Noble learned that McClellan entered into contingency fee agreements with AMI's clients and that McClellan was not an attorney. They settled a number of cases for AMI, and learned that McClellan processed settlements of AMI cases through his own bank account. Noble resigned from AMI in May 1991, after working there approximately six months.

In July 1991, McClellan hired Deloris Mullen as a paralegal. Mullen considered Jescavage to be her supervising attorney though Jescavage provided little supervision. Jescavage resigned from AMI in the first week of September 1991. McClellan told Mullen that her new supervising attorney would be James Bailey. Mullen did not immediately contact Bailey to confirm that he was her supervising attorney. He later told her he was not.

While at AMI, Mullen worked on approximately 50–60 cases, including those of plaintiffs Tegman, Leszynski[,] and Calixto. Mullen was aware of some of McClellan's questionable practices and knew that there were substantial improprieties involved with his operation. Mullen stopped working at AMI on December 6, 1991, when the situation became personally intolerable to her and she obtained direct knowledge that she was without a supervising attorney. When she left, she did not advise any of the plaintiffs about the problems at AMI. After Mullen left, McClellan settled each plaintiff's case for various amounts without their knowledge or consent, and deposited the funds in his general account by forging their names on the settlement checks.

In 1993, Calixto, Leszynski, and Tegman each individually sued McClellan, AMI, Mullen[,] and Jescavage. Tegman also sued Noble. Their complaints sought damages on various theories. The cases were consolidated. In the interim, McClellan pleaded guilty to mail fraud in United States District Court in 1997 and was sentenced to two years imprisonment. Also, this court affirmed a judgment by the same trial court in another case where McClellan settled a client's case without authorization and stole the proceeds. That judgment apportioned 20-percent fault to attorney James Bailey who, like Noble and Jescavage, had associated himself with AMI and failed to warn his clients of McClellan's improprieties.

In the present matter, the court entered summary judgment against McClellan and AMI on the issue of liability. After a six-day trial, the court held Mullen, Noble, and Jescavage liable for negligence and legal negligence, and awarded damages. Only Mullen and Noble appeal[ed]. Their appeals have been consolidated.

PARALEGAL NEGLIGENCE

Mullen, a paralegal, contends the court erred in finding her negligent. To establish the elements of an action for negligence, a plaintiff must show: (1) the existence of a duty owed, (2) breach of that duty, (3) a resulting injury, and (4) a proximate cause between the breach and the injury.

Non-attorneys who attempt to practice law will be held to the same standards of competence demanded of attorneys and will be liable for negligence if these standards are not met.

The "practice of law" clearly does not just mean appearing in court. In a larger sense, it includes "legal advice and counsel, and the preparation of legal instruments and contracts by which legal rights are secured."

Mullen contends that her status as a paralegal precludes a finding that she was engaged in the practice of law. She argues that a paralegal is, by definition, someone who works under the supervision of an attorney, and that it is necessarily the attorney, not the paralegal, who is practicing law and owes a duty to the clients. Her argument assumes that she had a supervising attorney. The trial court's determination that Mullen was negligent was dependent on the court's finding that Mullen knew, or should have known, that she did not have a supervising attorney over a period of several months while she was at AMI. "Had Mullen been properly supervised by an attorney at all times during her employment with AMI, plaintiffs presumably would have no case against her. Rather, her supervising attorney would be responsible for any alleged wrongdoing on her part."

We agree with the trial court's observation. The label "paralegal" is not in itself a shield from liability. A factual evaluation is necessary to distinguish a paralegal who is working under an attorney's supervision from one who is actually practicing law. A finding that a paralegal is practicing law will not be supported merely by evidence of infrequent contact with the supervising attorney. As long as the paralegal does in fact have a supervising attorney who is responsible for the case, any deficiency in the quality of the supervision or in the quality of the paralegal's work goes to the attorney's negligence, not the paralegal's. In this case, Mullen testified that she believed James Bailey was her supervising attorney after Jescavage left. The court found Mullen was not justified in that belief. Mullen assigns error to this finding, but the evidence supports it. Mullen testified that she had started to distrust McClellan before he informed her that Bailey would be her supervising attorney. Mullen also testified that she did not contact Bailey to confirm that he was supervising her. Bailey testified at a deposition that he did not share Mullen's clients and she did not consult him regarding any of her ongoing cases. He also said that one of the only conversations he remembers having with Mullen with respect to AMI is one where he told her that he was not her supervising attorney after she raised the issue with him. This testimony amply supports the trial court's finding that Mullen was unjustified in her belief that Bailey was her supervising attorney.

"It is the nature and character of the service performed which governs whether given activities constitute the practice of law, not the nature or status of the person performing the services". Hunt, 75 Wash. App. at 802, 880 P.2d 96. Mullen's status as a paralegal did not preclude the trial court from concluding that Mullen had engaged in the practice of law.

Contrary to Mullen's argument, such a conclusion does not require evidence that the paralegal called herself an attorney, entered appearances, or charged fees. Mullen testified that she negotiated settlements on behalf of the plaintiffs. She sent a letter rejecting, without Tegman's knowledge, a settlement offer made to Tegman. She continued to send out demand and representation letters after Jescavage left AMI. Letters written by Mullen before Jescavage's departure identify Mullen as a paralegal after her signature, whereas letters she wrote after Jescavage's departure lacked such identification. Even after Mullen discovered, in late November 1991, that Bailey was not her supervising attorney, she wrote letters identifying "this office" as representing the plaintiffs, neglecting to mention that she was a paralegal and that no attorney was responsible for the case. This evidence substantially supports the finding that Mullen engaged in the practice of law.

Mullen, because she is not an attorney, could not have attorney–client relationships. Nevertheless, as Bowers demonstrates, a layperson can logically be held to the standard of care of an attorney in a negligence action. The duty arises from the attempt to engage in the practice of law rather than from the professional status of the defendant. The trial court, covering all bases, held Mullen liable both for negligence and legal negligence.

While the "legal negligence" label may have been incorrect, any such error is immaterial because the negligence theory produces the same result and, as the trial court observed, for practical purposes the allegations are the same.

Accordingly, we conclude the trial court did not err in following Bowers and holding Mullen to the duty of an attorney. The duty of care owed by an attorney is that degree of care, skill, diligence, and knowledge commonly possessed and exercised by a reasonable, careful, and prudent lawyer in the practice of law in Washington.

Mullen challenges, as unsupported by the evidence, the trial court's key finding as to the duties that Mullen owed and breached. The court found that the standard of care owed by an attorney, and therefore also by Mullen, required her to notify the plaintiffs of: (1) the serious problems concerning the accessibility of their files to persons who had no right to see them, (2) the fact that client settlements were not processed through an attorney's trust account, but rather McClellan's own account, (3) the fact that McClellan and AMI, as non-lawyers, had no right to enter into contingent fee agreements with clients and receive contingent fees, (4) the fact that McClellan was, in fact, engaged in the unlawful practice of law, and that, generally, (5) the clients of McClellan and AMI were at substantial risk of financial harm as a result of their association with AMI. Mullen breached her duty to her clients in all of these particulars.

Although Mullen was a paralegal, she is held to an attorney's standard of care because she worked on the plaintiffs' cases during a period of several months when she had no supervising attorney. The fact that she did not render legal advice directly does not excuse her; in fact, her failure to advise the plaintiffs of the improper arrangements at AMI is the very omission that breached her duty. Under these circumstances it is not unjust to hold her accountable as a legal cause of the plaintiffs' injuries.

As all the elements of negligence have been established, we affirm the judgment against Mullen.

The judgments are affirmed.

Source: From Westlaw. Used with permission of Thomson/West.

Case Questions:

1. What facts brought the plaintiffs to seek assistance from the paralegals in this case?

2. Whom did paralegal Mullen consider to be her supervising attorney?

3. What other questionable or illegal practices were carried out by McClellan?

4. According to the court, what standard is used for paralegals who attempt to practice law?

5. What argument does Mullen offer against the court's position?

6. Is it a complete shield against civil liability for a person to refer to him- or herself as a "paralegal"?

person has financed a car and for how much. Does a defendant claim that he has no assets and therefore cannot pay a judgment? The UCC filings can show you that he recently purchased a boat or a recreational vehicle. Many deed rooms also maintain a record called Vital Statistics, or Birth and Death records. These records show the names of a person's children, if they were born in that county. They also show whether a person has been the beneficiary of a will. Attorneys

FIGURE 2.7
Contract of
Representation

STATE OF EDWARDS
COUNTY OF PLACID

EMPLOYMENT CONTRACT

THIS AGREEMENT, made and entered into this the _____ day of _____, 2005, by and between _____, hereinafter referred to as "Client"; and ALLISON ATTORNEY, P.A., hereinafter referred to as "Attorneys";

IN WITNESS OF THE FOLLOWING:

WHEREAS, Client has a claim against _____ arising out of an incident which occurred on or about the _____ day of _____, _____, and desires to employ the Attorneys on a contingent fee basis;

NOW, THEREFORE, the Attorneys agree to represent, through trial court, as attorney for the Client and the Client agrees to pay the Attorneys Thirty-Three and One-Third (33 1/3%) per cent of the amount recovered or which may be recovered in this matter, whether by compromise or settlement at any time before suit is instituted or by compromise, settlement or judgment after suit is instituted, plus expenses incurred in the preparation of the case. Both parties agree that neither party will compromise or settle this action without consent of the other party.

This the _____ day of _____, 2005.

_____
Attorney
ALLISON ATTORNEY, P.A.

often check these records—in what are called "asset searches"—before bringing a lawsuit to make sure that they can recover something from the other side. A defendant who has no assets cannot pay a judgment and may not be worth the trouble of suing.

Probate Court

probate court
The court empowered to settle estates for those individuals who have died with or without a will.

The **probate court** is responsible for administering the estates of people who have died in the county. If a person has had his or her estate probated in that county, you can locate a record of the will in the probate court, as well as the names of his or her beneficiaries and a list of what each beneficiary received. In many states, the probate court also keeps records of marriages.

Tax Office

The tax office is required to keep extensive records about real estate, and all of this information is available to the public. Many people never think about going to the tax office for information, but it has more raw data than any other office. Of course, the tax office keeps records about whether a person has paid his or her property taxes, but there also is a great deal of other data here. If you want to find a person's address, and his or her name doesn't appear in the telephone book, it's a simple matter to enter the name in the tax office database and find out where the person lives. Tax offices even keep information about the basic floor plan of a house and list how many bedrooms and bathrooms the house has. In some areas, the tax office has a digital photograph of every structure in the county, and you can view this photo simply by clicking on it. The tax office also maintains information about sales, acreage, and assessed value.

Eye on Ethics

FREELANCE PARALEGALS

The role of the paralegal in the United States has been slowly changing. The traditional arrangement, in which a paralegal works full-time for an attorney, is slowly giving way to independent contractors: freelance paralegals who hire themselves out to attorneys on a case-by-case basis. Freelance paralegals are part of a new movement of paralegals who take greater control of their own destinies.

Although becoming a freelance paralegal has many attractions, there are some downsides. For one thing, there is the issue of the unauthorized

practice of law. Freelance paralegals, especially those in more conservative parts of the country, have felt pressure from attorneys who do not like competition.

In some states, such as California, where paralegals are regulated and distinctions are made between document preparers and legal assistants, the rule about unauthorized practice of law remains the same. When it comes to giving legal advice, you just can't.

Legal document assistants are not permitted to practice law. They can help people complete legal forms, but they cannot give legal advice.

A Day in the Life: Darlene Burgess

Darlene Burgess has worked as a paralegal since she was 16 years old. She began her legal career by working with her mother, also a paralegal. "The attorney we worked for was blind," she explained, "and he often had me read the law to him." In addition to her reading duties, Burgess slowly worked her way up from answering the phones to handling increasingly more difficult and detailed activities at the firm.

These days, she works for the tax office, collecting delinquent real property taxes. In addition to working for the tax office, Burgess is also a certified legal assistant. Following the receipt of her bachelor's degree from a local college, she began teaching part-time in a paralegal program. She uses her legal education every day, not only in locating delinquent tax payers but also in training future paralegals.

During an average day, Burgess may visit several different parts of the courthouse. Although there is a wealth of information available in the tax office where she works, she may also visit the clerk's office, the deed room, and other departments. Here is a summary of the information that she can locate about another individual:

- Full legal name.
- Whether the person has a criminal record.
- Whether the person has ever been sued or brought a suit.
- The basic floor plan of the person's home.
- Maps of all of the person's real estate holdings.
- Whether the person has ever received property through probate.
- Information about the person's cars, boats, trailers, or other financed items.

This information is helpful not only to individuals who work for the tax office but also any legal professional who wishes to gather information about witnesses or simply wants to find out if a potential party to a civil suit has enough property or assets to pay a judgment.

Real Paralegal Life: Building a Skill Set

KEEPING TRACK OF YOUR TIME

Whether you are working for a plaintiff's firm or a defense firm, it is important for you to keep track of your billable hours. As we will see in a subsequent chapter, plaintiffs' firms are generally paid only when the case settles. Because the amount of payment does not depend on the hours billed, why would it be important to keep track of the hours you spent working on a particular case? The

(Continued)

(Continued)

simple answer is that by keeping track of your hours, you have a better idea of where you are spending a majority of your time and whether your activities ultimately benefit the firm. You may find, for example, that most of your time is spent dealing with clients on the telephone. Keeping track of your activities and the amount of time you spend on those activities will give you a better idea of how to streamline your workday and eliminate some nonproductive periods. This streamlining will help you become a better paralegal and thus even more indispensable to the firm.

BILLABLE HOURS AT DEFENSE FIRMS

When a paralegal works for a defense firm, keeping track of billable hours is often the only way to ensure that the firm is paid for its services. Defense firms are not paid on the basis of the ultimate settlement amount. Instead, most defense firms bill their clients with an hourly charge. In such a situation, the attorneys working at the firm will want to make sure that they bill for every possible activity. Some firms do this by requiring you to keep track of your activities and assigning not only how much time you spent on these particular activities but for whom the activity was conducted. For instance, you may have spent 30 minutes writing a letter for the *Joe Doe vs. Sue Doe* case. Most firms bill their clients on the basis of one-tenth of an hour. One-tenth of an hour equates to 6 minutes. Therefore, if you spend half an hour working on a letter, your time would appear as .5 hours. Defense firms spend a great deal of time and energy making sure that all activities at the firm are billed to the appropriate client.

 Career Prep

Visit your local courthouse and locate the various departments. Prepare a list showing the following:

- The name of a specific department, such as the tax office, land office, and so forth.
- The name of the person who heads this department.
- The phone number for this department.
- A contact person within the department.
- A summary of the public records stored there.

This list will come in handy later, when you begin your practice, to help you quickly and accurately locate pertinent information.

Summary

There are many participants in the American legal system. Judges are responsible for the administration of justice, maintaining order, and ruling on legal issues that arise in a court action. Judges act as impartial and neutral third parties in trials. They are employed by the government, and though they generally receive salaries that are less than those of prominent attorneys, a judgeship offers security and lighter workloads, as well as prestige in the community. Attorneys are also an important part of the American legal system. These days, a person becomes an attorney by attending law school and successfully passing the state bar examination. Once a person has been admitted to the state bar, he or she is entitled to practice any type of law. Most attorneys specialize in particular areas of law, such as civil litigation practice. Paralegals are legal professionals who work closely with attorneys. Paralegals carry out many of the daily activities in a legal practice, from drafting pleadings to conducting telephone conference calls to interacting with clients, to name just a few. Several states have recently passed laws to certify or license paralegals, in the same way that nurses and other professions are regulated. Other important participants in the American legal system include courthouse personnel, such as the clerk of court's office, which is responsible for maintaining public records of all pending cases; the land office or deed office, which stores records pertaining to real estate transactions; the probate office, which is responsible for administering wills and estates; and the tax office, which keeps extensive records on both personal and real property.

Key Terms

Judge, 22
Motion, 25
Disbarment, 25
Private reprimand, 26
Public reprimand, 26
Temporary suspension, 27

Commingling, 27
Bar examination, 28
State bar, 28
Paralegal, 30
Clerk, 33
Probate court, 36

Review Questions

1. What are some of the activities judges perform in civil cases?
2. What are some of the selection processes used in various states to appoint individuals to serve as judges?
3. What are some of the ethical guidelines that judges must follow?
4. What is a motion?
5. What are some considerations that judges must take into account when ruling on evidence?
6. How does a person become an attorney?
7. What is disbarment?
8. How long does a typical, full-time law school curriculum take?
9. What is the bar examination?
10. What is the difference between plaintiffs' attorneys and defendants' attorneys?
11. Why is it important for a paralegal to know and understand an attorney's code of ethics?
12. When did paralegals first begin to organize themselves on a national level?
13. In 2002, how many paralegals were there nationwide?
14. What are some of the daily activities of paralegals?
15. Explain the paralegal licensing and certification initiatives that have been passed in several states.
16. What is the function of the clerk of court?
17. What is the function of the deed office?
18. What kind of information can you learn at the tax office?
19. Explain the holding in this chapter's significant case as it applies to paralegals.

Discussion Questions

1. What are some of the arguments for and against state licensure of paralegals?
2. Based on the case provided in this chapter, what are some ways that you could avoid an allegation that you are practicing law without a license?
3. Are the restrictions governing paralegals a way to protect society from individuals who do not understand the legal implications of their actions or a way for attorneys to maintain a monopoly on the practice of law?
4. What are the ethical guidelines for paralegals and attorneys?
5. What is the attorney licensing and disciplinary process for your state?

Exercises: Skill Builders

Review the case provided in this chapter and research the question of the unauthorized practice of law. Prepare a checklist showing actions that are and are not permissible in your state by paralegals. For instance, may a paralegal prepare legal pleadings, child custody materials, settlement brochures, and so forth?

Portfolio Assignment

Portfolio Assignment 2-1: Most firms that bill clients do so in tenths of an hour. The basic premise behind billing is that you list, down to the tenths of an hour, exactly how much time you spent doing any particular task. Here is an example from a billing statement.

File No.	Activity	Amount	Entry
101-1231	Telephone call	.1	Confirmed witness for case

Breaking this entry down, we see that the first item is the file number assigned for this particular case and the entity that will be billed for this activity. The activity is a telephone call. The length of time for the telephone call is .1 hour. Because an hour is 60 minutes and computers like everything to be in decimals, law firms break down an hour into tenths, with one-tenth equal to 6 minutes. Most firms bill 6 minutes as the absolute minimum that it takes to do anything. When you create an itemized billing, your end product may look something like this:

File No. 101-1231
Activity: Researched legal issues in contributory negligence, especially concerning possible federal claim.
2.7 hours

Activity: Researched medical literature on possibility of recurrent amnesia for client injured in car wreck.
3.4 hours

Activity: Prepared brief to trial court on evidentiary issue of subsequent remedial measures for repairs to stairs completed after the client was injured.
1.4 hours

File No. 101-1231   Total billed: 7.5 hours

Portfolio Assignment 2-2: Research and discuss, in a three-page paper, the development of the paralegal profession from the 1970s to the certification and licensure movements of the early 2000s.

Vocabulary Builders

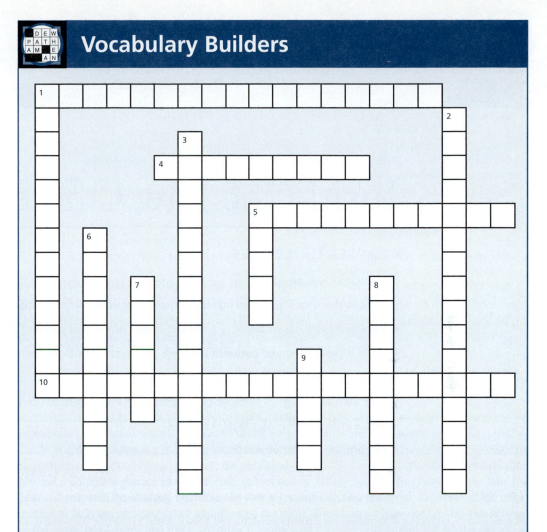

ACROSS

1 A private letter to an attorney advising of possible ethics violations.

4 A legal professional who handles many aspects of legal practice but is not authorized to give legal advice. Also know as a legal assistant.

5 Combining funds from different sources into one, such as using a client's money as the attorney's personal funds.

10 A sanction that prevents an attorney from practicing law for a specified period, usually because of a serious ethics violation.

DOWN

1 The court empowered to settle estates for those individuals who have died with or without a will.

2 A published notice concerning an attorney's ethical violation.

3 A test administered to graduates from approved law schools that determines the applicant's knowledge of the law and suitability to practice in the state.

5 A government official responsible for maintaining public records.

6 When an attorney's right to practice law is rescinded.

7 A request by a party to a judge.

8 The organization that licenses and oversees the practice of law and the conduct of attorneys in the state. An attorney must be a member of the state bar before he or she will be allowed to practice in that state.

9 A person either appointed or elected to serve as the final arbiter for legal questions in a court of law.

Chapter 3

Inside the Law Office

CHAPTER OBJECTIVES

The student will be able to:

- Explain the issues surrounding the formation of an attorney partnership.
- Discuss the clauses of a typical partnership agreement for running a law firm.
- Define the differences between partners and associate attorneys.
- Explain the role of the paralegal in a civil firm.
- Compare and contrast the role of the paralegal with other positions.
- Discuss the position of a legal secretary.
- Explain the role of other support staff in a law firm.
- Define the business models that a law firm may use to run its day-to-day business.
- Discuss the ethical implications of running a law firm.
- Explain the prohibition against "fee splitting."

This chapter examines the personnel and typical issues that arise in a private law firm. Although law is a profession that stretches back to the ancient Romans, it is also a modern business. Like any other business, it must make money to meet its financial obligations. In this chapter, we examine the internal organization of a civil law firm, not only from a business perspective—though that is vitally important—but also to show the roles played by various personnel in the office.

ORGANIZATION OF THE LAW OFFICE

We will assume for the purposes of this discussion that the firm we describe in this section exclusively handles civil litigation matters. There are many firms that limit themselves to civil matters, ranging from divorce to contract disputes. However, many other law firms are generalists and take on additional matters, including criminal matters, probate, and real estate issues. We will ignore the specialized issues raised by these other matters and concentrate exclusively on civil cases. This area is broad enough to encompass a huge variety of lawsuits and will also serve as a method to introduce various members of a typical law office and the actions they carry out on a daily basis.

In general, it should come as no surprise that an average law firm consists of lawyers and other support staff. There is only so much that a single attorney can do on a daily basis, and having support staff is essential if a lawyer wishes to expand his or her practice to a size that will generate substantial income. Within this general parameter of attorneys and support staff, there are numerous subcategories of specialized professions, including associate attorneys, legal secretaries, paralegals, clerks, private investigators, legal nurse consultants, and others.

Partners

partnership
Business enterprise owned by more than one person, entered into for profit.

Because the practice of law is both a noble profession and a business, the internal organization of a law office reflects both the hierarchy imposed on the legal field and the practical considerations of running a business for profit. The traditional organizational model for a law office is a **partnership**. The general definition of a partnership is a business run for the benefit or two or more individuals. A partnership provides distinct advantages that outweigh the prospects of a sole proprietorship. Business **partners** can pool their resources and share profits and losses. In its simplest form, a law partnership consists of two or more attorneys who share profits and losses.

partners
Attorneys who own the law firm and split the profits and losses.

Managing Partner

managing partner
A partner who has the additional responsibilities of handling policies, procedures, and personnel issues for the business.

Depending on the size of the firm, the partners may choose one of their number to serve as a **managing partner**. This person would have the responsibility of hiring and firing personnel, setting policies, and handling the large amount of administrative work, ranging from client billing to employee handbooks, that arises in the day-to-day practice of law. Although many law firms rely on a partner for these functions, just as many delegate these activities to an office manager, also known as a law office administrator. This position is normally filled by a non-lawyer who works closely with the partners to implement their policies and ensure the smooth operation of the office.

Splitting Profits and Losses from the Business

When an attorney is in a partnership with other attorneys, he or she pools the income from clients and other matters in a general fund that is used to pay financial obligations, from office rent to employee salaries. The remainder is then split evenly among the partners. Of course, if there are no profits after paying the firm's bills, then there is no income for a partner. This is a distinct possibility for a new firm with few or no clients and no source of income. Later, the opposite situation may prevail. For an established firm, the profits can be substantial, and the partners are each entitled to a share. Successful civil firms can generate huge incomes for the attorney-partners. Like any business, however, poor business decisions can hurt profits or even result in the firm going out of business or the dissolution of the partnership.

unlimited liability
A finding that a business owner's personal assets may be used to satisfy a judgment against the business.

Sharing profits and losses is a basic component of the legal definition of a partnership, and though this business model offers several distinct advantages over a single attorney acting alone, it also has inherent limitations. For one thing, one attorney cannot make unilateral decisions about the firm's business. All partners must consult with one another about decisions such as what clients the firm should take on, which additional employees should be hired (and whether some should be fired), and the myriad other details that go into running a business. Other disadvantages of a partnership include the concept of **unlimited liability**. Should the firm be sued (such as in a legal malpractice action), both the firm's assets and the individual partners' possessions could be used to satisfy the judgment. This is one of the biggest disadvantages of a law partnership: The attorneys use their personal resources to run the profession but risk losing them because of a business problem. This shortcoming is one reason law partnerships have morphed over the years into different business models, including limited liability companies and professional corporations, discussed later in this chapter. It also explains why attorneys seek out malpractice insurance to help defray the costs of any judgment.

Partnership Agreements

partnership agreement
The contract between the partners that creates duties, establishes responsibilities, and details benefits of the attorneys involved in the partnership.

A **partnership agreement** sets out the duties, responsibilities, and rights that attorney-partners gain from membership in the firm. In other businesses, there may be positions such as "silent partners" or inactive partners; such designations are usually not a feature of an attorney partnership. In large firms, there may be positions such as managing partners, but few distinctions exist beyond that. When an attorney becomes a partner in a law firm, he or she is generally entitled to a full and equal share of all profits. This is one reason so many attorneys who are employed by law firms want so desperately to be invited to become a partner.

The partnership agreement contains all of the provisions that govern how, when, and who may become a partner. Unlike other businesses, attorney partnerships have practical limitations. For instance, most states have provisions barring non-attorneys from occupying a partnership position in a law firm (though some allow non-attorneys to occupy other managerial positions in the firm). Interestingly enough, there is usually no provision that the partnership agreement must be in writing. Even among attorneys who routinely encourage their business clients to put their partnership agreements in writing, it is surprising to learn how many attorneys have no such written agreement with their own partners.

Provisions of the Partnership Agreement

Among the more important features of any partnership agreement are the details about the division of profits and the assessment of losses. However, a partnership agreement may contain many other provisions, including:

- Term of the partnership.
- Property rights of individual partners.
- Client lists.
- Dissolution of partnership.

Terms of the Partnership. Laws provide that partnerships can be formed to operate for a specified period of time. Although this is a perfectly acceptable provision, it is usually not a provision found in attorney partnership agreements. The exception is a partnership formed for the express purpose of carrying out a particular case. Once the case is concluded, the partnership dissolves.

Property Rights of the Individual Partners. Many partnership agreements provide not only for the division of profits and losses but also the rights of the partners to the personal property owned by the partnership. This property includes the desks, chairs, computers, printers, and other equipment needed for the day-to-day business of running a firm. The partnership agreement might include a provision specifying exactly how these articles will be divided by the attorneys in the event that the partnership is dissolved and whether the attorneys have the power to use any of the firm's property as collateral for loans.

Client Lists. Clients are the lifeblood of a law firm, and rights to those clients, commonly referred to as the *client list,* can be the most negotiated part of any partnership agreement. Many attorneys bring existing clients to a newly formed firm, and they will want to retain those clients in the event that the firm is dissolved. There are also provisions about who should keep those clients retained after the firm's establishment.

Dissolution of the Partnership. Finally, a partnership agreement will contain provisions detailing how the partnership can be dissolved. Dissolution is more complicated than a decision to simply split the partnership. Who will pay the firm's financial obligations? Which attorneys, if any, will remain on the lease's premises and which will leave? If the partnership has taken on business loans, how will these be resolved among the attorneys? As you can see, the issues involved in dissolving an attorney partnership can become very complicated, especially when you consider the issue of which attorneys will retain which support personnel.

Hiring Personnel

Once the decision to form an attorney partnership has been made and dispositions about purchasing equipment and leasing an office have been addressed, the next question involves hiring support personnel. These positions include:

- Associate attorneys
- Paralegals
- Legal secretaries
- Other support staff

associate attorney
An attorney who is an employee of an attorney partnership.

Associate Attorneys

An **associate attorney** is an employee of the firm, not a partner. As a result, the associate attorney has no say in the business dealings of the firm, has no authority to negotiate on behalf of the firm, and does not share in the profits. However, an associate attorney is also not obligated to pay any of the firm's debts. Associate attorneys are paid a salary, though many firms have provisions that provide for a base salary plus a percentage of profits from new clients that the associate brings to the firm. The associate attorney is usually someone who has recently graduated from law school and is learning his or her trade on the job. An associate's salary is not in the same realm as that received by a partner. In a successful firm, the associate's salary may be a fraction of the partner's income. Associates also work long hours and are expected to bill a minimum number of hours each year or bring in a minimum number of new clients each quarter. One might wonder why an attorney would accept a position as an associate, given the workload and the fact that the associate does not share in the firm's profits. The answer is simple: Most associates hope to become a partner. A successful associate will, one day, be invited to join the firm as a partner and then enjoy the fruits of all of his or her labors on behalf of the firm. Of course, an associate might just as easily be fired and replaced by another associate. This element of uncertainty contributes to a general sense of stress for associates.

Paralegals

paralegal
A person qualified to assist an attorney, under direct supervision, in all substantive legal matters with the exception of appearing in court and rendering legal advice.

It is not an overstatement to say that a **paralegal** is vital to the practice of law. Intimately involved in every aspect of a legal practice, paralegals can mean the difference between a good legal practice and a great one. They work on every phase of a case, from client intake to appeals, and must have a solid understanding of every stage of litigation, as well as of the more practical and often mundane matters, such as follow-up client telephone calls and proper billing practices.

The Day-to-Day Activities of Paralegals. This entire book is devoted to setting out the day-to-day activities of paralegals in civil practice, so we only touch on the fundamentals here. Paralegals may be present at the very first interview with a new client and take notes on the client's potential legal problems. The paralegal may also work with that new client to ferret out additional information and create documents to assist with those claims. In addition to client intake, paralegals play a central role in drafting motions, issuing subpoenas, reviewing correspondence, conducting legal research, filing documents at the courthouse, arranging depositions, preparing settlement brochures, and billing clients, to name just a few duties. We will discuss all of these topics and many others throughout this text. Before we can discuss the many activities carried out by paralegals though, we must address the concepts of licensure and certification.

licensure
The requirement of governmental approval before a person can practice a specific profession.

Licensure and Certification. **Licensure** is the process of requiring governmental approval of an individual before he or she is allowed to practice a profession. Doctors, lawyers, and many other professionals are required to possess a license, issued by the state, before they are allowed to practice. As we have already seen, the process for an attorney to become licensed involves graduation from a law school, a background investigation, and the successful completion of the state bar examination. It might seem odd then to consider that a process so much a part of an attorney's professional life is virtually nonexistent when it comes to paralegals. As of this writing, no state requires licensure of a paralegal before that person can work with an attorney. In fact, as you can see from Figure 3.1, the vast majority of states have no regulatory control over paralegals at all. In these states, the paralegal works under the direct supervision of the attorney, who still bears the full brunt of all legal responsibility for that work. However, that situation has begun to change. For instance, in Figure 3.1, you can also see that several states have enacted or have pending legislation that creates a voluntary certification program for paralegals.

 PRACTICE TIP

Whether you work as a paralegal in a small, medium, or large firm, it is important to review the office procedure manual to make sure that you stay in compliance with the firm's policies about client confidentiality, correspondence, billing, and the many other issues that arise in the day-to-day practice of law. Unfortunately, not all offices have such a manual, and the procedures may be ill defined. In such a situation, you may earn great esteem by suggesting that you help create an office procedure manual. You will also make yourself that much more invaluable to the firm by doing so.

FIGURE 3.1
Summary of Paralegal Certification Across the United States

State	Voluntary Certification	Mandatory Licensure	Neither Certified nor Licensed[1]
Alabama			X
Alaska			X
Arizona	Legal document preparers		
Arkansas			X
California	Paralegals & Legal document preparers		
Colorado			X
Connecticut			X
Delaware	X		
Florida	X		
Georgia			X
Hawaii			X
Idaho			X
Illinois			X
Indiana	("Registered paralegal")		
Iowa			X
Kansas			X
Kentucky	X		
Louisiana	X		
Maine			X
Maryland			X
Massachusetts			X
Michigan			X
Minnesota			X
Mississippi			X
Missouri			X
Montana			X
Nebraska			X
Nevada			X
New Hampshire			X
New Jersey			X
New Mexico			X
New York			X
North Carolina	X		
North Dakota			X
Ohio			X (Voluntary certification pending)
Oklahoma			X
Oregon			X
Pennsylvania			X
Rhode Island			X
South Carolina			X
South Dakota			X
Tennessee			X
Texas	X (6 different specialty areas)		
Utah			X
Vermont			X
Virginia			X
Washington	(pending)		
West Virginia			X
Wisconsin	(pending)		
Wyoming			X

[1]In these states, paralegals or legal assistants are considered to be working under the authority and direct supervision of attorneys who remain responsible for all legal work.

certification
The recognition of the attainment of a degree of academic and practical knowledge by a professional.

Certification. The biggest difference between **certification** and licensure, at least as these issues are defined for paralegals, concerns the mandatory nature of the proceeding. In states such as North Carolina, Delaware, Texas, and Louisiana, a person may register with a state agency and receive a designation of certified paralegal. Usually, this designation comes at the end of a registration process that requires graduation from an approved paralegal program and a minimum number of hours on the job, as well as continuing legal education requirements. Given the fact that certification in these states is voluntary, why would a paralegal even bother to go through the process? Even more startling, why do statistics show that in states where voluntary certification procedures have been set in place, applications have skyrocketed?

There are several possible answers. For one, paralegals have been organizing for several decades and are now beginning to exert some pressure on the legal field to receive the recognition they have long deserved. Certification is one way to address that issue. Paralegals may also wish to receive the personal recognition and satisfaction that state certification brings. Of course, there are also monetary issues to consider. A certified paralegal would be justified in demanding a higher salary than a noncertified paralegal. Finally, some paralegals may see certification as the first step down a long road toward licensure and believe that obtaining certification may give them a head start or even a possible waiver when the licensure process is finally instituted. Regardless of the reasons, there is slow but steady pressure building across the United States to recognize the critical role played by paralegals in the day-to-day practice of law.

unauthorized practice of law
Practicing law without proper authorization to do so.

Paralegal Ethics. An important component of any licensure or certification scheme is the implementation of a continuing education program that focuses on ethics. Even in states without any programs to recognize paralegals, ethics remains an extremely important topic. Ethical concerns point out the interdependence of attorneys and paralegals. Attorneys need paralegals to assist them with the practice of law, but the attorney is ultimately responsible for any legal malfeasance. Paralegals in nearly all states have no regulatory body that can revoke their license to practice as a legal professional when they violate ethical rules, but their unethical actions can have dire consequences for the attorneys with whom they work. This is only one reason ethical issues are addressed in every chapter of this text. Not only can an ethical violation result in a legal malpractice action against an attorney, but a paralegal who engages in some activities, such as giving legal advice, can find him- or herself the subject of a criminal prosecution. **Unauthorized practice of law** (UPL) is considered a misdemeanor offense in states such as California (California Business and Professions Code 6125-6133) and as a felony in states such as Texas (Tx. Govt. §83.001).

Other than criminal prosecution, paralegals in most states are regulated indirectly. The attorneys with whom they work are closely regulated by their state bar, and any unethical activities carried out by their staff, including paralegals, are imputed to them. In states that have a certification regime, unethical paralegals may have their certifications stripped away in much the same way that an attorney may be disbarred. Unlike attorneys, however, a paralegal that has lost his or her certification is not prohibited from working but may have greater difficulty securing employment when attorneys learn why the paralegal lost certification.

National Organizations. In addition to state-based certification and registration plans, there are several national organizations that offer voluntary certification programs. The National Association of Legal Assistants offers the Certified Legal Assistant program, and the National Federation of Paralegal Associations offers the PACE (Paralegal Advanced Competency Exam). Both organizations test applicants extensively in the law with an eye toward creating a comprehensive and reliable certification program. Although these organizations can boast membership in the tens of thousands, they are not the only national organizations dedicated to legal professionals. In fact, if you review the Web sites under the Cyber Trip feature, you will find several other organizations listed.

CYBER TRIP

National Federation of Paralegal Associations http://www.paralegals.org/
National Association of Legal Assistants www.nala.org
American Association for Paralegal Education www.aafpe.org

legal document assistant
A specialized type of paralegal, legally able to provide assistance to clients in preparing forms.

Legal Document Assistants

Some states, such as California, recognize another class of legal professionals: independent paralegals or **legal document assistants**. These individuals are authorized to assist members of the public who choose to represent themselves in litigation or who wish to file documents with the state. See Figure 3.2.

FIGURE 3.2
**Legal Document
Assistant (California)**
Source: CAL BUS. & PROF. D.
3, Ch. 5.5.

Definition:

(1) Any person who is not exempted under Section 6401 and who provides, or assists in providing, or offers to provide, or offers to assist in providing, for compensation, any self-help service to a member of the public who is representing himself or herself in a legal matter, or who holds himself or herself out as someone who offers that service or has that authority. This paragraph does not apply to any individual whose assistance consists merely of secretarial or receptionist services.

COMMUNICATION TIP

In the past, communicating with clients was limited to telephone calls and letters. However, the communication options available to modern legal professionals are almost mind boggling. In addition to faxes and email, there is text messaging, instant messaging, and blogs. All of these new media raise new concerns about one of the most important aspects of a legal practice: maintaining the confidentiality of client communications. Although we all tend to think of email as a medium that is in many ways identical to writing a letter, the legal implications are not similar at all. For one thing, courts consistently refuse to give email the same level of protection as a letter or a telephone call to a client. As a result, email communications with clients must be scrutinized closely. Revealing sensitive information in an email, text message, or other digital medium may waive the client's protections.

RESEARCH THIS!

Review recent decisions in your state's appellate courts that discuss aspects of legal malpractice. Why did these attorneys get into ethical trouble? Do any of these cases refer to the role of paralegals? If so, how was the paralegal involved? Summarize these cases by name and citation and provide a brief synopsis listing the unethical practice that resulted in attorney disciplinary actions. What general rules can you take away from these cases? Are there some simple rules that, if followed, would have helped these legal professionals avoid ethical violations?

LEGAL RESEARCH MAXIM

Whenever you conduct legal research into cases, such as the assignment that you find under "Research This," you must keep in mind that published cases are subject to modification by later cases. In previous decades, the best method to check on the status of a published decision was to view a publication called *Sheperd's Case Citator.* This volume provides a nationwide cross-reference of every published decision and the impact that later cases had on the opinion. For instance, if a subsequent state supreme court decision overturned a published opinion, *Sheperd's* would provide a summary of the case and answer the pressing question, "Is this case still good law?"

Nowadays, even though *Sheperd's* is still very much alive, there are other methods of achieving the same results. For instance, Westlaw offers a similar function, called Key Cite™, that also provides citing references for a case, showing when the published opinion was referred to by other cases or statutes and including any reference showing if the case was later overturned or overruled. A researcher can access Key Cite™ from the main tab page on Westlaw, from any displayed document in Westlaw, or by using the Key Cite™ Status Flag that appears in a frame next to a cited document.

Legal Secretaries

legal secretary
A secretary trained to perform specialized tasks directly related to the practice of law.

In addition to paralegals, the next most vitally important individual in the law office is the **legal secretary**. There are some attorneys who work with the same secretary for decades. In fact, in the early days of the paralegal profession, it was often difficult to distinguish between a legal secretary and a paralegal. These days, the lines of distinction are easier to draw. Legal secretaries prepare legal documents and other pleadings at the express direction of the attorney. They also coordinate meetings, spend a great deal of time on the telephone with other legal secretaries arranging court hearings, filing, and performing many of the other critical if mundane office procedures. Perhaps the easiest way to distinguish between a legal secretary and a paralegal is by the training that each receives. A paralegal may receive some training in word processing programs and filing, but the paralegal's primary emphasis is on an in-depth understanding of the legal process. A legal secretary's training focuses on office issues, from transcription to scheduling to creating a comprehensive calendar, and often serves as the all-important buffer between the attorney and the clamor of the outside world.

Other Support Staff

Paralegals and legal secretaries perform vital tasks inside and outside the law office, but there are several other important positions often found in any firm that specializes in litigation. These other positions include:

- Runners
- Clerks
- Process servers
- Accountants
- Private investigators
- File clerks

Runners. Although terminology varies across the country, a "runner" is a staff member who is primarily responsible for picking up and delivering important documents. In some cases, this position is merged with that of paralegal, whereas at other law firms, it is a separate and distinct position. A runner might be a high school or college student seeking to gain some insight into the practice of law or another individual who is only interested in part-time employment. In this era of faxes and email, such a position might seem redundant, but there are still many courthouses that will not or cannot accept pleadings filed electronically. Instead, the document must be filed in person, and that is where a runner earns every penny of his or her small salary.

Clerks. In the previous chapter, we discussed the role of clerks of court. However, there is another position also commonly referred to as "clerk." This position is often occupied by a law student or recent college graduate. This person performs basic legal research assignments, runs errands, and assists the attorney with activities that fall outside the purview of the paralegal. This position is also often filled by a person who is seeking to gain some experience in the practice of law before attending law school or by a law student who hopes to gain some practical experience before graduating.

process server
A person statutorily authorized to serve legal documents such as complaints.

Process Servers. A **process server** is a person who personally serves pleadings on parties to civil cases. Although some states limit this practice to sheriff's deputies or other law enforcement officers, many other states allow private individuals to act in the capacity of a process server. The job brings with it a certain amount of risk. A person who is served with a petition or complaint may not welcome the experience or look kindly on the person who delivers the bad news.

Accountants. In addition to the individuals who work more or less directly from the law office, there is also an obvious need for a professional to manage the financial affairs of the firm. In large firms, this position may be filled by an in-house accountant or even an entire accounting department. For smaller firms, these duties may fall to a single individual who works for the law firm on a periodic basis, perhaps once a week or even two or three times a month. A small firm usually cannot afford to pay for a full-time, in-house accountant, but any firm that operates completely without one is only asking for trouble.

SURF'S UP!

The Internet has made access to some public information much easier to obtain. Balanced against this new openness are the concerns that arose after September 11 to block access to potentially sensitive information. Even with the concerns about homeland security, it is still much easier to find public records online than it was even a few years ago. An entry such as "online public records" in any well-known search engine will provide a wealth of hits. But not all sites are created equal. If you plan on trying to save yourself some time by researching issues in online public records, there are a few things you must keep in mind. For instance:

1. Avoid pay sites, if possible.
2. Always go to the source.
3. Evaluate the site as well as the information.

AVOID PAY SITES

There are literally hundreds if not thousands of commercially available sites promising to provide you, for a fee, access to a wealth of public records. Whether these sites can actually deliver is another matter. Many sites provide teasers about information that they claim to have access to but require you to pay a monthly fee or a processing fee to obtain it. When you do, you find that the information is the same thing that you could have gotten from reviewing the telephone book. Beyond the issues surrounding access, there is a more fundamental question: Why pay for something that is already free? You might or might not get accurate information from a commercial site, but many courthouses now have direct Internet access.

ALWAYS GO TO THE SOURCE

In addition to the implications of paying for questionable information, consider the basic question of where these companies obtained their information. They probably went straight to the government site and downloaded it for free. Why bother to pay for something that you can also obtain for free? Most state and local governments now have Web sites, and many provide some form of access to public documents. After all, many of these records are open to the public, so there is no real privacy concern about making them available on the Internet. Of course, the opposite is also true: Matters that are not public record will not be available on the Internet if they are not already available at the courthouse. Another reason to go directly to the government site is that the information will have a greater degree of reliability. A private company might provide errors, but there is less of a chance of this happening if you go directly to the source.

EVALUATE THE SITE

Critical thinking skills and evaluation are as important on the Web as they are in any other aspect of life. In fact, you could argue that critical thinking skills are even more important on the Internet. While you are reviewing the information, note the source of the information. Is this actually a government site or a pseudo site? The URL will tell you a lot about the source of the information, but you should also check the bona fides of the site, often provided in a link such as "About . . . ." If such a link is not provided, you should spend more time evaluating the accuracy of the information provided.

Private Investigators. There are times when the firm may need the services of a private investigator. Like the position of accountant, the private investigator is almost always brought in on a case-by-case basis. Private investigators are licensed by the state and trained to obtain a wide variety of information. Attorneys rely on private investigators to locate witnesses, seek out financial data, document accident sites, and carry out a vast array of other functions that fall outside the expertise of a paralegal or legal secretary.

File Clerks. Some firms also hire individuals to handle the enormous quantity of paper generated by the modern practice of law. A file clerk is an individual who is responsible for filing all documents, letters, contracts, pleadings, and the myriad other materials that are either generated by the firm or received by it. Many client files can grow from a single manila file folder to reams and reams of expandable file folders. Tracking all of this information can be a formidable task. Many firms have begun using advanced technology to help with the process. For instance, the position of file clerk in a traditional firm has slowly transmuted from someone who handles paper to a position involving extensive computer databases. The goal of the paperless law office (where every document in a case is available on an in-house computer network) has not yet become a reality in most firms, but it remains the ultimate goal for many legal professionals. In firms that have made extensive use of imaging, anyone with access to the network can retrieve an important document, move it to a laptop to be taken to a courtroom, or use it as a person would use any digitally created document. Here, the role of file clerk more closely resembles a Web master or computer technician who is responsible for maintaining the entire computer system and ensuring that all files remain accessible to attorneys and staff and, just as important, inaccessible to outsiders.

COMPENSATING LEGAL PROFESSIONALS

We have already stated that the practice of law is a business, and as a businessperson, an attorney expects to be paid by his or her clients. This expectation holds whether the attorney represents plaintiffs or defendants. There are, however, some important differences in the way that attorneys who primarily represent plaintiffs are compensated compared with the common method for compensating attorneys who routinely represent defendants. The two primary methods are:

- Contingency fee
- Hourly rate

Contingency Fees

contingency fee
The attorney's fee calculated as a percentage of the final award in a civil case.

Although attorneys can represent plaintiffs or defendants in different cases, most attorneys specialize in one type or another. An attorney who regularly represents individuals injured in automobile collisions (the most common type of litigation) is commonly referred to as a "plaintiffs' attorney." These lawyers enter into an agreement with their clients called a **contingency fee** arrangement.

In the most common type of contingency fee agreement, the client signs a contract agreeing to pay the attorney one-third of the total recovery from the case. If the client eventually receives $10,000, for example, the attorney who represents him or her will receive $3,333. A contingency fee arrangement is often the only way that some individuals can afford legal representation. Of course, there is an element of risk in the arrangement. One-third of the total recovery sounds like an excellent relationship—as long as the final settlement amount is large. But one-third of nothing is nothing. If the client loses the case, the attorney will receive nothing.

In most situations, the contingency fee arrangement does not apply to routine costs, such as filing or copying fees, but will apply to the attorney and all costs incurred by the attorney's support staff. There are also certain types of cases for which contingency is either inappropriate or not permitted by state bar rules. In California, as in many other states, an attorney cannot enter into a contingency fee arrangement in a family law case, such as divorce or child custody. The contingency fee agreement (see Figure 3.3) can cause the attorney a great deal of stress, especially if the attorney is risk averse. However, some attorneys thrive on the prospect of a one-third recovery. For those who find the prospect daunting, there is the flip side of the coin: hourly billing.

Hourly Billing

PRACTICE TIP

Attorneys who work with insurance companies to represent policyholders are commonly referred to as "insurance defense" attorneys.

The attorneys who represent the defendants in a civil case generally charge by the hour. Contingency fees are rare for defendants' attorneys for the simple reason that most civil cases settle, and the settlement amount comes from the defendant's personal assets or the defendant's insurance policy. As a result, basing the defendant's fee on the final amount would not be a fair reflection of the attorney's work. Instead, the attorney may charge a flat fee or an hourly rate. Some attorneys charge extremely high hourly rates, such as $500 per hour. This rate does not mean that the attorney actually pockets $1,000 for two hours' work. The attorney's fee pays a portion of the firm's expenses, from the electric bill to the employee payroll. However, $500 per hour is still an excellent pay rate.

If we again return to the example of automobile collision (commonly called personal injury) cases, there is another reason for the defendant's attorney to bill by the hour. The defendant-driver is required to have an insurance policy covering collisions, and this policy provides for attorney expenses related to litigation following an accident. The attorney will bill the defendant's insurance company instead of the defendant, and insurance companies insist on accurate, itemized billing.

In addition to addressing the topic of how attorneys are compensated, it is just as important to note that paralegals also bill for their time. Whether the ultimate fee comes from a contingency fee agreement, flat fee, or hourly rate, paralegals must pay particular attention to itemized billing. A paralegal should track the time he or she spends on every activity related to a case. These itemized statements will help support the firm's claim for services to a client who is reluctant to pay and may also become an issue in litigation should the court find that the losing party must pay the winner's attorney's fees. Courts allow the imposition of fees to cover the activities of both attorneys and paralegals.

FIGURE 3.3
Contingency Fee
Agreement

THIS AGREEMENT, made this 7th day of April, 2007, between the foregoing named person(s) being herein called Client, and Allison Attorney, herein called "Attorney(s)". It is understood that litigation can be expensive, and that the Attorneys are prohibited by law from becoming liable for its costs, expenses, disbursements, and deposits. Attorneys may advance them, but they cannot become ultimately liable for them. The Client and the Attorneys have agreed as follows:

1. The Client this day retains, employs, and authorizes the Attorneys:

    (a) To prosecute, administratively and judicially, if necessary in his judgment, each of the Client's following claims;

    (b) To prosecute or defend any and all appeals that may be taken in connection with the Client's claims; and

    (c) To receive and collect any final recovery that may be realized on the Client's claims and to satisfy the same upon the records of the appropriate agency or court. The words "final recovery" when used anywhere in this Agreement means the total gross amount of any and all monies, property, and compensation of any and every kind whatsoever realized or received by any Client for any claim, whether realized as the result of settlement or litigation or otherwise, and shall include, but not be limited to, any and all monies, funds, awards, verdicts, judgments, determinations, damages, principal, interest of every kind and nature, penalties, allowances, costs, and any and all compensation of every kind, nature, and description; and

    (d) To deduct and retain their Attorneys' fees out of the proceeds of the final recovery, and to remit the balance, less their costs, expenses, disbursements, and deposits, to the Client.

2. The Client agrees to pay the Attorneys, and the Attorneys agree to accept for all of the legal services rendered in accordance with this Agreement, the following fee:

    (a) A contingent fee, paid within thirty (30) days of a final recovery or any portion thereof, computed as follows: thirty-three percent (33%) of any final recovery obtained if the claim is settled without suit.

IN WITNESS WHEREOF, the parties have executed this Agreement the day and year first above written.

_____   _____

CLIENT   Attorney

Sworn to and subscribed before me
this _____ day of _____, 200__

_____
Notary Public

PROFESSIONAL CORPORATIONS AND ASSOCIATIONS

professional corporation
Business form organized as a closely held group of professional intellectual employees such as doctors.

Corporations are business models that have many of the characteristics of natural persons. A corporation can own property, pay taxes, and engage in a wide variety of businesses. They are categorized as artificial persons. However, under the original legislation authorizing the creation of corporate structures in the United States, a corporation was prohibited from practicing a profession such as medicine or law. This rule prevented doctors and attorneys from taking advantage of some of the benefits of a corporate structure, including shielding personal assets from civil judgments.

In recent decades, all states have amended their rules about corporate law to allow attorneys to form some type of business model that closely resembles a corporation. In some instances,

CASE IN POINT

In re Oheb
L 1132036
(Cal. Bar Ct., 2006)

In this conviction referral proceeding, the State Bar sought our review of a hearing judge's decision recommending that respondent, Tamir Oheb, be placed on four years' stayed suspension and on four years' probation with conditions, including two years' actual suspension. On July 16, 2004, we filed our opinion in this case, concluding that summary disbarment was not authorized under Bus. & Prof.Code, § 6102(c), but finding that the facts and circumstances surrounding the conviction of respondent, Tamir Oheb, of violation of Penal Code, section 549 involved moral turpitude. We accordingly adopted the hearing judge's recommendation that respondent be suspended for four years, that execution be stayed and that respondent be actually suspended for two years, retroactive to October 1, 2001, the start of his interim suspension, and that his actual suspension should continue until he makes an acceptable showing under Standard 1.4(c)(ii), Standards for Attorney Sanctions for Professional Misconduct (Standards).

The State Bar sought Supreme Court review of our decision, arguing that disbarment is the appropriate discipline to recommend. In the alternative, the Bar sought a remand to us to reconsider the degree of discipline.

After an opportunity for the parties to brief the issue on remand, we have reconsidered our earlier discipline recommendation and now recommend, for the reasons stated, that respondent be disbarred.

I. PROCEDURAL HISTORY

In September 2000, after pleading nolo contendere, respondent was convicted in the Los Angeles Superior Court on two felony counts of violating Penal Code section 549 for accepting referrals of personal injury clients with reckless disregard for whether the referring party or the referred clients intended to make false or fraudulent insurance claims. Once the State Bar notified us of respondent's convictions, we filed an order in August 2001 that placed respondent on interim suspension because respondent's convictions were for (1) felony crimes and (2) crimes which there is probable cause to believe involve moral turpitude. In that same August 2001 order, following the customary practice for such crimes, we also referred respondent's convictions to the hearing department for a trial on the issues of whether the facts and circumstances surrounding the commission of the crimes involved moral turpitude.

After he was placed on interim suspension in California under our August 2001 order, respondent practiced law in Las Vegas until he was suspended in Nevada in February 2002, which was only about two months before the State Bar Court trial. The record does not indicate whether respondent was physically present in Las Vegas or anywhere else in Nevada when he practiced law after his interim suspension in California.

After a trial of almost five days, the hearing judge found that the circumstances surrounding respondent's crimes involved moral turpitude because respondent accepted personal injury cases with knowledge that they were being purchased and took steps to conceal the fact that he was splitting attorney's fees with a nonattorney. The hearing judge further found that the circumstances surrounding respondent's convictions also involved respondent's (1) willful violation of rule 1-311 of the Rules of Professional Conduct of the State Bar by employing a nonattorney whom respondent knew had previously resigned from the State Bar with disciplinary charges pending without complying with the requirements of rule 1-311, (2) willful violation of rule 1-320 by improperly entering into financial arrangements with nonattorneys to obtain clients, and (3) willful violation of rule 4-100(A) by making certain improper deposits into and payments from his client trust account.

FINDINGS OF FACT

Turning to the facts and circumstances surrounding respondent's conviction, our independent review causes us to make the following findings of fact, which are established by clear and convincing evidence.

Respondent personally kept his financial records, maintaining particularly meticulous bank records for each of his accounts, including his client trust account. For each bank account, he kept a file containing a copy of each check written on the account and another file containing a copy of each check deposited into the account. Respondent was the only one who wrote or signed checks on his bank accounts.

When a case settled, respondent personally prepared the "settlement sheet," which set forth the division of the settlement proceeds, i.e., between the client, respondent, medical providers, and any other party entitled to a portion of the proceeds. The client had to approve division of the settlement proceeds and sign the settlement sheet before respondent would pay out any proceeds.

One morning in October 1997, chiropractor Richard Monoson telephoned respondent. When Monoson telephoned respondent that morning in October 1997, he asked respondent to come to his chiropractic office in Encino that afternoon to meet Kenneth Gottlieb, whom Monoson described only as a former attorney who could increase respondent's practice. When respondent went to Monoson's office that afternoon, Monoson introduced him to Gottlieb as well as to Keith R. Ohanesian, a chiropractor with whom Monoson did business and who knew Gottlieb, and Tony Folgar, an investigator who worked with Gottlieb.

At the meeting, no one told respondent that Gottlieb resigned with disciplinary charges pending in July 1992 or that Gottlieb had a criminal record. After the introductions were made that afternoon, the men met for about 30 minutes. At that meeting, respondent learned that Monoson just met Gottlieb the day before; that Gottlieb was working with Attorney Ronald Hettena in Hettena's personal injury practice, but that Gottlieb was looking for another attorney to work with because Hettena was allegedly closing his practice and moving out of state; and that Gottlieb was going to keep and to continue working out of an office in Van Nuys, California[,] that he had shared with Hettena. In addition, respondent was told and believed that Gottlieb had been a very successful "attorney for 25 years plus, that [Gottlieb] was a litigator, [that Gottlieb] had worked for a number of famous attorneys," that Gottlieb had a "huge book of business" that he was willing to refer to respondent, and that he was willing to teach respondent how to litigate.

Respondent soon learned of Gottlieb's resignation when he looked Gottlieb's membership status up on the State Bar's web site. The State Bar's official public records, although not then available on its web site, disclosed that Gottlieb had been publicly reproved in May 1986 and that the disciplinary charges pending against Gottlieb involved both Gottlieb's September 1991 convictions on two counts of insurance fraud, two counts of grand theft, and two counts of forgery, and Gottlieb's failure to comply with rule 955 of the California Rules of Court as directed in an order we filed in fall 1991 placing Gottlieb on interim suspension.

As the hearing judge correctly found, the parties agreed at the meeting that Gottlieb would transfer all of the personal injury cases that he had with Attorney Hettena to respondent, that respondent would be substituted in place of Hettena as the attorney of record in those cases, that Gottlieb would find and, when necessary, buy new cases and refer them to respondent to be the attorney of record, that Gottlieb would work for respondent on the cases he referred to respondent, and that the clients would be sent to either Monoson or Ohanesian for treatment. Moreover, as the hearing judge correctly found, respondent and Gottlieb agreed at the meeting to split the attorney's fees on each case Gottlieb referred to respondent: 25 percent to respondent and 75 percent to Gottlieb whenever Gottlieb had to buy the case or otherwise had to pay money to someone in connection with the case, and 50 percent each whenever Gottlieb did not have to buy the case or otherwise have to pay for some expense related to the case or whenever Gottlieb bought the case from a specific individual who did not charge much for cases.

In sum, by the end of this 30-minute meeting, respondent had entered into a business relationship with Gottlieb, whom he had just met, in which Gottlieb would buy and refer cases to respondent, work on those cases with respondent, and teach respondent how to litigate and in which respondent was to pay Gottlieb, under their fee splitting agreement, either 75 or 50 percent of any attorney's fees recovered in each case Gottlieb brought into respondent's law office. Respondent did this even though he knew that his fee splitting agreement with Gottlieb violated the Rules of Professional Conduct and that he viewed fee splitting agreements with nonattorneys as "not legal." However, respondent did testify that his law practice had slowed down considerably by October 1997, causing him severe financial difficulties, a great deal of anxiety, and to become very scared that he and his parents would lose their homes.

Respondent admits that he agreed to permit Gottlieb, for the first couple of months of their business relationship, to operate his office in Van Nuys as an extension of respondent's law office and to work on the cases Gottlieb referred to him in that Van Nuys office without respondent's or another attorney's supervision. In fact, as late as February or March 1998, the name "Law Offices of Tamir Oheb" was still on the front door of Gottlieb's office and on the office building's central directory. About one month after the beginning of their relationship, i.e., about November 1997, and during the time Gottlieb was operating his

Van Nuys office as an extension of respondent's law office, three settlement checks for clients Gottlieb referred to respondent were sent to Gottlieb's office. Gottlieb stole those checks, forged respondent's signature on them, and attempted to cash them, but was unable to do so. Respondent became very upset when he learned of Gottlieb's theft and forgery. Respondent testified that Gottlieb pleaded that he was desperate and that he had been pressured into stealing the checks, forging respondent's signature, and trying to cash them. However, neither respondent nor Gottlieb offered any details of this pressure.

Monoson pleaded that he had provided treatments to and obtained x-rays on the clients in many of the cases that Gottlieb referred to respondent and that he, therefore, had a real financial interest in those cases, which would be jeopardized if respondent terminated his relationship with Gottlieb. Finally, at the meeting at Monoson's home, respondent asked Gottlieb to modify the fee splitting agreement to give respondent more than 25 percent of the recovered attorney's fees because it was respondent's law license. Gottlieb refused and again explained that he could not agree to give respondent anymore than 25 percent because Gottlieb had to pay for the cases out of his 75 percent share.

In total, Gottlieb referred 50 to 60 automobile accident injury cases involving about 150 plaintiffs to respondent. Virtually all of the Gottlieb referred cases were based on fraudulent insurance claims arising from staged automobile accidents under a sophisticated scheme involving, at least, Monoson, Ohanesian[, and] Gottlieb.

Once Gottlieb signed up a new client and set up the client's file, he took the file into respondent's Tarzana office and put it in the file cabinet drawers reserved for Gottlieb's referrals. Respondent testified that, at some point during his representation of each client, he reviewed the client's file in detail and never discovered anything that led him to believe that fraud might be involved in a case.

Respondent admitted that he often did not even meet the clients in the Gottlieb referred cases until an insurance company or someone wanted to take the clients' statements. However, respondent also admits that he was not always present when a client's statement was taken. Respondent explained that, whenever it was inconvenient for him to be present when a client's statement was taken, he sent Gottlieb to appear with the client.

Respondent permitted Gottlieb to work on the cases Gottlieb brought into the office with very little supervision or instruction. In addition to having Gottlieb appear with clients when their statements were taken, respondent had Gottlieb negotiate the settlements in the cases he brought in the office. Respondent asserts that he required Gottlieb to get his approval of any settlement offer before Gottlieb accepted it; however, the hearing judge made no finding on this issue. Moreover, as the State Bar points out, respondent testified that, because he thought that Gottlieb was such a good negotiator, he had Gottlieb call the insurance adjustor in one of respondent's own cases and that Gottlieb quickly negotiated a great settlement.

During his 14-month association with Gottlieb, respondent's practice increased substantially. During that time, respondent had somewhere between two and six individuals, excluding Gottlieb, working for him. Even though some of those individuals were independent contractors, others clearly were not.

In total, respondent paid Gottlieb about $148,300 as Gottlieb's 75 percent share of the attorney's fees recovered on the cases that he brought into respondent's office. Respondent paid Gottlieb as an independent contractor, and ordinarily paid him with checks that described the nature of the payment in the memo section of the checks by writing "independent contractor." However, respondent occasionally attempted to conceal the true nature of his payments to Gottlieb by writing in the memo section of the check entries such as reimbursement of travel expenses, advance of wages, or new car. Moreover, respondent admits that, once or twice when he had a case with a particularly large settlement, he attempted to conceal the nature of his payment to Gottlieb by writing an incorrect description of the payment in the memo section with the intent to disguise or hide his fee splitting from the State Bar. Respondent testified that, other than keeping copies of the checks, he did not keep any records with respect to any of his payments to Gottlieb.

On December 8, 1997, respondent, with Attorney Jeffery Sklan appearing with him, was interviewed about his relationship with Gottlieb by Kelly Mercer, a peace officer with the Insurance Fraud Division of the California Department of Insurance. Officer Mercer ask[ed] respondent whether he notified the State Bar of his employment of Gottlieb as required by rule 1-311. Respondent admits that he did not.

In mid-December 1998, both Hettena and Gottlieb were arrested. Hettena was apparently released relatively soon, but Gottlieb remained in jail until sometime around February 24, 1999. Respondent quickly learned of the arrests. It was not until after respondent learned that Gottlieb had been arrested in mid-December 1998 that respondent retained Jeffery Sklan as his criminal attorney. At that time, Sklan advised respondent to end his relationship with Gottlieb and to change his office locks, which respondent did after Gottlieb was released from jail.

Even after Hettena and Gottlieb were arrested, and respondent was interviewed by investigator Mercer, respondent neither investigated the disciplinary charges pending when Gottlieb resigned, e.g., by contacting the State Bar, nor investigated the extent and nature of the money laundering charge respondent was told was the basis of Gottlieb's incarceration.

In early 1999, the client or clients in the Deleon matter claimed that they had not been paid their share of the settlement proceeds in their case. When respondent pulled the Deleon matter file, there were copies of negotiated drafts in it. Respondent and Sklan met with Gottlieb in respondent's office on February 26, 1999, to confront Gottlieb on this payment problem. Gottlieb wore a "wire" so that officer Mercer could record the meeting. It was at this meeting that Gottlieb first told respondent that all the cases he brought into respondent's office were based on staged accidents.

Even though respondent and Sklan claimed not to know whether cases referred to Gottlieb involved staged accidents, Sklan advised respondent, after the February 26, 1999, meeting "to get rid of any pending cases" referred to respondent by Gottlieb. By the end of March 1999, respondent had "dropped" all such pending cases. However, respondent did not return the client files to clients when he "dropped" them. In fact, as late as June 1999[,] other attorneys were requesting, from respondent, the client files in cases respondent dropped.

Respondent was arrested on June 29, 1999, and charged with a total of 36 counts of making false insurance claims, conspiracy to commit grand theft, and capping. As noted ante, respondent pleaded nolo contendere to two felony counts of violating Penal Code section 549 for accepting referrals of personal injury clients with reckless disregard for whether the referring party or the referred clients intended to make false or fraudulent insurance claims.

Respondent completed all the terms of his sentence, and the superior court granted respondent's motion to reduce his convictions to misdemeanors, but it denied his motion to dismiss the case. In February 2004, the superior court terminated respondent's criminal probation, set aside his plea of guilty and his conviction, and dismissed the criminal proceedings in accordance with Penal Code section 1203.4.

CONCLUSIONS OF LAW

Respondent's many demonstrations of recklessness involved moral turpitude.

Respondent was reckless in entering his business relationship with Gottlieb without investigating him and in not seeking additional information on Gottlieb once he learned at the outset that Gottlieb resigned with disciplinary charges pending. At that point, respondent had a direct and easy opportunity to investigate Gottlieb's background and, with the most minimal of effort, to learn of Gottlieb's prior record of discipline and 1991 convictions for forgery, grand theft, and insurance fraud. Respondent's tolerance for Gottlieb should have ended completely when respondent later learned that Gottlieb stole and forged the three settlement checks.

Respondent knowingly permitted Gottlieb to, inter alia, interview and sign up clients without his knowledge or approval, and knowingly failed to monitor the cases Gottlieb referred to him, e.g., he did not review each Gottlieb referral when Gottlieb first brought it into the office. This conduct establishes "an habitual failure to give reasonable attention to the handling of the affairs of his clients rather than an isolated instance of carelessness followed by a firm determination to make amends." (*Waterman v. State Bar* (1936) 8 Cal.2d 17, 21.) Recklessness and gross carelessness in the practice of law, even if not deliberate or dishonest, violate "the oath of an attorney to discharge faithfully the duties of an attorney to the best of his knowledge and ability and involve moral turpitude, in that they are a breach of the fiduciary relation which binds him to the most conscientious fidelity to his clients' interests." (*Simmons v. State Bar* (1970) 2 Cal.3d 719, 729; accord, *Doyle v. State Bar* (1976) 15 Cal.3d 973, 978, and cases there cited.) Even repeated acts of mere negligence and omission can involve moral turpitude and "prove as great a lack of fitness to practice law as affirmative violations of duty." (*Bruns v. State Bar* (1941) 18 Cal.2d 667, 672.)

We hold that respondent's manner and method of practicing law, at least, during his 14-month association with Gottlieb, was reckless and, therefore, involved moral turpitude. Given the several opportunities respondent had to protect himself from Gottlieb early on, his failure to do so can only be seen as recklessness of the most acute nature.

Respondent's repeated failures to competently represent his clients involved moral turpitude.

As noted ante, we do not address the issue of when respondent learned that the Gottlieb referred cases were based on staged accidents because respondent should have proceeded as if he had known about the staged accidents no later than February 26, 1999, when Gottlieb told him of the staged accidents. Respondent should have, at a minimum, met with each client referred to him by Gottlieb, whether their case was then pending or had already been settled, and told him or her that respondent had substantial information suggesting, inter alia, that the client knowingly made a false claim based on a staged accident and on fraudulently obtained automobile insurance and then given him or her whatever legal counsel was appropriate, e.g., advising the client to seek advice from a criminal defense attorney. (Cf. *Nichols v. Keller* (1993) 15 Cal.App.4th 1672, 1684-1687 [duty to competently perform requires attorneys to alert clients to all reasonably apparent legal problems even when they fall outside the scope of attorney's retention and to the possible need for other counsel to address those problems]; In the Matter of Respondent G (Review Dept.1992) 2 Cal. State Bar Ct. Rptr. 175, 178-179 ["attorney's duty to the client can extend beyond the closing of the file."]) Respondent, however, did not do so even though it was readily apparent that his clients might have been included in the Department of Insurance fraud investigation involving Gottlieb and prosecuted for client insurance fraud. In sum, respondent's wholesale failure to competently represent these clients by providing them with competent legal advice after the February 26, 1999, meeting also involves moral turpitude.

We reject as meritless the contentions respondent asserted while testifying that, to contact his clients and provide them such advice would have been improper because it would amount to accusing them of committing fraud, which Sklan advised him he could not do; and that, in any event, such advice was unnecessary with respect to the Gottlieb referred cases that were already settled because the clients in those cases would have already signed some insurance company form of affidavit or release, which all contain fraud warning language. That contention reflects a failure to appreciate the duties he owed to his clients.

Finally, respondent's practice of deceit by falsely recording in his records the nature of his payments to Gottlieb, in order to conceal their illegal or unethical purpose, unquestionably involved intentional acts of moral turpitude.

When we review the numerous ways respondent committed moral turpitude, we can only conclude that his conviction for violating Penal Code section 549 was most serious for disciplinary purposes, fully warranting following the guidance of Standard 3.2 for disbarment. Indeed, "[D]isbarments, and not suspensions, have been the rule rather than the exception in cases of serious crimes involving moral turpitude."

We have assigned little weight to respondent's cooperation with the State Bar and to the evidence offered as to his character. Also, respondent's misconduct commenced less than five years after his admission to practice so that his lack of prior discipline was not entitled to mitigating credit. (E.g., *Amante v. State Bar* (1990) 50 Cal.3d 247, 255-256; In the Matter of Greenwood

(Review Dept.1998) 3 Cal. State Bar Ct. Rptr. 831, 837.) In contrast, the weight of aggravating circumstances decisively predominates. As we found ante, respondent engaged in multiple acts of misconduct, he profited from that misconduct, his conduct harmed insurers[,] and he either jeopardized legitimate clients or exposed persons engaged in potential or actual fraudulent conduct to even greater civil or criminal liability.

In this case, we find no grave or even serious doubts as to the propriety of the recommendation. It was purely fortuitous that more harm did not occur as a result of the facts and circumstances surrounding respondent's criminal offense, given especially that the accident claims pressed in the name of respondent's office appear to have arisen from fraud and that respondent's conduct was both grossly reckless in a number of ways and, by disguising financial entries, intentionally dishonest. As the overriding purposes of lawyer discipline are to protect the public, maintain high professional standards[,] and preserve the integrity of the legal profession (std.1.3), disbarment is appropriate based on applying the Standards to this case and also appropriate when measured against decisional law.

FORMAL RECOMMENDATION

For the foregoing reasons, we recommend that respondent, Tamir Oheb, be disbarred from the practice of law in this State and that his name be stricken from the roll of attorneys licensed to practice in the State.

Source: From Westlaw. Used with permission of Thomson/West.

Case Questions:

1. What actions are carried out by the attorney in this case that the court says justify his disbarment?

2. In what way was the attorney's fee-splitting arrangement considered unethical?

3. Was it improper for the attorney to work with another attorney who had been disbarred? Why or why not?

4. Does the attorney in this case have a legitimate claim that he had no knowledge of the illegal activities carried out by Gottlieb?

5. What should this attorney have done when originally approached by Dr. Monoson and Gottlieb?

they are referred to as **professional corporations** or professional associations (see Figure 3.4). These new rules allow attorneys to create business models that go far beyond the typical general partnership (*Street v. Sugarman*, 202 So. 2d 749 (D.C. Fla. 1967)).

FIGURE 3.4
Professional Corporations

Source: Florida Statute § 621.03.

The term "professional service" means any type of personal service to the public which requires as a condition precedent to the rendering of such service the obtaining of a license or other legal authorization. By way of example and without limiting the generality thereof, the personal services which come within the provisions of this act are the personal services rendered by certified public accountants, public accountants, chiropractic physicians, dentists, osteopathic physicians, physicians and surgeons, doctors of medicine, doctors of dentistry, podiatric physicians, chiropodists, architects, veterinarians, attorneys at law, and life insurance agents.

SPOT THE ISSUE!

Bart Barrister is visiting his chiropractor one day, and while he is adjusting Bart's spine, the chiropractor mentions that he has another patient who was recently involved in a car wreck. He offers to send the client to Bart on the condition that Bart pays the client's outstanding chiropractic bill of $150. Is this improper fee splitting, as that term is defined in this chapter's Case in Point? Discuss your answer.

Eye on Ethics

SPLITTING FEES

As you can see from this chapter's Case in Point, fee splitting can be an ethical minefield for attorneys. Why should this be the case? In other professions, it is common for individuals to share fees. A real estate broker might split a commission with another broker or an individual might request a "finder's fee" that is a percentage of the final sale price. What makes splitting fees such a problematic issue for attorneys? The answer goes to the heart of the attorney's duty to the client. The attorney–client relationship is not established by the payment of the fee, but it is simple common sense that an attorney will work harder for a paying versus a nonpaying client. When the attorney engages in fee splitting, he or she is placed in a potential ethical dilemma. Another party, someone who does not place the client's interests at the forefront, will put pressure on the attorney to settle the case as soon as possible so that he or she can receive a portion of the fee. It is not always advantageous to the

client to settle the case early, and this pressure splits the attorney's loyalty as surely as it does the final fee. For an attorney, whose responsibility is to represent the interests of the client zealously, this position attacks the basic premise of the attorney–client relationship. Anything that interferes with the attorney's responsibility to the client is an ethical problem, and fee splitting certainly creates this tension.

There is an important distinction between fee splitting and referral fees. A referral fee is a monetary amount paid from one attorney to another. When a lawyer receives a case that he or she is either unwilling or unable to take on, the attorney might pass the case to another attorney in exchange for a referral fee. The fee might simply be a flat fee agreed to between the attorneys or consist of a percentage of the final contingency fee payment. In either event, there is nothing unethical about attorneys charging fees to one another to refer a case. The ethical problem develops when an attorney engages in such a practice with a non-attorney.

A Day in the Life: Debra Holbrook

Debra Holbrook has been a paralegal for several years now. Her firm specializes in all aspects of civil litigation. On a daily basis, she deals with clients on the phone, handles billing questions, drafts pleadings, coordinates depositions, and carries out a seemingly endless series of other activities. According to Holbrook, one of the most important things that a new paralegal can do is to visit the local courthouse and make contacts there. "You'll want to know the basic layout of the building and learn a little bit about each of the clerks themselves," she says. "Try to develop a friendly contact in each office. Talk to them before you need them. Most people are pretty friendly, and if you take the time to learn something about them as human beings, you'll find that things will go a lot smoother for you later when you really need something."

Holbrook recommends getting direct-dial numbers for clerks and judge's secretaries, because "Once they know you, calling them up directly can save you a lot of time." Getting to know the people at the courthouse can also have unanticipated benefits, she notes: "When you have friends at the courthouse, they'll actually call you up sometimes with news about one of your cases. They can tell you right away when a defendant has been served or if a new motion has been filed in a case."

(Continued)

(Continued)

Debra Holbrook may go to the courthouse several times a week or only once a month. It all depends on what is happening in the pending cases. When she does go to the courthouse, she makes a habit of stopping by to say hello to as many different people in different departments as possible.

Why would a paralegal need to go to the courthouse? There are several reasons:

- File pleadings in a case.
- File materials requesting service of process on a defendant.
- Look up judgments against individuals.
- Try to locate addresses or other information about witnesses.
- Pull criminal histories on individuals.
- Locate information about what a potential defendant owns to judge his or her ability to pay a judgment.

 Real Paralegal Life: Building A Skill Set

CERTIFICATION

Review your state's law regarding paralegals and then prepare a summary, including any relevant cases and statutes that define exactly what a paralegal is in your state. Does your state offer a voluntary certification program? If so, describe it in detail.

 Career Prep

Receiving payment for services rendered is one of the most important practical concerns of any law office. When the payment arrangement is based on a contingency fee, the paralegal must be aware that though the ultimate fee is based on a percentage of the final award amount, there are certain fees that are factored into that figure. Filing fees and other administrative charges must be billed to the client directly, and it often falls to the paralegal to follow up with the client to make sure that these fees are paid.

When a paralegal works for a firm that primarily bills by the hour, the concerns are different. Of course the firm will still collect administrative and other fees from clients, but the focus is on what activities can be billed to the client on an hourly basis and which ones cannot. Because many firms ultimately send their bills to insurance companies, the activities must be carefully itemized and contain sufficient detail to justify final payment. In these firms, partners, associates, and paralegals prepare daily time sheets summarizing their actions for all clients and assessing these hourly rates to specific files. Specific and detailed records are critical in such firms.

OTHER BUSINESS MODELS FOR LAW OFFICES

In addition to professional corporations and associations, attorneys now have access to several other business models. In the past, an attorney who worked alone might simply organize his or her business as a sole proprietorship and not be able to shield any business or personal assets from lawsuits. The development of the professional corporation helped end this worry, but the professional corporation is hardly the only business model available to modern attorneys. Many states now allow attorneys to organize their firms as limited liability companies or professional limited liability companies. Similar to corporations, a limited liability company allows members to contribute to the business and share in profits but shields the extent of their liability to their contribution to the business. The final business model for any law firm will be the result of the personal inclinations of the member attorneys about how best to protect the firm and their personal assets.

Summary

It is important for any legal professional to understand the basic organization of a law office, especially if he or she plans to work in one. If the office is viewed as a hierarchy, then the attorney-partners would be at the top. These are the attorneys who actually own the firm and are entitled to share in all the firm's profits. They are also authorized to make decisions about hiring and firing staff and which clients and cases should be taken on. The downside of a partnership is that the partners also share in any losses. The individual partners are also subject to personal liability for judgments against the partnership.

Associate attorneys are employees of the firm. They receive a salary, or a salary plus incentives. They are not authorized to share in profits and do not bear the responsibility of the firm's losses. Their salary is much lower than that of a partner, and they work for the firm not only to earn income but also with the idea of one day being invited to become a partner at the firm and substantially boosting their salaries.

Paralegals are legal professionals who are involved in every phase of legal practice. They are essential to the smooth operation of a large firm and increasingly critical in small firms as well. Paralegals meet with clients, draft pleadings, and participate in every stage of a civil case. In recent years, the paralegal profession has received some long overdue attention, with national associations offering certifications in certain legal specialties and several states offering voluntary certification programs.

A law office also employs other support personnel, including the vital role of the legal secretary, who is responsible for the smooth routine of the office, from filing to preparing correspondence and pleadings to fielding telephone calls. In addition to legal secretaries, there are also several other positions commonly found in law offices, such as runners who pick and up deliver important legal documents, law clerks who run errands and do basic legal research, and private investigators who investigate accident scenes and locate potential witnesses.

Key Terms

Partnership, 43
Partner, 43
Managing partner, 43
Unlimited liability, 43
Partnership agreement, 43
Associate attorney, 44
Paralegal, 45
Licensure, 45

Certification, 47
Unauthorized practice of law, 47
Legal document assistant, 47
Legal secretary, 49
Process server, 49
Contingency fee, 51
Professional corporation, 52

Review Questions

1. Explain the organization of a typical law office.
2. What responsibilities and benefits does a partner in an attorney partnership enjoy?
3. Explain unlimited liability.
4. What is a partnership agreement?
5. What provisions are commonly found in an attorney partnership agreement?
6. Discuss the issues surrounding the firm's client list and the dissolution of the partnership.
7. Explain the duties of associate attorneys.
8. Compare and contrast the role of partners and associates in a typical law firm.
9. What duties are normally carried out by paralegals at a civil firm?
10. What national associations certify paralegals?
11. What is the difference between a certified paralegal and a licensed paralegal?
12. What are some of the duties carried out by legal secretaries?
13. What is a "runner" as that term applies to law firms?
14. What duties are normally carried out by clerks at law firms?

15. What are some of the other support staff that may be found at a law firm, and what activities do they perform?

16. Explain contingency fee arrangements.

17. Discuss the issues that arise in billing clients.

18. Why is fee splitting an ethical concern for attorneys?

Discussion Questions

1. Compare and contrast the various roles of support personnel in a typical law office.

2. Explain why fee splitting is an important ethical concern.

3. What are the advantages and disadvantages of being a partner at a law firm?

Exercises: Skill Builders

Contact a local law firm and request to speak with a paralegal who handles civil litigation. Identify yourself as a student and ask if you can have a few minutes of this person's time. Explain that you are completing an assignment to ask this paralegal some basic questions about civil practice. For instance, ask the paralegal what he or she likes and dislikes about civil practice. Ask this person about the biggest misconceptions about working for a law office. If this person could give one piece of advice to a paralegal student, what would it be? Follow up with any other questions you think are appropriate. You will often be surprised at how helpful practicing paralegals are to students. After all, they were once in the same position.

Portfolio Assignment

Portfolio Assignment 3-1: Research the issue of contingency fees in your state and locate a form that will serve as the basis for a contingency fee agreement. Fill out the form using the following information:

1. Client's name: Cal Client.

2. Matter: Litigation arising out of an automobile collision.

3. Client to pay all filing fees, fees to obtain medical and other records, and copying fees.

4. Attorney's Name: Allison Attorney.

5. Attorney's firm to receive one-third of the final settlement amount.

Portfolio Assignment 3-2: In a three-page, double-spaced, typed paper, discuss the various national paralegal associations, including their emphasis, total membership, and the specific certifications offered by each.

Vocabulary Builders

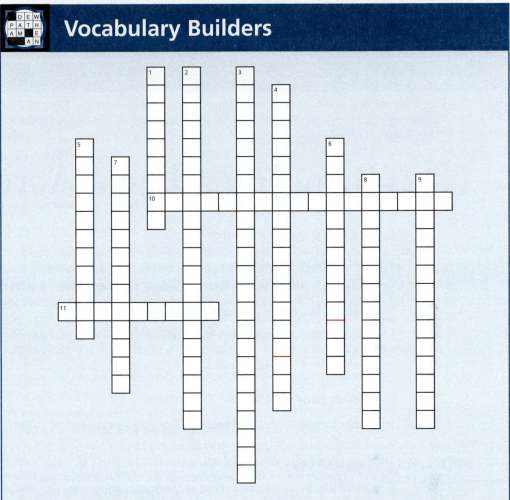

ACROSS

10 An attorney who is an employee of an attorney partnership.

11 The requirement of governmental approval before a person can practice a specific profession.

DOWN

1 A legal professional who handles many aspects of legal practice but is not authorized to give legal advice. Also known as a legal assistant.

2 The contract between the partners that creates duties, establishes responsibilities, and details benefits of the attorneys involved in the partnership.

3 A business model that is reserved for individuals who may form the corporation only after they are licensed by the state to practice their profession.

4 A finding that a business owner's personal assets may be used to satisfy a judgment against the business.

5 A business model where two or more individuals pool assets, run a business for profit, and share in the profits and losses of the business.

6 The recognition of the attainment of a degree of academic and practical knowledge by a professional.

7 A private individual who serves legal pleadings on the parties involved in a civil suit.

8 The attorney's fee calculated as a percentage of the final award in a civil case.

9 A secretary trained to perform specialized tasks directly related to the practice of law.

Chapter 4

Bringing a Legal Action

CHAPTER OBJECTIVES

The student will be able to:

- Explain the importance of determining a cause of action prior to filing a lawsuit.

- Describe the process of evaluating a potential civil case.

- Explain the legal requirement for an independent factual investigation prior to filing a claim.

- Document the significance of Rule 11 of the Rules of Civil Procedure.

- Explain cause of action.

- Describe the initial client meeting and important documentation that must occur therein.

- Prepare a basic client questionnaire.

- Detail the importance of client authorizations for release of records.

- Explain how witnesses should be interviewed about potential cases.

- Describe how a paralegal can conduct basic factual investigations.

This chapter discusses the process of evaluating a civil case and the preliminary investigation that is required before bringing an action. The steps preliminary to initiating a civil action are some of the most important that a paralegal can learn. There are many requirements that must be satisfied before a civil lawsuit can be brought against a defendant. We will discuss those numerous preliminary steps in this chapter, concentrating on not only the rules of civil procedure but also the practical aspects of research, investigation, and preparation that must occur.

EVALUATING A CIVIL CASE

In any civil practice, both paralegals and attorneys must develop the skill to evaluate a case. Evaluation takes into account not only the merits of the case, the law, and applicable statutes but also an in-depth analysis of the witnesses and client. Like any skill, the ability to analyze accurately the basic facts leading to a civil action takes time to develop. Why should anyone take this time? The simple answer is that the better paralegals are at evaluating cases, the better they are at their jobs. **Case evaluation** skills also make paralegals even more indispensable to the firm, helping them understand the legal elements of claims while also building important other skills that can be applied in different legal settings.

case evaluation
The process of investigating the facts, issues, and legal implications of a proposed lawsuit before it is ever filed.

What Is a Case Evaluation?

Evaluating a fact pattern is necessary because the firm must decide whether to represent a client in a particular action. It also helps the firm make a decision about the merits of a particular action and, in many instances, is a legal requirement. We discuss all of these aspects in this chapter, but first we must address a more fundamental question: How is a case evaluation conducted? Case evaluations take into account the following issues:

• The nature of the claim.

• The facts.

• The defendant's liability.

• The impact of the law.

• The likelihood of recovery.

• The extent of the plaintiff's injuries.

The Nature of the Claim

The nature of the claim is perhaps the single most important item in a case evaluation. We assume in this section that you are building your case evaluation skills by working for a firm that represents plaintiffs. The most typical way for a case to begin is when a person schedules an appointment with the firm to review a specific situation. Consider the following hypothetical:

> Martha is a single mother. Last month, as she was driving home from work, she was involved in a car wreck. On a rainy evening, around 8:00 p.m., Martha and her daughter Rachel were heading home. Martha was driving a route that she had traveled many times before. Martha had just picked up Rachel from a late basketball practice, and the two were talking as Martha came into a wide arc in the road that leads to their home. As Martha came to the midpoint of the curve, she noticed a large tractor-trailer rig in the oncoming lane. According to Martha, the truck had come into her lane as it negotiated the curve. Martha was unable to avoid a collision. The back end of the tractor-trailer rig sideswiped Martha's car, and the impact caused her car to go into a spin. Fortunately, the front air bags deployed, cushioning the impact as Martha's car ran off the road and struck a tree. Martha suffered several broken ribs, a broken wrist, and neck trauma. Her daughter suffered numerous scrapes and bruises but no major injuries. Martha and her daughter were taken to the hospital after the collision. Rachel was released within a few hours, but Martha remained in the hospital for three days. She lost time from work, has no medical insurance, and is still in constant pain. Today, she came to your firm with a very basic question: Is the defendant liable?

Before answering the client's question in the preceding hypothetical, the firm must evaluate the case. The evaluation must take into account the facts, the law, and many other issues. This is the skill that we focus on in this chapter.

The first question that must be answered regarding the facts presented in the hypothetical is: What type of case is being contemplated? As we have already seen, there are many different subspecialties in the law. Martha's claim appears to center on negligent driving by the truck driver, which would place it squarely in the field of personal injury or negligence law. However, there may be other theories that would allow Martha the right to recover. In future chapters, we will address concepts such as product liability, strict liability, and other actions that might be authorized according to these facts. For purposes of this chapter, we limit our discussion to a civil action based on negligence. Once the initial determination is made, the next question that must be answered in the case evaluation pertains to the facts.

The Facts

Injuries do not always equate to financial recovery. There are many injuries, from minor scrapes to accidental deaths, that do not provide a means to seek compensation from anyone. A person who is struck by lightening does not have the legal right to recover for an act of God. This is why the process of evaluating the facts is so important. Without the right set of facts, there is no case.

Factual analysis of any civil case must clearly demonstrate that someone other than the plaintiff is at fault. Without such a showing, there can be no lawsuit. Although an initial review of the facts in Martha's case seems to indicate a strong case against the truck driver, case evaluation requires a thorough check of all facts. Are there facts in this case that would have a dramatic effect on the outcome of the case? If it were proven that Martha was operating her car under the influence of alcohol or another drug, that she was in fact across the center line, or that she had lied about critical facts in this case, these elements would affect case analysis. Later in this chapter, we will examine, in detail, exactly how legal professionals gather pertinent information. Once the basic facts have been gleaned, the next step in a case analysis is legal research. Factual investigation will answer the question of the defendant's liability. Was the defendant clearly at fault? What evidence supports this contention? Are there witnesses to the incident? These and many other questions must be answered as part of the factual analysis. There is another important reason to conduct an investigation of the case before a lawsuit is filed: The law requires it.

The Legal Requirement to Investigate a Civil Case

Although it would seem obvious that a firm should investigate the basic facts of an incident before filing suit, recent decades have seen the steady expansion of the number of civil lawsuits filed. Some of these suits have involved frivolous or unfounded claims. Because such claims subject individuals to significant costs, even when the case is resolved in their favor, all states have created a rule that requires attorneys to investigate claims prior to filing suit. The most common version of this requirement is seen in **Rule 11** of the Federal Rules of Civil Procedure.

Rule 11
One of the major rules under the Rules of Civil Procedure; it requires an attorney to investigate an action before bringing it.

Rule 11 Requirements

The Federal Rules of Civil Procedure govern the conduct of all phases of a lawsuit, and Rule 11 specifically addresses the topic of how a civil case may begin. Rule 11 provides:

(a) *Signature.*
   Every pleading, written motion, and other paper shall be signed by at least one attorney of record in the attorney's individual name, or, if the party is not represented by an attorney, shall be signed by the party. Each paper shall state the signer's address and telephone number, if any. Except when otherwise specifically provided by rule or statute, pleadings need not be verified or accompanied by affidavit. An unsigned paper shall be stricken unless omission of the signature is corrected promptly after being called to the attention of attorney or party.

(b) *Representations to Court.*
   By presenting to the court (whether by signing, filing, submitting, or later advocating) a pleading, written motion, or other paper, an attorney or unrepresented party is certifying that to the best of the person's knowledge, information, and belief, formed after an inquiry reasonable under the circumstances,—
   (1) *It is not being presented for any improper purpose, such as to harass or to cause unnecessary delay or needless increase in the cost of litigation;*
   (2) *The claims, defenses, and other legal contentions therein are warranted by existing law or by a nonfrivolous argument for the extension, modification, or reversal of existing law or the establishment of new law;*
   (3) *The allegations and other factual contentions have evidentiary support or, if specifically so identified, are likely to have evidentiary support after a reasonable opportunity for further investigation or discovery; and*
   (4) *The denials of factual contentions are warranted on the evidence or, if specifically so identified, are reasonably based on a lack of information or belief.*

(c) *Sanctions.*
   If, after notice and a reasonable opportunity to respond, the court determines that subdivision (b) has been violated, the court may, subject to the conditions stated below, impose an appropriate sanction upon the attorneys, law firms, or parties that have violated subdivision (b) or are responsible for the violation.

Rule 11 has served as the model for various state sanctions for frivolous lawsuits. Consider Figure 4.1.

The provisions for Rule 11, whether based on state or federal rules, require that any attorney filing an action on behalf of another must have thoroughly investigated the claim and, by affixing his or her signature to the pleadings, attest to this prefiling investigation. As

FIGURE 4.1
Rule 11, Idaho Rules of Civil Procedure

Rule 11(a)(1). Signing of pleadings, motions, and other papers; sanctions.

Every pleading, motion, and other paper of a party represented by an attorney shall be signed by at least one (1) licensed attorney of record of the state of Idaho, in the attorney's individual name, whose address shall be stated before the same may be filed. A party who is not represented by an attorney shall sign the pleading, motion, or other paper and state the party's address. Except when otherwise specifically provided by rule or statute, pleadings need not be verified or accompanied by affidavit. The signature of an attorney or party constitutes a certificate that the attorney or party has read the pleading, motion, or other paper; that to the best of the signer's knowledge, information, and belief after reasonable inquiry it is well grounded in fact and is warranted by existing law or a good faith argument for the extension, modification, or reversal of existing law, and that it is not interposed for any improper purpose, such as to harass or to cause unnecessary delay or needless increase in the cost of litigation.

If a pleading, motion, or other paper is not signed, it shall be stricken unless it is signed promptly after the omission is called to the attention of the pleader or movant. If a pleading, motion, or other paper is signed in violation of this rule, the court, upon motion or upon its own initiative, shall impose upon the person who signed it, a represented party, or both, an appropriate sanction, which may include an order to pay to the other party or parties the amount of the reasonable expenses incurred because of the filing of the pleading, motion, or other paper, including a reasonable attorney's fee. Idaho R. Civ. Pro. Rule 11.

RESEARCH THIS!

Does your state have a corollary to Rule 11? If so, what does the rule say? Locate a copy of it. Then, research any cases under this rule.

Locate a case in which Rule 11 (or its equivalent in your state) played a major role in the case outcome.

LEGAL RESEARCH MAXIM

Remember that the adequate investigation of a case involves not only the facts but also the law. Does your state require specific affidavits or expert reports in certain types of cases? For instance, does your state require expert affidavits in medical malpractice cases prior to filing? Locate the applicable rules and summarize them.

you can see in Figure 4.1, Rule 11 also provides sanctions for attorneys and others who file frivolous, harassing, or groundless lawsuits. These sanctions include paying the other party's legal fees and expenses.

The Defendant's Liability

liability
A jury's determination that one party is responsible for injuries to another party; the basis for an award of damages.

One of the questions that should be answered early in the case evaluation process is, "Just how liable is the defendant?" If the case against the defendant is shaky, the rest of the evaluation will be affected. On the other hand, if the case against the defendant establishes a clear case of **liability**, then part of the legal evaluation will indicate a strong case against the defendant. The facts of the case are the most important aspect of the evaluation. Another important point is to ensure that the factual evaluation is both realistic and objective. In this situation, sympathy for the client can actually cause problems. Legal professionals must be able to take a cold, hard look at the facts presented and make a declarative statement about the extent of the defendant's liability. If the case against the defendant is weak, the final case evaluation must reflect it.

The Impact of the Law

A proper case evaluation must not only consider the facts of the possible case but also the applicable law. The first question that must be answered as part of the legal analysis is: Does the law provide a remedy for the plaintiff's injuries? If, as we have already seen, the plaintiff has suffered an act of God or cannot point to anyone else as the responsible agent for his or her injuries, the plaintiff has no legal option, no matter how severe the injuries. Legal research will focus on the basic facts of the case and whether the law grants a cause of action to the plaintiff.

cause of action
A personal, financial, or other injury for which the law gives a person the right to receive compensation.

Cause of Action. A **cause of action** is the right of the plaintiff to maintain an action against another for specific injuries. Researching a cause of action entails not only comparing the facts of the current case with prior cases but also reviewing cases and statutes. Depending on the nature of the claim, legal research might not only prevent a lawsuit, it might also point the litigants in certain directions. For instance, case law might demand that the case be brought in federal instead of state court, such as when the defendant is a citizen of another state or some other federal question is involved. Legal research into the cause of action not only answers the question of whether a civil action is authorized but also where the case should be filed.

Applicable law can have a drastic effect on the case. For instance, in the minority of states that follow a contributory negligence model, the plaintiff's fault might bar all possibility of recovery. This rule would bar Martha's recovery if the defense were able to show that she was also at fault during the collision, such as driving too fast for conditions. Other jurisdictions follow a comparative negligence rule, such that the plaintiff's recovery is reduced by the amount of her own negligence. Obviously, the legal research portion of case analysis must determine the applicable law and the possible impact on the case of various statutes, evidentiary standards, and prior cases.

There are many different types of causes of actions. Individuals involved in business relationships might bring a breach of contract action if one party alleges that the other failed to meet the obligations created by their contract. A person injured in an automobile accident might bring a personal injury or negligence suit against the person responsible for causing his or her injuries. A short list of causes of action includes:

- Invasion of privacy.
- Defamation.
- Tort.
- Medical malpractice.
- Wrongful death.
- Intentional infliction of emotional distress.

In each case, a plaintiff's cause of action is not only the basis for his or her claim for financial, emotional, or physical injuries; the plaintiff's legal theory about why he or she should prevail against the defendant serves as a basis as well. In this context, a cause of action becomes both the basis of the lawsuit and the theory setting out why the plaintiff is entitled to damages or equitable relief from the defendant. We will discuss cause of action in the next chapter and address damages and equitable relief in Chapter 11.

The Likelihood of Recovery

Although it might seem mercenary to include the extent of the defendant's assets as part of the decision to accept or reject a possible case, the likelihood of financial recovery is as critical a factor in case analysis as any other. Law firms are businesses and must generate income. For plaintiffs' firms, this income comes in the form of contingency fees, or a percentage of the plaintiff's recovery from the case. As we saw in the previous chapter, contingency fees are usually one-third of the total recovery. If the defendant is unable to pay a judgment after successful completion of the action, the firm will recover nothing for all of its efforts. Any plaintiff's firm that engaged in such practices would quickly declare bankruptcy. The investigation that goes into evaluating a potential case therefore must take into account the defendant's financial resources. This evaluation will center around the defendant's personal finances and whether the defendant is insured.

Insurance

Automobile insurance is required for motorists. In the facts set out in the hypothetical on page 63, the defendant likely has the statutorily required insurance. This fact can be established by reviewing the police and accident reports, discussed subsequently. When the defendant has insurance, it can increase the likelihood of recovery and be a positive factor in evaluating the case overall. We will examine issues related to insurance in greater detail in Chapter 8 (Discovery).

The Extent of the Plaintiff's Injuries

The last part of a case evaluation pertains to the extent of the plaintiff's injuries. Once the facts have been investigated and confirmed, the applicable law researched and found to be favorable, the defendant's liability clearly established, and the possibility of recovery verified, the question then turns to the plaintiff's injuries. Many people might be tempted to begin with this question rather than saving it for last. However, the other elements of a case evaluation must be established. If the other elements are either unclear or negative, the plaintiff's injuries, no matter how severe, will dictate that the firm should refuse to take the case.

The defendant's physical injuries should be listed in detail. All medical procedures, treatments, and any medical issues related to the plaintiff must be documented, including any prior injury that might have a bearing on the case. The best way to gather this information is through extended meetings with the client, followed by cross-referencing with all available records.

Initial Client Meeting

In the hypothetical on page 63, the factual situation concluded with Martha appearing at the firm to inquire about suing the truck driver who collided with her car. The **initial client meeting** is vital to establish a working relationship with the client, create an attorney–client relationship, and gather essential information about the case. One method that many legal professionals employ to ensure that all relevant information has been gathered is to use a client questionnaire (see Figure 4.2).

When a person meets with a law firm, he or she is often anxious and in trouble. People who have had no previous experience with lawyers and paralegals base their expectations on the wildly inaccurate view provided in the media.

Please review the client questionnaire in Figure 4.2. As you can see in that questionnaire, there is a great deal of information that can and must be gathered from the client. At a minimum, this information should include the client's full name, address, and home, work, and cell phone numbers. It is also important to note the client's email addresses, both at work and at home. When you need to contact the client on short notice, this information will come in handy.

Obtaining Authorizations from the Client

In addition to signing a contract of representation and gathering information about the client and the incident, the firm will usually obtain a series of signed medical authorizations from the client. A **medical authorization** is a legal document that gives a legal representative the right to

initial client meeting
The first meeting with a prospective client in which information will be gathered, additional information requested, and the attorney–client relationship formed.

medical authorization
A form, signed by the client, that allows the legal team to review and obtain copies of the client's medical records.

COMMUNICATION TIP

It is always important to create a written record of all meetings with clients because of the potential for allegations of legal malpractice. Such a claim could come years after the initial meeting with the client, and the paralegals and attorneys may be hard pressed to remember the specific details of that meeting, especially in the context of similar such meetings with hundreds of other clients. The best practice is to write a follow-up letter to the client as soon as possible after the meeting, detailing what was discussed, problems presented, potential issues, and any additional information that may be needed from the client. Such a letter is even more important when the firm decides not to accept representation of a client. The letter must be specific about why the firm has decided against taking on the case and set out any issues about impending statute of limitations concerns.

FIGURE 4.2
Client Questionnaire

CLIENT QUESTIONNAIRE

CLIENT'S NAME:

ADDRESS:

PHONE # WORK:

PHONE # HOME:

HOW LONG AT PRESENT ADDRESS?

WITH WHOM DOES CLIENT LIVE:

    SPOUSE:

CHILDREN: _____   AGE: _____

            _____   AGE: _____

            _____   AGE: _____

OTHER PRIOR RESIDENCES:

PERSONS CLIENT SUPPORTS: _____   AGE: _____

                         _____   AGE: _____

CLIENT'S AGE:

CLIENT'S DATE OF BIRTH:

CLIENT'S SOCIAL SECURITY NUMBER:

CLIENT'S PLACE OF BIRTH:

CLIENT'S EDUCATIONAL BACKGROUND:

CLIENT'S EMPLOYMENT HISTORY:

CLIENT'S CURRENT EMPLOYMENT:

    EMPLOYER:

    ADDRESS:

    SUPERVISOR:

    TYPE OF WORK:

    LENGTH OF EMPLOYMENT:

    PRESENT JOB STILL AVAILABLE?:

    PAY:

MILITARY HISTORY:

CLIENT EVER TREATED BY PSYCHIATRIST OR BEEN IN MENTAL INSTITUTION?

PHYSICAL AILMENTS?

PHYSICAL AILMENTS OF FAMILY MEMBERS?

OTHER NAMES BY WHICH CLIENT HAS BEEN KNOWN?

BRIEF EXPLANATION OF WHAT HAPPENED:

PRIOR ACCIDENTS/LAWSUITS?

YEAR	COURT	DISPOSITION	PARTY

FIGURE 4.3

Authorization Form for Medical Records (HIPAA Compliant)

To: Anywhere Medical Services, LLC

Re: Jane Doe

Address: 21 Maple Drive, Anywhere, AP 00030

I, Jane M. Doe, do hereby authorize the release of all medical documentation, including, but not limited to medical treatment, diagnosis, medical reports, medical billing, and all other health and medical information to which I am legally entitled, currently in the possession of:

Anywhere Medical Services, LLC

Anywhere, AP 00030

   I further authorize the release of said information in full knowledge of and in compliance with the Health Insurance Portability and Accountability Act of 1996 ("HIPAA") to: Smith and Jones, PC, my attorneys. Under the provisions of HIPAA I grant and authorize my attorneys full and immediate access to my medical records.

   Upon presentation of this medical authorization, you are hereby authorized to release any and all medical records of any kind to my attorneys.

_____

Jane M. Doe

_____

Date

obtain copies of the client's medical records. This information is confidential, and the only way that medical providers will release it to anyone other than the patient is through an authorization. These medical authorizations must comply with the requirements of state law and must also conform to the requirements imposed by the Health Insurance Portability and Accountability Act of 1996 (HIPAA).

HIPAA Concerns

The Health Insurance Portability and Accountability Act of 1996 imposed new requirements on health providers that limit the information they may release about a patient's condition or course of treatment. Any authorization obtained by the firm must take into account these stringent requirements. See Figure 4.3 for a sample authorization form. Many firms have the client sign several copies of these authorizations so that they can serve originals on medical providers. (Many will not accept copies.) In many situations, a HIPAA authorization may remain valid for only one year. In addition, the medical provider may require that the client sign an attorney designation statement, identifying the attorney and the law firm representing the client in a pending action.

Other Information from Clients

When questioning the client about the incident, do not neglect obvious points. Does the client know of any witnesses to the collision? Has anyone taken photos of the car the client was driving? Does the client know if the local press did a story about the wreck? The only way to find out this information is by asking.

   When a new client meets with a law firm, he or she can provide the basic facts of the incident. In the hypothetical, Martha could provide an overview of what happened but will probably not be able to provide the kind of detail that the firm must have before it can initiate a lawsuit. Sometimes, clients bring documentation with them, but most clients do not. What kind of information does the firm need to begin an investigation of a claim? At a minimum, the legal team needs the following:

- Details of the incident.
- The police report.
- Any investigative reports.
- Police accident reconstruction report (if any).
- Witness names and contact information.

Details of the Incident

The client should be questioned in detail about the incident. This is the time to pin down as many facts as possible. It is important to record all relevant data, not only because it is necessary to assist in further investigation but also as a way to confirm the client's version of the incident. If the client's narrative differs in significant ways from the details provided by others, it is a strong indicator that the client is either misinformed or actively deceiving the legal team.

Date and Time.   The most critical piece of information is the date and time of the incident. In Martha's collision, it is absolutely essential to confirm the date of the accident. This date determines the statute of limitations period.

statute of limitation
Establishes the applicable time limits for filing and responding to certain claims or legal actions.

Statute of Limitations Concerns.   A **statute of limitation** is a statutory time limit on legal actions (see Figure 4.4). Different causes of action have different statutes of limitation. In negligence cases, the statute of limitations may be as short as one or two years. In such a situation, the client must file an action before the statutory period expires. If no action is filed within this time period, the action is barred, and the client will have no recourse.

Police Reports

If the police were called to the scene of the accident or were in any other way involved, they will create a police report. The police report is an excellent resource because it is created by a neutral, third party with no vested interest in the outcome of a possible civil case. It also lists important details including the date, time, weather conditions, and other relevant data.

Investigative Reports

In some cases, a police officer or detective may generate a second report, referred to as an investigative report. This report differs from a traditional police report by showing follow-up investigations by the police department. Although investigative reports are common in criminal investigations, they are rare in situations involving routine traffic accidents. However, if such a report exists, it behooves the legal team to locate a copy of it and review it closely. An investigative report will provide additional details not found in the police report, including additional witness statements, forensic investigation, and additional evidence not mentioned in the original police report.

Police Accident Reconstruction Report

In the hypothetical case presented on page 63 of this chapter, we outlined a fairly routine traffic accident. These cases are all too common in the United States and one of the most common lawsuits in the American court system. Because of the frequency of automobile accidents, many police officers have received training in accident reconstruction. An accident reconstructionist can gather details from the scene of a car collision and prepare a report showing the most probable sequence of

FIGURE 4.4
Statute of Limitation for Personal Injury Cases (Illinois)
Source: IL ST CH 735 §5/13-202.

§ 13-202. Personal injury—Penalty. Actions for damages for an injury to the person, or for false imprisonment, or malicious prosecution . . . shall be commenced within 2 years next after the cause of action accrued.

events that led to the injuries. Police officers trained in accident reconstruction will measure skid marks, the pattern of glass shards from broken headlights and windshields, and the relative position of the automobiles, which they use to reach conclusions about which driver was at fault. These conclusions can be invaluable to a legal team considering bringing a lawsuit. If the conclusions of the accident reconstructionist run against the client, the legal team should reconsider bringing the case.

Witnesses

The police report often contains the names and contact information of any witnesses to the incident, but any good prefiling investigation will attempt to locate additional witnesses. The police may not have located all witnesses to the incident. The client may know of others who have information about the case. All of these individuals should be noted and marked for later interviews. Important witness information includes:

- Name.
- Address.
- Telephone numbers, including work, residence, and cell, if known.
- Place of work.
- General description (if name is incomplete or not known).

Other Critical Information

In addition to gathering all of this information, individual cases require additional specific information. There may be a need to gather specific information unique to each case. In Martha's case, for instance, it will be important to know if the truck driver was employed for a company at the time, whether he was on duty at the time of the incident, whether he was under the influence of alcohol, whether either driver was cited by the police, whether trucks were permitted on that particular section of road, and a host of other issues. As you can see, other critical information depends on the nature of the claim and the specifics surrounding the actual incident.

Client Intangibles

It also is important to understand that the initial and subsequent meetings with the client are not limited simply to gathering information about the case. There is another important evaluation that the legal team must take into account: the client. Under the heading of "Client Intangibles" fall such things as the client's personality, the client's background, previous medical history, and other factors.

Client Personality.   Why is the client's personality an important part of any case evaluation? The answer is simple: If the case goes to a jury, the client's personality will have a profound impact on the case. We would all like to believe that cases are decided solely on their factual and legal basis, but in truth, the personalities of the main players in the case are also critical. If the client has a pleasant disposition and will have a positive impact on the jury, the case will have a better chance of a positive resolution than a situation in which the client is rude, obnoxious, and annoying. One of the most important parts of the preliminary evaluation of the client involves the answer to a very basic question: Will the client make a good witness?

Will the Client Make a Good Witness?   If the case goes to trial, the client will take the stand. The client is a witness to the events in the case and must testify about important aspects of the case, including the incident and subsequent events. If the client is someone who will make a positive impression on the jury, this fact should be noted prominently in the materials used to record important details of the case. If, however, the client is someone who will obviously make a terrible impression on the jury, this fact should be noted just as prominently.

Cross-Referencing the Client's Version.   One of the final elements involved in evaluating the client is confirming the client's version of the facts with other sources. Does the client's version of the events correspond to the record? Are there significant discrepancies? If so, is there a good reason for these discrepancies? A client might, for example, have been so traumatized by the incident that his or her memory was affected. Alternatively, significant discrepancies might indicate a client who is either exaggerating injuries or actually trying to deceive the legal team. In any event, these discrepancies must be cleared up before the case is filed.

Information the Law Firm Provides to the Client

So far, we have limited our discussion to the information that the client provides to the legal team. But there is another important information exchange that must be addressed: the information that the firm provides to the client.

Court Procedures

The original reason that the client sought legal advice was to inquire about his or her rights and the possibility of bringing a lawsuit against another. The client may not have any experience with the court system and so may not understand many of the procedures. For instance, clients are often confused and frustrated by the length of time it takes from filing the complaint to actually trying the case. They do not understand why this process can take a year or more. Explaining it to them at this stage will often prevent a lot of the client's frustration later on. The legal team must explain the various stages involved in bringing a suit and also frame the process in such a way that the client understands that the court system has many other cases currently pending and that it may take months or years to resolve his or her case. The initial meetings with the client are the time to explain all of these aspects of bringing or defending a civil suit. Paralegals should keep in mind that many times a client will not ask basic questions out of a fear that he or she will appear stupid or misinformed. Take the time to explain the entire procedure of a civil case to the client and give the client numerous opportunities to ask questions.

Many law firms provide the client with a printed handout or brochure that explains the legal process in detail. The client can take the printed material home and review it later. If you are called upon to create such a brochure, it should spell out in uncomplicated terms exactly what happens at each stage of the lawsuit. When they are well written, these brochures can also serve as a marketing tool for the firm. When the case concludes, the satisfied client may give the brochure to a friend who has just been injured in a car wreck, generating additional income for the firm.

Videotapes.   There are currently several different professionally produced videotapes and DVDs that discuss all phases of civil litigation. Companies market these media to law firms, which in turn provide them to clients at no charge. They answer most of the common questions raised by new clients, and clients can watch them several times to better understand the legal process.

INVESTIGATING THE CLAIM

Now that we have established the need for a proper investigation of an incident before a lawsuit is ever filed, the next question becomes: How is such an investigation carried out? Although you might be tempted to think that attorneys hand the responsibility of the factual investigation off to a private detective, there are several reasons why this is not the case. For one thing, private detectives are expensive, and there are numerous cases for which this investment is simply not cost effective. A case that might potentially earn only a few thousand dollars would quickly turn into a losing proposition if a large chunk of that ultimate recovery went to pay a private detective's wages. Another consideration pertains to the timeline of the case. Although private detectives can do a great job locating witnesses, taking photographs, and interviewing witnesses, they might not enter the picture until months, or even years, after the event. It is extremely difficult to reconstruct the facts after so much time has passed.

As a general rule, both sides in a civil case, plaintiffs and defendants, simply wait too long before involving a private investigator in the case. Normally, the parties only justify the additional expense when the case is likely to go to trial, but that can be months or even years after the complaint was filed.

By the time a private investigator is brought into the case, critical information may already be lost. The road where the accident occurred could be paved over, so all evidence of skid marks are gone. Sometimes, the entire area has changed because of road or other construction. Both time and money considerations are reasons attorneys conduct their own investigations or insist that paralegals do so.

Career Prep

WHAT MAKES A GOOD INVESTIGATOR?

Deborah Reusher is a paralegal investigator for the Missouri Public Defender's Office in Kansas City, Missouri. She describes her responsibilities as follows: "We work on a case from the beginning, doing the prework for the trial, and then help out through the trial. We touch on all phases of a case." Her work involves going to the scenes of crimes, taking photos and video, and interviewing witnesses. According to Reusher, investigation is all about people: "To be a good investigator, bottom line, you need good people skills. You really have to know how to read people. You have to know what kind of situations to walk into, when to take a buddy with you."

Attorneys and Paralegals as Investigators

Having an attorney or paralegal conduct the preliminary investigation solves many of the problems created by using private detectives. For one thing, the legal professional is already on the payroll. For another, a paralegal can go to the accident scene within days of the initial client meeting. The photographs, videos, and witness contacts made at this early juncture can mean the difference between winning and losing a case at trial.

Paralegal Investigators

Although it is common for attorneys to conduct the prefiling investigation, it is becoming increasingly common for attorneys to entrust this duty to paralegals. The reason is simple economics: While the attorney is generating additional income by meeting with new clients, conducting depositions, or participating in a trial, the paralegal can do the basic investigative work and then present a complete picture to the attorney subsequently. Of course, the final decision to take the case will rest with the attorney, but it may be your responsibility, as a paralegal, to gather all the information to help the attorney make an informed decision. The attorney may not have the time to go to the scene right away, and there are other reasons why the attorney should not be the person to create certain forms of documentation. For example, if the attorney goes to the scene and learns something about the case, he or she cannot testify about it. Attorneys are legally barred from being both witnesses and advocates in the same case, which is one reason an attorney should not interview witnesses with no one else present. If the witness gives a statement and then later contradicts it, the attorney cannot take the stand and dispute it. But if the paralegal took that statement, the paralegal is perfectly capable of being sworn in and questioned about it. Therefore, paralegals must know the basics of investigating a case, including how to locate and interview witnesses, document testimony, and gather evidence.

Locating Witnesses

We have already seen that there are several potential resources for locating witnesses in civil cases. The client, for example, can provide names of witnesses. The names will also appear in police and accident reports. Once located, individual witnesses may be able to provide information about other witnesses. However, simply obtaining a person's name does not always mean that you will be able to find this person. Some witnesses are difficult to locate and may challenge your ability to track them down.

witness locator service
A company that provides information about a witness's former addresses, telephone numbers, employment, and current location.

skip tracing
A general term for tracking a person who has absconded or is attempting to avoid legal process.

Witness Locator Services.   A **witness locator service** is a company that locates people for a fee. They can be private investigators, "**skip tracing**" agencies, or other types of businesses that specialize in locating people who do not wish to be found. However, in most civil cases, a well-trained paralegal can find a witness without having to resort to such companies. How do you locate witnesses? Go to the witness's last reported address and talk to his or her neighbors. If you can locate family members, ask them. One person can often provide a goldmine of information about a person: an ex-wife or ex-husband. You can request a person's new address from the U.S. Post Office, though a written request, on office letterhead and signed by an attorney, is usually

SURF'S UP!

The widespread availability of the Internet has made it much easier to locate information, but that availability does not always guarantee the quality of the sources. The biggest problem with the Internet is that there is no method for ensuring the pedigree of a particular site. Web sites may offer substantial resources or simply be platforms for people to express radical views. As a general rule, legal professionals can trust Web sites established by government agencies or higher education institutes, but even these may not have the most up-to-date information. Your own critical thinking skills are still your best guide; you must be able to not only locate information online but also sort through sites for the best and most accurate data.

CYBER TRIP

Phone Directories Online
www.reversephone-directory.com
Locating individuals
www.peoplefind.com
people.yahoo.com
www.whowhere.com
www.infospace.com

required. The Internet offers several free services to locate people by last name, region, or other identifying information. Most public libraries have telephone books for cities across the nation. Look up the witness's name there; you might actually find it. If you have reason to believe that the person is actively avoiding being found, it may be necessary to resort to a professional service.

Internet Search.   In addition to hiring a witness locator service, it is also possible to glean a great deal of information about a person through a simple Internet search. Using Google or Yahoo! or any of a number of other online services, you can gather a lot of information about a person, including any references to a person mentioned in a newspaper article, address, telephone numbers, age, whether they have created their own Web site, and even a satellite image of their home (using Google Earth, at earth.google.com, for example).

Interviewing Witnesses

When it comes to talking to witnesses, keep your pen and paper handy. Although you might think that tape recording the person's statement would make better use of the interview time, many people become nervous and uncommunicative when a tape recorder comes out. Of course, you should never tape record a person's statement without his or her permission, so if the person does not wish to be tape recorded, the next best thing is to write out what the person tells you. It is important to record not only the data that the person provides but also the phrases and vocabulary that the witness uses to describe the incident. Later, you may need to type up your notes or even prepare an affidavit, and a witness is more likely to sign such a document when the writing actually sounds like the person.

Even if your tape recorder is working perfectly, you should still take notes. Good note taking is an important skill that pays off in many different contexts. When interviewing a witness, for example, keeping notes helps you stay focused on the important issues in the case, while giving you the opportunity to follow up on interesting points that the witness has raised during the interview. Having a prepared list of questions is a good starting point, but when it comes to interviewing, your best assets are your ability to take good notes and actually listen to what the witness has to say. You may find that the witness brings up issues that you had not considered when you originally created your list of questions. Sometimes, witnesses surprise you with information you never expected them to possess. Being able to track these issues with careful note taking can save a great deal of additional follow-up work.

Interviewing witnesses is a skill that only comes with practice. Establishing rapport with a person before getting him or her to provide details of the incident is often the best way to approach an interview. If you like to talk to people, you will probably make a good interviewer. Find a way to create common ground with a witness before asking the pertinent questions. People are reluctant to talk with lawyers or other legal professionals. A good paralegal investigator must overcome that hurdle and get the person to relax. An uncomfortable, nervous person will never provide as much information as a comfortable, relaxed person will. Hopefully, you will already have a copy of the police and accident reports with you that you can use to cross-reference what the witness tells you. You should also compare the information provided by the witness with what you have previously received from the client. Is there a disparity between the two? It is not unusual for witnesses to disagree about minor points in a story. However, the main points should

PRACTICE TIP

You can always get better ideas about how to research from speaking with police officers. Call a local detective and ask for pointers about how to do some basic investigative work in civil cases. Also make sure that you know what you can and cannot do under the law.

remain the same from witness to witness. For instance, they might disagree about the color of the cars, but there should not be any disagreement about the fact that there was a collision.

Interviewing Techniques

Interviewing others is both a skill and an art. It takes practice to master the ability to get people to speak to you, especially when they learn that you are a legal professional. The first reaction most people have is that they do not want to become involved in any legal action, even as a witness. You can explain that you are gathering information, but you should not promise that the person will never be called to testify. At this early point in the investigation, it is far too soon to rule anyone out as a potential witness at the trial. However, there is no reason to be overly aggressive. Most paralegals who interview witnesses try to be approachable and courteous. After all, you are simply doing a job that has been assigned to you, and this person may have information that is critical to your client's case.

When questioning witnesses, it is extremely important to let the witness tell his or her story. Allow the witness to recount the story in a narrative and then follow up with questions after the main facts have been provided. From the plaintiff's perspective, the important facts to be learned from a witness are those facts that either help the case or hurt it. Witnesses who corroborate the client's version of what happened are just as important as are witnesses who disagree with the client's version of the facts. Witnesses often know of other people with more information, and asking them about other witnesses is always an excellent idea. It also helps to visit the scene. Whether the scene is the site of a car wreck or the office layout in a sexual harassment case, knowing the "lay of the land" prior to talking with key witnesses helps the paralegal understand the facts being related. Such knowledge also helps when a witness begins to exaggerate or in the few occasions when a witness actually lies. In addition, the basic facts of the lawsuit—who, what, when, where, and why—should always be asked and recorded for later review. Any discrepancies among the versions provided by the witnesses should be prominently noted.

Of course, it is equally important for the paralegal to make sure that the witness is under no illusions about the role of the paralegal. Any paralegal conducting an investigation should always properly identify him- or herself as a paralegal, not as an attorney, private investigator, detective, or police officer. Such identification is an ethical requirement, and misidentifying yourself as a police officer or attorney is against the law.

Purposes of the Interview

The purpose of any witness interview is to learn as much information about the case as possible, as well as plan how the witness's testimony may be used. Will it be necessary to depose this witness? Is the witness likely to testify at trial? Although it is not possible to answer these questions conclusively in a preliminary investigation, there are times when the answers are plain. An eyewitness will almost certainly testify. During the interview, the paralegal should also make notations about the witness's attitude. The witness should be classified as friendly, neutral, or hostile. The witness's attitude will often determine to what extent the legal team will rely on that person's testimony in later hearings or at trial.

Deceitful Witnesses

It is an unfortunate fact of life that some witnesses shade, exaggerate, or deliberately lie about critical facts in a case. How can you tell when someone is lying to you? Even trained investigators sometimes have trouble spotting a lie. Usually, no single factor will demonstrate a person's credibility. For instance, if a witness fails to make eye contact with you, that could indicate deceit, or it might just as easily indicate a person who is anxious or nervous. Instead of looking for one telltale sign, weigh the person's entire story. Do the facts add up? Could the person have seen what he or she claims to have seen? Does this person have a vested interest in the outcome of the case? Do you, as the interviewer, have some reservations about the person's testimony? These are just some of the factors that go into evaluating the veracity of a person's statement.

Documenting the Scene

Another important aspect of a preliminary investigation relates to documenting the scene where the accident occurred. This step is important no matter what the issues are in the case. Obviously, the scene of an automobile accident will prove to be a critical element of a case, but the scene is just as important in other types of cases. As people move through their lives, they are constantly negotiating their way around other people and inanimate objects that affect their actions. In a sexual harassment case, for example, where does the plaintiff allege that the harassment occurred? Is this area secluded? Could others have witnessed the incident? In almost all civil and criminal cases, the location where the incident occurred is critical.

Accident scenes can change their appearance quickly. If you wait even a few weeks before going out to record the site, the scene may have changed dramatically. For instance, road crews may have come through and put up barriers where none existed before. A change in seasons can mean that the foliage and underbrush have changed their appearance. Skid marks and other evidence of the crash fade and disappear over time. All of these are excellent reasons to go to the scene as soon as possible.

Photographs

Photographs of the scene are absolutely essential and should be taken as soon as possible. When the client informs the legal team about the location of an accident, the paralegal should go to that scene armed with a still camera, a video camera, and some blank paper for drawing a diagram.

We have all heard the old maxim that a picture is worth a thousand words. In litigation, it can be worth thousands of dollars. The jury may not understand what happened from two hours of testimony, but a single snapshot can bring the case home for them. Photographs should take in all the available angles of the scene. When you are taking photographs, try to duplicate the conditions of the accident as close as possible. If the collision occurred in the morning, make sure that you go to the scene in the morning. Shadows, the angle of the sun, the position of trees, and more can have a huge impact on the case.

When in doubt, take your photographs with an eye toward what the jurors ultimately will see in the case. Remember that most jurors will be unfamiliar with the scene and may not have a frame of reference. You should take camera shots from as many different angles as possible, but do not neglect the obvious. Still shots are great for pinpointing exact details, but video can sometimes make or break a case.

Video

These days, there are a huge number of choices for capturing moving images. In addition to the traditional videotape, there is now digital video. For the sake of clarity, we refer to all of these formats as "video."

If a paralegal has taken still shots of the scene, why would it be necessary to also take video? Moving video is more interesting to watch, and jurors can get a better idea of what happened in the case by watching a moving picture. This is true for automobile accidents, but video is commonly used in other types of cases, too. For instance, plaintiffs' attorneys routinely present "day in the life" videos to support damage claims. A day in the life video follows the plaintiff through a normal day, showing how the plaintiff's injuries impact everyday activities, from getting out of bed to taking out the trash to going to work. Videos can have a huge impact on jurors.

Although it is always best to have a professional shoot your video footage, that is not always feasible. There may not be sufficient funds to hire a professional, and early in the case, while the firm is still evaluating the facts, the only person available to take video may be the paralegal. If you are the person called upon to shoot video of any scene, here are some guidelines:

- Move the camera slowly. Some people find this to be a lot more difficult than it sounds. We all have a natural tendency to aim the video camera at one thing and then at another. The problem with doing so is that when you view the tape later, your eyes get whiplash because the scene is changing so quickly.

- Hold the camera with a steady hand. Shaky video can be a terrible distraction and limit its effectiveness.

- Keep perspectives in mind. Start your video from a known landmark and follow a common-sense route, either right to left or left to right.

- Avoid comments. If your video camera has a way to mute the audio part of the recording, use it. Do not talk while the video is running. You should certainly avoid inserting comments such as, "Wow! Our guy must have really been speeding to go this far off the road!" For videos, the best course is no audio at all.

- Do not use dramatic effects. These days, many video cameras come with a host of special effects. Do not use them for your video. It might make the video more dramatic to put a warning sign in the shot that wasn't actually there when the accident occurred, but you are there to record, not to improvise. In the same vein, you should not rearrange the site to make it more picturesque or dramatic. Record the scene as it appears, not as you would like it to appear.

Diagramming the Scene

If you have taken the time to capture the scene in still photos and video, why do you need a diagram of the scene? A diagram gives you a different perspective on the scene, and you want as many different perspectives as possible. The time to draw your diagram is while you are still at the scene. You should not concern yourself with making the diagram to scale, but you should make sure that you capture important features, especially landmarks that are already on film or videotape. Later, you can compare the photos and video to the diagram. It should give you and your witnesses a better understanding of what the scene is like.

Gathering Evidence

When you collect photographs, videotape, and witness statements, you must save them for future use. Put everything in a clearly marked box in the firm's basement or in a storage unit that belongs to the office. Never store it in a box in your office. Somehow, when you need it, the box will mysteriously disappear. Worse, the cleaning crew might think that it is trash and throw it out for you. Of course, you should store all of this information in the case file, but you might also want to consider making backup copies of everything.

When you want to preserve evidence, take a cue from *CSI* or other law shows. The reason that they store evidence in plastic bags is to keep people from handling or tampering with it. Plastic bags are see-through, so you do not have to keep taking your evidence out of the bag to see what it is. *CSI* also provides a couple of other good tips; for example, label the bag with information such as:

- Who collected it.
- When it was collected.
- Where it was found.

Researching Public Records

When it comes to evaluating a case, it is also important to review the public records, which can provide valuable information about the defendant, the witnesses, and even your client.

 SPOT THE ISSUE!

THE GREAT CAT FOOD CAPER

A few years ago, a woman was getting ready to feed her cat. When she picked up the can of cat food, it exploded. She had severe injuries, and after numerous trips to the doctor, she sought a lawyer to sue the cat food company. The attorney was eager to take the case, seeing the possibility of a huge settlement against a multinational corporation. "So," he said, "where's the can?"

The woman looked at him blankly. "The can? Oh, I threw that away a long time ago."

You be the judge: What is the result? Can they bring their case? Why or why not?

FIGURE 4.5

Information That Can Be Developed about Witnesses

1. Full name, address, and telephone number. (clerk's office; deed room; tax office)

2. Where the house is located, what it looks like. (tax office)

3. A rough picture of finances. (clerk's office; UCC filings; deed room)

4. Does the person have a criminal record? (clerk's office; Internet)

5. Prior contact with the legal system; has the person ever been a plaintiff or a defendant in a civil suit? (clerk's office)

6. Any pending litigation, either civil or criminal. (clerk's office)

7. Does the person have a relationship with anyone else in this suit? (birth/death records, marriage records, probate court)

8. What kind of assets does this person own? (deed room; tax office)

9. What does the person do for a living? (neighbors; deed room)

10. Does the witness have anything in common with you? (all of the above)

See Figure 4.5. One of the best places to start a review of public records is the clerk of court's office.

The Clerk of Court's Office

The local clerk's office maintains records about all civil and criminal cases in the county. Most clerks' offices are now computerized, which speeds up information gathering tremendously. Using the computer databases, a paralegal can learn whether someone has been sued, divorced, or convicted of a crime. Some terminals can provide you with statewide information on both civil and criminal cases. If you want to know if one of your witnesses has a criminal record, the clerk's office is the best place to start. Private detectives use these resources all the time, but you do not have to be a licensed private investigator to get access.

Just around the corner is another information treasure trove: the deed room.

The Deed Room

Sometimes called the registrar's office or the land office, the deed room is where records of all real estate transactions are stored. Although it might not sound very promising, it is one of the best places to gather information about a person. In this office, for instance, a paralegal can find out what real estate a person owns (useful in evaluating the likelihood of enforcing a judgment). You can also find out how much this person paid for the property. Although in most cases the purchase amount is not stated directly on the deed, the tax assessed on the purchase can help you figure out the sale price. You can also find out if someone has recently transferred property out of his or her name into someone else's—a close family member, for instance. This common act in domestic cases occurs when someone is trying to shield assets. Most deed rooms also have plats or maps of the properties owned to help you locate exactly where the property is. Information also is available about first and second mortgages. How much does this person owe? Has he or she recently obtained a second or even third mortgage on the property? If so, it might indicate financial trouble.

UCC Filings

Other sources of information can help you build a picture of a witness or potential defendant. For instance, the Uniform Commercial Code filings, commonly referred to as UCC filings, are required for financed items like cars and boats. This information is free and open to the public. Has your witness purchased a boat lately, had a garage door installed, or purchased a new car? The UCC filings will tell you. You might think this information is not very helpful, but imagine that you are about to interview someone, and this person has critical information. Wouldn't it be a great icebreaker to mention in passing that you like to water ski, knowing full well that this witness just purchased a powerboat? Establishing rapport with a person is essential if you are going to get any information out of him or her. Obviously, this information also helps you build a better picture of the defendant's finances and his or her ability to pay a substantial civil judgment.

Birth, Marriage, and Death Records

It is always helpful to know who someone's family members are. You can get this information from birth and death records. In some states, this information is stored in the deed room; in others, it is in the probate court. Wherever they are stored, these records are worth a look. In the past, when people did not relocate as often as they do today, you could glean a person's entire history from these records alone. However, these records may be of limited use. People relocate so often now that is rare to find someone who has lived in the same area his or her entire life. The birth records will show the names of the person's parents and children but only if they were born in that county. In some states, this information is linked with probate records, which show if the person was the beneficiary of a will. Along with birth and death records, marriage licenses can tell you a lot about family relationships. These records, along with the others mentioned previously, are important for asset searches too. Knowing what someone owns is always helpful in determining if they should be sued in the first place.

Tax Office

The tax office is required to keep extensive records about real estate, and all of this information is open to the public. Many people never think about going to the tax office for information, but it has more raw data than any other office. The tax office is the perfect place to start if the only information you have on someone is his or her name. Most people do not realize just how extensive the tax office information is. The tax office can give the basic floor plan of the person's house, including the number of bedrooms and bathrooms; total square footage, including heated and unheated spaces; amenities like decks and pools; and even information about recent renovations. In some tax offices, you can see a digital photo of the house. In larger counties, such as metropolitan Atlanta, this information is available at public access terminals. A picture of the house and all of the details are just a mouse click away.

DETERMINING A CAUSE OF ACTION

The end result of all of the investigative work on a case is to build as complete a picture as possible of the facts of the case so that the attorneys can establish that a cause of action exists. We will examine other legal issues related to bringing a lawsuit in Chapter 5.

 SPOT THE ISSUE!

Your firm has scheduled a meeting with a potential new client. When you and the attorney meet with the client, he describes the following facts:

He works at a local factory and his boss, who is female, has on several occasions touched him in what he describes as inappropriate ways. She often tells him that his skin is beautiful and that his eyes are the bluest that she has ever seen. She has recently promoted him to become her office assistant, even though he has very little office training. She schedules late evening meetings and tries to give him back rubs. The entire situation has made him uncomfortable. When he complained to the department supervisor, the supervisor told him that he was crazy and that a man cannot bring a sexual harassment suit against a woman.

Is this a case for sexual harassment, based on your own state's decision on the topic? Do we advise this client that, on the basis of our review of the applicable law, this is a case we will take or one that we will turn down?

Kozar

v.

Bio-Medical Applications of Ohio, Inc.

L 2244482, 1-4

(Ohio App. 9 Dist., 2004)

[unreported case]

I.

The facts of this case are not in dispute. On January 28, 2002, Nicholas Kozar, age 84, died during kidney dialysis treatment at Bio-Medical Applications of Ohio. Coincidentally, an Ohio Edison power line failed, causing temporary, accidental and unexpected power outages at the center. The county medical examiner investigated a possible link between the power outage and Mr. Kozar's death, and reported that Mr. Kozar died of natural causes associated with chronic heart disease, with no causation attributed to the concurrent power outage.

Almost a year later, Peter M. Kozar contacted attorney Mark C. Cavanaugh, seeking to file a lawsuit and relating that an unnamed emergency room physician had alleged that the power outage caused his father's death. Relying on this information and without conducting any legal research, Cavanaugh rushed to file the complaint on January 27, 2003, naming Bio-Medical Applications of Ohio and Ohio Edison as joint defendants and claiming negligence.

On March 13, 2003, Ohio Edison's attorney called Cavanaugh to urge the dismissal of Ohio Edison, instructing him that his claim was baseless under prevailing law and informing him of the medical examiner's conclusion. The call was formalized in a follow-up letter, which detailed the deficiencies of Cavanaugh's claim and warned that a motion for sanctions would be forthcoming unless the suit was dismissed. In his defense, Cavanaugh has insisted that he would not dismiss an action merely on such threats, but also admitted that he did not investigate whether Ohio Edison's assertions had merit.

Ohio Edison moved to dismiss the action on the basis that, under established Ohio law, Ohio Edison owed no duty to Mr. Kozar, a non-customer. At a subsequent deposition, Cavanaugh testified that it was at this point that he did his first legal research. Yet, even with his own research, Ohio Edison's legally compelling motion and the prior warning of insufficiency, Cavanaugh refused to concede. Rather, he opposed the motion by arguing that utilities do owe a duty to non-customers and citing non-Ohio case law. Ohio Edison replied that even these cases were inapplicable, as they addressed intentional misconduct, not negligence. On June 20, 2003, the trial court granted Ohio Edison's motion.

As promised, Ohio Edison moved for attorney fees, under both Civ.R. 11 and R.C. 2323.51, alleging a frivolous claim. The trial court conducted a hearing, during which Ohio Edison entered evidence, without objection, of $12,683.15 in attorney fees resulting directly from the claim. The trial court denied the sanctions on January 6, 2004, but expressly ruled on only Civ.R. 11. The order concluded that it was a final appealable order with no just cause for delay, and it is from this order that Ohio Edison appeals.

Ohio Edison timely appealed, asserting two assignments of error for review. We reverse the order of the assignments of error to facilitate review.

II.

As a prelude to this analysis, we begin by noting that this Court has previously decided a case on point. See *Ceol v. Zion Industries, Inc.* (1992), 81 Ohio App.3d 286, 610 N.E.2d 1076. In *Ceol,* counsel for defendant Zion Industries wrote a letter early in the litigation articulating the insufficiency of plaintiff's evidence and the preclusive effect of the established law, and also offering to forgo a motion for sanctions if Mr. Ceol and his attorney would heed their warnings and dismiss the case. Id. at 288, 610 N.E.2d 1076. Mr. Ceol resisted, and upon obtaining summary judgment, Zion Industries moved for sanctions under both Civ.R. 11 and R.C. 2323.51. Id. The trial court denied the sanctions. Id. at 289, 610 N.E.2d 1076.

On review, this Court affirmed the denial under Civ.R. 11's subjective bad-faith standard, on the basis that the trial court's refusal to assign subjective bad faith to Mr. Ceol did not rise to the level of an abuse of discretion. Id. at 290-91, 610 N.E.2d 1076. However, this Court reversed the decision under R.C. 2323.51's objective measure of frivolous conduct, finding that the trial court erred as a matter of law by erroneously concluding that a misinterpretation of existing law was enough to meet the objective measure of good faith. Id. at 292-93, 610 N.E.2d 1076. The case was remanded for an award of attorney fees under R.C. 2323.51. Id. at 293, 610 N.E.2d 1076. The present case proceeds along similar lines, and stare decisis guides the outcome.

A.

First Assignment of Error

"THE TRIAL COURT ABUSED ITS DISCRETION IN FINDING THAT PLAINTIFF'S COUNSEL COMPLIED WITH CIVIL RULE 11[.]"

Ohio Edison challenges the trial court's finding that the evidence was insufficient to demonstrate Cavanaugh's subjective bad faith under Civ.R. 11. We disagree.

The trial court denied Ohio Edison's frivolous conduct claim under Civ.R. 11, and thus denied attorney fees. Civ.R. 11 expressly requires that the frivolous conduct must be willful; mere negligence is insufficient. *Riston v. Butler* (2002), 149 Ohio App.3d 390, 777 N.E.2d 857, 2002-Ohio-2308, at ¶ 9. We review a decision on Civ.R. 11 for abuse of discretion. *City of Lorain v. Elbert* (Apr. 22, 1998), 9th Dist. No. 97CA006747.

Regarding the factual inquiry, the trial court found that Cavanaugh relied on his client's story of an unnamed emergency room physician who claimed the power outage killed his father. An attorney's reasonable reliance on the client's representations does not constitute bad faith. See *Driskill v. Babai* (Mar. 26, 1997), 9th Dist. No. 17914. Regarding the legal inquiry, Cavanaugh's failure to research his claim, his unawareness of the law, and his collection of only inapplicable, out-of-state case law appears to rest in negligence rather than willfulness. The trial court could reasonably decide that the evidence was insufficient to establish subjective bad faith. Therefore, we cannot conclude that the trial court abused its discretion in reaching its decision with respect to the Civ.R. 11 claim.

Ohio Edison's first assignment of error is overruled.

Costs taxed to both parties equally.

Source: From Westlaw. Used with permission of Thomson/West.

Case Questions:

1. According to the patient's heirs, what impact did the power outage have on the decedent's medical care?

2. Did the plaintiff's attorney investigate the claims raised by Ohio Edison?

3. When was the first time that the plaintiff's attorney conducted legal research into the claim?

4. What impact did prior existing case law, directly on point, have on the outcome of this case?

5. According to the court, does a misrepresentation of existing law rise to the level of bad faith? If so, what impact does this have on the case?

 Eye on Ethics

CLIENTS

One area filled with potential problems is the initial meeting with the client. We have already mentioned the dangers involved in the unauthorized practice of law. This meeting is the most common place for a client to ask you a legal question, such as, "Does my case look good?" There is almost no way to answer this question without getting into some form of legal advice. When this question comes up, the safest course is to simply say that you cannot give legal advice and leave it at that. However, not all clients will let the issue go so easily. They will ask what you think when they really want some assurance that things are going to work out all right. If you understand the real reason behind this question is to seek assurance, you can speak to the client's real concerns and still avoid giving legal advice.

 A Day in the Life: Jane Huffman

For Jane Huffman, a litigation paralegal, preparing a case begins with a review of the police or accident reports. She reviews these reports extensively before speaking with any witnesses. "These reports can give you a lot of information about the case, and you can use it to test your witness's knowledge of the case. Before I speak with regular witnesses," says Huffman, "I try to speak with the police officers involved."

Interviewing the police officers offers several advantages. "For one thing," she says, "police officers are trained to remember and record details. They can give you a lot of information about the case in a short period of time." Huffman follows a regular procedure when speaking with police officers: "First, I introduce myself and tell them right up front that I'm a paralegal and we're thinking about bringing a suit for client X." After that, "I ask the police officer if he has any drawings or photographs that will help me understand what happened." She is often surprised how often they do. Then she tries to find out what they think about the case. A police officer may have developed a feel for the case by watching all of the people involved and can often tell a paralegal early on about a particular problem in the case.

Huffman finds that most police officers are easy to talk to, though "the attorney I work for has a good reputation in the community, and that helps." But there are some guidelines that she follows when she speaks with police officers. "For one thing," she says, "don't be too aggressive. Police officers, like everybody else, are turned off if you're too aggressive in your questions."

(Continued)

(Continued)

When Jane Huffman interviews witnesses in civil cases, she keeps in mind some basic rules: "First of all, always be honest and straightforward. I'll call the witness and tell them that the attorney asked me to call. I say we need some information about the case. Sometimes they talk to me and sometimes they don't. Sometimes I call just to find out if they're willing to speak with us at all."

There are some questions that a paralegal can always expect to get from a witness. One of them involves whether they will have to testify or not; Huffman says, "I always tell them that I don't know if the case is going to go to court or not." She never promises that the witness will not have to testify, because "at this stage, I don't know what is going to happen, and I tell them that. I try to get as much information as possible without pressing too hard. Some people just are not going to tell you anything." Later, the legal team may use subpoenas and scheduled deposition to uncover what these people know, but it is always helpful to get as much information as early as possible in the process.

Real Paralegal Life: Building a Skill Set

INVESTIGATING ACCIDENT SCENES

Go to the courthouse or your local paper and find a recent automobile accident. Investigate this case as though you were the paralegal assigned to it from your firm. What facts can you develop about the main players in the case? Is there a viable case? Would you recommend that your firm take this case? Provide specific examples and facts to justify your recommendation.

Career Prep

Whenever the firm considers representing a new client, one of the most important practical applications to follow is a conflicts check. A conflicts check is a review of the firm's current and past client list to make sure that the action brought by the new attorney will not affect a previous client. An attorney is barred from representing the plaintiff in one action and the defendant in another. This action raises the specter of a conflict of interest, in which the interests of one client are in direct conflict with the interests of another. This conflict places the attorney and the firm in an untenable position; they have access to privileged and sensitive information about a client who is now about to be sued by the firm. In such a situation, the attorney and firm should disqualify themselves from representing the new client when there is even a possibility that the new client's action will impinge on the interests of a previous client.

Summary

The process of evaluating a potential civil case involves many different elements. A case evaluation must take into account various factors, including the nature of the possible claim, the facts setting out the defendant's liability, the law, the likelihood of recovery, and the extent of the plaintiff's injuries. Rule 11 of the Federal Rules of Civil Procedure—and its analog found in most state court rules—requires that an attorney must investigate a claim before bringing it. This investigation must focus on not only the facts of the case but also a review of the applicable laws. Before a plaintiff can bring an action against a defendant, the plaintiff must have a cause of action. A cause of action is a legally recognized wrong committed against the plaintiff that entitles the plaintiff to recovery in a court of law.

To investigate a claim adequately, the law firm must first meet and consult with the client to gather as much information as possible. The initial client consultation involves obtaining extensive information from the client, including the details of the plaintiff's injury, background on the plaintiff, and additional details. At the initial client consultation, the law firm often obtains authorization forms that allow the firm to obtain copies of the client's medical and other personal files. This material is essential to an adequate review of the case. Additional investigations will be required before the lawsuit can be filed. Additional information will come in the form of reviews of accident or police reports, medical records, and interviews with witnesses, among other things. A paralegal must know some basic investigative techniques in the event that he or she is called on to go to the scene and record important details.

Key Terms

Case evaluation, 62
Rule 11, 64
Liability, 65
Cause of action, 66
Initial client meeting, 67

Medical authorization, 67
Statute of limitation, 70
Witness locator service, 73
Skip tracing, 73

Review Questions

1. What are the preliminary steps to bringing a lawsuit?
2. Why is it important to evaluate a civil case before bringing it?
3. Explain the steps involved in evaluating a case.
4. Why should the nature of the claim have an impact on the decision about whether the law firm should accept the case?
5. Explain the steps involved in a factual analysis of a potential lawsuit.
6. What legal requirements are imposed on attorneys to conduct a thorough evaluation of a case prior to filing?
7. What is Rule 11, and what impact does it have on filing a lawsuit?
8. Explain the sanctions that can be imposed for violations of Rule 11.
9. How does an investigation into the defendant's liability affect the decision about whether to file the case?
10. What is a cause of action?
11. Explain how the fact that there is very little likelihood of recovery can have a damaging effect on a case evaluation.
12. Discuss the impact that the existence or nonexistence of insurance has on a case evaluation.
13. How do the plaintiff's injuries influence the case evaluation?
14. What is an initial client meeting?
15. What kind of information should the legal team obtain from a client during the initial client meeting?
16. What are medical authorizations?
17. What is HIPAA, and what impact does it have on obtaining medical authorizations?
18. Explain the statute of limitation concerns in evaluating a case.
19. What kind of information can be gleaned from accident and police reports?
20. What information should be obtained from witnesses to the incident?

Discussion Questions

1. Why would states and federal courts impose such stringent requirements on attorneys to conduct a thorough investigation of a case before the case is filed? Wouldn't it make more sense for the facts to come out as the case proceeds?
2. Why would a paralegal be called on to conduct some basic investigation into a civil case? What type of investigation is detailed in this chapter? Would you feel confident conducting such investigations?

Locate a fellow student who has been involved in a car accident. Interview this person, using the details provided in this chapter as a guide to the comprehensive nature of your interview. Pretend that this student is a new client. Prepare a complete client questionnaire and prepare as much detail as possible about this incident.

 # Portfolio Assignment

Portfolio Assignment 4-1: Create a basic investigative toolkit. Before you can carry out some basic investigative work, you need the right tools. Here are the nine things you need in your investigative toolkit:

1. Tape recorder.
2. Still camera.
3. Video camera.
4. Hammer and nails.
5. Pen and paper.
6. 100 ft. tape measure.
7. 12 in. ruler.
8. Extra tapes and batteries for all your machines.
9. Latex or rubber gloves.

TAPE RECORDER

You should always have a tape recorder with you, even when you do not plan on talking to any witnesses. You will be surprised to learn how many times a little trip to the accident scene for a couple of photos will turn up additional witnesses to whom no one has spoken.

Not all witnesses like to be recorded, and you should not record anyone without permission. But tape recorders are not just for witness interviews. When you go to the scene, you may not always have the time to sit down and write out your impressions. Instead, you may have to dictate what you see and transcribe it later. Your next piece of equipment is equally valuable: a still camera.

PHOTOS AND VIDEO

We have already discussed the important need to document visually any scene that will have importance in a lawsuit. Although we tend to recognize the importance of photos and video in automobile accidents, visual documentation is important in almost all cases. In contract cases, the issues often center on performance or the lack thereof. A photo showing the level of completion can answer that question better than several live witnesses. In divorce cases, evidence of physical trauma from violence can offer dramatic testimony. Visual documentation should be an element of prefiling research in all cases.

As far as photographs go, paralegals should take lots of them. When you do, you will find that you can never shoot enough. Too much is better. Some paralegals deliberately fill an entire roll or two of film, just to make sure that every possible angle and element of the claim is documented.

HAMMER AND NAILS?

From the high-tech world we move to decidedly low-tech tools: a hammer and nails. Why should these be an important part of your investigative toolkit? Ask any private investigator. They routinely hammer a ten-penny nail at the beginning of a skid mark and put the other one at the end of the skid mark. That way, even if the road is later paved over, they can use a metal detector to find skid marks. A hammer is also a useful tool for brushing away debris and other items that you might not want to put your hands in.

(Continued)

(Continued)

OTHER ITEMS

Rounding out your investigative toolbox, we find some more obvious items. You should never go anywhere without pen and paper. A 100-foot tape measure comes in handy for measuring. But if you have a measuring tape, why do you need a ruler? The ruler is important to give you some measuring technique for close-up photographs. Suppose you want to show the size and indentation of a gouge in the roadway or the size of blood stains on the front of a car. The problem with close-up pictures is that it is hard to get any perspective. By placing a ruler in the picture, you give the viewer a frame of reference.

Finally, you always need extra film, tapes, batteries, and rechargers. Remember Murphy's Law of recording equipment: If something can go wrong, it will, and right when you are about to get something that will win the case. Finally, always have several pairs of surgical or rubber gloves handy. You never know when you may need to handle something that is either dirty or potentially harmful. Having several pairs of gloves handy will help keep your hands clean.

Portfolio Assignment 4-2: We have reviewed the case recently brought to us by Jane Doe. Our firm has reviewed the applicable law and does not feel that her claim of psychic distress, created by an overbearing boss and his obvious mental powers, is a sufficient cause of action. We must inform our client of this fact in such a way that she understands that we will not be representing her in this case but also inform her that the statute of limitations for such an action, at least as she has described it, will run out in three weeks. Create your own firm letterhead and draft a letter that explains these concerns, as well as our decision not to accept the case.

Vocabulary Builders

ACROSS

2 A jury's determination that one party is responsible for injuries to another party; the basis for an award of damages.

7 A personal, financial, or other injury for which the law gives a person the right to receive compensation.

8 One of the major rules under the Rules of Civil Procedure; it requires an attorney to investigate an action before bringing it.

DOWN

1 A company that provides information about a witness's former addresses, telephone numbers, employment, and current location.

3 The first meeting with a prospective client where information will be gathered, additional information requested, and the attorney–client relationship formed.

4 The process of investigating the facts, issues, and legal implications of a proposed lawsuit before it is ever filed.

5 A form, signed by the client, that allows the legal team to review and obtain copies of the client's medical records.

6 A statute that imposes a time limit on the initiation of a civil action.

Chapter 5

Civil Complaints

CHAPTER OBJECTIVES

The student will be able to:

- Identify the basic components of a complaint.
- Describe the important procedural rules that affect how complaints are drafted.
- Explain subject matter jurisdiction.
- Define the term "limited jurisdiction" and how it applies to federal courts.
- Explain the requirements of capacity and standing in civil suits.
- Define the "case or controversy" requirement.
- Identify the importance of the concepts of mootness and ripeness.
- Describe the caption or style of a complaint.
- Explain the importance of notice pleading.
- Define the role of factual allegations in a complaint.

In this chapter, we will examine the issues that surround commencing a civil action, including jurisdictional questions, standing, and other legal elements of complaints. We will also examine the elements of a complaint, explain the significance of each feature, and show how a complaint raises a legal claim against the defendant.

PARTIES

plaintiff
The party initiating legal action.

defendant
The party against whom a lawsuit is brought.

Before we can discuss the issues pertinent to filing a complaint, we must answer a basic question: Who are the parties to a lawsuit? The easiest answer is that the **plaintiff** is the party who files suit, and the **defendant** is the party who is served with the complaint. But that answer does not provide sufficient detail. How does someone become a plaintiff, and what rules govern how and when a person can be sued? We begin by defining the parties and then proceed to the issues that give a party the right to claim a legally recognized injury so that he or she may be called plaintiff.

Defining "Party"

Under the federal rules, the definition of a party is relatively simple. A party is one who seeks relief or against whom relief is brought. Under this definition, a party can be a person, a business, a governmental entity, or even a corporation. Any of these can sue or be sued. This definition also does not limit itself to the named plaintiffs and defendants. Anyone who has an interest in the proceedings can be a party in a federal civil action. As we will see in subsequent chapters, simply because a plaintiff brings suit against a specific defendant does not mean that other parties are barred from entering the action. Under the theories of cross-claims, interpleader, and impleader, additional parties may join the action. However, to become officially designated as a defendant, some procedural issues must be satisfied, including the service of process. We will discuss service of process later in this chapter.

Adverse Parties Are Required

In any lawsuit, there must be two adverse parties. If the court dismisses the case against the defendant, the suit is dismissed. The suit also is dismissed when there is more than one defendant and each is eliminated from the case. Without adverse parties, there can be no suit.

JURISDICTIONAL ISSUES IN CIVIL SUITS

One of the first issues that a plaintiff must establish is that a court has the power to hear the action contemplated. At its simplest level, jurisdiction refers to a court's power to make rulings that are binding on the parties involved. Jurisdiction comes in many forms. Before a court can make binding decisions, it must have two basic forms of jurisdiction: personal and subject matter.

Personal Jurisdiction

personal jurisdiction
A court's power over the individuals involved in the case; when a court has personal jurisdiction, it can compel attendance at court hearings and enter judgments against the parties.

Before a court can consider the issues involved in any suit, the judge must make a determination that he or she has **personal jurisdiction** over the parties. Personal jurisdiction is the power of the court to create binding decrees on the parties and enforce those court orders on all parties. A court does not acquire personal jurisdiction simply because the court exists. Instead, the plaintiff must establish that the court has personal jurisdiction over all of the parties. The plaintiff does this by investigating the issues in the case, carrying out legal research, and then alleging the basis of personal jurisdiction in the complaint.

Personal jurisdiction can be a complicated question. How, for instance, does a court acquire personal jurisdiction over the parties? Personal jurisdiction can be established by any of a number of methods. The most important basis of any allegation of personal jurisdiction is that, at some time, the defendant has had contact with the geographic area where the court is located. That geographic component gives the court the power to fashion orders that require the defendant to appear in court, answer pleadings, and, ultimately, pay any judgment assessed against him or her. Therefore, personal jurisdiction has a geographic and legal basis. The geographic basis, referred to as the **forum**, requires that the defendant must have lived, worked, or done business within the geographic boundaries of the court. Let's suppose that a particular court's forum is contained within a single county. For the court to exercise personal jurisdiction over the defendant, the plaintiff must show that the defendant has had a presence within that county. Doing so establishes the forum where the court's authority can be expressed. The legal basis of personal jurisdiction is the consideration of how the court can determine that the defendant had sufficient contacts within the county to make it fair to sue the defendant there and also to require the defendant to appear before that court. There are several different legal tests that courts can use to justify personal jurisdiction over the defendant. They include the defendant's

forum
The proper legal site or location.

- Presence
- Domicile
- Consent
- Minimum contacts

Presence

The simplest and most obvious way to establish that the court has personal jurisdiction over the defendant is for the defendant to be located physically within the court's forum. Physical presence automatically gives the court personal jurisdiction over the parties, even if the defendant is within the jurisdiction for only a limited period of time. If the plaintiff can show the defendant was served with a copy of the summons and complaint while the defendant was in the forum jurisdiction, the court has personal jurisdiction over the defendant. The court can then require that the defendant to appear for future court hearings and sanction the defendant if he or she fails to appear.

Domicile

domicile
The place where a person maintains a physical residence with the intent to permanently remain in that place; the permanent home of the party.

Another way that a plaintiff can establish the court's personal jurisdiction over the defendant is to prove that the defendant is domiciled in the forum jurisdiction. **Domicile** is the legal term for residence. If the defendant has a residence in the area, it can be sufficient to establish personal jurisdiction (*Milliken v. Meyer,* 311 U.S. 457, 61 S. Ct. 339, 85 L. Ed. 278 (1940)). A domicile is something more than mere presence in a state; to qualify, a person must reside in a specific location and have the intent to remain there indefinitely.

Consent

Another method to establish the court's personal jurisdiction over the defendant is by the defendant's consent. If the defendant agrees to appear in court and submits him- or herself to the court's authority, then the defendant has consented to personal jurisdiction and waived any objection.

Minimum Contacts

The last category used to establish personal jurisdiction over the defendant is based on a legal test created in the case that has been the bane of law students' existence for decades: *International Shoe Co. v. Washington,* 326 U.S. 310, 66 S. Ct. 154, 90 L. Ed. 95 (1945). In a long, complicated opinion, the U.S. Supreme Court established that a court could acquire personal jurisdiction over a commercial enterprise when it has had sufficient minimum contacts with the forum to make it reasonable for the defendant to answer lawsuits there. The premise is that the defendant has had business contacts within the forum, has had the advantage of profits, and has even paid taxes in the forum, and therefore, it is not unreasonable to require the defendant to answer a complaint in the same forum.

Special Appearance

special appearance
A term describing a defendant's contest of jurisdiction; the defendant enters the court for the limited purpose of contesting the case, but does not submit to the court's jurisdiction for other purposes.

A defendant who wishes to challenge a court's personal jurisdiction may do so through a **special appearance**. When the defendant comes before the court through the vehicle of a special appearance, he or she contests the court's power to enter any order in the matter, without simultaneously triggering personal jurisdiction through the appearance. Consider the implications for a defendant who, in contesting personal jurisdiction, unwittingly submits to it. By making a special appearance before the court, defendants insulate themselves from a claim that they have opened themselves to the court's personal jurisdiction simply by appearing before the court to contest its authority. Without this ability, a defendant would be faced with two grim possibilities: fail to appear in court, have judgment entered against him or her, and then attempt to attack the judgment

SURF'S UP!

There are many sources from which to obtain forms for nearly every type of civil filing it is possible to bring. You can search through various online search engines and find a plethora of forms. Some of these forms are in PDF format, provided by the local or state court system. Others are completed or sample legal filings. There are even companies that advertise sample civil forms that are "legal in all 50 states." With the exception of blank forms provided by the court system, you should view all other sample pleadings and forms with skepticism. The same holds true for the more traditional method of disseminating forms: form books. A form or sample

pleading is only as good as the person who put it together. Although you can certainly review sample pleadings in other cases as a guide in your own case, never rely on them exclusively, especially with any company producing forms that are valid throughout the country. There is such a wide variation in legal practice from state to state that it is virtually impossible to create any form that is valid in every state court from Alaska to Florida. In the end, you must rely on your own state or Federal Rules of Civil Procedure, statutes, and case law. There is no perfect sample pleading that will work in every case.

when the plaintiff seeks to enforce it or appear in court to contest the action and by so doing submit to the court's personal jurisdiction. A special appearance avoids both of these unpleasant alternatives. If a court should rule that it has no personal jurisdiction over the defendant, the defendant may have the case dismissed, and the plaintiff will be forced to refile in a jurisdiction that does have authority over the defendant.

Subject Matter Jurisdiction

subject matter jurisdiction
A court's authority over the res, the subject of the case.

In addition to establishing personal jurisdiction over the defendant, the plaintiff must also prove that the court has **subject matter jurisdiction** over the issues in the case. Subject matter jurisdiction is the power of the court to hear certain types of cases. Federal courts and many state courts are circumscribed by limited jurisdiction. They are permitted to hear only specific types of cases, and if the plaintiff cannot prove that the court is empowered to hear the issues in his or her case, the court will dismiss the suit.

General Jurisdiction Courts

All states have at least one court that is empowered to hear a broad range of lawsuits, from divorces to personal injury to contested wills. These are referred to as general jurisdiction courts. They have subject matter jurisdiction over a wide variety of cases. In many states, this court is referred to as superior court. The state legislature has granted superior courts this wide general jurisdiction to provide a mechanism for litigants. In some situations, the superior court may have transferred the authority to hear certain types of cases to other courts. For instance, when a superior court authorizes the creation of a small claims court, it transfers its jurisdictional power to that court. In situations involving claims below a specific amount, such as $1,000, small claims court would be authorized to hear those cases. If we were to diagram the subject matter jurisdiction of a superior court, we would see that it was originally vested with general jurisdiction, then transferred a portion of its jurisdictional power to another court, creating a court of limited jurisdiction.

Court of Limited Jurisdiction

A court of limited jurisdiction is empowered to hear only certain types of cases. On the state level, small claims court is an excellent example. When a person wishes to sue another for a small amount of money, he or she must take the case to small claims court, because this court is specifically empowered to hear such cases. If the litigants have a case involving other issues, they are required to file their suit in a court of general jurisdiction.

Limited jurisdiction courts are significant in that they can consider only specific issues. Although all states have at least one court of general jurisdiction, limited jurisdiction courts are the rule, not the exception, in federal courts.

Federal Court Jurisdiction

Article III of the U.S. Constitution authorizes the creation of the federal court system but also imposes restrictions on that system. For one thing, all federal courts are courts of limited jurisdiction. Federal courts are empowered to hear only those cases that fall within certain specified classifications, including:

- Federal questions
- Diversity of citizenship
- Amount in controversy

Federal Questions.   Federal courts are specifically authorized to consider questions involving the application of the U.S. Constitution or the U.S. Code. To bring a case within the confines of a federal court, the plaintiff must prove that the federal court has subject matter jurisdiction. The practical result of this rule is that the plaintiff's preliminary allegations in a federal complaint are more detailed than those typically found in a state court complaint. After all, the state court will often be a court of general jurisdiction, giving it broad discretion to hear a wide variety of issues. Federal courts, in contrast, have always been courts of limited jurisdiction, and given the general interpretation against granting federal jurisdiction, the plaintiff must prove federal jurisdiction at the outset of the lawsuit.

Diversity Jurisdiction.   Diversity cases involve lawsuits between citizens of different states or territories. Because of the potential for abuse and the wide disparity between state-based laws, requiring the suit to be brought in federal court makes sense. All federal courts follow the same procedures and are at least arguably free of local prejudices in favor of one litigant or the other.

The rules about establishing citizenship resemble and are actually based on the rules we previously discussed concerning domicile. If a plaintiff is domiciled in one state and the defendant is domiciled in another, it satisfies the diversity of citizenship rules to invoke federal court jurisdiction.

Amount in Controversy.   However, diversity of citizenship does not always guarantee that a federal court will accept a particular case. There are additional requirements. For instance, the plaintiff must also establish a minimum monetary threshold before the federal courts will become involved. To bring a case in federal court, the plaintiff must prove that the amount in controversy between the parties exceeds $75,000, not counting court costs and interest. The plaintiff must make an allegation in the complaint that his or her damages exceed this amount and that the parties are domiciled in different states before the federal court is authorized to hear the case.

When considering the complexities of federal cases, questions often arise about the interplay between subject matter jurisdiction and personal jurisdiction. Proof of one does not negate the requirement of proof of the other. The plaintiff must prove both subject matter and personal jurisdiction before federal court jurisdiction is triggered (see Figure 5.1). If a plaintiff can establish one but not the other, a federal judge must dismiss the plaintiff's complaint.

Hypothetical 5-1

Anna has a claim against Stewart. They are both citizens of different states and have clearly established domiciles in different states. Anna wishes to bring her claim in federal court because she has heard that these courts are generally more favorable to plaintiffs. Can Anna establish subject matter jurisdiction in federal court?

Answer: No. Anna must establish not only diversity of citizenship but also that her claim involves an amount of at least $75,000. Without such proof, a federal court will not consider the case.

Pendent and Ancillary Jurisdiction

What happens in cases in which there are multiple issues, some of which clearly fall within a federal court's jurisdiction and some that do not? Put another way, does the fact that some of the claims do not satisfy federal jurisdiction mean that none of the claims can be heard in federal court?

If a party can establish that some of his or her claims fall under federal subject matter, then that party can take advantage of the concepts of pendent and ancillary jurisdiction to have all claims heard in one court. This compromise negates the only other option: that the parties would litigate some of their claims in federal court and some in state court. That option would be an unnecessary duplication of effort and result in the unnecessary waste of time and effort, especially when the claims are all related.

FIGURE 5.1
Federal Court Jurisdiction
Source: 28 U.S.C. § 1332.

> (a) The district courts shall have original jurisdiction of all civil actions where the matter in controversy exceeds the sum or value of $75,000, exclusive of interest and costs, and is between—
>   (1) citizens of different States;
>   (2) citizens of a State and citizens or subjects of a foreign state;
>   (3) citizens of different States and in which citizens or subjects of a foreign state are additional parties; and
>   (4) a foreign state, defined in section *1603* (*a*) of this title, as plaintiff and citizens of a State or of different States.

Ancillary Jurisdiction. **Ancillary jurisdiction** is the power of a federal court to consider issues that do not technically fall within the court's subject matter jurisdiction but are part of other claims that do. In such a case, the court would be authorized to make rulings on closely related issues. Ancillary jurisdiction involves parties. As we have already seen, one of the basic requirements of a federal action is that diversity of citizenship exist between the parties. If a defendant wishes to bring a claim against a third party but that third party is a resident of the same state, ancillary jurisdiction allows cross-claims against persons who would ordinarily not meet the minimum federal requirements. In such a case, the plaintiff would be from State A, the defendant from State B, and the third party defendant also from State B. We will discuss third-party complaints and related issues in the next chapter.

Pendent Jurisdiction. Whereas ancillary jurisdiction focuses on the parties, **pendent jurisdiction** focuses on the nature of the claims. Once the plaintiff has established subject matter jurisdiction on some of the claims, he or she can rely on pendent jurisdiction to request that the court rule on other, closely linked issues, even when they do not technically meet the requirements of federal jurisdiction. Because the claims are closely linked, the court can rely on pendent jurisdiction to make final determinations on all. Both ancillary and pendent jurisdiction require that the claims be closely interlinked with one another. If they are not, the court will refuse to consider them and insist that the parties bring a separate, state action to resolve them.

Exclusive Jurisdiction

exclusive jurisdiction
Only one court has the authority to hear the specific case; for example, only a federal court can decide a bankruptcy case.

When we say that a court has **exclusive jurisdiction**, it means that a particular action must be brought in a specific court. When a business or person wishes to file bankruptcy, for example, the court with exclusive jurisdiction is the U.S. Bankruptcy Court. Similarly, on the state level, cases involving particular disputes, from child support to cases in which the amount in controversy is above a specific amount, must be brought in the court that possesses the appropriate exclusive jurisdiction.

Removal

removal
Moving a case from the state court to the federal court system.

In situations in which a state action has commenced but the state judge determines that the issues actually qualify under federal jurisdiction, the judge is authorized to transfer the case to federal court. This action is called **removal** (see Figure 5.2). A defendant has the right to file for removal by bringing a motion requesting it. This motion must allege that though the case was filed in state court, it properly requires federal court jurisdiction. A defendant might file a motion to remove a case when he or she is domiciled in another state and the claim involves $75,000 or more. In that case, the minimum federal threshold would be met, and the case would qualify for federal, not state, court.

In Rem Jurisdiction

Although our discussion has centered on personal and subject matter jurisdiction, it is important to note that though these are the most common bases of jurisdiction, they are not the only forms. For instance, in some situations, the fact that the defendant owns property in a particular venue may be enough to submit him or her to the jurisdiction of the court, at least for some matters. Basing jurisdiction on the location of real property is referred to as **in rem jurisdiction**.

in rem jurisdiction
A court's authority over claims affecting property.

Concurrent Jurisdiction

There are times when a party may have the right to bring an action in one of several possible courts. Suppose that a plaintiff located in one state wishes to bring a civil action against a

FIGURE 5.2
Actions Removable Generally
Source: 28 U.S.C. § 1441(a).

(a) Except as otherwise expressly provided by Act of Congress, any civil action brought in a State court of which the district courts of the United States have original jurisdiction, may be removed by the defendant or the defendants, to the district court of the United States for the district and division embracing the place where such action is pending. For purposes of removal under this chapter, the citizenship of defendants sued under fictitious names shall be disregarded.

defendant located in another state. The plaintiff may bring it as a federal action, based on diversity of citizenship, or may travel to the defendant's home state and bring the action there. **Concurrent jurisdiction** is a term that encompasses the situation in which more than one court has the power to hear a particular matter. In such a case, the plaintiff may decide to choose one court over another because the rules or applicable laws weigh more in the plaintiff's favor. As we have already seen, however, when a plaintiff brings a case in state court in which federal courts have concurrent jurisdiction, the defendant may have the case transferred to federal court.

concurrent jurisdiction
Jurisdiction over the subject matter exists in both state and federal court, unless statutorily prohibited.

CAPACITY AND STANDING

Once the jurisdictional issues have been resolved, a plaintiff must establish other legal prerequisites, including the parties' capacity and the plaintiff's standing to bring the suit.

Capacity

In all civil suits, the parties must have the capacity to know and understand the legal effect of the claim. Capacity is a word that is used in different ways in the law. Capacity to enter into a contract is not the same as the capacity necessary to make a will. Here, the word "capacity" takes on yet another meaning. To initiate a complaint, the plaintiff must establish that he, she, or it is free of a legal disability, such as insanity, incompetence, or infancy. In any of these situations, the plaintiff would be unable to prove the ability to know and understand the consequences of bringing suit. In situations in which the plaintiff has been declared mentally incompetent or is under the age of 18 years, the courts will presume that the plaintiff lacks capacity and dismiss the case.

Unlike most other aspects of a civil suit, there is no requirement to list a party's capacity in the complaint. See Figure 5.3. Instead, if capacity becomes an issue, the other party can raise it once the suit has commenced.

Capacity is listed as a separate element because courts consider it independently of other questions such as cause of action or other action. As often occurs in other situations, when a person lacks the ability to understand the legal action, the courts are short circuited from taking any further action. Before any developments in the case, the court must be satisfied the parties understand what is occurring (*Sun Pipe Line Co. v. Altes,* 511 F.2d 280 (8th Cir. 1975)).

Is capacity an issue when dealing with businesses? Certainly. A corporation that has been dissolved lacks the capacity to be sued in the same way that a natural person who has been declared mentally incompetent lacks the capacity to be sued (*Walder v. Paramount Publix Corp.,* 132 F. Supp. 912 (S.D.N.Y. 1955)). Because corporations are artificial persons, the fact that they no longer legally exist is an issue of capacity. Other business models, especially ones that do not enjoy the recognition of "artificial person" under statutory laws, have different capacity issues. In those situations, the plaintiff normally sues the natural persons who make up the business, not the business itself.

Suing through a Representative

When a plaintiff or defendant lacks capacity, it does not mean that he or she is unable to be a party in a suit; it simply means that he or she must have a representative appointed to represent his or her interests. A representative must be appointed by a court and must act with the party's best interests in mind.

FIGURE 5.3
Federal Rules of Civil Procedure, Rule 9(a) Capacity

It is not necessary to aver the capacity of a party to sue or be sued or the authority of a party to sue or be sued in a representative capacity or the legal existence of an organized association of persons that is made a party, except to the extent required to show the jurisdiction of the court. When a party desires to raise an issue as to the legal existence of any party or the capacity of any party to sue or be sued or the authority of a party to sue or be sued in a representative capacity, the party desiring to raise the issue shall do so by specific negative averment, which shall include such supporting particulars as are peculiarly within the pleader's knowledge.

PRACTICE TIP

Begin with the End in Mind

When your firm decides to take on a new case, you should always begin the case with the end in mind. For litigation purposes, the end is the trial. Your preparation should anticipate potential trial issues. Although most civil cases settle, you should act as though each case you handle will definitely go to trial. With that in mind, you will find yourself focusing on visual aids, such as photographs and diagrams that will show the jury important information. You also need to record as much detail as possible. If you receive evidence from a client, keep it in a safe place. It may be used during the trial, and there could be a question concerning tampering with the evidence. Prepare the client for the real prospect that the case will take a long time to resolve, especially if it goes to trial.

SPOT THE ISSUE!

Last week, Mrs. Rivera's neighbor, Kurt, smashed her back windshield with a tire iron. It caused $920 in damages, and Mrs. Rivera wants to sue Kurt for the damages. Kurt is in high school and has had trouble with the law before. Mrs. Rivera knows, for instance, that Kurt spent time in a youth detention facility last year. What jurisdictional and other issues does this case raise?

Standing

standing
Legally sufficient reason and right to object.

Standing is a separate issue from capacity to sue. When a person has standing, he or she can establish that a particular court has the constitutional power to hear the case and that one or more of the plaintiff's guaranteed rights have been infringed upon or that the plaintiff has a property interest that will suffer as a result of another's actions. Standing ensures that the persons who bring actions have some stake in the outcome. It is not enough for a party to claim that a court's decision might eventually impact his or her potential rights; the party must show that the certain, specific actions are having an adverse effect on the party. In federal court, establishing standing has two parts: The plaintiff must show that the federal court has the authority to resolve the dispute and that the party's constitutional, financial, or property rights are involved (*Kowalski v. Tesmer,* 125 S. Ct. 564 (U.S. 2004)). The reason that standing is required has more to do with the underlying theories of the separation of powers among the three branches of government. Requiring a party to establish standing places the court outside the realm of actively seeking potential governmental problems and hypothetical issues. Instead, the court concerns itself with concrete controversies between real parties and leaves it to the other branches to anticipate problems and create solutions for them (*Elk Grove Unified School Dist. v. Newdow,* 124 S. Ct. 2301, 159 L. Ed. 2d 98, 188 Ed. Law Rep. 17 (U.S. 2004)). Under these rules, a plaintiff must prove to the court three different elements. The first is that he or she has suffered an "injury in fact."

Injury in Fact

Courts have defined the concept of injury in fact as an invasion of a legally protected interest that is "concrete and particularized." This definition excludes hypothetical questions, advisory opinions, and other issues that have not yet been brought before the court by litigants (*Lujan v. Defenders of Wildlife,* 504 U.S. 555, 112 S. Ct. 2130 (U.S.Minn.1992)). See Figure 5.4. Other courts have defined standing as the requirement that the plaintiff must have suffered a distinct and palpable injury. Without such a showing, the plaintiff lacks standing, and the case will be dismissed. But simply showing an injury in fact is only the first step in establishing standing.

Once the plaintiff has established an injury in fact, the courts next look to the causal connection between the injury that the plaintiff is complaining about and the conduct that caused it. We

FIGURE 5.4

Standing—Rule 17. Federal Rules of Civil Procedure

(a) Real party in interest.

Every action shall be prosecuted in the name of the real party in interest. An executor, administrator, guardian, bailee, trustee of an express trust, a party with whom or in whose name a contract has been made for the benefit of another, or a party authorized by statute may sue in that person's own name without joining the party for whose benefit the action is brought; and when a statute of the United States so provides, an action for the use or benefit of another shall be brought in the name of the United States. No action shall be dismissed on the ground that it is not prosecuted in the name of the real party in interest until a reasonable time has been allowed after objection for ratification of commencement of the action by, or joinder or substitution of, the real party in interest; and such ratification, joinder, or substitution shall have the same effect as if the action had been commenced in the name of the real party in interest.

PRACTICE TIP

To establish standing, a party must have "alleged such a personal stake in the outcome of the controversy as to assure that concrete adverseness which sharpens the presentation of issues upon which the court so largely depends for illumination of difficult constitutional questions." (*Duke Power Co. v. Carolina Environmental Study Group, Inc.*, 98 S. Ct. 2620, 2630 (U.S.N.C. 1978)).

all know of situations in which people suffer terrible injuries, but there is no one for the plaintiff to sue. Natural disasters are an excellent example. A hurricane or earthquake can cause widespread and terrible damage, but at the end of the day, an injured person will be hard pressed to establish standing for a suit against a particular individual for these injuries.

The third and final element of standing involves the prospect that a court decision will likely resolve the issue. This requirement does not mean that the plaintiff must try his or her case before it has even begun, but the plaintiff must establish that a court decision will have an impact on the case. This third element explains why third parties cannot sue in the names of friends or relatives. The court's decision, whatever it might be, will have no direct effect on the third party. In such a case, the friend or family member must sue in his or her own name or through a personal representative appointed for that very purpose.

Hypothetical 5-2

Debbie and Dawn were married for two years under the provisions of New Hampshire's civil union statute. Last month, they were granted a final divorce by a local judge. A citizens' group filed suit against the judge, challenging the judicial decree on the basis that homosexual unions offend contemporary community standards. They based their standing on the fact that they are "concerned citizens." The judge has sought dismissal on the grounds that the group lacks standing. How is the court likely to rule?

Answer: The court will dismiss the suit because the citizens' group has failed to establish standing (*Alons v. Iowa Dist. Court for Woodbury County*, 698 N.W.2d 858 (Iowa 2005)).

Case or Controversy Requirement

Closely intertwined with the requirement of standing is the case or controversy requirement, one of the few guidelines provided to the federal court system in Article III of the U.S. Constitution. Under that article, which has been adopted in whole or in part by every state constitution, a court has the power to hear only "cases" or "controversies." These words have been interpreted to mean situations in which the parties have standing and the issue between the parties has reached a stage at which court intervention is proper. See Figure 5.5.

Thus, courts labor under specific limitations that prevent them from taking all cases filed. In addition to the requirement that the plaintiff prove standing, there are also the issues of ripeness and mootness.

Ripeness Doctrine

The ripeness doctrine requires that the issues in the case have reached a point that court intervention is proper. Federal courts and many state courts will refuse to hear hypothetical cases. They require that there be actual litigants with specific, concrete complaints against one another. Under the ripeness doctrine, if the issues have not progressed to such a point that a court order is warranted, the judge is authorized to dismiss the case and order the parties to refile in the future when the issues have progressed to that stage. Consider Hypothetical 5-3.

FIGURE 5.5
Article III, Section 2,
U.S. Constitution

The judicial power shall extend to all cases, in law and equity, arising under this Constitution, the laws of the United States, and treaties made, or which shall be made, under their authority;—to all cases affecting ambassadors, other public ministers and consuls;—to all cases of admiralty and maritime jurisdiction;—to controversies to which the United States shall be a party;—to controversies between two or more states;—between a state and citizens of another state;—between citizens of different states;—between citizens of the same state claiming lands under grants of different states, and between a state, or the citizens thereof, and foreign states, citizens or subjects.

Hypothetical 5-3

Mary and Andy are married but considering divorce. Andy files a petition seeking a court order establishing his rights to the vacation home that the couple owns. He would like to have his title established so that he will know for sure whether he owns half of the property. How does the court rule?

Answer: The court will refuse to rule because the issues in this case are not ripe. There is no divorce action pending, and until there is, the court will not rule on speculations. When the parties actually file a divorce action, the issues will be ripe, and the court can rule about the disposition of the marital property.

Mootness Doctrine

In many ways, mootness is the opposite of ripeness. Under the ripeness doctrine, a court will not consider issues until they are actually being litigated. Under the mootness doctrine, the court will refuse to hear a case if the issues have already been resolved. The court will base a decision to dismiss a case on mootness when there is no longer a valid, pending controversy between the parties. Consider Hypothetical 5-4.

Hypothetical 5-4

Terry has suffered irreparable brain damage and her husband wishes to take her off life support. Her parents sue to have the life support system left on, but while the case is pending, Terry dies. Terry's parents would still like the court to rule, because it would set a precedent for parental rights in other cases. What action does the court take?

Answer: The court dismisses the case because of mootness. Because Terry is no longer alive, the only issue pending in this case is now moot. The court will not continue to consider the matter, even if the case has broad national importance. Instead, the court will wait to tackle the issue in a future case in which the patient is still alive.

Advisory Opinions

Federal and most state courts also refuse to give advisory opinions, under the same principles that underlie ripeness and mootness doctrines. The courts have no desire to anticipate problems or commit themselves to rulings before litigants have actually brought them. Although there are some state appellate courts that will give advisory opinions in limited circumstances, the vast majority delay any ruling until the full facts and pleadings are presented to the court for review.

THE ELEMENTS OF A COMPLAINT

Our discussion so far has centered on the prerequisites of initiating a civil action. In the previous chapter, we examined the legal research and factual investigation that must be carried out to support a complaint. In the early part of this chapter, we saw that there are many different legal issues that must be established before the complaint can be brought. In this section, we examine the specific elements of a complaint. We analyze each aspect of a complaint, from beginning to end, and explain the significance of each and how these elements come together to initiate a civil suit.

The basis of our discussion centers on the complaint, a sample of which appears in Figure 5.16 on page 102. We use the example of a personal injury because such actions are among the most common types of lawsuits brought in the United States today and because these complaints do not raise too many complex issues. In subsequent chapters, we will discuss more detailed pleadings, including answers, cross-claims, counter-claims, interpleader, and impleader.

FIGURE 5.6
Caption with
Multiple Parties

IN THE SUPERIOR COURT OF BURKE COUNTY
STATE OF GRACE

CHARLES DICKENS,   )
)
        Plaintiff,   )   CIVIL ACTION NUMBER: _____
)
        vs.   )   **COMPLAINT**
)   **JURY TRIAL DEMANDED**
)
SCROOGE & MARLOWE, INC.   )
ROBERT CRATCHIT,   )
TIMOTHY CRATCHIT,   )
)
        Defendants.   )
)
_____   )

                        Complaint

FIGURE 5.7
§ 422.30. Names of
Parties in Complaint;
Names in Other
Pleadings (California)

Source: CAL. CIV. PRO.
§ 422.30.

In the complaint, the title of the action shall include the names of all the parties; but, except as otherwise provided by statute or rule of the Judicial Council, in other pleadings it is sufficient to state the name of the first party on each side with an appropriate indication of other parties.

Identification of Court

The first element of a complaint is the correct heading identifying the court where the action will be brought. This entry must list the court by its correct name.

Style or Caption of a Complaint

One of the first issues for the legal team is to determine the appropriate caption of the civil suit. In this regard, both the plaintiff and the defendant must be identified in the correct, legal capacity. For persons, this identification means their full legal name, whether as defendant or plaintiff. When there are multiple parties, all must be listed. See Figure 5.6. The caption of the complaint must set out and correctly identify all parties. However, the rules change slightly when there are multiple parties to be identified in other pleadings. In those situations, the legal team can simply list the full name of the plaintiff and defendant, as noted in Figure 5.7.

Caption

The purpose of the caption (or style) is to identify all parties to the action, both plaintiffs and defendants. As such, the caption must correctly spell and designate each party. As you will notice in Figure 5.8, each party is designated not only by full legal name but also with the suffix, "plaintiff" or "defendant." This designation eliminates any possibility of confusion about the precise parties in the case.

FIGURE 5.8
§ 422.30. Caption;
Contents (California)

Source: West's Ann. Cal.
C.C.P. § 422.30. Used with
permission from Thomson/
West.

(a) Every pleading shall contain a caption setting forth:
   (1) The name of the court and county in which the action is brought.
   (2) The title of the action.
(b) In a limited civil case, the caption shall state that the case is a limited civil case, and the clerk shall classify the case accordingly.

Businesses as Parties

Businesses can be parties in civil actions; however, the rules about naming businesses are more complicated than those that apply to persons. For instance, a business might be formed under one name but conduct business under another. In such a situation, the legal team must ensure that the proper name is used in the pleadings.

Plea of Misnomer

Later, we will address the issues that arise when a defendant is incorrectly named in the suit. A defendant has the right to file a motion with the court requesting dismissal or other appropriate remedy when the defendant has been incorrectly identified. We will discuss pleas of misnomer and other motions in Chapter 9.

Deceased Parties

Individuals cannot sue on behalf of deceased persons, nor can an action be brought against a person who has died (*Banakus v. United Aircraft Corp.,* 290 F. Supp. 259 (S.D.N.Y. 1968)). In either situation, the right to sue or be sued dies with the person—though states often have survivors' statutes that allow an heir or guardian to continue a case originally brought by a party who has since died. There are also situations in which family members and others can maintain an action based on the death of a person, such as a wrongful death claim. In such a situation, the person is suing based on the impact the other person's death has had on him or her, not because the dead person can maintain a suit.

Fugitives

In a similar vein, a fugitive from justice is not permitted to bring suit against another. To allow a contrary ruling would put the court in an unusual situation: On the one hand, there is an outstanding warrant for a person that must be served. On the other hand, the court would have to allow a person who has flaunted justice in one context to employ it in another. To avoid this dilemma, courts simply bar fugitives from bringing suit (*U.S. v. Forty-Five Thousand Nine Hundred Forty Dollars ($45,940) in U.S. Currency,* 739 F.2d 792 (2d Cir. 1984)).

Title of Action

Federal and state courts have adopted rules concerning "notice" pleading. Under these rules, a party must not only correctly entitle his or her action but also must provide sufficient detail to put the other party on notice as to the exact nature of the claim and the facts that support it. The first time that notice pleading rears its head in a complaint is with the title of the action.

The civil suit must be correctly identified. Although we have used the term "complaint" to describe the pleading that sets out the plaintiff's wrong against the defendant, not all jurisdictions follow this rule. For instance, in some states, the document filed by the plaintiff is referred to as a *petition*. By whatever name, the purpose of the pleading remains the same: to set out the claims against the defendant and the facts that the plaintiff claims support his or her demands against the defendant. For the sake of clarity, we use the term "complaint" to describe this document.

Allegation of Jurisdiction

The actual wording of the pleading is governed by Rule 8 or its state equivalent. Under that rule, pleadings must be short and concise and put the other party on notice of all the claims. As you can see in Figure 5.9, Rule 8 requires a "short and plain statement" setting out the court's jurisdiction and an equally short and plain statement regarding the claims and relief sought.

The basis of Rule 8 of the federal rules, and the various state rules that closely follow it, is that a party should receive as much information as possible from the pleading. Rather than waiting for trial to reveal the facts of the case, modern civil practice is based on a theory of learning as much as possible about the case prior to trial. This theory underlies not only notice pleadings but also the mechanics of discovery that we will examine in Chapter 8. This principle is amplified in other provisions of Rule 8, including (e). See Figure 5.10.

FIGURE 5.9
Rule 8. General Rules of Pleading
Source: Federal Rules of Civil Procedure, Rule 8(a).

Claims for Relief. A pleading which sets forth a claim for relief, whether an original claim, counterclaim, cross-claim, or third-party claim, shall contain (1) a short and plain statement of the grounds upon which the court's jurisdiction depends, unless the court already has jurisdiction and the claim needs no new grounds of jurisdiction to support it, (2) a short and plain statement of the claim showing that the pleader is entitled to relief, and (3) a demand for judgment for the relief the pleader seeks. Relief in the alternative or of several different types may be demanded.

FIGURE 5.10
Rule 8, Pleading to Be Concise and Direct; Consistency
Source: Federal Rules of Civil Procedure, Rule 8(e).

(1) Each averment of a pleading shall be simple, concise, and direct. No technical forms of pleading or motions are required.

Following the guidelines created in Rule 8, the first paragraph of a complaint sets out the plaintiff's contention that the court identified at the top of the document is the appropriate forum to consider the issues raised in the complaint. Because federal courts have limited jurisdiction, the plaintiff must set out specific allegations to satisfy the court that it does have such jurisdiction. In cases involving state courts, the plaintiff's jurisdictional allegation may contain only an allegation that the defendant is subject to the jurisdiction of the court because of domicile. See Figure 5.11.

Factual Contentions

In the next paragraphs of the complaint, which can vary in number considerably, the plaintiff slowly builds his or her case against the defendant by establishing the basic facts that the plaintiff contends resulted in his or her injury and that establish the defendant's legal responsibility for the action. The best practice in this regard is to separate different factual allegations into different paragraphs. For instance, consider Figure 5.12, in which the plaintiff's attorney sets out each disparate set of facts as separate paragraphs. This organization has the benefit of satisfying the requirements of Rule 8 while also narrowing down the elements of the plaintiff's claim.

The plaintiff's factual allegations must establish his or her cause of action and also provide sufficient notice of the relevant dates, times, and actions that the plaintiff states were committed by the defendant. Following the factual allegations, the plaintiff then proceeds to a theory of liability, again setting it out in specific, numbered allegations.

Liability Allegations

The plaintiff must not only set out the specific facts of the claim but also make a clear case for why the defendant is the person who is liable to the plaintiff for the injuries sustained. In the sample complaint that we are using in this chapter (see Figure 5.16), those allegations are paragraphs 10–13, with subparts.

FIGURE 5.11
Jurisdictional Allegations in Complaint

Complaint

Plaintiff, by and through his attorneys, complains of the defendant as follows:

1. Plaintiff is, and at all times hereafter was, a citizen and resident of the Town of New Haven, County of Berry, State of Anystate.

2. Plaintiff alleges upon information and belief that the defendant Rideway Transport Truck Company (Truck Company) is, and at all times hereafter was, a corporation organized and existing under the laws of the State of Anystate, licensed to do business, and in fact doing business, in the State of Anystate and having a registered agent for the service of process by the name of Darryl P. Putnam, located at 230 N. Tree Street, Suite 2000, New Haven, Anystate, 27401.

3. Plaintiff alleges upon information and belief that the defendant Martin W. Jerry is a citizen and resident of the County of Berry, State of Anystate.

FIGURE 5.12
Specific Factual Allegations from Plaintiff's Complaint

4. That at all times relevant to this Complaint the defendant Martin W. Jerry was an agent, servant, and employee of the defendant Rideway Transport Truck Company (Truck Company) and was acting within the course and scope of his employment with it.

5. Truck Company, at the time of the accident, owned, maintained, and used, a fourteen foot (14') tractor-trailer rig, license plate number PMH 3032, VIN JXR123456989.

6. Katie Street is a public street in the Town which runs in a north-south direction through the town of New Haven.

7. On May 23, of last year, at approximately 1:55 p.m., plaintiff was driving his automobile south on Katie Street. Defendant Martin Jerry was operating his tractor-trailer rig in the oncoming lane of traffic, in a northerly direction.

8. At approximately the point where Katie Street intersects with Ben Avenue, the tractor-trailer rig operated by Defendant Martin Jerry crossed over the double yellow lines and into the oncoming flow of traffic.

9. Truck Company's truck struck plaintiff's automobile with great force, causing substantial damage to the automobile.

prima facie
(Latin) "at first sight." A case with the required proof of elements in a tort cause of action; the elements of the plaintiff's (or prosecutor's) cause of action; what the plaintiff must prove; accepted on its face, but not indisputable.

PRACTICE TIP

A complaint that fails to meet the minimum requirements of notice pleading is subject to a dismissal for failure to state a claim (see *Xechem, Inc. v. Bristol-Myers Squibb Co.*, 274 F. Supp. 2d 937 (N.D. Ill. 2003)).

Sufficiency of the Allegations

How do the courts evaluate the sufficiency of the complaint? Put another way, how much information must the plaintiff provide to support his or her claims so that the plaintiff meets the threshold of Rule 8 (or its state equivalent)? The complaint must provide enough information on its own to withstand the court's scrutiny. The plaintiff must establish a **prima facie** case for jurisdiction, standing, and other issues without reliance on other pleadings. Case decisions have placed the burden squarely on the plaintiff to meet all of the material elements to place the defendant on notice of the claims against him or her, as well as the facts that support this claim. A complaint that fails to meet that standard is subject to dismissal. We will discuss how the defendant seeks to dismiss an insufficient complaint in the next chapter.

Demand for Judgment/Prayer for Relief

Once the plaintiff has made his or her case against the defendant, the plaintiff must make a specific request to the court. Here, the plaintiff requests that the court take some action, based on the contentions in the case. This section is referred to alternatively as the demand for judgment or the prayer for relief. By whatever name, the purpose is the same: The plaintiff requests that the court carry out an action to award the plaintiff compensation for the injuries alleged in the complaint. See Figure 5.13.

As you can see in Figure 5.13, the plaintiff requests a nonspecific sum but in excess of $10,000. The plaintiff also requests other relief, including a jury trial, that the defendant pay all costs associated with bringing the suit, and a final, catchall phrase, "for such other and further relief as the Court may deem just and proper." This phrase is inserted for the express purpose of allowing the plaintiff to receive any other compensation the court may deem proper. After all, if the plaintiff doesn't ask for all possible remedies, he or she may not receive them.

FIGURE 5.13
Prayer for Relief

WHEREFORE, the plaintiff prays the Court as follows:

1. That the plaintiff have and recover from the defendants, jointly and severally, a sum in excess of Ten Thousand Dollars ($10,000.00) for compensatory and punitive damages as alleged above.

2. That the plaintiff have and recover the costs of this action.

3. For a trial by jury.

4. For such other and further relief as the Court may deem just and proper.

FIGURE 5.14
Federal Rules of Civil
Procedure, Rule 9(g):
Special Damage

> When items of special damage are claimed, they shall be specifically stated.

Request for Damages

In addition to the other requirements listed above, a complaint must also contain a specific allegation about the damages that the plaintiff suffered and that the plaintiff is demanding from the defendant. On the federal level, the rule is that the plaintiffs must state their damages in "definite and certain" terms. For instance, a plaintiff might state that he or she has suffered damages in "excess of $1 million." The plaintiff also may simply allege a total or lump sum of the requested damages.

Pleading Special Damages

The rule about specifying damages is different when the plaintiff claims special damages. A "special damage" is a request for compensation for a specific out-of-pocket expense, such as medical bills, damage to personal property, and lost wages, among others (see Figure 5.14). When a claim involves a request for damages for these items, they must be pled with specificity. We will discuss possible damages in Chapter 11.

Jury Trial Demand

Among the demands raised by the plaintiff, there is usually a request that the case be heard before a jury. The rule in most states and on the federal level is simple with regard to jury trials: If a party does not request a jury, he or she will not receive one. To avoid any potential waivers on this point, attorneys usually figure their request for trial by jury prominently and in several different parts of the complaint. You will notice, for example, that the plaintiff's request for a jury trial in our sample complaint is mentioned twice: once at the beginning and again in the prayer for relief.

COMPLAINT ATTACHMENTS AND EXHIBITS

Now that we have addressed the common aspects of the body of a civil complaint, there are additional issues to consider. For instance, how common is it for a complaint to contain additional documents that seek to prove the plaintiff's allegations? This question brings us to the issues surrounding verifications, exhibits, and affidavits.

Verifications

verification
Acknowledgment by a party of the truthfulness of the information contained within a document.

As we saw in the last chapter, the attorney's signature on the complaint acts as his or her representation that the basic facts alleged in the complaint are true and that they were investigated. But are there additional requirements? In years past, many states required not only the attorney's signature but also a signed **verification** from the client. A verification is a sworn statement that the facts set out in the complaint are true. Verifications often followed the lines of the statement set out in Figure 5.15.

Rule 11 abolished the need for verifications in the vast majority of suits, though verifications remain a feature of specific types of pleadings, such as zoning ordinance actions, defamation, tortious interference with contract, and actions against the government.

Exhibits

exhibit
A document attached to a pleading that is incorporated by reference into the body of the pleading.

An **exhibit** is a document attached to a pleading that is referred to or incorporated into the main body of the pleading. Attaching exhibits to all types of pleadings, including complaints and answers, is common practice. Here, Rule 8 again requires that the wording of the complaint seek to establish the basic allegations made by the plaintiff and that exhibits help facilitate notice pleading. See Figure 5.16.

FIGURE 5.15
Verification

> I hereby declare, under penalty of perjury, that the foregoing facts and statements contained in this complaint are true and known to me of my own knowledge.

FIGURE 5.16
Complaint in a Car
Wreck Case

**STATE OF PLACID
DISTRICT COURT
LONDON COUNTY**

Sherlock Holmes (Plaintiff) v. Professor James Moriarty, individually and as owner, operator of Moriarty Transport Trucking Co. (Defendant)	CIVIL ACTION: 04-100 *COMPLAINT* (Jury Trial Requested)

JURISDICTIONAL ALLEGATIONS

1. The plaintiff, Sherlock Holmes, age 57, is a citizen and resident of London County, PLACID.

2. The defendant, Moriarty Transport Trucking Co., is a corporation organized under PLACID laws and headquartered in Lestrade, N.C. and doing business in PLACID in London County.

3. The cause of action happened in Baskerville, PL, in London County.

GENERAL ALLEGATIONS

4. On August 23, 2006, at approximately 3:30 P.M., the plaintiff was driving his car on Watson Street, in Baskerville, PL, with his wife, Irene Adler Holmes, in the passenger seat.

5. As he passed through the intersection of Watson Street and Roylott Avenue, a truck belonging to and owned and operated by the defendant failed to stop at a red light and caused a collision with the automobile driven by plaintiff.

6. Irene Adler Holmes died at the scene of the accident from injuries she sustained in the crash.

7. Mr. Holmes was seriously injured by the collision with defendant's truck. He suffered head wounds, broken bones, and internal injuries.

8. At the time of the accident Mr. Holmes was self-employed as a private consulting detective with a large client list. Since the collision, he has been unable to return to work.

9. Mr. Holmes has been severely disabled by the accident.

10. Mr. Holmes's quality of life has been severely diminished as a result of the accident injuries and the loss of his wife.

11. Mr. Holmes's life expectancy has been dramatically shortened as a result of the collision.

12. The injuries suffered by the defendant from the accident were caused by the defendant's negligence.

13. Defendant driver Moriarty failed to maintain a proper lookout.

14. Defendant driver Moriarty failed to abide by the rules of the road.

15. Defendant driver Moriarty was driving too fast for conditions prior to the collision.

PRAYER FOR RELIEF

The plaintiff incorporates by reference Paragraphs 1 through 21 in support of this claim for relief.

The plaintiff prays to the court for the following relief.

1. Judgment be made against the defendant for negligence described in Paragraphs 13–15.

2. Compensatory damages be awarded to the plaintiff in excess of $10,000.

3. The defendant be required to pay the costs of this action, including the attorney fees of the plaintiff.

4. For such other and further relief as the court may deem necessary and in the interests of justice.

5. The plaintiff requests that a jury trial be held.

November 18, 2007

Respectfully Submitted,

By: _____

_____
(PL. Bar No.)
Neal Bevans
Attorney for the Plaintiff

Bevans & Bevans, P.A.
1001 Burkemont Avenue
Bohemia, PL 28655
828-555-1212 (phone)
828-555-1213 (fax)

AFFIDAVIT OF VERIFICATION BY THE PLAINTIFF

I, Sherlock Holmes, do hereby swear that I have read and understand the attached complaint against the Moriarty Transport Trucking Co. and that the facts and allegations contained within this complaint are true except those matters stated to be upon information and belief, and as to those matters, I believe they are true.

_____

Date: November 18, 2007

Sherlock Holmes

STATE OF PLACID
COUNTY OF LONDON

On this day, November 18, 2007, Sherlock Holmes personally appeared before me and signed this affidavit.

_____

Notary Public

Notary Seal

My Commission expires _____.

RESEARCH THIS!

As you will see in this chapter's "Real Paralegal Life" section, many states now impose requirements on medical malpractice cases before they can be filed. For instance, a state might require an affidavit from a licensed doctor setting out a claim that the defendant-doctor in the complaint breached the standard of care. This affidavit is required to be filed with the complaint. Does your state have similar requirements? Research the issue and determine what limitations or requirements your state imposes on the filing of medical malpractice cases.

LEGAL RESEARCH MAXIM

Before you ever begin developing a case for possible litigation, it is important to have a solid grasp of the Rules of Civil Procedure. These rules exist on both state and federal levels, and you, like the attorney, must know every rule that has any bearing on your case. Failure to adhere strictly to the rules can have disastrous consequences, such as dismissal of pleadings in the case or court sanctions. Rules of Civil Procedure are available in print form, as part of your state code, and online. Many paralegals find it convenient to purchase a copy of the Rules of Civil Procedure as a separate printing, which makes it easier to locate specific rules and include your own notations beside the rules.

Affidavits

affidavit
A sworn statement.

Just as it is common to attach exhibits to a complaint, it is not unusual to attach an **affidavit** to a complaint. An affidavit is a written, sworn statement that declares certain facts to be true.

SUMMONS AND SERVICE OF PROCESS

CYBER TRIP

Legal Information Institute
http://www.law.cornell.edu/
Law Guru—General issues surrounding civil litigation
http://www.lawguru.com/faq/9.html
U.S. Department of Justice—Tobacco Litigation
http://www.usdoj.gov/civil/cases/tobacco2/
U.S. Department of Justice—Statistics on Civil Cases
http://www.ojp.gov/bjs/abstract/ctcvlc01.htm

Preparing the complaint is only the first step in beginning a lawsuit. Just as important are the considerations surrounding the summons and service of process. All states require that when a complaint is drafted, it must be served on the defendant. In this situation, service means that the defendant must receive a copy of the complaint and a summons directing the defendant to appear in court on a specific date and time. In this section, we discuss the issues that arise under the requirement of service of process.

Once the complaint has been drafted, the next issue for consideration by the legal team is the manner in which the defendant will be served with a copy. Only when the defendant has been physically served with the complaint will the lawsuit actually have commenced. Service often raises a host of issues. For instance, how is service actually accomplished? State and federal rules provide for several different mechanisms for serving defendants. See Figure 5.17. Local rules also dictate who is responsible for actually contacting the defendant.

In some states, private process servers are paid to locate defendants and physically hand them a copy of the complaint. There is a long history of case law regarding what is considered proper service. For instance, the defendant must receive a copy of the complaint, but there is no requirement that he or she must actually read it before the valid service has been performed. Defendants cannot avoid valid service by a claim that they refused to read the complaint. The certification by the process server, often referred to as proof of service, establishes that the defendant received a copy of the complaint on a particular date and time. Proof of service is essential because it determines when the lawsuit begins. Whereas some states use private process servers, many courts, including federal courts, rely on law enforcement officers to carry out service. Using police officers, marshals, and deputies tends to mitigate the violent reaction that a defendant often has to being presented with a lawsuit.

Service by Personal Delivery

Whether service of process is carried out by private individuals or law enforcement officers, the requirements are that the defendant must receive a copy of the complaint, along with any exhibits,

FIGURE 5.17
Rule 4.1. Service of Other Process

Source: Federal Rules of Civil Procedure, Rule 4.1.

(a) Generally. Process other than a summons as provided in Rule 4 or subpoena as provided in Rule 45 shall be served by a United States marshal, a deputy United States marshal, or a person specially appointed for that purpose, who shall make proof of service as provided in Rule 4(1). The process may be served anywhere within the territorial limits of the state in which the district court is located, and, when authorized by a statute of the United States, beyond the territorial limits of that state.

COMMUNICATION TIP

Memoranda to File

Whenever you speak with someone important to a case or discuss an issue that may have any significance to a client, always write up a memorandum about it. You might think that you will remember any significant conversation or discovery in a case, but the human memory is a great deal more fragile than most of us are willing to believe. Whenever you discuss anything of significance with a client, witness, judge's secretary, or anyone else having a bearing on a case, immediately create a memo and put it into the file. Save the digital version of the memo in the client's file on the computer or network, but also make a back-up hard copy. If this sounds like overkill, keep in mind that a short telephone conversation could become the major focus of a legal malpractice action several years from now. Being able to produce a contemporaneously written memo may short-circuit a potential claim and also assure others that you took the action that you claimed you took. In the era of ubiquitous computers, there is no reason not to create a quick memorandum to the file about any conversation. Consider this example:

Memorandum to File

TO: File

From: Paula Paralegal

RE: TC with John Smith

Date: May 24, 2006

I spoke with client John Smith this morning, and he said that he definitely does not want his Aunt, Myra Smith, called to testify in this case. I explained to him that Ms. Smith has critical information in this case and by not calling her, we put the entire case in jeopardy, but he was adamant. I discussed this decision with Allison Attorney, and she agreed that we would not call the client's aunt to the stand in this case. Ms. Attorney suggested that I send a letter to the client confirming this decision, and I followed up this conversation with a letter to Mr. Smith, setting out his decision.

verifications, and other attachments. Personal service means handing the complaint and related material to the defendant. It is not sufficient service to leave a copy with a friend or at the defendant's place of business. There are provisions that allow service of process by posting at the defendant's residence or by leaving it with the defendant's spouse, but the best means is by hand delivering it to the defendant. However, that is not always possible.

Service by Other Means

In situations in which the defendant cannot be located or is avoiding service of process, there are other provisions for service. For instance, a plaintiff might rely on a provision that allows proof of service by posting notice and summons in the local newspaper for successive weeks or by posting the service on the front door of the defendant's residence. However, the preference is always for physical delivery to the actual defendant.

Serving a Corporation or Government Entity

Service of process on corporations or other entities raises interesting questions. Because there is no human defendant, who must be served for the plaintiff to establish adequate service of process under the law? In these situations, service is accomplished by hand delivering a copy of the complaint and summons to a registered agent. As part of a corporation's registration with the state, it must designate a specific individual who will act as an agent for the corporation. This person's name and address remain on file with the state, and when a plaintiff wishes to sue a corporation or other entity, this person must be served with the appropriate paperwork. Once served, the registered agent forwards this information to the corporate directors and officers, but when proof of service is established for the registered agent, the lawsuit has commenced, regardless of how much or how little the actual corporate officers and directors know about the case.

Georgia Community Support & Solutions, Inc.

v.

Berryhill

275 Ga. App. 189, 620 S.E.2d 178 (2005)

PHIPPS, Judge.

Georgia Community Support and Solutions, Inc. (GCSS), a non-profit organization that assists disabled adults and their families, sued Shirley Berryhill, whose disabled son had used its services, for defamation and tortious interference with business relationships. The verified complaint alleged that Berryhill had maliciously published false information about GCSS and its executive director, Whitney Fuchs, in emails and on an internet website. The trial court dismissed the complaint under Georgia's anti-SLAPP (Strategic Lawsuits Against Public Participation) statute, OCGA § 9-11-11.1, finding that Berryhill's statements were privileged and that GCSS had brought the suit for the improper purpose of chilling her right to speak out on an issue of public concern. GCSS appeals, arguing that substantial evidence supported its claims and that Berryhill's statements were not privileged. Because the undisputed facts do not support the trial court's findings, we reverse.

The undisputed facts are as follows. Berryhill's adult son, Robert, suffers from mental retardation and requires constant supervision and care. In July 2000, GCSS placed him with an independently contracted home caregiver. On July 15, 2002, Berryhill posted a message on an internet website for families of disabled adults complaining about the quality of care her son had received from GCSS. In the message, Berryhill stated that her son had been "dumped" at a house where he slept on a "4-foot settee in a back corner, lost a rapid 35–40 pounds, [and] became afraid to speak to [his family]." She further stated that she could not locate him and that GCSS would not tell her where he was. Eventually, she found her son in a "converted single basement garage, with bars on the inner windows." According to the message, her son was not allowed in the house, had no clothes and no bed, had a shaved head, was left in the yard all day as punishment, and was fed chicken bones. A "football player" had punched him repeatedly in the back, shoulders, and head, until the caregiver called the police and had the "thug" arrested.

On February 12, 2003, Berryhill sent an email to about 40 people, including one who worked for the *Atlanta Journal-Constitution* and one who worked for the Georgia Department of Human Resources. In the email, Berryhill stated that while her son was in GCSS's care, GCSS had not told her where he was; that it had taken her two and a half months to find him; and that when she eventually located him, she learned that he had been kept in a backyard shed and beaten. Berryhill also posted the contents of this email message on the aforementioned website.

GCSS's lawyer sent Berryhill a letter demanding a retraction and apology. When neither was forthcoming, GCSS filed suit. It later submitted verifications from its attorney and Fuchs, as well as affidavits to support its allegations that Berryhill's statements were false. In response, Berryhill filed her own affidavit stating that she had made the statements in a good faith belief that they were true and that she had hoped that "the *Atlanta Journal-Constitution,* the Department of Human Resources, and other private individuals might be able to investigate the nature of my concerns about my son's treatment and care, and to remedy such concerns, if possible."

After a non-evidentiary hearing, the trial court granted Berryhill's motion to dismiss, finding that GCSS had not met the substantive verification requirements of the anti-SLAPP statute. In particular, the court found that Berryhill's statements were privileged communications and that GCSS had sued her for the improper purpose of preventing her "from bringing the plight of her son under the care of GCSS to the attention of the media, the government and the public at large."

The General Assembly enacted the anti-SLAPP statute to encourage Georgians to participate "in matters of public significance through the exercise of their constitutional rights of freedom of speech and the right to petition government for the redress of grievances." The statute requires, among other things, that a written verification under oath accompany any claim asserted against a person arising from an act "which could reasonably be construed as an act in furtherance of the right of free speech or the right to petition government for a redress of grievances." The statute defines such an act as any written or oral statement, writing, or petition made before or to a legislative, executive, or judicial proceeding, or any other official proceeding authorized by law, or any written or oral statement, writing, or petition made in connection with an issue under consideration or review by a legislative, executive, or judicial body, or any other official proceeding authorized by law.

The verification must certify that the party and his attorney have read the claim; that to the best of their knowledge, information, and belief formed after reasonable inquiry it is well grounded in fact and is warranted by existing law or a good faith argument for the extension, modification, or reversal of existing law; that the act forming the basis for the claim is not a privileged communication under paragraph (4) of Code Section 51-5-7; and that the claim is not interposed for any improper purpose . . .

OCGA § 51-5-7(4), in turn, provides that a statement is privileged if it was "made in good faith as part of an act in furtherance of the right of free speech or the right to petition government for a redress of grievances . . . in connection with an issue of public interest or concern. . . ."

In *Atlanta Humane Society v. Harkins,* our Supreme Court held that a trial court may dismiss a claim that has been falsely verified. First, the court must make a threshold finding that the anti-SLAPP statute applies and that verification was required; that is, it must find that "the claim involves statements in furtherance of the right of free speech or the right to petition the government, in connection with an issue under consideration or review by a governmental body." Second, the court must make a substantive, evidentiary determination that (a) the claimant or his attorney did not reasonably believe that the claim was well grounded in fact and that it was warranted by existing law or a good faith argument for the modification of existing law, (b) the claim was interposed for an improper purpose, or (c) the defendant's statements were privileged pursuant to OCGA § 51-5-7(4).

Although discovery is stayed upon the filing of a motion to dismiss for failure to comply with the anti-SLAPP statute's verification requirement, the trial court may nevertheless allow limited discovery to resolve the motion.

GCSS argues that the court failed to properly apply the *Atlanta Humane Society v. Harkins* two-step analysis before dismissing its complaint, and we agree. The court found that Berryhill's statements satisfied the threshold requirement for applicability of the anti-SLAPP statute because they "were made in furtherance of her right to free speech about an issue of public concern: the safety and care of adults with disabilities." That, however, is not the question. The anti-SLAPP statute does not encompass all statements that touch upon matters of public concern. Rather, by its terms, the statute's application is limited to statements made before or to a legislative, executive, or judicial proceeding, or any other official proceeding authorized by law, or any . . . statement . . . made in connection with an issue under consideration or review by a legislative, executive, or judicial body, or any other official proceeding authorized by law.

Although this description is broad, it does require that the statement in question be made in relation to some official proceeding. There is no evidence that any such proceeding was involved here, either before or after Berryhill's statements. Nor is there any evidence that Berryhill sought to initiate an official proceeding by making the statements. Although she stated in her affidavit that she hoped her emails would prompt the *Atlanta Journal-Constitution* and Georgia Department of Human Resources to look into GCSS's treatment and care of her son,

nothing in the emails can be construed as a request for any official investigation or other proceeding.

Accordingly, the trial court erred in concluding that the anti-SLAPP statute applied here. GCSS was not required to submit any verification; thus, its complaint could not be dismissed on the basis of alleged shortcomings in its verification.

GCSS also argues that its verification did comply with the anti-SLAPP statute and that the anti-SLAPP statute violates its constitutional rights to due process and equal protection of the laws. In light of our decision in Division (1), we do not reach these issues.

A substantial portion of Berryhill's appellate brief is devoted to the argument that her statements were not libelous as a matter of law because they were not about GCSS, they were opinion, they were not made maliciously, and they did not harm GCSS. The trial court, however, did not address these issues, which are better resolved on summary judgment or by the jury. Because its ruling was based on GCSS's alleged filing of a false verification under the anti-SLAPP statute, we confine our opinion to that issue, as well.

Judgment reversed.

Source: From Westlaw. Used with permission of Thomson/West.

Case Questions:

1. What were Berryhill's statements about GCSS?

2. What impact did Berryhill's verification have on this case?

3. According to the court, what is the significance of a verification when it accompanies a complaint?

4. What action should a court take when it appears that a verification has been filed falsely?

5. Why did a higher court conclude that the lower court was incorrect when it ruled that Georgia's anti-SLAPP statute applied to this case?

After meeting with a client, the legal team must carry out some basic investigations into the factual allegations raised by the client. What if the firm decides that there is not a sufficient basis to bring a suit? The firm must contact the client and inform him or her that the firm will not be handling the matter and advise the client of potential consequences. Consider the example in Figure 5.18.

Eye on Ethics: Cutting Corners in Complaints

When dealing with drafting and filing complaints, there are important ethical issues to consider. For instance, we have already seen that there are important rules that must be followed in not only drafting the complaint but in the way that it is served on the defendant. Here, a tendency to cut corners or make light of the rules can have drastic consequences for the client. If the complaint does not meet the minimum standards under your state's court rules, the judge may be authorized to strike some or all of the allegations. Therefore, your client would no longer have a legal recourse against the defendant. Of course, the client would have a legal malpractice against the firm, and that is something that should always be avoided. Strict adherence to the rules is not only a valuable ethical guideline but can also avoid some nasty and potentially devastating legal consequences.

FIGURE 5.18
Letter to Client
Declining
Representation

Allison Attorney & Associates
1001 Maple Street
Lake Placid, PL 22202
904-555-1212

May 24, 2006

Ms. Jane Marple
1001 Mary's Lane
St. Mary Mead, PL 22202

Dear Ms. Marple:

Thank you for meeting with me on February 12, 2006. At that time, you requested that I review the materials you provided me and reach a conclusion about the possibility of bringing an action against Detective John Slack. The materials you provided included:

• Newspaper clippings detailing your involvement in various criminal cases.

• Letters from local law enforcement praising you for your efforts.

• Character references from local community residents, detailing your high character and reputation for honesty.

• Your own scrapbook of cases in which you have been involved.

• An excerpt from the "St. Mary Mead Gazette," dated December 14, 2005, which includes statements by Det. Slack about you and your involvement in the recent investigation of the murder of Belle Girdler.

Based on our review of this case, we do not believe that there is sufficient evidence to support a claim of libel against Detective Slack. We do not believe that the statements rise to the level required by Placid law to bring such an action. The fact that you have become a celebrity in your own right substantially raises the bar for any slander or libel cases, and that requires a showing of actual malice on the part of Det. Slack that is not reflected in this newspaper clipping.

Please do not construe our decision as a reflection on the merits of your claim; our firm simply does not believe it can prevail in an action against Det. Slack. Feel free to consult with other attorneys. Keep in mind that the statute of limitations for a libel action is 12 months from the date of publication. In this case, that means that any action you intend to file against Det. Slack for his statement in the newspaper must be filed on or before December 14, 2006, or it will be barred forever.

I'm sorry that we cannot assist you with this case.

Sincerely,

Allison Attorney, Esq

Encl: Newspaper clippings, letters, scrapbook

Real Paralegal Life: Building a Skill Set

JOHN PURVIS

John Purvis is a senior legal assistant at a firm that specializes in civil litigation. He has worked there for years and spends a great deal of his time concentrating on medical malpractice cases. "When it comes to med/mal," he says, "we handle strictly plaintiff work in medical malpractice cases." When the firm decides to accept a case, Purvis's focus is investigation. According to him, "We have the client list of every physician they have ever seen; we have them execute medical authorization releases. We take that information and immediately send out requests to all medical providers for complete copies of all their records, diagnostics, lab reports, that type of thing. Depending on the type of injury, we may also request actual copies of x-rays, MRIs, CAT-scans, any diagnostic tool that may be useful in the ultimate evaluation and potential review by an expert."

At his firm, they use a team approach to litigation, so "when we take a case to trial, we use two or three attorneys, letting [the opposition] know that we are bringing the full resources of the firm to a case."

A Day in the Life: John Purvis

SCREENING CASES

John Purvis spends a large part of his day screening potential cases. He summarizes his screening duties as follows: "What usually happens is a possible client will call the office and I or one of the other legal assistants will screen the call. There are a multitude of calls that you are going to get. Many people will call up complaining about something that a doctor did. Seventy-five percent of those are things that are not actionable as medical malpractice claims. When we are screening calls, if a case sounds like one with real merit, we then present it to one or all of the partners. We usually have a weekly meeting where we go over all of the pending cases, their status, and any potential statutes of limitations problems. The attorneys then vote on whether or not it's a case that they want to investigate. Then we have the person come in and have a sit-down meeting with them. At the meeting there is at least one attorney and one legal assistant. We listen to what the person has to say about their medical treatment. Then we try to give them an overview of what is involved in bringing a medical malpractice case, what it takes to proceed on a case, and also inform them about the low likelihood of getting a recovery. The statistics show that only a small percentage of the medical malpractice cases that are brought are successful. If the client is willing to proceed and understands that there are risks associated with going forward, and that there will be expenses that they are going to incur in continuing with the action, then we agree to take the matter on an investigative review."

Real Paralegal Life: Building a Skill Set

CREATING AN EVIDENCE CHART

One item that helps in preparing a complaint is an evidence chart. Prepared either for the plaintiff or the defense, this chart shows all the elements of the claim, the evidence necessary to support that claim, and the identity of the witness or evidence that will prove this claim.

Obviously the evidence chart will look different depending on which side prepares it. When the plaintiff prepares an evidence chart, the essential elements include all of the basic claims of the complaint. When the defense prepares an evidence chart, it focuses on disproving the essential elements of the plaintiff's claim by attacking particular pieces of evidence.

EVIDENCE CHART

This is a sample evidence chart from a car wreck case. The allegations come directly from a complaint.

Allegation	Witness	Testimony (summary)	Physical Evidence
That on or about the 19th day of October 2000, at approximately 9:40 A.M., plaintiff was operating a motor vehicle traveling west on Maple Street in Anytown, Mason County, State of Anywhere.	Plaintiff: Jane Smith	That she was driving that day on that street and defendant ran red light and struck her car.	Photographs: check foundation questions and make sure that she can answer them; Model of the intersection, check foundation questions and make sure that witness can answer all.
The defendant driver admitted at the scene that she did not see plaintiff's vehicle before pulling out into the intersection.	Officer John Doe	Taking the statement from defendant after being called to the scene.	Possible hearsay objection; officer may have based his conclusions on secondhand info provided by witnesses, not his own observations.
That plaintiff was operating her vehicle below the posted speed limit of 35 mph.	Plaintiff: Jane Smith	Ms. Smith's testimony	Possible hearsay testimony; photo issues, etc.
	Accident reconstructionist: Dave Jones	His study of the scene; skid marks, point of impact from glass shards	Photographs, diagrams made by Dr. Jones, possible relevance objection: photos taken months after accident, does not fairly and accurately depict the scene as it appeared on the day of the accident; testimony based on hearsay.

Using the fact pattern provided in Appendix A, create an evidence chart for the Cherry case.

Career Prep

Locate a recent news report of an automobile accident and then prepare a legally sufficient complaint based on the report. Make sure that you not only make correct factual allegations but also allege the jurisdictional basis and satisfy the other required elements of a complaint. Finally, locate your state court rules on notice pleading and include copies of these rules with the final draft of your complaint.

Summary

There are many important considerations that go into creating a complaint in a civil case. First, the plaintiff must research the court's jurisdiction. Jurisdiction is the power of a court to enter judgments and compel parties. Before a plaintiff can file in a particular court, the plaintiff must establish that the court has both subject matter jurisdiction and personal jurisdiction. Subject matter jurisdiction refers to the power of the court to consider the specific issues raised in the case. Personal jurisdiction is the court's power to enter judgments against the parties involved. Some courts, particularly on the state level, are courts of general jurisdiction, meaning that they have broad power to hear a wide range of actions. Other courts, including all federal courts, are courts of limited jurisdiction. They are empowered to hear only specific types of actions. Federal courts are limited to considering cases involving federal questions, including the interpretation of the U.S. Constitution and U.S. statutes. In addition, the plaintiff must establish that there is diversity of citizenship between the parties and that the amount in controversy exceeds $75,000.

Whether a complaint is filed in federal or state court, it must have basic elements. All complaints have a caption or style that lists the names of the parties and the court. Complaints have internal requirements, including allegations concerning jurisdiction and the factual allegations that support the plaintiff's cause of action against the defendant. The plaintiff must have a prayer for relief, requesting damages to be assessed against the defendant.

Once drafted, a complaint must be served on the defendant, along with a summons directing the defendant to appear in court to answer the charges on a specific date and time. Service of process is often accomplished by law enforcement officers, though some states allow service by private individuals.

Key Terms

Plaintiff, 87
Defendant, 87
Personal jurisdiction, 88
Forum, 88
Domicile, 89
Special appearance, 89
Subject matter jurisdiction, 90
Ancillary jurisdiction, 92
Pendent jurisdiction, 92

Exclusive jurisdiction, 92
Removal, 92
In rem jurisdiction, 92
Concurrent jurisdiction, 93
Standing, 94
Prima facie, 100
Verification, 101
Exhibit, 101
Affidavit, 104

Review Questions

1. What are the terms that refer to the two main parties in a lawsuit?

2. How is a person defined as a "party" to a lawsuit?

3. What is personal jurisdiction?

4. What role does a paralegal have in drafting a complaint?

5. What is a forum, and what relation does it have to a court's jurisdictional power?

6. Compare and contrast obtaining personal jurisdiction through the defendant's presence in the forum and his or her domicile in the forum.

7. Explain how a forum can obtain personal jurisdiction over a defendant through minimum contacts under the *International Shoe* case.

8. Compare and contrast general jurisdiction courts with limited jurisdiction courts.

9. All federal courts are limited jurisdiction courts. Explain.

10. What is diversity of citizenship, and what impact does it have on jurisdictional issues in federal courts?

11. Explain "amount in controversy" and what it means to subject matter jurisdiction.

12. Compare and contrast pendent and ancillary jurisdiction.

13. What is "removal"?

14. Explain in rem jurisdiction.

15. What is "capacity"?

16. What is "standing," and why is it a requirement in a lawsuit?

17. What is the "case or controversy" requirement?

18. Compare and contrast ripeness and mootness.

19. List and describe the basic elements of a complaint.

20. What is "notice pleading"?

Discussion Questions

1. Compare and contrast the jurisdictional questions raised in federal and state courts.

2. Why have courts moved to a "notice pleading" requirement in complaints? What purpose is served by such a requirement?

Exercises: Skill Builders

TURN DOWN LETTER

Using the facts of the Cherry or Baker cases found in Appendixes A and B, respectively, draft a letter to the plaintiff declining representation on the grounds that the statute of limitations has run out on the cause of action.

Portfolio Assignment

Portfolio Assignment 5-1: Draft a complaint in the Cherry case. Using the facts set out in Appendix A, draft a complaint in the Cherry case.

Portfolio Assignment 5-2: Draft a letter to a client. Using the facts in the Baker case in Appendix B, draft a letter to Mr. Baker explaining that your firm has decided not to accept Mr. Baker's case and also explaining that the statute of limitations for Mr. Baker's action appears to have run out. Your letter should detail not only the firm's conclusion that the case should not be filed but also the meeting with Mr. Baker and the facts as the firm has come to understand them.

Vocabulary Builders

ACROSS

2 The requirement that a party to a suit have a legally recognized interest in the proceedings or that a party's rights will be infringed upon by the rulings in the litigation.

4 A sworn statement by a party attesting to the truth and accuracy of the statements made in a complaint.

6 The party who has a cause of action; the person who initiates a suit against another.

7 The party who is named in the complaint and against whom the plaintiff has a cause of action.

8 The transfer of a case from state court to the federal court.

10 A party's permanent residence, where the party has lived and where the party intends to return.

DOWN

1 The power of a court to exercise jurisdiction based on the location of real property within the forum.

2 The power of a court to entertain specific legal actions and to make rulings on those issues.

3 A court's power over the individuals involved in the case; it can compel attendance at court hearings and enter judgments against the parties.

5 A written statement, made under oath, that details specific facts.

9 (Latin) "at first sight"; the presentation of a minimum of evidence to establish the party's case.

Chapter 6

The Defendant's Answer

CHAPTER OBJECTIVES

The student will be able to:

- Explain the function of the defendant's answer.
- Describe how an answer matches the allegations of the plaintiff's complaint.
- Describe the minimum requirements of a legally valid answer.
- Explain the process of raising affirmative defenses in an answer.
- Define 12(b)(6) motions.
- Explain counterclaims.
- Discuss cross-claims.
- Compare and contrast impleader with interpleader.
- Discuss class-action lawsuits.
- Draft an answer containing a counterclaim.

In the previous chapter, we explored the world of the plaintiff's complaint, in which the plaintiff raises allegations against the defendant and seeks to build a case for compensation that should be paid by the defendant. In this chapter, we examine all of the aspects of the defendant's answer, including admissions, denials, the consequences for failing to deny the plaintiff's allegations, counterclaims, cross-claims, and other elements of third-party practices. Before we can address those other issues, we must first consider the question of what exactly an answer is.

THE ANSWER

answer
The defendant's response to the plaintiff's complaint.

The **answer** is the defendant's response to the allegations raised by the plaintiff. Rule 7 of the Federal Rules of Civil Procedure requires that the defendant submit an answer to the plaintiff's complaint. Not only must the defendant respond in writing to the complaint, the defendant must also answer each and every one of the plaintiff's allegations. Answers frequently contain denials of the plaintiff's allegations.

> *Rule 7. Pleadings Allowed; Form of Motions*
> *(a) Pleadings.*
> *There shall be a complaint and an answer.*

However, though Rule 7 creates the requirement for an answer, it is Rule 12 that frames the practical issues involved in drafting and filing the answer, including the time limits. We will discuss Rule 12 in greater detail when we consider the issues of defenses raised in answers. But first, we examine the basic function of an answer.

FIGURE 6.1

Rule 8(b) Defenses; Form of Denials

Source: Rule 8(b) Federal Rules of Civil Procedure.

A party shall state in short and plain terms the party's defenses to each claim asserted and shall admit or deny the averments upon which the adverse party relies. If a party is without knowledge or information sufficient to form a belief as to the truth of an averment, the party shall so state and this has the effect of a denial. Denials shall fairly meet the substance of the averments denied. When a pleader intends in good faith to deny only a part or a qualification of an averment, the pleader shall specify so much of it as is true and material and shall deny only the remainder. Unless the pleader intends in good faith to controvert all the averments of the preceding pleading, the pleader may make denials as specific denials of designated averments or paragraphs, or may generally deny all the averments except such designated averments or paragraphs as the pleader expressly admits; but, when the pleader does so intend to controvert all its averments, including averments of the grounds upon which the court's jurisdiction depends, the pleader may do so by general denial subject to the obligations set forth in Rule 11.

FIGURE 6.2

Components of an Answer

An answer will have three general components:

- A point-by-point response to each of the allegations raised in the complaint.
- Affirmative defenses and counterclaims against the plaintiff.
- Rule 12(b)(6) motion.

The Function of the Answer

The function of the answer is to allow the defendant to assert his or her defenses to the plaintiff's claims. Failure to do so results in a default judgment in the plaintiff's favor. But an answer serves more functions than simply providing the defendant with a forum to deny the plaintiff's claims. Answers contain not only denials but also admissions, defenses, and counterclaims against the plaintiff. For an example of a detailed answer, see Figure 6.22 at the conclusion of this chapter.

The Minimum Requirements of the Answer

A defendant's answer must conform to certain minimum requirements. These are set out in Rule 8(b). In that rule, the defendant must present his or her defenses in short and plain terms and either admit or deny each of the plaintiff's allegations in the complaint. Rule 8(b) requires short and plain terms in the answer (see Figures 6.1 and 6.2). An answer must admit, deny, or allege that the defendant is without knowledge or information sufficient to form a belief as to the truth of the answer.

Drafting the Answer

admit

To agree or stipulate to the allegations presented in a complaint.

deny

To disagree with or contest the allegations presented in a complaint.

The prime purpose of an answer is to either **admit** or **deny** the allegations in the complaint in such a way that it satisfies the requirements of Rule 8. If the defendant admits to the allegations contained in a particular paragraph, then those facts are deemed conclusively proven for the purposes of further litigation between the parties. There is no requirement for a plaintiff to present evidence about contentions that the defendant has admitted. When a defendant denies a particular allegation, it frames the issues in the litigation. The plaintiff must present proof to substantiate allegations that the defendant has denied in his or her answer. If a defendant fails to properly deny an allegation, it is deemed to be an admission and will carry the same weight and have the same consequences as if the defendant actually stated an admission in his or her answer. See Figure 6.3.

FIGURE 6.3

Rule 8(d). Effect of Failure to Deny

Source: Rule 8(d) Federal Rules of Civil Procedure.

Averments in a pleading to which a responsive pleading is required, other than those as to the amount of damage, are admitted when not denied in the responsive pleading. Averments in a pleading to which no responsive pleading is required or permitted shall be taken as denied or avoided.

FIGURE 6.4

Possible Defense Responses in an Answer

Defendant hereby responds to the allegations contained in the complaint as follows:

1. The allegations contained in paragraph 1 of the complaint are hereby admitted.

2. The allegations contained in paragraph 2 of the complaint are hereby denied.

3. The allegations contained in paragraph 3 of the complaint are admitted to the extent that the defendant admits that there was a collision on the second day of November, last year; as to all other allegations contained in this paragraph, denied.

4. As to the allegations contained in paragraph 4 of the complaint, defendant is without sufficient knowledge or information to form a belief as to the truth of the allegations and therefore denies each and every one contained therein.

The practical effect of an admission in the answer is that the defendant is then prevented from denying those facts during the trial. There is no requirement that a defendant must be consistent in his or her denials. A defendant is not prohibited from offering inconsistent replies to the plaintiff's complaint, even if this puts the defendant in the position of pleading inconsistent or alternative defenses.

As you can see in Figure 6.4, a defendant can admit to the plaintiff's allegations, deny them, offer a partial admission and denial, or claim that he or she is without sufficient information to form a belief about the veracity of the claim. This last phrase effectively denies the plaintiff's allegations but is offered as a way to avoid a claim of bad faith or frivolous legal maneuverings that can open the defendant to court-ordered sanctions. We will discuss those sanctions subsequently in this chapter.

Denying Claims

A defendant's denial of the allegations raised in the complaint serves to form the issues that will be litigated in the case. Unlike the issues that the defendant admitted, the plaintiff must present proof about any allegation denied by the defendant. The answer essentially creates the issues for trial. The defendant's admissions in the answer result in the parties taking as true the allegations made by the plaintiff in his or her complaint. The allegations denied by the defendant force the plaintiff to present testimony and evidence at trial to sustain the allegations. For an example of a plaintiff's factual allegations in a complaint and a defendant's corresponding denials in an answer, see Figure 6.5.

Other Responses in Answers

Defendants are not limited to giving only admissions or denials in answers. There may be some allegations the defendant can neither admit nor deny. For instance, the defendant may have no

PRACTICE TIP

When the legal team drafts the responses to the plaintiff's complaint, it must be precise and provide detailed responses, where appropriate. Denials should be specific, direct to the point, and not offer any argument. If there is some doubt about the wording of the corresponding paragraph in the complaint, then the denial should be phrased in such a way that there is no doubt about what is being denied and for what part some other averment is made. For instance, a complaint might contain the following language:

> 17. That the defendant did, on the day in question, recklessly drive his automobile, in disregard of the rules of the road, the good sense of man, and the established customs of worthwhile drivers.

This allegation contains some unusual statements. How should a defendant respond? One way is to offer the following:

> 17. (Defendant's answer). The defendant denies that, on the day in question, he did operate his automobile in a reckless manner; he also denies that he disregarded the rules of the road. Defendant is unable to either admit or deny the additional allegations contained in this paragraph as he is without knowledge of their substance or relation to the facts alleged. However, these additional statements are deemed denied by the defendant.

FIGURE 6.5
The Defendant's Answer

STATE OF PLACID
DISTRICT COURT
LONDON COUNTY

Sherlock Holmes (Plaintiff) v. Professor James Moriarty, individually and as owner, operator of Moriarty Transport Trucking Co. (Defendant)	CIVIL ACTION: 04-100 ***ANSWER*** (Jury Trial Requested)

COMES NOW, the defendants in the above-styled action and bring this their Answer to Complaint filed by Plaintiff Sherlock Holmes, hereafter referred to as Plaintiff. All responses are deemed made by Defendant James Moriarty (hereafter referred to as "Defendant") in his individual capacity and in his capacity as owner and operator of Moriarty Transport Trucking Company.

ANSWER BY DEFENDANT

1. The allegations contained in this paragraph are admitted.
2. The allegations contained in this paragraph are admitted.
3. The defendant denies that there is any cause of action in this case, either based in Baskerville, PL, or any other area in this state.
4. The allegations contained in this paragraph are admitted.
5. The allegations contained in this paragraph are denied.
6. Defendant is without any information as to the cause of death of Irene Adler Holmes and therefore denies the contentions of paragraph 6.
7. Defendant has no information about the extent of the plaintiff's injuries nor the cause thereof and therefore denies the contentions of paragraph 7.
8. Denied.
9. Denied.
10. Denied.
11. Denied.
12. Denied.
13. Denied.
14. Denied.
15. Denied.

DEFENDANT'S PRAYER FOR RELIEF

The defendant prays that the court:

1. Deny any compensation to the plaintiff.
2. Grant no award of damages to the plaintiff.
3. Make no award of costs to the plaintiff or plaintiff's attorney.
4. Dismiss the plaintiff's action for failure to state a ground upon which relief may be granted.
5. Grant the defendant's prayer for relief contained in Defendant's Counter-claim, set out below.

FIGURE 6.5
(*Continued*)

6. Award the defendant a jury trial on all triable issues.

7. Award the defendant any and all damages, compensation and other relief that justice may demand.

So submitted, this the 19th day of December, 2004.

By: _____

Deborah Bolstridge

_____

(PL. Bar No.)
Attorney for Defendant, James Moriarty

21 Robin's Wood Place
Bohemia, PL 28655
828-555-2121 (phone)
828-555-2123 (fax)

information about a particular allegation or be willing to admit a portion of the allegation but not the entirety. In such a situation, the defendant might admit part and deny the remainder of the allegation. Consider Hypothetical 6-1.

Hypothetical 6-1

Paragraph 17 of the plaintiff's complaint contains the following allegation:

> That, at the time of the collision, witness Nora Burke was an eyewitness to defendant's negligent driving and will testify thereto.

The defendant in this case is not sure how to respond to this allegation. How can the defendant say for sure what this witness saw or what the witness will testify to at trial? How does the defendant respond and still protect his or her legal interests?

Answer: The defendant will respond with the following phrase: "The defendant neither admits nor denies the allegations contained in paragraph 17; the defendant is without any information to form a belief as to the truth of the matter asserted."

As you can see in Hypothetical 6-1, when the defendant is presented with situations in which he or she is unaware of the facts surrounding a particular allegation, the only proper response is for the defendant to state that he or she lacks information about the accuracy of the allegation and can neither admit nor deny it for the purposes of the pleadings. In such a situation, the defendant's response would be deemed a denial, and the plaintiff would be required to present proof at trial to substantiate that claim.

Bad Faith

A question often arises when drafting complaints about admissions and denials. Why wouldn't a defendant simply deny all of the allegations raised in the complaint? After all, by denying everything, the defendant is forcing the plaintiff to present proof on all the allegations contained in the complaint, which would make the plaintiff's job harder at trial and might result in a favorable ruling for the defendant. To answer this question, we must first address ourselves to the rules. Rule 11 provides that the judge can impose sanctions on parties who act in **bad faith** (see Figure 6.6). This rule applies to both the plaintiff and the defendant. If the defendant interposes defenses or denies allegations out of bad faith or simply to harass or annoy the other party, the judge is authorized to impose sanctions including:

bad faith
Intentional misrepresentation, wanton disregard for truth, and/or fraudulent activity that can be the basis for an additional award of damages to the party that can establish such activity occurred.

• Attorneys' fees related to the litigation of the matter denied in bad faith.

• Monetary sanctions against the attorneys involved.

• Other sanctions approved by the court, including dismissal of some of the defendants' denials.

FIGURE 6.6

Sanctions for Bad Faith in Pleadings

Source: Rule 11(c) Federal Rules of Civil Procedure.

> (2) Nature of Sanction; Limitations. A sanction imposed for violation of this rule shall be limited to what is sufficient to deter repetition of such conduct or comparable conduct by others similarly situated. Subject to the limitations in subparagraphs (A) and (B), the sanction may consist of, or include, directives of a nonmonetary nature, an order to pay a penalty into court, or, if imposed on motion and warranted for effective deterrence, an order directing payment to the movant of some or all of the reasonable attorneys' fees and other expenses incurred as a direct result of the violation.
>
> (A) Monetary sanctions may not be awarded against a represented party for a violation of subdivision (b)(2).
>
> (B) Monetary sanctions may not be awarded on the court's initiative unless the court issues its order to show cause before a voluntary dismissal or settlement of the claims made by or against the party which is, or whose attorneys are, to be sanctioned.
>
> (3) Order. When imposing sanctions, the court shall describe the conduct determined.

FIGURE 6.7

Time Limits on Serving Answer

> (a) When Presented.
>
> (1) Unless a different time is prescribed in a statute of the United States, a defendant shall serve an answer
>
> (A) within 20 days after being served with the summons and complaint.

default judgment

A judgment entered by the court against the defendant for failure to respond to the plaintiff's complaint.

CYBER TRIP

Michigan Court System–Responding to a Complaint http://www.courts.michigan.gov/scao/selfhelp/general/answers.htm Wikipedia–Answers in Civil Cases http://en.wikipedia.org/wiki/Answer New Mexico–Judicial Education Center http://jec.unm.edu/resources/benchbooks/magistrate/1-2-3.htm

Serving the Answer on the Plaintiff

Under Rule 12(a), the defendant has 20 days from the date of service to file an answer. See Figure 6.7 for time limits. Calculating the actual due date is relatively simple. One must count all intervening days, including holidays and weekends, unless the final day falls on a weekend or a holiday. In that event, the actual deadline moves to the next business day that is not a holiday. Failure to file within the required time period will result in a default judgment against the defendant.

Failure to Respond to the Complaint

If a defendant fails to respond to the complaint, the judge is authorized to enter a **default judgment** against him or her. In a default judgment, the judge takes as true all of the allegations in the complaint and awards whatever damages the plaintiff has requested. Such a ruling can have obvious and devastating consequences for a defendant, which is one reason attorneys who represent defendants insist on getting a copy of the complaint as soon as possible. Many make it a part of their practice to file the answer early, to avoid even the prospect of a default judgment. Of course, a default judgment is authorized only when the plaintiff can prove adequate service of process. (See Chapter 5).

Failure to Respond to Allegations in the Complaint

As we have already seen, the defendant must respond to each allegation raised in the complaint. If the defendant fails to do so, then the Rules of Civil Procedure provide a single outcome: The facts, also known as averments, are deemed to be admitted (see Figure 6.8). In this situation, the plaintiff's contention about a specific set of facts will be taken as true, and deemed admitted by the defendant, for all issues raised throughout the remainder of the litigation. Consider Hypothetical 6-2.

Hypothetical 6-2

Plaintiff's Complaint, Paragraph 6, contains the following allegation:

> Defendant, did, on the 8th day of November, fail to keep a proper lookout and operated his car in a negligent manner to wit: operated his automobile too closely to the plaintiff's car, failed to maintain a safe distance and failed to obey the rules of the road.

FIGURE 6.8

Effect of Failure to Deny

> Averments in a pleading to which a responsive pleading is required, other than those as to the amount of damage, are admitted when not denied in the responsive pleading. Averments in a pleading to which no responsive pleading is required or permitted shall be taken as denied or avoided.

Defendant's answer to paragraph 6 contains the following statement:

Defendant denies that he failed to keep a proper lookout on the day of the accident.

What effect does this language have on the other allegations contained in the complaint?

Answer: Because the defendant did not specifically deny each and every allegation in paragraph 6, a judge is likely to rule that the defendant has admitted that he (1) operated his car in a negligent manner, (2) failed to maintain a safe distance, and (3) failed to obey the rules of the road.

DEFENSES

Answers not only provide the defendant with a forum to admit or deny the allegations in a complaint but also a method for the defendant to assert defenses and counterclaims. A defense to an action is a legally recognized excuse. If proven, the defense would entitle the defendant to a verdict in his or her favor or provide that the defendant is not obligated to pay any judgment to the plaintiff. We begin our discussion with affirmative defenses.

Affirmative Defenses

affirmative defense
An "excuse" by the opposing party that does not just simply negate the allegation, but puts forth a legal reason to avoid enforcement. These defenses are waived if not pleaded.

An **affirmative defense** is one that is not raised by the defendant's denials in the body of the answer. Instead, it must be raised separately and stated prominently in the answer. An affirmative defense entitles the defendant to a judgment against the plaintiff for specific matters. Rule 8(c) sets out the general categories of affirmative defenses that a defendant can raise in a civil case. See Figure 6.9.

Raising Affirmative Defenses

A defendant raises affirmative defenses in the latter portion of his or her answer. The first part of the answer is dedicated to responding to each and every one of the allegations raised in the complaint. After that, the defendant is free to raise affirmative defenses. Suppose, for example, that the defendant wishes to raise the affirmative defense of laches. Under the doctrine of laches, a person may waive a legal right by failing to assert it within a specific time period. Such a defense is similar to raising the issue of statutes of limitations. When a defendant raises the defense of laches, he or she is saying that the plaintiff is not entitled to any award of damages because the plaintiff has waited too long to raise objections to the defendant's actions. This defense is not assumed; it must be raised by the defendant in the answer.

Affirmative defenses provide the defendant with the mechanism to have the case dismissed. But there are situations in which the defendant actually has claims against the plaintiff. In that situation, instead of raising an affirmative defense, such as laches, the defendant may actually seek damages from the plaintiff in the form of a counterclaim. See Figure 6.10 for an example of an affirmative defense.

Counterclaims

counterclaim
A claim made by the defendant against the plaintiff—not a defense, but a new claim for damages, as if the defendant were the plaintiff in a separate suit; a countersuit brought by the defendant against the plaintiff.

Rule 13 sets out the basis for **counterclaims** and cross-claims. Under Rule 13, a counterclaim consists of "any claim which at the time of serving the pleading the pleader has against any opposing party, if it arises out of the transaction or occurrence that is the subject matter of the opposing party's claim and does not require for its adjudication the presence of third parties of whom the court cannot acquire jurisdiction" (Rule 13(a), Rules of Civil Procedure). Rule 13 allows the defendant to bring a claim against the plaintiff. In many ways, a counterclaim resembles the original complaint, except that it is brought by the defendant against the plaintiff. What are some circumstances in which a defendant might have a counterclaim against the plaintiff? Consider Hypothetical 6-3.

FIGURE 6.9
Rule 8(c) Affirmative Defenses

In pleading to a preceding pleading, a party shall set forth affirmatively accord and satisfaction, arbitration and award, assumption of risk, contributory negligence, discharge in bankruptcy, duress, estoppel, failure of consideration, fraud, illegality, injury by fellow servant, laches, license, payment, release, res judicata, statute of frauds, statute of limitations, waiver, and any other matter constituting an avoidance or affirmative defense. When a party has mistakenly designated a defense as a counterclaim or a counterclaim as a defense, the court on terms, if justice so requires, shall treat the pleading as if there had been a proper designation.

FIGURE 6.10
Example of an Affirmative Defense

> **Defendant's First Affirmative Defense**
>
> Plaintiff's claim for personal injury against defendant is barred by the applicable statute of limitations. PL § 5-2-13.
>
> **Defendant's Second Affirmative Defense**
>
> Plaintiff's claims against defendant are barred under the doctrine of assumption of risk. PL § 5-2-15(a).

RESEARCH THIS!

One of the most common types of lawsuits in the United States today is a personal injury action, usually brought by an individual motorist against another individual motorist. Because we have seen that statute of limitations can be brought as an affirmative defense in any action, it is always important to determine what the statute of limitations is for a particular action. Research personal injuries arising from automobile collisions and locate the statute in your state that provides exactly how long a plaintiff has to bring such an action before it is barred forever.

LEGAL RESEARCH MAXIM

When researching issues related to answers, keep in mind that though the rules of civil procedure for your jurisdiction are important, the case law that applies and develops these rules is just as important. The rule may provide the basic parameters for a particular action, such as setting a time limit of 20 days to file an answer, but it is the case law that applies this rule that explains how the time periods are calculated and also provides answers for unusual situations, including federal holidays not recognized in the state or other situations in which it is unclear from the wording in the rule exactly how a party should proceed.

Hypothetical 6-3

Maria is leaving work one day, and as she approaches an intersection, she notices that the traffic lights do not appear to be working. Motorists are attempting to cross through the intersection, but there is a great deal of confusion. Maria waits for an opportune moment and then proceeds through the intersection. William is driving a car that enters the intersection from Maria's right, and the two cars strike one another. A few days later, William drafts a complaint and serves it on Maria. She believes that William is responsible for the damages to her car and that he was at fault. In fact, she had been working with her attorney to draft a complaint against him. When he filed his complaint first, he became the plaintiff in the action. Maria wishes not only to deny William's allegations of her negligence but also to counterclaim against him for the damages that he caused to her car. In this situation, when Maria files her answer, she will include a counterclaim against William for the damages to her automobile.

Compulsory and Permissive Counterclaims

Rule 13 recognizes two different types of counterclaims: compulsory and permissive. A **compulsory counterclaim** is one that arises from the transaction that forms the basis of the complaint, whereas a **permissive counterclaim** may be raised either as part of the same case or in a separate action. In the hypothetical involving Maria and William, Maria must bring her counterclaim against William for the damages done to her car because it arises out of the same transaction as William's complaint. If Maria fails to bring this counterclaim, she has waived it. Under the rules of compulsory counterclaims, her failure to allege her counterclaim against William for the damages to her car would result in her being barred from bringing a separate action over this issue. A compulsory counterclaim must be brought in the same action or it is barred forever.

compulsory counterclaim
A counterclaim that is required to be pleaded because the facts relate to the same transaction as that set forth in the original complaint.

permissive counterclaim
A counterclaim that is not required to be filed with a complaint because the facts do not arise out of the same set of circumstances as the complaint.

COMMUNICATION TIP

There are times when a defendant may decide, though he or she has the basis for a counterclaim against the plaintiff, to waive it. Such a procedure, especially when it involves compulsory counterclaims, can result in a complete dismissal of one of the defendant's possible actions against the plaintiff. In such a situation, the legal team must ensure that the defendant is fully aware of the consequences of failing to file a counterclaim. The best way to do this is in writing. Compose a letter to the defendant detailing exactly what the nature of the counterclaim is, what the firm's opinion is regarding its classification as compulsory or permissive, and the fact that if the claim is not raised in the answer, the defendant may be waiving any right to bring the claim in the future. Some firms even go so far as to have the client sign an acknowledgement that he or she has been advised of the consequences and voluntarily agreed to forgo the counterclaim.

How do the courts determine when a counterclaim is compulsory or permissive? A compulsory counterclaim involves the same transaction that was raised by the plaintiff in the original complaint. In our hypothetical involving Maria and William, Maria's claim against William would be considered compulsory because it involves the same traffic collision. A court will insist that such a claim be brought in the original case to cut down on duplicative actions and for the practical reason that the same parties, witnesses, and issues are involved and the court can dispense with two claims in one action.

Res Judicata

res judicata
(Latin) "The thing has been adjudicated." The principle that a court's decision on a particular matter is binding on future litigation between the parties; sometimes referred to as "*res adjudicata.*"

There is an important legal principle that applies in situations involving counterclaims. ***Res judicata*** is the principle that a legal finding on an issue in one case may be dispositive of that issue in another case. For instance, if the same parties are involved in litigation and a court makes a final determination that one of the parties is liable, that determination may be binding on related cases. The principle of *res judicata* is based on conservation of resources. If all parties were present and litigated the question to a resolution, it makes very little sense to relitigate the same issue in another case. *Res judicata* is important in counterclaims because if the issues in the counterclaim are resolved against the defendant, he or she will be barred from bringing a new action that challenges that finding. The court will rule that the issue is now *res judicata,* and decided permanently, at least as it relates to the parties. *Res judicata* does not apply to other individuals who were not involved in the legal action; it only binds those who were named in the suit and had a chance to present evidence about the issue. When a defendant brings a counterclaim against the plaintiff and that issue is resolved in the plaintiff's favor, the defendant cannot bring a new action making the same allegation. The court will rule that the issues have been decided and that the defendant is barred from any further action on the issue because of *res judicata.*

A different rule applies to permissive counterclaims. Recall that a permissive counterclaim is a claim that one party has against the other that does not arise out of the transaction involved in the original complaint. Suppose, in our previous example, that Maria and William coincidentally had been involved in a business transaction together. Maria wishes to sue William for failure to comply with a business contract. This claim could be brought separately, but because Maria is already involved in a suit against William, she decides to allege it in her complaint involving the automobile collision. When we are discussing compulsory counterclaims, the inquiry centers on a single incident, in this case a motor vehicle accident between Maria and William. It will be ruled a compulsory counterclaim when the defendant has a claim against the plaintiff that arises from the same facts and circumstances as alleged in the complaint. However, the issues change when dealing with permissive counterclaims. For these, the defendant brings a claim against the plaintiff that is not related to the issues in the original complaint. Instead, the party brings the claim because it would be convenient to resolve both issues in a single case. However, because a permissive counterclaim involves situations that are not related to the main case, the counterclaim might cause confusion and result in a protracted case. A judge might decide to sever Maria's claim for a business transaction out of the main case. In such a situation, Maria would be required to bring a separate complaint against William, which would result in an entirely separate civil action. It is at the judge's discretion whether to permit a permissive counterclaim to remain

FIGURE 6.11
Reply to a
Counterclaim

STATE OF PLACID
DISTRICT COURT
LONDON COUNTY

Sherlock Holmes
(Plaintiff)

CIVIL ACTION: 04-100

v.

**REPLY TO DEFENDANT'S
COUNTERCLAIM**

Professor James Moriarty, individually
and as owner, operator of Moriarty
Transport Trucking Co. (Defendant)
CIVIL ACTION: 04-100

COMES NOW Plaintiff Sherlock Holmes and files this, his reply to Defendant's
Counterclaim.

1. The allegations contained in paragraph 1 of the Defendant's counterclaim are denied.

2. The allegations contained in paragraph 2 of the Defendant's counterclaim are denied.

3. The allegations contained in paragraph 3 of the Defendant's counterclaim are denied.

Respectfully submitted, this the 29th day of December, 2004.

By: _____
Neal Bevans

_____
(PL. Bar No.)
Attorney for the plaintiff

Bevans & Bevans, P.A.
1001 Burkemont Avenue
Bohemia, PL 28655
828-555-1212 (phone)
828-555-1213 (fax)

reply
The responsive pleading
provided in Rule 7 to a
counterclaim.

12(b)(6) motion
A motion under the
provisions of Rule 12 of the
Rules of Civil Procedure
that challenges the basis of
the complaint for failure to
state a claim upon which
relief can be granted.

in a case. The judge's final decision will be based on several factors, including the potential confusion and additional time that proving the permissive counterclaim would add to the trial. If the judge decides that this counterclaim does not involve an unnecessary protraction of the trial, the judge might decide to allow Maria to bring her permissive counterclaim against William based on the business contract.

Replies to Counterclaims

A **reply** is the pleading used to respond to the allegations of a counterclaim. The term "reply" is used to differentiate between this pleading and the answer, which the defendant uses to respond to the allegations made in the complaint. When a defendant serves a counterclaim on the plaintiff, the plaintiff responds with a pleading entitled, "Reply to Counterclaim." This pleading is very similar to an answer. It sets out the plaintiff's admissions, denials, and defenses to the counterclaim raised by the defendant. See Figure 6.11 for an example of a reply to a counterclaim.

RULE 12(b)(6) MOTIONS

The final aspect of the defendant's answer is not really part of the pleading itself. A **12(b)(6) motion** is a separate motion from the actual answer. See Figure 6.12 for an example. It is a motion that the defendant files that challenges the specific wording of the complaint.

FIGURE 6.12

Example of a Rule 12(b)(6) Motion

> "Paragraph 3 of the complaint fails to state a claim upon which relief can be granted."
>
> "This court lacks subject matter jurisdiction over the action contemplated in this case as the plaintiff's allegations fail to allege a minimum monetary amount of damages in excess of $10,000."

PRACTICE TIP

There are other motions authorized under Rule 12. However, a 12(b)(6) motion is one of the most common motions made in any civil case.

PRACTICE TIP

A 12(b)(6) motion can be raised not only against complaints but also against counterclaims, cross-claims, and third-party claims.

Purpose of the Rule 12(b)(6) Motion

The purpose of Rule 12(b)(6) is to provide the defendant with a mechanism to challenge the allegations raised in the plaintiff's complaint. A 12(b)(6) motion was never designed as a means to challenge the legal effect of the complaint. Instead, its primary purpose is based on the theory of notice pleadings. As we saw in our discussions of Rule 8 in Chapter 5, the plaintiff must make a short and plain statement of the claim against the defendant. When the defendant alleges that the complaint is confusing or fails to meet minimum notice requirements, the defendant is entitled to file a 12(b)(6) motion to challenge the allegations in the complaint. A 12(b)(6) motion has a very narrow focus: It challenges the allegations by stating that the plaintiff's wording fails to set out a legally recognized claim. If the defendant can convince the judge that the plaintiff's complaint fails to rise to the minimum level required under the Rules of Civil Procedure, the judge would be authorized to dismiss some or all of the allegations. Because of the potential benefit that a defendant would earn from such a ruling, it is routine for defendants in civil cases to file 12(b)(6) motions in all cases, whether or not they actually believe that the plaintiff's complaints are insufficient.

A 12(b)(6) motion also was never designed to act as a corrective measure for poor choice of wording in a complaint. The rule does not require perfect pleadings, only pleadings that put the defendant on notice as to what the claim is against him or her. If the wording in the complaint is ambiguous or subject to different interpretations, a 12(b)(6) motion is not the appropriate way to challenge that language. Instead, the defendant would be authorized to bring a motion for a more definite statement under the provisions of Rule 12(e) (see Figure 6.13). We will discuss these motions in greater detail in Chapter 9. If the defendant alleges that the complaint contains improper or redundant material, a 12(b)(6) motion is also not authorized. Instead, the defendant must file a motion under the provisions of Rule 12(f), also discussed in Chapter 9.

Instead, 12(b)(6) motions are designed to attack the very basis of the complaint by stating that there is no legally recognized action against the defendant. If the complaint fails to set out the basis of the plaintiff's legal claim against the defendant, a judge would be authorized to dismiss the complaint on the basis of Rule 12(b)(6). How does the court make this determination? The complaint must stand on its own. When a judge evaluates the complaint, he or she focuses on the language contained in that complaint, not any subsequent pleadings or other materials. There are provisions under Rule 12(b)(6) that allow a defendant to convert the motion into one for summary judgment. We do not discuss that aspect of the rule in this chapter but rather wait to explain summary judgment motions in greater detail in Chapter 9. A judge's determination of the sufficiency of the complaint must come from a review of the plaintiff's wording in that document. If, by reviewing the actual language, the judge is convinced that the complaint fails to meet the standard set out in Rule 12(b)(6), he or she is authorized to dismiss that contention. Because this dismissal can have dire consequences for the plaintiff, careful research and equally careful drafting will help avoid a 12(b)(6) motion.

When Can a Defendant File a Rule 12(b)(6) Motion?

The most common method, and the one suggested by the rules, is for the defendant to file a 12(b)(6) motion contemporaneously with his or her answer. A strict interpretation of the rule would suggest that a 12(b)(6) motion should be filed before the responsive pleading, but it is

FIGURE 6.13

Motion for a More Definite Statement

Source: Rule 12(e) Federal Rules of Civil Procedure.

> If a pleading to which a responsive pleading is permitted is so vague or ambiguous that a party cannot reasonably be required to frame a responsive pleading, the party may move for a more definite statement before interposing a responsive pleading. The motion shall point out the defects complained of and the details desired. If the motion is granted and the order of the court is not obeyed within 10 days after notice of the order or within such other time as the court may fix, the court may strike the pleading to which the motion was directed or make such order as it deems just.

FIGURE 6.14

Motion to Strike

Source: Rule 12(f) Federal Rules of Civil Procedure.

> Upon motion made by a party before responding to a pleading or, if no responsive pleading is permitted by these rules, upon motion made by a party within 20 days after the service of the pleading upon the party or upon the court's own initiative at any time, the court may order stricken from any pleading any insufficient defense or any redundant, immaterial, impertinent, or scandalous matter.

common practice for defendants to file them at the same time. In such situations, the court will usually infer that the 12(b)(6) motion was filed prior to filing of the answer. There is a practical reason a defendant might file both pleadings at the same time. If a defendant's 12(b)(6) motion is denied, then the next item of business for the court to consider is whether the defendant filed his or her answer within the statutorily required time period. Rather than run the risk of having the 12(b)(6) motion dismissed and then losing the case on a default judgment, attorneys for the defendant will file both the answer and the bagel motion. By doing so, they avoid a default judgment by ensuring that they answer within the statutorily required time limit and also reserve their right to have some or all of the allegations in the complaint dismissed.

If a party waits too long and files a 12(b)(6) motion after responsive pleadings, the court may still consider the issues but will view them as a motion for summary judgment instead of a 12(b)(6) motion. The conversion from a 12(b)(6) motion to a motion for summary judgment has important procedural aspects that we will discuss in Chapter 9.

Because answers must be filed within 20 days of service of process, the practical limitation on when a 12(b)(6) motion must be filed is also 20 days. After all, the 12(b)(6) motion must be filed before other responsive pleadings, and because it is common practice to file both the motion and the answer contemporaneously, the defendant has 20 days to put the motion together to file with the court. The time periods can vary depending on the nature of the 12(b)(6) motion. For instance, if the motion is interposed on a counterclaim, the time limit will be based on the time limits imposed on filing the reply to the counterclaim.

Motions to Strike

In addition to Rule 12(b)(6) motions, parties may bring several other motions under the authority of Rule 12 of the Federal Rules of Civil Procedure. For instance, it is quite common for a defendant to file a motion to strike some or all of a plaintiff's complaint based on Rule 12(f). Such a motion is referred to as a motion to strike, and a defendant may file such a motion when some portion of the plaintiff's complaint is impossible to understand, redundant, or inserts language that a court would deem scandalous (see Figure 6.14). In a recent case, for example, a court struck a portion of the plaintiff's complaint that relied on improperly obtained communications between an attorney and his client (*Emmanouil v. Roggio,* 2006 WL 2927621, *2 (D.N.J.) (D.N.J. 2006)).

CROSS-CLAIMS

cross-claim lawsuit
A lawsuit against a party of the same side; plaintiffs or defendants suing each other (defendant versus defendant or plaintiff versus plaintiff).

When a party has a claim against a co-party, he or she brings it as a **cross-claim**. The difference between counterclaims and cross-claims is that a counterclaim is brought against another party, such as a defendant against a plaintiff. A cross-claim, in contrast, is brought against a codefendant or a co-plaintiff. See Figure 6.15 for a diagram of the differences between counterclaims and cross-claims.

Just as we saw with counterclaims, a cross-claim must arise out of the same transaction or facts that form the basis of the original lawsuit. The theory behind cross-claims is very simple: If

FIGURE 6.15

Diagram of the Differences between Counterclaims and Cross-Claims

Counterclaim	Cross-Claim
Brought by defendant against plaintiff	Brought by defendant against codefendant or plaintiff against co-plaintiff
Divided into two categories: compulsory and permissive	Only one class
Requires reply by plaintiff	Requires reply by co-party

FIGURE 6.16
Cross-Claim against Co-Party

Source: Rule 13(g) Federal Rules of Civil Procedure.

> A pleading may state as a cross-claim any claim by one party against a co-party arising out of the transaction or occurrence that is the subject matter either of the original action or of a counterclaim therein or relating to any property that is the subject matter of the original action. Such cross-claim may include a claim that the party against whom it is asserted is or may be liable to the cross-claimant for all or part of a claim asserted in the action against the cross-claimant.

the court can dispose of several different actions within the context of the single civil case, it makes sense to do so. It will save on time and resources to adjudicate related claims all at the same time instead of forcing the parties to file multiple separate actions to litigate issues that are essentially based on a single occurrence. Because of this, courts have held that the rules about permitting cross-claims should be liberally construed to achieve the principle set out in Rule 13. However, even given a liberal approach to Rule 13, there are certain limitations on cross-claims. For one thing, a cross-claim is not authorized if brought by someone who is not a party to the action. Only plaintiffs or defendants who are already involved in the litigation can bring cross-claims against one another. Unlike counterclaims, cross-claims are always permissive. Therefore, if a co-party does not bring a cross-claim in the main case, he or she may still be able to bring that claim in a separate action. Like the other pleadings involved in the case, the cross-claim must also contain a short and plain statement of the claim made against the co-party. Cross-claims, like all other pleadings, must conform to the requirements of Rule 8 of the Federal Rules of Civil Procedure. They are also subject to bagel motions and therefore should be carefully crafted.

A party might bring a cross-claim against another party to allege that one party is more culpable in the action than the other. A codefendant, for instance, might bring a cross-claim to seek reimbursement for any judgments he or she is compelled to pay out as part of the main action.

Answers to Cross-Claims

PRACTICE TIP

The standard for asserting a cross-claim is that the claim rests on issues that have a strong relationship with the original action.

Just as we have seen with all previous pleadings, a party must respond to a cross-claim. In some states, the reply to a cross-claim is referred to as a reply—the same terminology used to respond to a counterclaim on the federal level. In other instances, the responsive pleading to a cross-claim is referred to as an answer. See Figure 6.16. Whatever the terminology, the response must meet the same requirements as any responsive pleading. It must admit or deny the allegations raised in the cross-claim. See Figure 6.17.

The practical result of the limitations on cross-claim actions is that when a party brings a counterclaim, he or she has greater flexibility than does a party who seeks to file a cross-claim. A counterclaim, for example, can involve the main transaction alleged in the complaint but also may involve unrelated matters. Cross-claims, in contrast, must involve the same subject matter as the original complaint and will be subject to dismissal if they are not.

There are other restrictions on cross-claims. Obviously, a cross-claim cannot be brought against a party on the other side of the action. This rule limits cross-claims to between plaintiffs or defendants, never between plaintiffs and defendants.

Time Limits for Cross-Claims

Interestingly enough, Rule 13 does not impose a time limit for bringing a cross-claim. As such, the claim may be brought at any point in the litigation, though it is always up to the judge to allow it. The judge's decision will be influenced by the time and resources necessary to adjudicate the cross-claim, balanced against a general approach that seeks to avoid multiple lawsuits on the same issues.

FIGURE 6.17
When Cross-Claims Are Allowed

> Rule 13(g) allows cross-claims against a co-party in the following situations:
>
> - When the claim arises out of the transaction or occurrence that forms the basis of the original complaint.
> - When the claim has the same subject matter as the original action.
> - When the claim is related to a counterclaim.
> - When the claim is related to property that is involved in the original action.

SPOT THE ISSUE!

On April 6, 2006, Manny is driving home and fails to pay attention to the upcoming intersection. He applies his brakes too late and rear-ends the car in front of him. The driver, Earl, gets out of his car, rushes to Manny's car, and strikes him in the face. Natasha, who is standing at the intersection, sees the entire incident. She has an irrational fear of violence and especially of blood, and when she sees Manny's nose bleeding, she passes out, striking her head on the ground and suffering a concussion. When the police arrive, they cite Manny for following too closely and Earl for battery. Earl claims that he has severe pain in his neck and is transported to the hospital, where he incurs $3,256 in medical bills. Manny is also taken to the hospital, where medical personnel discover that his nose is broken. He undergoes surgery to repair it. The bill for his medical treatment is $4,590. Earl is behind on his child support payments, for a total of $11,435, and his ex-wife, Myra, learns that he has hired an attorney who is drafting a complaint against Manny based on the accident.

Which of these parties, if any, have cross-claims or counterclaims against one another? Should any of the parties be brought into the case through impleader? Are there any parties who might wish to interplead in the case? For an explanation of these terms, please see the next section.

impleader
The involuntary addition of a new party to the litigation; a party without whom all issues raised in the case could not be resolved.

THIRD-PARTY CLAIMS

PRACTICE TIP

Impleader is based on an old common law practice first recognized in England, called "vouching to warranty." There, a defendant who was sued for the return of property could bring in a third party who had given the defendant warranty on the title to the property. The defendant could bring in this third party to prove that he had legitimate title to the disputed property.

So far, our discussion has centered on the claims brought by the original parties to a suit between and against one another. However, there are provisions that allow the addition of third parties to the action, individuals who were not originally parties to the litigation but whose presence may be necessary to bring about a final adjudication of all claims in the case. There are three methods that can be used to bring in third parties to a lawsuit. They include:

• Impleader
• Interpleader
• Intervention

Impleader

Impleader is authorized under Rule 14 of the Federal Rules of Civil Procedure. Also known as third-party practice, impleader is the process of bringing a new party to the action. When a current defendant impleads a third-party defendant, this new party is added to the action as though he or she were one of the original parties. A defendant might implead a third-party defendant when he or she alleges that this third party is responsible for some or all of the plaintiff's claims against the original defendant. See Figure 6.18.

Although impleader originally required the trial judge's approval, modern practice allows a defendant to implead a third-party defendant within 10 days of the filing of the defendant's answer. The judge still retains the authority to strike the third-party complaint and sever out the claim to be brought as a separate action.

When a defendant brings in a third-party defendant, he or she does so with a third-party complaint. This complaint resembles the original complaint that initially began the case, but it is brought by a defendant against a person that the defendant claims is essential to resolve the issues in the main case. This third-party defendant has the right to file a third-party answer, alleging the defenses that any defendant would have, as well as cross-claims and counterclaims. As you can see, third-party practice can swiftly make the issues in the case very complicated. See this chapter's "Case in Point" for an example of issues involving third-party practice.

interpleader
The deposit of contested funds with the court, followed by the removal of the filing party from other action in the suit.

Interpleader

Interpleader involves an action in which one party owes money to another party but is not sure to whom it should be paid. It applies to insurance proceeds, devises under wills, and other

FIGURE 6.18 **Third-Party Complaint Form: Defendant Impleads a Third-Party Defendant**

STATE OF PLACID
DISTRICT COURT
LONDON COUNTY

Professor James Moriarty, individually and as owner, operator of Moriarty Transport Trucking Co. (Third-Party Plaintiff) v. Dr. John Watson (Third-Party Defendant)	**CIVIL ACTION: 04-100** **Third Party Complaint**

Pursuant to PL Rules of Civil Procedure 14, James Moriarty, Defendant in Civil Action No. 04-100 (hereafter "Moriarty"), brings this Third-Party Complaint against Dr. John Watson, Third-Party Defendant (hereafter "Watson") and as grounds therefore shows the following:

1. Moriarty is named as defendant in the original complaint in this action.
2. Although Moriarty in no way admits to any extent of liability in the underlying Complaint and Answer, Moriarty shows that Watson is liable to Moriarty for all alleged liability and damages complained of by Plaintiff Holmes.
3. The presence of Watson in this suit is indispensable to the proper administration of justice in the underlying suit.
4. Third-party plaintiff Moriarty has been served and has responded to a Complaint filed in London County.
5. Moriarty has submitted to the personal and subject matter jurisdiction of this court.
6. On August 23, 2003, on or about 3:30 p.m., Watson was waiting for Plaintiff Holmes at the intersection of Carbuncle and Watson Street.
7. Watson flagged down the automobile operated by Plaintiff Holmes.
8. The automobile driven by Holmes came to a sudden and abrupt stop.
9. Plaintiff Holmes made no indications of his proposed stop.
10. Plaintiff Holmes was not responding to any traffic signs or signals.
11. Plaintiff Holmes's automobile blocked traffic in both lanes of traffic.
12. Upon seeing Moriarty, Watson drew a revolver and pointed it in Moriarty's direction.
13. Moriarty, in an attempt to avoid being shot, swerved into Plaintiff Holmes's vehicle.
14. Moriarty was severely injured in the crash and has incurred substantial medical bills.
15. Moriarty has been unable to return to his former employment as Professor of Mathematics at Oxford University.
16. Third-Party Defendant Watson was the sole, proximate, and legal cause of the injuries to both Moriarty and Plaintiff Holmes.

WHEREFORE,

Third-Party Plaintiff Moriarty prays that this court:

1. Have judgment against third-party defendant Watson for damages in excess of $10,000.
2. Order all necessary damages, equitable relief, and any other relief that the court may deem just and proper.
3. Permit a jury trial on the issues raised by Third-Party Plaintiff on his Third-Party Complaint.

Respectfully submitted,

January 15, 2005

By: _____
Deborah Bolstridge

_____
(PL. Bar No.)

Attorney for Defendant, James Moriarty

21 Robin's Wood Place
Bohemia, PL 28655
828-555-2121 (phone)
828-555-2123 (fax)

FIGURE 6.19
Intervention

Rule 24. Intervention

(a) Intervention of Right.
Upon timely application anyone shall be permitted to intervene in an action: (1) when a statute of the United States confers an unconditional right to intervene; or (2) when the applicant claims an interest relating to the property or transaction which is the subject of the action and the applicant is so situated that the disposition of the action may as a practical matter impair or impede the applicant's ability to protect that interest, unless the applicant's interest is adequately represented by existing parties.

(b) Permissive Intervention.
Upon timely application anyone may be permitted to intervene in an action: (1) when a statute of the United States confers a conditional right to intervene; or (2) when an applicant's claim or defense and the main action have a question of law or fact in common. When a party to an action relies for ground of claim or defense upon any statute or executive order administered by a federal or state governmental officer or agency or upon any regulation, order, requirement, or agreement issued or made pursuant to the statute or executive order, the officer or agency upon timely application may be permitted to intervene in the action. In exercising its discretion the court shall consider whether the intervention will unduly delay or prejudice the adjudication of the rights of the original parties.

(c) Procedure.
A person desiring to intervene shall serve a motion to intervene upon the parties as provided in *Rule 5.* The motion shall state the grounds therefor and shall be accompanied by a pleading setting forth the claim or defense for which intervention is sought. The same procedure shall be followed when a statute of the United States gives a right to intervene. When the constitutionality of an act of Congress affecting the public interest is drawn in question in any action in which the United States or an officer, agency, or employee thereof is not a party, the court shall notify the Attorney General of the United States as provided in *Title 28, U.S.C. § 2403.* When the constitutionality of any statute of a State affecting the public interest is drawn in question in any action in which that State or any agency, officer, or employee thereof is not a party, the court shall notify the attorney general of the State as provided in *Title 28, U.S.C. § 2403.* A party challenging the constitutionality of legislation should call the attention of the court to its consequential duty, but failure to do so is not a waiver of any constitutional right otherwise timely asserted.

situations in which there is no dispute about the fact that money is owed but no certainty about who should receive it. In such a case, the party who owes money files an interpleader complaint and deposits the money with the court. The complaint must be as legally sufficient as any other and must also be served on all interested parties. However, interpleader is different in that once the party has deposited the contested funds with the court, his or her involvement in the case is essentially at an end. From that point onward, it is up to the court to decide among the contesting defendants who should receive the funds. Interpleader is governed by Rule 22 of Federal Rules of Civil Procedure.

Intervention

There are situations in which individuals who are not involved in the original action seek to interject themselves. In such a case, the party would comply with Rule 24 of the Federal Rules of Civil Procedure by filing a motion to intervene (see Figure 6.19). However, Rule 24 applies strict standards to those who seek to enter pending litigation. For instance, the party seeking to intervene must show one of the following elements:

- That a United States statute gives the party an unconditional right to intervene, or
- That the party claims interest in the litigation and that resolution of the case without the party's presence may affect his or her property rights.

Although the first basis for **intervention**, reliance on a federal statute, is rare, the second grounds is not. Various court decisions have determined that if a person has a direct, substantial, or significant property interest in the case, that party will be allowed to intervene in the action. See Figure 6.20.

STATE OF PLACID
DISTRICT COURT
LONDON COUNTY

Sherlock Holmes
(Plaintiff)
and
United States of America,
Plaintiff-Intervenor

    v.

Professor James Moriarty, individually and as owner, operator of Moriarty Transport Trucking Co. (Defendant)
Professor James Moriarty, individually and as owner, operator of Moriarty Transport Trucking Co.
(Defendant)

CIVIL ACTION: 04-100

United States' Motion to Intervene as Plaintiff-Intervenor

UNITED STATES' MOTION TO INTERVENE AS PLAINTIFF-INTERVENOR

COMES NOW the United States of America and for the reasons set out below, moves this court for an order permitting it to intervene as Plaintiff in the above styled action, pursuant to Rule 24 of the Federal Rules of Civil Procedure. In support of this motion, the United States submits:

1. Plaintiff Holmes filed a complaint against Defendant Moriarty on November 18, 2004.
2. Plaintiff's allegations against Defendant include a demand for a jury trial and an award of damages for Defendant's alleged negligence.
3. On August 13, 2006, Defendant Moriarty entered the Federal Witness Protection under agreement to testify against alleged co-conspirators in federal indictment U.S. CR 124-47874.
4. On October 2, 2006, an attempt was made to murder Defendant in his home in London County.
5. Defendant's physical presence in or near the London County Courthouse to respond to the allegations of the Plaintiff will jeopardize the physical safety of the defendant and hamper the government's ability to prosecute a serious criminal threat to the people of the United States.

WHEREFORE, the United States of America moves this court for an order dismissing the allegations of the Complaint by Plaintiff CV 04-100 or, in the alternative, to order that the trial of said case be postponed until the completion of the criminal action pending in Indictment U.S. CR 124-47874.

    Respectfully submitted,

Elliott S. Ness, Assistant Attorney General
United States Department of Justice
601 D Street, N.W., Suite 4300
Washington, DC 20530
(202) 514-4092

SURF'S UP!

CASE MANAGEMENT SYSTEMS

In the next few chapters, we will discuss various software packages that provide case, client, or litigation support (and some that provide all three). In this chapter, we discuss Abacus Law.

Many legal malpractice insurers now require law offices to have some kind of case management system to avoid the prospect of missing an important deadline, especially running into the statute of limitations for a particular claim. Failing to file before the statute runs out is a surefire way for the attorney to be sued for legal malpractice. Abacus Law is a case management program that allows a law office to create calendars showing when clients are scheduled to come to the office, when the attorneys must appear in

court, and a wide variety of other activities. It also provides a platform for instant messaging to everyone on the network inside the office. Abacus Law also allows individual users to check for conflicts of interest by reviewing current and past clients. It generates to-do lists and timelines and gives instant access to a broad range of client information. Like many case management programs, Abacus Law has its proponents and its critics. Some find that it suits their practice perfectly, whereas others prefer other programs. One of its best features is the broad database it provides not only for clients but also for opposing counsel, paralegals, judges' secretaries, clerks, and many others with whom a legal professional deals on a daily basis.

Source: Abacus Law, www.abacuslaw.com.

CLASS ACTIONS

class action
A lawsuit involving a large group of plaintiffs who have been certified by a court as having mutual interests, common claims, and a representative plaintiff who will pursue the action on the basis of the entire group.

There are provisions that allow dozens or even hundreds of plaintiffs to bring suit against a defendant. Such a case is referred to as a **class action**, but before a court will allow a large group of plaintiffs to pool their resources in a suit against a defendant, the plaintiffs must meet four prerequisites. They are set out in Figure 6.21.

Under Rule 23, before a group can bring a class action, it must first establish that the number of plaintiffs is so large that following a traditional civil case would be impractical. The plaintiffs must also show that there are questions of law or fact common to all of the plaintiffs and that the representative plaintiffs have claims and defenses that are similar to the entire class. Finally, they must show that the representative plaintiffs will be fair and adequately protect the interests of the entire group.

When the plaintiffs can establish these minimum requirements, the court will certify a class and allow the case to proceed as a class action. Once the class has been certified, all plaintiffs are grouped together as a single action. This grouping has the advantage of resolving hundreds, and sometimes thousands, of cases in a single suit. Recent examples of major class-action lawsuits include actions against Firestone Tire Company for producing defective tires and against the manufacturers of breast implants for creating faulty products.

A class-action case proceeds through the representative plaintiffs who act on behalf of the entire class. If the case is settled prior to trial, the judge must make a determination that the settlement is in the best interests of the class and what amount each plaintiff will receive to terminate the case.

FIGURE 6.21
Rule 23. Class Actions

(a) Prerequisites to a Class Action.
One or more members of a class may sue or be sued as representative parties on behalf of all only if (1) the class is so numerous that joinder of all members is impracticable, (2) there are questions of law or fact common to the class, (3) the claims or defenses of the representative parties are typical of the claims or defenses of the class, and (4) the representative parties will fairly and adequately protect the interests of the class.

FIGURE 6.22 Answer

STATE OF PLACID
DISTRICT COURT
LONDON COUNTY

Sherlock Holmes (Plaintiff)	CIVIL ACTION: 04-100
v.	*Answer of Defendant*
Professor James Moriarty, individually and as owner, operator of Moriarty Transport Trucking Co. (Defendant)	

COMES NOW the defendant in the above-styled action, James Moriarty and files this his Answer and Counterclaim against the plaintiff.

JURISDICTIONAL ALLEGATIONS

1. James Moriarty, hereafter referred to as "the defendant," hereby alleges that he is without information as to the plaintiff's residence, citizenship, or age.
2. James Moriarty is president, founder, and majority stockholder of Moriarty Transport Trucking Co. The remainder of the plaintiff's allegations in this paragraph are hereby ADMITTED.
3. Defendant denies that there is any cause of action; therefore this paragraph is deemed DENIED.

GENERAL ALLEGATIONS

4. The allegations in this paragraph are ADMITTED.
5. The allegations contained in this paragraph are admitted to the extent that defendant was the driver of a truck owned and operated by Moriarty Transport Trucking Co. The remaining allegations in this paragraph are DENIED.
6. Defendant is without sufficient knowledge to either admit or deny the allegations in this paragraph.
7. Defendant is without sufficient knowledge to either admit or deny the allegations in this paragraph.
8. Defendant is without sufficient knowledge to either admit or deny the allegations in this paragraph.
9. Defendant is without sufficient knowledge to either admit or deny the allegations in this paragraph.
10. Defendant is without sufficient knowledge to either admit or deny the allegations in this paragraph.
11. Defendant is without sufficient knowledge to either admit or deny the allegations in this paragraph.
12. The allegations contained in this paragraph are DENIED.
13. The allegations contained in this paragraph are DENIED.
14. The allegations contained in this paragraph are DENIED.
15. The allegations contained in this paragraph are DENIED.

REQUEST FOR JURY TRIAL

Defendant requests a trial by jury for all allegations raised in the pleadings by plaintiff and defendant.

AFFIRMATIVE DEFENSES

1. The plaintiff's allegations are barred by the statute of limitations.
2. The plaintiff's allegations are based on the plaintiff's own contributory negligence.
3. The plaintiff's allegations are based on fraud.
4. The plaintiff assumed the risk of any injuries he may have received on the date of the collision (as set out in the plaintiff's complaint) by undertaking a career as a self-proclaimed "investigative consultant."
5. The plaintiff's claims are barred by *res judicata.*

COUNTERCLAIM AGAINST PLAINTIFF
Counterclaim I

The defendant incorporates here by reference all previous paragraphs and further brings the following counterclaim against plaintiff:

1. That the plaintiff was, on the day of collision set out in paragraph 4 of the plaintiff's complaint, operating his automobile in an erratic manner.
2. That the plaintiff put his car in reverse as the defendant approached the intersection.
3. That the plaintiff caused the collision between the two vehicles by deliberately backing into the defendant's automobile.
4. That the defendant suffered personal injuries as a result of the plaintiff's negligent conduct.
5. That the defendant suffered property losses in excess of $10,000 by the plaintiff's conduct.

WHEREFORE, defendant prays:

1. That the plaintiff have and receive nothing from his claim against the defendant.
2. That the plaintiff be ordered to pay all of the defendant's medical, property, and other damages directly tied to the collision alleged in the plaintiff's complaint.
3. That the plaintiff be ordered to pay all costs, including defendant's attorney's fees, for the defense of this action.
4. That the defendant should receive whatever compensation, awards, and equitable relief that the court may deem just and proper.

Counterclaim II

The defendant incorporates by reference all previous paragraphs alleged by him in this Answer and Counterclaim. Defendant further brings this second counterclaim against the plaintiff, to wit:

1. That the plaintiff has, on numerous occasions, accused the defendant of unethical, immoral, and illegal conduct.
2. That the plaintiff has communicated these unethical, immoral, and illegal accusations to others, including police officers.
3. That the defendant's reputation has been damaged by the plaintiff's allegations.
4. That the allegations are untrue.
5. That the plaintiff has engaged in these statements as a result of malice and a generalized hatred of the defendant.

WHEREFORE, the defendant prays:

1. That the plaintiff have and receive nothing from his claim against the defendant.
2. That the plaintiff be assessed general and special damages for his slander of the defendant's reputation.
3. That the plaintiff be enjoined from issuing such statements in the future.
4. That the defendant should receive whatever compensation, awards, and equitable relief that the court may deem just and proper.

PRAYER FOR RELIEF
Defendant requests:

1. That the plaintiff have and receive nothing from the defendant for any count alleged in plaintiff's complaint.
2. That the defendant's counterclaims be granted against the plaintiff.
3. That the costs of this action be assessed against plaintiff.
4. That the plaintiff be assessed for bad faith damages.
5. That the defendant's prayers for equitable relief should be granted.
6. That the defendant's prayers for monetary relief be granted.
7. That the court provide any additional relief, award, equitable relief, sanctions, or other remedies in accord with its own findings and in the interests of justice.

Respectfully submitted, this the ___ day of December, 2004.

_____

Deborah Bolstridge
Attorney for Defendant
21 Robin's Wood Place
Bohemia, PL 28655
828-555-1212
State Bar No. 00666

CASE IN POINT

Smith v. Figa and Burns
69 Fed. Appx. 922, RICO Bus. Disp. Guide 10,500
HENRY, Circuit Judge.

In this appeal, plaintiff Mary Julia Hook appeals four rulings by the district court: (1) denial of plaintiffs' request that Judge Downes disqualify himself; (2) grant of partial summary judgment dismissing plaintiff David L. Smith's legal malpractice claims; (3) dismissal of plaintiffs' RICO claims; and (4) remand of defendants' remaining contract claim to state court. We affirm the district court's judgment and dismissal because the district court judge was well within his discretion in refusing to recuse himself and in remanding the remaining contract claim to state court after dismissal of the federal claims, and the RICO claims were not pled with sufficient particularity to avoid dismissal. We dismiss the appeal of the judgment in favor of defendants on Mr. Smith's legal malpractice claims because Ms. Hook lacks standing to appeal those claims.

I. BACKGROUND

Mr. Smith brought an action in state court alleging legal malpractice against his former attorney, Mr. Figa, and Mr. Figa's law firm. The defendants counterclaimed against Mr. Smith for breach of contract, joining Ms. Hook as a counterclaim defendant because she was a party to the agreement for payment of the firm's fees incurred in its representation of Mr. Smith. Mr. Smith and Ms. Hook then brought additional claims against defendants, alleging RICO violations in connection with the law firm's billing practices. Upon introduction of the federal RICO claims, defendants removed the case to federal district court.

After the case was removed, Mr. Smith and Ms. Hook filed a motion to disqualify Judge Downes, which he denied. The district court went on to grant partial summary judgment in favor of defendants on Mr. Smith's legal malpractice claims, dismiss Mr. Smith and Ms. Hook's RICO claims under Fed. R.Civ.P. 12(b)(6) and 9(b), and remand defendants' remaining contract claim to state court. Mr. Smith and Ms. Hook appealed these rulings. At the outset of this appeal, Mr. Smith was ordered to show cause why he should not be dismissed as a party to the appeal, pursuant to a previous order of this court restricting Mr. Smith's ability to pursue pro se appeals in this court. After considering Mr. Smith's response to the order to show cause, the Chief Judge of this court issued an order denying Mr. Smith permission to proceed pro se and dismissing him from this appeal. Consequently, Ms. Hook is the only appellant in this matter.

II. DISCUSSION

1. Disqualification.

Ms. Hook argues that the district court erred in denying the motion to recuse on account of bias, a ruling we review for abuse of discretion. Generally, Ms. Hook argues that Judge Downes' "ob-

vious" bias against Mr. Smith was transferred to her by association. Aplt. Br. at 11. Specifically, she cites "numerous delays" and "unreasonable rulings" as evidence of Judge Downes' bias against her.

An unsubstantiated allegation of bias is insufficient to mandate recusal. That is precisely the nature of Ms. Hook's allegation that the court's bias against Mr. Smith was conferred upon her. She states no facts "concerning [Judge Downes'] demeanor that would cause a reasonable man to doubt the judge's impartiality." And her characterization of adverse rulings as evidence of the judge's impartiality is insufficient to establish bias. A motion to recuse cannot be based solely on adverse rulings. Further, her passing reference to delayed rulings as evidence of bias is completely unsupported by any facts and must fail. For these reasons, we conclude that Judge Downes did not abuse his discretion in denying the motion to disqualify.

2. Legal Malpractice Claims.

The district court granted defendants' motion for partial summary judgment on Mr. Smith's legal malpractice claims. Ms. Hook appeals this ruling—something she must have standing to do.

This "irreducible constitutional minimum" of standing requires: (1) that the plaintiff have suffered an "injury in fact"—an invasion of a judicially cognizable interest which is (a) concrete and particularized and (b) actual or imminent, not conjectural or hypothetical; (2) that there be a causal connection between the injury and the conduct complained of—the injury must be fairly traceable to the challenged action of the defendant, and not the result of the independent action of some third party not before the court; and (3) that it be likely, as opposed to merely speculative, that the injury will be redressed by a favorable decision. The same constitutional minima for standing to sue, i.e., injury in fact, causation, and redressibility are also required for standing to appeal. In the appellate context, "one must be aggrieved by the order from which appeal is taken." And "the law is well-settled that a party is generally not aggrieved by, and thus lacks standing to appeal from, a judgment rendered against a co-party." Here, the legal malpractice claims were brought by Mr. Smith before Ms. Hook was a party to the suit. And it follows that the judgment on those claims was entered against the party who brought them, Mr. Smith. Although defendants joined Ms. Hook as a defendant on their contract claim before judgment on the malpractice claims was entered, that did not change the fact that the judgment on the malpractice claims was entered not against Ms. Hook, but against her co-party. To overcome this standing obstacle, Ms. Hook makes a narrow argument attempting to show she was aggrieved by the judgment against her co-party.

In support of her standing, Ms. Hook points to her potential liability as a party to the fee agreement for defendants' legal representation of Mr. Smith. She argues that she is aggrieved by the dismissal of Mr. Smith's malpractice claims because it may affect her ability to allege defendants' malpractice in defense of their fee-contract claim, which was remanded to state court. Because injury-in-fact requires an invasion of a legally protected interest that is actual or imminent, and not conjectural or hypothetical, "this court's focus is on past and present injury; possible future injury is insufficient to create standing." And while unrealized but imminent harm can satisfy the injury-in-fact element, the Supreme Court has cautioned that the concept of imminence "cannot be stretched beyond its purpose, which is to ensure that the alleged injury is not too speculative for Article III purposes—that the injury is certainly impending."

The injury that Ms. Hook alleges cannot establish her standing because it is "indirect and consequential, rather than direct and immediate." In fact, the possible injury is so theoretical and hypothetical that it hinges on the assumption, as Ms. Hook herself recognizes, that any court hearing the fee-contract dispute would apply finality principles inappropriately. The injury she alleges is too conjectural and hypothetical to have conferred standing upon her to bring the malpractice claims in the first instance, and, for the same reason, she is not aggrieved by the judgment. Ms. Hook has no standing to appeal the district court's ruling on the malpractice claims brought by Mr. Smith.

3. RICO Claims.

Ms. Hook counterclaimed against defendants, alleging that they violated the Racketeer Influenced and Corrupt Organizations Act (RICO), 18 U.S.C. § 1962(c), (d). To survive a motion to dismiss pursuant to Fed. R.Civ.P. 12(b)(6), "a civil RICO claim must allege (1) conduct (2) of an enterprise (3) through a pattern (4) of racketeering activity." This court has held that RICO predicate acts based on fraud must be stated with the particularity required by Fed. R.Civ.P. 9(b). This requirement is to ensure that defendant and the trial court have "clear notice of the factual basis of the predicate acts," and it is especially important, as here, "where the predicate fraud allegations provide the only link to federal jurisdiction."

The district court found that the two RICO claims based on mail and wire fraud were lacking in the required specificity, and after de novo review, we agree. The "cross claim" states that "on numerous occasions in 1993, 1994, and 1995, Mr. Figa unlawfully used the United States mail and made wire communications in furtherance of a scheme to engage in fraudulent billing practices (including extortionate payment demands) based on outrageously excessive fees, costs and expenses." Reply to Counterclaim, Affirmative Defenses and Mitigating Circumstances, and Cross Claims, dated January 6, 1997. This allegation contains no details or specifics of the predicate mail/wire fraud acts: there are no details about the nature of the fraudulent billing practices or when they occurred. The pleading does not allege what the billing practices were, let alone how they were fraudulent: the allegations fall well short of the particularity requirements for pleading fraud.

The RICO claims also fail to adequately allege a pattern of racketeering activity. The statute requires at least two acts of racketeering activity, and, "while two acts are necessary, they may not be sufficient." Because the allegations include absolutely no details about the timing and nature of the predicate acts, it is impossible to tell from the pleading whether there were two acts, what those two acts were, or if they were sufficiently related and continuous as to constitute a pattern.

In addition to the substantive RICO claim, the "cross claim" also alleged conspiracy to violate § 1962(c), which is a violation of 18 U.S.C. § 1962(d). The district court was correct to dismiss the § 1962(c) RICO claim for lack of particularity and detail, and it follows that dismissal of the conspiracy claim was also correct.

III. MOTION FOR COSTS

Defendants filed a motion requesting damages and costs pursuant to Fed. R.App. P. 38, which permits sanctions for frivolous appeals. "An appeal is frivolous when the result is obvious, or the appellant's arguments of error are wholly without merit." Although Ms. Hook's appeal of the insufficiently pled RICO claims may border on frivolous, we are not prepared to say that, on the whole, the result in this appeal was obvious or that the appeal was wholly without merit. Ms. Hook was joined as a party to this action on account of her alleged contractual liability for Mr. Smith's legal fees. Although her argument to establish her standing to appeal the district court's ruling on legal malpractice claims was unsuccessful, we cannot say that it was frivolous. And we are not prepared to label her substantive arguments in attempting to appeal the legal malpractice claims as completely lacking in merit, since we did not consider them.

IV. CONCLUSION

We AFFIRM the judgment of the district court insofar as it denied the motion to disqualify, dismissed the RICO claims, and remanded the remaining claim to state court. Because Ms. Hook lacks standing to appeal the grant of summary judgment in favor of defendants on the legal malpractice claims, we DISMISS her appeal of the district court's judgment on those claims. Defendants' motion for award of just damages and single or double costs is DENIED.

Source: From Westlaw. Used with permission of Thomson/West.

Case Questions:

1. What are the four grounds that the plaintiff is raising in her appeal?

2. What was the basis for removal to federal court?

3. Why does Ms. Hook lack standing to appeal the partial summary judgment on Mr. Smith's legal malpractice claim?

4. How does standing to sue compare with standing to appeal?

5. Explain the basis of Ms. Hook's counterclaim against the defendant and the RICO allegation.

Eye on Ethics

BAD FAITH

As we have seen in this chapter, attorneys who interpose frivolous defenses or engage in bad faith in the claims raised in answers are subject to sanctions by the court. The sanctions include not only monetary fines but also the possibility that a client's defenses may be struck from the answer. Such an action would have drastic consequences for the client and no doubt result in a legal malpractice action against the attorney should the client lose the case. These are all excellent reasons to be familiar with the Rules of Civil Procedure for the jurisdiction in which you practice and also to avoid any pressure from the client to interpose frivolous or harassing claims in answers as part of a misguided attempt to seek revenge or punishment on the other party. Such practices often misfire and have negative consequences for both the law firm and the client.

Real Paralegal Life: Building a Skill Set

DEBRA HOLBROOK

Debra Holbrook is a paralegal at a firm that handles a wide variety of cases, including "some real estate, some bankruptcy, criminal, business litigation, and corporate law." She finds that the variety keeps her stimulated, because "Although it can be a little overwhelming, it's never boring." In addition to her duties of monitoring files and keeping up with clients and schedules, she has many other duties. "On any given day, you'll find me doing payables [tracking client fees]. I'm putting memos in the file, making sure that bills go out. In a small office, you never get bored, because there is always so much to do. I'm always involved in several different things at the same time. I don't have time to get bored. I'm kind of the office manager and the accountant and the investigator and the secretary all rolled into one," she admits.

A Day in the Life

CASE MANAGEMENT SOFTWARE AND THE PARALEGAL

Debra Holbrook's firm uses Abacus Law as its case management system "to help keep track of client appointments. Using Abacus, you can link all of your various client documents together. You can look up clients by name, for instance, and find more information about them. We assign our client file number simply by year and number. As a paralegal, there is an awful lot of interaction with the client, and having all of your information in one place makes it a lot easier to dig out a telephone number or an address."

Real Paralegal Life: Building a Skill Set

RULES CONCERNING ANSWERS AND OTHER CLAIMS

Locate copies of your State Rules of Civil Procedure concerning answers, especially the form of an answer, the rules regarding compulsory and permissive counterclaims, the rules about cross-claims, and the rules pertaining to third-party practices. Make copies of all these rules and place them in your trial notebook.

Career Prep

For the complaint that you prepared for Chapter 5's "Career Prep," prepare an answer that provides a legally sufficient response to each allegation raised. If the facts of your case suggest a counterclaim, include that information as well.

Summary

Once a complaint has been served on a defendant, he or she has a specific time period to file a response. This response is usually known as an answer. In most situations, the defendant has 20 days to file the answer and serve it on the plaintiff. The actual method for computing the time period is important for any legal professional to know and understand. Generally, intervening weekends and holidays are not counted for the purposes of computing the time limit, but if the final day falls on a weekend or recognized state or federal holiday, it will be due on the next business day. An answer contains the defendant's response to each of the allegations raised by the plaintiff in the complaint. The answer must either admit or deny the contentions raised in the complaint. The defendant is also permitted to allege that he or she is without knowledge about a particular contention.

In addition to responding to the plaintiff's allegations in the complaint, the defendant's answer must also set out specific defenses. Some defenses, referred to as affirmative defenses, must be stated in the complaint. Examples of affirmative defenses include *res judicata* and statutes of limitations, to name just two. In addition to raising affirmative defenses, a defendant is allowed to bring a counterclaim against the plaintiff for any injuries that the defendant claims were committed by the plaintiff. A compulsory counterclaim involves the same facts and circumstances as the complaint, whereas a permissive counterclaim is not factually tied to the complaint.

An answer may also raise other issues, including the provision for a 12(b)(6) motion. Such a motion challenges the actual wording of the complaint by claiming that it fails to state a claim upon which relief can be granted by a court.

Defendants also have additional options when it comes to pleadings. They can bring other individuals into the suit through impleader. Persons who want to insert themselves into the litigation and who satisfy the applicable legal requirements are entitled to do so through intervention.

Key Terms

Answer, 114
Admit, 115
Deny, 115
Bad faith, 118
Default judgment, 119
Affirmative defense, 120
Counterclaim, 120
Compulsory counterclaim, 121
Permissive counterclaim, 121

Res judicata, 122
Reply, 123
12(b)(6) motion, 123
Cross-claim lawsuit, 125
Impleader, 127
Interpleader, 127
Intervention, 130
Class action, 131

Review Questions

1. What is the purpose of the defendant's answer?

2. What are the minimum requirements for a legally sufficient answer?

3. What are the consequences of an admission in an answer?

4. What are the three possible statements that a defendant can give to the allegations in the plaintiff's complaint?

5. What are the consequences to the defendant when he or she fails to respond to an allegation in the complaint?

6. What are the consequences when a court determines that the defendant has acted in bad faith in drafting his or her answer?

7. What is the normal time limit for a defendant to serve an answer on the plaintiff?

8. What are affirmative defenses?

9. How does a defendant raise an affirmative defense?

10. What is a counterclaim?

11. What is the difference between a compulsory counterclaim and a permissive counterclaim?

12. What is *res judicata*?

13. What is a 12(b)(6) motion?

14. When is a defendant authorized to bring a 12(b)(6) motion?

15. What is a cross-claim?

16. Compare and contrast counterclaims and cross-claims.

17. What is impleader?

18. What is interpleader?

19. Explain intervention.

20. Explain how a court determines that a class is certified in a class-action suit.

Discussion Question

1. Explain the differences among compulsory counterclaims, permissive counterclaims, and cross-claims. How does the principle of *res judicata* interact with these various actions?

Exercises: Skill Builders

Allison rents an apartment and lives on the second floor of a unit owned by Landlord Inc. One day, as she is leaving for work, the stairs give way beneath her; she falls through and is severely injured. She brings a complaint against Landlord Inc. In her complaint, she alleges that recent repairs done to the stairway were incomplete and resulted in dangerous conditions. Acme Construction Company performed the work. Allison is also two months behind on her rent. Diagram the possible claims that these parties may bring against one another.

Portfolio Assignment

Portfolio Assignment 6-1: Draft an answer containing a counterclaim. Using the complaint you prepared in Chapter 5, draft an answer in the Cherry case in Appendix A. Also include in that answer a counterclaim against the plaintiff.

Portfolio Assignment 6-2: Review your state rules and case law on cross-claims and counterclaims and then compare and contrast these two types of claims. When and where are they brought? What is the primary difference between a counterclaim and a cross-claim? What is the significance of permissive versus compulsory counterclaims? How do these claims relate to interpleader and impleader?

Vocabulary Builders

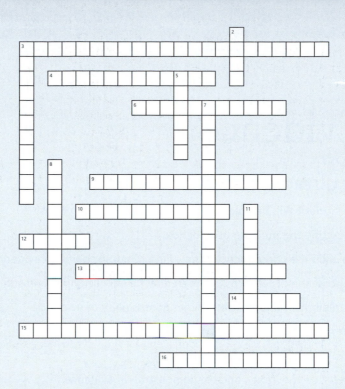

ACROSS

3 A claim by the defendant against the plaintiff that must be raised in the case or it will be barred.

4 A claim by the defendant against the plaintiff where the defendant seeks damages.

6 A lawsuit involving a large group of plaintiffs who have been certified by a court as having mutual interest, common claims, and a representative plaintiff who will pursue the action on the basis of the entire group.

9 A motion under the provisions of Rule 12 of the Rules of Civil Procedure that challenges the basis of the complaint for failure to state a claim upon which relief can be granted.

10 (Lat) "The thing has been adjudicated"; the principle that a court's decision on a particular matter is binding on future litigation between the parties; sometimes referred to as "*res adjudicata.*"

12 The responsive pleading provided in Rule 7 to a counter-claim.

13 A judgment entered against a defendant who has failed to file an answer to the plaintiff's complaint.

14 To agree or stipulate to the allegations presented in a complaint.

15 A claim by the defendant against the plaintiff that may be raised in the case; it may also be brought as a separate action.

16 The voluntary insertion of a third party into a pending civil action, often to resolve issues directly related to the third party's interests.

DOWN

2 To disagree with or contest the allegations presented in a complaint.

3 A claim by one party against another party on the same side of the action. Example: plaintiff against another plaintiff or defendant against a codefendant.

5 The document filed by the defendant in a civil action that responds to each of the allegations raised in the plaintiff's complaint (or petition), denies or admits to the factual allegations, and denies or admits to responsibility for the plaintiff's injuries.

7 A defense that goes beyond a simple denial; states that the defendant is entitled to judgment in his or her favor for specific reasons; it would entitle the defendant to a verdict in his or her favor, if proven.

8 The deposit of contested funds with the court, followed by the removal of the filing party from other action in the suit.

11 The involuntary addition of a new party to the litigation; a party without whom all issues raised in the case could not be resolved.

Chapter 7

Evidence

CHAPTER OBJECTIVES

The student will be able to:

- Describe the purpose of evidence.

- Explain the consequences of a ruling of admissibility on evidence.

- Discuss the differences between direct evidence and circumstantial evidence.

- Explain how a judge determines admissibility of evidence.

- Describe the process of laying the foundation of evidence.

- Explain hearsay and its exceptions.

- Describe the importance of demonstrative evidence.

- Distinguish between physical evidence and documentary evidence.

- Explain how the paralegal can be involved in gathering evidence.

- Explain the best evidence rule.

The importance of evidence, including direct and circumstantial evidence, is examined in depth in this chapter.

We discuss the rules of evidence as they apply to civil pleadings and trials. Although we base our discussion on the Federal Rules of Evidence, many states have followed the federal rules as their template for enacting their own evidentiary rules. Learning the rules of evidence is important for all paralegals. However, it would be optimistic to think that all of the complexities of evidentiary law could be expressed in a single chapter. There are huge, multivolume treatises written on the topic. Although attorneys spend their entire legal careers dealing with evidentiary issues, there are still many fine points that require them to engage in additional research. We begin our discussion of evidentiary law by first explaining how evidence is used in civil cases and how various types of evidence are used to support the contentions in a civil case and then addressing important evidentiary rules, such as hearsay.

THE ROLE OF EVIDENCE

evidence
Any fact, testimony, or physical object that tends to prove or disprove allegations raised in a case; must be reasonably calculated to lead to the discovery of admissible evidence.

Evidence consists of oral testimony, documentary evidence, physical evidence, and many other types, all presented by the various parties at trial to support their contentions or detract from their opponents' claims. The purpose of evidence is clear: It is the way that the parties prove their allegations. When a plaintiff drafts a complaint, for instance, the plaintiff's attorney and paralegal must be mindful of the evidence that will be used to support each and every allegation contained in the complaint. Without evidence to support the contentions, the claim will be dismissed. A plaintiff without evidence is a plaintiff without a case. Another important point to keep in mind about evidence is that attorneys are not allowed to testify about the merits of their case. Attorneys

Is evidence the same thing as "fact"? Although we often tend to think of the terms "evidence" and "facts" as interchangeable, as far as the law is concerned, they are two quite separate entities. A fact is any data, whether admissible or not. Evidence is something that tends to prove or disprove allegations in a trial.

relevance
Reasonably related or associated with the ultimate facts and legal theories.

cannot, for example, present evidence to the jury on their own. Instead, evidence must come through a sponsoring witness or through some other source. Therefore, if the attorney wishes to introduce a photograph of the plaintiff's wrecked car, for example, the attorney must put a witness on the stand and ask that witness basic questions to establish relevancy, laying the proper foundation to prove that the photograph is admissible. Once that phase is complete, the attorney must request that the judge rule on the admissibility of the evidence.

All of these elements require attorneys and paralegals to be very knowledgeable about the use of evidence.

Use of evidence is not limited to trials. Evidence is an important feature of all types of legal proceedings. The importance of evidence law explains why it is a significant course in every law school student's curriculum. In fact, most law schools devote an entire academic year to the topic.

The basic definition of evidence is that it is any item that tends to prove or disprove any fact in contention between the parties. As such, evidence includes witness testimony, documentary evidence, physical evidence, and a wide variety of other types. Evidence can be classified into three broad categories—direct, circumstantial, and documentary—but before it can be used, it must be shown to have relevance to the issues being litigated. Before we can address the broad classifications of evidence and demonstrate how it is used at trial, we must first address a more fundamental question: What is relevance?

Relevance

Just as all facts do not constitute evidence, not all evidence is admissible during a trial. Courts require that the party offering evidence satisfy some minimal criteria, the most important of which is **relevance**. Evidence is relevant if it tends to prove or disprove an allegation by the parties. Under this test, there are many different types of evidence that might be interesting to the parties but that would not be admissible. Consider the facts in Hypothetical 7-1.

Hypothetical 7-1

Maria has brought suit against a local newspaper for incorrectly placing a caption under her photograph as "Maria Collins, recently convicted of forgery." Maria's last name is not Collins, and she was not convicted of forgery. Unfortunately, the newspaper incorrectly switched photos of the real convicted felon with an article about winners of a recent pie bake off. In Maria's suit for defamation of character against the newspaper, the attorney representing the paper has learned that Maria actually came in second at the pie contest, not first. Is this evidence admissible during Maria's trial for defamation?

Answer: No. The facts surrounding the pie contest are not under consideration in this case. If the attorney attempted to admit this evidence, the judge would likely rule that it had no relevance to the issues and would not allow the attorney to present it.

The Federal Rules of Evidence embody the concept of relevance in Rule 401. The Federal Rules of Evidence bind all federal courts and obviously play an important role throughout the country, but the rules also serve an additional function. The federal rules have served as a template for evidentiary rules in dozens of states. Each state has its own evidentiary code, and many have changed theirs over the years to follow the federal model. The advantages of using the

 PRACTICE TIP

Although it is always a good practice to read recent appellate decisions from both state and federal appellate courts, some opinions are more valuable than others. For instance, if you focus on litigation, you might consider creating a separate reference that contains evidentiary opinions only. Any time a new appellate case discusses, amplifies, or changes an existing evidentiary rule, place a synopsis of this case in your reference. This reference file could be a notebook containing print copies, an easily accessible computer file, or even a database cross-referenced with other material. Some attorneys copy out the case synopsis on 3 × 5 cards, label them, and store them alphabetically in a file. However you decide to track these cases, find a way that works for you. Inevitably, an issue will arise in a future case, and your ready access to the answer will prove invaluable.

FIGURE 7.1

Rule 401. Definition of "Relevant Evidence"

"Relevant evidence" means evidence having any tendency to make the existence of any fact that is of consequence to the determination of the action more probable or less probable than it would be without the evidence.

PRACTICE TIP

We tend to think of evidence as tangible objects—murder weapons, photographs, fingerprints, and DNA—but the legal definition is much more broad. Other examples of evidence include a person's testimony on the stand, a contract clause, and a medical analysis, among many other examples.

federal rules as a model are that they provide a ready-made framework for the myriad evidentiary issues that federal jurisdictions have already considered, and they allow practitioners to rely on well-thought-out decisions by appellate courts regarding the use of various kinds of evidence. Practitioners who routinely appear in federal courts can readily grasp the concepts of state evidentiary law when that law is based on federal rules.

Whether using the federal rules as a model or not, all states have their own rules of evidence. Practitioners in those states must be intimately knowledgeable about those rules or face disastrous consequences at trial. No matter which model is followed, all jurisdictions require that a party intending to present evidence at trial must establish that the evidence is relevant to the issues. If we rely on the federal definition, relevance has a particular meaning. Relevant evidence is anything that has a tendency to make the existence of a fact under contention more or less likely to be true (see Figure 7.1). Under this definition, the parties are limited to presenting evidence that tends to prove or disprove the allegations in the case. They cannot present evidence wholly unrelated to the issues raised in the complaint and answer.

Hypothetical 7-2

Officer Baker is on the stand, being cross-examined about arriving at the scene of an accident. The plaintiff is alleging that the defendant was driving negligently and rear-ended her car.

> Officer: I was dispatched to the scene of an accident. When I arrived, there were two cars in the middle of the intersection of Tango and Cash streets. The front of the defendant's car was smashed in and so was the back of the plaintiff's car. I made sure that everyone was safe and asked if anyone needed medical attention, and then began taking statements.

At this point, the defense attorney then asks the officer:

> Attorney: You've had family members who've been in trouble with the police, haven't you?
>
> Plaintiff's Attorney: Objection! Relevance.

How is the court likely to rule?

Answer: The judge will almost certainly rule that this question is not relevant to the proceedings and instruct the attorney to move on to a topic that has something to do with the allegations in the case.

Competence

In addition to a showing of relevance, the rules of evidence also require a showing of competency. In this regard, "competency" has a special meaning. It refers to the fact that the evidence presented tends to prove the facts in dispute and is not based on conjecture, guesswork, or mere speculation. Competent evidence must be based on a solid foundation—and on the witness's personal knowledge. Consider Hypothetical 7-3.

Hypothetical 7-3

Jane is on the stand and testifying under oath. She witnessed a car wreck last year, and the plaintiff's attorney asks her, "Did you see the color of the traffic light shortly before the defendant drove through that intersection?"

A: "Yes, I did."
Q: "What was the color of that light?"
A: "It was red for the drivers coming from the defendant's direction."

Confident of winning his case, the plaintiff's attorney then asks,

Q: "And how can you be so sure of the color of the light?"

A: "Well, it had to be. The plaintiff was moving through the intersection and she wouldn't have driven through a red light, so her light was green. Therefore, the defendant's light must have been red."

Is Jane's testimony competent?

Answer: No. Although it initially appeared that Jane based her testimony on her personal observations of the accident (which would have been competent evidence), she has revealed that her testimony is based on conjecture or guesswork. Such testimony is not admissible. If the defense attorney requests that the judge strike her testimony and instruct the jury to ignore it, the judge will probably comply.

In their testimony, most witnesses are limited to describing experiences that they actually perceived, not what they assume or guess must have happened. The practical result is that a witness is generally prohibited from testifying to facts and situations that he or she did not actually experience. There is at least one important exception to that rule: expert testimony. We will discuss that topic later in this chapter.

Admissibility

admissibility
A ruling on whether the jury will be allowed to view proffered evidence.

A judge rules on the **admissibility** of evidence during the trial. If a judge rules that certain evidence is admissible, the jury will be allowed to see it or hear it. When the evidence consists of physical objects such as weapons or any other physical evidence, a ruling of admissibility means that the evidence will go into the jury room with the jurors when they deliberate at the end of the case. They will be permitted to handle the evidence and examine it for themselves. However, a judge might rule that particular evidence is inadmissible, meaning that the jury will not be permitted to see it or hear it. Evidence can be ruled inadmissible for a wide variety of reasons. The judge might decide that the evidence is not relevant to the issues in the case or that the evidence is too prejudicial and would result in an unfair trial if the jurors were to see it.

Hypothetical 7-4

Consider the following transcript of testimony from a recent medical malpractice case:

Plaintiff's Attorney: Doctor, I'm handing you what has been marked as "Plaintiff's Exhibit Number One." Would you describe it to the jury?
Witness: Yes. It appears to be a picture of the plaintiff when he was a child. He is smiling and being held by his mother.
Defense Attorney: Objection! Relevance.
Judge: What is the relevance of this evidence?
Plaintiff's Attorney: I'm attempting to show that the plaintiff had a nice childhood.
Judge: The plaintiff is 60 years old, counsel. The issue is not relevant to a medical malpractice case.
Judge (to the defense attorney): Your objection is sustained.

sustain
A judge's ruling in agreement with the party who raised the objection.

In Hypothetical 7-4, the judge has ruled that the question is not relevant and will not be allowed. When the judge says that the objection is **sustained**, it means the judge is in agreement with the basis of the objection and has ruled in favor of the party who raised it. If the judge had decided for some reason to allow the testimony, then the judge would have said that the objection was **overruled**. If sustained, the objection would effectively preclude the party from asking further questions about the evidence. If overruled, the original party would be permitted to continue questioning the witness.

overrule
A judge's ruling in disagreement with the party who raised the objection.

Laying the Foundation

lay the foundation
The presentation of sufficient background material to establish the relevancy and competency of a particular piece of evidence.

Many attorneys view the process of presenting a case as analogous to building a house. To have a solid structure, the foundation must be properly constructed. Courts have often extended the construction metaphor to presenting evidence at trial. Before counsel can request a court to rule on the admissibility of an item of evidence, the attorney must establish relevance and competency. These two items are the cornerstone of admissibility. A case is built up, fact by fact, until an entire, complete version is presented to the jury. If the legal team skimps on the basics, the result is just as bad as what happens when a house is built on a shaky foundation: The case falls apart.

To show that a particular fact has relevance, the attorney must **lay the foundation**. The attorney must establish relevance by asking specific questions of a witness. Because attorneys cannot testify about facts themselves, one of the few ways of presenting facts to the jury is by asking witnesses questions to show the relevance and competency of any particular piece of evidence. Failure to lay the foundation properly could result in a ruling of inadmissibility.

RESEARCH THIS!

It is always important to know what foundation questions are needed to admit different types of evidence. Locate your state's legal index, encyclopedia, and any other sources that will provide you with specific foundation questions to admit evidence such as audio tapes, videotapes, and photographs. What prominent cases provide the parameters for using this evidence? Are there cases that limit how new technology, such as computer animation, may be used at trial?

LEGAL RESEARCH MAXIM

Whenever you are researching evidentiary questions, keep in mind that there are several national treatises and publications on evidentiary issues that can provide you with valuable guidance. One such source is *American Law Reports* (ALR). Published by Thomson-West, this continuing, multivolume set analyzes every aspect of the law, especially recent case decisions and their impact on specific legal topics. ALR is also an excellent overview of specific types of evidence and provides foundation questions and other material that can be very helpful to a practitioner. ALR's *Proof of Facts* provides specific foundation questions and checklists and details exactly what evidence must be admitted during the trial to prove a contested fact conclusively.

Suppose that the plaintiff is testifying, and his or her attorney wants the jury to see a photograph of the intersection where the collision occurred. The attorney cannot simply walk over to the jurors and hand them a photo. The judge would never allow such a serious breach of protocol. Before the jury may see the photo, the attorney must prove that it is relevant and competent. How does the attorney accomplish this? He or she must question the plaintiff. That testimony might go something like this:

Hypothetical 7-5

Attorney: Mr. Wilson, I'm handing you what has been labeled as "Plaintiff's Exhibit Number One." What is it?
Wilson: It's a photograph.
Attorney: What does the photograph show?
Wilson: That's the intersection where the accident occurred. You can clearly see the traffic light and the gas station on the corner.
Attorney: Does that photograph accurately reflect how the intersection looked on the day of the accident?
Plaintiff: Yes, it does.
Attorney: Has that photograph been altered or changed in any way to change the actual appearance of the intersection?
Plaintiff: No, it hasn't been altered or tampered with.
Attorney: Is that how the intersection actually looked from your perspective as you were approaching it on the day of the collision?
Plaintiff: Yes.
Attorney: Your Honor, I move to admit Plaintiff's Exhibit Number One.

In the exchange between the attorney and witness in Hypothetical 7-5, several important things have happened. First of all, the attorney asked open-ended questions. The attorney is not permitted to simply tell the witness what the evidence is. Instead, the attorney must draw the information from the witness. That accounts for the questions about what the exhibit is and what it shows. You will also notice that the attorney didn't simply start asking questions about the collision and how the photo proved the case. Before he or she can do that, the attorney must first prove that this photograph is relevant. The attorney does so by first

COMMUNICATION TIP

You should always be prepared to explain to clients the importance of locating and retaining important evidence. Many paralegals take care of this point by incorporating it into the follow-up letter sent to the client after the initial meeting. They include a paragraph that might go something like this:

"As we discussed, it is absolutely essential to your case that we immediately take possession of any evidence in your case so that we may hold it for safe keeping and retain it for any further purposes, including pretrial motions, settlement discussions, and possible admission at trial. If you know of any evidence that pertains to any issues in this case, whether it is in your possession or anyone else's, please notify us immediately so that we may begin the process of obtaining it. In some cases, it may be necessary to issue subpoenas to recover the evidence, so do not delay in listing all sources of medical and employment records, photographs, diagrams, or any other object that we touched on during our discussions when you came to our office."

establishing that the photograph shows the intersection where the collision occurred. In addition to those questions, the attorney also asks questions establishing that the photograph has not been altered in a way that emphasizes certain features at the expense of others. A photograph must accurately reflect the reality of the scene. If it has been altered, it is not admissible. Photographs, like many other types of evidence, have specific types of foundation questions that have been established over the years. In this case, the attorney must ask if the photograph was altered or tampered with. If the attorney were presenting another type of evidence, such as a videotape or the cast of a footprint, the attorney's foundation questions would have been different.

Tendering Evidence

You will also notice that after the attorney asked the witness what the attorney believed were sufficient questions to establish relevance and competence, the attorney then requested the court to rule on the photograph. The attorney did this by stating: "Your Honor, I move to admit Plaintiff's Exhibit Number One."

tendering
The process of admitting evidence in a trial by asking the court to rule on relevance.

This statement is referred to as **tendering** the evidence. What the attorney is doing here is asking the judge to rule on the admissibility of the evidence. The attorney could simply ask, "Judge, will you say that it is admissible?" But the traditions that have developed over centuries of trials require that the question be asked in this way. Once the attorney makes this request, the judge will then refer to opposing counsel for any objections to the use of the evidence. Once all objections and arguments have been heard about the evidence, the judge rules on the admissibility of the item. Consider Hypothetical 7-6.

Hypothetical 7-6

This hypothetical is a continuation of the transcript shown in Hypothetical 7-5.

Judge: Ms. Hershey, do you have any objections to Plaintiff's Exhibit Number 1, the photograph of the intersection?
Hershey: Yes, Your Honor, insufficient foundation.

Will this objection be sustained or overruled?
Answer: To answer this question, we must first decipher the nature of the attorney's objection. Essentially, the attorney's objection states that the plaintiff's attorney has failed to prove enough relevance or competence of the evidence. The shorthand way of stating this is to simply say, "Insufficient foundation." Then the judge is left with the decision of whether to admit it.
Is there sufficient foundation for the photograph? The plaintiff's attorney has shown that the photo accurately shows the intersection as it appeared on the day of the collision, and the photo certainly seems to satisfy the requirements of relevance and competence. In this case, the judge will almost certainly overrule the defense attorney's objection. Most likely, the judge will make the following announcement:
Judge: Exhibit Number 1 admitted over objection.

The protocol followed in admitting evidence always calls for the judge to refer to opposing counsel before admitting evidence. This step gives the opposing attorney a chance to lodge an objection to the evidence and preserve the objection for appeal. In some cases, the objection may be properly raised, and the judge may refuse to admit the evidence. In such a case, the plaintiff's attorney would be barred from referring to it in any way. Finally, the judge announces his or her decision because everything that is said in the courtroom is being taken down by a court reporter, and therefore, the judge's decision on the point is preserved for later review.

Objecting to Evidence

There are numerous objections that can be raised to evidence tendered to the court. Although we have focused on foundation and hearsay issues, it is important to note that trial counsel may object to evidence on numerous other grounds. The attorney may wish to object on the basis of any of the following (offered only as a summary of the vast array of potential objections):

- Improper conclusion
- Attorney–client privilege
- Relevance
- Prejudice
- Other issues

Improper Conclusion

An attorney's objection about a witness or other testimony in which he or she calls for an "improper conclusion" is shorthand for an objection that is actually more extensive. In essence, this objection goes to the very heart of a jury trial. When attorneys present testimony, documentary, or physical evidence to a jury, they are asking the jury to reach a conclusion about the impact of this evidence on the issues in the case. Because it is the jury's responsibility to allocate importance to each piece of evidence to achieve an overall cohesive conclusion about the case, it is improper for a witness to tell the jury the significance of any evidence. For instance, suppose that a witness testifies that the defendant's negligent driving was the cause of the accident. The attorney representing the defendant would object, pointing out that it is not for the witness to reach this conclusion, but instead for the jury. In such a case, the judge would almost certainly sustain such an objection, direct the witness not to make such statements, and instruct the jury to disregard the witness's testimony. The judge might even go further and remind the jury that it is the responsibility of the individual jurors to determine the importance of each piece of evidence, not a witness.

In a subsequent chapter, we will see that this rule has one important exception. Expert witnesses, once qualified, may give conclusions about specific facts in the case, primarily because the issues about which they testify are beyond the knowledge and training of the average juror.

Attorney–Client Privilege

As we will see in Chapter 10, privilege is a right that can be interposed by a witness when a question asks for communications between a person and specifically enumerated professionals. For instance, a witness cannot be compelled to testify about communications between physicians and patients, attorneys and clients, or pastors and penitents. In each situation, the parties involved are protected by an evidentiary privilege that exempts them from doing what all other witnesses must do: answer questions posed to them by the attorneys. There are numerous privileges, including husband–wife, attorney–client, pastor–penitent, and physician–patient, as well as others recognized by individual states, including accountant–client.

Relevance

An objection of relevance goes to the very heart of the purpose of evidence: It must bear on an issue pending in the case. When an attorney raises an objection of relevance, he or she is saying that the evidence sought to be admitted does not serve that critical function. If the judge rules that an item of evidence is not relevant, the court is essentially denying the usefulness of the evidence to assist the jury in resolving any of the issues raised in the case.

Prejudice

An objection based on the prejudicial impact of evidence is one that may agree to the relevance of the evidence but object because the evidence will have an effect on the jury that outweighs other evidence. Autopsy photos, for instance, may have relevance to the issues surrounding the decedent's injuries but may be so gruesome that jurors will have a difficult time giving other evidence as much credence and attention. Although prejudice is an objection that can be raised for any evidence, it is often seen in the context of gruesome photos or other visual media or concerning an individual's past actions, including conviction of a crime. These issues might tend to overly sway the jury, and because of this, courts are reluctant to admit highly controversial evidence unless the party offering it can show that there is no other way to have the jury consider the facts.

Other Issues

There are so many other grounds for objection to evidence that entire books have been written on this topic alone. Objections run the gamut from hearsay to impeachment to trade secrets. Paralegals should be aware of any potential objections to evidence that the legal team intends to use at trial. Simply because the opposition objects to the admission of specific evidence does not mean that the judge will sustain that objection. A paralegal who has thoroughly researched the legal issues surrounding the evidence intended to be used at trial can be an invaluable asset in helping the legal team convince a judge to rule in its favor.

TYPES OF EVIDENCE

Now that we have discussed how evidence is admitted at trial, we must address the various types of evidence used in civil cases. Evidence can be classified into three broad categories: direct (real) evidence, circumstantial evidence, and documentary evidence.

Direct Evidence

direct evidence
Evidence that establishes a particular fact without resort to other testimony or evidence.

Direct evidence is also known as real evidence. Direct evidence is anything that is conclusive proof of a particular fact. It proves the point of contention between the parties. See Figure 7.2 for examples of direct evidence. For example, suppose that in a personal injury lawsuit, the plaintiff offers evidence of the impact of the defendant's car with his own car. The plaintiff removes the car door and brings it to court. Anyone can clearly see a terrible gash in the door. The direct evidence of the damage would come from actually looking at the car door in the courtroom. If the attorney representing the plaintiff wishes to prove just how damaged the door was, the best option is to bring the door into the courtroom and have the jury look at it. That would be direct evidence of the damage. However, direct evidence is sometimes neither practical nor possible. In those cases, such as when the car has been destroyed, the second best option would be to present a photograph of the car door. However, as we will shortly see, a photograph is not direct evidence; it is documentary evidence. In the first situation, producing the actual door is direct evidence of the damage done to it. It demonstrates that the plaintiff's car door was damaged but does not, of course, prove who damaged it. That determination is left to the jury. Another common example of direct evidence is eyewitness testimony.

Eyewitness Testimony

Both criminal cases and civil cases rely on eyewitness testimony in nearly every case. There is something very compelling about hearing someone say, "I saw the defendant do it." Direct testimony, offered on the stand, is very convincing, which explains why attorneys for both sides often try to find witnesses who can testify about their direct experiences. Suppose, for example, that the

FIGURE 7.2
Examples of Direct Evidence

- Eyewitness testimony.
- Photographs of plaintiff's injuries.
- Video or audiotapes of conversations.
- Objects relevant to issues in the case.
- Written statements.
- Documents.

defense team in a car wreck case has located a witness who will testify that the plaintiff ignored the red light and actually caused the collision that he is now blaming on the defendant. When this witness takes the stand and testifies, his or her testimony is direct evidence that the plaintiff was at fault in the accident, which will be devastating to the plaintiff's case. We have all heard the old maxim, "Seeing is believing." This maxim applies indirectly to jury trials. There, the fact that the witness saw it is enough for the jury to believe it.

Many legal commentators and average jurors have a strong bias toward direct evidence. When in doubt, they would much prefer to be presented with eyewitness testimony or physical objects that substantiate the claims in the case. However, that is not always possible. Sometimes, the evidence presented falls into the category of circumstantial evidence.

Circumstantial Evidence

circumstantial evidence
Evidence that suggests a conclusion.

If direct evidence is proof of a fact, then **circumstantial evidence** suggests a conclusion about a fact. Generations of law students have been presented with the famous example of finding "a trout in the milk." In the example, a person finds a fish in a glass of milk. The conclusion: Someone put it there. The reason this qualifies as circumstantial evidence is that if this were your glass of milk, you could not conclusively say that you saw a person put the fish in the glass but you could certainly draw the conclusion that someone must have done so.

Circumstantial evidence suggests a conclusion, but the reason that circumstantial evidence is considered weaker than direct evidence is because circumstantial evidence is often open to interpretation. Consider Hypothetical 7-7.

Hypothetical 7-7

It's winter. Just before you fall asleep, you happen to look out your bedroom window and notice that the first snowfall of the season has started. In the morning, you look out at the back yard and see footprints in the snow. When you get up and go to the kitchen, you see your child's boots next to the door, covered in snow. You draw a conclusion that your son got up early and went out to play in the snow before you woke up. Your conclusion is based on circumstantial evidence. After all, you didn't actually see your son playing in the snow, so you don't have any direct evidence, but it is a reasonable conclusion based on the facts at hand. This is circumstantial evidence because there are other possible explanations. For instance, someone else could have made the footprints. The snow dripping off your child's boots could have come from the front yard or might not even be snow, but the more reasonable conclusion is the one that you've drawn.

Simply because evidence falls into the category of circumstantial does not mean that it is somehow defective. Entire cases can be constructed on circumstantial evidence. However, there is an important problem that arises in basing a case exclusively on circumstantial evidence: The conclusion suggested from the evidence must support the allegations. The more that the evidence is open to interpretation, the more likely it is that the judge and jury may draw a contrary conclusion.

In the real world of litigation, most cases are a blend of both direct and circumstantial evidence. In a personal injury case, for example, the damages to the plaintiff's automobile and her scarring from injuries received qualify as direct evidence, whereas a witness's testimony about hearing a crash and then seeing the plaintiff climbing out of her car would be circumstantial evidence that the crash had just occurred.

Hypothetical 7-8

Ron is running late one day and fails to stop for a red light. He runs his car into the back of the car in front of him. Sue is at the wheel of the other car, and she sustains severe neck injuries. She is also knocked unconscious at the wreck and is later unable to testify about the facts immediately prior to the collision. There are no eyewitnesses. At trial, Ron claims that the light was green and that he never saw Sue's car. The damage to the front of Ron's car is extensive. There are also skid marks from Ron's wheels.

What is the direct evidence and what is the circumstantial evidence in this case? Sue's medical injuries are direct evidence of the extent of her injuries sustained in the car crash. Is there any circumstantial evidence in this case? As a matter of fact, there is. What about the skid marks from Ron's car? Taken by themselves, you could consider them as direct evidence that Ron put on the brakes. But this evidence is also circumstantial in that it suggests a possible conclusion. What is that conclusion? If Ron claims that he never saw Sue's car, then there should have been no reason for him to hit the brakes, and therefore, he's not telling the truth. If he never saw Sue's car, he would never have applied the brakes, and there would be no skid marks. Circumstantial evidence in this case suggests that Ron saw Sue's car, hit the brakes, went into a skid, and plowed into the back of her car.

As you can see from Hypothetical 7-8, almost all cases have both direct evidence and circumstantial evidence in them. But there are also many cases that involve the third major classification of evidence: documentary evidence.

Documentary Evidence

documentary evidence
Any document or paper offered to prove a matter in contention in a trial.

The third broad category of evidence is **documentary evidence**. Documentary evidence refers to any evidence recorded in a medium. Evidence is classified as documentary when it records significant events but does not qualify as evidence itself. A contract is an example of documentary evidence. It records the details of the agreement between the parties. A photograph is also documentary evidence. It records details and facts about a particular scene, but it is not the scene itself. It is a representation, in the same way that a drawing or a digital cell phone picture is a representation.

Documentary evidence raises several important considerations. Because this evidence is not direct evidence (it is not the actual evidence but a representation of that evidence), it resembles circumstantial evidence. But classifying documentary evidence as circumstantial evidence creates confusion. After all, the wording of a document or the photograph of a scene would appear to represent a fact in itself, not open the evidence to other possible considerations. As a result, documentary evidence falls into a middle ground, which accounts for the special rules involved in presenting it, such as the best evidence rule, discussed subsequently in this chapter.

When a paralegal subpoenas documents, he or she should obtain a declaration from the custodian of the records that the records produced are complete and accurate. That way, the paralegal may have some indication that the request has been fully complied with.

Other Categories of Evidence

In addition to direct, circumstantial, and documentary evidence, there are several other classifications of evidence that are important in any civil case. They include:

- Testimonial evidence
- Demonstrative evidence
- Scientific or expert evidence

Testimonial Evidence

testimonial evidence
Oral statements made by a witness under oath.

Testimonial evidence refers to statements by witnesses from the witness stand while they are under oath. During the trial, a witness will be called to the stand by either the plaintiff or the defendant and questioned on direct examination. The attorney will ask the witness questions about the incident to prove one or more allegations in the case. The witness may have been present when the incident occurred, may have additional information, may be an expert, or may even be the plaintiff. In every situation, the witness must give truthful testimony, and when the attorney has finished asking questions, he or she is subject to cross-examination by the opposing attorney. Testimonial evidence carries the same weight as any other testimony but is often the most powerful evidence given at trial. After all, the jurors are far more likely to be swayed by the statement of a person than the words in a document. Because of the power of testimonial evidence, attorneys work very hard to locate as many witnesses as possible to help carry their burden of proving the elements in their pleadings.

Demonstrative Evidence

demonstrative evidence
Any object, visual aid, model, scale drawing, or other exhibit designed to help clarify points in the trial.

Attorneys and paralegals often prepare charts and diagrams to help them explain specific points to the jury. The question often arises: How should such a chart or diagram be classified as evidence? Generally speaking, a visual aid prepared by one of the attorneys falls into the category of **demonstrative evidence**. This evidence can be used in the courtroom to help present the party's case and can be relied on by witnesses and even the attorney during the closing argument, but such evidence usually does not go out with the jurors when they deliberate on the case. Because the parties prepared it, it is not given the same weight as the direct and circumstantial evidence presented at trial. After all, this evidence was prepared as an **exhibit** by one side to help prove its case and, as such, has inherent problems of bias and subjectivity.

exhibit
A document attached to a pleading that is incorporated by reference into the body of the pleading.

Hypothetical 7-9

The plaintiff's attorney has asked a paralegal (or someone else, such as a legal nurse consultant) to go through all of the medical records in a case and prepare a chronology of medical treatments. This chronology lists every procedure carried out on the plaintiff after he was admitted to the hospital. The attorney has blown up the chronology so that it is now six feet tall and three feet wide. She has done this so that the jury can easily see it from across the room. However, before the attorney can show it to the jury, she must establish relevance and have the judge rule that it is admissible.

The first issue that the attorney must resolve is which witness she will use to get the evidence admitted. She must use someone who knows about the exhibit and will be able to answer the foundation questions. Could she use the plaintiff? The problem with using the plaintiff is that he may not know the answers to some of the foundation questions. The attorney cannot give the questions and answers herself, because she is barred from giving such testimony during the trial. So, whom should she call to the stand to testify about this medical chronology? The best choice is either a paralegal or some medical professional, such as the legal nurse consultant who actually prepared the chronology in the first place. The foundation questions for this demonstrative evidence will probably go something like this:

Attorney: Ms. Doe, did you prepare the medical chronology in this case?
Witness: Yes, I did.
Attorney: Would you tell the court how you prepared this medical chronology?
Witness: I sifted through all of the medical reports, bills, medical diagnoses, charts, nurses' notes, and the complete medical file and then prepared a day-by-day account of what happened to the plaintiff from all of these various sources.
Attorney: Does this medical chronology fairly and accurately depict all of the plaintiff's treatment, procedures, and medicines administered, and all of the people who were involved in the plaintiff's treatment?
Witness: Yes, it does.
Attorney: Your Honor, I move to admit Plaintiff's Exhibit Number Two.

Has the attorney laid a sufficient foundation to have this evidence admitted at trial?
Answer: Yes. The attorney has laid sufficient foundation for this demonstrative evidence. When the judge admits it, the attorney can refer to it throughout the rest of the trial as a way of helping witnesses and the jury understand specific points in the case.

Scientific Evidence

There are times when the parties must present complicated, technical, or scientific evidence. In such a case, the parties will usually rely on the services of an expert witness. A person qualifies as an expert when he or she has knowledge that is beyond the normal experience and education of average jurors. Expert witnesses are permitted to reach conclusions and can base their testimony on conjecture, in direct opposition to the rules that prohibit similar tactics by lay witnesses. We will discuss expert witnesses in greater detail in the next chapter.

 SURF'S UP!

COMPUTER-AIDED EVIDENTIARY PRESENTATIONS

In the age of the Internet and the widespread availability of computer networked law offices, several companies specialize in providing assistance to attorneys preparing to try a civil case. Visual aids are important for juries, whether it is simply providing the details of the accident site or laying out the complexities of a medical malpractice case. Today, companies offer a broad range of services, from simple aids to computer animation. Examples of companies that provide these services include Insight Legal Graphics and Animation (www.insightlegalgraphics.com) or High Impact Litigation, Inc. (www.highimpactlit.com), both of which specialize in assisting attorneys preparing for trial by generating a wide variety of exhibits, diagrams, graphic designs, computer animation, PowerPoint slides, and nearly every type of trial aid imaginable. Other companies, such as Power Graphics, Inc. (www.power-graphics.com), concentrate on taking the various evidentiary exhibits in a case and presenting them in as dramatic a fashion as possible. For instance, these companies can blow up an important photograph or diagram so that it is truly enormous—making it much easier for the jury to see all of the important details.

FIGURE 7.3
Rule 1002.
Requirement of
Original

> To prove the content of a writing, recording, or photograph, the original writing, recording, or photograph is required, except as otherwise provided in these rules or by statute.

SPECIFIC EVIDENTIARY RULES

Whenever we discuss the topic of evidence, there are specific evidentiary issues that arise. Some of the most important of these rules pertain to the admissibility of original copies of documents, the use of hearsay at trial, and issues surrounding the authentication of the evidence used at trial.

The Best Evidence Rule

Whenever an attorney must use a document at trial, such as a medical report, the rules of evidence require that the original must be presented (see Figure 7.3). Copies are generally not admissible, unless the party can show the original has been destroyed. The reason for the requirement of the original, also known under the slightly misleading name "the best evidence rule," goes back to the circumstances when the document was created. The original document was the one actually handled by the parties and the one upon which the agreement was reached. In these days of nearly perfect copies, the best evidence rule continues to have important consequences. The original may bear handwritten notes or other modifications that a freshly printed document would not contain.

Hearsay

The topic of hearsay can be very complicated. The basic definition of hearsay is an out-of-court statement offered to prove the matter asserted. Unfortunately, that definition fails to clarify exactly what hearsay is. At its simplest, hearsay consists of a statement repeated on the witness stand by someone who did not originally make it. The most common circumstance in which hearsay arises is when a witness is asked a question while he or she is testifying in court and the witness's answer encompasses a statement made by someone else. Consider Hypothetical 7-10.

Hypothetical 7-10

Rosario is on the witness stand testifying about a car collision. The plaintiff's attorney asks Rosario what happened immediately after the collision. Rosario testifies, "I got out of my car and a man was standing there. He turned to me and said, 'that other guy ran the red light.'"

At this point, the defense attorney objects that the statement is hearsay. Is it?

Answer: If hearsay consists of one witness testifying about what another person said, then this would qualify as hearsay. The rules of evidence bar the use of this statement, and the witness's testimony about the other man's statement would be stricken from the record, if not from the jurors' minds.

The reason that hearsay is considered objectionable is that when one person repeats what another person has said, it is impossible to question the witness on the stand about the conditions in which that statement was made. For instance, the attorney cannot question the witness who repeated the statement about the other person's motivations, prejudices, or biases. The attorney cannot question the witness on the stand about what the other witness could or could not have seen. As a result, courts restrict the use of hearsay statements. Rather than using a hearsay statement, courts much prefer that the attorneys produce the original witness who made the statement. In addition, hearsay statements are considered inherently unreliable. When a statement qualifies as hearsay, and an objection is raised, the court will instruct the witness not to repeat what someone else said.

Does the prohibition against hearsay mean that the witness can't repeat something that he or she said? No. If the witness made a statement and repeats it on the stand, then it does not qualify as hearsay. The person who made the statement can be questioned about it, and the accuracy of the statement can be assessed because the person who made it is currently on the stand.

Hearsay in Documents

Hearsay is not limited to oral statements by witnesses; it also applies to documents. When documentary evidence contains statements by witnesses, it satisfies the definition of hearsay in the same way that a live witness would. That explains why typical documents such as police reports, medical narratives, and other records qualify as hearsay and cannot be used at trial, unless they fall under some exception. Consider Hypothetical 7-11.

COMMUNICATION TIP

If the purpose of putting people up on the stand, swearing them in, and then asking them questions under oath is to get truthful testimony, then that whole process gets shot in the foot when the witness repeats what someone else says. How can you test the accuracy of a statement made by someone else? How can you be sure that the statement was repeated correctly? How can you be sure that the statement was ever even made?

Hypothetical 7-11

Terry was admitted to the hospital last year with classic symptoms of appendicitis: referred pain on the left side, fever, vomiting, and a high white blood cell count. Unfortunately, he was incorrectly diagnosed with gastroenteritis. Later, his appendix burst, and he had a severe case of peritonitis. He has brought a medical malpractice action against the doctor who originally saw him at the emergency room. You are working for the plaintiff's attorney. As you go through the file, you discover a note, made by the admitting nurse, that says, "Classic case of appendicitis."

When it comes time for the trial, can the attorney simply use the nurse's note as evidence of the doctor's malpractice?

Answer: No. The note is hearsay. Nurses' notes, police reports, and other documents are all technically classified as hearsay. Unless the note comes under an exception to the hearsay rule, it cannot be used. Instead, the nurse who made the notation must be called to the stand and questioned about the note. Without that authentication, the note is inadmissible.

Exceptions to the Hearsay Rule

Although we have seen that any out-of-court statement that is repeated on the stand or presented to the jury technically qualifies as hearsay, there are numerous exceptions to the hearsay rule that allow hearsay testimony to be used. In each of the exceptions, there are other indicators that the hearsay statement was made under conditions that give it some reliability. All of the exceptions to the hearsay rule are based on the premise that a particular statement has a greater degree of credibility because of when or who made it. This rationale explains why statements made as excited utterances, as part of business records, or in connection with medical diagnoses are all admissible as exceptions to the hearsay rule.

The first exception to the use of hearsay statements is not really an exception at all. When a witness is testifying about what one of the parties to the case said, the hearsay rule does not apply. Suppose, for example, that a witness repeats what the plaintiff said at the time of the accident. Because both the plaintiff and defendant are present in the courtroom and can refute any such statement, statements by parties are not considered hearsay.

The Federal Rules of Evidence recognize 23 separate exceptions to the use of hearsay statements. They range from present-tense impressions to civil judgments concerning family history. For the sake of clarity, we address the most commonly used exceptions, including:

- Excited utterances.
- Business records.
- Statements for purpose of medical diagnosis.

Excited Utterances.   The basic premise behind not allowing hearsay statements to be repeated in court is that they are inherently unreliable. However, what if a person has no time or inclination to think up an unreliable statement? The premise behind the excited utterance is that a person blurts out a statement after being confronted with an unexpected and sudden surprise. Under these circumstances, courts assume that the statement is probably true. As a result, it can be used at trial.

To qualify a statement as an excited utterance, the attorney seeking to use the statement must establish the conditions shortly before the statement was made. The attorney must show that there was a sudden and unexpected event, one that shocked or surprised the speaker.

Hypothetical 7-12

Witness: The wreck had just happened, and I jumped out of my car. The passenger was sitting in one of the cars and said, "That guy should have been watching the road."

Ordinarily, the statement in Hypothetical 7-12 would be hearsay and inadmissible at trial; however, because it is an excited utterance, it will be allowed into evidence. The premise behind the excited utterance exception is that when a person is confronted with a sudden, dangerous situation, anything that he or she might blurt out is probably not a lie (see Figure 7.4).

FIGURE 7.4
Excited Utterance Exception to Hearsay

Source: Rule 803(2) Federal Rules of Evidence.

> The following are not excluded by the hearsay rule, even though the declarant is available as a witness:
>
> (2) Excited utterance. A statement relating to a startling event or condition made while the declarant was under the stress of excitement caused by the event or condition.

(6) Records of regularly conducted activity. A memorandum, report, record, or data compilation, in any form, of acts, events, conditions, opinions, or diagnoses, made at or near the time by, or from information transmitted by, a person with knowledge, if kept in the course of a regularly conducted business activity, and if it was the regular practice of that business activity to make the memorandum, report, record, or data compilation, all as shown by the testimony of the custodian or other qualified witness, or by certification that complies with Rule 902(11), Rule 902(12), or a statute permitting certification, unless the source of information or the method or circumstances of preparation indicate lack of trustworthiness. The term "business" as used in this paragraph includes business, institution, association, profession, occupation, and calling of every kind, whether or not conducted for profit.

Statements made for purposes of medical diagnosis or treatment and describing medical history, or past or present symptoms, pain, or sensations, or the inception or general character of the cause or external source thereof insofar as reasonably pertinent to diagnosis or treatment.

Business Records.   The premise behind the business records exception to hearsay is similar to that for the excited utterance exception. When a person writes comments in business records, especially comments written before there is a lawsuit, the court may allow a witness to repeat what the business records contain. Again, because the statement is made in such a way as to be reliable, it is an exception to the general rule against the use of hearsay statements (see Figure 7.5). In our previous example involving the nurse's note, would the notation, "Classic case of appendicitis" be admissible as a business record? The answer is probably yes.

Statements for the Purpose of Medical Diagnosis.   Another exception to the hearsay rule concerns statements made for the purpose of medical diagnosis (see Figure 7.6). Here again, the idea of inherent reliability makes the statement more likely to be true. After all, giving false information to a medical provider could have disastrous consequences. These statements, assuming that they are not protected by an evidentiary privilege, are admissible as an exception to the hearsay rule.

Authentication

One issue that often comes up in presenting evidence at trial is how to authenticate the item. **Authentication** is actually a feature of competence, but is often dealt with as a separate concern (see Figure 7.7). We have already encountered a species of authentication in the best evidence rule. There, we saw that when a document is in dispute, the only way to prove its contents is to present the original. That is a form of authentication, or proof of the document's origin and provenance. But what happens when the parties are faced with presenting facts that we all know to be true? Do the rules of authentication require witnesses to testify about those issues as well?

authentication
Proof by an officer, witness, or certifying document that evidence is what it is claimed to be.

Judicial Notice

So far, our discussions about evidence have revealed that the most common method for offering such evidence is by a sponsoring witness or, as we will discuss in the next section, through a self-authenticating document. However, there are provisions that allow the parties to simply request the court to take **judicial notice** of a particular fact without the necessity of presenting proof to support it. When a court takes judicial notice of a fact, the fact is assumed to be true for purposes of the litigation, and neither party must present evidence to prove it (see Figure 7.8). Courts are limited in the ways that they may take judicial notice of facts. A court cannot, for example, take judicial notice of the fact that the defendant is liable to the plaintiff. Such a ruling would invade

judicial notice
A request that a court accept evidence as fact without the necessity of further proof.

(a) General provision.
The requirement of authentication or identification as a condition precedent to admissibility is satisfied by evidence sufficient to support a finding that the matter in question is what its proponent claims.

SPOT THE ISSUE!

Review the Baker complaint in Appendix B. Locate the two paragraphs in the complaint that contain hearsay statements. Do either of those statements fall under the exceptions to hearsay rules? Explain your answer.

FIGURE 7.8
Federal Rules of Evidence: Judicial Notice

Rule 201(b). A judicially noticed fact must be one not subject to reasonable dispute in that it is either (1) generally known within the territorial jurisdiction of the trial court or (2) capable of accurate and ready determination by resort to sources whose accuracy cannot reasonably be questioned.

CYBER TRIP

American Association of Law Libraries http://www.aallnet.org/sis/lisp/research.htm
Cornell Law School–Overview of Evidence Law http://www.law.cornell.edu/wex/index.php/Evidence
The Evidence Site–University of Michigan http://www.law.umich.edu/thayer/
The Jurist–Evidence Law, University of Pittsburgh School of Law http://jurist.law.pitt.edu/sg_evid.htm

self-authenticating document
A document that is authorized by statute and that can be used without additional offer of proof.

the province of the jury and no doubt be overturned on appeal. Traditionally, trial judges are reluctant to take judicial notice of all but the most obvious facts. For instance, a court would be authorized to take judicial notice of the fact that a particular city is the state capitol. It would be a waste of the court's time if the parties were required to present live witness to testify about this fact when it is well known to everyone. Judicial notice is generally limited to such obvious facts and rarely extended to the issue in contention between the parties.

Hypothetical 7-13

During a trial involving medical malpractice allegations, the plaintiff's attorney requests that the judge take judicial notice of the fact that children have thinner bones than adults. The defense attorney objects to judicial notice on this fact and requests that the plaintiff present evidence to support it. How does the judge rule?

Answer: Because judicial notice is generally reserved for facts that are common knowledge, and the thickness of children's bones compared with adult bones is not a matter of common knowledge, the judge will most likely refuse to give judicial notice to the plaintiff's request and will require the plaintiff to present evidence to support the allegations.

Self-Authenticating Document

A **self-authenticating document**, also known as a self-proving document, is an official document that provides for its own authentication (see Figure 7.9). Such documents are usually issued by the state and can be as simple as a certified copy. When the clerk of court issues a certified copy of a public document, the certification is authorized by law and avoids the necessity of issuing a subpoena of someone in the courthouse to testify that the document is a correct copy. Self-authenticating documents are often the product of special enabling legislation that specifically provides that documents bearing government seals do not require sponsoring witnesses. At trial, the party with such a document may simply present it to the court, note the self-authentication feature, and move to admit it. As long as the document satisfies relevancy, the judge must admit it.

Privilege

In most situations, a person can be subpoenaed to the stand and questioned about his or her actions, including conversations that the witness had with other people. A witness can be asked what he or she said to another person and must divulge the contents of that conversation, even

FIGURE 7.9
Rule 902. Self-Authentication

Extrinsic evidence of authenticity as a condition precedent to admissibility is not required with respect to the following:
(1) Domestic public documents under seal. A document bearing a seal purporting to be that of the United States, or of any State, district, Commonwealth, territory, or insular possession thereof, or the Panama Canal Zone, or the Trust Territory of the Pacific Islands, or of a political subdivision, department, officer, or agency thereof, and a signature purporting to be an attestation or execution.

when the subject is embarrassing. However, a certain class of individuals is protected from being forced to reveal the contents of their conversations with others. The ability to refuse to answer specific types of questions has long been referred to as **privilege**. Only certain individuals enjoy this privilege. The idea behind protecting certain forms of communication is that, even though it might hurt a particular case, society as a whole is protected by making certain conversations off-limits. For instance, suppose that you visit a member of the clergy and discuss some personal problems. Later, this person is called to the stand and asked to repeat that conversation. The clergy member can refuse to answer the question and cannot be compelled to answer because the clergy is protected by evidentiary privilege. The judge cannot hold the witness in contempt for failing to answer the question, and no other court can compel the witness to discuss conversations that occurred within the bonds of that relationship.

privilege
Reasonable expectation of privacy and confidentiality for communications in furtherance of the relationship such as attorney–client, doctor–patient, husband–wife, psychotherapist–patient, and priest–penitent.

Evidentiary privileges are granted only to specific professions and only under certain types of circumstances. The most commonly recognized evidentiary privileges include:

- Husband–wife (known as marital privilege).
- Attorney–client.
- Physician–patient.
- Clergyman–communicant.
- Psychologist–patient.
- School counselor (in some states and only under certain circumstances).
- Family therapist.
- Social worker.

You will notice that certain professions are not listed here. For instance, most states do not recognize accountant–client evidentiary privileges. In most states, an accountant can be summoned to the stand and asked to repeat a conversation that he or she had with a party. However, if a party's attorney, physician, psychiatrist, or social worker is summoned to the stand, that person can refuse to answer any questions about confidential communications. Privilege is a very powerful protection. The premise behind this privilege is that without it, a person might be reluctant to share vital information with the very person who can provide the best assistance. If a person believed that a conversation with a doctor might later be repeated, the person might not be willing to share enough information to receive proper treatment.

Marital Privilege

marital privilege
An evidentiary protection that permits married individuals to refuse to testify against one another.

Husband–wife privilege, or **marital privilege**, is one of the most misunderstood of all the evidentiary privileges. Although legally married spouses cannot be compelled to testify against each other, this privilege only protects the spouse that has been called to the stand. The other spouse cannot assert it to prevent the spouse from testifying. A wife is always free to testify against her husband, if that is her wish. The evidentiary privilege was created to prevent others from forcing a spouse to testify, not to prevent spouses from voluntarily doing so. In divorce actions, for example, spouses routinely testify against each other. The reason for the privilege is that society has made a determination that it is more important to respect the private communications between spouses than to force them to testify against each other, with devastating results to the marriage.

Attorney–Client Privilege

attorney–client privilege
The legal relationship established between attorney and client allowing for free exchange of information without fear of disclosure.

The **attorney–client privilege** has been called the most important aspect of the attorney and paralegal's role. The privilege is not only important for attorneys but also for paralegals, legal assistants, and legal secretaries. Any of these individuals may inadvertently waive the protection by repeating confidential matters to others.

When a client has a confidential meeting with his or her attorney, for instance, neither party can be compelled to reveal what was discussed. If the witness is asked about this conversation, he or she can invoke an evidentiary privilege that prevents any further questions. The attorney can also invoke this protection if the attorney is subpoenaed to testify. This privilege against revealing any details of the conversation applies to any communication between an attorney and a client, whether it is a telephone call, a face-to-face meeting, a letter, a fax, or even an email.

Papach
v.
Mercy Suburban Hosp. 2005
WL 2517100, 19
(Pa. Super., 2005)
MCEWEN, P.J.E.

This appeal has been taken from the judgment entered in this medical malpractice action on the jury verdict which absolved the then remaining defendants, appellees Mercy Suburban Hospital, Edward F. Schrieber, D.O., Kevin McAveney, D.O., and Frank DuPont, III, M.D., of any negligence in connection with the death of Christopher Haws. Appellant, the mother of Christopher Haws, contends in this appeal that a new trial is required due to the admission of prejudicial hearsay. We agree with appellant that the trial court erred when it overruled certain objections to the use of an EMS report. As a result, we vacate the judgment entered in favor of all appellees.

The events immediately preceding the untimely death of Christopher Haws on August 23, 1999, were described at trial by Mark Thompson who had accompanied Christopher on a motorcycle ride on an unpaved trail along high tension line towers on the evening of August 19, 1999:

[BY MR. HAINES:]

Q. Well, let me get to it. August 19th, were you with Chris on that night?

A. Yes.

Q. And had the two of you ridden together the night before that?

A. Yes, we had.

Q. Mr. Thompson, were you with Chris on the 6th [of August] when he was riding?

A. No, I was not.

Q. Did you ride with him between [August] the 6th and the 18th?

A. No, we did not.

Q. Do you know why? I mean was there a particular reason that you were not riding at that point?

A. Well, because of the time from his first incident, you know, we were allotted a few weeks not to ride, so we abstained from riding.

Q. Keep your voice up, Mr. Thompson.

A. I'm sorry. We stopped. We didn't ride for that period of time just because of his previous injury.

Q. When did you first learn about the accident of the 6th?

A. When Cindy and I returned home from Maryland she went into the house before I did and when I came back into the house she told me there was a message on the answering machine that Chris had been in an accident. To the best of my recollection, that's how it went.

Q. Okay. Did you and Chris ever discuss that accident, that first accident on the 6th?

A. Yes, we did.

Q. Did Chris describe to you what had happened?

A. Yes, he did.

Q. What did he tell you happened?

A. Chris told me that he was riding one way on a trail and it was at a point of a fairly, like a hairpin, like a sharp turn back the other direction and another rider was coming that direction and that they just kind of met in the middle, just type of terrain didn't allow the evasive action and they collided.

Q. The two of you went out on the 18th and then the 19th; is that right?

A. That's correct.

Q. Tell us where you went on the 18th, how long you rode, what you did.

A. On the 18th we got together basically to go out and get some fresh air. It was just pure relaxation kind of thing. That might sound kind of relax riding what it really was and we went to a local area that a local group of guys, friends of ours and his, get together and practice riding. I mean it's a practice area that we usually use.

Q. How long did you ride on the 18th?

A. We were only at that area for probably—from the time we got in to the time we left, 45 minutes maybe, but, actual riding time, it couldn't have been more than 20 minutes probably.

Q. Was there a particular reason that you only rode 20 minutes?

A. As a matter of fact, we were asked to leave that day. Somebody had complained about the noise or something and the owner came over and asked us to cut it short.

Q. Are you aware of anything, any incident involving Chris and his bike on the 18th, a fall, an accident, or anything like that?

A. On the 18th, no.

Q. Did you see the picture, were you able to see the picture of Chris this morning when we showed it in his gear?

A. In gear, yes.

Q. When you went riding on the 18th, was he dressed like that?

A. Absolutely.

Q. The 19th, you went riding again; is that right?

A. Yes, that's correct.

Q. Where did you go?

A. We went to another local spot where guys go to ride and down off of Conshohocken Road in I think it's Plymouth Township.

Q. What time was that?

A. Let's see, it was probably between 5:00 and 6 o'clock.

Q. Because it was a summer night—

A. It was after work, so it had to be after 5:00.

Q. What happened?

A. We got there, unloaded the bikes, and started riding a little bit. It wasn't a real big area, so it was a type of strip of power lines, so it's not real giant sprawling and wide area and it's a fairly good road except for the actual trail you're riding on, which is maybe ten or 15 feet wide at that time and we had only been riding at that point for, let's see, it was like not long at all, five, ten minutes, and the way that place is laid out is it's along power lines, so you can go along the power lines for a fairly long distance straight away and there are certain cuts back to where the parking lot is, what we call kind of home base, and you can cut back and shoot back down towards home base and he was ahead of me and he turned and I kept continued on forward and I took a larger loop than he did and when I came back around from my loop, just there at the parking lot, you known, you turn, you go back up again and around. When I came—you know, the terrain sort of comes down. The elevation from the parking lot to where we were was maybe 20 feet, but it's a fairly long rise, so it's not like it's real steep or anything, but I went down and came back up and around and there on the side of the trail was Chris.

Q. Can you describe what you saw?

A. It was kind of strange the way he was laying there. He was laying flat on his face with his arms down at his side, palms up, and his head was turned to the right and the front tire of his motorcycle was in perfect line with him and the front tire of the motorcycle was just laid over his riding boot by maybe a foot and I stopped alongside of him and he was a terrible practical joker, I actually, you know, booted him in the foot and said, "Hey, come on, quit messing around," and when he didn't respond, that's when I, you know, I didn't know what to think, so I got off my motorcycle and pulled his back, you know, dumped it back off to the side of him, and at that point he was—it was kind of like he was asleep, he was actually snoring, and I turned to see if, you know, for some reason turned around in the parking lot was another rider and I yelled to him, hey, go in my truck which was parked right there and get my cell phone and get up here and that's what he did and that's when I called 911.

Q. When you found Chris, did he have his helmet on?

A. Yes, he did.

Q. All of his gear on?

A. Complete gear.

Q. I'm sorry?

A. He had every piece of gear you can imagine on.

Q. Okay.

A. I dialed 911. The other rider that brought me the telephone, I handed him the telephone. That was the first time that I had been at that location was on the 19th and so I wasn't real familiar how to tell the emergency personnel how to get where we were, so I handed the phone off to him and he gave him directions to get there and I stayed with Chris until the paramedics arrived and before they arrived Chris had started to have a—well, actually let's back up a minute. After—all right. Let me just back up just a minute. When the gentleman, the other rider was bringing my phone up the hill to me, I started to dial 911. At that point Chris came around.

Q. What do you mean came around?

A. He started to wake up.

Q. Okay.

A. So he said, well, hold on a minute, he's coming around, he's coming around, so I said okay, and I stopped with the 911 call. Chris sat up, and he kind of flailed his arm around a little bit. You could see his motor skills were out of whack somewhat because his arm just didn't bend right. He was trying to undo his gloves. The gloves have like a big nylon strap that holds them on and he was having difficulty taking that glove off and so I asked him, "Chris, are you okay, do you need an ambulance?" And he was not able to vocally tell me yes or no, he just kind of moaned a little bit and I asked him a second time after—at that point, rather, I helped him take his helmet off and I asked him again, "Chris, do you need an ambulance, are you okay," and at that point he raised his hand to his forehead and just let out a moan and he just laid back down and that to my knowledge was the last time I saw him conscious or that he was conscious period and so at that point I dialed 911 again and that's when I handed the phone to the guy to direct the emergency personnel in. Shortly thereafter while we were waiting for the ambulance people to show up, Chris went into somewhat of a seizure.

Q. What do you mean he went into a seizure?

A. Well, he just started flailing around on the ground unconscious, and so I just basically got on top of him and held him still until the paramedics arrived.

Q. Why did you do that?

A. Because he was really thrashing around on the ground. His head was weaving and bobbing and he was having problems.

Q. You said you took his helmet off?

A. Yes, I did.

Q. Did you see any evidence of any cut or bruise on him anywhere?

A. No, not at that time.

Q. Did you notice anything torn or ripped about his clothes?

A. No.

Q. Did you observe anything that would explain or suggest what had happened?

A. To this day I can't explain what happened. I've been over it a hundred times in my head, I've been back to the site numerous times and I just can't explain why he was down in that location the way he was laid out. I can't explain it.

Thirteen days prior to the events of August 19, 1999, on August 6, 1999, Christopher had sustained a head injury while riding his motorcycle and had visited the emergency room of appellee Mercy Suburban Hospital.

According to Cynthia Papach, Christopher's mother, she was away the weekend of the accident and learned of it when she came home and had a phone message to call Mercy Suburban Hospital. When she returned that call on Sunday, August 8, an unidentified physician told her only that some shadow had been seen on the x-ray and there was nothing to worry about. She also testified that she was told that Christopher should probably stay off his bike for several weeks.

At trial plaintiff presented evidence that the CT scan performed on August 6 and interpreted remotely by Dr. Frank DuPont, III, M.D., should have been interpreted as demonstrating the presence of a subdural hematoma when it was read remotely. Plaintiff's expert, Dr. Carlos Martinez, M.D., testified that Christopher's hematoma was one that should have been identified, even accepting that teleradiology has inherent limitations of interpretation and reported as a bleed on the brain before [Christopher] left the hospital to insure proper care and management of his injury.

Dr. Stephen Levine, an expert neurologist, testified that the injury that Christopher suffered on August 6 was one that not only required follow-up, but also warranted Christopher abandoning his dirt-bike riding for a significant period of time. According to Dr. Levine, the events and injury that Christopher suffered on August 6 were causally related to the further injury that Christopher suffered on August 19 when he experienced either a reoccurrence, continuation or aggravation of his original injury. It was Dr. Levine's opinion that the original injury was causally related to [Christopher's] second injury and, ultimately, to Christopher's death.

While no one witnessed the second event of August 19, which immediately led to Christopher's death, Mark Thompson testified that he and Christopher had agreed to go riding at a practice area that evening after they were done with work. According to Mr. Thompson, it was only a few minutes after they had begun riding that Christopher got ahead of Mr. Thompson. Mr. Thompson explained that he came over a small rise along the trail they were using and saw Christopher lying in the path next to his bike. There was no one else on the trail with whom Christopher could have collided. There were no obstacles on or along the path to explain why Christopher may have fallen. There was no evidence of any accident. The way in which Christopher was laying next to his bike was inconsistent with his being thrown from the bike or his losing control of the bike while it was moving. It appeared to Mr. Thompson that Christopher had stopped his bike and either lay down next to it or fallen from a standstill. There were no cuts or bruises that Mr. Thompson noticed and no damage to the bike or unusual marks on it. According to Mr. Thompson, Christopher appeared to be either unconscious or semiconscious when he found him. Mr. Thompson was able to arouse Christopher briefly, only to have him lapse into unconsciousness and begin to shake violently as if he were suffering a seizure. Christopher appeared to be having difficulty breathing.

The first people to attend to Christopher were members of an ambulance crew from Plymouth Community Ambulance. Mark Thompson testified to their presence, but there was no identification before or at trial as to who any of the individuals associated with the company were, what experience, if any, they had with the emergency they faced, or what training they had in emergency medical care. A [typed EMS form] report offered at trial, contains only a description of what occurred in some sort of chronology and a narrative statement prepared without the name of any of the individuals who were part of the crew or the person making the report. There is nothing identifying the author of the document or providing any information about anyone who was at the scene or involved with attending to Christopher.

The description of the scene, the events that transpired, and Christopher's condition that is contained in the "ambulance report" is widely different from any other description provided by Mr. Thompson in his trial testimony or in the subsequent

medical records from the Hospital of the University of Pennsylvania. In addition to containing a description of Christopher that is wholly inconsistent with those prepared by any of the medical personnel from the hospital, the written chronology from Plymouth Community Ambulance indicates that they found Chris having difficulty breathing, but were unable to perform even the fundamental task of intubation. It was only after the arrival of a med-evac helicopter from the Hospital of the University of Pennsylvania that the doctors who apparently were a part of that team were able to quickly intubate Christopher to assist his breathing. That fact alone suggests that no experienced medical person was a part of the ambulance crew.

At the Hospital of the University of Pennsylvania, a CT scan revealed the presence of a subdural hematoma as well as massive swelling of the brain, causing herniation of the brain. Grant P. Sinson, M.D., a neurosurgeon at the Hospital of the University of Pennsylvania, immediately took Christopher to surgery to relieve the pressure on his brain. Appellees contended at trial that there were two separate hematomas, a small, resolving hematoma resulting from the accident of August 6 and a new one from August 19, and argued that the swelling was not related to the hematomas but rather to a recent, forceful blow to the side of Christopher's head.

At trial, the main theory of the defense was that Christopher had sustained a serious injury on August 19th, wholly unrelated to the injury sustained on August 6th, and died as a result of massive edema of the brain which occurred on August 19th. Appellees made extensive use at trial of the EMS report to establish that Christopher had "crashed" his motorcycle on August 19th rather than, as argued by appellant, laying it down due to symptoms he was experiencing related to his subdural hematoma.

Appellant presented expert testimony from Dr. Steven Levine, Dr. Gregory Jay, and Dr. Carlos Martinez at trial. Dr. Levine testified that the failure to order a repeat CT scan once the hematoma had been identified the next morning by the on-site radiologist constituted negligence. Dr. Levine also testified that Christopher should have been admitted to the hospital on August 6 for observation in light of his symptoms.

Dr. Levine testified that once the subdural hematoma had been diagnosed, Christopher should have been told to return to the hospital to be seen by a neurosurgeon and that the instruction to obtain follow-up care from his family doctor was below the applicable standard of care.

Dr. Martinez, a neuroradiologist, testified that the CT scan performed on August 6, 1999, clearly showed the subdural hematoma and that it was below the standard of care for the radiologist to fail to immediately identify the subdural hematoma.

I. Admissibility of EMS Report

Appellant claims that the appellees' extensive use at trial of the six-page Plymouth Community Ambulance EMS Report, over the objections of appellant, requires the award of a new trial. The trial court originally sustained hearsay objections to introduction of the comments contained in the EMS report, but later in the trial overruled those same hearsay objections, resulting in the admission of all of the hearsay statements contained in the report.

Our standard of review of an evidentiary ruling made by the trial court is extremely narrow.

"The admission or exclusion of evidence is a matter within the sound discretion of the trial court, which may only be reversed upon a showing of a manifest abuse of discretion." *Eichman v. McKeon,* 824 A.2d 305, 319 (Pa.Super.2003) (citation omitted). "To constitute reversible error, an evidentiary ruling must not only be erroneous, but also harmful or prejudicial to the complaining party." We find ourselves unable to agree with the learned trial court that the EMS report was admissible as an exception to the prohibition against hearsay.

The EMS form contains the following recitation of the events of August 19th:

Scene: Arrived to find 24 yoa male, approx. 90 Kg., lying supine at top of hill with motorcycle lying in front of pt near pt.s right leg. PD and bystanders on scene with pt. Noted that pt did not have a helmet on upon EMS arriving at the scene.

Primary: Pt unresponsive, ABC's beginning to compromise/ distress noted; pt. has aginal respirations 8-10 minute, pt still has good color. HPI: Friend of pt. was riding in front of him when he heard a crash behind him. Friend then turned his bike around to see his friend lying at the top of the hill motionless. Pt.s friend then went for help. Pt. was riding his dirt bike behind some bldg.s in the industrial park at this location when somehow he lost control of the bike but there is no witness to tell exactly what happened or what caused the accident.

PE: Pt began to have seizure activity again and was given 5 mg of Valium, IV push. After pt. was suctioned, pt was Hyperventilated with BVM and 02 before ET attempt made. Pt. exposed to look for further injuries, but did not find bruising or deformity to chest or abdomen. Abdomen still rigid upon palpation. After approx. 1 min. of drug administration pt.s seizure activity stopped and his jaw became unclenched. . . .

Flight crew entered ambulance and was given report of pt. assessment, pt condition and treatment rendered. Pt. intubated with 7.5 ET that measured 24 mm at the lips and was secured. IV attempt made with 16G in L-ACF, obtained flash but site infiltrated. Pt. was then suctioned again from ET tube obtaining approx. 300 cc's more frothy blood. IV attempt made with 16G, right ACF, unsuccessful. Pt. continually monitored and reassessed while waiting to transfer to flight crew for transport.

Pt transported class 1 to LZ at Fire Academy. Pt care transferred to Penn Star flight crew for transport back to HUP. JMZ-040981

Crew signatures:

Despite the area designated for "crew signatures", no signatures of any kind are affixed to the report—nor are the members of the crew identified in the report by name.

The trial transcript clearly evidences that appellees sought and did on numerous occasions in the presentation of the defense utilize the EMS report to establish that Christopher was, on August 19, 1999, involved in a serious accident which resulted in trauma to his head, abdomen and hand which trauma resulted in his death. Thus, appellees sought to introduce the report as proof of the matter asserted therein, namely, that Christopher had sustained serious injuries to his head, abdomen and hand, in a motorcycle accident. Because the report itself was clearly hearsay, it could be properly introduced into evidence only if it was an exception to the hearsay rule. Appellees posit two arguments in support of their claim that the report was admissible.

A. Pa.R.E. 803(6)
Appellees first claim the report is admissible pursuant to Pa.R.E. 803(6). The EMS report was obtained by the appellees from the Plymouth Ambulance Corps pursuant to a subpoena. At trial, and in the appeal to this Court, appellees argue that the report was admissible pursuant to Pa.R.E. 803(6) Records of Regularly Conducted Activity, which provides:

A memorandum, report, record, or data compilation in any form, of acts, events, or conditions, made at or near the time by, or from information transmitted by, a person with knowledge, if kept in the course of a regularly conducted business activity, and if it was the regular practice of that business activity to make the memorandum, report, record, or data compilation, all as shown by the testimony of the custodian or other qualified witness, or by certification that complies with Rule 902(11), Rule 902(12), or a statute permitting certification, unless the sources of information or other circumstances indicate lack of trustworthiness. The term "business" as used in this paragraph includes business, institution, association, profession, occupation, and calling of every kind, whether or not conducted for profit. Pa.R.E. 803(6).

The Comment to Pa.R.E. 803(6) recites that the Pennsylvania Rule is similar to F.R.E. 803(6), but with two differences. One difference is that Pa.R.E. 803(6) does not include opinions and diagnoses. This is consistent with prior Pennsylvania case law. The second difference is that Pa.R.E. 803(6) allows the court to exclude business records that would otherwise qualify for exception to the hearsay rule if the "sources of information or other circumstances indicate lack of trustworthiness." The Federal rule allows the court to do so only if "the source of information or the method or circumstances of preparation indicate lack of trustworthiness."

Appellees contend that the EMS report, made in the regular course of the ambulance service's business, qualified for admission into evidence under Rule 803(6), since the report was certified by the custodian of the records of the ambulance service pursuant to Pa.R.E. 902(11).

The EMS report at issue is in many respects similar to a police accident report as it contains what appears to be both first-hand observations by members of the crew as well as statements obtained from individuals at the scene. Police accident reports are hearsay under Pennsylvania law, not admissible under Rule 803(6).

Pennsylvania Rule of Evidence 802 provides that hearsay is not admissible unless some exception applies. "A police report prepared by an officer who is not a witness to the accident is inadmissible hearsay evidence and should not be admitted into evidence. Nor should a party be able to get such a report into evidence in an indirect manner."

The argument of appellees that the report is admissible pursuant to Rule 803(6), because it was made in the regular course of business by the ambulance corps, overlooks the requirement: either (1) that the author of the document had personal knowledge of the matters reported, or (2) that the information he reported was transmitted by another person who had personal knowledge, acting in the course of a regularly conducted activity, or (3) that it was the author's regular practice to record information transmitted by persons who had personal knowledge.

Rule 803(6) requires that all persons involved in the compilation of the data be acting in the course of a regularly conducted activity. Witnesses to and bystanders at accident scenes are not then engaged in the regular course of business.

The justification for this exception [Rule 803(6)] is that business records have a high degree of accuracy because the nation's business demands it, because the records are customarily checked for correctness, and because record keepers are trained in habits of precision. Double hearsay exists when a business record is prepared by one employee from information supplied by another employee. If both the source and the records of the information, as well as every other participant in the chain producing the record, are acting in the regular course of business, the multiple hearsay is excused by Rule 803(6). HOWEVER, IF THE SOURCE OF THE INFORMATION IS AN OUTSIDER, RULE 803(6) DOES NOT, BY ITSELF, PERMIT THE ADMISSION OF THE BUSINESS RECORD. The outsider's statement must fall within another hearsay exception to be admissible because it does not have the presumption of accuracy that statements made during the regular course of business have.

The Plymouth Ambulance EMS report, however, was clearly cobbled from information provided by bystanders not engaged in the course and scope of the business which compiled the report, the Plymouth Ambulance Service, as well as from the personal observations of the members of the ambulance crew.

A medical report is admissible under the business records exception to the hearsay rule if the report: (1) was made contemporaneously with the events it purports to relate, (2) at the time the report was prepared, it was impossible to anticipate reasons which might arise in the future for making a false entry in the original, and (3) the person responsible for the statements contained in the report is known.

There is a complete absence of any such indicia of trustworthiness in this case for no one knows who supplied the information concerning the alleged incident to the treating physician. "The problem is, however, that no party to the action nor any other person responsible for the hospital entries in question is known to have given the information on which the histories were based." Thus, we have no hesitation in concluding that the EMS report was not admissible under Pa. R.E. 803(6), as the statements at issue were provided by individuals who were not acting in the course of their employment.

We are, therefore, compelled to award appellant a new trial as to Mercy Suburban Hospital, Edward Schrieber, D.O., Kevin M. McAveney, D.O., and Frank DuPont, III, M.D., as our review of the record provides no basis upon which to conclude that the error was harmless.

Source: From Westlaw. Used with permission of Thomson/West.

Case Questions:

1. In this case, why is it important that the plaintiff's decedent had been in a prior accident and may have received a subdural hematoma?

2. Why was the EMS report considered to be hearsay?

3. Would the EMS report have been admissible if it had been signed by the crew?

4. Does the EMS report qualify as a "business record"? Why or why not?

5. According to the court, are police accident reports also considered hearsay?

6. What is "double hearsay"?

Eye on Ethics: Preserving Attorney–Client Privilege

When an attorney advises a client about a legal matter, the substance of that conversation is protected by law by an evidentiary privilege. This privilege protects the client's privacy. An attorney who is called to the stand and asked to testify about a conversation with a client can legally refuse to answer any questions. The attorney cannot be held in contempt or otherwise prosecuted for failure to answer such questions. Are legal assistants and paralegals protected by a similar privilege? The answer is no. There are some jurisdictions that have held that the presence of a third party during an attorney–client discussion may actually waive or eliminate the privilege. However, other states have included paralegals under a kind of pseudo-protection, extending the attorney's privilege to the conversation because the paralegal or legal assistant is an integral part of the legal team. However, a paralegal might not be protected by the privilege in specific instances. If that is true, then the paralegal cannot refuse to answer questions about conversations with a client. Because the conversations between the attorney and the client are supposed to be private, you should make sure that they remain so. The best way to do this is not to discuss any client business away from the office. Unless given permission to do so, it is a good idea even to refuse to give out information that the attorney represents a particular person.

Real Paralegal Life: Building a Skill Set

CYNDY ADAMS

Cyndy Adams began her legal career 28 years ago at one of the largest firms in the state at that time. She recounts, "My mentors were the two senior members, both of whom are well-respected CPA's and attorneys." Since 1992, she has worked as a paralegal specializing in domestic law. While working as a paralegal, she also attended college and completed an Associate's Degree in Paralegal Studies in 2006. Her practical experience proved to be a great asset in her classes, because "When other students were struggling with drafting pleadings in Civil Litigation I," she said, "I found the assignments easy. I often received e-mails from fellow students with questions about homework. With each semester that passed and with every class that I successfully completed, my level of confidence increased."

Adams continued, "My current and immediate past bosses have both been extremely supportive of me during my time at college. I have recently been congratulated on my achievements by judges, clerks, fellow paralegals, attorneys, clients, my church, and my family. But in the end, nothing makes my day like being told by a client that I have done a good job for them or that I helped them through a difficult situation in their legal situation. It is with a great sense of pride, commitment and responsibility that I continue my career as a paralegal. A very wise attorney told me many years ago that I had 'found my niche in life,' and I do believe he was correct."

A Day in the Life: Organizing Evidence

One aspect of Cyndy Adams's job that she likes best is attending a trial with her attorney. However, before that can happen, a lot of work must go into the case. One of the most important aspects is gathering and organizing the evidence.

"It is important to make a minimum of four copies of evidence to be presented, which is one for the Court, one for your attorney, one for the opposing attorney, and one for the paralegal. If there is a jury, make additional copies for them. Never give the original of anything to your boss, though, because it may get introduced into evidence and become lost in the abyss. However, it is a good idea to have the original in the trial notebook, clearly labeled as such, in the event the Court requires an original document. Keep a list of evidence introduced at trial, by number, description, date and approximate time submitted."

"Place photographic evidence into clear sheet protectors for ease of handling, with notes made on the back of your attorney's copy as to the subject matter of the picture. If a PowerPoint presentation is used, review it numerous times before Court, time it, and make sure that no typographical errors appear and that the flow of the slides is right. Take along a back-up CD in case the first one gets scratched or becomes corrupted. Print an outline of the PowerPoint presentation too, so that if the worst happens and the presentation, computer, or power fails, the attorney has something to rely on as a back-up."

Real Paralegal Life: Building a Skill Set

CLASSIFYING EVIDENCE

In a medical malpractice case, classify the following types of evidence:

- The doctor's narrative medical report.
- The admission forms for the plaintiff's trip to the emergency room.
- The attending nurse's testimony about the treatment that the plaintiff received.
- The plaintiff's medical bills.
- Photographs of the plaintiff's injuries.
- A charge showing the comprehensive care received by the plaintiff during his illness, prepared by the plaintiff's attorney.
- A video showing the impact of the injuries on the plaintiff's day-to-day activities.
- Testimony by the plaintiff's family about how the plaintiff has changed since his illness.

Career Prep

In Hypothetical 7-4, the plaintiff's attorney presented the doctor with a photograph of the plaintiff as a child. Is there a way that you could lay a proper foundation to have this photograph admitted? Would it be helpful if the issues in this case involved a claim of botched plastic surgery? Can you create a scenario in which such a photograph would be admissible?

Summary

An understanding of evidentiary law is extremely important for any legal profession. Evidence consists of physical items, testimony, documents, and other data presented to prove or disprove essential allegations in a civil or criminal case. The plaintiff must present evidence to support the claims made in the complaint, and the defendant will often present evidence to refute those same claims. Before evidence can be used at trial, it must be shown to be relevant and competent. An attorney who intends to present evidence must lay a proper foundation showing how the evidence is relevant and then request a ruling on admissibility by the trial court judge to allow the jury to see the evidence.

Evidence can be classified in several ways. The most common methodology used to classify evidence is by direct evidence, circumstantial evidence, or documentary evidence. Direct evidence consists of physical objects and testimony that can establish a specific fact. Direct evidence involves no inferences or presumptions; it is a conclusion in itself. Circumstantial evidence, in contrast, suggests a possible conclusion but is not definitive of that conclusion. The most common example of circumstantial evidence is footprints in the snow. Although the witness cannot testify that he or she specifically saw a person walking in the snow, the footprints suggest a conclusion. Documentary evidence consists of written documents, photographs, and any other media that can record information about a particular event. There are several important rules that govern evidence, including the best evidence rule. This rule requires that when the contents of the document are in dispute, the parties must present the original. Hearsay is another important rule. A hearsay statement is an out-of-court statement repeated by the witness on the witness stand. Hearsay statements are inherently unreliable and therefore inadmissible. However, there are many important exceptions to hearsay, including statements made to medical professionals, statements against interest, business records, and excited utterances. Paralegals are often involved in gathering evidence and preserving it for trial and must be aware of the evidentiary rules to make sure that none of them are violated, resulting in a ruling that the evidence is no longer admissible.

Key Terms

Evidence, 140
Relevance, 141
Admissibility, 143
Sustain, 143
Overrule, 143
Lay the foundation, 143
Tendering, 145
Direct evidence, 147
Circumstantial evidence, 148
Documentary evidence, 149

Testimonial evidence, 149
Demonstrative evidence, 149
Exhibit, 149
Authentication, 153
Judicial notice, 153
Self-authenticating document, 155
Privilege, 155
Marital privilege, 155
Attorney–client privilege, 155

Review Questions

1. Explain admissibility of evidence.

2. Discuss how the jury uses evidence in reaching its conclusions in a civil case.

3. What is physical evidence?

4. Discuss the differences between documentary evidence and physical evidence.

5. Is witness testimony considered evidence? Explain your answer.

6. Explain circumstantial evidence.

7. Compare and contrast direct evidence with circumstantial evidence.

8. What is relevance?

9. Explain hearsay.

10. List and explain some of the exceptions to the hearsay rule.

11. Explain how paralegals can gather evidence.

12. What is demonstrative evidence?

13. Explain "tendering" of evidence.

14. What is laying the foundation?

15. What is the best evidence rule?

16. Explain the business records exception to the hearsay rule.

17. Explain the excited utterance exception to the hearsay rule.

18. Provide some examples of documentary evidence.

19. Explain privilege.

Discussion Questions

1. Federal and state rules of evidence recognize numerous exceptions to the hearsay rule. Have the exceptions essentially swallowed up the entire reason for the objection to hearsay in the first place? Explain your answer.

2. In the era of digital storage of media, does the best evidence rule continue to make sense? Why or why not?

Exercises: Skill Builders

Go through the Baker case in Appendix B and classify the various types of evidence suggested in that factual scenario. Prepare a checklist showing the classification of each type of evidence and how it will be used.

Portfolio Assignment

Portfolio Assignment 7-1: Create an evidence checklist. Go through the sample complaint and answer in Chapters 5 and 6, respectively, and prepare an evidence chart listing the types of evidence that both the plaintiff and defendant must use to prove or disprove their allegations. Prepare an evidence chart listing each allegation and the type of evidence necessary to sustain it.

Portfolio Assignment 7-2: Understand your state's evidentiary rules. Prepare a three-page, double-spaced paper discussing your state's rules of evidence, including the definition of relevance, the classification and different types of evidence, the hearsay rule, and important exceptions to the hearsay rule.

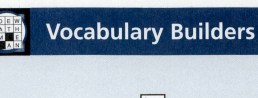

Vocabulary Builders

ACROSS

3 An out-of-court statement offered to prove a matter in contention in the lawsuit.

7 A judge's ruling in agreement with the party who raised the objection.

8 Evidence that establishes a particular fact without resort to other testimony or evidence.

9 Any fact, testimony, or physical object that tends to prove or disprove allegations raised in a case.

DOWN

1 Evidence that suggests a conclusion.

2 Any object, visual aid, model, scale drawing, or other exhibit designed to help clarify points in the trial.

4 An exception to the hearsay rule that allows a statement made spontaneously after a shocking event to be admissible at trial.

5 A judge's ruling in disagreement with the party who raised the objection.

6 A ruling on whether the jury will be allowed to view proffered evidence.

Chapter 8

Discovery

CHAPTER OBJECTIVES

The student will be able to:

- Explain the purpose of discovery.

- Provide a historical background of the development of discovery rules.

- Describe the sequence normally followed in civil discovery.

- Compare and contrast the use of depositions and interrogatories in civil discovery.

- Prepare a deposition digest.

- Explain how a paralegal participates in discovery.

- Describe the drafting of and responses to interrogatories.

- Explain the sanctions available for parties who fail to comply with discovery.

- Describe the use of protective orders in discovery.

This chapter discusses the purpose of and means to carry out discovery in civil cases.

INTRODUCTION TO DISCOVERY

discovery
The pretrial investigation process authorized and governed by the Rules of Civil Procedure; the process of investigation and collection of evidence by litigants; process in which the opposing parties obtain information about the case from each other; the process of investigation and collection of evidence by litigants.

Once the pleadings have been filed and both sides have considered the evidence that they will need to prove the allegations in the case, the next phase in civil litigation is **discovery**. In the discovery phase, both sides can learn essentially everything about the case before going to trial. Through the exchange of information, both sides can question witnesses, ask questions of the opposition, and demand the production of critical documents relied on by the opposition in proving its case. The modern approach to civil discovery is very liberal and requires the parties to produce nearly everything that they will rely on during a trial. Discovery takes place months and sometimes years before the case is ever called for trial. During the discovery phase, the parties schedule depositions, exchange interrogatories, and file additional discovery requests. For attorneys in civil cases, there are few, if any, surprises during a civil case. There are no unexpected witnesses, no undisclosed evidence, and no dramatic events. The discovery rules were drafted in such a way that they encourage the parties to know as much as possible about the case prior to trial. The reason for this is commonsense: The courts reason that if both parties know everything about the case prior to trial, they might be less inclined to bring questionable cases to a jury. Whether or not that theory holds water is still an open question.

PURPOSE OF DISCOVERY

The basic purpose of discovery is to learn the facts of a case, but discovery actually serves several different functions, including:

- Clarification of the facts.
- Preservation of testimony for later use.
- Avoiding surprise at trial.
- Narrowing the issues.

Clarification of the Facts

Although the plaintiff's attorney is required to conduct an investigation before filing the complaint, this investigation is hardly exhaustive. Once the case has begun in earnest, it is time for the plaintiff to clarify every vital fact in the case. This process includes pinning down witness testimony, questioning the defendant, and examining every pertinent document. Before the pleadings are filed, the plaintiff's legal team is limited in the depth of its investigation for the simple reason that many of the discovery tools are not available until the complaint and answer have been served. Like the plaintiff, the defendant will also wish to conduct a thorough investigation and actively participate in all phases of discovery. Obviously, the focus of each party is different. The plaintiff will seek out any and all evidence that supports the claims of the complaint, while keeping an eye out for negative or damaging facts. The defendant will attempt to learn as many details about the case as possible to attack the allegations raised in the plaintiff's complaint. The defendant will also stay alert to potentially damaging information that might push the case toward settlement instead of trial. In either event, discovery is the vehicle to clarify all positive and negative facts in the case for both parties.

Preservation of Testimony for Later Use

Another important aspect of discovery is the preservation of witness testimony. In civil discovery, the parties are allowed to question witnesses thoroughly weeks or even months before the trial is ever scheduled. If a witness should become unavailable at the actual trial, the Rules of Civil Procedure permit the parties to present the transcript of that question-and-answer session instead of the live witness. Although presenting a live person is always better and more effective than simply reading a transcript to a jury, in some cases it is unavoidable. Preserving this testimony allows both parties to proceed to trial in the event that a witness is no longer available to testify.

Avoiding Surprise at Trial

We have all watched TV court dramas in which a surprise witness suddenly appears and completely changes the dynamics of a case. Although this makes for exciting television, in the real world of civil litigation, such an event should be rare if not completely impossible. A party who conducts thorough discovery should know the names, addresses, and substantial testimony of all witnesses in the case. If not, then the failing is with the legal team, not the justice process. Although it takes much of the drama out of the trial, an attorney handling a modern civil case should have no surprises when it comes to trial.

Narrowing the Issues

Discovery is also a powerful tool that allows all parties to narrow the disputed issues prior to trial. By pinpointing the precise issues in contention, and by forcing parties to agree on others, discovery techniques bring out the main points in contention in the case and eliminate redundant or uncontested issues. At the conclusion of discovery, all parties in the case will be aware of exactly what the opposition claims are the facts in contention and, just as important, what they are willing to stipulate. Here, a **stipulation** refers to facts, evidence, or testimony that a party is willing to adopt as true without the need for further proof.

stipulation
An agreement between attorneys and parties in a case about a procedural or factual issue.

SHORT HISTORY OF DISCOVERY

The rules governing discovery in civil cases have changed dramatically in the past 100 years. Prior to the creation of modern discovery statutes and rules, it was quite common for the opposing parties in civil cases to conceal evidence, hide witnesses, and engage in a wide variety of practices that modern practitioners would consider unethical (if not illegal). However, from an efficiency standpoint, such practices also committed the sin of wasting a considerable amount of the court's time. A surprise witness who debunks the plaintiff's entire case might make for an exciting spectacle, but such testimony should have been discovered long before the case ever came to trial. Proper discovery has more to do with saving time and resources by forcing the parties to learn as much as possible about the case before it is ever scheduled for a jury trial.

However, coming around to the modern approach to civil discovery took considerable time and faced tremendous opposition. Parties were (and remain) reluctant to share damaging information in a civil case, knowing full well that it will be used against them. Many attorneys might be more than willing to learn as much about the opposing witnesses as possible but are considerably less enthusiastic about the opposition learning as much about their own.

Discovery rules, which began to be seriously reconsidered and redrafted in the middle of the 20th century, provided for more extensive exchange of information than had ever been seen before. In addition to requiring that the parties freely exchange witness names, documents, and all other evidence, the revised discovery rules also provided courts with the authority to impose sanctions against non-complying parties, including striking provisions of pleadings, disallowing specific claims or defenses, and even dismissing the case in its entirety.

Under modern discovery rules, all parties have the duty to engage in an open exchange of information. This duty is continuous throughout the litigation. If a party receives updates on information, it must provide those updates to the opposition. Some states continue to require that the parties file copies of all discovery obtained with the court, whereas other states have abolished this requirement.

Hypothetical 8-1

Carla is a witness for the plaintiff. She recently changed her address and moved out of state. If the defendant is not informed, he will attempt to serve a trial subpoena on Carla at the wrong address, and she will not be located. In that case, Carla will not give testimony that is potentially harmful to the plaintiff. Does the plaintiff have a duty to provide Carla's new address to the defendant, even though he could conceivably find her himself?

Answer: The plaintiff must provide Carla's new address as soon as the plaintiff learns that she has moved. The discovery rules are clear on this point: A party has a continuous duty to update information prior to trial, and even though her testimony is potentially damaging, the failure to update her address would violate the discovery rules and could open the plaintiff to court-ordered sanctions.

Modern Approaches to Discovery

Under the modern rules of discovery, an attorney can request information and receive it even though it may not be admissible at trial. The opposing party must disclose the information, even though there may be a sound objection to it on the grounds of relevance, prejudice, or some other matter. Modern discovery rules provide that the parties may argue about admissibility at trial but not during the discovery process. The premise behind current discovery rules is that nearly anything can be requested and produced, with a few important exceptions. This approach is most clearly enumerated in the Federal Rules of Civil Procedure.

Rules of Civil Procedure

The Federal Rules of Civil Procedure are embodied in Title 28 of the United States Code and govern civil actions in federal courts across the nation. The federal rules have created an orderly and systematic approach to the many issues that arise in civil actions, not the least of which involves discovery. In the federal rules, the discovery rules are found in Rules 26–37 and govern issues as disparate as the duty of disclosure to the sanctions that a judge can impose for a party's failure to comply with discovery. Because so many states have adopted these rules, in whole or in part, we rely on the federal discovery rules throughout the rest of this chapter.

DISCOVERY IN MODERN CIVIL PRACTICE

In modern practice, attorneys routinely file discovery requests along with the initial pleadings. Discovery has become very much a drill that is followed in every case, despite the wide variety of issues addressed in civil cases. Although the rules do not create any set pattern for discovery activities, modern practitioners generally follow a similar pattern.

Sequence of Discovery

Once the pleadings in a civil case have been filed and served on opposing parties, the discovery phase begins. As we will shortly see, there are many different vehicles for discovering facts about a case, but most practitioners follow a similar pattern based on the information that can be developed through the different discovery techniques. For instance, many attorneys use the following sequence:

1. Interrogatories are filed on opposing party.
2. Request for production of documents.
3. Depositions.
4. Request for physical examination.
5. Request to admit.

This sequence is followed, even though the rules set no pattern for discovery requests and certainly set no order among the various methods to gather information, as Figure 8.1 shows. This sequence offers several advantages. The practitioner can learn specific answers to questions from interrogatories, follow up with requests to produce the documents on which these answers are based, and then use both to question witnesses in the case. Following that, the attorney can decide if a physical examination is needed and finally pin down testimony that both sides can agree to through a request to admit.

Supplementing Discovery Responses

As we have already seen, modern discovery rules not only allow parties to request and receive a wide variety of information but also impose on the parties the obligation to supplement discovery responses as new information becomes available (see Figure 8.2).

The rule about supplementation of information applies not only to witnesses and discovery responses, but also particularly to expert witnesses. (See Figure 8.5.)

FIGURE 8.1
Timing and Sequence of Discovery

Unless the court upon motion, for the convenience of parties and witnesses and in the interests of justice, orders otherwise, methods of discovery may be used in any sequence, and the fact that a party is conducting discovery, whether by deposition or otherwise, does not operate to delay any other party's discovery.

FIGURE 8.2
Supplementation of Disclosures and Responses

Source: Rule 26(e) Federal Rules of Civil Procedure.

A party who has made a disclosure under subdivision (a) or responded to a request for discovery with a disclosure or response is under a duty to supplement or correct the disclosure or response to include information thereafter acquired if ordered by the court or in the following circumstances:

(1) A party is under a duty to supplement at appropriate intervals its disclosures under subdivision (a) if the party learns that in some material respect the information disclosed is incomplete or incorrect and if the additional or corrective information has not otherwise been made known to the other parties during the discovery process or in writing.

(2) A party is under a duty seasonably to amend a prior response to an interrogatory, request for production, or request for admission if the party learns that the response is in some material respect incomplete or incorrect and if the additional or corrective information has not otherwise been made known to the other parties during the discovery process or in writing.

FIGURE 8.3
Meeting of Parties;
Planning for
Discovery

Source: Rule 26(f) Federal
Rules of Civil Procedure.

> Except in categories of proceedings exempted from initial disclosure under Rule 26(a)(1)(E) or when otherwise ordered, the parties must, as soon as practicable and in any event at least 21 days before a scheduling conference is held or a scheduling order is due under Rule 16(b), confer to consider the nature and basis of their claims and defenses and the possibilities for a prompt settlement or resolution of the case, to make or arrange for the disclosures required by Rule 26(a)(1), and to develop a proposed discovery plan that indicates the parties' views and proposals.

Duty of Disclosure

Under Rule 26(f), the parties in a civil suit must meet or otherwise arrange a plan of discovery that they will follow throughout this phase of the lawsuit. Among the items that they must arrange during this conference are:

- Changes in the timing, sequence, or requirement of disclosure.
- Subjects on which discovery may be needed.
- A schedule for completing all discovery.
- What, if any, limitations should be imposed on discovery (see Figure 8.3).

Expert Witnesses in Modern Discovery

Under the rules of discovery, an opposing party is permitted to learn not only the identity of any expert witness relied on by the other side but also the pertinent details of this expert's proposed testimony. A party must release the subject matter about which the expert is expected to testify and the substance of the expert's testimony.

Discovery rules essentially create two classifications of experts: those who will testify and those who will not. (See Figure 8.4.) For witnesses who will testify, the party must provide the following:

- The full name of the expert witness.
- Address and telephone numbers.
- The subject matter about which the expert is expected to testify.
- The substance of the expert's testimony, including the expert's ultimate opinion about these matters.
- A summary of the expert's conclusions.

The rules change, however, when the expert is simply sought out for advice and will not be used at trial. In that situation, the party must simply identify the expert. No further information is required.

Electronic Discovery

Some studies show that up to 90% of all documents produced by businesses, law firms, and individuals are created on a computer. Traditional discovery has always focused on documents, especially those that reside in files; however, with modern technology, it is just as

FIGURE 8.4
Discovery Rules
Regarding Experts

Source: Rule 26(e) Federal
Rules of Civil Procedure.

> With respect to testimony of an expert from whom a report is required under subdivision (a)(2)(B) the duty extends both to information contained in the report and to information provided through a deposition of the expert, and any additions or other changes to this information shall be disclosed by the time the party's disclosures under Rule 26(a)(3) are due.

FIGURE 8.5
Duty to Supplement
Discovery Responses

> A party is under a duty to supplement discovery responses when the party:
>
> - Obtains new information that shows that a previous response was incorrect.
> - Obtains new information that makes the previous response incorrect, even though it was correct at the time that it was made.

likely that an important memorandum or other piece of writing resides on a computer hard drive, which is one reason electronic discovery has become such an important part of any discovery phase. Attorneys and paralegals must adapt their discovery processes to take into account that some of the information they will need for trial will come from someone's computer. This need forces legal professionals to think like computer forensic experts. These individuals are skilled in data retrieval, even from devices on which portions of the material have been written over or damaged. However, before a paralegal can start sifting through computer files, it is important to realize that the legal team must first get access to the data files, which is not always a simple process. Unlike law enforcement officials who can simply seize computers and hard drives, civil litigants must use traditional discovery tools to retrieve advanced data. Whenever the attorney and paralegal have reason to believe that important information may be stored on a computer, the legal team should notify the person in possession that it may contain evidence that will be used in litigation. Such a letter may contain a demand that the person preserve the data intact and not seek to destroy it. Using various discovery techniques, including requests to produce, the legal team may then obtain access to the computer files and make back-up copies of the data contained in those files.

DISCOVERY METHODS

In civil cases, there are several different methods that parties can use to learn more detail about the case. These include:

- Depositions.
- Interrogatories.
- Requests for production of documents.
- Request for physical and/or mental examination.
- Request to admit.

Depositions

deposition
A discovery tool in a question-and-answer format in which the attorney verbally questions a party or a witness under oath.

A **deposition** is a face-to-face session between the attorneys in the case and a witness. The witness is sworn in and then asked general questions about the issues surrounding the litigation. The questions and answers are taken down by a **court reporter** and later printed off in a transcript. If the witness becomes unavailable to testify during the trial, the transcript of the deposition can be read instead. Although depositions are common in civil cases, they are rarely used in criminal cases. In criminal cases, the defendant has the right to face his or her accusers, and therefore, depositions are of little use. In a civil deposition, attorneys for both sides can ask broad-ranging questions, not only about the accident itself but also about any potential bias on the part of the witness or any other matter related to the case.

court reporter
Individual who transcribes the court proceedings and certifies their authenticity.

Types of Depositions

The rules provide for two different types of depositions: oral and written. Depositions on written questions are relatively rare and consist of one party sending written questions to witnesses in the case. Oral depositions are far more common. These depositions are governed by Rule 30 and its various subparts.

Preparing for a Deposition

A deposition is, in many ways, similar to the testimony that a witness will give at trial. The witness will be asked questions on direct examination, and the opposing attorney has the right to cross-examine the witness. However, the similarities between trial testimony and deposition testimony end there. Depositions are much more relaxed affairs than trial testimony. For one thing, they are rarely held in courthouses. The most common place to conduct a deposition is at one of the attorneys' offices, though almost any venue will serve. Before questioning can begin, the attorney must prepare. Preparation for a deposition includes a close review of all relevant facts of the case, as well as a review of the pleadings, other witness statements, and any other sources that can provide details. Many attorneys also rely on general question forms to make sure they ask sufficient

FIGURE 8.6
Rule 30. Deposition Upon Oral Examination

Source: Rule 30 Federal Rules of Civil Procedure.

(a) When Depositions May Be Taken; When Leave Required.
(1) A party may take the testimony of any person, including a party, by deposition upon oral examination without leave of court except as provided in paragraph (2). The attendance of witnesses may be compelled by subpoena as provided in Rule 45.

questions. There are also some basic guidelines that most attorneys adhere to in fashioning questions for witnesses in a deposition, including:

- The questions must be clear.
- The attorney should avoid questions that require yes/no answers.
- The attorney should ask the deponent to specify the information source for his or her replies.

Setting a Deposition

Setting a deposition can be as simple as issuing a Notice of Deposition for a specific date and time and waiting for the witness and other attorneys to appear. However, the real world of litigation follows a more complicated system. Attorneys often attempt to work out the time and place of a deposition around their schedules and those of the opposing attorneys, considered common courtesy among professionals. The job of coordinating the date and time of the deposition usually falls to the attorney's paralegal, who may need to call the other attorneys' offices several times before arriving at a mutually convenient time. Generally, the witness is not given such a courtesy (see Figure 8.6).

Notice of Deposition

A Notice of Deposition, also called a Notice of Examination, is a simple form that sets the date, time, and place for a deposition (see Figures 8.7 and 8.8). In some states, it may be issued in conjunction with a witness subpoena to appear for a deposition. In any event, the notice serves to

FIGURE 8.7
Notice of Deposition Form

STATE OF PLACID
DISTRICT COURT
LONDON COUNTY

Sherlock Holmes
(Plaintiff)

CIVIL ACTION: 04-100

v.

Professor James Moriarty, individually
and as owner, operator of Moriarty
Transport Trucking Co. (Defendant)

TO: Mrs. Joan Hudson
      221 B Baker Street
      London, PL 28655

PLEASE TAKE NOTICE that at 9:00 a.m. on April 10, 2006, at the offices of Deborah L. Bolstridge, Attorney at Law, 21 Robin's Wood Place, Bohemia, PL 28655, the Plaintiff in the above-entitled action will take the videotaped deposition of Madge Manager, as witness upon oral examination, pursuant to Rule 30 of the Placid Rules of Civil Procedure, before a Court Reporter or before some other person authorized by law to administer oaths. The oral examination will begin at 9:00 a.m. and will continue from day to day until completed. The oral examination will be videotaped. You are invited to attend and cross-examine.

This the 6th day of March, 2006.

FIGURE 8.8
Rule 30. Notice of Deposition

Source: Rule 30(b) Federal Rules of Civil Procedure.

(b) Notice of Examination
(1) A party desiring to take the deposition of any person upon oral examination shall give reasonable notice in writing to every other party to the action. The notice shall state the time and place for taking the deposition and the name and address of each person to be examined, if known, and, if the name is not known, a general description sufficient to identify the person or the particular class or group to which the person belongs. If a subpoena duces tecum is to be served on the person to be examined, the designation of the materials to be produced as set forth in the subpoena shall be attached to, or included in, the notice.

alert all parties that a deposition has been set and that they should attend if they want the opportunity to question the witness thoroughly.

Conducting the Deposition

The rules provide that any person can be deposed, whether the person is a witness or a party. In a civil case, both the plaintiff and the defendant will be deposed, as well as any other witnesses with information about any aspect of the case.

 COMMUNICATION TIP

On a daily basis, a paralegal will find that he or she spends a great deal of time on the telephone speaking with other legal professionals, many of whom represent opposing parties in pending cases. Most of these individuals are honest, hardworking, and perfectly reputable. However, there will be times when you come in contact with legal professionals who are not as scrupulous as you might like. Many attorneys and paralegals make it a habit to follow up any verbal communication with a confirming letter. In fact, setting up the template for a letter is remarkably easy given the availability of word processing programs. The follow-up letter can be as simple as confirming the details of a telephone call, but it can have dramatic effects on the case. Suppose, for instance, that the attorney in this chapter's "Case in Point," had listed the April 4 report as part of what he was providing to the opposing party. He might easily have avoided paying $1,750 in fines. Here is a sample confirming letter:

Allison Attorney, Attorney at Law
100 Maple Street
Placid City, PC 00550

June 5, 2006

Re: Calvin Client v. Darrell Defendant
Case No. 07CV9786

Laura Lawyer
1020 Legal Place
Placid City, PL 00550

Dear Ms. Lawyer,

This letter will confirm our conversation today in which you kindly agreed to our request to schedule the deposition for our client on a Thursday or Friday afternoon in the next two weeks. As I understand our conversation, you will need to check with Judge Roberts to see if you are scheduled for trial next week and, if you are not, then we will schedule the deposition of our client, Calvin Client, at your office either Thursday, June 8, or Friday, June 9, any time between 1:00 p.m. and 5:00 p.m. If those dates are not convenient, we will then schedule the deposition for Thursday, June 15, or Friday, June 16.

Thank you for your cooperation in this matter. If I have misstated any portion of our conversation, please contact me at 555-1212 to discuss the matter.

Sincerely,

Paul Paralegal
Legal Assistant for Allison Attorney, Esq.

FIGURE 8.9

Rule 29. Stipulations Regarding Discovery Procedure

Source: Rule 29 Federal Rules of Civil Procedure.

> Unless otherwise directed by the court, the parties may by written stipulation (1) provide that depositions may be taken before any person, at any time or place, upon any notice, and in any manner and when so taken may be used like other depositions, and (2) modify other procedures governing or limitations placed upon discovery, except that stipulations extending the time provided in Rules 33, 34, and 36 for responses to discovery may, if they would interfere with any time set for completion of discovery, for hearing of a motion, or for trial, be made only with the approval of the court.

FIGURE 8.10

Rule 30. Schedule and Duration; Motion to Terminate or Limit Examination

Source: Rule 30(d) Federal Rules of Civil Procedure.

> (1) Any objection during a deposition must be stated concisely and in a non-argumentative and non-suggestive manner. A person may instruct a deponent not to answer only when necessary to preserve a privilege, to enforce a limitation directed by the court, or to present a motion under Rule 30(d)(4).

Opening Stipulations

When the day of the deposition arrives, the attorneys usually meet beforehand to work out some stipulations (see Figure 8.9). A stipulation is an agreement about facts or issues. For a deposition, the parties might enter into several stipulations regarding the admissibility of the testimony, including:

- That any question or answer deemed objectionable shall be reserved for argument at trial.
- That the parties have not waived attorney–client privilege.
- That the witness waives his or her right to review the transcript of the deposition.

Reserving Objections

Because the deposition is taken weeks or months before the trial, attorneys routinely reserve the right to object to the questions offered during a deposition. Because the rules about deposition questions are so liberal and essentially allow the attorneys to ask any question, whether relevant or not, the attorneys generally begin the deposition by reserving their right to challenge testimony at a later date. Simply because an attorney can ask about a matter during a deposition does not mean that that same testimony will be admissible during the trial. By reserving an objection, the attorney assures that he or she will be able to challenge the testimony before the jury hears it. (See Figure 8.10.)

Permissible Questions

The rules about questions in a deposition are extraordinarily liberal. Essentially, the attorneys can ask the witness anything, while recognizing that some of the answers may not be admissible later at trial (see Figure 8.11). Attorneys are free to ask questions only tangentially connected to the case. The only exception is when the question crosses into privileged matters.

A witness cannot be compelled to answer questions protected by the attorney–client privilege or any legally recognized privilege. If such a question is asked, the witness may simply refuse to answer it. Unlike other refusals that may lead to court sanctions, a witness who refuses to reveal privileged information cannot be punished for doing so. Recognized privileges include:

- Attorney–client privilege
- Pastor–penitent privilege
- Marital privilege
- Doctor–patient privilege

FIGURE 8.11

Scope of Questions in Depositions

Source: Rule 26(b)(1) Federal Rules of Civil Procedure.

> Parties may obtain discovery regarding any matter, not privileged, that is relevant to the claim or defense of any party, including the existence, description, nature, custody, condition, and location of any books, documents, or other tangible things and the identity and location of persons having knowledge of any discoverable matter.

SPOT THE ISSUE!

Wally Whistleblower was fired last year by Spurious, Inc. Wally alleges that he was fired when he brought the company's questionable accounting practices to the attention of the shareholders. He has brought a wrongful termination suit against Spurious, Inc. Wally's attorney, Laura Litigator, is questioning a Spurious employee at a deposition. Also present at the deposition is Barry Barrister, representing Spurious, Inc. Laura asks the following question:

Q: At any point in your employment with Spurious, did you ever observe any accounting practices that you thought were questionable, unethical, or illegal?

A: Well, I would have to say—

Mr. Barrister: Objection. This question goes into privileged matter. I direct the witness not to answer this question.

Is this question objectionable? What privilege could Mr. Barrister be asserting in this case? Is this a legitimate objection or could it be subject to a motion for sanctions under the discovery rules?

Cross-Examining a Witness during the Deposition

The opposing attorney is also permitted to question the witness during the deposition (see Figure 8.12). Technically, this process qualifies as cross-examination and can, in some instances, become quite heated. The attorney for the opposition has the same latitude in questioning the witness as the other attorney, and cross-examining a witness during a deposition makes a great deal of sense. It is better to pin down all possible points at this stage rather than wait for surprises at trial.

Use of Exhibits

Attorneys and witnesses can use exhibits during the trial, including photographs, diagrams, and anything else to help illuminate the witness's testimony. When the deposition has been concluded, the court reporter will include the exhibit with the transcript.

Persons Present at the Deposition

Whenever a deposition is scheduled, there are several people present. They include:

- The deponent
- The attorneys
- The court reporter
- The parties

deponent
The party or witness who is questioned during a deposition.

Witness. The witness or **deponent** is always present at the deposition. Although there are provisions that allow attorneys to conduct depositions over the telephone, the most common practice is for all parties to be physically present.

Attorneys. Attorneys are the persons who request the deposition, and therefore, they are present to ask questions. Generally, a legal representative for each party in the case will be present. Both the plaintiff's and the defendant's attorneys are permitted to ask questions during the deposition, with the attorney who set the deposition beginning the questioning and then turning the witness over to the opposing attorney for cross-examination.

FIGURE 8.12
Rule 30. Cross-Examination at Deposition
Source: Rule 30(c) Federal Rules of Civil Procedure.

(c) Examination and Cross-Examination; Record of Examination; Oath; Objections

Examination and cross-examination of witnesses may proceed as permitted at the trial under the provisions of the Federal Rules of Evidence except Rules 103 and 615. The officer before whom the deposition is to be taken shall put the witness on oath or affirmation and shall personally, or by someone acting under the officer's direction and in the officer's presence, record the testimony of the witness.

FIGURE 8.13

Rule 30. Court Reporter

Source: Rule 30(b)(4) Federal Rules of Civil Procedure.

(4) Unless otherwise agreed by the parties, a deposition shall be conducted before an officer appointed or designated under Rule 28 and shall begin with a statement on the record by the officer that includes (A) the officer's name and business address; (B) the date, time and place of the deposition; (C) the name of the deponent; (D) the administration of the oath or affirmation to the deponent; and (E) an identification of all persons present.

Court Reporter.   A court reporter is a person who has been trained to record testimony, usually on a stenograph machine (see Figure 8.13). A court reporter takes down everything said at the deposition, no matter who is speaking. Modern stenograph machines come with computer hardware and software programs that allow the court reporter to convert shorthand script to readable English. The court reporter is also the person who swears in the witness before the deposition begins.

Parties.   The parties are also permitted to be present when others are being deposed. However, in most cases, the attorney will suggest that the party not attend the deposition. The client may need to work or attend to other responsibilities, and sometimes having the client present is more of a distraction to the attorney than assistance.

Duration of the Deposition

The Federal Rules of Civil Procedure limit the duration of a deposition to seven hours during one day (see Figure 8.14). If an attorney needs additional time, he or she must petition the judge for an extension. There are times when it is reasonable for a deposition to last longer than a single day. Consider the issues raised in class-action lawsuits or highly complicated civil actions. In those cases, attorneys routinely request additional time to conduct depositions of the main witnesses in the case.

After the Deposition

Once the deposition has been completed, the court reporter gathers together all notes and records and prepares a transcript. Preparing the transcript sometimes takes days or even weeks, even in this era of computer stenograph machines. The court reporter must go through the entire transcript and ensure that there are no errors.

Transcript

Once completed, the transcript is sent to the attorneys who attended the deposition and the witness who was questioned. See Figure 8.15.

Reviewing the Transcript.   The Rules of Civil Procedure allow a witness to review the transcript of the deposition and make changes in the wording, but only in limited contexts. The witness cannot, for example, change the substance of the testimony but can correct typographical errors or words that were transcribed incorrectly (see Figure 8.16). The rules provide a 30-day time period for a witness to correct the transcript once it has been completed. After that time, the witness is not permitted to make any changes.

Deposition Digest

deposition digest
A summary of deposition testimony of a witness.

Once the transcript has been generated, it usually falls to the paralegal to prepare a **deposition digest** or deposition summary (see Figure 8.17). This document summarizes the critical points raised in the deposition and cross-references them by the page number on which they appear in the transcript. Deposition transcripts are useful tools that help attorneys and others understand the important points in a witness's testimony without having to read the entire transcript to ferret them out. You will find an example of a deposition digest at the end of this chapter.

FIGURE 8.14

Time Limits on Depositions

Source: Rule 30(d)(2) Federal Rules of Civil Procedure.

(2) Unless otherwise authorized by the court or stipulated by the parties, a deposition is limited to one day of seven hours. The court must allow additional time consistent with Rule 26(b)(2) if needed for a fair examination of the deponent or if the deponent or another person, or other circumstance, impedes or delays the examination.

FIGURE 8.15
First Page of Transcript

STATE OF COLUMBIA
COUNTY OF HALEY
CHARLES REGINALD,

    Plaintiff,

    vs.

COLUMBIA RAILWAY LINES
RAILWAY COMPANY, TOWN OF CLING,
and STEVE W. BLUE,
    Defendant.

IN THE GENERAL COURT OF JUSTICE
SUPERIOR COURT DIVISION
FILE NUMBER: 98 CVS 1001

DEPOSITION OF BENNIE HALL

March 29, 1994

APPEARANCES:

For the Plaintiff: I. M. Lawyer
DEWEY, EATHAM AND HOWE, P.A.
89 N. Montford Street
Morganton, NC 28655
(704) 438-6153

For the Defendants: Rip Offe
Offe & Going
800 Spruce St.
Cling, NC 28777
704-555-1000

Hugh Burpe
Eaten, Swallow & Burpe
900 Apple Tree St.
Asheville, NC 28801
704-555-9999

Interrogatories

interrogatories
A discovery tool in the form of a series of written questions that are answered by the party in writing, to be answered under oath.

Interrogatories are written questions sent to the parties in the case. The party must respond in writing and thoroughly answer the questions. Whereas depositions can be used on both parties and witnesses, interrogatories are reserved for parties only.

What Are Interrogatories?

Interrogatories are official documents served by one party on another that ask a series of questions. These questions must be thoroughly answered and returned to the requesting party within a specific

FIGURE 8.16
Review by Witness; Changes; Signing
Source: Rule 30(e) Federal Rules of Civil Procedure.

If requested by the deponent or a party before completion of the deposition, the deponent shall have 30 days after being notified by the officer that the transcript or recording is available in which to review the transcript or recording and, if there are changes in form or substance, to sign a statement reciting such changes and the reasons given by the deponent for making them. The officer shall indicate in the certificate prescribed by subdivision (f)(1) whether any review was requested and, if so, shall append any changes made by the deponent during the period allowed.

FIGURE 8.17
Deposition Digest

Deposition Summary
Howell v. Howell
11-6-05

DIGEST TO DEPOSITION OF **Ruth Bowles Lee** October 28, 2005

Page#   Testimony:

3-4   Witness resides at 6 Bluebird Road, Morganton, NC; she is married to lawyer Phil Lee and is self-employed. She runs a business called Appraiser's, Inc., for personal property appraisals and runs a space in an antique mall. She has a second business, Antique Estimates, Inc,; she has a partner and has operated this for 22 years doing estate auctions and estate sales.

4   She has been in the appraisal business almost 23 years. 12 years previously, she took the exam for The American Society of Appraisers and passed it. When she took the exam she had already been in business 10 years.

5   She has to be re-certified with 100 classroom hours every 5 years and standards examinations; she was re-certified in February 2005. She also keeps current with periodicals, trade journals, etc. She keeps current publications for American/English antiques and popular collectibles and orders new publications as her business requires.

6   Discussion of her exam to be certified in antiques, decorative arts, and residential contents.

7   She is certified in all these areas.

7   On July 20, 2005, she appraised personal items at 10 Beaver View Court, Morganton; some items, boxed in the garage, she did not appraise.

7-9   Discussion of review of home contents with Mrs. Howell and access; also, her written report.

9-10   Discussion of first three items, Franklin Mint Plate through Danbury Mint Plates. She has valued these kinds of items many times. Although these producers publish catalogues discussing values of their items, she knows from her experience that the items are a "hard sell" and the value deflates terrifically after purchase. The values the publications would show are not "real-world" values.

SURF'S UP!

VIDEO DEPOSITIONS

Although this chapter discusses the more traditional approach to depositions—that is, oral questions taken before a court reporter or stenographer—there is a growing trend of using video depositions. Companies all over the United States specialize in providing professional video deposition services. Companies such as Affordable Video Solutions (www.affordablevideosolutions.com) and Video Resources (www.videoresources.com) specialize in setting up, recording, and then indexing video depositions. A deposition recorded in this manner has several distinct advantages over the traditional method. For one thing, if the witness becomes unavailable, the party seeking to admit the testimony can simply play the video for the jury. Under the old system, the only way to get the absent witness's testimony before the jury would be to have the attorney or someone else read it aloud. No matter how well a person reads a transcript, jurors become quickly bored. When they can actually see the person as he or she appeared at the deposition, they pay closer attention. Video depositions also help capture a witness's demeanor, allow the witness to present visual aids, and give the attorney the option of a dramatic presentation during the trial. These days, companies not only offer a video service but also the possibility of indexing various videos, recording them in digital format for quick retrieval, and even juxtaposing one video segment with another (such as showing how the witness contradicted his or her own previous testimony).

FIGURE 8.18

Rule 33. Interrogatories to Parties

Source: Rule 33(a) Federal Rules of Civil Procedure.

> Without leave of court or written stipulation, any party may serve upon any other party written interrogatories, not exceeding 25 in number including all discrete subparts, to be answered by the party served or, if the party served is a public or private corporation or a partnership or association or governmental agency, by any officer or agent, who shall furnish such information as is available to the party.

time period (see Figure 8.18). If filed by the plaintiff along with the complaint, the defendant has 45 days to file an answer. Otherwise, a party must reply within 30 days. Interrogatories are governed by Rule 33 of the Federal Rules of Civil Procedure.

Who Can Receive Interrogatories?

Only parties to the suit are authorized to send or receive interrogatories. Witnesses cannot be served with interrogatories. The party to whom the interrogatories are sent must answer the questions in writing. Usually, the legal team works with the client to fashion answers and then takes responsibility for preparing them in their final form. Clients usually sign a verification that accompanies the interrogatory answers. The verification is the client's personal oath that the answers contain true and correct information (see Figure 8.19).

Limitations on Interrogatories

Just as we saw with depositions, a party can object to a question posed in an interrogatory on the basis of privilege. However, a party can also raise additional challenges to interrogatories, including the following:

- The information sought is unreasonably cumulative or duplicative.
- Discovery is unduly burdensome and expensive.
- General grounds, including specific objections to individual questions.

FIGURE 8.19

Interrogatory Verification

> ### STATE OF PLACID
> ### DISTRICT COURT
> ### LONDON COUNTY
>
> Sherlock Holmes (Plaintiff)   **CIVIL ACTION: 04-100**
>
> v.
>
> Professor James Moriarty,
> individually and as owner,
> operator of Moriarty
> Transport Trucking Co.
> (Defendant)
>
> To: Neal Bevans
>   Attorney for Plaintiff Sherlock Holmes
>
> VERIFICATION
>
> I hereby certify and attest upon my oath, that the following answers to Plaintiff's First Interrogatories are complete and truthful to the best of my knowledge.
>
> _____
>
>   Professor James Moriarty, Defendant
>   This the ___ day of February, 2005

FIGURE 8.20
Objecting to Interrogatory Questions

Source: Rule 33(b)(4) Federal Rules of Civil Procedure.

> (4) All grounds for an objection to an interrogatory shall be stated with specificity. Any ground not stated in a timely objection is waived unless the party's failure to object is excused by the court for good cause shown.

Unreasonably Cumulative or Burdensome. As we will see subsequently in this chapter, a party is always free to interpose the objection to a discovery device that it is unduly burdensome. When the opposing party has already obtained the information or is simply posing questions to harass or wear down the party, the client can object to the judge. This objection can apply to the entire set of interrogatories.

Objections to Specific Questions. In addition to a general objection about the burdensome nature of the interrogatories, the party can object to the issues raised in specific questions, again based on the burdensomeness of the question or because it infringes on some legally protected interest, such as privilege (see Figure 8.20).

Drafting Interrogatories

The best place to start when drafting interrogatory questions is with the complaint. This document sets out the main issues raised by the plaintiff and therefore serves as a good starting point for both parties. See Figures 8.21 and 8.22 for frequent topics contained in interrogatories and a sample caption page. The plaintiff asks questions related to proving the elements of the complaint, whereas the defendant poses questions attempting to disprove it. After that, a party who is drafting interrogatories reviews the answer. These two pleadings provide the issues in the case and serve as the bedrock for the interrogatory questions that must be posed to both the plaintiff and defendant.

These days, it is very common for law offices to have forms of interrogatories ready to go at the click of a mouse. However, simply because there is a computer-generated form does not mean that the form will comply with the facts of the case. Forms can provide a good starting point, but they are no substitute for clear thinking and processing of the information provided in a specific case.

In addition to relying on the pleadings and forms, legal practitioners who draft interrogatories refer to form books, similar files, and even recent appellate cases. All of these provide guidelines for the types of questions that should be asked. However, it is always best to keep in mind the unique features of the individual case and tailor questions to meet those demands.

Answering Interrogatories

When the party answers interrogatory questions, he or she must provide verification or post that the answers provided are truthful. See Figure 8.23. Dishonesty or deceit in answering interrogatory questions can have disastrous consequences for the party. (See this chapter's Eye on Ethics.)

In general practice, it is very common for attorneys and paralegals to give the client an artificial date to respond to the interrogatories. This date is usually a week to 10 days prior to the actual due date. Because many people tend to procrastinate, giving the client an artificially early date gives the law firm sufficient time to collate the answers, type them up, and serve them on the requesting party. Obviously, the client must respond to all questions, and if there are any gaps or omissions in the answers, these must be called to the attention of the attorney immediately. Many states impose numeric limitations on interrogatories, such as limiting a practitioner to 25–50

FIGURE 8.21
Frequent Topics in Interrogatories

- Identity of the person answering the interrogatories.
- Identity of witnesses.
- Information about expert witnesses.
- Information about documents relied upon in the case.
- Complete details of the other parties' version of the facts.
- Specification of the amount/type of damages.
- Insurance coverage and liability amounts.

FIGURE 8.22
Interrogatories—
Caption Page

STATE OF COLUMBIA
COUNTY OF BURNETT
IN THE GENERAL COURT OF JUSTICE

SUPERIOR COURT DIVISION
FILE NUMBER: _____

ALVIN REGINALD,
  (Plaintiff)

      vs.   INTERROGATORIES

COLUMBIA RAILWAY LINES,
  Defendant.

To: _____

  I herewith serve upon you the following written interrogatories under the provisions of Rule 33 of the Rules of Civil Procedure.

  You are required to answer these interrogatories separately and fully in writing under oath and to serve a copy of your answers undersigned within 30 days after service hereof.

  These interrogatories shall be continuing in nature until the date of trial and you are required to serve supplemental answers as additional information may become available to you.

    1. State the name and address of each person whom you expect to call as an expert witness at trial, and state the subject matter on which the expert is expected to testify, and for each such expert identified, state the following:

      (a) The substance of the facts and opinions to which the expert is expected to testify, and a summary of the grounds for each opinion;

      (b) The identity of any and all documents submitted or supplied to the expert in connection with his or her opinions and testimony; and

      (c) The qualifications of each such expert, listing the schools attended, years of attendance, degrees received, experience in any particular field of specialization or expertise, all publications authored, including the title of the work and the book or journal in which it was published and the date of publication.

questions in total. For the purposes of counting the questions, a sentence that ends with a question mark might constitute more than one question. For example, the following question might easily be construed as three questions instead of one:

> *Was there anyone else in the car with you, how fast were you going, and did you see anyone who was a witness to the collision between your car and the plaintiff's?*

Because these three questions cover three separate topics, a party might contest the number of interrogatories by asking the court to rule that this single question qualifies as three and thus the total number of the party's interrogatories exceeds the permissible limit. In such a case, the court might rule that the party is only required to answer the first 50, and the others are deemed withdrawn. Different jurisdictions deal with this issue in a variety of ways, and you should be aware of the possible complexities in drafting interrogatory questions.

FIGURE 8.23

**Answering
Interrogatories**

Source: Rule 33(b)(1) Federal
Rules of Civil Procedure.

(1) Each interrogatory shall be answered separately and fully in writing under oath, unless it is objected to, in which event the objecting party shall state the reasons for objection and shall answer to the extent the interrogatory is not objectionable.

FIGURE 8.24
**Time Limits on
Interrogatory Answers**
Source: Rule 33(b)(3) Federal
Rules of Civil Procedure.

> The party upon whom the interrogatories have been served shall serve a copy of the answers, and objections if any, within 30 days after the service of the interrogatories. A shorter or longer time may be directed by the court or, in the absence of such an order, agreed to in writing by the parties subject to Rule 29.

FIGURE 8.25
**Request for
Production of
Documents**
Source: Rule 34(a) Federal
Rules of Civil Procedure.

> Any party may serve on any other party a request (1) to produce and permit the party making the request, or someone acting on the requestor's behalf, to inspect and copy, any designated documents (including writings, drawings, graphs, charts, photographs, phonorecords, and other data compilations from which information can be obtained, translated, if necessary, by the respondent through detection devices into reasonably usable form), or to inspect and copy, test, or sample any tangible things which constitute or contain matters within the scope of Rule 26(b) and which are in the possession, custody or control of the party upon whom the request is served.

Time Limits on Interrogatories

Once served, a party has 30 days to respond to the interrogatories. Failure to serve answers will subject the party to sanctions (see Figure 8.24). We discuss discovery sanctions subsequently in this chapter.

Request for Production of Documents and Things

request to produce
A discovery device that
requests the production of
certain items, such as
photographs, papers,
reports, and physical
evidence; must specify the
document sought.

Another discovery method is to serve a **request to produce** from the opposing side. This request asks for copies of all relevant documents, including photographs, videotapes, and any other evidence in the case (see Figure 8.25). When this request has been filed, the other party must produce the evidence or risk sanctions by the court.

One of the best sources to determine the existence of critical documents about the case is the client. The legal team should always thoroughly question the client about any potential documents, photographs, written reports, or any other documents that might serve as the basis for any contention in the case. The legal team can then file a request for production on the opposing side. The Federal Rules of Civil Procedure do not require the party to give a reason for the request. Once made, the opposing party must comply or raise an authorized objection to producing the documents. The request can also be fashioned in such a way as to allow the parties to inspect physical items that are impossible to either move or reproduce in some other form. In fact, the rules even allow the parties to enter real estate to examine specific items.

In many ways, a request for production of documents resembles and is often served along with the interrogatories in the case. (See Figure 8.26.) However, whereas interrogatories request answers, requests for production require physical objects. A request for production should specify a date, time, and location for inspecting and copying the requested material. In large lawsuits, the production of documents is a huge undertaking that may require thousands of man-hours and a team of clerical assistants who help gather and copy documents. In responding to a request for documents, the legal team may be required to go through clients' files at their offices or warehouses and often find themselves dealing with less-than-perfect filing systems. Before documents are turned over to the opposition, the legal team must review them to make sure that information of a confidential or privileged nature is not included.

**subpoena duces
tecum**
A type of subpoena that
requests a witness to
produce documents.

Subpoena Duces Tecum

Although frequently discussed within the context of a request for production of documents and things, a **subpoena duces tecum** is a court order compelling a witness to appear at a specific date and time and for the witness to bring specific documents and other evidence to a court. Such

FIGURE 8.26
**Procedure for Request
for Documents**
Source: Rule 34(b) Federal
Rules of Civil Procedure.

> The request shall set forth, either by individual item or by category, the items to be inspected, and describe each with reasonable particularity. The request shall specify a reasonable time, place, and manner of making the inspection and performing the related acts.

PRACTICE TIP

As the paralegal featured in this chapter's "A Day in the Life" suggests, it is always a good idea to protect the original version of any document or other evidence to be used at trial. There are many times when the court will allow the parties to use a copy of a document but only when it has been clearly established that the original is available or there is a good explanation for the disappearance of the original. Sloppy recordkeeping is not considered a good excuse. Many paralegals protect original documents by placing them in plastic protectors or otherwise placing them where they are accessible, but not readily so. If a person must work to obtain the original, there is less chance that the original will be used as scratch paper for notes or simply misplaced in a pile of other papers.

a subpoena can be used within the context of a civil trial but differs in important ways from a request for production of documents. Normally, a request for production of documents compels one party to serve documents and evidence on another party, whereas a subpoena duces tecum requires a witness to bring items to court and present them to the judge.

Request for Physical and/or Mental Examination

A request for a physical and/or mental examination is often raised in situations in which the condition of one of the parties is a central issue in the case (see Figure 8.27). A request for a physical examination can be made by the defendant in a personal injury case to have the plaintiff evaluated by the defendant's doctors to determine the extent of the plaintiff's physical injuries. Mental examinations are less frequent under the rule but are also permissible. Before such an examination is authorized, the parties must show good cause to require it. Physical and mental evaluations are not a common feature in all cases but are used when a party's condition is a central point of the case, especially in medical malpractice or personal injury cases.

Request to Admit Facts

In every case, there are always certain facts that are beyond dispute between the parties. A request for admission of facts allows the parties to stipulate to these undisputed facts and then concentrate their time and resources on the contested issues. A request to admit facts helps the parties focus on the important issues raised in the case. Examples of issues that are commonly raised within the confines of a request to admit are set out in Figure 8.28 and Figure 8.29.

FIGURE 8.27
Request for Physical or Mental Examination
Source: Rule 35(a) Federal Rules of Civil Procedure.

When the mental or physical condition (including the blood group) of a party or of a person in the custody or under the legal control of a party is in controversy, the court in which the action is pending may order the party to submit to a physical or mental examination by a suitably licensed or certified examiner or to produce for examination the person in the party's custody or legal control.

FIGURE 8.28
Undisputed Facts that Are Commonly Raised in Requests to Admit

- Date of the incident
- Location of the incident
- Location of corporate headquarters

FIGURE 8.29
Request to Admit Facts
Source: Rule 36(a) Federal Rules of Civil Procedure.

A party may serve upon any other party a written request for the admission, for purposes of the pending action only, of the truth of any matters within the scope of Rule 26(b)(1) set forth in the request that relate to statements or opinions of fact or of the application of law to fact, including the genuineness of any documents described in the request.

Objections to Discovery Requests

As we have already seen in several contexts, a party or witness can object to discovery requests on the grounds of privilege or some other legally recognized excuse. We have discussed examples of the attorney–client privilege usurping a discovery request. But there are additional grounds for objections to discovery requests, including:

- Work product.
- Unduly burdensome, cumulative, and/or expensive.
- Constitutional rights.
- Trade secrets.

Work Product Objections

work product
An attorney's written notes, impressions, charts, diagrams, and other material used by him or her to prepare strategy and tactics for trial.

Work product refers to the mental impressions, conclusions, strategy, opinions, and legal theories about the case put together by the parties' attorneys. This material is not discoverable because it reflects the essence of what the attorney does for the client, using his or her talents and skills to provide the best possible outcome. In many ways, the work product privilege is an offshoot of the attorney–client privilege. The very substance of what an attorney does is reflected in work product, and a requirement to give the other side a complete overview of the legal team's theory of the case would be unreasonable and substantially damage the relationship between attorney and client.

Unduly Burdensome, Cumulative, and/or Expensive Objections

We have already provided examples of a party interposing an objection of unduly burdensome, cumulative, or expensive in responding to interrogatories and requests for production of documents. If a party believes that the opposition's request falls into any of these categories, it can petition the court for relief. The party cannot, however, simply ignore the discovery request and hope that the court eventually will rule in its favor. Such actions would doubtless result in court-ordered sanctions for the failure to comply with discovery requests.

Constitutional Rights Objections

There are times when a person may refuse to respond to discovery requests because the information requested infringes on a constitutionally guaranteed right. A party might refuse to answer certain questions because they cause the person to incriminate him- or herself in a crime, in violation of the Fifth Amendment.

Hypothetical 8-2

Anne is being deposed about a car wreck last year. The allegation is that Anne was intoxicated at the time, crossed the centerline, and had a head-on collision with the plaintiff. Anne was cited for driving under the influence, but her case has not yet been adjudicated. At her deposition, Anne is asked:

Q: How many drinks had you had that night?
A: I refuse to answer on the grounds that the answer might tend to incriminate me.

Is Anne's failure to answer grounds for sanctions, or is she protected?

Answer: She is protected under the Fifth Amendment.

Hypothetical 8-3

Several months after the first deposition, attorneys are again questioning Anne. This time, she has entered a plea of guilty to one count of driving under the influence. As part of her guilty plea, Anne waived her Fifth Amendment rights. When she is questioned at the deposition, she again raises the same objection.

Is Anne protected by the Constitution from having to answer this question?

Answer: No. Anne waived her Fifth Amendment protections when she pled guilty. She can now be questioned thoroughly about the incident and must answer the questions.

Trade Secrets Objections

In addition to interposing objections to discovery requests on the basis of privilege, work product, or constitutional rights, a party may also object to discovery requests that demand information

FIGURE 8.30
Examples of Requests that Would Justify a Discovery Protective Order

- Information requested is protected under trademark or copyright.
- Discovery request is too broad.
- Discovery request is designed to harass or annoy the other party.
- The information requested would unnecessarily delay the proceedings.
- The discovery request is overly expensive or time-consuming.
- The request would endanger the health of the party (physical examination).

about trade secrets. Revealing such secrets could provide competitors with everything that they need to launch a similar product. As a result, courts generally guard trade secrets and prevent parties from requesting this information in a civil suit.

Protective Orders

In situations in which a party believes that the opposition is acting in bad faith or that he or she has a legally recognized interest in protecting certain information, the party can move for a discovery protective order that bars the opposition from receiving specific information. To receive such a protective order, the party who is subject to the request must file a petition with the court, and the judge must make specific findings before invoking the order (see Figures 8.30 and 8.31).

FIGURE 8.31
Motion for Protective Order

STATE OF COLUMBIA
COUNTY OF BURNETT
IN THE GENERAL COURT OF JUSTICE

SUPERIOR COURT DIVISION
FILE NUMBER: _____

ALVIN REGINALD,
   Plaintiff

     vs.

COLUMBIA RAILWAY LINES,
   Defendant.

Motion for Protective Order

    Now comes Darrell Defendant, pursuant to Rule 26 and 45 of the State Rules of Civil Procedure, and hereby moves the court for order of quashing the subpoena attached hereto as Exhibit a, and also for a protective order from the court prohibiting the plaintiff from obtaining the discovery sought in the subpoena, and an order specifying that all parties cannot be questioned nor shall be required to answer questions regarding the material presented in Exhibit a and in support of this motion Darrell Defendant hereby respectfully shows the court that the documents and records requested are not relevant to any matter in this action, that the material requested cannot reasonably lead to the discovery of any other relevant material, that the materials requested are privileged under the attorney–client relationship, that the material requested is also protected under the work product rule, and that the request is designed harass, intimidate, and annoy the defendant.

    WHEREFORE, Darrell Defendant requests that the court issue an order quashing the subpoena in this case, and also entering a protective order specifying that the plaintiff, the plaintiff's attorney, and any party associated with the plaintiff is hereby prohibited from requesting, demanding, posing questions regarding, or otherwise using discovery rules to request information contained in Exhibit a. Defendant also requests that the costs of this action be assessed against the plaintiff, including reasonable attorney's fees that were incurred in researching, preparing, and presenting this motion to the court, and for such other and further relief as the court may deem appropriate and just.

    This the 12th day of October, 2006.

_____
Attorney for Darrell Defendant

FIGURE 8.32
Failure to Attend or to Serve Subpoena; Expenses

Source: Rule 30(g)(1) Federal Rules of Civil Procedure.

> (1) If the party giving the notice of the taking of a deposition fails to attend and proceed therewith and another party attends in person or by attorney pursuant to the notice, the court may order the party giving the notice to pay to such other party the reasonable expenses incurred by that party and that party's attorney in attending, including reasonable attorney's fees.

A court may issue a discovery protective order when the opposition's request is overly broad or irrelevant, the opposition is requesting material it has already received, the material requested is protected by trademark or other legal provision, or the discovery request is designed to be abusive or harassing.

Professional Courtesy

Some states have held that an attorney's request for a protective order or sanctions against the opposing side will not be upheld when the attorney has failed to exercise the courtesy of advising opposing counsel of his or her intention not to appear at a deposition or to comply with discovery requests.

Failure to Respond to Discovery Requests

The Rules of Civil Procedure provide a broad range of sanctions against a party or witness who fails to comply with discovery requests. If a witness fails to appear for a deposition, for instance, he or she can be required to pay all reasonable fees incurred by the party who set it, including attorneys' fees (see Figure 8.32). Other sanctions that a court can impose for failure to comply with discovery include:

- An order by the court taking as truth the facts alleged by the opposing party in its pleadings.
- A court order prohibiting the non-complying party to present evidence to support its case.
- A court order striking all or a portion of the non-complying party's pleadings.
- A court order prohibiting the party from presenting a particular defense.
- Dismissal of the action.
- Default judgment against the party.

 RESEARCH THIS!

According to your state's rules of civil procedure, what sanctions are available to a trial court for violations of discovery rules? Can judges in your state impose monetary fines as the court does in this chapter's "Case in Point"? What other sanctions are courts in your state authorized to impose?

 LEGAL RESEARCH MAXIM

Whenever there is an issue surrounding discovery, it is always best to begin with the rules of discovery, usually found in the Rules of Civil Procedure. However, you must keep in mind that these rules may be supplemented, enacted, or otherwise modified by statutes. You should review the rules, the statutes, and case law to have a solid understanding of discovery issues.

FIGURE 8.33
Motion to Compel Discovery

Source: Rule 37(a) Federal Rules of Civil Procedure.

> A party, upon reasonable notice to other parties and all persons affected thereby, may apply for an order compelling disclosure.

FIGURE 8.34
Sanctions for Failure to Comply with Discovery

Source: Rule 37(a)(4)(A) Federal Rules of Civil Procedure.

> (4) Expenses and Sanctions.
> (A) If the motion is granted or if the disclosure or requested discovery is provided after the motion was filed, the court shall, after affording an opportunity to be heard, require the party or deponent whose conduct necessitated the motion or the party or attorney advising such conduct or both of them to pay to the moving party the reasonable expenses incurred in making the motion, including attorney's fees, unless the court finds that the motion was filed without the movant's first making a good faith effort to obtain the disclosure or discovery without court action, or that the opposing party's nondisclosure, response, or objection was substantially justified, or that other circumstances make an award of expenses unjust.

CYBER TRIP

Federal Rules of Discovery—Cornell Law School
http://www.law.cornell.edu/rules/frcp/
'Lectric Law Library—Discovery sanctions
http://www.lectlaw.com/def2/s113.htm
Federal Rules of Civil Procedure
http://judiciary.house.gov/media/pdfs/printers/109th/civil2005.pdf
Litigation Overview—University of Pennsylvania
http://www.upenn.edu/ogc/legal/lit.html

Compelling Discovery

A party who believes that the opposing party is acting in bad faith in failing to respond to discovery requests is also entitled to file a motion to compel discovery (see Figure 8.33). Such a motion lists the specific failures of the opposing party to comply and requests that the court impose sanctions against the non-complying party (see Figure 8.34). For an example of a motion to compel discovery, see Appendix C.

Software that Assists in Discovery

Given the sheer bulk of documents and other material that can be generated in contemporary litigation, it is no wonder that some companies have designed litigation software packages specifically targeted at lawyers and paralegals. These programs, such as Summation® and Concordance®, among many others, allow attorneys and paralegals to scan, organize, label, and categorize the hundreds or even thousands of documents that can be produced in a single lawsuit. This software even allows the legal team to cross-reference documents with deposition transcripts, motions, and other forms of discovery to produce a coherent picture of the facts supporting particular points in the complaint or answer.

 Eye on Ethics

HIDING DAMAGING INFORMATION

Individuals have a natural tendency to try to conceal personal information from others—especially during the discovery phase of a civil case. Many times, clients will wish to conceal or at least "spin" details about their personal lives, work history, or the details of the incident that forms the basis of the civil suit. The problem with all of these approaches is that when a client conceals information in the discovery process, it can have dire consequences for the case. The opposing attorney may use the fact of the concealment to show that the client is unworthy of belief or even move for sanctions. Legal professionals must be ready to explain to clients the benefits of being forthright and honest, even when doing so involves revealing details that may be embarrassing or humiliating. The modern rules of discovery place a high premium on complete disclosure, and courts are always ready to impose sanctions against parties who have failed to live up to that standard. This chapter's "Case in Point" is a prime example of the dangers of concealing or withholding damaging evidence.

CASE IN POINT

Maynard

v.

Nygren,

332 F.3d 462 (C.A. 7 (Ill.), 2003),

Cudahy, Circuit Judge.

Corrections officer Harry Maynard sued his former employer, the McHenry County Sheriff, alleging a violation of the Americans with Disabilities Act (ADA), 42 U.S.C. §§ 12101–213. On February 14, 2002, the district court, finding discovery violations, Fed.R.Civ.P. 37(c), granted the defendant Sheriff's motion to dismiss and assessed monetary sanctions against Maynard and his counsel, attorneys Dennis Favaro and Patricia Jochum and the firm of Favaro, Buzek & Groman, Ltd. Maynard and his counsel appeal on the ground that the trial court failed [to] make a finding of a discovery violation sufficient to sustain the sanction of dismissal. The appellants also claim that part of the monetary sanctions were improper and that there was insufficient cause to sanction counsel. The appellants ask us to vacate the district court order and remand to a different district judge under 28 U.S.C. § 455(a). The Sheriff cross-appeals, requesting additional attorney's fees from the appellants. We affirm in part and reverse in part and remand for reconsideration.

I.

Harry Maynard began working as a corrections officer at the McHenry County Sheriff's Department in 1992. In February 1996, Maynard was hospitalized and diagnosed with multiple sclerosis. Following his hospital stay, he presented his supervisor, Chief Maire, with a report (dated March 4) from his doctor, David Martinez, allowing him to return to work. However, Maynard was told by Maire that he would not be allowed to return to work because the report stated that he could have recurrent episodes of weakness and unsteadiness. Maynard met with Dr. Martinez to discuss Maynard's displeasure with the content of the March 4th report, and they arranged for Maynard to meet with a neurologist. On March 25, Benjamin Nager, a neurologist, wrote to Dr. Martinez confirming that Maynard should not be released back to work without restrictions. Based on this letter, Dr. Martinez wrote a second report on April 4, stating that Maynard was not then able to perform the functions of his job, but that he might become able within ninety days. Where this April 4th report ended up, and did not end up, lies at the root of Maynard's troubles; what is known is that the Sheriff was not given a copy of this report until this lawsuit was well underway.

The Sheriff's lawyer wrote Maynard in November 1996 to advise him that, as an alternative to releasing his medical records (something he was not legally obligated to do), Maynard could submit himself to an examination by an Independent Medical Examiner in order to determine his ability to return to work. In January 1997, Maynard met with Dr. Pradip Sethi, who confirmed that there was no guarantee that Maynard would be symptom-free or that he could perform all his job functions at all times. Based on Dr. Sethi's reports, the Sheriff terminated Maynard. This lawsuit alleging refusal to provide a reasonable accommodation under the ADA followed.

The Complaint and the Amended Complaint in this action failed to mention the existence of the second, April 4th, report of

Dr. Martinez. Nor did the April 4th report appear during discovery, although Maynard's counsel forwarded to the Sheriff what was supposed to be all of Maynard's medical records from Dr. Martinez's file. The Sheriff finally learned of the April 4th report and received a copy of it from Dr. Martinez in January 2002, shortly before the trial date. The Sheriff then filed an emergency motion seeking involuntary dismissal and sanctions under Fed.R.Civ.P. 37(c)(1) for Maynard's failure to disclose the document. The trial judge held an evidentiary hearing to explore exactly what had happened to the April 4th report.

At the hearing, Dr. Martinez testified that he had prepared the April 4th report at Maynard's urgent request. Jeanne Gannon, Dr. Martinez's assistant, testified that she had typed the report and left it hanging in a public area of the office to be picked up. While she did not witness Maynard picking up the report, she concluded that the report had been picked up since the original was not returned to Maynard's medical file. On the other hand, there was no note in Maynard's chart showing that he had requested such a report (as there ordinarily would be), and Maynard denied that he had requested or received the report. Cynthia Kroncke, Dr. Martinez's former medical assistant, also testified. She said that she had copied the entire Maynard file and had sent copies to Maynard's counsel in February 1999. In view of Dr. Martinez's testimony that a copy of the April 4th report was in the file in 2002, it appeared that Maynard's counsel had received the April 4th report during discovery, but somehow had failed to forward it to the Sheriff's counsel.

Judge Reinhard found that Maynard's denials were not credible, and that he had intentionally withheld the April 4th report. Judge Reinhard also noted that Maynard had lied in his Amended Complaint and in an affidavit by stating that Dr. Martinez would not change the original, March 4th report. Am. Compl. at 4, para. 18 ("Maynard tried unsuccessfully to obtain a different release, but the physician would not change the wording from the original release."); Maynard Aff., Pl.'s Resp. to Def.'s Emergency Mot. for Involuntary Dismissal Ex. G, at 1 ("I had never seen Dr. Martinez's April 4, 1996 letter until January 25, 2002 when it was provided to me by my counsel."). The judge dismissed Maynard's suit, awarded the Sheriff attorney's fees and costs incurred in bringing the emergency motion and assessed a fine of $3500 payable to the court for the time spent on the motion. Judge Reinhard also found that the April 4th report had been provided to Maynard's counsel, but he did not believe that counsel had deliberately withheld the letter, positing instead that the letter was either lost in the office or removed from the office, possibly by Maynard. Nonetheless, the monetary sanctions were divided evenly between Maynard and his counsel because the judge felt that the situation could have been avoided had counsel been more careful with the discovery documents or more diligent in investigating their client's testimony.

The court enters the following sanctions against plaintiff/his counsel: (1) This case is dismissed with prejudice for discovery violation; (2) Defendant is awarded reasonable attorney fees, expenses,

187

and costs incurred in bringing this emergency motion (1/2 to be paid by the plaintiff and 1/2 to be paid by plaintiff's counsel); and (3) an additional sanction of $3,500 to be paid to the Clerk of Court for the court's time incurred on this emergency motion (1/2 to be paid by plaintiff and 1/2 to be paid by plaintiff's counsel).

II.

Discovery sanctions are reviewed for abuse of discretion. Under this standard, we uphold any exercise of the district court's discretion that could be considered reasonable, even if we might have resolved the question differently. However, a district court by definition abuses its discretion when it makes an error of law, and, while factual findings are generally reviewed only for clear error, findings which are tainted by the application of an inapposite standard are subject to fuller review. In cases of mixed questions of law and fact the standard is oftentimes clear error (or abuse of discretion), though plenary review may be used when certain factors indicate it is warranted or needed.

We must first clarify the law of this circuit on the weight of evidence necessary to support dismissal as a discovery sanction. Then, we will consider the appropriateness of the other sanctions ordered by the district judge.

A.

Of all possible sanctions, dismissal is considered "draconian," and we must be "vigilant" in our review. Because of its severity, we have circumscribed the range of cases in which dismissal may be used as a sanction. Looking at the case law, we find two different standards for determining whether a case can properly be dismissed. Some of our cases have held that actions can be dismissed "when there is a clear record of delay or contumacious conduct, or when other less drastic sanctions have proven unavailing." This appears to be the standard used when cases are dismissed for want of prosecution or failure to comply with orders of the court, Fed.R.Civ.P. 41(b). A slightly different requirement—a finding of willfulness, bad faith or fault—comes into play when dismissals are used specifically as a discovery sanction under Fed.R.Civ.P. 37. That is, even without "a clear record of delay, contumacious conduct or prior failed sanctions," a court can apply the sanction of dismissal for Rule 37 violations with a finding of willfulness, bad faith or fault, as long as it first considers and explains why lesser sanctions would be inappropriate.

We have not yet answered the question of what burden of proof is necessary to sustain a Rule 37 dismissal based on willfulness, bad faith or fault. For Rule 41(b) dismissals, the record of delay, contumacious conduct or prior failed sanctions must be "clear." Is there a similar requirement for the evidence supporting a finding of willfulness, bad faith or fault? The Sheriff argues that a preponderance of the evidence suffices, while Maynard argues that there must be clear and convincing evidence before a case is dismissed for a discovery violation. We agree with the appellants that, considering the severe and punitive nature of dismissal as a discovery sanction, a court must have clear and convincing evidence of willfulness, bad faith or fault before dismissing a case.

Working without the benefit of a clear pronouncement from this court on the appropriate burden of proof, the district judge did not specify which standard he was applying. We are left to deduce from the record which standard was applied. We agree with the appellants that the district court may have applied a preponderance standard. This belief is grounded principally on the portions of the ruling which deal with Maynard's counsel's culpability. On two occasions, the district judge noted that it was "more likely" than not that the April 4th report was sent to coun-

sel. We also note the circumstantial nature of much of the evidence, which makes this perhaps a closer case than some. While we cannot conclude with certainty that a preponderance, rather than a clear and convincing, standard was applied, the absence of any assurance that the higher burden of proof was considered advises us to assume for the purpose of this appeal that the lower threshold was used.

The Sheriff argues now that, regardless of the standard used below, the evidence is in fact clear and convincing, and that we should affirm the dismissal. And the evidence does appear to support the Sheriff's positions and the district court's conclusions quite strongly. The court reasonably relied on the persuasive testimony of Dr. Martinez and his staff in finding that Maynard had acted in bad faith in concealing evidence during pleadings and discovery. However, especially because factual determinations such as these are the special province of the trial judge, we must defer to the trial judge and allow him to reconsider the evidence in light of the standard announced here. In remanding the case, we do not find appropriate the recusal of Judge Reinhard, and are confident that he will approach this determination without preconception. Nothing in the record persuades us otherwise.

B.

Even if the district court upon reconsideration declines to dismiss this lawsuit—and we make no recommendation on the matter— there remain the other, non-dismissal sanctions, which are generally permissible even without clear and convincing evidence. The monetary sanctions imposed by the district judge included both attorney's fees to the Sheriff and a $3500 fine for the court's time. Half of these amounts was to be paid by Maynard and half by Maynard's counsel. The appellants argue that the $3500 fine was an abuse of discretion, as was any sanction against counsel.

As to the $3500 fine, the appellants provide no case law that supports their argument. On the contrary, there is ample case law validating the use of fines, especially where they are "remedial" and correspond to some real cost (here, the court's time at $500 per hour). While fines are not specifically included in the non-exclusive list of sanctions in Rule 37(b)(2), they are among the tools available to trial courts to remedy the harms of discovery violations. Such a fine was within the discretion of the district judge.

The second question demands more analysis. We see two potential bases for upholding the district court's sanction against Maynard's counsel: the Federal Rules of Civil Procedure and the inherent powers of the court. Reading the transcript of the proceedings below, it is not clear on which the district court was basing the sanctions; thus, we consider whether the sanctions against Maynard's counsel would have been permissible under either authority.

We agree with the appellants that *Insurance Benefit Administrators v. Martin*, 871 F.2d 1354, 1360 (7th Cir.1989), does not permit the imposition of Rule 37(c) sanctions on attorneys. In IBA, we held that attorneys can be sanctioned for failure-to-disclose violations only under Rule 26(g)(3), which authorizes sanctions against attorneys who certify discovery disclosures in violation of the rules. In the case at hand, because the court found that counsel had no knowledge that the discovery response was inadequate, there is no ground for a sanction under Rule 26(g), which applies only to knowing violations of the rules. Any sanction against Maynard's counsel based on Rule 37(c) or 26(g) was improper.

The district judge's finding of no willfulness also precludes any sanction against counsel under the inherent powers of the court. While generally the inherent powers of the court can extend beyond those powers granted in the Federal Rules of Civil Procedure, the assessment of fees against counsel under the inherent powers of the court is permitted only when there is a finding of willful disobedience or bad faith. Here, however, the district judge found explicitly that counsel did not willfully withhold the document—the judge blamed the document's disappearance on negligent mishandling. There is no authority under the Rules or under the inherent powers of the court to sanction attorneys for mere negligence, and so sanctions must be reversed as applied to Maynard's counsel.

III.

The Sheriff cross-appeals, arguing that he should have been awarded all his attorney's fees, and not merely those incurred in bringing the successful motion for dismissal. The Sheriff argues that such full reimbursement is required by the text of Rule 37. However, Rule 37 supports only the reimbursement of fees resulting from the discovery violation. As long as the suit as a whole was not frivolous, and we have no reason to believe that it was, the remaining attorney's fees would have been incurred even without the discovery violation; thus, the causality requirement was not met. The Sheriff also argues that attorney's fees are required under Rule 41, under which a dismissal not otherwise grounded "operates as an adjudication on the merits." However, the American Rule is generally that prevailing parties are not entitled to fees, even where a full adjudication on the merits has

taken place. The Sheriff's claim under the ADA, 42 U.S.C. § 12205, also fails since there was no finding that Maynard's claim was frivolous, unreasonable or without foundation. None of the bases for cross-appeal are therefore valid.

IV.

For the foregoing reasons, the judgment of the district court is REVERSED in part and AFFIRMED in part.

Source: From Westlaw. Used with permission of Thomson/West.

Case Questions:

1. Explain the significance of the second letter by Dr. Martinez about Maynard's condition.

2. What is the basis of the suit by Maynard against the Sheriff?

3. According to the trial court, why was it likely that Maynard had intentionally withheld the April 4 report?

4. Why were both Maynard and his attorney fined?

5. What view does the appellate court take of dismissing a civil action? Why?

6. According to the appellate court, is it proper for a trial court to impose monetary fines for abuse of discovery?

Real Paralegal Life: Building a Skill Set

Jane Huffman has been working as a paralegal for several years. "I enjoy working in the legal field," she says. "In fact, now that I've gotten my bachelor's degree, I actually teach part time at the college where I originally got my associate's degree. You never know what doors will open to you once you enter the law." She works on all facets of a case, from the initial meeting with the client to preparing and reviewing discovery materials to preparing settlement brochures. "The law can be very consuming," she notes. "Some days, you'll look up and say, 'What happened to the day?' I guess that's a good thing. I've worked in jobs where you just watched the clock. There's always plenty to do in a law office."

A Day in the Life: Jone Huffman

One of Jane Huffman's favorite parts of a civil case is going through discovery materials: "When I organize discovery, I dig through everything that we've received. I pull out every relevant document produced and go through it with a fine-tooth comb. I make four copies of everything: one for attorney, one for judge, one for opposition, and one for the witness. I organize our attorney's copy first. I put it in an order that makes sense. I like to have a clean set of discovery. The attorneys tend to make notes on their copies, so I always keep a clean set that hasn't been marked. It's a lot harder to get a document admitted at trial if it's got handwritten notes written across it.

"Once I've gone through the discovery, I start working the file to get it ready for trial. You can't start too soon for that. I put together a list of the evidence that we'll be using at trial and put it in a notebook. That way, when the witness is on the stand, we can just hand them the notebook, or even leave it on the witness stand and just ask them to turn to a specific page."

After the first round of discovery, there is usually a follow up, which Huffman calls "the second round of discovery, I follow up on the stuff we get in the first round. I review what the other side has given us for completeness and objections. If they've raised an objection and I don't think it's legitimate, we'll point it out and cite a statute or case law showing how the objection isn't legitimate."

Real Paralegal Life: Building a Skill Set

PREPARING A DEPOSITION DIGEST

Review the deposition provided in the Apple case (Appendix C) and prepare a deposition digest of that testimony.

Career Prep

Suppose that you have been handed a case involving a typical automobile accident. Defendant B rear-ended Plaintiff A at a red light. Compose 20 interrogatory questions that the plaintiff should serve on the defendant, making sure that they abide by your state's limitations on interrogatories and that they do not request privileged information.

Summary

Discovery is the exchange of information between opposing sides in a civil case. Although the historical approach to discovery was to limit information exchange, modern approaches to discovery rules have liberalized the approach and require parties to exchange as much information as possible prior to trial. The modern discovery rules are based on the premise that the parties should know everything about the case before the trial ever begins. Discovery methods include depositions, interrogatories, requests for production documents, requests to admit, and requests for physical and/or mental examination. Depositions are oral questions of witnesses taken under oath. Interrogatories are written questions posed to parties that must be answered within a specified time period. Requests for production of documents require opposing parties to produce any written document or thing that will form the basis of any contention raised in the case. A request to admit facts is posed by one party to another to request that the party stipulate to an undisputed fact, thus eliminating the necessity of presenting evidence to support it. Discovery requests must be reasonable, but the party who receives a request may move for a protective order if the information requested is excessive, is overly broad, or infringes on a privilege, such as attorney–client privilege.

Key Terms

Discovery, 165
Stipulation, 166
Deposition, 170
Court reporter, 170
Deponent, 174

Deposition digest, 175
Interrogatories, 176
Request to produce, 181
Subpoena duces tecum, 181
Work product, 183

Review Questions

1. What is the purpose of discovery?

2. Explain the historical approach to discovery and how it has changed over time.

3. What approach do the Federal Rules of Civil Procedure take regarding revealing information to opposing sides?

4. Is there a typical sequence followed in civil discovery? Explain.

5. What are depositions?

6. What are the two types of depositions that are permissible in civil cases?

7. What are interrogatories?

8. What is a deposition digest?

9. Explain how a deposition is conducted.

10. What is the time limit imposed on answering interrogatories?

11. What sanctions can be imposed against a party that fails to comply with discovery?

12. What are requests for production of documents?

13. What are requests to admit?

14. What types of objections can a party raise to a discovery request?

15. What is a discovery protective order?

16. Which individuals are normally present at a deposition?

17. Explain the type of information that must be revealed about expert witnesses in civil discovery.

18. Create a timeline of the civil process, beginning with the service of the complaint and continuing through discovery.

Discussion Questions

1. How has the modern approach to civil discovery changed the process of exchanging information in civil cases?

2. Have the discovery rules increased the chance that civil cases will be settled prior to trial? Explain your answer.

Exercises: Skill Builders

Visit your local courthouse and locate a civil case. What discovery is available in the file? Were there motions to compel discovery or to move for sanctions for discovery violations? If so, what were the outcomes of these motions?

Portfolio Assignment

Portfolio Assignment 8-1: Draft interrogatories. Our client, Joe Doe and his wife Flo were driving through their hometown on their way to go out to dinner. The restaurant was on the other side of the railroad tracks that run through the town. As they approached the intersection of the track with the road, Joe Doe thinks he looked both ways and didn't see anything but isn't sure because of his injuries.

It is undisputed that just as the car Doe was driving began to cross the tracks, it was struck by a southbound train, owned and operated by Columbo Railway. The force of the impact impaled Doe's car on the front of the engine, and the car was dragged 242 feet down the track before the car fell off to the side.

Flo Doe was killed at the scene, and Joe Doe was severely injured, requiring hospitalization for four months before he was released, in a wheelchair, never to walk again. Joe came to our firm, wanting to sue, because the trees that grow next to the track block anyone's view and everybody in town knows it.

We have filed a Wrongful Death action on behalf of Flo and a separate action for damages for Joe's injuries. We are now at the stage where interrogatories are to be filed. Draft 10 questions for the railroad company.

Portfolio Assignment 8-2: Learn discovery rules. Review your state's discovery rules and then prepare a paper discussing the following:

- When, where, and who may be deposed?

- What issues can and cannot be raised in interrogatories?

- What can be produced through requests to produce?

- What privileges protect the production of materials through any type of discovery device?

- What rules expand or limit the use of depositions, interrogatories, and requests to produce in civil cases?

Vocabulary Builders

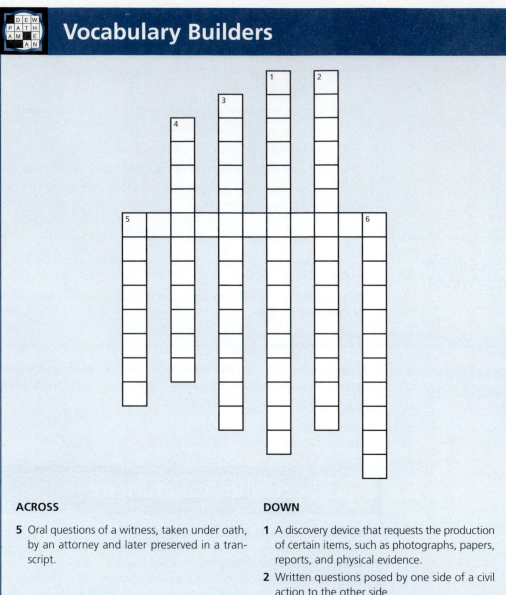

ACROSS

5 Oral questions of a witness, taken under oath, by an attorney and later preserved in a transcript.

DOWN

1 A discovery device that requests the production of certain items, such as photographs, papers, reports, and physical evidence.

2 Written questions posed by one side of a civil action to the other side.

3 A discovery tool that seeks admissions from the opposing side about uncontested facts.

4 An attorney's written notes, impressions, charts, diagrams, and other material used by him or her to prepare strategy and tactics for trial.

5 The person questioned during a deposition.

6 An agreement between attorneys and parties about a procedural or factual issue in a case.

Chapter 9

Motions Practice

CHAPTER OBJECTIVES

The student will be able to:

- Explain the importance of motions in civil practice.

- Describe how a motion is prepared.

- Define how a motion is served on opposing parties.

- Compare and contrast a notice of motion with a certificate of service.

- Explain the role of the judge in granting or denying motions.

- Describe the function of a motion for summary judgment.

- Explain the significance of a motion for a more definite statement.

- Describe the significance of a judgment on the pleadings.

- Define the role of a 12(b)(6) motion.

- Explain how attorneys use motions to clarify the issues in a civil case.

motion
A procedural request or application presented by the attorney in court.

Motions practice is as critical to a legal practitioner as is the ability to draft legal pleadings and prepare for trial. At its simplest, a **motion** addresses a specific issue and clarifies it for trial. There are several different types of motions, including those directed at specific evidence and motions that seek to dismiss the entire case. We will address all of these motions in this chapter.

BRINGING A MOTION

A party may file a motion in a civil case for any of a number of reasons. The plaintiff might bring a motion to prevent the defense from bringing up prejudicial and inflammatory evidence during the trial. A defendant might move for summary judgment, requesting that the case be dismissed for the failure of the plaintiff to state a legally recognized claim. Other motions may be more narrowly focused on specific legal or evidentiary issues. Consider Hypothetical 9-1.

Hypothetical 9-1

In a personal injury case, the defendant does not want the jury to hear that the defendant has been involved in other litigation. The defendant's attorney believes that if the jury should hear about the defendant's contentious divorce, the jury might be more inclined to rule against the defendant. To avoid anyone bringing up such evidence, the defense attorney files a motion with the court, seeking an order directing all parties to refrain from mentioning the defendant's divorce.

When the judge receives this motion, he or she confers with all parties and, if satisfied, enters an order doing precisely what the defendant requests.

SPOT THE ISSUE!

In the case of *Smith v. Gonzalez*, Mr. Smith is representing himself. One afternoon, the attorney representing Ms. Gonzalez receives a handwritten document from Mr. Smith that states:

"The plaintiff, being sui juris and independent of any governmental authority and acting pursuant to his rights granted by birth in a free nation and being therefore a person with sufficient qualities recognized under the legal preeminence of the United States hereby requests that the defendant's Answer be struck and replaced with the allegations found in the plaintiff's complaint. This motion is made under authority of the Rules of Civil Procedure to which the plaintiff refers, but does not adhere to."

"This the 10th day of June 2006."

This document was also filed at the courthouse and includes a Notice of Motion for the first Monday in August. How should Ms. Gonzalez's attorney respond?

PRACTICE TIP

In previous decades, a motion might be dismissed because of a technical failure to allege the appropriate wording or a failure to include the correct formulation of words. That approach is no longer followed.

Construing the Language in a Motion

The rules about how to interpret the language in a motion are very broad. In previous centuries, a party's motion might be denied for failure to apply the correct formulation of words, but such rulings have fallen by the wayside. These days, courts liberally interpret the language of a motion and, as long as the intent can be discerned, do not require specific legal language before considering the merits of the motion.

Drafting a Motion

The legal test used to determine the intent of a motion is whether or not the wording puts the opposing party on notice about the claims being raised and the action requested. If a motion satisfies these two conditions, the court will consider it. Whether or not the motion is granted, however, is an entirely separate issue.

Once the party conceives of an issue that would be appropriately dealt with through a motion, the next step is to draft it. Drafting a motion might be as simple as a one-sentence request. Consider Figure 9.1.

FIGURE 9.1
Plaintiff's Motion

STATE OF PLACID   IN THE SUPERIOR COURT
COUNTY OF BURKE   FILE NUMBER: 06 CV 2121

INGRED SVENSON,   )
)
      Plaintiff,   )
)
      vs.   )
)
)
JANE MARPLE   )
)
      Defendant.   )
)
_____   )

The plaintiff hereby requests that the parties be allowed to adjourn at 4:30 PM each day of the trial, in order to give counsel sufficient time to notify witnesses to appear for the following day's testimony.

Respectfully submitted, this the 6th day of June, 2007.

                                          _____

                                          Laura Lawyer
                                          Attorney for Plaintiff

RESEARCH THIS!

Some court systems not only have statewide rules regarding motions but also "local rules" governing the filing of motions and related activities. Does your court system have local rules? If so, what do they provide for filing motions for summary judgment? For instance, do your local rules require that an affidavit supporting the motion must be filed with the motion? Do the local rules make any other changes to the general requirements under your state's rules of civil procedure?

LEGAL RESEARCH MAXIM

In this chapter, we discuss that a motion makes certain assumptions. For instance, in a motion for summary judgment, the opposing party claims that taking all of the movant's contentions as true, the law still requires that the judge rule in the opposing party's favor. However, simply because a judge grants a motion does not automatically mean that the case will be appealed. There are many instances in which the judge may make a ruling and the case will continue to trial on other issues. When there are remaining issues in the case, the parties are prevented from taking the case up on appeal. However, when a motion for summary judgment dismisses all pending issues in the case, the losing party is entitled to bring an appeal; for this reason, you will often find cases brought on appeal on the grounds of "an order granting appellant's motion for summary judgment."

Although drafting a motion may be as simple as presenting a request to adjourn at a specific time each day, many motions require extensive legal research and keen attention to drafting. A motion for summary judgment, for example, might require several days' attention before it is ready to be served on the opposing side.

Serving a Motion

Once drafted, the next step for the party seeking court intervention is to serve a copy of the motion on the opposition. All parties, including codefendants and co-plaintiffs, must be served with a copy of the motion. Service can be accomplished by having the motion hand-delivered to the offices of the attorneys who represent the various parties, or it can simply be mailed. In either event, the party presenting the motion proves service by creating a certificate of service to accompany the motion.

Certificate of Service

certificate of service
Verification by attorney that pleadings or court documents were sent to the opposing counsel in a case.

A **certificate of service** is the party's proof that a copy of the motion has been served on all parties. Whether the motion was hand-delivered or mailed, the party will sign the certificate of service indicating exactly how the other parties were served and when this service took place. A certificate of service is considered to be sufficient proof that the service took place as alleged, and such certificates are rarely challenged. Obviously, an attorney or other legal professional that creates fraudulent certificates of service is violating ethical rules. The purpose of the certificate of service is to document actions taken by the attorneys in the case. Whenever an attorney creates a motion or other pleading, it must be served on the opposing attorneys as well as filed in the courthouse. The failure to complete either step may render the entire motion null and void. A court may, for instance, refuse to consider a motion filed by one party that has not been filed on the other party or that the moving party cannot prove was served on the opposition. For this reason, certificates of service can be pivotal in deciding issues in a case even before the court reaches conclusions about the merits of the actual motion. See Figure 9.2.

Attaching Affidavits to the Motion

affidavit
A sworn statement.

In addition to the actual motion, a party might also include exhibits to accompany the motion. The most common exhibit is an **affidavit** by a party or a witness attesting to the facts raised in

FIGURE 9.2
Certificate of Service

Certificate of Service

 This is to certify that the undersigned has on the date set out below served a copy of this Motion for Summary Judgment on the plaintiff's attorney, to wit:

Linda Lawyer
200 Elm Street
Placid City, PL 25360

 By depositing same, postage prepaid, in the United States Mail.
This the 9th day of May, 2007.

_____

Clarence D. Arrow
Attorney for Defendant
100 Maple Ave.
Placid City, PL 25360
(555)555-1212
State Bar No. 004562

---

the motion. (See Figure 9.3.) Attaching an affidavit in this situation helps the party prove the facts associated with its request. In some circumstances, the accompanying affidavit may serve as verification of the facts and claims contained in the motion. (See Figure 9.4.) In addition to an affidavit, a party may, in some jurisdictions, be required to file additional supplementation, including a memorandum of the legal points raised in the motion, the legal authority that

FIGURE 9.3
Affidavit

STATE OF PLACID	IN THE SUPERIOR COURT
	SUPERIOR COURT FILE NO. _____

COUNTY OF BURKE

JANE DOE,   )   AFFIDAVIT
)
 Plaintiff   )
)
vs.   )
)
NICHOLAS CHARLES,   )
 Defendant.   )
)

Date: _____

Affidavit of Nicholas D. Charles

Nicholas D. Charles, having been duly sworn, says:

1. Affiant is the defendant in the above action and makes this affidavit based upon personal knowledge.

2. Affiant has personally reviewed plaintiff's complaint filed in the above action and is familiar with its content.

3. Affiant was not personally involved nor did affiant participate in the alleged acts and/or omissions which form the factual basis for plaintiff's complaint in the above action.

4. Affiant was not present at the date and time alleged by the plaintiff as the occurrence for the underlying action in this case.

5. Affiant, if called to testify as a witness, will give sworn testimony to the points raised in paragraphs numbered 1-4.

                 _____
                 Affiant

Subscribed to and sworn before
me on _____

_____
Notary Public

My commission expires: _____

FIGURE 9.4

Affidavits

Source: Rule 56(f) Federal Rules of Civil Procedure.

> Should it appear from the affidavits of a party opposing the motion that the party cannot for reasons stated present by affidavit facts essential to justify the party's opposition, the court may refuse the application for judgment or may order a continuance to permit affidavits to be obtained or depositions to be taken or discovery to be had or may make such other order as is just.

PRACTICE TIP

If the facts supporting the motion are already a matter of record, there may be no requirement to file a supporting affidavit (*Muller v. Reagh*, 173 Cal. App. 2d 1, 343 P.2d 135 (1st Dist. 1959)).

supports the motion, or the movant's theory about how the facts and legal authorities support its position.

Filing a Motion

Once served on all parties, the motion is then filed with the court. Filing may be as simple as presenting the document to the clerk of court and having it inserted in the file. Most attorneys bring at least two copies to the courthouse, one for the clerk's file and one that can be dated and time stamped so that they have independent proof that the motion was correctly filed.

Responding to a Motion

Unlike pleadings, a motion generally does not require a response. After all, the motion is the written embodiment of the party's request for a judge to take some action and assumes that the points of the motion will be discussed at a hearing. At this hearing, the opposing party will have the right to contest the issues, raise additional points, and even present evidence in opposition to the motion. As a result, unless specifically ordered to do so by the trial court, the opposing side is not required to file a written motion in opposition to the original motion (*Driver v. Driver*, 148 Vt. 560, 536 A.2d 557 (1987)). However, having said that, many practitioners often feel that providing a written explanation of their opposition to the motion gives the judge something to review as well as something that will remind the judge of the opposition's points if the judge chooses to review written materials before coming to a decision.

Arguing a Motion

Simply serving a motion and filing it does not complete the motion process. To have the judge rule on the motion, the attorney must usually request a court hearing to present the motion formally to the judge and seek a ruling on the issues it contains. Although some courts routinely set aside a specific date for the argument of all motions pending in the case, many attorneys must contact the court administrator and specifically request such a hearing to make sure that the motion is heard.

Once the hearing date is set, the attorney notifies all other parties about the day and time that the motion will be heard. The right of parties to have an opportunity to appear and argue a motion is considered one of the central rights in a civil or criminal case (*Craver v. Craver*, 298 N.C. 231, 258 S.E.2d 357 (1979)). The most common way to alert other parties to the motion hearing date is by a Notice of Motion. See Figure 9.5.

SURFS UP!

AUTOMATING DOCUMENTS

In this chapter, you will find a discussion of how to create your own "motions bank." By taking copies of motions created in other cases and storing them in a central location, you can often save time when it comes to creating similar documents in the future. However, there are also companies that offer the same process. Companies such as Word Automation (www.wordautomation.com) and Thuriam (www.thuriam.com) allow users to create templates for a huge variety of documents, including legal pleadings and motions. Instead of copying and pasting from old documents, automated documents pull up the basic structure of the proposed motion and ask you for details, often by requesting

that you fill in material in a discussion box. Once completed, the program fills in the rest of the information, generating all of the standard language and preparing a completed form in seconds. The advantage of word automation programs is that they also generate ancillary documents, including certificates of service, affidavit forms, court cover sheets, and any other forms required. Then, the programs can print all of this material for you. In a few seconds, you can produce everything you need to file and serve a motion, right down to the envelope and signature pages for attorneys. However, you should always keep in mind that no matter how great a program is at taking the drudgery out of drafting, serving, and filing motions, there is still no substitute for thought and analysis in deciding to bring one.

FIGURE 9.5 Notice of Motion

IN THE SUPERIOR COURT
BURKE COUNTY
STATE OF PLACID

SUPERIOR COURT DIVISION
FILE NUMBER: _____

JANE DOE,)
)
Plaintiff,)
) NOTICE OF MOTION
vs.)
)
NICHOLAS D. CHARLES)
)
Defendant.)
)
_____)

TO: Linda Lawyer
200 Elm Street
Placid City, PL 25360

THIS MATTER having been brought before the court on its Motion for Summary Judgment by Clarence D. Arrow, attorney for defendant, for an order dismissing the plaintiff's complaint by and through a Motion for Summary Judgment filed by Defendant Nicholas D. Charles, hereinafter referred to as "Defendant" and notice having been given to all parties, the Defendant's Motion for Summary Judgment is set for argument on the 8th day of July, 2007, at 1 p.m. in Courtroom 1A, Burke County Superior Court, 100 Courthouse Lane, Placid City, PL before Judge Hancock.

PLEASE TAKE notice that attorney for the defendant has requested oral argument on his Motion for Summary Judgment.

PLEASE TAKE FURTHER NOTICE that, in support of his motion, defendant will rely on Plaintiff's First Interrogatories to Defendant, and Defendant's Response to Plaintiff's First Interrogatories to Defendant, Defendant's Request for Admission to Plaintiff, and Plaintiff's Response to Defendant's Request for Admission to Plaintiff.

This the 19th day of June, 2007
Respectfully submitted,

_____
Clarence D. Arrow
Attorney for Defendant
100 Maple Ave.
Placid City, PL 25360
(555)555-1212
State Bar No. 004562

Certificate of Service

This is to certify that the undersigned has on the date set out below served a copy of this Notice of Motion on the plaintiff's attorney, to wit:

Linda Lawyer
200 Elm Street
Placid City, PL 25360

By depositing same, postage prepaid, in the United States Mail.

This the 9th day of May, 2007.

_____
Clarence D. Arrow
Attorney for Defendant
100 Maple Ave.
Placid City, PL 25360
(555)555-1212
State Bar No. 004562

On the day of the hearing, the party who initially filed the motion has the burden of presenting an argument and perhaps even testimony to support his or her contentions. Attorneys can simply argue many motions, but some require the attorneys to present live testimony to bolster the attorney's position. We will discuss the details of how specific motions are argued subsequently in this chapter.

Ruling on a Motion

The ultimate ruling on a motion is always left up to the judge. Juries are not allowed to consider motions for the simple reason that the jurors are the final arbiters of the facts of the case, whereas the judge has the final say about legal issues.

Written Motions

The rules governing motions, specifically Rule 12 and case law interpreting the Rules of Civil Procedure, provide that motions may be made orally or in writing, but most courts prefer written motions. Although modern courts allow greater latitude in how the written motion may be presented, most prefer that any motion raising substantive issues or affirmative defenses be written, served on opposing counsel, and filed with the court. However, that is not to say that there are no provisions for oral motions.

Oral Motions

motion in limine
A request that certain evidence not be raised at trial, as it is arguably prejudicial, irrelevant, or legally inadmissible evidence.

There are many circumstances in which an oral motion is permissible. A party may bring such a motion within the context of a hearing, while arguing another motion, and also during the trial itself. A **motion in limine**, for example, is usually an oral motion made at the commencement of the trial. Such a motion might request a ruling on a particular item of evidence sought to be admitted later in the trial by one of the parties. In addition to motions in limine, it is common practice for defense attorneys to use an oral motion to request a JNOV ruling at the conclusion of the plaintiff's case. (We discuss such motions in Chapter 10.)

ISSUES THAT CAN BE ADDRESSED IN A MOTION

Motions can be used to address a wide variety of issues, from correcting errors in the original pleadings to requesting that the entire case against the defendant be dismissed. Under the Federal Rules of Civil Procedure, Rule 12 governs the issues that can be raised in motions. (See Figure 9.6.) They include:

- Summary judgment.
- Partial summary judgment.
- Judgment on the pleadings.
- Affirmative defenses, including:
  - Lack of jurisdiction over the subject matter,
  - Lack of jurisdiction over the person,
  - Improper venue,
  - Insufficiency of process,
  - Insufficiency of service of process,
  - Failure to state a claim upon which relief can be granted, and
  - Failure to join a party under Rule 19.

FIGURE 9.6
Presenting Motions under Rule 12

Source: Rule 12(b) Federal Rules of Civil Procedure.

Every defense, in law or fact, to a claim for relief in any pleading, whether a claim, counterclaim, cross-claim, or third-party claim, shall be asserted in the responsive pleading thereto if one is required, except that the following defenses may at the option of the pleader be made by motion: (1) lack of jurisdiction over the subject matter, (2) lack of jurisdiction over the person, (3) improper venue, (4) insufficiency of process, (5) insufficiency of service of process, (6) failure to state a claim upon which relief can be granted, (7) failure to join a party under Rule 19.

The general purpose of Rule 12 is to provide practitioners with a vehicle through which they can dispose of the case early in the litigation process, when it is clear that a legal element is missing from the pleadings. As a result, Rule 12, which has been the template used by many states, provides a number of grounds that a party can raise in a motion that may dispose of all issues pending in the case. Therefore, motions under Rule 12 are commonly referred to as **dispositive motions**. It is important to keep in mind that the burden of proof is always on the party bringing such a motion. The party who files a motion for summary judgment or any of the many other motions that may be brought in a case has the burden of proof and the burden of persuasion. The first requires satisfying the court of the merits of the legal claim, whereas the second requires the party to persuade the court of the rationale for bringing the motion.

dispositive motion
A motion that terminates some or all of the pending issues in a case.

Motion for Summary Judgment

motion for summary judgment
A motion by either party for judgment based on all court documents.

A **motion for summary judgment** is a request by one party for a complete disposition of the case without ever taking it to trial. A party who moves for a summary judgment alleges that, taking all facts as true, the opposing party is not entitled to any legal relief. If a party can show that there are no undisputed material facts, that party can argue that there is no need for a jury to intervene in the case. The jury's function is to determine the facts, and if the important details of this case are not contested, there is no need for a jury. The stated purpose of a motion for summary judgment is to eliminate the expense and drain on resources of trials for which there are no contestable issues between the parties. Parties routinely file motions for summary judgment when they believe that the opposition has raised frivolous claims. Because such claims are not based on legally recognized issues, a judge would be authorized to dismiss the case. However, simply because a party moves for summary judgment does not mean the party will actually have the motion granted. Unlike other motions we discuss in this chapter, a motion for summary judgment falls under the jurisdiction of Rule 56 of the Federal Rules of Civil Procedure. (See Figure 9.7.)

There is a huge body of cases that stands for the proposition that granting a summary judgment is a drastic action that should occur only when the court has determined that the original claim is frivolous, that there are no genuine issues to be determined in the case, or that the claim is brought for the purposes of harassing or annoying the other party. Courts are required to be cautious before granting a summary judgment because such an order removes a party's right to seek compensation in a case (*Venti v. EDS,* 236 F. Supp. 2d 264 (W.D. N.Y. 2002)). The purpose of a motion for summary judgment is to resolve questions of law, not fact. Essentially, a party requesting a motion for summary judgment states that, taking all of the facts raised by the opposition as true, that party is still entitled to win (*Dalton v. Camp,* 353 N.C. 647, 548 S.E.2d 704 (2001)). When there are no factual disputes for the jury to resolve, it becomes the judge's duty to rule on the legal issues. If the judge finds that the law is squarely in one side's favor, he or she is obligated to rule in conformance with that legal authority. For an example of a motion for summary judgment, see Figure 9.8.

Because the ultimate decision in a motion for summary judgment may be the dismissal of a party's case, judges should act with caution in ordering it. Many court decisions have held that a trial judge must strictly comply with the provisions of the law, especially Rule 56, in granting such a motion (*Manchester Memorial Hospital v. Whitney,* 6 Conn. Cir. Ct. 212, 269 A.2d 300 (App. Div. 1969), *petition denied,* 158 Conn. 667, 259 A.2d 648 (1969)).

FIGURE 9.7
Motion for Summary Judgment

Source: Rule 56 Federal Rules of Civil Procedure

(a) For Claimant.
A party seeking to recover upon a claim, counterclaim, or cross-claim or to obtain a declaratory judgment may, at any time after the expiration of 20 days from the commencement of the action or after service of a motion for summary judgment by the adverse party, move with or without supporting affidavits for a summary judgment in the party's favor upon all or any part thereof.

(b) For Defending Party.
A party against whom a claim, counterclaim, or cross-claim is asserted or a declaratory judgment is sought may, at any time, move with or without supporting affidavits for a summary judgment in the party's favor as to all or any part thereof.

FIGURE 9.8   Example of Motion for Summary Judgment

IN THE SUPERIOR COURT
BURKE COUNTY
STATE OF PLACID

SUPERIOR COURT DIVISION
FILE NUMBER: _____

JANE DOE,   )
)
       Plaintiff,   )
)
       vs.   )
)
NICHOLAS D. CHARLES   )
)
       Defendant.   )
)
_____   )

Motion for Summary Judgment

COMES NOW the defendant, hereinafter referred to as Defendant Charles and files this his motion for summary judgment pursuant to PL R. Civ. P. 56 and as grounds therefore shows that there is no genuine issue as to any material fact and Defendant Charles is entitled to judgment as a matter of law. Defendant Charles respectfully shows the court the following in support of his motion:

1.   This is an action for slander.

2.   Interrogatories served and filed by plaintiff Doe and answers filed by Defendant Charles establish the following facts:

(a) Interrogatory No. 12
Question: List any incident in which you referred to the plaintiff in any manner to any third person.
    Answer to Interrogatory No. 12
"Defendant has, to his knowledge, never referred to, mentioned, or otherwise discussed the plaintiff in any manner. Defendant denies any knowledge of the plaintiff's existence prior to the filing of this action."

(b) Interrogatory No. 33
Question: List any communications between yourself and third parties, including, but not limited to, newspaper reporters, journalists, writers, and television reporters concerning the plaintiff.
    Answer to Interrogatory No. 33
"Defendant has, to his knowledge, never discussed the plaintiff with any other person, including the list promulgated by the plaintiff. Defendant denies any knowledge of the plaintiff prior to the filing of this action."

3.   Requests for admissions were filed by defendant and served on plaintiff on March 3, 2007, and answers to admissions were filed by plaintiff on April 4, 2007, admitting the following facts:

(a) Request for Admission No. 2
The plaintiff is unable to produce any witness, other than herself, to substantiate the slanderous statements allegedly made by the defendant.

Response to Request for Admission No. 2
"Plaintiff has not located any witness, to date, who can substantiate the defendant's slanderous comments about the plaintiff. However, plaintiff's investigation is proceeding."

Plaintiff is, as a matter of law, unable to meet the elements of slander in that she is unable to produce a third party who overhead or had communicated to any supposedly slanderous statement by defendant. Defendant Charles requests that the court enter judgment in his favor, together with the costs of this action.

This the 9th day of May, 2007.

Respectfully submitted,

_____
Clarence D. Arrow
Attorney for Defendant
100 Maple Ave.
Placid City, PL 25360
(555)555-1212
State Bar No. 004562

FIGURE 9.8 *(continued)*

Certificate of Service

This is to certify that the undersigned has on the date set out below served a copy of this Motion for Summary Judgment on the plaintiff's attorney, to wit:

Linda Lawyer
200 Elm Street
Placid City, PL 25360

By depositing same, postage prepaid, in the United States Mail.

This the 9th day of May, 2007.

_____

Clarence D. Arrow
Attorney for Defendant
100 Maple Ave.
Placid City, PL 25360
(555)555-1212
State Bar No. 004562

Motion for Partial Summary Judgment

When a party moves for partial summary judgment, he or she requests a ruling on specific issues in the case and does not seek the disposition of the entire case. A motion for partial summary judgment is usually addressed at a specific contention in the complaint or answer. The movant requests the court to dismiss the allegation and, in support of the motion, shows that there is no genuine dispute about the facts surrounding this issue. If the court grants a partial summary judgment, the particular claim will be struck, and the jury will not consider it at trial.

Judgment on the Pleadings

judgment on the pleadings
A motion that alleges that if all of the allegations raised in the pleadings are true and correct, the movant would still be entitled to a ruling in his favor and a dismissal of the opposition's pleadings.

A **judgment on the pleadings** is a motion filed by either party that essentially requests the judge to make a ruling that, even if the court takes all of the opposition's allegations as true, the party has failed to allege any legally recognized injury. This motion falls under the jurisdiction of Rule 12(c) of the Federal Rules of Civil Procedure. A motion for judgment pleadings is usually reserved for cases in which legally recognized defenses are not pled, including statutes of limitation. A party facing the prospect of having the pleadings dismissed because of an obvious omission can move under Rule 15 of the Federal Rules of Civil Procedure to amend the pleadings to correct the error.

PRACTICE TIP

Given that attorneys often concentrate on certain areas of litigation, there is a strong potential for the legal team to face the same legal issues over and over. A firm that specializes in medical malpractice defense, for example, may find itself filing motions for summary judgment on statute of limitations issues in nearly all of its cases. As a result, both defense and plaintiffs' firms maintain a "motions bank," a file containing motions filed in other cases. In the days before computers, it actually was a file, often an over-stuffed manila file folder with copies of old motions. These days, it is far more common to find the files on computer hard drives and disks. Once drafted, a motion can be redone with relatively minor work and put to use in a current case. Of course, because no case is ever identical to another, it is a good idea to use this practice with caution. Every motion filed in every case should be closely reviewed, not only from the standpoint of whether it is justified by the law but also by the standard of whether it is a legitimate motion or simply "filler."

FIGURE 9.9
Judgment on the Pleadings

Source: Rule 12(c) Federal Rules of Civil Procedure.

> After the pleadings are closed but within such time as not to delay the trial, any party may move for judgment on the pleadings. If, on a motion for judgment on the pleadings, matters outside the pleadings are presented to and not excluded by the court, the motion shall be treated as one for summary judgment and disposed of as provided in Rule 56, and all parties shall be given reasonable opportunity to present all material made pertinent to such a motion by Rule 56.

The essence of a motion for judgment on the pleadings is that they are so defective that even if taken at face value, they do not make a case for the legal liability of the other party. Motions for judgment on the pleadings are often mentioned in conjunction with motions for summary judgment for the simple reason that they are linked by the express wording of Rule 12(c) and by the fact that the point of the motion is to attack the basis of a party's contention. When one party challenges the legal sufficiency of the other side's claim, that action begins to resemble the legal definition of a motion for summary judgment. As you can see from reading Rule 12(c), a motion for judgment on the pleadings can easily convert to a motion for summary judgment, but only when the issues and evidence not expressly provided in the pleadings are to be considered. (See Figure 9.9.)

Affirmative Defenses

affirmative defense

An "excuse" by the opposing party that does not just simply negate the allegation, but puts forth a legal reason to avoid enforcement. These defenses are waived if not pleaded.

In addition to motions for summary judgment and a motion for a judgment on the pleadings, parties are also entitled to raise various **affirmative defenses** in motions. Under Rule 12 of the Federal Rules of Civil Procedure, parties may raise affirmative defenses in their response to pleadings or by motion. Among these affirmative defenses are:

1. Lack of jurisdiction over the subject matter.
2. Lack of jurisdiction over the person.
3. Improper venue.
4. Insufficiency of process.
5. Insufficiency of service of process.
6. Failure to state a claim upon which relief can be granted.
7. Failure to join a party under Rule 19.

Lack of Jurisdiction over the Subject Matter

If the court lacks subject matter jurisdiction, it is not empowered to hear any of the issues raised in the complaint and answer. As a result, if a party can successfully claim lack of subject matter jurisdiction, the court has no option but to dismiss the case or transfer it to a court that does have appropriate jurisdiction.

Lack of Jurisdiction over the Person

A motion under Rule 12(b)(2) makes an allegation similar to lack of jurisdiction over the subject matter. In this situation, the party alleges that the court has no jurisdiction over one or both parties involved in the case and that the court is therefore unable to enter a legally binding decision. If a court determines that it lacks personal jurisdiction over the parties, the court must again dismiss the case or remove it to the appropriate forum.

Improper Venue

Venue refers to the locale where the trial occurs. Like personal jurisdiction and subject matter jurisdiction, the trial must occur in an appropriate venue. Venue is determined by state statute. If the court determines that the trial is located in the incorrect county, the action must be transferred to the appropriate venue.

Insufficiency of Process and Service of Process

Categories 4 and 5 under Rule 12 are directed to two different aspects of the same action. Insufficiency of process refers to some error or defect that occurred in drafting the summons

FIGURE 9.10
Grounds for
Granting a 12(b)(6)
Motion

- The complaint sets out no valid legal theory to support the plaintiff's request.
- The complaint fails to allege an essential fact, required for the court to rule in the plaintiff's favor.
- The complaint contradicts its own allegations by providing a bar to the plaintiff's claim. Example: The complaint clearly alleges that the claim is barred by the statute of limitations.

that accompanied the complaint. Insufficiency of service of process refers to some error that occurred in actually serving the defendant with a copy of the summons and complaint.

Failure to Join a Necessary Party under Rule 19

Rule 19 of the Rules of Civil Procedure provides that all parties who have an interest in the litigation must be joined as plaintiffs or defendants in the action. Interested parties are often described as "necessary parties" and must be parties to the action. If they are not, the original parties or interested parties may file motions to have them added to the case.

You may have noticed that we skipped Rule 12(b)(6); that is because a motion under this subpart to Rule 12 deserves separate treatment.

12(b)(6) Motion

It is very common for a party to file a 12(b)(6) motion. In fact, it is one of the most commonly filed motions and goes to the very heart of the issues raised in the case. Many defense attorneys make it part of their routine motions. The purpose of such a motion is to challenge the basis of the complaint by stating that it fails to allege a legally recognized wrong and should therefore be dismissed. Although this motion is common, actually succeeding on the motion is rare. Because most states have adopted notice pleading as the basis for all of their civil actions, the question often arises: What makes a complaint so vague or lacking in factual detail that it fails to state a claim upon which relief can be granted? For instance, if the defendant alleges that the allegation lacks sufficient detail to put him or her on notice of claim, the appropriate vehicle to challenge the wording of the complaint is a motion for a more definite statement. The standard that courts use in evaluating a 12(b)(6) motion is to consider the facts pled by the plaintiff as true and determine whether, given the veracity of those facts, the plaintiff's claim alleges a legally recognized wrong. Another way to approach a 12(b)(6) motion is to ask whether, taking all of the plaintiff's allegations as true, the complaint fails to allege sufficient grounds to entitle the plaintiff to a recovery. Examples of deficiencies that would authorize a court to grant a 12(b)(6) motion are set out in Figure 9.10.

Motion for More Definite Statement

motion for more definite statement
A request by a defendant for additional specificity of plaintiff's complaint.

If the defendant believes that the complaint is so vague or ambiguous that it fails to place the defendant on adequate notice about the nature of the plaintiff's claim, the defendant is authorized to bring a **motion for more definite statement** under Rule 12(e). (See Figure 9.11.) That rule provides that a party may request the opposing party to supplement the wording of its pleading with additional details that the party claims are specifically lacking. (See Figure 9.12.)

Motion for Default Judgment

default judgment
A judgment entered by the court against the defendant for failure to respond to the plaintiff's complaint.

A plaintiff is also authorized to move for a **default judgment** when the defendant fails to respond to the complaint. A motion for default judgment is commonly raised when the defendant fails to file an answer or fails to appear for a scheduled court date. In such a case, the plaintiff would win the case by default and could then request the court to award damages.

FIGURE 9.11
**Motion for a More
Definite Statement**
Source: Rule 12(e) Federal
Rules of Civil Procedure.

If a pleading to which a responsive pleading is permitted is so vague or ambiguous that a party cannot reasonably be required to frame a responsive pleading, the party may move for a more definite statement before interposing a responsive pleading. The motion shall point out the defects complained of and the details desired. If the motion is granted and the order of the court is not obeyed within 10 days after notice of the order or within such other time as the court may fix, the court may strike the pleading to which the motion was directed or make such order as it deems just.

FIGURE 9.12   **Example of Motion for a More Definite Statement**

IN THE SUPERIOR COURT
BURKE COUNTY
STATE OF PLACID

SUPERIOR COURT DIVISION
FILE NUMBER: _____

JANE DOE,

      Plaintiff,

      vs.

NICHOLAS D. CHARLES

      Defendant.

)
)
)
)
)
)
)
)
)
)
)

Motion for More Definite Statement

    Defendant, by counsel, pursuant to PL R. Civ. P. 8(e), moves the court to grant its motion requiring the plaintiff, Jane Doe, to file with the court and serve on the defendant a more definite statement, based on the following reasons:

    1. Plaintiff's complaint is so vague and ambiguous that it fails to comply with the court rules in the following respects:

    a. It violates PL Rules of Civil Procedure, Rule 8, in that it fails to contain an affidavit by a third party establishing that the party heard or had communicated to it a slanderous statement supposedly made by the defendant concerning the plaintiff.

    b. It violates PL STAT. ANN. 23-21-06, in that it fails to allege that the statements supposedly made by the defendant concerned the plaintiff's professional status, a crime involving moral turpitude, a sexually transmitted disease, or the plaintiff's mental incompetence.

    Defendant requests that this court enter an order requiring plaintiff to file and serve a more definite statement. This the 9th day of May, 2007.
    Respectfully submitted,

_____

Clarence D. Arrow
Attorney for Defendant
100 Maple Ave.
Placid City, PL 25360
(555)555-1212
State Bar No. 004562

Certificate of Service

    This is to certify that the undersigned has on the date set out below served a copy of this Motion for Summary Judgment on the plaintiff's attorney, to wit:

Linda Lawyer
200 Elm Street
Placid City, PL 25360

By depositing same, postage prepaid, in the United States Mail.
This the 9th day of May, 2007.

_____

Clarence D. Arrow
Attorney for Defendant
100 Maple Ave.
Placid City, PL 25360
(555)555-1212
State Bar No. 004562

COMMUNICATION TIP

Although it is possible for one party in a civil case to schedule a motion unilaterally by the use of a Notice of Motion, it is far more common for the parties to work with one another and the judge's office to schedule the motion at a convenient time. People who are unfamiliar with the legal profession are often surprised by how much opposing sides in a civil case accommodate one another with issues such as scheduling discovery and hearing motions. Setting a date to argue a series of motions may involve a lot of telephone calls between the parties to find a time that is convenient. Although it is not always possible, especially if the court has a rigid schedule about when it hears motions, it is always good practice to work with the opposing legal team as much as possible. Much of this pre-filing communication is usually documented only in memoranda to the file. Only the final agreement is written up in a confirming letter.

THE JUDGE'S ROLE IN CONSIDERING MOTIONS

CYBER TRIP

'Lectric Law Library—Motion for Summary Judgment http://www.lectlaw.com/def2/m043.htm Tech Law Journal—Motion for Summary Judgment http://www.techlawjournal.com/glossary/legal/summary.htm Motion for Default Judgment—Federal Court, filing instructions http://www.deb.uscourts.gov/Attorney/Motion_For_Default_Judgment.htm Cornell University—Motion for more definite statement http://www.law.cornell.edu/uscode/html/uscode26a/usc_sec_26a_00000051----000-.html

So far, we have discussed the role of the parties in bringing and arguing motions, but it is just as important to understand the role of the judge in the process. We have already seen that a motion for summary judgment assumes that certain facts are true and that, given these facts, the plaintiff is not legally entitled to win. What exactly does that mean? Are there situations in which the judge can take all of the plaintiff's allegations as true and still rule for the defendant? Consider Hypothetical 9-2.

Hypothetical 9-2

Two years ago, John Doe sought medical treatment from Dr. Medico. Unfortunately, Dr. Medico did not follow the prescribed standard of care, and John's original injury was aggravated. Eventually, John had to undergo surgery on the affected area and was left with a terrible scar. He has brought suit against Dr. Medico, alleging medical malpractice. Dr. Medico answers the complaint, denying any responsibility. There is some brief discovery in the case, and then Dr. Medico files a motion for summary judgment, alleging that the statute of limitations for such an action is one year and that Doe's complaint is barred.

Will the judge grant the motion for summary judgment?

To answer the question posed in Hypothetical 9-2, we must address the basic issue of the contested facts in the case of *Doe v. Medico*. What Dr. Medico is saying in his motion for summary judgment is that there are no contested facts in this case. Dr. Medico does not challenge Doe's version of the facts and even, for the purposes of the motion only, will agree that they are valid. However, the defendant states that the law on this issue is clear: The plaintiff must bring a claim of medical malpractice within one year of the injury.

Motions for Summary Judgment

When a trial judge is presented with a motion for summary judgment, the first question that must be answered pertains to the contested facts. If there are any genuine issues of fact to be resolved, the judge is barred from making a ruling on the motion. If the judge were to make a ruling when the facts were not clear, the judge would be invading the authority reserved for the jury. It is for the jurors to determine which party's version of the facts is the more reasonable, and judges are usually more than willing to let them carry out this function. Even more important, at least from the judge's perspective, if a judge does invade the **province of the jury**, the judgment is likely to be overturned on appeal. The judge must therefore determine if there are contested facts in the case. However, because parties can always find some facts upon which they disagree, the law establishes a standard that the trial

province of the jury
An issue that is exclusively the responsibility of the jury to determine.

judge must apply to the motion for summary judgment: Are there genuine issues concerning material facts?

material fact
A fact that is essential to the case and its holding; a fact that, if different, might alter the entire outcome of the case.

A **material fact** is one that is so vital to the allegations that without it, the case fails. When a court considers a motion for summary judgment, the judge makes this determination by reviewing the written motions filed by the parties and all accompanying information, including affidavits and excerpts from discovery. If a judge finds that there are genuine issues about the important facts in this case, he or she must deny the motion and allow it to go to trial, during which the jurors will consider all of the evidence and reach their own conclusions. However, if there are no genuine issues, then the only remaining points in the case involve interpretations of the law, and that is the exclusive province of the judge.

Questions of law are resolved by the judge, not by juries. It is not for the jurors in the case of *Doe v. Medico* to say whether the statute of limitations applies. The trial judge makes that determination. If the judge rules that the defendant's motion for summary judgment is valid, and that there are no triable issues left in the case, the judge must grant the motion.

Hypothetical 9-2, Part II

Does John Doe have any possible defense to the claim that the statute of limitations has run out? On the face of the matter, Dr. Medico seems to have a solid case. The statute provides that Doe must have brought his case within one year, and it was actually brought two years later. However, the law on the statute of limitations, especially when it involves medical malpractice cases, is rarely so black and white. For one thing, most states have provisions in their statutes allowing a tolling (or temporary suspension of the running of the time limit) of the statute until the patient becomes aware of the condition or, by reasonable procedures, would have become aware of the condition. In such a situation, Doe's claim may not be barred by the statute of limitations.

USING MOTIONS TO CLARIFY ISSUES IN LITIGATION

Because various motions can resolve or even completely dismiss a pending case, it should come as no surprise that parties in civil cases routinely file many motions in their cases. Whether requesting a default judgment, a dismissal of the case, sanctions for improper activities during discovery, or a partial summary judgment, motions are important for any of a number of issues in a case. Civil practitioners also use motions as a way of honing their case. By filing a wide variety of motions, the parties can help shake loose any minor issues and force the court, and later the jury, to focus on a few specific points. When a judge grants a motion for partial summary judgment, for example, the issues addressed in that motion will never be presented to the jury. The parties can then present testimony and evidence on the remaining issues. Attorneys often file a broad spectrum of motions with this end game in mind: By resolving many of the issues prior to trial, the motions will help clarify the remaining issues in the case, saving time and resources.

PRETRIAL, TRIAL, AND POST-TRIAL MOTIONS

One way of categorizing motions is by grouping them in terms of when they are likely to be brought during the course of litigation. For instance, if we were to arrange motions into the broad categories of pretrial, trial, and post-trial motions, we might come up with the following headings:

Pretrial Motions

- Summary judgment.
- Partial summary judgment.
- Judgment on the pleadings.
- Affirmative defenses.

- 12(b)(6) motion.
- Motion for more definite statement.
- Motion for default judgment.

Trial Motions

- Motion for continuance.
- Motion in limine.

Post-Trial Motions

- JNOV.
- Motion for directed verdict.
- Motion for a new trial.

We have addressed both pretrial and trial motions but have not considered the issues surrounding post-trial motions. For instance, one motion that is frequently brought at the conclusion of a jury trial is a JNOV motion.

JNOV Motions

JNOV (judgment notwithstanding the verdict)
Asks the judge to reverse the jury verdict based on the inadequacy of the evidence presented to support the law and the verdict.

The abbreviation **JNOV** stands for the Latin phrase, "judgment non obstante verdicto," or a judgment not withstanding the verdict. When the jury returns its verdict, the losing party is permitted to file a JNOV motion requesting that the jury's decision be overturned and replaced with a verdict in favor of the moving party. The losing party might justify this request on the grounds that no reasonable jury hearing the evidence presented in the case could rule as the present jury has done. The party might also claim that the verdict is against the weight of both the law and the facts and ask that the judge reverse the jury's verdict. Although this motion is made at the conclusion of many civil trials, it is rarely granted. To justify reversing the jury, the trial judge must reach the conclusion that the jury's finding is not supported by the evidence and that no reasonable jury could reach such a conclusion. Given the hotly contested nature of most civil suits, there is usually more than sufficient grounds for the jury's decision in favor of either party.

Motion for Directed Verdict

motion for directed verdict
A request by a party for a judgment because the other side has not met its burden of proof.

Another motion that is commonly brought at the conclusion of one or more phases of a trial is a **motion for directed verdict**. This motion may come at the conclusion of the plaintiff's case in chief and may be renewed at the conclusion of the trial. Here, a party moves the court to enter a verdict in its favor without resorting to jury deliberations. A defendant might move for a directed verdict at the conclusion of the plaintiff's case when the plaintiff has failed to prove some essential element of his or her case. The defendant is also free to renew the motion at the conclusion of the trial. The plaintiff is also permitted to move for a directed verdict against the defendant, especially when the defendant has filed counterclaims and failed to present any evidence to support them. Directed verdicts can also be granted for specific issues, while leaving others for the jury's consideration.

Motion for New Trial

motion for new trial
Post-trial relief that requests a new trial on the same issues for specific reasons that must be clearly explained and argued in the motion.

Although we discuss **motions for new trial** in greater depth in Chapter 13, a word about them here is also helpful. Let us suppose that at the end of a trial, the jury finds for the plaintiff and assesses damages against the culpable defendant. In such a situation, the defendant would file a motion for new trial, alleging any possible improprieties that may have occurred during the trial. If the judge grants the motion, which is rare, the parties must retry the case before a different jury. If the judge denies the motion, then that denial allows the defendant to begin the appellate process.

CASE IN POINT

Davidson

v.

Castner-Knott Dry Goods Co., Inc.

L 1114043, 1-8 (Ky. App., 2006)

Taja Davidson appeals from a January 28, 2005[,] order of the Warren Circuit Court granting summary judgment to Castner-Knott Dry Goods Co., Inc.[,] as to Davidson's malicious prosecution claim. Upon review, we reverse and remand for further proceedings.

On October 2, 1997, Davidson reported to the Nashville Metropolitan Police Department that checks on her account at First Union National Bank of Tennessee had been stolen, and that her account there had been closed for approximately one year. The report resulted from Davidson's discovery that two of those checks had been presented to a grocery store and a Wal-Mart in Nashville.

On November 28, 1997, Castner-Knott accepted a check in the amount of $349.79 drawn on Davidson's First Union account. The check was dishonored by the bank and returned to Castner-Knott marked "Account Closed." Subsequently, on or about March 5, 1998, Timothy Bush—a loss prevention employee at Castner-Knott—appeared at the Warren County Attorney's office and signed a criminal complaint against Davidson. On April 8, 1998, the Warren County Grand Jury reported a True Bill against Davidson charging her with Theft by Deception over $300.00, and a bench warrant was issued for her arrest.

On July 21, 2001, Davidson was a passenger in a car that was stopped in Blue Ash, Ohio, for an alleged traffic violation. A record check disclosed the Warren County bench warrant, and Davidson was arrested. Several days later, she appeared in court in Hamilton County, Ohio, where she waived extradition before being taken to Warren County by sheriff's deputies. She was subsequently arraigned and released from custody on July 27, 2001, by Warren Circuit Court Judge Thomas R. Lewis.

On August 29, 2001, the Commonwealth Attorney filed a written motion to dismiss the indictment against Davidson without prejudice. On September 4, 2001, at the scheduled pretrial conference, the Commonwealth Attorney told Judge Lewis that he sought to dismiss the case due to (1) Davidson's police report indicating that her checks had been stolen, and (2) the fact that Castner-Knott no longer did business in Warren County, so the Commonwealth did not have a witness. In response to the Commonwealth's motion to dismiss, counsel for Davidson moved the court to dismiss the indictment with prejudice, citing the Commonwealth's inability to go forward with the case and the injustice that had been caused to Davidson. On September 5, 2001, the court entered an order dismissing the indictment without prejudice, in accordance with the Commonwealth's request.

On August 30, 2002, Davidson filed suit against Castner-Knott in Warren Circuit Court alleging malicious prosecution and abuse of process. On July 24, 2003, Castner-Knott moved for summary judgment on the malicious prosecution claim on the basis that Davidson could not prove that the underlying criminal proceeding terminated in her favor, in part because she allegedly agreed to the Commonwealth's motion to dismiss without prejudice. On September 2, 2003, Judge Lewis entered an order denying the motion. Castner-

Knott appealed the denial to this court and then to the Kentucky Supreme Court, but the appeal was rejected in both cases.

On September 29, 2004, following Judge Lewis' retirement, Castner-Knott renewed its motion for summary judgment. It reiterated the arguments made in its previous motion and additionally contended that Timothy Bush had probable cause to swear out a complaint against Davidson. Following an October 26, 2004[,] hearing and extensive briefing, Judge John R. Grise indicated that he would grant the motion at a December 16, 2004[,] pretrial conference. A written order to this effect was entered on January 28, 2005.

In this order, the trial court concluded that "Castner-Knott is entitled to summary judgment because Ms. Davidson has failed to show that the dismissal without prejudice of the indictment constitutes a termination of criminal proceedings in her favor." First—relying primarily upon *Van Arsdale v. Caswell*, 311 S.W.2d 404 (Ky.1958)—the trial court held that, although a dismissal without prejudice is not final for purposes of the tort of malicious prosecution, Davidson still could have appealed the dismissal without prejudice. It also noted that a formal objection to the dismissal without prejudice is nowhere to be found in the record.

The trial court then disagreed with Davidson's argument that a dismissal without prejudice was a termination in her favor, citing to a passage in 52 Am.Jur.2d Malicious Prosecution § 40 (2000) that states: "Some types of terminations that do not satisfy the requirement for a favorable termination include . . . the striking of the case from the criminal docket with leave to reinstate." The court also cited to 52 Am.Jur.2d Malicious Prosecution § 34 and *Van Arsdale* for the proposition that "an indefinite continuance does not amount to an abandonment of prosecution that would permit maintenance of a malicious prosecution action."

The court also found—pointing to § 660(c) of the Restatement (Second) of Torts while indicating that it has never been adopted by a Kentucky appellate court—that Davidson was not entitled to relief because her indictment was not withdrawn because the Commonwealth thought she was innocent; instead, it "was dismissed because attainment of evidence necessary to fully prosecute her was not readily available." The court further held— citing this same provision—that Davidson's indictment "was not abandoned out of mercy requested or accepted by the accused." In this context, the court concluded that the Commonwealth had to believe that Davidson was guilty; otherwise, it would not have dismissed her indictment without prejudice.

Consequently, the trial court held that "Davidson will not be able to prove that the indictment that was dismissed without prejudice constitutes a termination of proceedings in her favor, even if the facts indicate that the Commonwealth will more than likely never re-indict her." It continued: "From the Kentucky case law cited above, there are no genuine issues of material fact as to whether the 'filing away' of an indictment constitutes nothing more than in [sic] indefinite continuance of the state's prerogative to bring charges against Ms. Davidson at a later date." The court finally concluded: "A dismissal without prejudice is neither final nor in Ms. Davidson's favor. Therefore, summary judgment in favor of Castner-Knott should be granted." This appeal followed.

On appeal, Davidson first argues that Castner-Knott's renewed summary judgment motion and the trial court's order granting it violate the "law of the case" doctrine. She specifically contends that the original order from Judge Lewis denying summary judgment was the "law of the case" pursuant to CR 54.02(1).

As a general rule, "the doctrine of law of the case establishes a presumption that a ruling made at one stage of a lawsuit will be adhered to throughout the lawsuit." *Hallahan v. The Courier Journal*, 138 S.W.3d 699, 705 n. 4 (Ky.App.2004). However, a judge does have the discretionary authority to reconsider a ruling. Id. "Generally, a judge may reexamine an earlier ruling and rescind it if he has a reasonable conviction that it was wrong and it would not cause undue prejudice to the party that benefited from it." Id. Moreover, and of particular relevance here, "it is well established that a trial court may reconsider and grant summary judgment to a party subsequent to an earlier denial." Id.

We review a decision to reconsider under an abuse of discretion standard. Id. "The test for abuse of discretion is whether the trial judge's decision was arbitrary, unreasonable, unfair, or unsupported by sound legal principles." Sexton v. Sexton, 125 S.W.3d 258, 272 (Ky.2004); see also *Kuprion v. Fitzgerald*, 888 S.W.2d 679, 684 (Ky.1994). After examining the record and the arguments of both parties, we do not believe that the trial court abused its discretion in deciding to reconsider its previous ruling. Judge Grise obviously felt that Judge Lewis' previous decision was wrong, and we do not believe that Davidson has produced enough substantive evidence of undue prejudice to merit a reversal on this ground. Accordingly, we turn to her remaining arguments.

Our standard of review as to cases where a summary judgment has been granted is "whether the trial court correctly found that there were no genuine issues as to any material fact and that the moving party was entitled to judgment as a matter of law." *Scifres v. Kraft*, 916 S.W.2d 779, 781 (Ky.App.1996); CR 56.03. Summary judgment "is proper only where the movant shows that the adverse party could not prevail under any circumstances." *Steelvest, Inc. v. Scansteel Service Center, Inc.*, 807 S.W.2d 476, 479 (Ky.1991). And, "because summary judgments involve no fact finding, this Court reviews them de novo, in the sense that we owe no deference to the conclusions of the trial court." *Blevins v. Moran*, 12 S.W.3d 698, 700 (Ky.App.2000).

"There are six basic elements necessary to the maintenance of an action for malicious prosecution, in response to both criminal prosecutions and civil action." *Raine v. Drasin*, 621 S.W.2d 895, 899 (Ky.1981). They include: "(1) the institution or continuation of original judicial proceedings, either civil or criminal, or of administrative or disciplinary proceedings, (2) by, or at the instance, of the plaintiff, (3) the termination of such proceedings in defendant's favor, (4) malice in the institution of such proceeding, (5) want or lack of probable cause for the proceeding, and (6) the suffering of damage as a result of the proceeding." Id. Historically, the tort of malicious prosecution is one that has not been favored in the law. *Prewitt v. Sexton*, 777 S.W.2d 891, 895 (Ky.1989); *Reid v. True*, 302 S.W.2d 846, 847-48 (Ky.1957). Accordingly, one claiming malicious prosecution must strictly comply with the elements of the tort. *See Prewitt*, 777 S.W.2d at 895; *Raine*, 621 S.W.2d at 899. In reviewing the record here, we find that the trial court's decision to grant summary judgment was predicated entirely upon its conclusion that Davidson could not satisfy the third prong of this test; that is, she could not prove a termination of the proceedings in her favor.

Although we find the trial court's order to be somewhat unclear as to the issue, Castner-Knott submits, and we agree, that the court concluded—relying on *Van Arsdale v. Caswell*, supra—that dismissing a criminal complaint without prejudice is the same as "filing away" a complaint. Therefore, such a dismissal "is not a final determination thereof but is an indefinite continuance of the case which may be reinstated on the docket upon reasonable notice at any time after such order is entered." *Van Arsdale*, 311 S.W.2d at 408.

Consequently, the first question we must consider is whether a dismissal without prejudice is the same as "filing away" a complaint for the purposes of a malicious prosecution claim. After reviewing the applicable case law, we believe that the answer is "No." Indeed, that law directly refutes the trial court's conclusion. For example, in *Hoskins v. Maricle*, 150 S.W.3d 1 (Ky.2004), our Supreme Court stated that the procedure of "filing away" a complaint was commonly used when, after issuance of an indictment, "the defendant cannot be found within the jurisdiction, witnesses are unavailable, or it is deemed appropriate to abate the prosecution conditioned upon the defendant's compliance with certain requirements." Id. at 13 n. 8. The Court then noted: "The practice is regarded not as a dismissal, which would require a reindictment, but as an indefinite continuance." Id., citing *Commonwealth v. Bottoms*, 105 Ky. 222, 48 S.W. 974, 975 (1899) (Italics added). Indeed, even *Van Arsdale* cites to case law pointing out this fact. Van Arsdale, 311 S.W.2d at 407 (*citing Jones v. Commonwealth*, 114 Ky. 599, 71 S.W. 643 (1903), for the proposition that "a 'filing away' order does not operate as a dismissal of the indictment but is only an indefinite continuance."). Accordingly, there is an obvious distinction between the dismissal of an indictment and simply "filing it away." The latter is considered an "indefinite continuance," while the former is not. The trial court's suggestion otherwise was in error.

With this point established, the question then becomes whether a dismissal without prejudice can be considered a "final termination" for purposes of malicious prosecution. In addressing this problem, we first note that our courts established long ago that the termination of a prosecution "by final trial, or dismissal by the prosecuting authorities or by the prosecutor himself, and without the voluntary procurement of the defendant in the prosecution" constitutes a final termination for purposes of a malicious prosecution suit. *Davis v. Brady*, 218 Ky. 384, 291 S.W. 412, 413 (1927) (Italics added). The point made by Castner-Knott here, however, is that a dismissal without prejudice—unlike a dismissal with prejudice—is not sufficiently final to meet this requirement. Davidson, of course, disagrees.

We believe that this question can be resolved by reference to *Commonwealth v. Sowell*, 157 S.W.3d 616 (Ky.2005). In *Sowell*, our Supreme Court reiterated its long-held position that a dismissal without prejudice is a final and appealable order. Id. at 617, citing *Wood v. Downing's* Admr., 110 Ky. 656, 62 S.W. 487, 488 (1901); *C.I.T. Corp. v. Teague*, 293 Ky. 521, 169 S.W.2d 593, 593 (1943); *Grubbs v. Slater & Gilroy, Inc.*, 267 S.W.2d 754, 755 (Ky.1954). Citing in particular to *Wood v. Downing's* Admr., the Court noted that an order dismissing without prejudice "fixed absolutely and finally the rights of the parties in this suit in relation to the subject matter of the litigation, and put an end to the suit. It was a final appealable order." Id., citing *Wood*, 110 Ky. 656, 62 S.W. at 488. Moreover, "notwithstanding the 'without prejudice' language, an order of dismissal adjudicates all rights. Nothing remains to be done." Id.

Castner-Knott argues, however, that *Sowell* supports the idea that a dismissal without prejudice does not constitute a "final termination" because it "does not bar another indictment or prosecution." Id. at 619. However, upon much consideration, we do not believe that such a bar is necessary for "finality" in malicious prosecution cases, as our law in this area only requires that a particular proceeding be terminated in a claimant's favor. As our Supreme Court further provided in *Sowell*, again citing *Commonwealth v. Smith*:

> When an indictment is dismissed, unless the matter be then referred to the grand jury, it is a final order in that case. After the term at which the order is entered, the court has not the power to set it aside. Should the court or the prosecution desire to retain control of the case after the term, it may be done by an order filing the indictment away, to be redocketed on motion of the commonwealth. But, without such reservation, an unconditional dismissal is an end of that case. If, therefore, the commonwealth desires to reinstate the prosecution, it may do so by procuring another indictment, or by warrant of arrest sworn out before an examining magistrate, and then proceed as in other original prosecutions. Id. at 618-19, citing *Smith*, 140 Ky. 580, 131 S.W. at 392.

While *Sowell* was not rendered in the context of a malicious prosecution case, we believe that its conclusions support our position that a dismissal of a case—whether it be with or without prejudice—constitutes a "final termination" for purposes of the tort. Once a case is dismissed without prejudice, the proceedings in which it occurred are final and concluded as a matter of law. In order for the case to be prosecuted again, an entirely new set of proceedings must be instituted and the prosecuting party must "proceed as in other original prosecutions." Id. at 619.

With this said, the third prong of our malicious prosecution test also requires that the termination be favorable to the accused. *Raine*, 621 S.W.2d at 899. In *Alcorn v. Gordon*, 762 S. W.2d 809 (Ky.App.1988), a panel of this court cited to Comment a to the Restatement (Second) of Torts § 660 for the proposition that "proceedings are 'terminated in favor of the accused' as that phrase is used in § 653 and throughout this Topic, only when their final disposition is such as to indicate the innocence of the accused." Id. at 811-12. Further citing to *Lackner v. LaCroix*, 25 Cal.3d 747, 159 Cal.Rptr. 693, 602 P.2d 393 (1979), we elaborated on this principle, stating:

> It is apparent "favorable" termination does not occur merely because a party complained against has prevailed in an underlying action. While the fact he has prevailed is an ingredient of a favorable termination, such termination must further reflect on his innocence of the alleged wrongful conduct. If the termination does not relate to the merits--reflecting on neither innocence of nor responsibility for the alleged misconduct--the termination is not favorable in the

sense it would support a subsequent action for malicious prosecution. Id. at 812, citing Lackner, 159 Cal.Rptr. at 695, 602 P.2d at 395.

We therefore concluded that "dismissal of a suit for technical or procedural reasons that do not reflect on the merits of the case is not a favorable termination of the action." Id.

Although we are hesitant to rule as a matter of law that the termination of Davidson's indictment was on the merits from the record that stands before us, we believe that the record clearly indicates that summary judgment as to this issue was inappropriate, particularly as we must consider all facts in a light most favorable to Davidson. We also note that if further discovery—for example, a sworn deposition of the Commonwealth Attorney who originally handled Davidson's indictment—supports the current record's strong suggestion that the Commonwealth's prosecution was abandoned, even in part, because of Davidson's report of stolen checks, the dismissal must be considered favorable to Davidson. While reaching such a conclusion requires further factual development, the determination of whether a termination is sufficiently favorable ultimately rests with the trial court as a matter of law, absent a factual dispute relative to the circumstances of the dismissal.

With this said, as this case is to be remanded, we believe it will be of some benefit to the trial court if we clear up one possible misconception raised by the parties' briefs. Castner-Knott argues that the Warren County grand jury's finding of probable cause to issue an indictment defeats Davidson's claim as a matter of law. However, Kentucky courts have expressed the role of a grand jury indictment as to the element of probable cause in malicious prosecution cases many times: "When a grand jury, upon other testimony than that of the prosecutor alone, find[s] an indictment to be a true bill, the presumption is prima facie that, as they, on their oaths, have said that the person indicted is guilty, the prosecutor had reasonable grounds for the prosecution." *Conder v. Morrison*, 275 Ky. 360, 121 S.W.2d 930, 931 (1938); see also *Schott v. Indiana Nat. Life Insurance Co.*, 160 Ky. 533, 535, 169 S.W. 1023 (1914); *Garrard v. Willet*, 27 Ky. (4 J.J. Marsh.) 628, 630 (1830). Consequently, while a grand jury indictment raises a presumption of probable cause, this presumption can be rebutted by the plaintiff. *Conder*, 121 S.W.2d at 931-32.

Accordingly, we reverse the Warren Circuit Court's entry of summary judgment against Taja Davidson and remand for proceedings consistent with this opinion.

DYCHE, Judge, concurs.

COMBS, Chief Judge, concurs and files separate opinion.

Source: From Westlaw. Used with permission of Thomson/West.

Case Questions:

1. The trial court ruled that Davidson was unable to establish a basic component of her case. What was it?

2. What is the "law of the case" doctrine?

3. Did the appellate court find that the trial judge has abused his discretion? Explain.

4. What is the standard that a moving party must show to prevail on a motion for summary judgment in Kentucky?

5. What are the six basic elements of a cause of action for malicious prosecution?

Eye on Ethics

BAD FAITH AFFIDAVITS

The Federal Rules of Civil Procedure, and the various state rules modeled closely on them, permit trial judges to impose a wide variety of sanctions against parties who file affidavits in bad faith or affidavits simply to delay the court's procedures. In such a situation, the court is empowered under Rule 12(g), as follows:

> (g) Affidavits Made in Bad Faith. Should it appear to the satisfaction of the court at any time that any of the affidavits presented pursuant to this rule are presented in bad faith or solely for the purpose of delay, the court shall forthwith order the party employing them to pay to the other party the amount of the reasonable expenses which

the filing of the affidavits caused the other party to incur, including reasonable attorney's fees, and any offending party or attorney may be adjudged guilty of contempt.

Under this rule, the judge can assess attorney's fees against the party who filed or participated in the filing of the bad faith affidavit. The court's power also includes contempt powers, which can result in monetary sanctions or even a finding that a party's willful acts deserve a few days in jail. As a result, it is important for all legal professionals to be aware of and discourage clients from attempting to file bogus or disingenuous affidavits. A party might wish to harass or annoy the other party, but using court procedures or sworn affidavits to do so can result in harsh actions by the trial judge.

A Day in the Life: Carmen Brown

Carmen Brown has always wanted to be an attorney. Several years ago, she decided to start by obtaining a degree from a paralegal program, because "Attending a Paralegal program would allow me to gain the foundation of law that would inevitably help me in law school." Completing the program was no easy matter because she worked full time, but she finished her Associate's degree in two years. The program offered her a chance to work as an intern at the local courthouse, an opportunity that "allowed me to gain a lot of useful knowledge in the field of law. [It] allowed me to actually have hands-on experience, which to me is the best. It also allowed me the opportunity to meet people within my field of interest. The internship was a very valuable experience."

Brown works full-time as a paralegal, specializing in personal injury cases. But she also finds herself working on other types of cases, including domestic and medical malpractice cases. "I love my job!" she exclaims. "Being a paralegal is a lot of work but it is very interesting work."

Carmen Brown believes that two things are essential to the day-to-day work of a paralegal: organization and attention to detail: "The largest amount of work done in a law firm is done by the paralegal. It is critical that the paralegal invest all of his or her attention to every aspect of a client's file, not just the document at hand. This is where good organization is a must. Organization within a file eliminates time wasted and allows one the ability to quickly answer any question posed regarding the file. Organization is critical!

"A paralegal's daily tasks vary from day to day. I may come in to work and be prepared to work on a certain file and may or may not get to work on [it]," she notes. On any given day, a paralegal might help draft a complaint, compile documents for a settlement brochure, prepare interrogatories, or research issues related to motions in the case.

Real Paralegal Life: Building a Skill Set

PREPARE a 12(b)(6) MOTION

Review the Apple complaint in Appendix C and prepare a 12(b)(6) motion requesting that the court dismiss counts one, two, and three of that complaint. Your motion must include a certificate of service and a notice of hearing or notice of motion setting a day in the future when the motion will be argued.

Career Prep

Prepare a table in which the first column contains a list of the motions authorized under your state's rules of civil procedure, and then summarize what each motion does.

Summary

A motion is a party's request to a trial judge for a specific ruling. Motions can be raised about a wide variety of issues. Parties may file motions to exclude evidence from the trial, request commendations, or even dismiss the entire case. A motion in limine is usually an oral motion made during the course of the trial that requests the court to make a specific evidentiary ruling, usually to exclude evidence. A motion for summary judgment is normally made prior to trial and filed by the defendant. This motion requests that the judge dismiss the entire case because there are no genuine issues of fact remaining for a jury to consider. In addition to filing a motion for summary judgment, a party may move for partial summary judgment to request the dismissal of a specific count of the complaint. Parties may also request courts to order the opposing party to clarify its wording in its pleadings through the vehicle of a motion for a more definite statement. A motion for judgment on the pleadings is similar to a motion for summary judgment, in that the party alleges there are no genuine issues of fact remaining in the case and that one side is entitled to a verdict in its favor. A 12(b)(6) motion is a motion based on Rule 12 of the Federal Rules of Civil Procedure. This motion alleges that the plaintiff has failed to state a legally recognized claim in his or her complaint and therefore that the defendant is entitled to a dismissal of the action. Although motions can be filed as separate documents, many modern practitioners include motions in their responsive pleadings.

Key Terms

Motion, 193
Certificate of service, 195
Affidavit, 195
Motion in limine, 199
Dispositive motions, 200
Motion for summary judgment, 200
Judgment on the pleadings, 202
Affirmative defense, 203

Motion for more definite statement, 204
Default judgment, 204
Province of the jury, 206
Material fact, 206
JNOV, 208
Motion for directed verdict, 208
Motion for new trial, 208

Review Questions

1. What is the purpose of a motion?
2. How do parties prepare motions?
3. What is a notice of motion?
4. What is a certificate of service?
5. Explain the function of motions for summary judgment.
6. What is a motion for partial summary judgment?
7. Explain the purpose of a motion for a more definite statement.
8. What is a judgment on the pleadings?
9. What is a motion in limine?
10. Explain the function of affidavits when they are included with a motion.
11. What is a notice of motion?
12. Explain how a party argues a motion before the court.

13. What is the judge's role in considering a motion?

14. How might a party seek to clarify issues in the case through the use of motions?

15. What are some of the issues that can be addressed through motions?

16. Explain the affirmative defenses that can be brought through a motion.

Discussion Questions

1. Why is it important for a legal professional to avoid allowing a client to file an affidavit in bad faith?

2. What basic holding can you describe from this chapter's "Case in Point"?

Exercises: Skill Builders

Prepare a notice of motion, based on the form provided in this chapter, to argue a motion for summary judgment in the Apple case (see Appendix C) for the first Tuesday of next month. Remember to include a time and location for the argument of the motion.

Portfolio Assignment

Portfolio Assignment 9-1: Prepare a motion for summary judgment. Based on the materials found in the Baker file (Appendix B), including the depositions, affidavits, and pleadings, prepare a motion for summary judgment requesting that the plaintiff's first count be dismissed.

Portfolio Assignment 9-2: Prepare motions. Prepare a series of motions on behalf of the plaintiff in the Apple case (Appendix C), including a motion in limine to restrict the defense witnesses from referring to the plaintiff's prior and unrelated marital trouble, including the filing of charges involving domestic violence; a motion for partial summary judgment alleging that the second count is legally insufficient; and a judgment on the pleadings for the entire complaint.

Vocabulary Builders

ACROSS

8 A defense that goes beyond a simple denial; it states that the defendant is entitled to judgment in his or her favor for specific reasons; it would entitle the defendant to a verdict in his or her favor, if proven.

9 A request by a party made to a judge requesting a specific action.

DOWN

1 A written motion filed by a party requesting a ruling in its favor and dismissal of the opposition's claims.

2 A motion that cites specific deficiencies in a pleading and requests a court order that the judge force the opposition to provide additional detail to support the claim.

3 A party's verification that a copy of a pleading or necessary document was served on the opposing party, either through the U.S. postal system or by personal hand delivery.

4 A judgment entered against a defendant who has failed to file an answer to the plaintiff's complaint.

5 A motion at the outset of a trial, often made orally, that may request a wide variety of forms of relief, including a ruling on evidentiary matters.

6 A contested fact in litigation; a fact that, if different, might alter the entire outcome of the case.

7 A motion that alleges that if all of the allegations raised in the pleadings are true and correct, the movant would still be entitled to a ruling in his or her favor and a dismissal of the opposition's pleadings.

Chapter 10

Preparing for and Conducting the Trial

CHAPTER OBJECTIVES

The student will be able to:

- Explain how legal professionals prepare for trials.

- Explain the role of the trial paralegal.

- Discuss how the case file is organized prior to trial.

- Explain the function of the trial notebook.

- Discuss the ethical concerns involved in preparing witnesses to testify.

- Describe the various phases of a civil trial.

- Explain the difference between direct and cross-examination.

- Discuss the importance of the charge conference.

- Explain the role of suggested pattern jury instructions.

- Describe the process through which a jury determines its verdict.

Trials are some of the most dramatic events in law. Television viewers tune in almost every night to see depictions of civil and criminal trials. There is something electric about that moment when the bailiff steps into the courtroom and announces, "The jury has a verdict!" At that moment, everything seems to kick into high gear. The judge returns to the bench. The jury returns to the jury box. The parties return to the courtroom and take their seats. It is time for the jury to announce its verdict. This is the moment when the parties find out if all of their hard work has paid off.

Trial work is stressful for everyone involved. Witnesses are scared about testifying. Attorneys, even those who have being doing trial work for years, are usually tense and nervous before a trial starts. Paralegals who may have been working in the field for years will also be anxious both before and during the trial.

In this chapter, we examine the various phases of a trial and emphasize the paralegal's increasingly vital role in helping prepare for and participate in the presentation of a civil case. We also note that as a paralegal, you may be the main contact point for clients and witnesses who need information about the trial, including when they are scheduled to testify and how they should act when they are on the witness stand.

PREPARING FOR TRIAL

Thorough preparation is always a requirement for both sides of a civil case. Attorneys who represent the parties must know every aspect of the case to make sure that there are no surprises and to ensure that they give their clients the best possible representation. The paralegals who work with these attorneys should know the case file, evidence, and witness statements as well as the attorneys.

Some of the work that goes into preparing for a trial casts paralegals in the role of private detectives. In big cases, the firm will often retain a real private detective, but in smaller cases, there may not be sufficient resources to justify the expense. In that situation, the investigative work often falls to the trial paralegal. You must be able to locate witnesses and track down judgments, criminal histories, and any other important information. In modern trial practice, attorneys and paralegals should know how to do some basic investigation.

In addition to assisting the attorney with gathering evidence, researching legal issues, tracking down witnesses, and preparing documentation for trial, the work of a trial paralegal sometimes involves unusual activities, such as reconnaissance work. As we saw in a previous chapter, you may need to go to the scene of the accident or locate a witness. Part of your reconnaissance work may involve a trip to the courthouse to examine the courtroom where the trial will be held. This trip may be necessary so that you can tell witnesses where they will be sitting, make sure that there is enough seating for the parties, and even ensure that there are sufficient electrical outlets for the attorneys' laptops, projectors, and other electrical equipment.

Many paralegals who specialize in litigation are drawn to the work because of the excitement and the element of unexpected developments. Trial work can be very exciting; it can also be very draining. There is a rush of adrenalin as the attorneys and paralegals must adjust to sudden changes in testimony, witness availability, and adverse rulings. Trial attorneys and paralegals must be able to think quickly on their feet. They must be able to readjust their plans, rethink their strategy, and work closely with one another to ensure that the case goes smoothly.

The Attorney's Role

The attorney's role in preparing for trial consists of reviewing all pleadings, discovery, and witness statements and preparing a strategy to win the case. The plaintiff's attorney must build the case from the bottom up, using witness testimony and evidence to support every contention in the complaint. Without such support, the case will fall apart. On the other side, the attorney representing the defendant will engage in a similar process but with a different orientation. That attorney will attempt to show that the plaintiff's allegations are groundless and use testimony and evidence to destroy the plaintiff's case. If the defendant also has counterclaims against the plaintiff, the attorney will carry out two actions: attack the merits of the plaintiff's case while proving the defendant's counterclaims. All of this requires a great deal of time and

 SPOT THE ISSUE!

Next week, your firm has a case that is likely to go to trial. The plaintiff is a young man who was struck by a delivery truck owned by the national corporation Get It There Deliveries. You have just met with the plaintiff and two of the people who were in the car with him at the time of the accident. During his deposition, several months ago, the plaintiff claimed that the delivery truck driver came up to him after the accident and admitted fault, saying that he failed to yield and thus caused the accident. When Al Able and Billy Better were originally deposed, they said that they had not heard any statement by the delivery truck driver. Before your firm's meeting with the three men, you saw them talking with another attorney who has only recently come to work for the firm. During the meeting, Al and Billy suddenly changed their story and said that they had heard the delivery man make a statement. You and your supervising attorney separated the men and asked them about this statement. In both circumstances, the men made identical statements, saying, "The driver came up to the car and said, 'Hey, I was at fault. I should have yielded. I'm to blame.'"

What, if anything, should you do about this new evidence?

energy. Attorneys must know every piece of evidence, every witness transcript, every pleading, and every item produced through discovery. In a large case, this can be a daunting task. Later, we will discuss how software developers have attempted to take some of the drudgery out of the process by creating ways for attorneys to track all the necessary information. But it is important for paralegals to understand that an attorney facing trial will be completely wrapped up in a case. It is often the only way to learn everything that the attorney needs to know to be successful at trial.

Added to this burden is the very real possibility of losing the trial. For the plaintiff's attorney, a loss means that all of the time and energy put into the case will have been for nothing. For the defense attorney, a loss is also painful. The defendant may have to pay a hefty monetary judgment to the plaintiff, in addition to the money that the defendant will pay to his or her attorney.

For attorneys representing plaintiffs or defendants, participating in a trial is a lot like doing a play, except that there is no script and the other actors are working against you. Although trial attorneys frequently find the process of trying a case to be stimulating and exciting, there is no question about one fact: Trials are stressful. Stress brings out both the good and the bad in people—more often the bad. When an attorney is getting ready for trial, he or she may get anxious and worried. A paralegal must be aware that in addition to the intensive preparation and concentration necessary to prepare for trial, an attorney may also be anxious or worried about participating in the trial. People suffering from anxiety are not always the easiest individuals to be around.

The Paralegal's Role

Attorneys are not the only professionals devoting tremendous time and energy to prepare for a trial. For a trial paralegal, intensive preparation is also the order of the day. Most paralegals follow a standard pattern when they begin preparing a case for trial. We outline that procedure in this section. In general, a trial paralegal starts trial preparation by first going through the pleadings and then every item of discovery produced by all parties, including their own. Trial paralegals sift through all of these documents and create several aids for the trial, including:

- Chronology of events
- Master index
- Issue table
- Witness cross-reference
- Witness summaries
- Trial timetable
- Organized client file
- Trial notebook

Chronology of Events

One of the best ways to start organizing a case for trial is to prepare an overall chronology of the events in the case. A chronology is useful because it frames the case by explaining exactly what happened, step by step, from beginning to end. Because this organization is how most people tell stories to one another, a detailed chronology can help the entire legal team see the case as a whole. A chronology has other advantages. By meticulously reviewing the case for each event and putting it in its proper sequence, the legal team can quickly see when specific areas have been neglected and develop additional information to explain gaps in the timeline. Many paralegals begin creating a case chronology as soon as the complaint and answer have been filed in the case. The chronology will then help guide the discovery process, as well as help the legal team prepare for the trial.

Creating a chronology requires careful review of all documents and testimony in the case. A paralegal must review the deposition transcripts, statements, affidavits, interrogatory answers, pleadings, and any other evidence in the case to be able to create a detailed and understandable chronology of events. See Figure 10.1 for an example of a case chronology.

When you create a chronology, there are some simple rules to keep in mind. First, the chronology must be accurate. If it is impossible to know a specific fact absolutely, then the entry should

FIGURE 10.1
Chronology of Events
Brown v. Dangerous

Collision between Mary Brown and Danny Dangerous
Date of collision: May 15, 2006
Location: Intersection of Burnett and Burke Streets (Elizabeth County, Placid)
Civil File No.:   06-1007

May 15, 2006

Time	Summary of Activity
9:15 a.m. (approx.)	Plaintiff Mary Brown leaves her home to drive to grocery store. She is alone in car.
9:20 a.m (approx.)	Plaintiff heads west on Burke Street, approaches traffic light at Burke and Burnett, and stops for red light. She is first in line. There is a car behind her and some traffic in oncoming lane.
9:21 a.m. (approx.)	Red light on Burke Street changes to green; she slowly proceeds into intersection.
9:21 a.m (approx.)	D runs red light on Burnett Street and hits passenger side of P's car. P's car is rammed across intersection and into light pole. P briefly loses consciousness.
9:25 a.m.	Officer Mark Williams receives call of accident at Burke and Burnett and logs call.
9:32 a.m.	Officer Williams arrives at scene. Finds P trapped in her car. D is standing next to his truck. Sees that P is trapped in her car and calls for Med/Vac and Fire & Rescue.
9: 41 a.m.	Fire & Rescue arrives, begins working on P's car door to free her.
10:14 a.m.	P freed from her car by Fire & Rescue; placed on spine board and transported to Memorial Hospital Emergency Room.
10:18 a.m.	P evaluated in ER, intubated, sedated. Dr. Wade is on-call physician. Begins her assessment. Notes broken ribs, dislocated shoulder, facial bruising, concussion. P sent to Surgery to drain fluid from base of brain.
May 15–18	P in intensive care.
May 18	P's status changed from critical to serious. Moved to private room.
June 1	P discharged from hospital.

reflect this fact. In Figure 10.1, the plaintiff was not sure about the time that she left her house for her trip to the grocery store, so the time entry is listed as "approximate." Second, the chronology should be simple and not overloaded with details. What a chronology records are events, not the issues surrounding those events. Third, a chronology must list every important detail in the case. Obviously, the date, time, and place of the accident are important, but in a case in which the plaintiff is suing for physical injuries, specific details about her treatment, including admission to the critical care unit and finally being released to go home, are also important points for a chronology.

Master Index

A master index is a general guide to all of the major points to be found in the client's file. A master index should direct the reader to the location of all important documents, discovery, pleadings, orders, and other materials. There are several ways to create a master index. A paralegal might simply bind all documents in the case together, number them consecutively, and then prepare an index similar to a table of contents for a book. See Figure 10.2.

The "table of contents" approach to a master index suffers from specific drawbacks. If additional material must be added, the page numbers may be altered, or the paralegal may need to add letters to the numbers, such as 32a, 32b, 32c, and so forth, to reflect the additional materials.

FIGURE 10.2

Master Index,
Version 1

Complaint	1–14
Answer	15–32
Plaintiff's First Interrogatories to Defendant	33–56
Defendant's Answers to Plaintiff's First Interrogatories	57–94
Plaintiff's First Request for Production of Documents to Defendant	95–99
Defendant's Response to Plaintiff's First Request for Production of Documents to Defendant	100–256

Another approach to creating a master index is to create clearly marked tabs for all important information. The tab method allows anyone reviewing the file to locate specific material quickly, without having to refer to a list with corresponding page numbers. It also frees the plaintiff from the drudgery of numbering consecutive pages for documents that were originally created independently of one another.

Issue Table

An "issue table" goes by many different names. Some attorneys refer to it as an "issue breakdown" or "count-by-count" summary. No matter what name is used, the purpose of an issue table is to summarize each of the key issues in the case according to the evidence and testimony to support or detract from it. By focusing on specific issues, the legal team can evaluate the possibilities of proving (or disproving) the claim at trial. In Figure 10.3, you will find an issue table for the proof of the plaintiff's financial losses in an automobile accident.

An issue table is one way for the legal team to double-check each issue in the case and make sure that there is sufficient evidence to prove it. Without a system for double-checking the issues and related proof, the legal team might easily fail to gather sufficient evidence to prove the point at trial.

Witness Cross-Reference

As a paralegal prepares a case for trial, it is important to focus on specific issues raised by the various witnesses and compare what each witness has to say about that specific point. Suppose, for example, that your firm is representing the plaintiff in an automobile accident case. The allegation is that the defendant ran a red light and rammed into the plaintiff's car. Obviously, the issue about the color of the traffic light when the defendant passed through it is going to be a key issue in the case. A witness cross-reference sheet compares the testimony of all relevant witnesses to this one issue. The process of creating such a sheet involves going through police reports, statements, and deposition transcripts. What you are looking for in a witness cross-reference are any discrepancies between the witnesses, or even discrepancies in the comments of one witness.

FIGURE 10.3

Issue: Plaintiff's
Financial Damages

Item	Proof
How much did the plaintiff earn in previous years?	Plaintiff's W-2, income tax returns from 2001, 2002, 2003, 2004, 2005
How much did plaintiff earn after the accident?	W-2 for 2006; return for 2006
What insurance and other benefits received following accident? (Collateral source)	Copies of checks from Everyone State Insurance Company
Property damages to plaintiff's car?	Photographs P's testimony Expert witness T. Holden, fair market value of car after accident = $0
Effect of her injuries on ability to earn future income	Dr. Marshall's testimony re: long-term prognosis
Future medical treatments, costs	Dr. Marshall

FIGURE 10.4
Witness Cross-Reference Sheet

Time delay between light change for plaintiff and defendant hitting plaintiff's car.

Summaries marked in **bold** indicate discrepancy between witnesses.

Witness	Testimony	Transcript X-Ref
John Doe	That he was sitting across intersection in oncoming lane; saw defendant's car from left, driving at high speed; that his light turned green and defendant kept coming; **about ten seconds between light change and the collision,** saw D's car hit PL on passenger side.	Doe, pp. 4, 5, 6–9, 23, 27, 28–34
Jane Roe	That she was behind PL, going in same direction; that the light turned green and PL pulled out; didn't actually see collision, but looked up immediately after; **not sure of time interval between light change and collision; maybe two seconds;** that D said, **"I'm so sorry; I knew it was red. I just couldn't stop."**	Roe, pp. 2–7, 13, 14–17
Officer Mark Williams	That he arrived on scene approx 15 minutes after collision; that **D refused to give a specific answer about color of light;** that PL was definite that light was green for her (hearsay); that John Doe was in far right lane, about to turn in same direction as D was coming; that D was charged with failure to yield.	Williams, pp. 4, 5–6.
Plaintiff	That she was stopped at red light, first in line; that Jane Roe was behind her; that John Doe was across intersection facing her; that D came from right, failed to stop; **less than five seconds between light change and collision;** effects of crash, terrible pain, taken from scene in ambulance; questioning by police, consistent statement at the scene as now.	PL, pp. 3, 4, 5, 6, 7–23, 42, 45, 71–73, 86–101

PRACTICE TIP

If you ever encounter a situation in which two or more witnesses agree point by point to a description of an event, it should make you cautious. Identical testimony almost always means that someone has rehearsed the witnesses about what they will say, and that smacks of witness coaching, which is unethical and may also be illegal. (See this chapter's "Eye on Ethics.")

Compare times, dates, events, and the timing of events to compare how each witness stacks up. The one thing you can be sure of when you compare the recollections of different people about the same event is that they will all be different. It is axiomatic that no two people remember an event in exactly the same way. What you are looking for when you create a witness cross-reference is the extent of the differences. (See Figure 10.4.)

Hypothetical 10-1

Last year, Mary Brown was involved in a traffic accident. According to her, she was stopped at a red light, and when the light changed, she pulled out into the intersection and was struck by a car driven by defendant Darryl Dangerous. Mary says that it was about five seconds between the time that the light changed and she pulled into the intersection. This assertion refutes some claims that she was traveling at an excessive speed when she approached the intersection and ran a red light herself. We need to know what the other witnesses say about the time delay between the light change and the impact. Prepare a witness cross-reference sheet on this point.

When creating a witness cross-reference sheet, it is often helpful to select a landscape layout on your printer. The result is much easier to read than a standard 8 1/2 × 11 sheet of paper. You should create a witness cross-reference sheet or chart for every major issue in the case. That way, the legal team can quickly cross-check the testimony of every witness with every critical point in the case. This system also makes it easy for the team to see what points are weaker than others. These weak points may require additional investigation or development before the trial begins.

As a paralegal prepares a witness cross-reference sheet, he or she will go through deposition digests prepared from transcripts. Important pages from the transcripts should be copied and attached to the witness cross-reference sheet for future reference.

FIGURE 10.5
Witness Summary

Witness	Summary
Plaintiff	That she was involved in an automobile accident; that she was stopped for a red light; that the defendant ran the red light; that she was taken to the hospital; that she suffered pain and financial loss as a result; bills paid.
John Doe	That he witnessed the collision and that the defendant ran the red light.
Jane Roe	That she was behind the P; that they were both stopped at a red light at intersection of Burnett and Burke; that D made statement that he had run a red light.
Officer Mark Williams	That he was dispatched to scene; that he diagrammed scene; that he took photos of the damage to both cars; that he has been trained as an accident reconstructionist; that it is his opinion that the defendant was traveling at 45 mph when he came through the intersection; that P was traveling 5 mph.
Dr. Marshall	P's injuries; P's prognosis; P's ability to work in the future.

Witness Summaries

A witness summary provides a general overview of what a witness will say in the trial. It is left deliberately general and created simply as a quick reference guide to double-check the purpose that the witness will serve in the trial. Many paralegals create a general witness summary, listing each witness and what this witness will testify to at trial. See Figure 10.5.

Trial Timetable

Another important entry in the client's file is a summary of the important dates and deadlines in the case. This timetable is usually a one-page sheet that details specific events in the case and their concomitant dates. This listing helps remind the legal team about looming deadlines in the case. See Figure 10.6.

Organized Client File

Organizing a file for trial is a process that varies considerably depending on the type of case, the amount of evidence, and the personal preferences of the attorneys involved. Some attorneys

FIGURE 10.6
Trial Timetable

Mary Brown v. Darryl Dangerous
Civil File No.:   06-1007
(All dates calculated in accordance with Rule 23-12, Placid State Rules of Civil Procedure)

Event	Date
Complaint filed and served	June 12, 2006
Discovery scheduled to end (6 months after complaint filed)	November 12, 2006
Motions deadline	December 1, 2006
Pre-Trial Conference scheduled	January 23, 2007
Trial date	Not yet set
Final Pretrial Order due (10 days prior to trial date)	Not set
Final attorney conference (at least 20 days prior to trial date)	Not set
All exhibits, evidence exchanged no later than (30 days prior to trial date)	Not set

organize their cases using manila file folders, each containing information specific to a particular issue or witness. Other attorneys rely on trial notebooks that contain internal sections reserved for evidentiary issues, witness transcripts, evidence, pleadings, and discovery. Some general categories will appear in nearly every case, including pleadings, correspondence, and discovery. Beyond that basic file structure, there are as many methods for organizing files as there are attorneys. An important tip for any paralegal is to learn the method used by the attorney with whom you work and follow it. There is nothing more frustrating for an attorney than to look for a crucial document or pleading at a critical point in a trial and not be able to locate it in the section where the attorney believes it should be.

Trial Notebook

A trial notebook is a handy reference guide that is filled with all of the legal topics and questions that an attorney will need at trial. We use the term "notebook" here broadly. Some attorneys use a system of file folders containing all of the information that they will need for trial, whereas others actually use a series of three-ring binders. The benefit of the binder system is that the pages can be securely fastened inside the cover. Manila file folders have a tendency to become lost, almost always when they are needed most. Trial notebooks help attorneys stay focused and organized during the course of a trial. A good trial notebook should contain:

- Jury materials, including voir dire questions.
- Motions in limine.
- Trial briefs.
- Notes for opening statements.
- Witness list.
- Direct or cross-examination points to be raised with specific witnesses.
- Evidence to be admitted during the direct examination of specific witnesses, along with any foundational questions required for specific evidence.
- Evidence list.
- Exhibit list.
- Foundational questions for specific types of evidence.
- Relevant pleadings, including the complaint, answer, counterclaim, and cross-claim.
- Witness deposition excerpts and summaries.
- Medical summaries and crucial medical records.
- Relevant case law, usually about issues that the attorney anticipates will arise during trial.
- Equipment.

Many attorneys have a standard format for a trial notebook. This format may be unique to the particular attorney, so a trial paralegal should always take the extra time to learn the attorney's system. For instance, some attorneys might group discovery responses under a general "Discovery" heading, whereas others might associate different responses with witness statements and other evidence in the case.

It is usually helpful to have all of the items contained in a single notebook. Large documents, such as lengthy depositions, can be held in separate files. The crucial points of a deposition transcript can be copied as single pages and placed under the heading for that witness.

Paralegal Trial Notebook

In addition to the attorney's notebook, a paralegal should have a trial notebook as well. What types of information should you have in your trial notebook? If you are attending the trial with the attorney, your focus will be slightly different than that of the attorney. You are there to provide logistical support and anticipate problems. Trying a case is a stressful event, and it often brings out the worst (though sometimes the best) in an attorney. Anything that you can do to eliminate complications will help alleviate that stress (and make you that much more valuable to the attorney). See Figure 10.7.

FIGURE 10.7
Minimum Materials
for Paralegal Trial
Notebook

A paralegal trial notebook should contain:

- General overview of the case.
- Trial timesheet.
- Voir dire questions for jury.
- Jury instructions.
- Foundational questions for specific evidence.
- Photos of scene.
- Witness list.
- Exhibit lists.
- Contact information.
- Courthouse layout.

A paralegal trial notebook is built on the premise of avoiding problems at trial or being able to handle them as expeditiously as possible. Your notebook therefore should contain:

- Contact information, including witness telephone, cell phone, and beeper numbers (for those occasions when you must contact a witness immediately).
- Basic information about the case, such as case file number, important filing dates, copies of the complaint and answer (unmarked), and your own highlighted copy of both documents.
- Evidence checklist, cross-referenced by witness and foundational questions.
- Jury charts, juror questions, and a section listing improper questions that may be asked by the opposing counsel with the cases that clearly state such questions are improper.
- Order of witnesses who will testify and the evidence that should be admitted during each witness's testimony.
- Telephone numbers, beeper numbers, cell phone numbers, and email addresses of:
  - Opposing counsel.
  - Opposing counsel's paralegal/legal assistant/legal secretary (who usually knows how to get in contact with the attorney better than anyone else).
  - The judge's secretary, law clerk, and other staff, as well as their direct dial numbers. (Sometimes it is easier to contact these people with a cell phone call in the courthouse hallway than trying to talk to them personally.)
  - The client, as well as any other telephone numbers where he or she can be reached, including email addresses and contact numbers for friends and relatives. (You never know whom you may have to speak with to track down a missing client.)
- Names, addresses, and telephone numbers for special witnesses, such as expert witnesses or investigators.
- Names and contact information for any support personnel, such as FedEx, UPS, court reporters, computer technicians, network administrators, and even the attorney's laptop manufacturer. (Remember Murphy's Law: Anything that can go wrong will go wrong and at the worst possible moment.)
- Home telephone numbers of all trial team members, including attorneys, paralegals, runners, and anyone else who might be useful.
- Complete list of all equipment needed for the trial, as well as a checklist showing that each piece of equipment has been tested and confirmed to work.
- Backup light bulbs for projectors, dark-colored duct tape (for emergency patches and to hold down pesky wires and electrical cords).
- Diagram of the courthouse, showing the location of bathrooms, vending machines, and water fountains. (Also include designated smoking areas for clients who smoke.)

Preparing Exhibits

The preparation of exhibits is one of the most important aspects of trial preparation. In recent decades, the importance of exhibits has become more and more obvious. Attorneys often rely on charts, diagrams, scale models, and a wide range of other exhibits to help bring home certain key points during the trial. The availability of copy machines and copying businesses such as Kinko's have made it far easier to get certain documents blown up to emphasize a particular aspect. It is also a great deal easier to blow up photographs and diagrams to a size that jurors can see easily. These days, exhibits are not just limited to drawings, models, and enlarged photographs. Computer generated animation has also become a feature in many civil cases. These programs allow the parties to use video to create a mini-movie that describes the party's version of what happened in the case. Such evidence can have a tremendous impact on the jury. Visual aids are always important. You should consider using diagrams and models to explain any aspect of the case that might be difficult for jurors to understand.

Using Software to Develop Exhibits

In addition to the tried-and-true methods of creating exhibits, such as enlarging photographs or hiring artists to render the scene of an accident, commonly available software packages are now making it possible for paralegals to perform a great deal of exhibit preparation right on their office computers. For instance, any drawing program will allow a paralegal to create diagrams, often to scale. Video editing software can even turn a paralegal into a video production team who can edit together various videos to present to the jury. There are also relatively inexpensive methods to scan in thousands of pages of documents and then reproduce them on a computer projector, thus saving a lot of time shuffling through stacks of documents during the trial.

Preparing Witnesses for the Trial

Preparing a witness for testifying at trial is one of the most important aspects of trial preparation and should never be skipped. Witnesses are often very nervous about testifying. They are afraid of looking foolish in front of a large group of strangers. They are afraid that the opposing attorney will yell at them or try to confuse or embarrass them. Make sure that the witness has a copy of his or her deposition transcript before the witness testifies. Tell the witness to read through the transcript, even if the witness claims to be able to remember the event clearly. The deposition was given much closer in time to the event than the witness's testimony, and a witness will invariably forget some minor points—and sometimes even major ones. However, the process of preparing a witness to testify at trial raises some potential ethical issues. See this chapter's "Eye on Ethics."

Reviewing Deposition Testimony

The first place that many paralegals start when they prepare a witness for trial is the deposition transcript. If this person is going to testify in a civil trial, he or she should have been deposed. Have the witness read over the deposition transcript. This is a great way to remind them about their testimony. It may have been months (or even years) since they last spoke about this case. Having them read their deposition transcript reminds them about all the big and little facts in the case.

Double- and Triple-Check Documentation

Once the witness has read the deposition transcript, go over the documentation. If the witness is someone who prepared notes to accompany a medical file, go back over these notes with the witness. Double-check the dates and times with him or her. Make sure that you both have a solid understanding of exactly what happened and when. Cross-reference the documentation with the deposition transcript. Does everything gibe? If it doesn't, you can bet that the other side has picked up on it too. How does your witness explain any discrepancies? Once you've double-checked the documentation, do it again: Triple-check it. Wait a couple of days and go over it with the witness again. You'd be surprised how much detail will bubble to the surface of a person's mind once they have started thinking about the case again. Take advantage of this phenomenon and go over everything again.

What to Tell Witnesses about Testifying

Witnesses always want to know what to expect. They don't like surprises. Sometimes, it helps calm a witness down simply to visit the courtroom before the trial ever starts. You can take the witness there on a non-court day and let the witness take in the entire layout. Tell the witness where he or she will be sitting. If the courtroom is vacant, take the witness to the stand and have the witness sit in the box. This simple process can help alleviate many of the anxieties that witnesses have about taking the stand. Of course, they will still be nervous, but they may be a little less nervous after they have seen the courtroom and gained some idea of what to expect.

In addition to being able to tell witnesses about the layout of the courtroom, your early reconnaissance work will help you tell witnesses where they should park. Remember to tell witnesses where the bathrooms are; people always need to go to the bathroom right before they testify.

When you are working with expert witnesses, you will not be required to spend this extra time calming them down and helping with their anxieties. Expert witnesses have done this kind of thing dozens of times before, and they are professionals. However, with all other witnesses, you should take them through the list of "Dos and Don'ts" found in Figure 10.8.

Review the File

Witnesses should always review the file. It helps them remember the facts, and it makes them feel a little more comfortable about testifying. However, the witness should never take the file to the witness stand. If the witness has given more than one statement, the witness should review them all. The witness should compare statements made in a deposition with statements contained in other documents. Are there discrepancies? Can these discrepancies be explained? Reviewing the file helps the witness anticipate the questions that the attorneys will ask and how he or she will answer them.

Dress Professionally

Always tell witnesses to dress professionally. If the witness wears scrubs to work every day, then tell him or her to wear a suit. It isn't always a successful strategy to tell witnesses to dress as though they were going to a wedding or a religious event. Dress codes for these events can vary drastically. Instead, tell the witness that a courtroom is a very formal place, and the witness should dress accordingly.

Make Eye Contact

Witnesses should make eye contact with the most important people in the courtroom: the jury. When they are answering questions, they should address their answers to the jury. We all tend to pay closer attention to someone who is making eye contact with us, and jurors are no exception.

FIGURE 10.8
Dos and Don'ts for All Witnesses

Do

- Review the file.
- Dress professionally.
- Make eye contact with the jurors.
- Be polite.
- Tell the truth.

Don't

- Guess.
- Get angry.
- Use sarcasm.
- Take the file with you to the stand.
- Answer questions you don't understand.

Be Polite

It is not always easy for a witness to be polite during a trial, especially when he or she is being cross-examined by opposing counsel. You should tell witnesses that they should try to remain calm and polite, even when the other attorney is being rude. When a person is polite in the face of rude tactics, the jury naturally sides with the polite person. Tell witnesses to remain polite even when they would rather snap at the opposing attorney. A witness should also never show any disrespect to a judge. In addition to the fact that the judge has the power to throw a witness in jail for contempt, the jury takes its cues on how to behave from the judge. If the judge rebukes a witness, the jury may discount anything that the witness has to say.

Tell the Truth

The final advice to witnesses is also the first thing that they should hear: No matter what, tell the truth. The witness is testifying under oath, and knowingly giving false testimony is perjury. Even when the facts are not that flattering, a witness should always tell the truth. Evasion, shading, or outright lying will invariably be found out, and the witness's credibility will be destroyed. Once a witness has been proven to be untruthful about one point, the jury tends to discredit anything else that he or she has to say.

Guessing

Just as important as telling witnesses what they should do is telling them what they should not do. For instance, witnesses should always avoid guessing to answer a question. If the opposing attorney asks, "Just how far is it from the witness stand to the back of the courtroom?" and the witness does not know, the best answer is, "I don't know." We all have a natural tendency to please, and saying "I don't know" makes us feel that we are creating a bad impression. But this is a trial, not a social gathering. Guessing can get a witness into a lot of trouble, especially when he or she guesses wrong.

Anger

Angry people say stupid things. Attorneys know this, and it is a time-honored technique for an attorney to try to get a witness angry. Tell your witnesses to work hard at maintaining their composure. Tell them that once they get off the stand, they can express their anger outside the courthouse, but they should try to remain as calm as possible on the witness stand.

Taking Notes to the Witness Stand

Witnesses are always surprised when they hear that they should not take notes or files with them to the stand. We all want something to hide behind, and a big piece of paper is as good as anything else. But if a witness takes notes to the stand, the opposing attorney has the right to take them away, read them, and even question the witness about the notes. Suppose that the witness has a note that reads, "Don't forget: Light was red!" The attorney can do a lot with a statement like that. Consider Hypothetical 10-2.

Hypothetical 10-2

Andrew is a witness in a case involving the defendant running a red light. He takes some notes with him to the stand and handles direct examination quite easily. However, cross-examination goes differently:

Attorney: I noticed that you've been referring to some notes in your hands. May I see them?
Witness: Yes.

Attorney: It says here, "Don't forget: The light was red!" Is that what this note says?
Witness: Yes.

Attorney: You mean that without this note, you wouldn't have remembered that the light was red? Did someone tell you to say this on the stand today?

Preparing the Paralegal for Trial

So far, our discussion has focused on preparing witnesses for the impending trial. But it is just as important to prepare yourself for the trial. Preparing the file, going through the documentation, and summarizing depositions will give you a feel for the case, but a trial is about more than technical points. In this section, we discuss how a paralegal prepares for the activities associated with the trial.

Reconnoiter the Courtroom

As it becomes more and more likely that a particular case is actually going to go to trial, it is time for you to get into "trial mode." If you think of a trial as if it were a battle (and, in many ways, it is), you should do what military professionals do: reconnaissance work. Go to the courthouse and find out which courtroom is reserved for your case. If the courtroom is locked, ask courthouse personnel to open it for you. Explain to them that you are there getting ready for trial.

Once you are inside the courtroom, draw a basic diagram of the room. Locate the witness stand, the judge's bench, and the attorney tables. The plaintiff usually has the table closest to the jury box. Sit in the jury box and look at the room from the jurors' perspective. If you have a friend with you, have the friend talk in a normal tone of voice from the witness stand. Can you hear him or her? If not, is there a microphone? These are the things that you can tell witnesses later.

Next, locate electrical outlets. These days, attorneys and paralegals often bring laptop computers, overhead projectors, and even printers into the courtroom. Are there enough plugs to accommodate all of these devices? If not, will you need a power strip or extension cords? Will you need to tape the cords down so that people will not trip on them?

If the attorney wants to write out notes for the jury during an opening or closing argument, is there a chalkboard, whiteboard, or easel available? Even if something is available, make sure that you have backup supplies. Do not rely on courthouse personnel to supply you with a dry-erase marker, for instance, when the one in the courtroom goes dry just as the attorney is starting his or her closing argument.

Rehearse Your Equipment

According to Murphy's Law, anything that can go wrong will go wrong, and at the worst possible moment. Keep this in mind if your team is going to be using any equipment during the trial, such as an overhead projector. Do a dry run with the device shortly before the trial. If it is a digital projector, does it actually work with the attorney's laptop? Try it and see. Do you have backup light bulbs and the right cable connectors? If possible, rehearse the presentation right in the actual courtroom. Is there a screen for the projection? If not, where will the attorney beam the projection so that the jury can see it? These are all questions that should be answered long before the trial starts.

Learn the Layout of the Courthouse

As part of your reconnaissance work at the courthouse, don't neglect the layout of the building outside the courtroom. If you are unfamiliar with the building, draw a map of the facility. You are going to have witnesses waiting around to testify. Where are they going to sit? What if they need to go to the bathroom or want to get a quick snack? If you know where the restroom and the snack bar are, you can direct them—and you will also know where to look for those witnesses if they disappear.

Master the Trial Notebook and the Case Files

By the time the case is actually about to go to trial, you should know the case file as well as the attorney does, if not better. Test yourself: Can you find any particular medical record, bill, summary, or doctor's note in less than 10 seconds? If you can, you know the file; if you can't, you have more work to do.

At some point in the trial, something unexpected will happen, and the attorney will need a document that the team had not anticipated would be needed. Can you find it immediately? There is nothing more frustrating (or nerve wracking) than floundering about in the middle of a cross-examination because a particular document is lost.

Get Ready for Stress

If you are good at handling stress, then you are in the right business. Unfortunately, most people are not. Trials are stressful events. The stress you will feel will be different from the stress that attorneys feel. In many ways, you will find yourself constantly trying to anticipate where the case

SURF'S UP!

CREATING TIMELINES

There are numerous programs available to assist you in creating a realistic timeline, as suggested in this chapter's discussion on creating chronologies of the events in a civil case. Internet search engines offer dozens of programs that can provide simple to highly complex timelines, permitting entries for each second or dragging the timeline out to cover decades. However, there is nothing that says that preparing a chronology requires expensive software. Many word processing programs provide templates that can just as easily serve the purpose. Even if you do not choose to use these ready-made templates, the simplest way to create a chronology is with a table. A simple two-column table will serve as a rudimentary timeline. Consider the following example:

Time	Event

In a table like this one, you can add, edit, or delete events as you gather information. Done correctly, you can even add the details as you discover them and then use the table sort feature to track the dates and times for you.

is going so that you can be ready with the right thing at the right time. There are ways that you can reduce the stress—such as by following the tips set out here—but there is no way to get rid of all of the stress.

Because you know that both you and the attorney will be under a great deal of stress, prepare with ways to deal with it. If you like to exercise, do not neglect it during the trial. At least take a break at the end of the day to take a walk or do something else that you find enjoyable. Unfortunately, too many stressed-out people turn to alcohol or food or some other unhealthy diversion. Over time, these short-term responses take their toll. The longer the trial, the more stress on everyone involved. It is not a wise move to stay up late every night of the trial, going over items. Regular sleep is one of the best ways to maintain physical and mental health, and anyone who neglects it, especially during a trial, is only asking for trouble.

Anticipate Problems

Anticipating a problem is different than worrying. An anticipated problem can be dealt with and resolved; a worry can never be. One way of anticipating problems is by visualizing the trial, step by step. What exhibits will the attorney need for each witness? Are those exhibits available? By tracing out each phase of the trial and working out the details associated with each, many potential problems can be solved before they ever arise.

Mock Trials

Many attorneys use juror simulations or mock trials to help prepare for the trial. Some attorneys are reluctant to use the actual witnesses to testify at a mock trial, reasoning that if the witness makes a statement contrary to a statement already provided to the opposing side, then this new statement might have to be provided to the opposing side through discovery. As we saw in the previous chapter, an attorney has a continuing obligation to update witness statements, and a contradictory statement at a mock trial would probably qualify under that rule. Instead, many attorneys use actors to portray key witnesses or show the videotaped deposition of crucial witnesses at the mock trial. The jurors are selected from the community at large, usually from the juror lists of dismissed panels from two or three prior court sessions. Because these individuals have already completed their jury duty, the attorney can be confident that this group of people will not be called for jury duty in the present case.

At the mock trial, the attorneys present their case to a jury and then gauge the jurors' reactions. This approach can be a very effective tool for trying out a risky trial strategy or assessing how well, or how poorly, a real jury may receive the attorney's case. Attorneys sometimes use the results of a mock trial to encourage their clients to settle a case, which is far easier when a mock jury has rendered a verdict against the client. We will discuss other aspects of settling a case in the next chapter.

Litigation-Trained Paralegals

In the actual trial, a growing number of attorneys are relying on litigation-trained paralegals to assist them during the trial. A paralegal with a broad knowledge of the trial process and a specific knowledge of the case can be a tremendous asset at trial. A well-trained paralegal can often anticipate an attorney's need for a document or file and thus become invaluable.

PHASES OF THE TRIAL

In this section, we discuss the various stages of a civil trial, beginning with the pretrial conference and ending with the jury's verdict and the entry of a judgment against one party by the presiding judge.

Pretrial Conference

pretrial conference
The meeting between the parties and the judge to identify legal issues, stipulate to uncontested matters, and encourage settlement.

Pretrial conferences are scheduled so that the judge can meet with all parties, discuss the basic framework of the action, and settle some of the ground rules for the subsequent trial. Rule 16 of the Federal Rules of Civil Procedure governs pretrial conferences. That rule authorizes a judge to direct the attorneys for the parties to appear before him or her for a conference to consider numerous issues. Some of these issues include discussions about simplifying or streamlining the issues in the suit, whether or not pleadings should be amended, and the possibility of obtaining admissions of fact to help narrow the issues that need to be proven at trial. In addition to these issues, the judge will also inquire about the number of witnesses and their potential areas of testimony. The judge will often attempt to boil issues down at a pretrial conference and thus limit the overall number of witnesses, especially expert witnesses who often testify for lengthy periods of time.

At the pretrial conference, the attorneys for the parties will often exchange witness and exhibit lists. The matters resolved will be reduced to writing in a **pretrial order**. See Figure 10.9.

pretrial order
An order, prepared by the trial judge with the input of the parties, that summarizes key issues in the case, including witness order, evidence, and other critical concerns.

In many jurisdictions, judges now require that attorneys appear at the pretrial conference with a draft of the pretrial order in their possession. Some even go so far as to require that the attorneys have the proposed order in both print and digital media. This requirement makes the job for the judge's secretary considerably easier; the secretary can simply copy and paste the relevant parts into the final order. In creating a proposed pretrial order, the judge will require each party to prepare the portions relevant to their presentation.

RESEARCH THIS!

What are the rules about the preparation, timing, and final presentation of pretrial orders in your state?

LEGAL RESEARCH MAXIM

We have seen that jury instructions are often prepared prior to trial. Although there are publications that contain jury instructions, this is not the only way to find them. In fact, one of the best ways of coming up with jury instructions about specific points in a case is to research the case law in your state or federal jurisdiction for recent appellate decisions on specific issues. A court's holding on an issue can serve as the basis for a very effective jury instruction.

FIGURE 10.9
Pretrial Order

STATE OF PLACID

COUNTY OF BURKE

JANE DOE,

    Plaintiff

vs.

NICHOLAS CHARLES,
    Defendant.

IN THE SUPERIOR COURT
SUPERIOR COURT FILE NO. _____

Pretrial Order

Order on Final Pretrial Conference between Plaintiff and Defendants

Pursuant to the provisions of PL. R. CIV. P. 16, and Rule 7 of the Placid General Rules of Practice, a final pretrial conference was held in the above-entitled cause on April 1, 2007. Allison Attorney, (PL Bar # 9999) appeared as counsel for the plaintiff; Clarence D. Arrow (PL Bar # 1999) appeared as counsel for defendant, Nicholas Charles.

(1) It is stipulated that all parties are properly before the court, and that the court has jurisdiction of the parties and of the subject matter.

(2) In addition to the other stipulations contained in this order, the parties stipulate and agree with respect to the following undisputed facts:
    a) Ms. Doe was severely injured in an automobile accident on May 15, 2005, in Placid City, PL.
    b) The weather was clear.
    c) Nicholas Charles owned and operated the 2005 Ford Spitfire involved in the accident.
    d) Nicholas Charles was driving on the day of the collision.
    e) Ms. Doe was the sole occupant and driver of her automobile.
    f) Ms. Doe was driving her car south on Burke Street and Nicholas Charles was coming from the east.
    g) Mr. Charles's car struck Ms. Doe's car on the passenger side of Ms. Doe's car.
    h) Before the accident, Ms. Doe worked as a supervisor at Knight Manufacturing Co.
    i) Ms. Doe has not been able to return to work since the accident.

(3) A list and description of all known exhibits plaintiff Doe may offer at trial are attached and marked as plaintiff Doe's pretrial exhibits. It is stipulated and agreed that opposing counsel has been furnished a copy of each exhibit listed by the plaintiff.

(4) It is stipulated and agreed that each of the exhibits identified by plaintiff Doe is genuine and, if relevant and material, may be received in evidence without further identification or proof.

(5) A list and description of all known exhibits defendant Nicholas Charles may offer at trial are attached and marked as defendant Nicholas Charles's pretrial exhibits. It is stipulated and agreed that opposing counsel has been furnished a copy of each exhibit listed by defendant except:

[List exceptions].

(6) It is stipulated and agreed that each of the exhibits identified by defendant Nicholas Charles is genuine and, if relevant and material, may be received in evidence without further identification or proof, except:

[List exceptions].

(7) A list of the names and addresses of all known witnesses plaintiff Doe may offer at trial is attached and marked as plaintiff Doe's proposed witnesses. A list of names and addresses of all known witnesses defendant Nicholas Charles may offer at trial is attached and marked as defendant Nicholas Charles's proposed witnesses. Counsel shall immediately notify opposing counsel if the names of additional witnesses are discovered after the preparation of this order.

(8) There are no pending motions, and neither party desires further amendments to the pleadings, except:

    a) Motion for More Definite Statement by defendant, Nicholas Charles.

    b) Motion to Strike by defendant, Nicholas Charles.

(9) Additional consideration has been given to a separation of the triable issues, and counsel for all parties are of the opinion that a separation of issues in this particular case would not be feasible.

(10) The plaintiff Doe contends that the contested issues to be tried by the jury are as follows:

    a) Defendant, Nicholas Charles, is negligent for failing to maintain a proper lookout.

    b) Defendant, Nicholas Charles, was negligent for failing to abide by the rules of the road.

    c) Defendant, Nicholas Charles, was negligent for failing to stop for a red light in his line of travel at the intersection of Burke and Burnett Streets.

    d) These instances of negligence by the defendant were the cause of the automobile accident and of Ms. Doe's injuries.

(11) The defendant Nicholas Charles contends that the contested issues to be tried by the jury are as follows:

[List contested issues].

(12) Counsel for the parties announced that all witnesses are available and the case is in all respects ready for trial. The probable length of the trial is estimated to be one week.

(13) Counsel for the parties represent to the court that, in advance of the preparation of this order, there was a full and frank discussion of settlement possibilities. Counsel for the plaintiff will immediately notify the clerk in the event of a material change in settlement prospects.

(15) Plaintiff Doe's Exhibits

    a) Photos of intersection of Burke St. and Burnett St.

    b) Diagrams of the intersection

    c) Accident reports

    d) Medical bills and reports

    e) Photographs of plaintiff's injuries

    f) "Day in the Life" video detailing plaintiff's daily activities following the collision

(16) Plaintiff Doe's Witnesses

    a) Mr. Warren Green, West Placid, PL

    b) Dr. Expert, Raleigh, PL

    c) Clara Hodges, West Placid, PL

    d) Steve Blue, Asheville, PL

    e) Officer Law, West Placid, PL

By:_____

Neal Bevans

PL Bar # 9999

Attorney for Plaintiff

By:_____

Clarence D. Arrow

PL Bar #1999

Attorney for Defendant Nicholas Charles

Approved, ordered, and filed:

This the 4th day of November, 2007.

Hon. A. Clayton Powell

Court Judge Presiding

FIGURE 10.10
The Phases of a Trial

The phases of the trial are:

- Calendar call.
- Jury selection.
- Opening statements.
- Presentation of the case.
- Closing arguments and jury instructions.
- The jury deliberation and verdict.

The Trial

Following the pretrial conference, the next stage in the litigation is scheduling the case for trial. Parties must appear at a calendar call to find out exactly when their cases will be called for trial. See Figure 10.10.

Calendar Call

calendar call
A mandatory court hearing in which the judge inquires about the readiness of the parties to go to trial; also known as a docket call.

On the first day of the week reserved for trials, judges have what is referred to as a **calendar call** or docket call. In this hearing, the parties in all pending cases are made to appear to give status reports. If a plaintiff fails to appear for the calendar call, the judge may dismiss the suit, which makes calendar calls very important. If the attorney representing the plaintiff has more than one courtroom to be in on the same day (a common experience), then the attorney will file a **conflict letter** with the court listing the various court appearances and requesting permission to report later in the day.

conflict letter
A letter sent by an attorney to the judge explaining that the attorney has several different appearances scheduled for the same date and detailing which courts the attorney will go to first.

When the parties announce that they are ready for trial, the judge often schedules them to appear later that week. Suppose that there are 60 cases on the current calendar. It should go without saying that it would be impossible to hold trials in all 60 cases with just one week reserved for jury trials. However, by requiring the parties to appear for the calendar call, the judge can exert some subtle (and sometimes not-so-subtle) pressure on the parties to settle the case.

Jury Selection

panel
A group of people who have been called for jury duty; the final jury will be selected from this group; also known as venire.

Once the case has been called and both parties have announced that they are ready for trial, the next step is jury selection. In the American legal system, it is inaccurate to say that a jury is selected. What actually happens is that a group of citizens is brought in, and members of the panel are eliminated until 12 remain. Those 12 will sit on the jury and consider the issues raised in the case.

Before we can discuss the details of jury selection, it is important to emphasize some of the terminology used during this process. For instance, when citizens are called in for jury duty, they appear in court as part of a **panel** or venire. Panel members are removed until 12 people remain. Those 12 people are then called **jurors**. The process of carrying out jury selection is often referred to as **voir dire**.

jurors
Those people who have been selected to sit on a jury; they will consider the evidence and reach a verdict in the case.

During the voir dire process, the various members of the panel are questioned about their life experiences, their knowledge of the case and the parties, and any other relevant issues. The attorneys then evaluate these answers to decide which members of the panel should be removed or challenged.

Trial Paralegals and Jury Selection

voir dire
The process of selecting a jury for trial.

A well-trained trial paralegal can be an invaluable asset during jury selection. A paralegal can assist the attorney by keeping track of panel members' responses to questions, noting unusual or interesting information about particular panel members, and even doing little things such as noticing the facial expressions of panel members when they think that they are not being observed. See Figure 10.11 for a jury information sheet.

When it comes time to actually select the jury, the attorneys are permitted to use jury strikes or challenges to remove panel members until 12 remain. There are two types of jury challenges: peremptory and cause.

jury strike
The removal of a jury panel member, also known as a jury challenge.

Peremptory Jury Strikes. Both sides in a jury trial have a minimum number of **jury strikes** or challenges that they may use to remove panel members. Suppose, for example, that in a civil case both the plaintiff and the defense have 10 strikes. If the panel consists of 32 persons and both

FIGURE 10.11
Jury Information Sheet

Jury Information Sheet

Juror No. _____

Positive response to questions: 1 2 3 4 5 6 7 8 9 10 11 12 13

Negative response to questions: 1 2 3 4 5 6 7 8 9 10 11 12 13

Notes: _____

_____

_____

_____

Strike for cause? Y/N Why? _____

_____

Strike? _____

peremptory jury strike

An attorney's elimination of a prospective juror without giving a reason; limited to a specific number of strikes.

sides use all their strikes, the result will be a 12-person jury. Such strikes are called **peremptory jury strikes** because the sides may use them in any manner they see fit to remove panel members.

The number of strikes that the parties may use varies depending on the type of case. In some cases, the parties have equal numbers of strikes, but in other jurisdictions, the plaintiff may have a slight numeric advantage.

Hypothetical 10-3

On the day of the trial, 42 panel members are brought in to go through jury selection in a civil case. The defense has a total of 15 strikes that it may use, and the plaintiff also has 15. When they use all of their strikes, 12 jurors will remain.

In the past, there were no limitations on the use of peremptory strikes. However, in recent decades, the United States Supreme Court has begun limiting a party's ability to use peremptory strikes especially when the strike is based on race.

challenge

An attorney's objection, during voir dire, to the inclusion of a specific person on the jury.

Challenges.   There is a second method that parties can use to remove panel members. When a party makes a **challenge** (sometimes referred to as a challenge for cause), it is requesting the judge to remove the panel member. A party might make this request for several reasons. For example, if a panel member has stated in open court that he or she will not obey the court's orders, will not actively participate in the jury deliberations, or has religious objections to being seated on a jury, a party might make a challenge for cause. If the judge accepts the challenge, the panel member is removed, and the removal is not assessed against any side's allotted number of peremptory strikes.

Once a jury has been selected to serve on the case, the next step is opening statements.

PRACTICE TIP

In some jurisdictions, peremptory removal of a juror is called a strike, whereas in other jurisdictions, it is called a challenge. The terms are used interchangeably throughout this chapter.

Opening Statements

An opening statement is a brief speech made by the attorneys for the plaintiff and the defendant during which they outline what will happen in the case and what evidence the jury can expect to see. The purpose of an opening statement is to provide some framework for the jurors. After all, the jurors have no independent knowledge of the case, and the attorneys use the opening statement to explain the issues to them. Attorneys use opening statements as a roadmap of where the trial will go and which witnesses will testify. Although opening statements are often depicted on television as dramatic presentations in which attorneys forcefully argue major points in their cases, the reality is that opening statements are usually dry and formal. Attorneys are barred from arguing points; the best that they can do is provide a foretaste of what will happen in the course of the trial.

In a civil case, the plaintiff's attorney presents opening statements first. The reason for this is simple: The plaintiff is the person who brought the allegations and must now prove them. Once the plaintiff has given an opening statement, the defendant is permitted to address the jury.

Although a defense attorney may wait to give his or her opening statement until after the plaintiff's case has been presented, the common practice is for both attorneys to address the jury shortly after jury selection. Once the opening statements have been given, the next phase is the presentation of the plaintiff's case.

Direct and Cross-Examination of Witnesses

The plaintiff has the burden of going first in a civil case. The plaintiff presents its case through two primary methods: witnesses and evidence. Attorneys are not allowed to address the jury and tell them about pertinent evidence or offer opinions about the legal position of their client. Instead, the attorneys must prove their case through witnesses.

Witnesses.   We have all seen movies and television dramas in which witnesses testify. Although some of the fictional accounts may be overly dramatic, the basics are usually correct. When a witness testifies, he or she is called to the stand, sworn in, and then asked questions. This process is called **direct examination**.

Witnesses who testify on direct examination are usually friendly to the plaintiff, or at least neutral about the outcome of the case. Consider Hypothetical 10-4.

direct examination
Occurs when the attorney questions his or her own witness.

Hypothetical 10-4

Maria was injured in a car wreck when the defendant, Jonathan Journeyman, ran a red light and struck Maria's car broadside. Maria brought suit against Jonathan Journeyman, and the trial has now begun. After giving her opening statement, Maria's attorney calls her first witness. In this case, there was another driver at the intersection that day who saw the entire incident. Maria's attorney, Lucy Lawyer, calls Wanda Witness to the stand and begins asking her questions. The direct examination went something like this:

Lawyer: Please state your name for the record.
Witness: My name is Wanda Witness.

Lawyer: Ms. Witness, were you present at the intersection of Elm Street and First Street in this city on May 1st of last year?
Witness: Yes, I was.

Lawyer: What, if anything, did you see that day?
Witness: I saw the defendant fail to stop at the red light and strike the car driven by that lady over there.

Lawyer: Let the record reflect that the witness has identified the plaintiff in this case. Ms. Witness, how can you be so sure that the defendant ran the red light that day?
Witness: Well, I was in the car right behind him, and I saw the light turn red. I turned to my daughter, who was in the car with me, and I said, "That guy's crazy. He's running a red light."

Lawyer: What happened after the defendant ran the red light?
Witness: He slammed into that lady's car, and both cars sort of rolled sideways.

Lawyer: What did you do then?
Witness: I parked my car and ran to the lady's car. I asked her if she was okay. That man, the defendant, had already gotten there.

Lawyer: Did the defendant say anything to you?
Witness: Yes, he said that he should have been paying attention and that he hoped he hadn't killed someone.

You will notice that the way that the attorney phrases questions on direct examination is different from the way a person would question the witness on the street. The lawyer uses stilted questions such as, "What, if anything, did you see that day?" The reason that attorneys phrase questions that way is that direct examination has strict limits on how attorneys may question witnesses. For one thing, attorneys are not allowed to testify for the witness; the witness must tell his or her own story. If the attorney puts words in the witness's mouth (called "leading" a witness), the other attorney may object.

cross-examination
Occurs when the opposing attorney asks the witness questions.

When the plaintiff's attorney has asked the witness all the questions he or she thinks are necessary, the plaintiff's attorney turns the questioning over to the defendant's attorney. This stage is called **cross-examination**.

COMMUNICATION TIP

One of the most important things you, as a trial paralegal, can do immediately before and during a trial is to maintain contact with your various witnesses. Tell the witnesses what is happening and when they are likely to be needed. Do not commit yourself to an absolute time and explain that no one can ever be sure exactly when a witness will take the stand, but by keeping them advised of the proceedings, you can lessen some of their anxiety. By staying in contact with them, you also make sure that you can reach them, should you need to do so at a moment's notice. Do not forget to call the witnesses when the case is over and tell them what happened. You never know when you might deal with that person again, and witnesses are always curious to know what happened—and if their testimony assisted in the resolution.

Cross-examination occurs after direct examination and is always done by the other side's attorney. The rules about asking questions on cross-examination are much more liberal than the rules governing attorneys on direct examination. Attorneys are allowed to ask leading questions, such as, "You weren't even looking at the light, were you?" Attorneys are also allowed to be more confrontational with witnesses on cross-examination. Cross-examination is more dramatic, which is probably why you are more likely to see it depicted on television courtroom dramas than direct examination.

Attorneys also are allowed to explore a witness's potential biases or lack of knowledge during cross-examination. The attorneys can impeach a witness by showing that the witness is not someone who should be believed. Impeachment can occur through a demonstration that the witness has no knowledge of the event, such as the fact that the witness was not at the scene on the day of the accident or has been convicted of a crime involving dishonesty, such as perjury.

Paralegal Assistance during the Testimony Phase of the Trial

A paralegal who has mastered all of the other skills that a trial paralegal needs must also work to develop a sixth sense about trial work. You must stay alert for the little things that could prove to be important later. Consider Hypothetical 10-5.

Hypothetical 10-5

Mary testifies that her husband kept her locked up in a room for 12 hours and wouldn't let her leave. The attorney had painstakingly gone through the entire episode, proving all of the elements and establishing the husband's pattern of abuse. At the end of direct examination, he turns to his trial paralegal with the question that attorneys often ask of their assistants: "Anything else?" Fortunately for this attorney, the trial paralegal had been involved in the case from the outset and had been paying attention. She scrawled a quick note on a piece of paper and handed it to the attorney. The note read: *When did she go to the bathroom?* The attorney shrugged and then asked the question. The witness explained that she had had to urinate in a bottle in the room.

Later, when they'd won the case, the attorney spoke with the jurors. The foreperson said, "I wasn't sure about the case until you asked about going to the bathroom. When I heard that, I knew she was telling the truth."

Resting the Case

The plaintiff's attorney will proceed through his or her case, calling witnesses and presenting evidence until he or she believes that all of the allegations against the defendant have been proven. When he or she is finished, the attorney will announce, "Your Honor, the Plaintiff rests."

This announcement informs the court that the plaintiff does not plan on presenting any additional witnesses or evidence and that the plaintiff is finished with its side of the case. At this point, the focus turns to the defendant, who is free to present evidence and witnesses. However, before the defendant begins his or her case, it is common for the defense attorney to raise a motion.

Motion for Directed Verdict

A **motion for directed verdict** comes at the end of the plaintiff's case, shortly after that party has announced that it rests. When a defendant brings a motion for directed verdict, he or she is saying

motion for directed verdict

A request by a party for a judgment because the other side has not met its burden of proof.

PRACTICE TIP

Throughout this chapter, we have examined the issues surrounding the presentation of a trial. It is one thing to talk about a trial and quite another to actually participate in one. One of the best things you can ever do, if you plan on a career in litigation, is to take the time to watch others present a trial. The local courthouse will have trials scheduled constantly. Find a case and sit in on the proceedings. The public is allowed to attend nearly all trials, and observing can be an invaluable learning tool. Try to watch every phase of the trial and see how the attorneys, witnesses, paralegals, judges, bailiffs, and others interact with one another. This type of hands-on experience will serve you well in the future when you are standing on the other side of the bar.

that the plaintiff has failed to prove all of the allegations raised in the complaint. Because the plaintiff has failed to prove its case, the defendant is entitled to a verdict entered by the judge that essentially dismisses the case and ends the trial. This is a directed verdict. Motions for directed verdict are routine in civil cases. Defendants raise these motions because there is no reason not to. If the defendant brings the motion and the judge denies it, the defendant is in no worse position than he or she was before. However, if the judge sustains the motion, the trial will end, and the defendant wins. Given that situation, it is little wonder that defense attorneys routinely bring a motion for directed verdict at the conclusion of the other side's case.

When the plaintiff has rested its case, the defendant is permitted to present his or her own case. The rules for the defendant's case are identical to those that bound the plaintiff. The defendant can present witnesses and testimony to attempt to disprove the plaintiff's allegations.

Presenting the Defense

In a civil case, though the defense is under no obligation to present a case, most defense attorneys do. The defense reasons that if the jurors hear only the plaintiff's version of the case, they will probably reach a verdict favorable to the plaintiff. The defendant will present witness testimony and evidence that tends to disprove, or mitigate, the defendant's liability.

Defense Witnesses

Like the plaintiff, the defendant must also present oral testimony from witnesses to prove its allegations or disprove the plaintiff's allegations. Just as we saw in the plaintiff's case, the defendant will call witnesses and conduct a direct examination. Afterward, the plaintiff's attorney is free to conduct a cross-examination of the defense witnesses.

Resting the Defense Case

Once the defendant has presented its case, the defense attorney also makes the announcement, "The Defense rests." This sentence signals that the defendant has no additional testimony or witnesses. The trial will now move into its final phase. At this point, the jury is usually sent back to the jury room or given a recess while the court conducts a charge conference.

Charge Conference

A charge conference is a meeting between the judge and the attorneys for both sides during which they discuss the type of instructions that will be given to the jury. As we will see, the judge always gives the jurors instructions about what they should do as they deliberate in the case and how they should announce that they are finished. The charge conference is when the judge gives the attorneys for both sides the opportunity to suggest specific types of instructions for the jury.

Attorneys know that in addition to the judge's instructions about what they should do in the jury room, jurors also receive instructions about what the law is pertaining to particular topics. The attorneys will research different cases, hoping that the judge will use language in his or her instructions to the jury that might slightly favor their side over the other. Consider the following jury instruction:

Plaintiff's Suggested Jury Charge #1.

Ladies and Gentlemen of the jury, I charge you that the defendant has been impeached by proof of a crime of dishonesty. Impeachment suggests that the witness is not capable of being believed. How much weight you give to that testimony is for you to decide.

Consider the defendant's suggested jury charge on the same topic:

Defendant's Suggested Jury Charge #1.
   Ladies and Gentlemen of the jury, I charge you that whether or not a person has been impeached in this case is solely a matter for you to decide.

You will notice that though both suggested jury charges state the same basic idea, the way that the defendant has worded the charge lessens the impact on the defense, whereas the plaintiff's suggested charge focuses attention on the defendant's testimony. The difference may be simple semantics, but attorneys do not take anything for granted. The entire case may hinge on how the jury considers this one issue.

The judge is free to accept or reject any of the parties' proposed jury charges. Once the court has considered all suggested jury instructions, the judge will call for the jury to return and announce that closing arguments may commence. See Figure 10.12.

Closing Argument

In a closing argument, the attorneys summarize their cases and show the jury why they should win. Unlike opening statements, attorneys are free to engage in the full range of dramatic presentations to sway the jury to their side. Attorneys can appeal not only to logic but also to emotion. They can argue that the verdict they want is good not only for their clients but also for society in general. Closing arguments in real cases have come to resemble their fictional counterparts on television,

FIGURE 10.12
Suggested Jury
Charge Cover Sheet

STATE OF PLACID	IN THE SUPERIOR COURT
COUNTY OF BURKE	SUPERIOR COURT FILE NO. _____
JANE DOE,	Jury Charge
Plaintiff	
vs.	
NICHOLAS CHARLES,	
Defendant.	

PLAINTIFF'S REQUESTS TO CHARGE NUMBER 1 THROUGH 4
Comes now the Plaintiff, Jane Doe, by and through Allison Barrister, Attorney for Plaintiff, and submits the attached requests to charge number 1 through _____.
Respectfully submitted, this 10th day of April, 2007.

_____

   Allison Barrister
   Attorney for Plaintiff Jane Doe

PLAINTIFF'S REQUEST TO CHARGE NO. 1
All drivers must obey traffic signs and electronic devices.
P.C.A. section 16-5-40

PLAINTIFF'S REQUEST TO CHARGE NO. 2
A driver who is cited for violation of a traffic device is presumed negligent. *Brown v. Simms*, 132 Pl. App. 399, 208 S.E.2d 183 (1974).

PLAINTIFF'S REQUEST TO CHARGE NO. 3
The plaintiff has the burden of proof in a civil case and when the plaintiff presents a preponderance of evidence, the burden shifts to the defendant to disprove the material allegations of the complaint.
Helton v. Plate, 166 Pl. App. 662, 305 S.E.2d 592 (1983).

PLAINTIFF'S REQUEST TO CHARGE NO. 4
A defendant has the obligation of proving the counterclaims raised in the answer and if the defendant fails to do so, the jury is authorized to find for the plaintiff on each and every unproven counterclaim.
P.C.A. section 16-5-23

with attorneys pulling out all the stops to convince the jurors that they should win. Unlike fictional trials, however, most real closing arguments last a lot longer than the few seconds that they take up on television. In many cases, attorneys have an hour or more to sum up their case. In previous decades, attorneys might have taken several days to complete a closing argument.

Just as we saw in opening statements, the plaintiff goes first in presenting a closing argument. When the plaintiff is finished, the defense gives its closing argument.

Jury Instructions

jury charge
Directions for the jury regarding what law applies and how it applies to the facts of a case; also known as *points of charge*.

When the closing arguments are complete, the judge then reads the **jury charge**. Among other things, the judge's charge instructs the jury what they must do in the jury room. For instance, a judge might read, "Once you have retired to the jury room, your first task will be to select one member of the jury to act as foreperson. This person will act as the jury spokesperson for any questions the jury might have and any communications, such as requests for breaks or meals, that the jury might need to make to the court."

In addition to instructing the jury about the practical matters about how to deliberate, the judge also instructs the jury about the law. The judge might instruct the jury about the burden on the plaintiff to prove the case against the defendant and that if the jurors feel that the plaintiff has failed to prove the case, they should return a verdict for the defendant.

A jury charge in a complex case could easily last for several hours. The court must go over not only procedural matters, such as where the jurors should write their verdict, but also the full range of legal issues that have arisen in the case.

Jury Deliberation

PRACTICE TIP

If the jurors are unable to reach a unanimous verdict, the judge will declare a mistrial. The jury will be referred to as a "hung" jury, and the case will be tried again before a different jury.

When the jury charge is complete, the jurors are led from the courtroom to the jury room where they can finally discuss the case among themselves. Jury deliberations are private; no one other than jury members is permitted to be inside the jury room while they deliberate. How does a jury actually deliberate on a case? The most common approach is for the jurors to discuss the case and then vote, often by secret ballot, which side they believe should win. The foreperson collects the ballots and then tabulates them. In most cases, the final verdict must be unanimous, so if the majority votes for one party and two or three people vote for the other, the majority will then spend some time trying to talk the minority over to their side. This process can take minutes, hours, or even days. Although the length of the trial is an indication of how long the jury will deliberate (longer trials usually result in longer deliberations), there are no rules when it comes to juries. Any trial attorney who has been involved in numerous trials will be quick to tell a client that there are no guarantees with jurors. For this reason, many trial attorneys refer to jury deliberations as "rolling the dice."

When the jurors finally reach a unanimous verdict, the jury spokesperson will knock on the jury room door and tell the court bailiff that they are ready to make their announcement. The bailiff will not ask about the verdict. Instead, he or she will conduct the jury back into the courtroom, where the judge will ask about the final verdict.

Verdict

In civil cases, when the plaintiff wins, the jury's announcement will be, "We find for the plaintiff." If they have decided that the defendant should win, their verdict will be, "We find for the defendant." If the jury has decided to make a monetary award, the jury spokesperson will then announce the amount and the party to whom it is awarded.

Judgment

judgment
The court's final decision regarding the rights and claims of the parties.

After the jury has announced its verdict, the judge officially enters this verdict as the final outcome in the case. This is referred to as the **judgment**. The jurors are released from jury duty and are now free to discuss the case with anyone they wish. Entering judgment has several important consequences. For one, the entry of judgment gives the winning party in a civil case the right to collect the amount awarded by the jury. It also gives the losing party the right to file an appeal.

Enforcing the Judgment

Once the case has concluded and the judge has entered judgment against one party, the other party may use various means to enforce that judgment. If the final judgment is that the defendant is liable to the plaintiff for specific damages, the plaintiff can use the judgment to enforce payment and even use the judgment to compel the defendant to sell off assets to pay the judgment.

CASE IN POINT

In re Lowell
14 A.D.3d 41, 784 N.Y.S.2d 69 (N.Y.A.D. 1 Dept., 2004)
Per Curiam.

Respondent Melinda E. Lowell was admitted to the practice of law in the State of New York by the Third Judicial Department on June 26, 1980, under the name Melinda Eilene Lowell. From 1996 to the present, she has maintained an office for the practice of law within the First Judicial Department. Respondent was also admitted to the bar in New Jersey in 1981, and at all relevant times herein, maintained an office for the practice of law there.

The Departmental Disciplinary Committee now seeks an order, pursuant to 22 NYCRR 603.3, suspending respondent for three years predicated upon similar discipline issued by the Supreme Court of New Jersey by an order filed November 25, 2003, imposing a three year suspension, retroactive to May 30, 2002. In the alternative, the Committee seeks an order sanctioning respondent as this Court deems appropriate. Respondent does not object to the imposition of reciprocal discipline but urges that such discipline should be coterminous with the disciplinary term imposed in New Jersey.

The New Jersey District II-B Ethics Committee served respondent with two separate disciplinary complaints and an amended complaint charging 48 counts and violations of various Rules of Professional Conduct. Most of the counts involved the charging of excessive fees. The remaining charges alleged that respondent engaged in a course of misconduct over a period of several years which included creating false documents which she then submitted to a court; counseling a client to lie in a certification and to disobey a court order; directing an employee to work on a client's case and charge the client after the client had discharged her; eliciting false testimony from a witness during trial; making misrepresentations to clients, the court and third parties; failing to refund the unearned portion of a retainer; failing to file a motion for pendente lite relief as requested by a client; failing to notify her adversary of the submission of an insertion made to a stipulation; directing a paralegal in her employ, who formerly worked for respondent's adversary in a pending case, to work on that case, even questioning the paralegal about her adversary's litigation strategy; and billing clients for work done by paralegals at the higher attorney billable rate.

Respondent answered the complaints and six days of hearings, between July 6, 2000[,] and August 8, 2000, were held before a Special Master at which respondent, represented by counsel, testified.

While the Special Master did not sustain all of the charges against respondent, he sustained 14 of them. In sustaining these charges, the Special Master reported that:

> I find that [respondent] has no appreciation of the inappropriateness of her conduct. I find that her testimony throughout the hearing was evasive and not credible. She neither expressed remorse nor did she accept any responsibility for her conduct. She attempted to challenge each of the allegations of misconduct by blaming others, including employees and associates of her firm or her adversaries. I find that her inability to recognize neither the nature nor the severity of her actions to be an aggravating factor.

The Special Master recommended a three-year suspension.

Upon a de novo review of the matter, the Disciplinary Review Board issued a lengthy decision dated October 26, 2001, recommending respondent's disbarment. This sanction was imposed after the Review Board thoroughly discussed the charges and findings against respondent.

Respondent represented the husband in a matrimonial matter. The Disciplinary Review Board found that by submitting to the court an order concerning a psychological exam of the parties' children without notifying the wife's attorney of its terms, she deliberately tried to circumvent the court rules so that her adversary could not object to the order, thereby violating Rules of Professional Conduct 3.4(c) [knowingly disobeying an obligation under the rules of a tribunal]. Although respondent was not charged with violating Rules of Professional Conduct 8.4(d) [engaging in conduct prejudicial to the administration of justice], the Disciplinary Review Board nevertheless found that her conduct violated this rule and amended the complaint to conform to the proof.

Also in this matrimonial action, respondent employed a paralegal who had formerly worked for the law firm which represented the wife. The Disciplinary Review Board found that by requiring the paralegal to work on this case and even questioning her about her adversary's litigation strategies, respondent breached the "screen" between the paralegal and the legal matter in violation of Advisory Committee Professional Ethics Opinion 665. This opinion requires the creation and maintenance of a "Chinese wall" separating the paralegal from any association with the matrimonial matter while in respondent's office.

In another matrimonial case, respondent added a sentence to a stipulation signed by her adversary and directed another attorney who worked for her to sign the stipulation containing the addition and to file it with the court, without advising the adversary of the addition. Respondent's associate refused, and the Disciplinary Review Board found that respondent attempted to pressure the associate to alter the stipulation and file it and, but for her refusal, it would have been filed with the court. Therefore, respondent violated Rules of Professional Conduct 8.4(a) [knowingly assisting or inducing another to violate the Rules of Professional Conduct] by her attempt to violate Rule 8.4(d).

In another matter, respondent stipulated and the Disciplinary Review Board concluded that by having her secretary sign her paralegal's name on a certification and then filing the certification with the court without the paralegal's consent[,] respondent violated Rules of Professional Conduct 3.4(c).

In 1996, a client paid respondent $5,000 to file a divorce complaint in New York and move for pendente lite support. Respondent never filed a pendente lite motion and was discharged in July 1996. The Disciplinary Review Board found that after her discharge, respondent instructed her paralegal to draft a pendente lite motion, place it in the file and deliver it to the client. Respondent then billed her former client for 15.4 hours of work including four hours for a "draft" of that motion and "review of financials." The Disciplinary Review Board concluded that respondent's conduct violated Rules of Professional Conduct 8.4(c) [conduct involving dishonesty, fraud, deceit or misrepresentation], that her failure to file the motion despite her client's request violated Rule 1.3 [lack of diligence], and by failing to return the unearned portion of the retainer she violated Rule 1.16(d) [failure to return unearned retainer on termination of representation].

In 1991, respondent filed an application for pendente lite relief for another client alleging that the client's father had lent her some $110,000, and attached six promissory notes to that effect. The husband claimed the notes were shams and the money was given to the couple as gifts. The Disciplinary Review Board found that respondent had her client sign fraudulent promissory notes and false certifications which respondent then filed with the court. In addition, respondent elicited false testimony from the wife's father at the divorce trial that the funds were loans and not gifts. By the foregoing conduct, the Review Board found that respondent violated Rules of Professional Conduct 1.2(d) [counseling or assisting a client in conduct the lawyer knows is illegal, criminal, or fraudulent], Rule 3.3(a)(1) [knowingly making a false statement of a material fact to a tribunal], Rule 3.3(a)(4) [offering evidence known to be false or failing to take remedial measures after learning that false evidence has been offered], [and] Rule 8.4(c).

On a separate issue, although the court had issued an order restraining the parties from transferring or dissipating assets, respondent assisted her client in cashing bearer bonds in order to pay her legal bill. The Disciplinary Review Board found respondent violated RPC 8.4(d).

While representing the wife in another matrimonial action, respondent filed a complaint in May 1997 against the husband seeking unpaid support. The husband was in the process of selling his house and respondent sent a letter to the broker stating that she represented the wife in a pending action and advised the broker that all proceeds from the sale must be held in escrow. However, there was no court order requiring that the proceeds be escrowed and respondent's subsequent application for such an order was denied. The Disciplinary Review Board concluded that respondent's conduct violated RPC 4.1(a)(1) [making a false statement of material fact or law to a third person] and Rule 8.4(c).

While the Disciplinary Review Board did not sustain 38 counts of charging clients with excessive fees, it did find that respondent billed various clients for work performed by paralegals at the higher attorney rate. The Review Board characterized this conduct as "misrepresentations" on clients' bills in violation of Rule 8.4(c) [engaging in conduct involving dishonesty, fraud, deceit, or misrepresentation].

Respondent did not present any evidence in mitigation.

In initially recommending disbarment, the Disciplinary Review Board found respondent's conduct "so egregious" that her "pervasive pattern of deceit and deficiency of character" warranted the most severe discipline. Specifically, the Review Board wrote in its report that:

> [Respondent] displayed an alarming lack of probity in these matters. Furthermore, she showed no appreciation for the basic trust that must exist between opposing counsel. The record is clear that, even at the ethics hearing, [respondent] displayed an arrogant, discourteous attitude toward the presenter, the witnesses and even the district ethics committee that docketed the grievances.

The Review Board also agreed with the Special Master that respondent had no appreciation of the inappropriateness of her behavior, failed to accept responsibility for her actions by blaming everyone but herself, and relentlessly browbeat her employees until they agreed to do things they otherwise would not have done.

Accordingly, the Disciplinary Review Board found that respondent had violated at least 10 provisions of the Rules of Professional Conduct as well as an Advisory Committee Opinion and recommended disbarment.

Thereafter, respondent moved to supplement the record with a report from her treating psychiatrist, letters from family members, attorneys and clients attesting to her reputation and character. In particular, respondent wished to address the Review Board's statements that at the hearing she was "arrogant" and "discourteous" and showed no appreciation that her behavior was inappropriate. The New Jersey Supreme Court granted respondent's motion and remanded the matter back to the Disciplinary Review Board for reconsideration of the record as supplemented. In addition, the court permitted the Office of Attorney Ethics to make its own submissions. The court also directed respondent, who had represented that she was not practicing law, to refrain from doing so until further order of the court.

Specifically, respondent's psychiatric expert explained in his report that at the time of respondent's hearing (summer 2000), she was on five different large doses of medication since she was suffering from "major depressive disorder, recurrent" and, as of the spring 2002, her major depressive disorder was in "partial remission". Respondent's doctor opined that respondent's medications and condition contributed to the way she projected to others during the hearing. While the psychiatric expert retained by the Office of Attorney Ethics shared the same diagnosis, he concluded that respondent's behavior during the hearing "were manifestations of [her] style of advocacy and presentation as an attorney, and not inevitable and invariable manifestations of her underlying psychiatric disorder."

The Disciplinary Review Board made no finding that respondent's mental condition caused any of the underlying misconduct. Rather, it was offered only to explain her behavior at the hearing before the Special Master and her then apparent lack of appreciation for her wrongdoing or acceptance of responsibility.

Upon reconsideration and by supplemental decision dated October 8, 2003, the Disciplinary Review Board did not modify its decision as to liability. However, with no new evidence submitted with respect to her conduct relating to the underlying charges, the Review Board nevertheless changed its sanction recommendation from disbarment to a three-year suspension. In recommending the reduced sanction, the Review Board considered these factors: respondent had failed to present any mitigating circumstances when the matter was first before the Review Board, the character letters submitted, the evidence of respondent's "severe psychiatric and emotional problems during the ethics hearing," and the Office of Attorney Ethic's recommendation of a three year suspension. Given these factors, the Review Board was no longer convinced that respondent could never again conform her conduct to the high standards required of an attorney, but that her misconduct warranted a lengthy suspension and that, prior to reinstatement, she should submit proof of her mental fitness.

Upon receipt of the Disciplinary Review Board's Supplemental Decision, the New Jersey Supreme Court issued an order, retroactively suspending respondent for three years from May 30, 2002.

The Departmental Disciplinary Committee now seeks an order finding respondent guilty of misconduct pursuant to 22 NYCRR 603.3(c) based upon the findings of misconduct made in the New Jersey disciplinary proceeding. Respondent was provided with sufficient notice that the Departmental Disciplinary Committee was seeking "an order, pursuant to 22 NYCRR 603.3, suspending [respondent] predicated upon similar discipline issued by a foreign jurisdiction, or, in the alternative, sanctioning respondent as this Court deems appropriate, or granting any other and further relief that is just and proper." She submitted a response in which she concedes none of the defenses enumerated in 22 NYCRR 603.3(c) are available to her and does not object to the imposition of reciprocal discipline. The findings of misconduct are supported by the record and are accepted by this Court. However, we cannot agree that the sanction New Jersey has imposed is appropriate under these circumstances.

We recognize and support the generally accepted and well reasoned principle that the jurisdiction where a respondent lives and actively practices law at the time of the offense has the greatest interest in the issue and the public policy considerations relevant to such disciplinary actions (see Matter of Yagman, 263 A.D.2d 151, 698 N.Y.S.2d 224 [1999]; Matter of Reiss, 119 A.D.2d 1, 505 N.Y.S.2d 604 [1986]). However, while we respect this long standing policy and tradition, and we always or virtually always impose a reciprocal sanction, we most respectfully—and indeed with some reluctance to deviate from our consistent adherence to the sound policy of reciprocal discipline—must decline to follow the doctrine of reciprocal discipline in this particular matter (see Matter of Gilbert, 268 A.D.2d 67, 707 N.Y.S.2d 394 [2000] [Committee's petition for more severe sanction of six months suspension rather than three months imposed in New Jersey granted]). Rather, we find ourselves in complete agreement with the original sanction which the New Jersey Disciplinary Review Board imposed because it is completely in accord with our own precedent in matters involving such egregious patterns of violations of legal and ethical obligations (see Matter of Heller, 9 A.D.3d 221, 780 N.Y.S.2d 314 [2004], lv. denied 3 N.Y.3d 607, 785 N.Y.S.2d 25, 818 N.E.2d 667 [2004] [11 counts of professional misconduct involving conduct prejudicial to the administration of justice, falsely testifying at a deposition, falsely submitting to the Supreme Court a post-trial affidavit, and intentionally engaging in conduct involving fraud, dishonestly, deceit and misrepresentation warranted disbarment over Committee's recommendation of suspension]; Matter of Weinstein, 4 A.D.3d 29, 772 N.Y.S.2d 275 [2004], lv. denied 3 N.Y.3d 608, 785 N.Y.S.2d 26, 818 N.E.2d 668 [2004] [professional misconduct which included converting and failing to return client funds, drafting and filing false petitions and affidavits, engaging in improper solicitations and charging and collecting excessive fees, despite otherwise unblemished record and character evidence, warranted disbarment]; Matter of Gadye, 283 A.D.2d 1, 726 N.Y.S.2d 401 [2001] [where attorney neglected numerous client matters, engaged in bad faith court filings, failed to comply with court orders, failed to advise clients of conflict of interest issues, and committed acts of fraud, dishonesty, and misrepresentation, disbarment appropriate sanction]; Matter of Brooks, 271 A.D.2d 127, 708 N.Y.S.2d 22 [2000], lv. dismissed 95 N.Y.2d 955, 722 N.Y.S.2d 468, 745 N.E.2d 388 [2000] [attorney who neglected legal matters, engaged in dishonesty involving clients, fabricated three orders and a bond, neglected numerous client matters, repeatedly failed to comply with court orders and directives, advancing claims he knew were unwarranted,

filing documents with false information and false notarization was disbarred]; Matter of Feldman, 252 A.D.2d 76, 682 N.Y.S.2d 204 [1998] [attorney disbarred when, over course of seven years involving four separate matters, he neglected legal matters entrusted to him and engaged in acts of misrepresentation, deceit and forgery in attempting to conceal behavior]; Matter of Goffe, 209 A.D.2d 124, 624 N.Y.S.2d 592 [1995] [under doctrine of reciprocal discipline, attorney disbarred where he was found to have engaged in conduct involving dishonesty, fraud, deceit and misrepresentation, conduct prejudicial to the administration of justice, proffered fabricated or altered evidence to the IRS and the United States Tax Court and lied under oath before the Tax Court]).

Respondent had the opportunity to put in evidence at the original hearing and again thereafter at the supplemental proceeding. Based on the record respondent developed, we find that the higher sanction is appropriate (see Matter of Gilbert, supra; Matter of Dinhofer, 257 A.D.2d 326, 690 N.Y.S.2d 245 [1999]; Matter of Aschheim, 224 A.D.2d 149, 647 N.Y.S.2d 221 [1996]). In reaching this determination, we note that the evidence respondent submitted to supplement the record does not address the underlying conduct giving rise to the charges of professional misconduct. Rather, it was offered only to explain her negative behavior at the hearing. As such, it cannot serve to lessen the sanction for an underlying pattern of conduct as egregious and dishonest as was otherwise established against this respondent. We add and emphasize that we have reached this conclusion only with the greatest regard for our sister state's disciplinary system on the one hand, but with a sincere, profound and respectful disagreement with its supplemental decision reducing respondent's sanction from disbarment to a three year suspension.

Accordingly, the Committee's petition should be denied to the extent that it seeks to impose a sanction of a suspension of three years and granted to the extent that it seeks findings of misconduct and an alternate sanction, and respondent should be disbarred and her name stricken from the roll of attorneys.

Respondent's name was stricken from the roll of attorneys and counselors-at-law in the State of New York, effective December 9, 2004.

Source: From Westlaw. Used with permission of Thomson/West.

Case Questions:

1. Although there are numerous charges of misconduct against the attorney in this case, explain the allegations concerning falsifying court documents and eliciting false testimony from a witness at trial.

2. The attorney in this case also tried to get her paralegal to engage in several unethical practices. What were they?

3. The court refers to the fact that the attorney lacked a basic understanding of the trust that must exist between an attorney and her clients. Explain what the court means by this statement.

4. Does the fact that the attorney here was suffering from depression and was on medication mitigate her actions? Why or why not?

5. How would you, as a paralegal, conduct your own affairs if you had found yourself working for this attorney?

Eye on Ethics

ETHICAL CONCERNS IN PREPARING WITNESSES FOR TRIAL

One of the issues that always arises when working with witnesses who will testify at trial concerns the difference between coaching a witness and preparing a witness. Coaching a witness is telling the witness what he or she should say and is not only unethical but may fall under the crime of tampering with a witness. Preparing a witness is not considered to be an ethical or a legal violation. The question often arises: What is the difference? A legal professional coaches a witness by taking that witness through questions that will likely be asked at trial and telling the witness how he or she should respond. Legal professionals are sometimes tempted to take these issues in their own hands, especially when they are dealing with reluctant or overly shy witnesses. But attorneys and paralegals are barred from providing witnesses with their answers. Preparing a witness for trial involves asking the witness questions that he or she might be asked at trial and then determining how the witness will respond. In the first example, the legal professional is providing the answers; in the second, the legal professional is noting what the witness's response will be. The best approach to take with witnesses is to advise them to tell their own story and that the story should be the truth. Witness coaching often backfires on the legal team when the witness suddenly reveals that one side scripted his or her responses. The jury will usually disregard the witness's entire testimony, and the judge will probably contact the state bar.

A Day in the Life: Cheryl Jones

Cheryl Jones has worked as a paralegal for over 11 years, primarily for a prominent attorney in a small community. "I specialize primarily in domestic law and criminal law," she says. "My personal motto has always been the attorney (or firm) is only as good as his/her paralegals. When the paralegal's work is below par, the attorney's reputation and business may suffer. Let's face it—clients interact more often with the paralegal than the attorney. I strive for perfection or pretty darn close in every task I tackle, whether answering the phone or assisting in trial. I believe the quality and professionalism of my work assisted me in obtaining and maintaining respect and a personal yet professional rapport with the judges, court personnel, attorneys, and other paralegals. A great paralegal should exude confidence as well as knowledge and should learn how to professionally compliment the attorney.

"In my experience," she continues, "it is imperative that new paralegals familiarize themselves and know the Local Rules of Court. In my experience, I have learned that attorneys generally know the Rules of Civil Procedure, but most depend on their paralegals to thoroughly know the Local Rules of Court and procedures to enforce the Local Rules of Court."

When Cheryl Jones prepares for trial, she does her homework because "I believe the most important aspect in assisting at trial happens before the trial. All paralegals should know the contents of the file, especially discovery. While in trial, I have developed the art of intense listening while multitasking. My goal is to listen to my attorney's line of questioning and predict where his questioning is going—doing this makes you and your attorney appear competent and professional in the eyes of a jury. About 99.9% of the time, I know the direction my attorney is taking the witness during direct or cross-examination and know what document or exhibit to pull out of the file for his use before he asks for it. Some attorneys and prosecutors pre-label exhibits and follow outlines, but my attorney does everything 'off the cuff,' which makes my job crucial.

"Another important aspect of being a litigation paralegal is effective legal research skills. On one occasion, I had to leave the courtroom and travel back to the office to pull supporting case law. When I returned to the courtroom and handed the cases to my attorney, he asked if the cases were in our favor and I gave him an affirmative nod. Because of his confidence in my abilities, he was able to hand the Court and opposing counsel copies of the case law without fully reviewing it first."

Real Paralegal Life: Building a Skill Set

PREPARING WITNESSES TO TESTIFY

It is often extremely helpful to prepare a small demonstration of how the direct and cross-examination of a witness is most likely to proceed. Go over the questions with the witness to let him or her know what will be asked on direct and what kinds of questions he or she can expect on cross-examination. Take the witness to the actual courthouse several days before the trial begins and show him or her where the courtroom is and how it is laid out. Indicate where the witness will be seated and how he or she should speak into the microphone, if one is provided. Witnesses who go through this process are often a great deal less anxious about testifying. Courthouse personnel are often quite accommodating and will allow access to the courtroom when court is not in session if you call ahead and ask for permission.

Trials are often rescheduled at the last moment. It is common for a trial to be continued until next week or next month. You must be adept at shifting gears at a moment's notice and be able to explain these changes to witnesses and clients.

Many people respond to anxiety with unreasonable demands and anger. You must be able to recognize that these mood swings are in direct response to the growing anxiety about the upcoming trial. Working with witnesses is often a challenge to your people skills, but if handled well, it can make the difference between winning and losing a case.

Career Prep

Prepare an issue table for the major issues presented in the Baker case, which you will find in Appendix B.

Summary

The trial is the culmination of months or even years of preparatory work that has included discovery, investigation, and drafting of pleadings. Preparing for a trial is absolutely necessary to assure that both parties have the evidence and witness testimony that they need to proceed on their claims. The actual trial begins with jury selection. Parties are given a specific number of peremptory jury strikes that they may use to remove panel members for any reason. If a juror indicates that he or she is unable to follow the court's directions, that panel member may be removed for cause. After the jury is selected, the parties proceed to opening statements, during which they outline facts in the case and what they intend to prove at trial. Once opening statements have concluded, the plaintiff presents his or her case, proceeding from witness to witness and offering evidence until the plaintiff believes that he or she has presented sufficient proof to prove the allegations in the complaint. At the conclusion of the plaintiff's case, the defendant is permitted to move for a directed verdict. If the judge grants this motion, the plaintiff's case will be dismissed, and the judge will enter a verdict in the defendant's favor. If the motion is denied, the defendant is free to present his or her own case, including witness testimony and evidence. At the conclusion of the defense case, the parties meet in a brief charge conference, during which they discuss the jury instructions that the jury will receive at the conclusion of the case. Following the charge conference, the parties engage in closing arguments, which summarize their perspectives on the case and request the jury to vote in their favor. At this point, the judge will read the jury instructions and then release the members of the jury to confer with one another in the jury room. The jury's decision is the verdict. When the jury announces its verdict, the judge imposes the jury's decision on the parties through a judgment.

Key Terms

Pretrial conference, 230
Pretrial order, 230
Calendar call, 233
Conflict letter, 233
Panel, 233
Jurors, 233
Voir dire, 233
Jury strike, 233

Peremptory jury strike, 234
Challenge, 234
Direct examination, 235
Cross-examination, 235
Motion for directed verdict, 236
Jury charge, 239
Judgment, 239

Review Questions

1. Explain the importance of preparing for trial.
2. What role can a paralegal play in trial preparation?
3. Explain how exhibits can be used in a trial.
4. Why is it necessary to organize the case file prior to trial?
5. What is a trial notebook?
6. What is a charge conference?
7. Describe a motion for a directed verdict.
8. Describe how a juror would be struck for cause.
9. Describe peremptory jury strikes.
10. List the various phases of the civil trial.
11. Describe the process of selecting a jury.
12. What is the purpose of an opening statement?
13. Compare and contrast direct and cross-examination.
14. Why would an attorney conduct a mock trial before the actual trial?
15. Explain the function of the closing argument.
16. What are jury instructions?
17. What is a verdict?
18. Compare and contrast verdicts and judgments.

Discussion Question

1. Are all of the various phases of a civil trial actually necessary? Is there a way to streamline or even eliminate some of these phases? Explain your answer.

Exercises: Skill Builders

Prepare a chronology of events in the Baker (Appendix B) and Apple (Appendix C) cases.

Portfolio Assignment

Portfolio Assignment 10-1: Prepare jury charges in a personal injury case. Review the pleadings in the Baker case, and then prepare at least 10 possible jury charges that the plaintiff would most likely submit to the judge.

Portfolio Assignment 10-2: List paralegal activities. Discuss the important activities that a paralegal carries out, from the initial meeting with a client to the day before a jury trial.

Vocabulary Builders

ACROSS

1 The removal of a jury panel member for any legally permissible reason, also known as a peremptory jury challenge.

9 The questioning of a witness to show bias, prejudice, or lack of knowledge.

12 The removal of a jury panel member, also known as a jury challenge.

13 An order, prepared by the trial judge with the input of the parties, that summarizes key issues in the case, including witness order, evidence, and other critical concerns.

DOWN

1 A conference between the judge, plaintiff, and defendant before the trial commences; the parties discuss witness issues and evidence and finalize their agreements in a pretrial order.

2 A motion by the defense that asks the court to enter a verdict in the defendant's favor because the plaintiff has failed to prove all material allegations against the defendant.

3 Oral instructions given by the judge to the jury about how they should deliberate and what law they should follow.

4 A mandatory court hearing in which the judge inquires about the readiness of the parties to go to trial; also known as a docket call.

5 When a panel member is removed because he or she cannot sit on the jury.

6 (Fr) To look; to speak. The process of questioning jurors about their potential biases in the case.

7 A group of people who have been called for jury duty; the final jury will be selected from this group; also known as venire.

8 The questioning of a witness by the side who called the witness to the stand.

10 A letter sent by an attorney to the judge explaining that the attorney has several different appearances scheduled for the same date and detailing which courts the attorney will go to first.

11 Those people who have been selected to sit on a jury; they will consider the evidence and reach a verdict in the case.

Chapter 11

Damages

CHAPTER OBJECTIVES

The student will be able to:

- Explain the difference between compensatory damages and punitive damages.

- Compare and contrast general damages with special damages.

- Create a list of specific types of damages and categorize them.

- Describe how attorneys present damages to juries.

- Describe how to measure future lost income.

- Explain how attorneys prove damages at trial.

- Define the importance of fair market value in property losses.

- Explain the collateral source rule.

- Describe the doctrine of mitigation of damages.

- Define a court's equity power.

damages
Money paid to compensate for loss or injury.

The many different forms of damages, including general, special, and punitive, are discussed in this chapter. In any civil case, the plaintiff must prove not only that the defendant is liable for the plaintiff's loss but also the extent of that loss. **Damages** refer to the monetary, property, or personal losses suffered by the plaintiff. The point of an award of damages is to restore the plaintiff to the condition he or she was in prior to the injury, if that is possible. Damages are also designed to punish the defendant for the defendant's willful actions or wanton disregard for the safety of others. Because civil damages serve so many functions, we begin this chapter with a general discussion of what damages are and then address the specific types of damages available in civil cases.

Requiring one party to pay another for the injuries he or she inflicts is not a new idea. As far back as the Old Testament, there were provisions that a person who injured another must pay a fee. This fee varied according to the type of injury, with the loss of a hand valued higher than the loss of a finger. Rather than impose an eye for an eye, societies realized that it made more sense, and caused much less violence, to impose a monetary fine for the negligent behavior of others (see John M. P. Smith, *Origin and History of Hebrew Law*, Hyperion Press, 1990).

In the previous few chapters, we outlined the various steps involved in bringing and proving a suit. Now we shall address the concept of proof of damages: In a basic civil suit, the plaintiff files a complaint and alleges a loss that might be financial, physical, or emotional and also alleges that the defendant is responsible for that loss. Proof of the defendant's proximate cause for that loss is only the first step. Next, the plaintiff must establish that he or she has suffered a legally recognized wrong. According to the Restatement of Torts, damages are defined as "a sum of money awarded to a person injured by a tort of another" (Restatement of Torts, 2d § 902). This definition provides an excellent summary of the purpose of awarding damages. If the jury determines that the defendant is liable, then the jury is empowered to award damages to the plaintiff. However, if the jury determines that the defendant is not liable, there is no consideration of damages. Determining the type of damages, and how best to prove these at trial, are the main considerations of the attorneys for both the plaintiff and the defendant. Whereas the plaintiff's legal team will focus on how best to show the jury that the plaintiff has suffered a legal wrong, the defendant's attorney focuses on any evidence that tends to mitigate or completely cancel out the defendant's responsibility for paying such damages.

TYPES OF DAMAGES

The damages available in civil cases are often classified into three broad categories:

- Compensatory damages
- Punitive damages
- Nominal damages

Compensatory Damages

compensatory damages
A payment to make up for a wrong committed and return the nonbreaching party to a position where the effect or the breach has been neutralized.

Compensatory damages are designed to do exactly what their name suggests: compensate the victim for losses caused by the defendant's negligent conduct. The stated purpose of compensatory damages is to place the plaintiff in the condition he or she was in prior to the injury. Of course, that is often impossible. In such situations, compensatory damages are designed to compensate the plaintiff for the change in his or her condition. Some jurisdictions define compensatory damages as the monetary assessments paid by the defendant to "make the plaintiff whole" again. These assessments usually take the form of monetary payments made by the defendant to the plaintiff to compensate the plaintiff for injuries or property and other losses. Compensatory damages are usually broken into two separate categories: general and special.

When the plaintiff's injuries are financial, the jury's award of money is designed to put the plaintiff back in the situation he or she was in before the defendant's actions took place. When the plaintiff's injuries are physical, money is regarded as a form of compensation for the aggravation, pain and suffering, and other losses, even when these conditions are not easy to assess on a monetary scale. The plaintiff can recover for all harm: past, present, and future.

General Damages

general damages
Those that normally would be anticipated in a similar action.

General damages are those payments by the defendant to the plaintiff that are most closely associated with the defendant's act. One example of general damages is pain and suffering. General damages are difficult to quantify. Just how much is a person's pain and suffering worth? Obviously different people will have different answers to this question, and any of the plaintiff's requests that fall into the category of subjective injury usually qualify as general damages. In such cases, jurors are often called on to use their own life experiences to determine an amount. Although calculating such damages is difficult and varies considerably from jury to jury, and even region to region, there are some basic guidelines. The more severe the injury, the more money the jury is likely to award. A scar on a person's face will justify a much larger award than a similar scar on a person's leg. However, because the very nature of general damages is so subjective, these awards have come under increasing criticism. The fact that similar cases can have such divergent results is often perceived as one of the primary weaknesses of the American civil justice system. Further complicating the issues in such cases is the fact that most jurisdictions do not require the plaintiff to state a specific amount sought for general damages. Instead, plaintiffs leave the final determination up to the jury.

Pain and Suffering. One of the most hotly contested issues in civil cases pertains to the issue of the plaintiff's claim for compensation for pain and suffering. What precisely qualifies under this definition? The law is vague, perhaps deliberately so. Most jurisdictions follow a formula that allows the jury to assess a sum that a "reasonable person" would find acceptable to compensate the plaintiff for the constant pain and suffering caused by an injury. Of course, the very vagueness of the definition often results in widely divergent jury awards.

PRACTICE TIP

The Restatement of Torts defines general damages as those injuries that result so frequently from most negligence and other tort actions that their existence can be assumed and their amount can be proven at trial.

per diem
(Latin) "by the day" or daily.

special damages
Those damages incurred beyond and in addition to the general damages suffered and expected in similar cases.

Because general damages are, by their very nature, difficult to quantify, attorneys have developed several different presentation styles to sway the jury to award pain and suffering compensation to plaintiffs. For example, an attorney might make a per diem argument.

A **per diem** argument is based on a simple calculation: How much would it be worth to a person, on a daily basis, to forgo specific pain? An attorney might argue that any reasonable person might be willing to pay $5 a day not to have the persistent ache from the injury in a car wreck or from a botched medical procedure. Applying the $5 per day formula for 365 days in a year equals $1,825. The best estimates show that the plaintiff might live as long as 30 additional years. Multiplying the per diem by that lifespan equals an award of $54,750. The attorney would then argue that the only reasonable award in this case would be an award in excess of $50,000 for the plaintiff's suffering, in addition to any other awards that the jury might make.

Of course, there is nothing predetermined about the attorney's argument. The defense attorney might easily argue that the plaintiff is not entitled to any pain and suffering, let alone a daily charge for the rest of the plaintiff's life to put up with pain that has already faded away. There is no state that imposes a per diem formula in any personal injury case.

Special Damages

Special damages are those damages that are usually easier to quantify because they have specific amounts. Examples of special damages are items such as the plaintiff's total medical bill for the injuries sustained in a car wreck, the additional fees that the plaintiff was charged by other doctors to repair the damage in a medical malpractice case, or even the total time that the plaintiff lost from work while recuperating from his or her injuries. Plaintiffs routinely plead the specific amounts of medical bills and other special damages in their complaints. At trial, the plaintiff will be required to present proof of the amount of his or her special damages before the jury will be authorized to make an award of special damages.

Lost Wages.   A prime example of special damages is lost wages. When the plaintiff alleges that the injuries caused by the defendant's actions resulted in the plaintiff's lost time from work, the plaintiff must present something more than the bald assertion of how much he or she would have made had that person worked. As we will see later in this chapter, actually proving losses can involve complicated testimony. Lost wages are an excellent example of how in-depth the plaintiff's attorney must get to plead this issue successfully to the jury.

To prove the plaintiff's lost wages, the plaintiff's attorney must present tax returns, paycheck stubs, affidavits from employers or clients, and other information, including IRS 1099 forms and similar items. The plaintiff's paralegal is usually the person responsible for gathering and organizing all of this information for use at trial.

Medical Bills.   Medical bills are another example of special damages. In personal injury and medical malpractice cases, the client may have amassed enormous medical bills and will request that the defendant pay all of those directly related to the defendant's negligence. Plaintiffs are often anxious about pending medical bills. They may be receiving telephone calls from bill collectors and letters in the mail from medical providers demanding payment. The best practice is for the plaintiff's attorney to intercede on the client's behalf and contact all medical providers

**PRACTICE
TIP**

When organizing a case for trial, keep a separate section for the damages. All medical bills, payment stubs, expert analyses, lost wages, and the dozens of other documents related to proof of damages at trial should be categorized, recorded, and calculated. You should also include a master list of all of these items so that you can double-check with the client that all bills have been listed.

 COMMUNICATION TIP

Because gathering all of the material together to prove civil damages can be a time-consuming project, it is important for you to communicate with the client the necessity of tracking down every bill. Unfortunately, clients are not always as organized as we would like them to be. You may send home questionnaires and checklists, but some clients lack the diligence to complete them. In the end, you may find that your attempts to communicate the importance of finding all of the bills fall on deaf ears. In some cases, you may find yourself going through the client's records yourself, just to be absolutely sure that all documents required to prove the damages at trial have been produced.

SPOT THE ISSUE!

Last year, Mary was admitted to the hospital with chest pain. The doctor diagnosed her problem as acid reflux and sent her home with some antacids. Because Mary is a self-employed graphic artist, she only gets paid when she completes projects. Her continuing chest pain prevented her from completing an assignment, and the client fired her and went with another company. That cost her a $5,000 fee. Two weeks after first reporting to the hospital with chest pain, Mary lost consciousness and was taken to the Emergency Room in cardiac arrest. She is now completely unable to work. Before the first incident, Mary earned about $3,000 per month. She is now on disability. Beyond that, her marriage has suffered, which has contributed to a bout of depression. Categorize all of Mary's potential damage claims and put as many dollar amounts to them as possible.

to inform them that the case has gone to litigation. This notice often results in the creditors waiting until the resolution of the case before making additional demands. In modern practice, it is usually the paralegal who must meet with the client, sort through the medical bills, and then organize them all to make sure that the plaintiff is requesting payment for every bill. These amounts will then be listed in the complaint.

Future Losses

A plaintiff is permitted to seek recovery for future medical services that are "reasonably certain" to be needed for the plaintiff's future care. The award for future losses is designed to anticipate all reasonable expenses connected with future medical care, including charges by doctors, nurses, therapists, and medical supplies. The plaintiff is also entitled to compensation for being required to hire someone else to perform a job while he or she is incapacitated. However, a plaintiff is not legally entitled to compensation for lost "time," that is, the time lost from leisure activities while he or she was recuperating from injuries.

Measuring Future Lost Income.   At the end of the trial, the jurors will be instructed that before they can determine an amount of future lost income, they must calculate the difference between what the plaintiff's future income would have been before he or she was injured and what it will be now that he or she has been injured. Proving lost future income usually involves expert testimony. The expert will calculate future lost income on the basis of complicated formulas involving the plaintiff's past income, his or her education, likelihood of promotion, probable lifespan, and a wide range of other factors.

Proving Damages

We now know that the plaintiff must present proof of his or her damages at trial, but that spurs an additional question: How much proof is required? Can the plaintiff simply make a broad allegation that he or she is entitled to X amount of dollars, or is more required? If more is required, how much more?

The general rules about proof of damages are that the same degree of proof is required to prove losses as was required for the plaintiff to prove the other elements of the case. In many jurisdictions, the plaintiff must present proof to a preponderance of the evidence that he or she is entitled to an award. The practical side of this burden of proof is that the plaintiff must prove not only that the defendant was the cause of the plaintiff's injuries but also the nature, extent, and full amount of the financial, property, and emotional losses suffered by the plaintiff as a result of the defendant's actions.

Courts also require certainty in calculating damages. A trial judge will not authorize damages when the plaintiff's claim is based on mere conjecture or a vague idea of what his or her injuries are. Trial judges are also authorized to overturn a jury's award of damages if the judge believes that the jury did not rely on testimony and evidence and instead simply voted their feelings (*Walston v. Greene*, 246 N.C. 617, 99 S.E.2d 805 (1957)).

Distinguishing between General and Special Damages

Why is there a distinction between general and special damages? The first answer to this question goes to the practical difficulties of presenting evidence about both at the trial. General damages, because they are difficult to quantify, are harder to prove than special damages. After all, special damages involve specific and quantified items, such as medical bills, whereas general damages involve intangibles such as pain and suffering and loss of emotional support. Proving these damages often involves testimony from the plaintiff's friends and family about the effect that the accident has had. This testimony is, by its very nature, purely subjective. In contrast, special damages involve presentations of bills and other hard evidence that are not subjective and are presented to the jury with a straightforward proposition. If the jurors believe that the defendant is responsible for the plaintiff's damages, they will usually award special damages with little difficulty. It should come as no surprise then that another important difference between general and special damages is that an award of general damages is more easily appealed than an award of special damages.

Presenting Proof at Trial

Because of the inherent difficulties in proving general damages, attorneys have been very creative over the years in attempting to show the jury why the plaintiff is entitled to general damages. One excellent presentation tool is the "day in the life" video.

A day in the life video is a professional presentation that tracks the plaintiff's activities during the day, following him or her from the moment that the plaintiff wakes up, through bathing, eating, and driving to see doctors. A day in the life video can be a powerful evidentiary tool, especially when the plaintiff suffers from terrible injuries. The jury can actually see just how difficult common tasks have become for the plaintiff. The video will also show the plaintiff interacting with others, such as home health care nurses. As a visual aid, these videos are unsurpassed for giving the jury an accurate, and often unforgettable, view of the plaintiff's life. The final award in the case usually justifies the added expense of creating it.

Proving Property Losses

Different types of evidence are required to prove the existence of different types of damages. Property losses, for example, are handled differently than the evidence presented to prove pain and suffering.

When the plaintiff claims damage to or a reduction in value of his or her property, he or she also must present some evidence showing what the value of the property was before the defendant's actions and what the value of the property is after the defendant's negligence. This proof

---

SURF'S UP!

DAY IN THE LIFE VIDEO

This chapter mentions the use of so-called day in the life videos as a way to show the jury exactly what a typical day is like for an injured plaintiff. Such videos can have a dramatic effect on the jury. Instead of simply hearing about how difficult it is for someone without the use of his or her legs to get out of bed, put on clothes, make breakfast, and go to work, the jury can actually see it. They can hear the plaintiff grunt with effort when climbing into a wheelchair, see the plaintiff navigate through a house that was never designed with a handicapped person in mind, and get an idea of the thousand little indignities such a handicap can bring.

If your firm is considering the use of a day in the life video, it is important to do the preparation work necessary to pull it all together. Long before the cameras come out, spend some time with the plaintiff going through his or her daily activities and make extensive notes. The videographer will need this information to set up the cameras, lights, and microphones. Shooting a day in the life video isn't as simple as following the plaintiff around with a camera. For the jury to see and understand what is happening, it is often necessary for the videographer to shoot a scene from several different angles, which means using more than one camera or having the plaintiff reenact certain actions from different viewpoints. Both you and the plaintiff must be aware of the procedures involved. If you are in doubt, talk with the videographer long before the day of the shooting. It will make for a much smoother process, with less stress on the client.

fair market value
The amount that a willing buyer would pay for an item that a willing seller would accept.

often involves calculations of the "fair market value" of the property. **Fair market value** is usually determined by an appraiser, someone who is an expert in the field and can give an accurate estimate of the property's value. Consider Hypothetical 11-1.

Hypothetical 11-1

Juan was recently in a car wreck. His car was rear-ended by the defendant while Juan was waiting for a traffic light to change. The damage to Juan's car was drastic, and an appraiser has set the value at $100. Before the accident, Juan was in negotiations to sell the car to a friend. The final sale price they had reached was $5,500. The appraiser agrees that the value of the car prior to the accident was probably at least $5,500. How much in property damages can Juan request in his complaint against the defendant?

   Answer: Juan's property damages will be $5,500. Because an expert can testify that the sale price Juan and his friend had agreed to was approximately what the fair market value would have been, Juan can request that amount. If he receives it, the jury will deduct $100 from the total amount. Why?

The Collateral Source Rule

collateral source rule
A rule of evidence rule that prohibits the jury from being informed about the plaintiff's other sources of compensation, such as insurance, worker's compensation, etc.

There are some important legal doctrines that can affect the total amount that a plaintiff may receive. One such critical doctrine is the **collateral source rule** (see Figure 11.1). When a jurisdiction follows the collateral source rule, it means that the jury cannot be told that the plaintiff has already been compensated for part of his or her loss through insurance or other benefits. The theory is that the plaintiff should not be penalized for a reduction in the final award simply because he or she has taken the precaution of obtaining insurance or receiving some other form of compensation for injuries received. Many states follow the collateral source rule, believing that if the jury knows that the plaintiff has already been compensated by other sources, it may reduce the total amount of the damage award to the plaintiff. Proponents of the collateral source rule say that a plaintiff who has taken the precautions of acquiring health, auto, and life insurance is punished by his or her thoughtfulness. A plaintiff who was fully insured against potential losses will end up with a smaller award than a plaintiff who failed to take such reasonable precautions. The proponents of the collateral source rule also point out that if the jury does award a plaintiff damages for which he or she has already been compensated, the plaintiff is not permitted to keep them. Instead, any excess will go to the plaintiff's insurers to defray their costs for compensating the plaintiff in the first place.

subrogation
The right to sue in the name of another.

   In cases in which an insurance company has compensated the plaintiff for his or her injuries, the company is entitled to seek payment of those damages from the defendant through the principle of **subrogation**. When an insurance company brings a subrogation action against the defendant, it is entitled to sue in the plaintiff's place for reimbursement for the funds paid out to the plaintiff under the insurance policy.

mitigation of damages
The obligation to offset or otherwise engage in curative measures to stop accrual of unreasonable economic damages; that is, to minimize the damage incurred through affirmative actions.

Mitigation of Damages

In addition to the collateral source rule, there are other important legal principles that often come into play in assessing damages. For example, the concept of **mitigation of damages** often plays an important role in determining a final award amount.

   Under the doctrine of mitigation of damages, a plaintiff is required to lessen his or her damages whenever reasonably possible. Therefore, the plaintiff is not permitted to refuse medical treatment

FIGURE 11.1
Collateral Source Rule

Source: Wilson v. Burch Farms, Inc. 627 S.E.2d 249 (N.C. App., 2006).

> "The purpose of the collateral source rule is to exclude evidence of payments made to the plaintiff by sources other than the defendant when this evidence is offered for the purpose of diminishing the defendant's liability to the injured plaintiff. The policy behind the rule is to prevent a tortfeasor from reducing his own liability for damages by the amount of compensation the injured party receives from an independent source. This rule is punitive in nature, and is intended to prevent the tortfeasor from a windfall when a portion of the plaintiff's damages have been paid by a collateral source."

for the injuries caused by the defendant's negligence or allow property to be destroyed when the plaintiff could have taken reasonable steps to protect it. The consequences for failing to mitigate damages are that the plaintiff's ultimate monetary award at trial will be reduced. Consider Hypothetical 11-2.

Hypothetical 11-2

When Juan was injured in his car wreck, he refused medical treatment. His back continued to ache, but he ignored all advice to seek medical help. Two weeks later, in unbearable pain, a doctor at the Emergency Room diagnosed Juan with an aggravated and herniated disk in his spine. The disk would not have been in such bad shape had Juan gone to the hospital immediately after the accident and been put into a proper restraint. At trial, the defendant alleges that he should not be liable for the additional medical bills related to Juan's failure to seek medical assistance. Will the defendant be successful?

Answer: Yes. Because Juan, like all plaintiffs, is required to mitigate his damages when reasonable, his failure to seek medical aid appears to be a clear case in which the doctrine of mitigation will affect his total amount of damages. However, is there an argument that Juan might be able to make to explain his failure to seek medical assistance?

Although we have framed the issues surrounding mitigation in terms of medical treatment, the concept also holds true for other civil disputes. In contract litigation, for example, a vendor has the obligation to sell perishable merchandise to other customers, even when the original customer wrongfully refuses to buy. Without such action, the vendor would be barred from seeking damages for the loss of the entire order. Of course, the vendor can always sue the original customer for the difference between what it would have gotten from the original transaction and the lower amount the vendor received when it was forced to sell to another (*International Correspondence School, Inc. v. Crabtree*, 162 Tenn. 70, 34 S.W.2d 447 (1931)).

Emotional Distress

The rules about suing for emotional distress vary from state to state. Although most states allow some claim for the emotional and mental impact of the injuries sustained by the defendant's actions, not all of them allow psychic injuries.

In many jurisdictions, a plaintiff is not allowed to recover for purely psychological injuries. In those jurisdictions, the emotional impact must be coupled with some physical impact. For instance, a plaintiff cannot request damages when the defendant's actions cause the plaintiff to lose sleep or feel anxious but not because of any other physical injury. In many other jurisdictions, this requirement of physical trauma has either slowly eroded away or been replaced entirely with actions allowing recovery for purely emotional or psychological injuries (*Tancredi v. Dive Makai Charters*, 823 F. Supp. 778 (D.C. Hawaii 1993)). An award of damages for emotional distress, or mental anguish, can include not only the plaintiff's sufferings in the past but also any mental distress the plaintiff is likely to endure in the future (*Davis v. Green*, 188 F. Supp. 808 (W.D. Ark.,1960)).

Loss of Consortium

loss of consortium
A claim filed by the plaintiff's spouse for the loss of companionship in the marriage caused by the injuries.

Another type of damage that falls into a special category is a **loss of consortium** claim, which is a claim raised not by the injured plaintiff but by his or her spouse. This claim states that when the plaintiff was injured, the marital relations between the plaintiff and spouse were also injured. In all jurisdictions, the spouse is entitled to file some form of loss of consortium claim. The spouse is entitled to damages for the loss of companionship, affection, sexual relations, and other losses that frequently occur when one spouse is incapacitated. At trial, the plaintiff's legal team will be required to present evidence to support the spouse's claim, which often comes in the form of the oral testimony of the spouse, who takes the stand and discusses the marital relationship prior to the injury and the state of the relationship post-injury. Some of this testimony will involve intimate details about the couple's sexual history before and after the incident.

With recent developments in the law of marriage, it is currently an open question if a loss of consortium claim could be sustained by a gay married couple or individuals who have entered into a civil union.

Prior Injuries

One of the most effective attacks that the defendant's attorney can mount against the plaintiff is a claim that the plaintiff was actually injured in a prior accident and that this prior accident is what caused his or her pain, not the incident involving the defendant in this case. A paralegal should always ask the plaintiff about any prior medical problems, including prior accidents or collisions. Any prior injury that is even vaguely like the current injury should be closely documented. At trial, the plaintiff's attorney will have to address this issue of prior injuries to make sure that the jury comprehends the difference in the injuries received in the pending case and those suffered by the plaintiff in other situations.

Bad Faith Damages

Often confused with punitive damages (discussed subsequently), bad faith damages generally do not involve the facts of the case. Instead, bad faith damages involve a specific party's conduct during the litigation. For instance, if a plaintiff brings a lawsuit solely for the purposes of harassing the defendant, the plaintiff may be subject to bad faith damages. In such a situation, the court might order that the plaintiff pay the costs of the action and the defendant's attorney fee. Normally, the losing party in a suit is not required to pay the fees of the opposing attorney. However, when a party files frivolous claims or has engaged in unethical or unfair tactics, a judge is authorized to make such an award (*Edwards-Warren Tire Co. v. Coble*, 102 Ga. App. 106, 115 S.E.2d 852 (1960)). Bad faith damages are not seen in all cases and are actually awarded in a minority of cases, but they have become important in recent decades and are certainly more prevalent than they were 25 years ago.

Punitive Damages

punitive damages
An amount of money awarded to a non-breaching party that is not based on the actual losses incurred by that party, but as a punishment to the breaching party for the commission of an intentional wrong.

Punitive damages are a category of damages separate from the compensatory damage issues we have addressed so far. All compensatory damages are designed to serve the same function: to reimburse the plaintiff for losses, even when these losses are difficult to quantify. But punitive damages serve a completely different purpose. If requested by the plaintiff, an award of punitive damages against a defendant is the jury's way of punishing the defendant for particular actions. They are awarded in addition to compensatory damages. Punitive damages are sometimes called "exemplary damages," "vindictive damages," or even "smart money" damages. When the jury awards punitive damages, the jurors are sending a message to the defendant and the rest of society that the defendant's conduct in the case was unacceptable. A jury might award punitive damages when it is obvious that the defendant acted in wanton disregard for the safety of others or engaged in willfully dangerous conduct that caused injury to others. Because the jury in a civil case is not empowered to request jail time for the defendant, the only real punitive action the jury can take is financial.

Tort Reform and Punitive Damages

Many states have passed so-called tort reform statutes that target punitive damages. In these states, it is common for a statute to limit the total punitive damages to some specified determination. The typical formula limits punitive damages to an amount that is three times the total of all compensatory damages. If the defendant were awarded compensatory damages totaling $1,500, then the most that the jury could assess against the defendant would be $4,500. This amount would be added to the award for compensatory damages and result in a total award of $6,000.

Hypothetical 11-3

Micah has brought suit against Reginald, alleging that Reginald willfully endangered him by driving down a sidewalk one evening. Micah managed to jump out of the way of the speeding car and thankfully only received a scratch on his face. He has sued Reginald for emotional distress, negligence, and lost time from work and is seeking compensatory damages in the amount of $5,000. He has also requested that the jury assess punitive damages against Reginald. Micah's case is brought in a state that has recently enacted a treble maximum award on punitive damages. The jury determines that Reginald's actions were particularly dangerous and assesses a $1 million award for punitive damages. The jury also finds that Micah should receive compensatory damages in the amount of $500. Will Reginald be able to reduce the total award when he appeals the case?

RESEARCH THIS!

Has your state imposed limitations or caps on punitive damages awards? If so, what are these limitations? Copy out the statute, summarize it, and place it in your portfolio.

LEGAL RESEARCH MAXIM

When courts review the award of damages in civil cases, they will first summarize the important facts and then the plaintiff's injuries. Many times, you can anticipate the court's final decision in the case by examining the court's word choice early in the opinion. If the court downplays the plaintiff's injuries or focuses on the failure of the plaintiff to preserve certain issues for appeal, you can often see the writing on the wall regarding the ultimate decision. This language is important not only because it signals the outcome but also because it gives you a checklist of what not to do in your own cases.

Answer: Yes. Because this is a tort reform state, the most that the jury can award, even in an egregious case, is three times the total of the compensatory damages. Micah's compensatory damages were only $500; therefore, the total punitive damages are limited to three times that amount or $1,500.

Nominal Damages

The final category of monetary damages is nominal damages. A nominal damage is the jury's award of a small amount of money to the plaintiff. In some cases, the plaintiff may have received a legal injury, but the jury does not believe that a large payment is either warranted or justified. In such a case, the jury may award the plaintiff the amount of $1 to show that though the plaintiff presented a technically proficient case, as far as the jury is concerned, the plaintiff's actual injuries are nonexistent.

EQUITABLE REMEDIES

equity
The doctrine of fairness and justice; the process of making things balance or be equal between parties.

In addition to requesting an award of monetary damages, a plaintiff is also allowed to request specific actions by the court. There are times when a plaintiff's demand cannot be satisfied by monetary damages. Instead, the plaintiff might request an injunction to prevent the defendant from taking some action. Courts in the United States have the power to both assess monetary damages and use their **equity** power to force individuals to do (or in some cases not do) specific actions. Equity power refers to a court's power to enforce justice through a wide variety of means, including contempt powers, injunctions, and other mechanisms. Although the U.S. court system is closely patterned on the English judicial system, the early colonies made some important changes. For one thing, they combined two different courts into one. In the English system, a party was forced to go to one court to request an equitable action, such as an injunction, and another court to request an award of monetary damages. Our system combined these powers into one court, thus giving American judges judicial and equitable powers. Consider Hypothetical 11-4.

Hypothetical 11-4

Carl believes that a recent development in his area of town has endangered the water supply and violated state and federal environmental laws. He brings suit but is not requesting money. Instead, he wants the court to order a halt to all new sewer hook-ups until the county complies with statutes to undertake an environmental impact study on the rapid growth in the area. Does the court have the power to order such an action?

Answer: Assuming that Carl brings his suit in the correct court, yes, the trial judge can order an injunction that bars any new sewage hook-ups in the county (effectively bringing all new building to a halt) until the county complies with the judge's order.

injunction
A court order that requires a party to refrain from acting in a certain way to prevent harm to the requesting party.

When a plaintiff brings suit requesting an **injunction**, as Carl is doing in Hypothetical 11-4, the plaintiff is asking the court for an order specifically directing someone to stop doing a specific action. In this case, the court could order that the county cease issuing new sewage permits until an environmental study has been completed. If that order is not followed, the judge has the power to impose a wide variety of sanctions, including daily fines and possible jail time under the court's contempt powers. Of course, we have oversimplified the issues raised in Hypothetical 11-4. A court generally would hold a hearing before ordering any injunction and would give county officials the opportunity to address the issues raised in Carl's suit.

declaratory judgment
The court's determination of the rights and responsibilities of a party with respect to the subject matter of the controversy.

A court's equity power can be exercised alongside its normal powers. For example, it is common for the parties in a personal injury suit to seek a **declaratory judgment** about a particular issue in the case. An insurance company might file such an action to determine if it is legally bound to provide (and pay for) a legal defense when their insured is sued.

temporary restraining order
A court order barring a person from harassing or harming another.

Another example of an equitable remedy is a **temporary restraining order**. This order specifically directs a person to stop doing a specific action and sets a date for a full-blown court hearing on the plaintiff's request. Temporary restraining orders are usually seen in situations where immediate action is required and there is no time to set a later court date. They are a common feature in domestic violence cases.

EVALUATING POTENTIAL DAMAGES

One of the first questions that a plaintiff usually asks an attorney once the lawsuit is under way is, "How much money am I going to get from this case?" The defendant similarly might ask, "How much am I likely to lose?" Unfortunately, there is no perfect formula for predicting the answer to this question. An attorney can often give a ballpark estimate but certainly cannot promise an outcome. The final award in any case is a result of a variety of almost innumerable factors and is what makes litigation such an exciting field. No one can predict what a jury will do; the best that the legal team can do is prepare for every possible contingency and keep the client as informed as possible.

However, this is not to say that it is impossible to evaluate a case for a likely outcome. Whether you are the paralegal for the plaintiff or the defense, it makes sense to understand some of the factors that go into evaluating a case.

Evaluating a Case

Case evaluations are not an exact science. They rely on both objective facts and an intuitive understanding of judges and juries. The most important starting point for any case evaluation involves an objective and hard-nosed review of the facts.

Reviewing the Facts of a Case

Even before you review the plaintiff's injuries, you should first pay careful attention to the defendant's liability. Without a clear showing that the defendant is responsible for the plaintiff's injuries, it is unlikely that the plaintiff will recover anything, no matter how severe his or her injuries. The defendant must be the person against whom the jury imposes an award, and if the jury does not find the defendant liable, there is no possibility of a judgment in the plaintiff's favor.

Most case evaluations begin at the end of the case and center on the likelihood of actually recovering anything from the defendant. There are times when the case against the defendant is easy to prove but the defendant has no assets. Pursuing such a claim would only be an exercise in futility. No matter how good the case against the defendant, if he or she has no financial resources, it is ultimately going to be a waste of time to bring a lawsuit against him. These are inescapable facts of modern legal finances. The practice of law is a business, and no attorney can afford to take on cases in which a win is not balanced by a large payday.

Asset Searches

Most case evaluations begin with an asset search. The plaintiff's legal team digs into public records and other sources to get a rough picture of the defendant's financial resources. This

CYBER TRIP

search is actually much easier than you might imagine. If the defendant is covered by an insurance policy, then knowing the policy limits is an important consideration (if they can be learned prior to filing the complaint). In the practical world that legal professionals must inhabit, a seemingly great case could easily become one that an attorney passes up for the simple reason that the defendant has no financial resources and is unable to pay any judgment (commonly referred to as "judgment-proof"). Such a defendant has no assets, no insurance coverage, and no other way of paying any damages assessed against him or her by the jury. In such a case, an asset search prior to filing would be an excellent precaution.

Conducting an Asset Search

The simplest method to conduct an asset search is to review public records. The local courthouse offers a tremendous amount of data about people, including recent lawsuits, UCC filings, and other information that can provide an indication of the defendant's wealth, including his or her real estate holdings, the value of his or her home, and other resources.

The Jury's Role

In a jury trial, the jury has two purposes: It must first determine liability and then move to the issue of damages. If the jury determines that the defendant is not liable, it is not empowered to assess damages against the defendant. When the jury's verdict finds the defendant liable for the plaintiff's injuries, the next stage in the deliberations is to consider how large an award to make to the plaintiff. See Figure 11.3 on page 258. Judges give jurors legal instructions about not only how they should conduct their deliberations but also the rules that govern how they should make awards. Jury instructions always come at the end of the trial and are read to the jurors before they leave the courtroom to deliberate. (See the previous chapter for a complete discussion of the jury deliberation process.)

Not all cases are heard before juries. In some cases, the parties may request a bench trial. In that situation, the judge acts as both the final determiner of the legal issues in the case and the fact finder. The judge will consider whether or not the defendant is liable and to what extent.

Jury Instructions

Before the jurors retire to consider the verdict, the judge will inform them about the law in the case. This is called a "jury charge" or "jury instruction." In a jury charge, the judge reads the applicable law to the jurors to help guide them in their deliberations. For instance, suppose that the plaintiff has requested punitive damages. The jury instruction in that case might read something like the charge provided in Figure 11.2.

FIGURE 11.2
Jury Instruction for Punitive Damages

"Ladies and Gentlemen of the jury, I hereby instruct you that you are authorized to award punitive damages, but only if you find by a preponderance of the evidence that the conduct of the defendant was intentional, malicious, or in reckless disregard of the safety of others."

FIGURE 11.3
Jury's Verdict in a
Civil Case

Doe v. Charles
Jury Verdict Form
(Circle the party indicated) We the jury in this action find for the plaintiff Jane Doe/defendant Nicholas Charles

QUESTION 1: Do you find in favor of the plaintiff and against the defendant as to the claim of Count One, negligence?
Answer "yes" or "no"
Answer _____

Proceed to the next question.
QUESTION 2: Do you find in favor of the plaintiff and against the defendant as to the claim of Count Two, willful failure to obey the rules of the road?
Answer "yes" or "no"
Answer _____

If you answered any of the above questions "yes" proceed to VERDICT FORM

VERDICT FORM
We, the jury in this action, having found for the plaintiff, Jane Doe, and against the defendant, assess the total amount of Jane Doe's damages at $42,234 broken down as follows:

Past damages $8,213
Future damages .. $34,021

This the 18th day of November, 2007.
/s/ Leslie McKesson
FOREPERSON

JNOV (judgment notwithstanding the verdict)
Asks the judge to reverse the jury verdict based on the inadequacy of the evidence presented to support the law and the verdict.

JNOV

In most civil cases, the judge has the power to overturn the jury's verdict and award of damages. A judge can issue a **JNOV** or a *judgment non obstante verdicto* (a judgment "notwithstanding the verdict"). The judge can make such a ruling after a motion by the losing party in the case or initiate the decision on his or her own authority.

 ## Eye on Ethics

WHEN THE CLIENT EXAGGERATES INJURIES

There are times when the legal team representing the plaintiff has reason to believe that the plaintiff may be exaggerating the extent of his or her injuries. The plaintiff may feel that by exaggerating the injuries in a case, he or she will receive a much larger award. However, gross exaggeration is equivalent to deceiving the court, and no legal professional should agree to work in conjunction with the client to carry out fraud. The same rule applies if the client is attempting to hide the fact that he or she has previous injuries. In either case, it is a violation of ethical rules to deceive the court. There are methods to double-check the veracity of the client's claims. For instance, if the reported symptoms are out of proportion with the client's injuries and medical professionals in the case suggest that the client is exaggerating, it may be time for a frank discussion with the plaintiff. Better to resolve these issues prior to trial and in the safety and security of the attorney's office than on the witness stand. If the jury becomes aware that the client is exaggerating the extent of his or her injuries, it may refuse to award any damages to the plaintiff, even if the initial complaint is proven.

CASE IN POINT

Zak v. Riffel (115 P.3d 165 (Kan. App., 2005))
before Malone, P. J., Green and Buser, J. J.
Malone, P. J.

Kathleen S. Zak filed a medical negligence case seeking damages for the wrongful death of her husband, Michael Zak, a 48-year-old business executive, from dilated cardiomyopathy. The case proceeded to trial against only Dr. Lawrence D. Riffel. The jury returned a verdict finding Dr. Riffel to be 51% at fault and Michael to be 49% at fault. The jury awarded $100,000 in total damages. The primary issue we will address on appeal is whether the trial court erred by giving an instruction which allowed the jury to allocate fault to Michael because of his "obesity and lifestyle." We will also address whether the trial court violated the collateral source rule by admitting evidence of a $262,500 payment made to Kathleen by Michael's employer after Michael's death.

FACTUAL AND PROCEDURAL BACKGROUND

In 1988, Michael became a patient of Dr. Fred Farris at the Kenyon Clinic. In 1992, Michael was diagnosed with aortic stenosis, a congenital defect in one of the valves of his heart. Michael underwent surgery for an aortic valve replacement on April 2, 1992. As a result of the damage due to the defective valve, however, Michael was left with a chronic condition known as left ventricular dysfunction in which the left ventricle of the heart was unable to pump the normal amount of blood from that chamber. Michael was obese and significant weight loss and lifestyle adjustments were suggested as a way to manage the left ventricular dysfunction.

In May 1996, Dr. Farris referred Michael to his partner, Dr. Riffel, for evaluation and consultation regarding weight loss. On May 30, 1996, at the time of the initial consultation with Dr. Riffel, Michael weighed 309 pounds and had borderline elevated blood pressure. Michael's cholesterol, triglycerides, and LDL cholesterol were all high. In a letter memorializing the consultation, Dr. Riffel advised that Michael's chest x-ray appeared normal and his electrocardiogram (EKG) was unchanged from previous EKG's in 1992 and 1994. The letter concluded that Michael was in good health and an excellent candidate for the weight loss program.

Dr. Riffel put Michael on a weight loss program of diet, exercise, and medication, which included a prescription for phentermine. Michael's goal was to lose about 80 pounds. The weight loss program was initially successful. Michael lost 89 pounds to a weight of 220 pounds. Blood pressure and cholesterol readings were down, and the weight loss program was stopped in May 1997.

By the time of his annual physical on November 25, 1997, Michael had regained 18 pounds. Dr. Riffel concluded that Michael was in excellent health, but he stressed the importance of continuing to exercise and watching his diet. In February 1998, Michael saw Dr. Riffel because he was concerned and upset that he was gaining weight despite exercising regularly. Dr. Riffel gave Michael another prescription for phentermine, but he did not continue taking the prescription beyond 30 days.

On December 21, 1998, Michael had his annual physical. Dr. Riffel noted that Michael's weight had gradually increased to 265 pounds. Michael reported that his appetite had been difficult to control. Michael's blood pressure, cholesterol, and LDL

cholesterol were elevated. Dr. Riffel concluded that Michael's chest x-ray was clear and his EKG had not changed significantly. He did not refer Michael to a cardiologist because he felt comfortable managing the left ventricular dysfunction.

On February 12, 1999, Michael went to the St. Joseph Health Center Emergency Room after he woke up experiencing chest pain and shortness of breath. Dr. Michael Reilly performed an examination and ordered a chest x-ray and EKG. Dr. Reilly reported the results of the tests as normal and diagnosed Michael with gastritis. He was given a gastrointestinal cocktail and discharged with a 10-day supply of Prevacid. The next day, Michael and Kathleen left for a scheduled vacation to Hawaii after reporting the emergency room visit to Dr. Riffel.

On February 22, 1999, after returning from vacation, Michael saw Dr. Riffel. Michael informed Dr. Riffel of the details of the emergency room visit on February 12, 1999. Michael also related to Dr. Riffel that he had several episodes of mild chest discomfort in the middle of the night while on vacation. Michael told Dr. Riffel that he had never had symptoms like this before. Dr. Riffel examined Michael and concluded he had gastroesophageal reflux disease (GERD). He continued the Prevacid medication.

On March 17, 1999, Michael left work early because he was not feeling well. On March 18, 1999, Michael again came home from work early and told Kathleen he was not feeling well. About 9:45 p.m., Michael began to have problems breathing, and Kathleen called 911. The paramedics arrived and found Michael in respiratory arrest. Efforts to resuscitate began, and Michael was transported to the hospital. After resuscitation efforts failed at the hospital, Michael was pronounced dead at 10:37 p.m., by Dr. Kevin Koch. Dr. Koch concluded that Michael had a cardiopulmonary arrest with pulmonary edema and called the coroner's office to schedule an autopsy.

Dr. Michael Handler conducted the autopsy and concluded that Michael died of an arrhythmia due to an enlarged heart, or dilated cardiomyopathy culminating in a cardiac arrest. Dr. Handler testified that Michael's heart weighed 880 grams at the time of the autopsy where a normal heart would weigh 350–420 grams. Any heart weighing over 600 grams is considered electrically unstable. Based on the scar tissue found on the heart, Dr. Handler believed that Michael had two previous heart attacks, but he could not date the attacks. At the time of his death, Michael weighed 272 pounds.

Kathleen filed her petition for medical negligence and wrongful death on March 15, 2001. Kathleen originally brought her lawsuit against Dr. Riffel and several other providers. Prior to trial, settlement agreements were reached and all the other providers were dismissed with prejudice, leaving Dr. Riffel as the sole defendant. Kathleen alleged that Dr. Riffel failed to properly diagnose and manage Michael's heart condition, failed to refer Michael to a cardiologist for treatment, and failed to advise Michael of the abnormal tests performed at the Kenyon Clinic.

On June 16, 2003, the case was tried to a jury. Dr. John Daniels, Kathleen's internal medicine expert, testified that Michael's EKG was "very abnormal," and his chest x-ray taken by Dr. Riffel in 1996 showed an enlarged heart at that time. Dr. Daniels testified that the standard of care required that Dr. Riffel place Michael on an ACE Inhibitor rather than prescribing phentermine as part of a weight loss plan. An ACE Inhibitor operates to decrease the workload on the heart, and Dr. Daniels testified it was standard therapy to use ACE Inhibitors on patients with left ventricular dysfunction by the mid-1990's. Dr. Daniels noted that phentermine was contraindicated for individuals with cardiac disease.

Based upon his review of the test results from Michael's December 21, 1998, annual physical, Dr. Daniels concluded that Michael had substantial left ventricular dysfunction that presented a life-threatening problem requiring treatment. Dr. Daniels testified the results from the December 1998 echocardiogram indicated that the heart was getting larger and the disease process was getting worse. Dr. Daniels opined that the standard of care required Dr. Riffel to have referred Michael to a cardiologist at that time.

Based upon his review of the records from Michael's emergency room visit on February 12, 1999, Dr. Daniels concluded that Michael was clearly in congestive heart failure. Dr. Daniels stated that Michael's further complaints of pain while on vacation should have alerted Dr. Riffel to be suspicious of the GERD diagnosis. According to Dr. Daniels, Michael required an urgent cardiac evaluation at that time, and Dr. Riffel's failure to provide proper management of Michael's condition contributed to his death. He believed that Dr. Riffel's failure to manage Michael's heart condition reduced his life expectancy by 5 to 10 years. Dr. Bresnahan opined Michael's life expectancy could have been 7 to 10 years with proper care.

At trial, Dr. Riffel admitted that Michael's chest x-ray and EKG results were abnormal. He testified that his entries in the medical records to the contrary meant that the results were "normal for Michael's condition." Dr. Riffel did not believe that Michael's heart condition was getting worse because he had not developed any symptoms of heart failure.

Dr. Riffel's experts testified that the use of ACE Inhibitors was not the standard of care for asymptomatic left ventricular dysfunction. They testified that weight loss and lifestyle changes were effective treatment for the condition. They also testified there was no indication in Michael's medical history which should have alerted Dr. Riffel to refer Michael to a cardiologist.

Dr. John Ward, economist, testified regarding a calculation of lost wages. Michael was an executive with BHA Group at the time of his death. Dr. Ward testified that BHA Group was a rapidly growing company from 1996 to 1998. Michael earned $592,000 in 1996, $363,000 in 1997, and $693,000 in 1998. According to Dr. Ward, total wage loss for a 5-year life expectancy was $1,077,737; total loss for a 10-year life expectancy was $2,132,797.

Prior to trial, Kathleen filed a motion in limine to exclude evidence of the $262,500 payment on the grounds that it constituted a collateral source payment. Dr. Riffel argued that he should be allowed to cross-examine Dr. Ward regarding this information because Dr. Ward had not counted the payment in his calculations and conclusions regarding economic loss. According to Dr. Riffel, this omission showed a bias by Dr. Ward which affected his credibility as a witness. The trial court ruled that it would allow the evidence of the $262,500 payment to be presented to the jury for the limited purpose of laying a foundation for the defense to cross-examine Dr. Ward about his report.

At the conclusion of the trial, the district court instructed the jury to compare fault between Michael and Dr. Riffel. The jury returned a verdict, finding Dr. Riffel to be 51% at fault and Michael to be 49% at fault. The jury awarded $100,000 in total damages, which included $25,000 for medical expenses and $75,000 for past economic loss. The jury did not award any damages for past or future noneconomic loss, past or future loss or impairment of services, or future economic loss. Kathleen filed a motion for a new trial which was denied. She timely appeals.

Kathleen raises five issues on appeal: (1) the trial court violated the collateral source rule by admitting evidence of the $262,500 payment; (2) the trial court erred by giving Instruction No. 14 because it allowed the jury to allocate fault to Michael because of his obesity and lifestyle; (3) Kathleen was denied a fair trial due to juror misconduct; (4) the damage award was inadequate and contrary to undisputed evidence; and (5) the trial court erred in limiting the cross-examination of an expert witness regarding Dr. Riffel's prescription for phentermine as part of Michael's weight loss program. We will begin with the claimed error involving Instruction No. 14.

INSTRUCTION NO. 14

Kathleen claims the trial court erred by giving jury Instruction No. 14 because it allowed the jury to allocate fault to Michael because of his obesity and lifestyle. Kathleen had objected to the instruction at trial on the basis that it was not supported by the evidence.

> "The trial court is required to properly instruct the jury on a party's theory of the case. Errors regarding jury instructions will not demand reversal unless they result in prejudice to the appealing party. Instructions in any particular action are to be considered together and read as a whole, and where they fairly instruct the jury on the law governing the case, error in an isolated instruction may be disregarded as harmless. If the instructions are substantially correct and the jury could not reasonably have been misled by them, the instructions will be approved on appeal." *Wood v. Groh,* 269 Kan. 420, 423-24, 7 P.3d 1163 (2000).

The trial court gave Instruction No. 14 to the jury which identified the party's "claims and defenses" as follows:

"Issues-Plaintiff's Claim

"The plaintiff, Kathy Zak, claims that she sustained damages as a result of the death of her husband and due to the fault of the defendant.

"The plaintiff claims that she sustained damage due to the fault of the defendant, Dr. Lawrence Riffel, in:

1. Failing to properly manage Michael Zak's heart condition;

2. Failing to refer Michael Zak to a cardiologist; and,

3. Failing to advise Michael Zak of the abnormal diagnostic test results performed at the Kenyon Clinic.

"Burden of Proof-Plaintiff's Claim

"The plaintiff has the burden to prove that it is more probably true than not true that she sustained damages caused by any one or more of the claimed negligent acts or omissions of the defendant. When more than one specified negligent act or omission is alleged against a defendant, agreement as to which specific act or omission is not required.

"Issues-Defendant's Admissions and Denials

"The defendant denies any and all claims of negligence asserted against him by plaintiff, and specifically, denies that he departed from acceptable standards of medical care with respect to the care and treatment provided to Michael Zak by him under the circumstances of this case. This defendant asserts that the care and treatment provided by this defendant was within acceptable standards of care for similarly situated physicians given the circumstances of this case.

"This defendant asserts that the death of Michael Zak was not the result of, or caused by, any act or omission on the part of this defendant. Instead, the death of Michael Zak was the result of a pre-existing cardiomyopathy that was aggravated by Michael Zak's obesity and lifestyle.

"This defendant denies the nature and extent of the damages alleged to have been sustained by the plaintiff."

Instruction No. 14 provided the basis for the trial court to further instruct the jury on the comparative fault of Michael and Dr. Riffel. Kathleen failed to object to any of the comparative fault instructions except for Instruction No. 14. However, the standard of review requires us to view the instructions as a whole in order to establish whether they are substantially correct.

Michael was obese and had a heart condition. However, a patient's prior condition which required him to be under a physician's care cannot be a basis for comparative fault in a negligence claim against the physician:

"Conduct prior to an injury or death is not legally significant in an action for damages, unless it is a legal or proximate cause of the injury or death. It is inconsistent with the reasonable and normal expectations for the court to excuse or reduce the medical provider's liability simply because it was the patient's own fault that he or she required care in the first place." *Huffman v. Thomas,* 26 Kan.App.2d 685, Syl. ¶ 2, 994 P.2d 1072, rev. denied 268 Kan. 846 (1999).

On appeal, Dr. Riffel asserts the basis for the jury to assess fault against Michael was his failure to follow Dr. Riffel's reasonable treatment advice. Kansas law recognizes a patient's duty to follow reasonable directions and advice given to the patient by a health care provider. See *Cox v. Lesko,* 263 Kan. 805, 819-20, 953 P.2d 1033 (1998) (patient failed to complete her physician-ordered physical therapy); *Wisker v. Hart,* 244 Kan. 36, 39-41, 766 P.2d 168 (1988) (patient disregarded his physician's warnings to refrain from strenuous work and returned to his physically demanding job soon after he suffered internal injuries in a motorcycle accident).

However, the evidence at trial supporting Dr. Riffel's assertion that Michael failed to follow reasonable treatment advice was tenuous. The only specific evidence cited by Dr. Riffel to support this claim was Michael's failure to keep his weight down and his failure to renew the phentermine prescription in 1998. The evidence was undisputed that Michael was overweight. However, the mere fact that Michael regained much of the weight that he had initially lost does not prove that Michael failed to follow Dr. Riffel's treatment advice. To the contrary, the testimony supported the fact that Michael continued to watch his diet and exercised regularly. In fact, Dr. Riffel testified that Michael was

an "excellent patient," and Dr. Riffel was shocked when he learned of Michael's death. Furthermore, Michael's failure to renew his prescription for phentermine could hardly be considered as fault in light of the evidence that phentermine was contraindicated for individuals with cardiac disease.

During the closing argument, Dr. Riffel's counsel never even asserted Michael was at fault for his injuries and death. To the contrary, defense counsel described Michael's conduct as follows:

"What else is going on at that time with Michael Zak? He is starting to eat better, and I think we have heard it from just about every witness who knew him in this trial, including Dr. Riffel, he was exercising much, much more, which is also in and of itself good for the heart and good for a heart with left ventricular dysfunction."

In summing up the case for the jury, defense counsel stated:

"I think we can conclude that nobody is at fault here. This was a death that was very unfortunate, tragic. Mr. Zak was taken way before his time, everybody agrees, but is it anybody's fault? . . .

"And my suggestion to you would be that when you go back to the jury room, that you answer question number one, no. No fault; nobody caused Michael Zak's death. That's the most appropriate and the fairest answer based on the evidence."

Clearly Dr. Riffel's trial strategy was to convince the jury that no one was at fault for Michael's death. In any event, whether there was sufficient evidence at trial to support a comparison of fault between Michael and Dr. Riffel is not the issue in this appeal. The real question we must decide is whether Instruction No. 14 adequately apprised the jury of each party's claims and affirmative defenses concerning fault. Regarding Dr. Riffel's contentions, we conclude Instruction No. 14 was fatally defective in two respects. First, Instruction No. 14 failed to specify any allegations of fault on Michael's part. Second, the instruction failed to set forth Dr. Riffel's burden of proof on this issue.

Kathleen's claims against Dr. Riffel were clearly identified in Instruction No. 14. She made three specific allegations of fault against Dr. Riffel. The instruction further informed the jury that Kathleen had the burden to prove that her allegations of fault were more probably true than not true. The instruction did not contain the same information regarding Dr. Riffel's claims, if any, against Michael.

The instruction stated that "defendant asserts that the death of Michael Zak was not the result of, or caused by, any act or omission on the part of this defendant. Instead, the death of Michael Zak was the result of a pre-existing cardiomyopathy that was aggravated by Michael Zak's obesity and lifestyle." At best, this language constituted a claim that Michael's death was caused by his obesity and lifestyle. However, causation is only one component of fault. The instruction did not include any specific allegations of fault against Michael which could be compared with the specific allegations of fault that had been made against Dr. Riffel. Although the jury was informed in another instruction that a patient has a duty to follow his or her physician's reasonable treatment advice, the jury was not given any guidance in the instructions as to what advice Michael failed to follow. This problem was exacerbated by the fact that defense counsel never pointed to any specific allegations of fault against Michael during the closing argument.

More importantly, Instruction No. 14 was fatally defective because it failed to inform the jury that Dr. Riffel shouldered the burden of proof to establish Michael's comparative fault. The trial court instructed the jury that Kathleen had the burden to prove her claims of fault against Dr. Riffel, but Instruction No. 14 never informed the jury that Dr. Riffel had a similar burden to prove any claim of fault against Michael. In another instruction, the jury was informed that "a party who has the burden of proof must persuade you that his claim is more probably true than not true." However, this instruction would be meaningless to the jury unless at some point the jury was informed Dr. Riffel had the burden to prove his claims. This important information was not contained anywhere in the entire set of instructions given by the trial court, and this omission resulted in the instructions as a whole being clearly erroneous.

PIK Civ.3d 106.01 provides that in outlining affirmative defenses, the defendant should "set forth concisely the defendant's specific grounds of negligence that are supported by the evidence." Also, PIK Civ.3d 106.01 includes a statement that "the defendant has the burden to prove that any of (his)(her) claims of fault on the part of the plaintiff are more probably true than not true." The use of PIK instructions by trial courts is strongly recommended. *State v. Kleypas,* 272 Kan. 894, 1035, 40 P.3d 139 (2001), cert. denied 537 U.S. 834, 123 S.Ct. 144, 154 L.Ed.2d 53 (2002), overruled on other grounds *State v. Marsh,* 278 Kan. 520, 102 P.3d 445 (2004).

Here, Instruction No. 14 did not include specific allegations of Michael's fault, nor did it set forth Dr. Riffel's burden of proof. The instructions as a whole were not substantially correct, and the jury could have reasonably been misled by them. We conclude the trial court committed reversible error in instructing the jury and, as a result, the case must be remanded for a new trial. Upon retrial, we make no determination whether Michael's alleged fault can be compared with Dr. Riffel's. That will depend on the evidence presented at trial. However, an assertion of fault based only upon Michael's "obesity and lifestyle" would be legally deficient because that is what required Michael to seek medical care in the first place. Furthermore, if fault is to be compared, the trial court must correctly instruct the jury on the specific claims of fault by each party and the respective burdens of proof pursuant to PIK Civ.3d 106.01.

COLLATERAL SOURCE BENEFIT

Kathleen also claims the trial court erred by admitting evidence of a $262,500 payment by BHA Group after Michael's death because the admission of the evidence violated the collateral source rule. The trial court admitted the evidence for the limited purpose of laying a foundation for the defense to cross-examine Dr. Ward about his report. We will address this issue because it is likely to be raised upon a retrial of the case.

Generally, the admission of evidence lies within the sound discretion of the trial court. An appellate court's standard of review regarding a trial court's admission of evidence is abuse of discretion. *Wendt v. University of Kansas Med. Center,* 274 Kan. 966, 975, 59 P.3d 325 (2002). An abuse of discretion must be shown by the party attacking the evidentiary ruling and exists only when no reasonable person would take the view adopted by the trial court. *Jenkins v. T.S.I. Holdings, Inc.,* 268 Kan. 623, 633-34, 1 P.3d 891 (2000). However, an abuse of discretion has occurred where the trial court clearly erred or ventured beyond the limits of permissible choice under the circumstances. *Unwitting Victim v. C.S.,* 273 Kan. 937, 944, 47 P.3d 392 (2002).

"'The collateral source rule provides that benefits received by the plaintiff from a source wholly independent of and collateral to the wrongdoer will not diminish the damages otherwise recoverable from the wrongdoer.'" *Farley v. Engelken,* 241 Kan. 663, 666, 740 P.2d 1058 (1987) (quoting *Allman v. Holleman,* 233 Kan. 781, Syl. ¶ 8, 667 P.2d 296 1983). The purpose of the collateral source rule is to prevent the tortfeasor from escaping full liability resulting from his or her actions by requiring the tortfeasor to compensate the injured party for all of the harm, not just the net loss. *Rose v. Via Christi Health System, Inc.,* 276 Kan. 539, 544, 78 P.3d 798 (2003), modified on rehearing 279 Kan. —, 113 P.3d 241 (2005).

> "A benefit secured by the injured party either through insurance contracts, advantageous employment arrangements, or gratuity from family or friends should not benefit the tortfeasor by reducing his or her liability for damages. If there is to be a windfall, it should benefit the injured party rather than the tortfeasor." (Emphasis added.) 276 Kan. at 544, 78 P.3d 798.

Dr. Riffel disputes the fact that the $262,500 payment from BHA Group to Kathleen constituted a collateral source payment and claims this was a factual issue for the jury to decide. He argues BHA Group's promise that Michael's salary would be continued for 1 year from the date of his death indicated that the payment was compensation to Michael rather than a death benefit. He also points to the fact that the payment was recorded in the company books as a payment from a "bonus account," to which payments of cash bonuses to employees were ascribed.

However, it was the trial court's function to determine whether the payment received by Kathleen constituted collateral source evidence. The testimony established that both BHA Group and Kathleen considered the payment to be a death benefit. It was irrelevant whether the payment was based upon BHA Group's promise to continue Michael's salary for 1 year from the date of his death. Even if this evidence is taken at face value, it was apparent that the payment was not compensation earned by Michael during his lifetime. Rather, it was a benefit paid upon his death. Furthermore, it was irrelevant whether the payment was voluntary or an obligation. The collateral source rule applies to payments received gratuitously as well as those received as a result of an obligation. *Johnson v. Baker,* 11 Kan.App.2d 274, 278, 719 P.2d 752 (1986). The evidence was undisputed that the $262,500 payment was a death benefit received by Kathleen as a result of an advantageous employment arrangement between BHA Group and Michael. This constituted inadmissible collateral source evidence as a matter of law. See *Rose,* 276 Kan. at 544, 78 P.3d 798.

Dr. Riffel also asserts that the evidence of the $262,500 payment was admissible to impeach the credibility of Dr. Ward because he had failed to account for the payment in his damages calculations. According to Dr. Riffel, this omission provided evidence that Dr. Ward's calculations were biased and not credible.

Dr. Riffel is correct in asserting that although evidence of a collateral source payment is generally inadmissible as a matter of law, such evidence may be admissible if it "'carries probative value on an issue not inherently related to measurement of damages.'" *Wentling v. Medical Anesthesia Services,* 237 Kan. 503, 515, 701 P.2d 939 (1985). Apparently the trial court adopted this reasoning when it ruled that evidence of the $262,500 payment would be admissible for the limited purpose of laying a foundation for the defense to impeach Dr. Ward.

Prior to allowing the jury to hear evidence of the $262,500 payment, the trial court gave the following limiting instruction to the jury:

> "Members of the jury, we are about to receive some evidence which is going to be received for a limited purpose only. This is evidence concerning some compensation that was paid by Mr. Zak's employer to Ms. Zak as his surviving spouse, and this evidence is being introduced, and I'm permitting it to be introduced solely for the purpose of being used in examination of an expert witness that's going to testify tomorrow, and it will become apparent which expert witness and what . . . it's being considered for when it happens.
>
> "This evidence is not being admitted for the purpose of permitting you to understand or in any way diminish or reduce the economic losses suffered by Ms. Zak, if any, as a result of Mr. Zak's death due to the negligence of the defendant.
>
> "In other words, later in this case you are going to have to determine the amount of damages that the plaintiff has suffered because of the negligence of the defendant and to the extent that you determine those amounts, this evidence is not being offered. It's being offered but not being received for the purpose of using that to reduce or to diminish the amount of damages that you may find Ms. Zak may be recovering.
>
> "It's only being used and received for the purpose of laying a foundation for some questions and calculations made by an expert witness who is going to testify presumably tomorrow, and so you are to consider it, and remember that it's being received only for that purpose."

After evidence regarding the payment was presented to the jury, the trial court again admonished the jury:

> "Members of the jury, these two exhibits that we have just been talking about, Exhibits 139 and 140, were received in evidence by me earlier this afternoon for the limited purposes that I have talked about before. They are merely being introduced for the purpose of laying a foundation to determine some calculations that have been made by an expert witness who will testify tomorrow. They are not received for the purpose of presenting evidence to diminish the amount of economic loss, if any, that the plaintiff has suffered as a result of the defendant's negligence."

The problem in this case is that the limited purpose for which the trial court admitted the collateral source evidence never became clear to the jury. After successfully convincing the trial court that the evidence of the payment should be admitted for the limited purpose of impeaching Dr. Ward, defense counsel failed to use the evidence for this purpose. Dr. Ward was never cross-examined about the $262,500 payment. After evidence of the payment was initially presented to the jury, the subject was not addressed throughout the remainder of the trial. Although the trial court had admonished the jury that it was hearing the evidence for a limited purpose that would "become apparent" in later testimony, no evidence was ever presented for the jury to make a connection. The jury could only have been confused by the limiting instruction given by the court.

Furthermore, the evidence of the $262,500 payment had no probative value on any issue other than the measurement of damages. As previously discussed, the question of whether the payment was compensation or a death benefit was not a factual issue for the jury to decide. The payment was collateral source evidence as a matter of law. Dr. Ward was correct in not including the payment in his calculations, and his failure to do so could not have properly been used to show bias by Dr. Ward. Thus, although collateral source evidence may be admissible in certain instances if relevant to an issue other than the measurement of damages, this case does not present such an instance.

Finally, Dr. Riffel argues that Kathleen should have filed a motion to strike the testimony regarding the $262,500 payment once Dr. Ward was not cross-examined on the issue. However, the burden was not on Kathleen to file such a motion, and it may have only caused further prejudice by reemphasizing the collateral source evidence. Furthermore, Instruction No. 5A, which instructed the jury that evidence admitted for one purpose should not be considered for any other purpose, did not cure the error because the limited purpose that the evidence was admitted in this case never became clear to the jury.

We conclude the $262,500 payment from BHA Group to Kathleen constituted inadmissible collateral source evidence as a matter of law. The trial court abused its discretion in admitting this evidence. Upon retrial, the evidence should not be admitted even for the limited purpose of impeaching Dr. Ward.

We recognize that Kathleen has raised other significant issues on appeal. Because we are already remanding this case for a new trial, we will not address the remaining issues.

Reversed and remanded.

Source: From Westlaw. Used with permission of Thomson/West.

Case Questions:

1. How did Michael's physical condition and lifestyle affect his medical condition?

2. How did the doctors treat Michael's reports of chest pain?

3. According to expert testimony, how did the doctor's negligence affect Michael's life expectancy?

4. What were the calculations concerning Michael's income and his future damages?

5. Did the jury award damages for future loss?

6. Explain the court's decision based on the collateral source rule.

Real Paralegal Life: Building a Skill Set

DANA MARTIN

Dana Martin is a paralegal for the national law firm of Greenbaum, Doll & McDonald. She likes to emphasize the importance of technology in the everyday practice of law. For instance, she uses a Blackberry, a handheld device that offers wireless access to email, calendar functions, and a host of other software, to keep herself organized and calls it her "'little pest.' A Blackberry is a wireless connection to your email, calendar; it's like a cell phone for your computer. We have Microsoft Outlook and it gives wireless access to Outlook, my address book, everything. It provides a satellite connection to my computer at the office. Say if I was on the road and I wanted to check my email, then I'd just look at my Blackberry. If I wanted to send a message, I'd send it on my Blackberry. It's small; it's got a very small keyboard. It's RIM technology; wireless technology, like a cell phone. With a Blackberry, it's just like I was in my office. If I had an event on my calendar, my office computer would beep me, but so would my Blackberry. It's maybe 2 × 3 inches. I can carry it in my purse or I can clip it to my belt. It's like a very hi-tech beeper."

Using a Blackberry makes Martin more efficient at her job, but it does cause some unforeseen problems, because "low-tech people are kind of distracted by it. They think it's kind of rude to take notes on it. It's still not well accepted. If I were going to a seminar, I've heard speakers say that they are offended by it; they don't think you're paying attention if you take notes on it. It's got a very small keyboard and you kind of type with your thumbs. It's still kind of a 'wave of the future' kind of thing."

A Day in the LIfe: Dana Martin

Dana Martin works for a large firm that is "extremely high-tech and cutting edge. All of our offices are connected. We all use the wireless, Blackberry technology. Our professional staff has access to our network.

"We have a very complex piece of software that keeps track of client information, accounting and billing software. Our whole office is really tied together. We have offices in Louisville, Lexington, Frankfurt, Cincinnati, Atlanta, and Washington, DC. We are a regional firm. Everybody can get to the same documents. They can work from their home computer and access our system from a secure network.

"Here's an attitude that paralegals don't need to have: It is silly nowadays for people to be afraid of a keyboard. Typing skills are important for any professional to have these days. They shouldn't be offended by that. Typing skills aren't just for secretaries. All professionals need to know a keyboard. They need to know the basics of computers. They need to know Windows. They need to understand operating systems. What are icons? They need to know the basics of the Microsoft Office package. It used to be that Word Perfect was the standard; people are going over to Microsoft packages. They're going to have a leg up if they know Microsoft. They're going to need to know something about Adobe Acrobat, especially in the litigation area.

"Federal courts are requiring briefs to be filed in Adobe Acrobat. The day-to-day life of a paralegal is filled with technology, and if you're going to get a good job, you need to know all about it."

Real Paralegal Life: Building a Skill Set

DAMAGES

Based on the deposition transcripts, medical bills, lost wages, and other information provided in the Apple case (located in Appendix C), prepare an exhibit summarizing all of the plaintiff's damages and categorizing them as general or special.

Career Prep

Go through the Baker case (Appendix B) and prepare a summary of all medical bills incurred by the client. Create a list showing the name of the provider and the amount. What is the total for the medical bills?

Summary

When the plaintiff files a complaint, he or she includes a demand for an award of damages. Damages are the payments by the defendant to the plaintiff to compensate the plaintiff for physical, financial, or emotional losses. Damages come in several different forms, including general damages for unspecified or difficult-to-quantify losses suffered by the plaintiff. Examples of general damages include pain and suffering and emotional distress. Special damages, in contrast, refer to specific losses, such as medical bills, lost time from work, and other specific and identifiable economic losses. To prevail at trial, a plaintiff must not only prove that the defendant is liable but also that the defendant is responsible for paying the plaintiff's damages. There are provisions that allow the plaintiff to seek additional damages against the defendant. Punitive damages are a prime example. When the plaintiff seeks punitive damages against the defendant, the plaintiff requests the court to make an example of the defendant and punish him or her by assessing additional monetary fines because of the defendant's conduct. Not all cases involve claims for punitive damages. The plaintiff may prove a case for liability against the defendant but then fail to show any significant loss. In such an event, the plaintiff might receive nominal damages, or a token award from the jury.

In addition to requesting monetary reimbursement, a plaintiff may also request that the court exercise its equity powers. Equitable remedies include declaratory judgments, injunctions, and other mechanisms through which the court can order a defendant to cease certain activity or dismiss specific claims in the case. Both the plaintiff's attorney and the defendant's attorney will evaluate a civil case prior to trial and make an assessment about possible damages that could be awarded. The plaintiff's attorney will make this assessment to ensure that there are sufficient damages to justify the plaintiff's contingency fee. The defense attorney will evaluate the case for damages to represent his or her client adequately and advise the client about possible losses. In most cases, the jury assesses final damage awards, but the trial judge also has a supervisory role in the process and may overturn an excessive award.

Key Terms

Damages, 247
Compensatory damages, 248
General damages, 248
Per diem, 249
Special damages, 249
Fair market value, 252
Collateral source rule, 252
Subrogation, 252

Mitigation of damages, 252
Loss of consortium, 253
Punitive damages, 254
Equity, 255
Injunction, 256
Declaratory judgment, 256
Temporary restraining order, 256
JNOV, 258

Review Questions

1. What is the function of compensatory damages?
2. Define general damages.
3. Explain "pain and suffering" damages.
4. Explain how an attorney would raise a per diem argument to a jury for an assessment of damages.

5. What are special damages?

6. How would you classify lost wages and medical bills? Are they general damages or special damages?

7. Can a plaintiff recover for future losses? Explain your answer.

8. What is the function of a "day in the life" video?

9. What is the collateral source rule?

10. Explain mitigation of damages.

11. In what circumstances can a plaintiff recover for emotional distress?

12. What is loss of consortium?

13. What are "bad faith" damages?

14. Explain punitive damages.

15. What are nominal damages?

16. What are equitable remedies?

17. What is a court's power of equity?

18. Explain circumstances that would justify a declaratory judgment.

19. Explain how legal professionals evaluate cases for possible damage awards.

20. What is the purpose of an asset search?

21. What is the role of the jury in assessing damages?

22. How does the attorney present damages to the jury?

23. What are arguments for and against punitive damages?

Discussion Question

1. Many states have passed tort reform statutes that limit punitive damages or prohibit them in certain types of cases. Have these statutes gone too far or not far enough? Justify your answer.

Exercises: Skill Builders

Review the Baker case in Appendix B and then prepare an evaluation of the case based on the material in this chapter. Is there a strong possibility of proving damages in this case? Is it likely that the jury will find the defendant liable for these damages? Can the defendant pay a large judgment? You should consider these and additional factors in preparing your Baker case evaluation.

Portfolio Assignment

Portfolio Assignment 11-1: Give jury instructions regarding general, special, and punitive damages. Review your state's statutes on general, special, and punitive damages and prepare jury instructions for the plaintiff in the Baker case (located in Appendix B). What issues does this case suggest that would be a factor in an award of general or special damages? Is this case appropriate for a request of punitive damages?

Portfolio Assignment 11-2: Compare and contrast damages. Prepare a three-page, double-spaced report discussing the differences and similarities between compensatory damages and punitive damages. Include references to special and general damages, future damages, punitive damage caps, and how these damages are proved at trial.

Vocabulary Builders

ACROSS

3 (Lat) "by the day" or daily.

5 A claim filed by the plaintiff's spouse for the loss of companionship in the marriage caused by the injuries.

13 A rule of evidence that allows the jury to be informed about the plaintiff's other sources of compensation, such as insurance, worker's compensation, etc.

14 A court order dismissing the jury's verdict and award of damages and entering an entirely different finding.

15 Monetary assessments by the jury against a party that are designed to punish or make an example of the party for others.

DOWN

1 An award by the jury (or judge) designed to compensate the plaintiff for physical or financial losses.

2 A type of injunction issued by the court without benefit of a hearing; it specifically describes actions that a person is barred from carrying out and sets a hearing date so that the parties can address the court.

4 A court order that specifies the duties and obligations of a party.

6 The doctrine that holds that it is the responsibility of the plaintiff to lessen his or her potential injuries or losses by taking reasonable actions to seek medical treatment or take other precautions when a reasonable person in the same situation would have done so.

7 The amount that a willing buyer would pay for an item that a willing seller would accept.

8 Monetary awards by a jury (or judge) that are closely tied to the defendant's actions but have no preset or easily quantifiable amount.

9 A court order that demands a certain action or prohibits a certain action.

10 Monetary payments assessed against a party who has been deemed liable to another party in a civil case.

11 Damages, such as lost wages or medical bills, that can be calculated with specificity.

12 The doctrine of fairness and justice; the process of making things balance or be equal between parties.

Chapter 12

Arbitration, Mediation, and Settlement

CHAPTER OBJECTIVES

The student will be able to:

- Explain the importance of alternative dispute resolution.

- Describe the difference between arbitration and mediation.

- Explain how an arbitration hearing is held.

- Discuss the differences between common law arbitration and statutory arbitration.

- Describe the duties of the arbitrator.

- Explain how a mediator's role is different than that of an arbitrator.

- Describe the significance of an offer of judgment.

- Explain the purpose of a settlement brochure.

- Describe how a settlement brochure is created and what it contains.

- Define "dismissal with prejudice."

In this chapter, we address the issues surrounding mediation and arbitration and the effect that they have on modern litigation practices, as well as the topic of resolving a case prior to trial. Resolution may come in the form of alternative dispute resolution, primarily through the means of arbitration and mediation. But a case may also be resolved through settlement. In each of these instances, the case never reaches trial because of the actions of the parties to resolve all outstanding claims and end the case before a jury has the opportunity to hear the case. We begin our discussion with the topic of alternative dispute resolution, concentrating particularly on arbitration and mediation, and then move on to the separate issue of settlement.

ALTERNATIVE DISPUTE RESOLUTION

Most civil cases do not reach trial. Many are settled prior to trial through negotiations between the parties. Other cases may be settled through mediation or arbitration.

Arbitration

Arbitration is similar to mediation in many ways. When a case is arbitrated, a third party attempts to get the parties to reach a settlement of the case. The purpose of arbitration is clear: It avoids the lengthy process of taking a case to trial. It also saves the court money and personnel and helps

arbitration
Alternative dispute resolution method mediated or supervised by a neutral third party who imposes a recommendation for resolution, after hearing evidence from both parties and the parties participated in reaching, that is fully enforceable and treated in the courts the same as a judicial order.

alleviate a court's backlog of pending cases. In addition, arbitration may save the client a great deal of expense by resolving the case prior to trial, thus avoiding additional attorneys' fees, expert fees, and the multitude of other charges that build up as a case readies for a presentation to a jury.

Arbitration is a separate proceeding from other types of alternative dispute resolution, such as mediation and appraisal. It is not a judicial proceeding and therefore is not required to follow judicial procedures that you would normally find in a courtroom. Arbitration rules were specifically designed to be less formal and complicated than the procedures followed in a courtroom. It truly is an alternative to a judicial proceeding, and that alternative applies equally well to the procedures used as well as the eventual outcome of the case.

The History of Arbitration

It should come as no surprise that there is a long history of parties with disputes submitting them to a third party for resolution. Arbitration has a long common law history and has always been seen as a way to resolve issues between contesting parties instead of taking the case to trial. In many ways, arbitration resembles a contractual agreement between the parties. The parties agree to submit their claims to a third party for a complete resolution of all issues and also agree to be bound by the arbitrator's final decision.

Arbitration has gained a strong foothold in the legal community in the last few decades. Many contracts, including credit card agreements, mortgages, car financing, and a wide range of other consumer relationships, involve some form of arbitration agreement. Taking a case through arbitration is seen as an advancement of public policy to lessen the burden on the court system and encourage the parties to reach agreements among themselves (*Weeks v. Harden Mfg. Corp.*, 291 F.3d 1307 (11th Cir. 2002)).

To further public policy favoring arbitration agreements, courts will generally uphold them unless the parties can show some irregularity in creating them. If the parties voluntarily agree to arbitration when they create their agreement, chances are that they will get it (*Hart v. McChristian*, 344 Ark. 656, 42 S.W.3d 552 (2001)).

The federal approach found in the Federal Arbitration Act that clearly favors arbitration is also reflected in the law of the states (*Allstate Ins. Co. v. Stinebaugh*, 374 Md. 631, 824 A.2d 87 (2003)). Arbitration is now a universally accepted medium for resolving a wide variety of cases.

Arbitration is a voluntary process and cannot be compelled. The parties must have agreed to enter into arbitration. This agreement can occur in the form of a contract clause in the original agreement between the parties. Consider Hypothetical 12-1.

Hypothetical 12-1

Irving applied for a credit card last year. When he signed the credit card agreement, he did not read the provisions very closely. One of the clauses provided for mandatory arbitration of any dispute between Irving and the credit card company. Last week, Irving received a credit card statement that contained errors. He has tried to work out this disagreement with the credit card company, but it has been unwilling to compromise. Irving wishes to bring a civil suit against the credit card company. The company has recently pointed out the arbitration clause and is now saying that Irving must submit to binding arbitration and cannot proceed with a civil suit. Is it correct?

Answer: Yes. Because Irving signed a credit card agreement and entered into a contractual relationship with the credit card company, and because one of the provisions of that agreement was Irving's consent to submit challenges and controversies to arbitration, he cannot attempt to bypass that provision. This is true even though Irving did not read the agreement very closely.

The Federal Arbitration Act

The Federal Arbitration Act was first enacted in 1925 but has been revised several times since then. It provides the general framework, procedures, rights, and obligations of parties seeking arbitration. The act also clearly establishes the right of the parties to seek arbitration and places it on the same level as jury trials and mediation as a legitimate way of avoiding lengthy court battles and reaching a fair and just resolution in civil cases (9 U.S.C. § 1-14).

The Federal Arbitration Act has been held to preempt state law, because the agreement falls under the Commerce Clause of the U.S. Constitution. Because there is such a diversity of transactions that potentially fall under interstate commerce, the Federal Arbitration Act can apply to a vast array of agreements (*Ex parte Ephraim,* 806 So. 2d 352 (Ala. 2001)).

States have followed the federal example and enacted their own alternative dispute resolution (ADR) laws that specifically authorize arbitration and mediation in specific types of cases. Most states that have created their own ADR schemes have based their legislation in whole or in part on the Uniform Arbitration Act.

Comparing Arbitration with Other Forms of ADR

Arbitration is only one type of alternative dispute resolution. Other types include mediation and appraisal. We discuss mediation in the next section, but we should also briefly discuss appraisal.

appraisal
The evaluation by an expert of the cash value of a contested item.

Appraisal v. Arbitration.   An **appraisal** is an informal investigation carried out by experts to evaluate the value of a particular item. It is not a form of arbitration; it merely sets value. Arbitration, in contrast, determines rights, liabilities, and the final outcome in a case.

Arbitration as a Contractual Agreement

Arbitration is a contractual proceeding, whereby the parties to any controversy or dispute, to obtain an inexpensive and speedy final disposition of the matter involved, select judges of their own choice and by consent submit their controversy to such judges for determination, in the place of the tribunals provided by the ordinary processes of law (*Gates v. Arizona Brewing Co.,* 54 Ariz. 266 (Ariz. 1939)). At its simplest, arbitration is a consensual agreement and cannot be forced on a party. Generally, the agreement to arbitrate comes about as one of the clauses in the general agreement between the parties to engage in a particular activity.

Two Types of Arbitration

There are two types of arbitration: common law and statutory. Under common law, it was considered a violation of the court's power to require that all contentions and claims between the parties be resolved by arbitration. But these limits were slowly eroded by acts of state legislatures, which gradually expanded the statutory right of arbitration in a wide variety of cases.

Common law arbitration can be triggered by the express agreement of the parties or when they fail to meet the minimum requirements set out in state law (*Beattie v. Autostyle Plastics, Inc.,* 217 Mich. App. 572, 552 N.W.2d 181 (1996)).

Arbitrations based on state statute can change the basic formula between the parties. For instance, a statute might require arbitration of specific types of disputes, even when the agreement between the parties does not provide for it (*Malted Mousse, Inc. v. Steinmetz,* 150 Wash. 2d 518, 79 P.3d 1154 (2003)).

Statutes that provide for compulsory or mandatory arbitration often provide mechanisms for appellate review of the arbitrator's decision and may even provide that the party disputing the final arbitration award may take the case to court (*Dearborn Fire Fighters Union Local No. 412, IAFF v. City of Dearborn,* 42 Mich. App. 51, 201 N.W.2d 650 (1972)).

Whether a particular action falls under the provisions of voluntary arbitration or mandatory arbitration depends on the applicable statutes. When the state requires arbitration, it must also provide a mechanism for appealing the final award (*Mount St. Mary's Hospital of Niagara Falls v. Catherwood,* 26 N.Y.2d 493, 311 N.Y.S.2d 863, 260 N.E.2d 508 (1970)).

Binding Arbitration

Binding arbitration is a clause found in many contracts that requires the parties to submit their dispute to arbitration instead of bringing a civil suit. In such a situation, as long as the provisions do not violate state or federal law, one party can compel the other to submit any disputes to an arbitrator and bar that party from bringing a civil suit. See Figure 12.1 for the New York Arbitration Statute.

Issues that Can Be Submitted to Arbitration

When there is no specified limitation, nearly any dispute can be submitted to mandatory arbitration, including medical malpractice cases, divorces, and even crimes (*American Safety Equipment Corp. v. J. P. Maguire & Co.,* 391 F.2d 821, 3 A.L.R. Fed. 901 (2d Cir. 1968)). Arbitration actions can be directed solely to the interpretation of statutes or to determine facts and the law that applies to them.

FIGURE 12.1
New York Arbitration
Statute
Source: 22 N.Y. A.D.C. 28.2.

Section 28.2 Mandatory submission of actions to arbitration.

(a) The Chief Administrator may establish in any trial court in any county the arbitration program authorized by this Part.

(b) In each county where an arbitration program is established by order of the Chief Administrator, all civil actions for a sum of money only, except those commenced in small claims parts and not subsequently transferred to a regular part of court, that are noticed for trial or commenced in the Supreme Court, County Court, the Civil Court of the City of New York, a District Court or a City Court, on or after the effective date of the order where recovery sought for each cause of action is $6,000 or less, or $10,000 or less in the Civil Court of the City of New York, or such other sum as may be authorized by law, exclusive of costs and interest, shall be heard and decided by a panel of arbitrators. The Chief Administrator may also, at any time, upon the establishment of the program in any particular court or county or thereafter, provide for the submission to arbitration of actions, seeking recovery of such sums, that are pending for trial in those courts on the effective date of the order.

Examples of cases that may be required to be submitted to arbitration include:

- Malpractice cases (medical and legal malpractice).
- Disputes between contractors and third parties in highway construction.
- Negligence claims against the state highway system.
- Wills.
- Torts.
- The construction of a statute.
- Spousal support payments.
- The effect of bankruptcy on other actions.

Limitations on Arbitration Cases

Although the general approach is to enforce arbitration agreements, there are some exceptions. For instance, the courts will not compel a party to go through arbitration when that party did not originally agree to the process (*Commonwealth Equity Services, Inc. v. Messick*, 152 Md. App. 381, 831 A.2d 1144 (2003), cert. denied, 378 Md. 614, 837 A.2d 926 (2003)). Similarly, if the parties clearly intended that arbitration would not be an option for disputes between them, the courts will not force them to go through it (*Board of Water & Sewer Com'rs of City of Mobile v. Bill Harbert Const. Co.*, 870 So. 2d 699 (Ala. 2003)).

Courts have generally been very liberal in allowing parties to negotiate arbitration provisions among themselves, but there are some limitations. Certain issues have been determined inappropriate for an arbitration hearing, including:

- The right of a person to enter into a profession, such as law or medicine.
- Custody and visitation rights for minor children.
- An interpretation of the state or federal Constitution.
- An action based on a criminal enterprise or invalid contract.

Arbitrators

The parties generally select the arbitrator, either by express terms of the agreement or with the consent of the parties prior to the arbitration hearing.

Scope of the Arbitrator's Authority.   The authority of the arbitrator flows from the contractual terms between the parties in which the original provision authorizing arbitration is found. Therefore, an arbitrator may have limited powers and authority that varies considerably from case to case. However, this is not true when the arbitration process is mandatory under state statutes. In those situations, all arbitrators have the same authority: to decide the issues pending between the parties and make a final determination that resolves the case.

Umpires

There also are provisions for selecting an **umpire** to decide a dispute. Not all states use this terminology, but for those that do, an umpire is a person who acts alone in deciding an issue, often after the original arbitrator has been unable to reach a decision.

The Arbitration Agreement

The agreement to arbitrate is often referred to as a **submission**, or an agreement for submission. This agreement is central to the determination that the parties voluntarily entered into an arbitration agreement. At its most basic, the submission is the agreement by which the parties specifically agree to submit their dispute to a third party who will make a determination about the case and also make a final award (*Schoolnick v. Finman*, 108 Conn. 478, 144 A. 41 (1928)).

The submission, like the original agreement between the parties, is a contract and enforced and evaluated under contract law principles. Therefore, the submission must meet the same criteria for any contract, including meeting of the minds, mutual assent, consideration, and capacity.

Mediation

In the 1980s and 1990s, many states began adopting statewide mediation programs to help with the backlog of cases pending in civil courts. In states that adopted mandatory mediation, statistics show that nearly 50 percent of all cases referred to medication were resolved successfully. Mediation saves precious court time and resources by encouraging parties to settle before the case comes to trial.

Mediation differs from arbitration in several important ways. The first is that arbitration is a process selected by the parties long before there is ever a dispute between them. The contract will usually set out the requirement to submit disputes to an arbitrator and even create the procedure for doing so. In contrast, the court often suggests mediation after litigation has begun. It is a mutual attempt to resolve difficulties and conclude a case. Arbitration is the process of using a neutral third party to determine issues in the case and make a final determination. If we were to compare arbitration, mediation, and the judicial process, we would have to say that arbitration most closely resembles the hearing it is designed to avoid. An arbitrator has the right to evaluate the evidence, listen to witnesses, and reach a binding result. A mediator, however, works with the parties to help them reach a voluntary agreement among themselves. If the parties are unwilling or unable to work out an agreement, then they go back to the litigation process.

State Mediation Programs

All states have enacted some form of mediation program. The most typical provisions provide that judges can send specific types of cases to nonbinding mediation, where there is a good chance that the case will be resolved and removed from the court's dockets. If the parties are unable to work out an agreement, they are in no worse a position than they were before and can still proceed on to litigation. See Figure 12.2 for Maryland's definition of mediation.

Certified Mediators

In states that have mediation programs, there are certified mediators. These are individuals who have qualified as mediators with the state. They are often attorneys, counselors, psychologists, or others who have received state training. Certified mediators understand the

---

umpire
A person with greater authority than an arbitrator; this person has the authority to make a final and binding decision when an arbitrator has been unable to do so.

submission
The agreement to arbitrate a specific matter or issue raised between the parties.

mediation
The process of submitting a claim to a neutral third party who then makes a determination about the ultimate liability and award in a civil case.

FIGURE 12.2
Mediation Defined (Maryland)

Source: Md. R. A.D.R. Rule 17-101.

(d) Mediation. "Mediation" means a process in which the parties work with one or more impartial mediators who, without providing legal advice, assist the parties in reaching their own voluntary agreement for the resolution of the dispute or issues in the dispute. A mediator may identify issues and options, assist the parties or their attorneys in exploring the needs underlying their respective positions, and, upon request, record points of agreement reached by the parties. While acting as a mediator, the mediator does not engage in arbitration, neutral case evaluation, neutral fact-finding, or other alternative dispute resolution processes and does not recommend the terms of an agreement.

RESEARCH THIS!

What is the law in your state regarding mediators? Is there a board that certifies mediators? Are they required to go through specific educa- tion before they can qualify as mediators for the court? Is there a certification process? How are mediators paid?

LEGAL RESEARCH MAXIM

You should always keep in mind that different states have different rules regarding arbitration and media- tion. Some states, for instance, require mandatory, binding mediation for certain types of cases. You should review your state's statutes to find out if a particular case is obliged to go through mediation.

PRACTICE TIP

Mediators are protected by judicial immunity in the same way as a trial court judge.

CYBER TRIP

Hieros Gamos—Arbitra- tion and mediation http://www.hg.org/adr. html American Arbitration Association http://www.adr.org/ Global Arbitration Mediation Association http://www.gama.com/ Connecticut Board of Mediation and Arbitration http://www.ctdol.state. ct.us/medarb/regs.htm

limited role that they can play in mediation. They cannot, for example, give legal advice to either side, reach binding decisions, or enforce a particular approach. What they can do is work with the parties to help them reach an agreement themselves. This is perhaps the biggest and most important difference between mediation and arbitration. An arbitrator can reach conclusions and enforce them against the parties, even when the parties do not like the result. This is not true in mediation. A successful mediation session results in a mutual agreement between the parties to resolve the case.

Selecting a Mediator

Before mediation begins, the parties are allowed to select a mediator. They can choose from a wide variety of individuals, including former judges, currently practicing attorneys, and other professionals who have been certified by the state board, including paralegals. Most states also have provisions that allow the parties to choose someone who is not board certified. If the parties find it impossible to select a mediator on their own, the court may select one for them. Mediators are paid a fee for their services. A typical fee is $100 per hour.

The Mediation Conference

The mediation settlement conference can be scheduled at the courthouse or any other public building. Responsibility for actually reserving the place and making arrangements for the confer- ence falls on the mediator. The mediator is also responsible for setting the time and date of the hearing and notifying all parties to make sure that they can attend.

Persons Required to Be Present at the Mediation

Before the mediation can begin, there are several persons who are required to be present. They include:

- The parties
- Insurance company representative(s)
- Attorneys

The plaintiff and defendant must be present to proceed with mediation for the simple reason that they will be actively involved in reaching an agreement. They will have input during the process and final approval over any deal reached during mediation. Simply put, if the parties do not agree to the proposed solution, there is none.

Insurance company representatives are often required to be present at mediations because they provide the pool of funds that will provide some of or the entire settlement amount. In a typical automobile collision case, for example, the defendant's insurance company will pay the final settlement to the plaintiff. Therefore, a representative from the insurance company is required to be present and actively involved in the mediation process. Obviously, the insurance representative will attempt to reserve as much of his or her company's money as possible. The most that the insurance company will be required to pay out is the policy limit on the defendant's insurance policy.

The parties will also have their attorneys present to provide them with legal advice and other counseling. The mediator is specifically barred from giving legal advice and therefore cannot advise a party about the legal consequences of the agreement. But the party's attorney can provide that information. In situations in which one of the parties is not represented, he or she bears the burden of the legal consequences, because there is no one present at the mediation who can provide legal advice to that person.

The Mediator's Authority

A mediator is the person responsible for controlling the conference and setting the procedures to be followed during the hearing (see Figure 12.3). Mediators are authorized to meet privately with any of the parties or attorneys prior to or during the conference. They can work behind the scenes to encourage a settlement and can shuttle back and forth between the parties with various proposals to move the process of settlement along.

Impasse

impasse
The declaration by the mediator that the parties are unable to reach an agreement.

The mediator has the final responsibility for declaring an **impasse** in a hearing. An impasse occurs when the parties are unable to reach an agreement and the mediator determines that there is no possibility of a mutual agreement by extending the hearing. Once an impasse has been declared, the case is sent back to the trial docket where it will be rescheduled for trial. None of the conversations that occurred during the mediation can be repeated in the trial, and the mediator cannot be compelled to testify about the settlement discussions. As far as the trial is concerned, the mediation never happened.

Statements made by the parties at the mediation hearing are not admissible at trial. This protection allows the parties to engage in frank discussions without the fear that anything they say at the mediation hearing might be used against them during the trial. This policy also explains why mediators cannot be called to testify about discussions held at the mediation. Without such protection, there would be very little that the parties would be willing to communicate during the mediation.

FIGURE 12.3
Duties of the Mediator

The mediator has the following duties:

- Setting the procedures at the hearing.
- Explaining the differences between mediation and other forms of alternative dispute resolution, such as arbitration.
- Explaining that the mediation conference is not a trial, the mediator is not a judge and does not have judicial power, and the parties retain their right to trial if they do not reach a settlement in the mediation hearing.
- Explaining that the agreement reached will be by mutual consent of the parties.

PRACTICE TIP

Before going to a mediation or arbitration hearing, it is always wise to try a dress rehearsal. Bring in the client and any others who will participate in the actual hearing and do a run through. Have someone play the role of the mediator. Do you have all of the exhibits and material that the legal team plans on presenting at the hearing? If not, where is this material? Present your case to the mediator and see what problems arise. Better to have a misstep here than at the actual hearing.

 SPOT THE ISSUE!

Mary and Jorge have entered into a partnership to run a small craft store. Part of their agreement provides that any issue arising out of the partnership will be resolved through arbitration, much like the provisions found in this chapter's "Case in Point." However, after working closely for several months, Mary and Jorge fall in love and get married. Six months later, the marriage ends, and Mary files for divorce. The biggest asset of the marriage is the business. Do Mary and Jorge have to go through arbitration, or can they apportion the assets through a divorce proceeding?

SETTLEMENT

settlement
A negotiated termination of a case prior to a trial or jury verdict.

When a case is settled, it means that the parties have reached an agreement about terminating the case. A case can be settled at any point in the litigation process, though most do so shortly before the trial begins. There is something about the looming prospect of a jury trial that tends to make parties begin to see reason. **Settlement** often involves payment by the defendant to the plaintiff in exchange for the plaintiff dismissing his or her claim. When the case is dismissed through settlement, it cannot be brought against the defendant at a future date.

Settlements Are Contracts

When both sides to a suit seek to settle a case, they are actually engaging in a form of contract. The plaintiff agrees to dismiss his or her complaint against the defendant in exchange for the defendant's agreement to pay the plaintiff a sum of money. Because it is a contract, the agreement must meet all of the minimum requirements of any contract, including:

- Mutual assent
- Capacity
- Consideration
- Legality

Mutual Assent

Mutual assent is the contract requirement that the parties to the contract have a "meeting of the minds" about the details provided in the agreement. They must know and understand what they are agreeing to and have an understanding about the basic arrangements involved in the contract.

Capacity

Capacity is the requirement that a party to a contract knows and understands the consequences of creating a legally binding agreement. A party who lacks capacity cannot enter into any contract, including one to settle a case. Examples of individuals who lack capacity include individuals under the age of 18 years, persons who have been declared mentally incompetent, persons acting under the influence of drugs, or persons suffering from a physical impairment that prevents them from understanding what they are doing.

Consideration

Consideration is the contract requirement that both parties to the agreement surrender something of value in exchange for receiving something else of value. The idea behind consideration is simple: It ensures that both parties have a vested interest in the contract. A contract that obligates only one party is not a contract at all. In the typical settlement agreement, the plaintiff surrenders his or her right to continue with a suit in exchange for a monetary payment. The defendant surrenders money in exchange for the benefit of having the suit dismissed.

Legality

The fourth and most obvious element of any contract is that the agreement must be legal or in accord with public policy. Courts will not enforce contracts for illegal subjects, such as to carry out a crime. Contracts that are considered to be in violation of public policy will also not be enforceable through the court system. An example of such an agreement would be one party's insistence that the other party surrender all possible rights before the contract could be carried out. Such a sweeping provision is a violation of public policy, and any settlement agreement that imposed such a requirement would be deemed void for public policy reasons and considered unenforceable.

Defining "Settlement"

The concept underlying a settlement is similar to other legal concepts, including accord and satisfaction, novation, and release. Accord and satisfaction is a term usually reserved for the negotiations between debtors and creditors. Novation is a term used by contracting parties to substitute one contract provision for a new one. Release is a term even more closely associated with settlement. In a release, a party surrenders a specific right, often in exchange for something of value.

A good working definition of settlement is the dismissal of the plaintiff's suit against the defendant in exchange for a monetary payment by the defendant. There is a strong public policy argument in favor of allowing the parties to settle their differences prior to trial. In fact, courts are encouraged to allow the parties to work out any agreement that they find satisfactory and enforce that agreement, as long as it does not violate the basic legal requirements of contract law (*Gates Corp. v. Bando Chemical Industries, Ltd.*, 4 F. App'x 676 (10th Cir. 2001)). Judges must enforce the provisions of a settlement as long as they do not violate other laws or a public policy concern. Consider Hypothetical 12-2.

Hypothetical 12-2

Carla was in a car wreck last year. A large delivery truck, owned and operated by Fuzzy Cola and driven by Randy, ran a red light and smashed into her car. She was severely injured and brought suit earlier this year, seeking several million dollars in damages. Fuzzy Cola representatives have recently approached Carla with a settlement proposal: They will pay her $1.2 million in exchange for her dismissing her suit and agreeing not to testify against Randy in the upcoming criminal action. It seems that Randy was cited for failure to stop at the red light, and the company is concerned about bad press as a result. Is this settlement agreement in violation of public policy?

Answer: Yes. The parties can certainly agree to settle the case for money and a dismissal of the suit, but the company cannot insist that Carla refuse to testify in a criminal action. Paying a person to refuse to testify could be considered witness tampering. At the least, it is a violation of public policy to encourage witnesses not to testify, but it is also a possible criminal action. When it comes to enforcing the settlement, a judge will undoubtedly refuse to implement that provision.

Procedures in Bringing About a Settlement

Settlement discussions can occur at any time during the litigation. The parties might discuss settlement before the plaintiff ever files suit or they could be discussing settlement as the jurors file into the courtroom at the beginning of the trial. There are several compelling reasons that would make both parties interested in bringing about a settlement of the case before it goes to trial.

Reasons to Settle a Case

For the plaintiff, there are several important reasons to settle a case before it goes to trial. First, even if the plaintiff believes that he or she has a strong case, there are no guarantees with jury trials. A strong case for the plaintiff could easily result in a verdict for the defendant, and a weak case might just as easily go the other way. It is virtually impossible to predict what a jury will do in any given case, and because of that uncertainty, the plaintiff's attorney often advises the client to take a certain sum of money instead of gambling on receiving more at trial. Second, in addition to the inherent risks of taking a case to trial, there are other reasons to settle. Prior to this point, the plaintiff and attorney have invested a great deal of time in the case. There have been depositions to attend, interrogatory questions to answer, and a host of pretrial issues to address. But the trial will take up even more time, and after months of dealing with the case, the plaintiff may just be tired of the whole thing. A large check and a resolution might be very attractive at this point, especially when the plaintiff considers even more lost time to attend the trial and putting his or her life on hold for an additional period of time.

On the defendant's side, the pressures to settle the case are similar. The defendant is also facing the possibility of a jury decision that could go either way. Of course, for the defendant, a loss could equate to a huge jury award. Rather than face that possibility, a defendant might be willing to pay an amount upfront to avoid the whole possibility of a huge jury award and the lengthy process of appealing the case. The defendant may also be facing litigation fatigue and want a resolution of the case just as much as the plaintiff.

You will notice that in our discussions of the reasons to settle a case, we did not include the preferences of the individual attorneys. Both the plaintiff's and the defense's attorneys might want a resolution of the case before trial, but their needs are always secondary to those of the client. The client has the final say in whether to settle the case or not, and even if the attorney believes that taking the case to trial is a bad idea, if that is the client's decision, that is what the attorney will do.

Settlement Brochure

At some point in the litigation process, the plaintiff's attorney may prepare a settlement proposal or settlement brochure and forward it to the defendant. No matter what name is used to describe this document, the basic purpose remains the same: The plaintiff makes his or her case against the defendant and suggests a figure that, if paid, will result in a dismissal of the suit.

Typical settlement brochures will contain several sections, including:

- The factual basis of the plaintiff's claim.
- A summary of the plaintiff's physical, financial, and emotional injuries.
- An overview of the law as it applies to the issues in the case.
- A summary of recent jury awards.
- An offer to settle the case for a specific sum.

The Factual Basis of the Plaintiff's Claim.   The settlement brochure will present an overview of the plaintiff's claim against the defendant. A settlement brochure is a one-sided affair; it does not seek to present the defendant's version of the case. Instead, it provides the best possible face on the plaintiff's claims. The defendant might well dispute some of the assertions, but the factual statements contained in the settlement brochure are at least one possible interpretation that the jury could bring to the case.

A Summary of the Plaintiff's Damages.   In addition to presenting the factual basis of the plaintiff's claim, the settlement brochure sets out the plaintiff's physical injuries, financial losses, and any claims for mental distress. Again, these are points seen in the best possible light and may not necessarily be how the case will be presented to the jury or even how the jury might view the claims. The plaintiff presents a strong case for damages in the settlement brochure to put psychological pressure on the defendant to settle the case. After reviewing the damages, the defendant might decide that it would be cheaper to settle the case early in the litigation process than spend money throughout the discovery and pretrial phases and still risk a large verdict in the plaintiff's favor at trial.

An Overview of the Law.   Although not all settlement brochures contain an overview of applicable law, there are times when it is appropriate. If a recent appellate decision clearly favors the plaintiff's case, the plaintiff's attorney would be well advised to include it in the materials. This inclusion is more for the defendant than the defendant's attorney. The attorney is probably already aware of this case and any others that have a direct bearing on the issues in the case, but the defendant might review this recent decision and begin to think the case law is against his or her position. After reviewing an overview of the law on the issues in the case, the plaintiff's attorney hopes that the defendant will begin to feel that the appellate courts will favor the plaintiff in this case, which is all the more reason to settle now rather than risk losing on appeal.

A Summary of Recent Jury Awards. A good settlement brochure will also include a section about recent jury awards from similar cases. This information can have a devastating impact on the defendant, especially if the plaintiff can point to recent jury awards in the millions of dollars. A defendant might easily conclude that it would be far cheaper to settle the case before trial than risk a similar jury award in the present case.

The question often arises: Where does the plaintiff obtain information about recent jury awards? In the past, researching these details was often difficult. A paralegal might be required to read dozens of appellate decisions and even go to courthouses around the state to discover exactly what a jury's award was in a particular case. However, these days, there are companies that do such research for legal professionals and are willing to share it, for a fee. Companies such as Jury Verdict Research have researchers scattered across the country who review this information and provide it to the company's database. Some companies provide this service as a regular publication, whereas others provide data on a case-by-case basis.

Offer to Settle. After setting out all of this information, the settlement brochure concludes with an offer to settle the case for a specific sum. This offer often contains a deadline. If the defendant fails to respond by the deadline or fails to make a serious counteroffer by the time indicated, the plaintiff will proceed to trial. For an example of a demand letter, see Figure 12.4.

Demand Letter. In some cases, a full-blown settlement brochure would be considered overkill. Cases involving smaller amounts of money might involve something as simple as a demand letter. In this letter, the plaintiff's attorney follows some of the same conventions as a settlement brochure but simplifies and shortens them. A demand letter serves the same function as a settlement brochure: It offers to settle the case for a specific sum of money. See Figure 12.4.

Offers of Judgment

In some states, there is a more formalized approach to settling cases. These states use a document referred to as an offer of judgment (see Figure 12.5). Like the settlement brochure and the demand letter, an offer of judgment seeks to settle the case without taking it to trial. However, unlike those two devices, the offer of judgment comes from the defendant. Offers of judgment are governed by the Rules of Civil Procedure. In the federal courts (and many state courts), Rule 68 of the Rules of Civil Procedure expressly authorizes a party defending a suit to serve on the opposing side an offer to settle the case by use of an offer of judgment. The rule provides that a party defending a claim may serve an offer of judgment 10 days or more prior to trial.

Offers of judgment have two aspects. If the offer is accepted, the clerk may then enter the offer of judgment as the final resolution in the case and mark it closed. If an offer is not accepted within 10 days, it is considered withdrawn. When the case is ultimately resolved, if the final verdict is less than what the party would have received had he or she accepted the offer of judgment, then the party who refused must pay the opposition's attorney's fees and other costs.

Rule 68 encourages parties to be reasonable and seek settlements of their lawsuits before the case actually goes to trial; it also puts some teeth into the process by creating monetary penalties when parties fail to do so. It assesses costs against the party that could have accepted an offer that was greater than what he or she ended up receiving after a long and expensive trial. This rule also encourages parties to settle their cases by an assessment of interest charges (see Figure 12.6). There are statutory provisions that allow increases or decreases in prejudgment interest rates depending on whether an offer of judgment was tendered or accepted.

Confessions of Judgment

In some states, there is another option for defendants that is closely associated with offers of judgment: confession of judgment. In a confession of judgment, a defendant who does not wish to contest a lawsuit is not required to do so. Instead, he or she can file with the clerk of the superior court a confession of judgment. A confession of judgment is a statement in writing, signed and verified, authorizing the entry of judgment for the amount stated in the complaint. Confessions

FIGURE 12.4 Demand Letter

Bevans & Bevans, P.A.
1001 Burkemont Avenue
Bohemia, PL 28655
828-555-1212 (phone)
828-555-1213 (fax)

April 24, 2006

Allnation Insurance Company
300 Money Street
Capitol City, PL 28888

Re: Claimant: Sherlock Holmes
            Insured: James Moriarty
            Date of Loss: August 23, 2003
            Claim No.:   665421-1457

Dear Sir or Madam:

I have been retained by Mr. Sherlock Holmes with respect to recovery of damages due to personal injuries suffered by Mr. Holmes in a train collision which occurred on August 23, 2003, and which involved your insured, James Moriarty.

I have been directed to do everything that is necessary to present, settle, and collect this claim for damages.

I have evaluated this claim for settlement purposes. This letter and the enclosures are presented to you for the purpose of attempting to settle this claim.

I. Liability

James Moriarty is owner and operator of Moriarty Trucking Company. On the 23rd day of August 2003, Mr. Moriarty disregarded a red traffic light in his lane of traffic and negligently crashed his truck into the 2002 Honda Civic owned by my client and driven by his wife, Irene Adler Holmes. The force of the impact caused severe physical and psychological damages to my client and ended the life of his beloved wife.

Numerous witnesses can testify that your client failed to stop for a red light in his lane of traffic and that he acted in disregard of the rules of the road. Traffic reconstruction testimony also shows that Mr. Moriarty failed to apply his brakes before striking the vehicle occupied by the plaintiff and his wife.

II. General Damages

As a result of the incident, Mr. Holmes has suffered a number of injuries, endured medical examinations, and suffered short-term and long-term health consequences. Injuries resulting from the collision include a closed-head injury, fractured left tibia, internal hemorrhaging, hemo-pneumothorax, and severe abdominal trauma. In addition, he had five broken ribs and a left hip fracture. Seven days after the collision, Mr. Holmes had a tracheostomy placed. Infection set in thereafter, causing acute and chronic bronchitis.

For several weeks after the collision, Mr. Holmes remained in a coma, with his breathing controlled by mechanical ventilation. It took several weeks after coming out of the coma for Mr. Holmes to reorient himself to his surroundings. Doctors noted that Mr. Holmes suffered from short-term memory loss.

In November 2003, Mr. Holmes began suffering severe and debilitating migraine headaches from which he has been unable to receive any relief. Mr. Holmes did not suffer from migraines prior to the accident, and medical diagnosis has determined that the head trauma he received has caused these painful migraine headaches. As a result, Mr. Holmes has been unable to return to his former profession, that of professional consulting private detective.

III. Loss of Consortium

As a result of the collision, Irene Adler Holmes, Mr. Holmes's wife of many years, was killed. Because of her death, Mr. Holmes is without her companionship and assistance in his own recovery. He has lost her companionship and affection forever.

IV. Enclosures

Enclosed are the following records and reports for your review:

1. Emergency Room Record, London County Hospital

2. Operative Report, London County Hospital

3. Medical Report from Dr. Thorne M.D., London County Hospital

4. Medical Report from Dr. Kaitland Burnett, King's Road Rehabilitative Hospital

V. Settlement

If this case can be resolved within 30 days and without the expense of litigation, I would recommend settlement in the amount of $3,000,000.00

Very truly yours,

_____

Neal Bevans
Attorney for Plaintiff Sherlock Holmes

FIGURE 12.5
Rule 68. Offer of Judgment

At any time more than 10 days before the trial begins, a party defending against a claim may serve upon the adverse party an offer to allow judgment to be taken against the defending party for the money or property or to the effect specified in the offer, with costs then accrued. If within 10 days after the service of the offer the adverse party serves written notice that the offer is accepted, either party may then file the offer and notice of acceptance together with proof of service thereof and thereupon the clerk shall enter judgment. An offer not accepted shall be deemed withdrawn and evidence thereof is not admissible except in a proceeding to determine costs. If the judgment finally obtained by the offeree is not more favorable than the offer, the offeree must pay the costs incurred after the making of the offer. The fact that an offer is made but not accepted does not preclude a subsequent offer. When the liability of one party to another has been determined by verdict or order or judgment, but the amount or extent of the liability remains to be determined by further proceedings, the party adjudged liable may make an offer of judgment, which shall have the same effect as an offer made before trial if it is served within a reasonable time not less than 10 days prior to the commencement of hearings to determine the amount or extent of liability.

FIGURE 12.6
Prejudgment and Judgment Interest

Source: N.C.G.S.A. § 1C-1828.

(a) Except as provided in subsection (b) of this section, recovery of prejudgment or pre-award interest and the rate of interest to be applied in the action or distribution proceeding shall be determined by the substantive law governing the right to recovery under the conflict of laws rules of this State.

(b) The court or arbitrator shall increase or decrease the amount of prejudgment or pre-award interest otherwise payable in a judgment or award in foreign money to the extent required by the law of this State governing a failure to make or accept an offer of settlement or offer of judgment, or conduct by a party or its attorney causing undue delay or expense.

of judgment are often seen in foreclosure proceedings in which the homeowner chooses not to contest the action and simply allows the house to be turned over to the mortgage lender.

Releases

release
A discharge from the parties' performance obligations that acknowledges the dispute but forgoes contractual remedies.

Once a case is settled, the parties release one another from the claims in the lawsuit. A **release** is an official relinquishment of the plaintiff's claim against the defendant, in exchange for the monetary payment through the settlement. When a party signs a release, he or she is forgoing all possible actions against the other party. The end result of the settlement is a complete dismissal of the complaint, often in the form of a dismissal with prejudice (though it may be called by another name in some jurisdictions). Once filed, a dismissal with prejudice means that the plaintiff is relinquishing any right to renew the action. A dismissal without prejudice gives the plaintiff the right to revive the action at a future date. Obviously, a defendant who negotiates the settlement of a case would require a dismissal with prejudice.

 SURF'S UP!

DIGITIZING FILES

With the widespread availability of computers, scanners, and huge storage capacities, it is natural to assume that law offices are swiftly moving away from the use of paper. However, practitioners are not seeing a move toward "paperless pleadings." Simply because it is possible to make digital copies of nearly every aspect of a case does not mean that digital files will replace paper. In fact, some legal professionals have begun seeing more paper produced rather than less. According to Dana Martin (profiled in Chapter 11

under "Real Paralegal Life"), "I love technology, but I've seen more paper since technology has been the thing. I've seen more copies of things since we became high-tech than I did before. Now, it's on the computer, and everybody wants their own copy. So instead of seeing two copies of a thing, now I'm seeing eight copies. Because everybody has to touch it."

Although it is always a good idea to back up all computer files, do not make the mistake of thinking that the days of paper are ending. Digital files and hard copies will probably coexist in the legal field for years to come.

Weitz v. Hudson (262 Va. 224, *224-229, 546 S.E.2d
732, **733-735 (Va., 2001))
Kinser, Justice.

Pursuant to Code § 8.01-581.016, this case is an interlocutory appeal from an order denying an application to compel arbitration. Because we conclude that the specific controversy alleged in a motion for judgment is covered by an arbitration clause in a limited partnership agreement, we will reverse the judgment of the circuit court.

FACTS AND MATERIAL PROCEEDINGS

The appellee, Donald E. Hudson, and the appellant, Benjamin B. Weitz, were general partners in a limited partnership formed under the laws of the State of Maryland and known as Leesburg Manor Associates Limited Partnership (Leesburg Manor). Weitz also served as the managing general partner. The limited partnership agreement, entered into in April 1972, contained two provisions that are at issue in this appeal. The first provision, paragraph 20, addresses the arbitration of disputes:

> Any dispute or controversy arising under, out of, in connection with, or in relation to this Agreement, and any amendments or proposed amendments hereto, shall be determined and settled by arbitration in Baltimore, Maryland[,] pursuant to the Rules of the American Arbitration Association then obtaining. Any award rendered therein shall be final and binding upon the parties hereto, and judgment may be entered thereon in any court of competent jurisdiction.

The second relevant paragraph, number 16(b), establishes the order of distributing proceeds from the liquidation of Leesburg Manor's assets. That paragraph provides that, after the payment of all debts and liabilities, such proceeds shall be applied to the setting up of any reserves which the General Partners or special liquidator may deem reasonably necessary for any contingent or unforeseen liabilities or obligations of the Partnership or of the General Partners arising out of or in connection with the Partnership or its liquidation.

In February 1999, Leesburg Manor sold its principal asset, an apartment complex. A distribution of the proceeds from that sale indicated that Hudson was to receive the sum of $51,884. However, Weitz allegedly withheld Hudson's share of the proceeds and placed the money in an "interest bearing escrow account," telling Hudson that he had done so to assure "that [Hudson's] indemnification liability to [Weitz and another general partner] will be met in small part."

Hudson then filed a motion for judgment against Weitz, alleging wrongful conversion and misappropriation of Hudson's share of those sale proceeds. Hudson alleges that Weitz's decision to escrow those funds has nothing to do with Leesburg Manor. Instead, he claims that Weitz acted in retaliation against Hudson because of Hudson's cooperation with limited partners in other partnerships in which both Hudson and Weitz were general partners. Therefore, Hudson contends that Weitz illegally converted the funds.

Pursuant to Code § 8.01-581.02(A), Weitz filed an application to compel arbitration. At a subsequent hearing on Weitz's application, the court declined to receive any evidence, but heard argument of counsel. During that hearing, the court indicated that it would grant the application if Weitz agreed that he would not present any affirmative defenses to the arbitrator or explain why he escrowed the funds. The court stated:

> On application of a party showing an agreement described in § 8.01-581.01, and the opposing party's refusal to arbitrate, the court shall order the parties to proceed with arbitration. However, if the opposing party denies the existence of the agreement to arbitrate, the court shall proceed summarily to the determination of the issue of the existence of an agreement and shall order arbitration only if found for the moving party.
>
> If Mr. Weitz will agree for purposes of this suit that his sole defense is he was acting within his authority under the agreement . . . then I'll send it to arbitration. But if he wants to argue other things[,] . . . about six or seven . . . affirmative defenses[,] . . . then the motion for arbitration is denied. . . .

The court opined that Weitz's assertion that he escrowed the funds because he was afraid that Hudson would move to Florida and leave Weitz solely responsible for the partnership's liabilities has nothing to do with the partnership agreement.

Weitz declined to limit his defense before the arbitrator. Accordingly, the court entered an order denying his application to compel arbitration. Weitz appeals from that order.

ANALYSIS

The dispositive question on appeal is whether the specific controversy alleged in Hudson's motion for judgment is subject to arbitration under paragraph 20 of the partnership agreement. Hudson answers this question in the negative because he claims that this case is just about the conversion or misappropriation of funds and that the arbitration clause does not encompass intentional torts. According to Hudson, the dispute is not between two general partners. Instead, Hudson asserts that the controversy is between two individuals who were general partners in several partnerships, and involves an act of revenge or "self-help personal financial protection" by Weitz. Finally, Hudson argues that there is no provision of the partnership agreement to which the parties must refer in order to resolve the dispute alleged in the motion for judgment. We do not agree with Hudson's arguments.

As we have said previously, a party cannot be compelled to arbitrate a question that is not arbitrable under the agreement between the parties. *Doyle & Russell, Inc. v. Roanoke Hosp.*, Assoc., 213 Va. 489, 494, 193 S.E.2d 662, 666 (1973). "The extent of the duty to arbitrate, just as the initial duty to arbitrate at all, arises from contractual undertakings." Id. Thus, we begin our analysis of the question before us by considering the language of the parties' contract, specifically paragraph 20 of the partnership agreement.

According to the terms of that paragraph, the parties agreed to arbitrate "any dispute or controversy" that arises either "under, out of, in connection with" or "in relation to" the partnership agreement. This Court has described language that is strikingly similar to, and perhaps even less expansive than, the terms of paragraph 20 as "very broad in its coverage." *Waterfront Marine Constr., Inc. v. North End 49ers Sandbridge Bulkhead Groups A, B and C,* 251 Va. 417, 426, 468 S.E.2d 894, 899 (1996) (citing *McMullin v. Union Land & Mgmt. Co.,* 242 Va. 337, 341, 410 S.E.2d 636, 639 (1991)). In *McMullin,* the contract language required arbitration of "any claim or controversy arising out of or relating to" the parties' agreement. 242 Va. at 340, 410 S.E.2d at 638. In discussing the arbitration clause in *McMullin,* we stated that "'broad language of this nature covers contract-generated or contract-related disputes between the parties however labeled.'" 242 Va. at 341, 410 S.E.2d at 639 (quoting *Maldonado v. PPG Indus., Inc.,* 514 F.2d 614, 616 n. 6 (1st Cir.1975)). We further recognized that "'an arbitration clause covering claims "relating to" a contract is broader than a clause covering claims "arising out of" a contract.'" 242 Va. at 341, 410 S.E.2d at 639 (quoting *International Talent Group, Inc. v. Copyright Management, Inc.,* 629 F.Supp. 587, 592 (S.D.N.Y.1986)).

Based on our prior cases and the terms employed in paragraph 20, we conclude that the specific controversy alleged in the motion for judgment is a dispute "in relation to" the partnership agreement. Hudson alleges that Weitz converted funds belonging to Hudson, but Weitz asserts that he had a right, as the managing general partner, to escrow those funds from the sale of Leesburg Manor's asset. Weitz relies on paragraph 16(b) as the source of his authority. That provision authorizes a reserve fund to be set up "for any contingent or unforeseen liabilities or obligations of the Partnership or of the General Partners arising out of or in connection with the Partnership or its liquidation." Thus, to resolve the contro-

versy, paragraph 16(b) will need to be construed or applied to determine whether Weitz converted the funds at issue or properly escrowed them. See *McMullin,* 242 Va. at 342, 410 S.E.2d at 639 (because parties had to refer to agreement to resolve controversy, dispute was one "relating to" agreement).

CONCLUSION

For these reasons, we conclude that the circuit court erred in denying Weitz's application to compel arbitration. Accordingly, we will reverse the judgment of the circuit court and remand for further proceedings consistent with this opinion and in accordance with the Uniform Arbitration Act, Code §§ 8.01-581.01 through -581.016. [FN7] On remand, the circuit court must determine whether any new issues raised in the amended motion for judgment are subject to arbitration, and if not, whether they are severable or subject to the stay. See Code § 8.01-581.01 through -581.016.

Source: From Westlaw. Used with permission of Thomson/West.

Case Questions:

1. What provisions did the limited partnership agreement have regarding arbitration?

2. What were the grounds of Hudson's motion for summary judgment against Weitz?

3. What order did the trial court enter regarding arbitration?

4. What argument does Hudson offer to support his contention that arbitration is not required in this case?

5. According to the court, is the dispute between Hudson and Weitz a disagreement that falls under the arbitration clause? Why or why not?

 Eye on Ethics

FRIVOLOUS LAWSUITS

One ethical challenge that constantly taxes legal professionals is the specter of frivolous lawsuits. There is a small percentage of plaintiffs who bring cases just on the off chance of receiving a large award from a defendant, either because of a sympathetic jury or, more likely, because the defendant is willing to settle the case prior to trial to avoid additional expenses. The problem with such suits is that bringing them is a violation of ethical rules. A claim that has no basis in law or fact is one that should never be brought in the first place. In situations in which the legal team only realizes after the pleadings have been filed that the case lacks merit, this fact should be pointed out to the attorney handling the case as soon as possible. Maintaining a frivolous lawsuit

can result in legal penalties, including bad faith damages and the award of attorneys' fees for the opposition. More important, a firm that makes a habit of bringing groundless lawsuits will soon lose the respect of others in the legal field. Beyond simply losing prestige, this lack of respect will be reflected in more concrete ways, including a sudden unwillingness of other law firms to accommodate the firm for scheduling depositions, requesting extensions on the deadlines for pleadings, and to cooperate in general. Although these results may not sound like such a bad thing, in the real world, they can have a cumulative effect and eventually drive a law firm out of business. No matter how big the city, the legal community is always small and close knit. Word of unscrupulous or unethical behavior by one firm spreads quickly in this community.

Real Paralegal Life: Building a Skill Set

JEAN JURASIN

Jean Jurasin started in the legal field when she was 15 years old, taking "a secretarial program in high school, and part of the curriculum called for an internship at the local courthouse. I worked for the local prosecutor, a couple of hours a day, ten hours a week. It was a great job. I learned that when you work for a team, everybody has to pull their weight. I typed up pleadings, did filing, answered the phone, and even took out the trash."

These days, technology has made huge inroads in the practice of law; "We're living in a cell phone world. Everything is done so quickly. Email, faxes, scanners, makes for a more stressful world, because everybody waits until the last minute. You're always rushing to get it done. One of our biggest concerns is email. You have to be real careful about email. Our firm includes a provision in the fee agreement that the client has no objection to being contacted by email. If the client objects, we don't use it. For a lot of clients, it's easier. We worry all the time about someone intercepting communications from our clients. You can't be too careful."

A Day in the Life: Jean Jurasin

"Some of what we do can be very boring," says Jean Jurasin. "You have to be detail oriented with your cases. Keeping track of all the evidence and exhibits in a case is so important because they get so jumbled up all the time. The attorney is constantly pulling things out of the client file to review it, and it doesn't always get back where it belongs. That's where you come in. You have to know where everything is. On top of that, you are also dealing with a dozen other things going on at the same time. It's my job to do anything to make my lawyer's life easier. I don't think that [the attorney] should have to worry about anything other than what she's been trained to do."

Real Paralegal Life: Building a Skill Set

OFFERS OF JUDGMENT AND SETTLEMENT ISSUE RULES

Research your state's laws and prepare excerpts to include in your trial notebook that list all applicable rules of civil procedure governing settlements, including offers of judgment, pre- and post-trial interest rates on judgments, and the various methods used to enforce judgments.

Career Prep

Discuss alternative dispute resolution, with a particular emphasis on the similarities and differences between arbitration and mediation.

Summary

Alternative dispute resolution has become very prominent in the last few decades. It is now a common practice to have disputes between parties referred to arbitration instead of proceeding through the court system. Many contracts, including many consumer agreements, have arbitration provisions in them as a matter of course. When a case is referred to arbitration, the arbitrator is authorized to make a final and binding decision about the issues pending between the parties. Another form of alternative dispute resolution is mediation. Unlike arbitration, mediation is a consensual process in which a mediator works with the parties to help them resolve the issues between them. Mediators cannot impose rulings; they help the parties resolve the issues on their own. Many states now require mediation for many different types of lawsuits. If the parties are unable to work out a case through mediation, it simply returns to the docket with other cases pending for trial.

Settlement is the resolution of the case between the plaintiff and the defendant. The most common method of settlement is for the defendant to pay a monetary amount to the plaintiff in exchange for the plaintiff's dismissal of his or her case. Plaintiffs often send settlement offers to defendants that set out the basis of the plaintiff's claim against the defendant and request a specific amount that the plaintiff will accept to dismiss the case. Settlement offers can come in the form of settlement brochures, demand letters, or simple negotiations between the parties. A plaintiff will usually sign a release and file a dismissal with prejudice of all claims pending against the defendant in exchange for the defendant's payment.

Key Terms

Arbitration, 268
Appraisal, 270
Umpire, 272
Submission, 272

Mediation, 272
Impasse, 274
Settlement, 275
Release, 280

Review Questions

1. What is alternative dispute resolution?
2. Why has ADR become popular in recent years?
3. What is arbitration?
4. Describe the history of arbitration.
5. What is the Federal Arbitration Act?
6. Compare and contrast appraisal and arbitration.
7. What are the two types of arbitration?
8. What are some examples of issues that commonly result in arbitration?
9. Explain the limitations on the issues that can be submitted to arbitration.
10. What is the scope of the arbitrator's authority?
11. What is "submission" of an arbitration agreement?
12. What is mediation?
13. Compare and contrast mediation and arbitration.
14. Why have many states adopted mandatory mediation programs?
15. What is a certified mediator?
16. Who is normally required to be present at a mediation hearing?
17. What are the normal duties of a mediator?
18. What is an "impasse" as that term applies to mediation?
19. What is a settlement?
20. Explain the contractual elements of a settlement agreement.
21. What are some of the reasons that a plaintiff and defendant would wish to settle a case?

22. What is a settlement brochure?

23. What is a demand letter?

24. What is an offer of judgment?

25. What is a confession of judgment?

Discussion Questions

1. Discuss the reasons the parties might actually seek a settlement instead of taking the case before a jury.

2. Does the modern settlement process encourage frivolous lawsuits? Explain your answer.

Exercises: Skill Builders

Contact your state's board or organization that regulates mediators. What standards are mediators required to follow during their hearings? Can anyone be a mediator? When and where can a mediation hearing be presented? What rules govern a mediation hearing? Locate these rules and place a copy of them in your portfolio.

Portfolio Assignment

Portfolio Assignment 12-1: Create a settlement brochure. Based on the Cherry documents that you find in Appendix A, prepare a settlement brochure based on the example provided in this chapter and the details discussed. What is the final amount that the plaintiff will offer to settle the case? That amount should figure prominently in your settlement brochure. Remember to summarize the important facts, the plaintiff's damages, and any relevant case law from your state that would help sway the defendant toward settling the case prior to trial.

Portfolio Assignment 12-2: Create an offer. Create an offer of settlement in the Baker case (Appendix B). What would the plaintiff propose if she genuinely wished to settle the case prior to trial? What justifies the amount of your proposed offer?

Vocabulary Builders

ACROSS

5 The declaration by the mediator that the parties are unable to reach an agreement.

7 The process of bringing both sides in a civil suit together to negotiate a resolution.

8 A negotiated termination of a case prior to a trial or jury verdict.

DOWN

1 The agreement to arbitrate a specific matter or issue raised between the parties.

2 To surrender a legal right to sue another, often in exchange for monetary payment.

3 A person with greater authority than an arbitrator; this person has the authority to make a final and binding decision when an arbitrator has been unable to do so.

4 The evaluation by an expert of the cash value of a contested item.

6 The process of submitting a claim to a neutral third party who then makes a determination about the ultimate liability and award in a civil case.

Chapter 13

Appeals

CHAPTER OBJECTIVES

The student will be able to:

- Explain the function of a motion for new trial.

- Describe the basis of appellate jurisdiction.

- Explain the purpose of the record.

- Define certiorari.

- List and describe the contents of an appellate brief.

- Explain a notice of appeal.

- Describe why a state supreme court would grant certiorari in a particular case.

- Explain the actions that an appellate court can take with a case on appeal.

In this final chapter, we examine when and how a party may appeal an adverse ruling from a trial court to an appellate court.

At the end of a civil trial, there is always a winner and a loser. The party that loses has the right to appeal the verdict to a higher court. In this chapter, we examine the issues that arise on appeal, explain how appellate courts are organized, and examine the actions that these courts are authorized to take.

STARTING AN APPEAL

Before a party can appeal to a higher court, there must be some final determination in the trial court. Parties are barred from taking up issues until the trial phase is over. A final determination in a case can come from the jury's verdict, but it can also come from a judge's decision granting a summary judgment or any other ruling that effectively ends the case. For purposes of simplicity, we will phrase our discussion about appeals using the facts found in Hypothetical 13-1.

Hypothetical 13-1

Kara was a smoker for over 30 years and 2 years ago was diagnosed with lung cancer. She brought suit against the manufacturer of the brand of cigarettes that she smoked for those three decades: Smokey Smokes, Inc. At trial, Kara produced testimony that the officers of the company knew that their product probably caused lung cancer but continued to market their "low tar" cigarettes as safer than the other brands. Kara's theory at trial was that Smokey Smokes violated her state's Consumer Protection Statute by failing to disclose the dangers of cigarette smoking and by marketing low tar cigarettes with an implied message that they were somehow safer and thus less likely to cause lung cancer.

At trial, the jury awards Kara a total of $1.14 million. Smokey Smokes intends to appeal.

Motion for New Trial

In Chapter 10, we examined the trial of a civil case. There, we saw that when a jury returns a verdict, the judge enters that finding as the official judgment of the court. What we did not point out is that the official entry of judgment is the trigger point for the next round of litigation in the case: the appeal.

motion for new trial
Post-trial relief that requests a new trial on the same issues for specific reasons that must be clearly explained and argued in the motion.

When a judge enters the judgment in the case, the losing party has the right to file a **motion for new trial**. This request is actually the first step in beginning the appellate process. If the motion is denied, the party then has the right to invoke the jurisdiction of the appellate court and begin the long process of appealing a case. However, if the party's request for a new trial is granted, there is no need for an appeal. Instead, the parties will return to a pretrial footing, and everyone must behave as though the first trial never occurred. It will be retried with the same witnesses and evidence introduced. Only a small percentage of motions for new trial are actually granted. In the vast majority of cases, the trial judge denies the motion, and the parties then move to an appellate footing.

In Hypothetical 13-1, Smokey Smokes filed a request for a new trial, citing several instances in the trial that it believed were unfair. For one, Smokey Smokes alleges that Kara's reliance on the state's Consumer Protection Statute was inappropriate, because the company complied with all of the provisions of that law, at least as they existed at the time that Kara was smoking. The trial judge disagrees and denies the motion for new trial. At this point, the jurisdiction in the case shifts to the appellate courts, and the appeal has begun.

APPELLATE COURTS

jurisdiction
The power or authority of the court to hear a particular classification of case.

Jurisdiction is an important term for any court proceeding. In the hypothetical involving Kara and Smokey Smokes, the trial judge's ruling denying the motion for new trial triggers appellate jurisdiction, which has more than record-keeping consequences. At the point that appellate courts obtain jurisdiction, the trial judge is no longer empowered to make any additional rulings in the case. All issues are now pending in the appellate courts, and the parties must go to that court to seek any relief or further rulings in the case.

With the trial judge's denial of the motion for new trial, the losing party can file a notice of appeal with the appellate court.

Notice of Appeal

The court systems in the United States are often compared to a pyramid, with the base composed of the numerous trial courts. In the center of the pyramid are the intermediate appellate courts, and at the top sits the supreme court. This metaphor is instructive whether we discuss the state or the federal appellate court system. On the state level, the trial courts must give way to the greater authority of the state court of appeals (though it is not called this in every state). That court must cede authority to the state supreme court (which also goes by slightly different names in different states). What this pyramid structure means is that each court occupying the lower tier of the pyramid must respect the authority and rulings of the next highest court. Trial courts are bound by the decisions of the court of appeals, which is bound by the decisions of the state supreme court.

notice of appeal
Puts the trial court, the appeals court, and the opposing party on notice that the judgment entered is challenged.

This model is instructive when we discuss the appeal mentioned in Hypothetical 13-1. Smokey Smokes filed a motion for new trial, and that motion was denied. Now, it must file a **notice of appeal** to begin the appellate process (see Figure 13.1). That notice must be filed in the state court of appeals.

A notice of appeal contains some basic information about the case and a request that the appellate court assume jurisdiction in the case. Filing the notice also has important consequences for deadlines. For instance, the party filing the notice of appeal now has a specific period of time

FIGURE 13.1
Contents of a Notice of Appeal

A typical notice of appeal contains:

- The names of the parties.
- A brief statement establishing appellate jurisdiction.
- A request that the jurisdiction be transferred to the state court of appeals.

FIGURE 13.2
Allegation of
**Appellate Jurisdiction
in Notice of Appeal by
Smokey Smokes**

> Appellant, Smokey Smokes, Inc., now alleges that jurisdiction is proper in this Court because of a final judgment entered on the jury's verdict for the Appellee, dated May 15, 2005. With this verdict, all issues pending between the parties were resolved, leaving no further issues pending in the trial court, and jurisdiction is proper in this court according to Rule 10, Appellate Rules of Procedure.

to file its briefs in support of its contentions that the trial court's ruling must be overturned. The notice of appeal will also be filed on the opposing party, and that party will have a specific time period to reply to the briefs filed by the opposition.

One of the most important elements in a notice of appeal is the allegation establishing appellate jurisdiction. The party on appeal must explain to the appellate court why it has jurisdiction in the case. If the party fails to do so, the appellate court might refuse to hear the case. See Figure 13.2 for an example of the phrasing that a party might use in alleging appellate jurisdiction and Figure 13.3 for a notice of appeal.

Terminology on Appeal

appellant
The party filing the appeal; that is, bringing the case to the appeals court.

When a case goes to an appellate court, there are some important changes in terminology that we must address here before we can proceed to other points. At the trial level, the party bringing the claim is usually referred to as the plaintiff and the person against whom the suit is brought is referred to as the defendant. However, on appeal, these terms change. The party bringing the appeal is referred to as the **appellant**, and the party against whom the appeal is brought is referred to as the **appellee**.

appellee
The prevailing party in the lower court, who will respond to the appellant's argument.

Hypothetical 13-2

In the case involving Kara and Smokey Smokes, which party is the appellant and which is the appellee?

Answer: Because Smokey Smokes lost on the trial level and has filed a notice of appeal, the company is the appellant and Kara is the appellee.

FIGURE 13.3
Notice of Appeal

> STATE OF PLACID
> DISTRICT COURT
> LONDON COUNTY
>
> Sherlock Holmes
> (Plaintiff)
>
> v.   File No.: _____
>
> Professor James Moriarty, individually and
> as owner, operator of Moriarty Transport
> Trucking Co. (Defendant)
>
> <u>NOTICE OF APPEAL</u>
>
> Notice is hereby given to Plaintiff Sherlock Holmes that the Defendant in the above-styled action, James Moriarty in his individual capacity and as owner and operator of Moriarty Transport Trucking Company, hereby appeals to the Placid State Court of Appeals from the final judgment and verdict entered against the defendant on December 1, 2006.
>
> _____
> Deborah Bolstridge
> Attorney for Defendant James Moriarty

The Record

The notice of appeal not only informs the appellate court that an appeal will be forthcoming but also requests that the trial court forward the **record** to the appellate court. The record consists of all the evidence and pleadings that have been admitted at trial. This record, along with the transcript of the witness testimony, will be sent to the appellate court and docketed there during the time that the appeal is pending.

Appellate Docket Number

When a case is filed with the state court of appeals, it is immediately assigned a docket number that must be used on all subsequent pleadings or filings by the parties. This docket number is similar to and serves the same purpose as the case file number originally assigned to the case in the trial court. It identifies the case and ensures that anything filed in the case will be stored in the appropriate file for later review.

BRIEFS

Once a notice of appeal has been filed and the case has been assigned a docket number, the next event in the appeal is the filing of briefs by both sides. The appellant usually has 30–60 days from the date that the case was docketed to file a brief with the court. After that, the appellee typically has 30 days to file a responding brief.

Appellant's Brief

The purpose of the appellant's brief is to explain the party's position and advocate a position, namely, that the ruling against the party in the lower court was wrong and should be overturned. The appellant's brief will have a very stylized and formal presentation, containing not only an analysis of the factual elements of the plaintiff's case but also a summary of the court's rulings and a position statement by the appellant declaring why these actions were clearly in contravention to prevailing legal authority. Appellate court briefs have a specified format, often set out in the state's Rules of Appellate Procedure (see Figure 13.4).

RESEARCH THIS!

Before you begin to draft a brief for an appellate court, make sure that you have the most up-to-date rules from that court. The rules govern a wide variety of activities associated with bringing an appeal, including the formatting of the actual documents, when and where they should be filed, how many copies should be filed, and even the font size that should be used in printing the briefs themselves.

LEGAL RESEARCH MAXIM

Online pay sites, such as Westlaw, offer briefs that accompany the final appellate opinions presented. Often, it is very instructive to review the briefs along with the court's final decision.

FIGURE 13.4
Appellate Court Rules: Format and Appearance of Appellate Briefs

Source: Ga. Sup. Ct. Rules, Rule 18.

> All briefs and responses shall be typed or printed on letter size (8½″ × 11″) paper with covers on the front and back, STAPLED on the left-hand side in booklet form. Covers shall be of recyclable paper, heavier than regular stationery, and shall bear the style of the case, the case number, and the name or names of the persons preparing the brief, along with their bar numbers, if attorneys.

FIGURE 13.5
Appellate Brief Title
Page

IN THE COURT OF APPEALS
FOR THE STATE OF ANYWHERE

Smokey Smokes, Inc.,
Appellant,

vs.   Docket No: 2005-1232

Kara Smoker,
Appellee

BRIEF OF APPELLANT

Contents of an Appellate Brief

An appellate brief has specific subsections, including:

- Title page
- Statement of facts
- Enumerations of error
- Argument
- Conclusion

Title Page. A brief must have a title or cover page, listing the names of the parties, the appellate docket number, and the name of the court (see Figure 13.5).

Statement of Facts. After the cover sheet, the next part of an appellate brief is the statement of facts. This section describes the underlying claim and any relevant facts that figured prominently in the lawsuit and that have implications on appeal. The purpose of the statement of facts is to apprise the court of appeals about the relevant events in the case, but most attorneys draft their statement of facts so that they also emphasize the client's points on appeal. See Figure 13.6 for a sample statement of facts.

As you can see, the appellant's statement of facts not only sets out specific incidents but also cross-references these details to the transcript of the trial. This cross-referencing makes it easier for the appellate justices to double-check facts and locate specific testimony. While presenting accurate information, the statement of facts also plays up critical features of the appellant's case.

Enumerations of Error. Once the appellant has drafted the statement of facts, the next part of the brief is the enumerations of error. These are usually single paragraphs, set off in bold face and indented to make them easy to find and even easier to read (see Figure 13.7). The enumerations of error specify the appellant's points about the errors that occurred at trial and why these errors should result in the appellate court overturning the trial court's decision.

FIGURE 13.6
Statement of Facts by
Smokey Smokes

STATEMENT OF FACTS

Appellant Smokey Smokes, hereafter referred to as Appellant, was in the business of manufacturing and marketing cigarettes. (Answer, p. 4) All phases of the production cycle were under the close scrutiny of government inspectors, and Appellant complied with all state and federal laws in producing its product. (Trial transcript, p. 208). Appellant complied with all requirements under this State's Consumer Protection statutes, including a filing specifying the dangers of smoking and its tendency to result in addiction to nicotine, including "low tar" varieties. (Trial transcript, p. 45).

BRIEF OF APPELLANT

FIGURE 13.7
Enumeration of Error
by Smokey Smokes

ENUMERATION OF ERROR

I. The trial court committed reversible error when it ruled that the state Consumer Protection Statute did not create an exemption for the Appellant, even after the Appellant followed all procedures set out by the statute.

An appeal can have dozens of enumerations of error, but for the purposes of simplicity, we limit our discussion to the single enumeration set out in Figure 13.7. As you can see, an enumeration is something more than a bare allegation that something at the trial was incorrect. In its own way, the enumeration also urges a particular point of view. The appellant could simply have stated, "trial court committed error in its ruling on the Consumer Protection Statute." Although that would have been technically correct, a brief is not simply a recitation of facts. At every point in the brief, the legal team seeks to argue its position, which accounts for the additional language in the enumeration that the appellant "followed all procedures set out by the statute." This is both an enumeration of error and an argument.

Argument. Following the enumeration of error, the appellant argues its position. The argument portion of a brief brings together the facts, the law, and the position urged by the appellant. The argument must be based on a solid foundation of legal research and an equally firm grasp of the facts in the case.

Essentially, the argument is based on a simple principle referred to as *stare decisis*. This principle is one of the most important and pervasive in the American judicial system.

stare decisis

(Latin) "Stand by the decision." Decisions from a court with substantially the same set of facts should be followed by that court and all lower courts under it; the judicial process of adhering to prior case decisions; the doctrine of precedent whereby once a court has decided a specific issue one way in the past, it and other courts in the same jurisdiction are obligated to follow that earlier decision in deciding cases with similar issues in the future.

Stare decisis is a Latin term for "stand by the decision." It indicates that all courts are bound by the principle that similar cases with similar facts should result in similar rulings. For instance, if the state supreme court has recently decided a case that has similar issues and similar facts to a case currently pending before the state court of appeals, that court should rule in exactly the same way as the state supreme court's decision. Of course, if things were that simple, there would be very little for appellate courts to do. After several centuries of running a legal system, most of the issues that a party could bring on appeal should already have been decided at some point or other. However, language is open to interpretation, and attorneys and judges are constantly inventing new ways of approaching a legal concept. These shifts result in an ever-growing slew of cases pending before the various appellate courts.

For instance, in Figure 13.7, we saw the enumeration of error raised by Smokey Smokes. How would Kara's brief handle the same issue? See Figure 13.8 for an example.

As you can see, the parties have very different approaches to these issues, and it is up to the appellate court to evaluate the merits of both arguments, review the applicable law, and reach its decision, with justification based on the facts in the case and the requirements of *stare decisis*.

Conclusion. The conclusion is usually a brief statement at the end of the brief that reiterates the party's position and requests specific relief (see Figure 13.9). It will emphasize what the party wants the appellate court to do.

FIGURE 13.8
Appellee's
Enumeration of
Error

ENUMERATION OF ERROR

I. The trial court did not commit reversible error when it ruled that the state Consumer Protection Statute did not create an exemption for the Appellant because courts in this state have been consistent that the statute does not apply to tobacco companies.

FIGURE 13.9
Conclusion

For all of the foregoing reasons, appellant urges the Court to reverse the decision of the trial court and order a new trial.

SPOT THE ISSUE!

Danny recently lost his case against his ex-wife. He had alleged that she had, on several occasions, slandered him by reporting him to the police. Apparently, Danny has been stalking his ex-wife for several months and has been arrested on more than one occasion. Danny's ex-wife moved for summary judgment on his action for slander, and the motion was granted. Danny filed a proper motion for new trial that was denied. To protest, Danny wrote his appellate brief to the state court of appeals on tissue paper. Will the court consider the merits of Danny's appeal?

SURF'S UP!

ELECTRONIC FILING

Because most federal (and many state) courts have gone to electronic filing, it is absolutely essential for all legal professionals to know and understand how to use programs such as Adobe Acrobat and others. Electronic filing allows an attorney to file a pleading over the Internet instead of the old-fashioned method of driving over to the courthouse and presenting a hard copy of the pleading or brief to a clerk. Electronic filing has obvious advantages: It saves time and money and, in some cases, allows a party to file as late as 11:59 p.m. instead of 5:00 p.m. An attorney can file a pleading while he or she is sitting on the beach in Hawaii just as easily as if he or she were sitting behind a desk at the firm. But there are complications to electronic filing. Many appellate courts still do not allow the practice, and many require that the firm establish an account, with a log-in name and password, before the first filing. The firm's bank account is then debited for the cost of the filing. If a deadline is approaching quickly, it is not the time to try to learn the complexities of electronic filing. However, it is obvious that more and more courts will move to this format, thus behooving all legal professionals to learn how the process works.

Filing Deadlines

Both parties on appeal have strict time limits for preparing and submitting their briefs. Failure to do so will often result in the appeal being dismissed or some other sanction.

Serving Copy on Appellee

Once the appellant's brief has been written, copies are served on the appellee and filed in the clerk of appellate court's office. The appellee then has a specific time in which to respond to the appellant's brief. This time period varies but is usually 30 days.

Appellee's Brief

The appellee's brief will be very similar in appearance to the appellant's brief. It will contain the same elements but have a very different approach to the law and the facts. For instance, the appellee's statement of facts will tend to emphasize its argument and also reiterate that the trial

PRACTICE TIP

It is always a smart idea to maintain a brief bank. A brief bank consists of previously written briefs in a wide variety of cases. Storing all of these briefs in the same location has obvious advantages. If you have a new case that raises issues similar to those of a previous case, you have a ready source of information, case law, and reasoning on which to draw. A brief bank also gives you a practical example of what a brief should look like and has already taken into account the formatting and other issues required by the appellate court.

court was correct in its rulings. The appellee's argument will obviously argue that the trial court's decision against the appellant was correct under the principle of *stare decisis*.

Oral Argument

Most appeals before the state court of appeals are conducted in writing. Although appellate rules allow for oral arguments, most parties do not request them. Oral arguments are usually reserved for unusual cases, in which the parties feel that a face-to-face meeting with the justices will somehow be beneficial to them. There are also times when the justices require oral arguments to consider an unusual appeal.

If an oral argument is scheduled for a case on appeal, the attorneys representing the parties will travel to the court of appeals courthouse, usually located in the state capitol. There, they will present their arguments to the justices in a very stylized and formal appearance. Witnesses do not testify at appellate court hearings, and attorneys are not allowed to present any evidence that is not already part of the record. The attorneys argue their positions from podiums in the large appellate chambers. Justices can interrupt the attorneys' presentations at any point, asking questions to clarify specific points or obtain additional information. When the presentations are concluded, the justices retire to consider their decision and may not actually announce it for months. Given the restrictions and pressure of oral arguments, most attorneys opt out of them and rely on their written briefs to make their points.

THE POWERS OF THE APPELLATE COURTS

Although we have said that the court system is organized as a pyramid, with the trial courts at the bottom and the appellate courts at the top, this metaphor oversimplifies the organization and powers of these courts. Appellate courts are higher courts, but they have greater restrictions than one might assume. These courts have very limited options in what they can do with a case on appeal. The decisions for appellate courts are limited to the following rulings on an appellate case:

- Affirming the lower court's decision.
- Reversing the lower court's decision.
- Modifying the lower court's decision.
- Remanding a case for further proceedings.

Affirming the Lower Court's Decision

affirm
Disposition in which the appellate court agrees with the trial court.

Returning to our hypothetical case of Kara v. Smokey Smokes, the cigarette company has now appealed its case to the state court of appeals. If that court agrees with the decision in the lower court, it will issue an order and **affirm** the decision. When a higher court affirms a lower court decision, it leaves it intact and does not change it. An order affirming the lower court ruling would be a loss for the cigarette company.

Reversing the Lower Court's Decision

reverse
Disposition in which the appellate court disagrees with the trial court.

When a higher court **reverses** a lower court ruling, it issues an order overturning that court's decision and making the appellant the winner in the case. If the court of appeals were to do so in the case involving Kara and Smokey Smokes, it would be a clear win for the cigarette company.

Modifying a Decision

Appellate courts are also authorized to create a hybrid decision that partly affirms and partly reverses a lower court's decision. This action is common when there are numerous issues in the appeal. Although we have only addressed a single enumeration of error in the case of Kara v. Smokey Smokes, there likely would be numerous issues, so the most likely result would be a series of decisions by the court of appeals, some of which affirm and some that reverse.

Remanding a Case

remand
Disposition in which the appellate court sends the case back to the lower court for further action.

If an appellate court requires additional information, such as witness testimony or evidence, the only option for the court is to **remand** the case to the trial court for additional hearings. Appellate courts are not equipped to hear new testimony. They are not trial courts, and no one ever testifies

COMMUNICATION TIP

As you stay abreast of recent appellate decisions, keep a list of pending issues from current client files. As you come across a case that has particular relevance to a client's case, send the client a letter describing the case and attaching a copy of the case to the letter. This communication helps the client know that you are actively involved in pursuing the client's legal matters and also gives the client a better feel for the legal complexities involved in bringing the case. One of the biggest complaints that clients have about attorneys and other legal professionals is that they fail to communicate on a regular basis. Letting the client know about recent appellate decisions is one way of staying in constant contact with the client.

before these courts. When an appellate court remands a case, it returns it to the trial court with directions that the court hold a hearing on specific issues.

ORGANIZATION OF THE APPELLATE COURT SYSTEM

If the court system in the United States is a pyramid with the trial courts at the bottom, that must mean that there is a court occupying the top position. On the state level, that court is usually named the state supreme court. This court has the final say on all issues involving the interpretation of state law and cases. In fact, almost all states have three levels to their court systems: the trial courts at the bottom, the state court of appeals in the middle, and the state supreme court at the top. We have discussed the function and limitations of the court of appeals; now we focus on the role played by the state supreme court.

The State Supreme Court

If Smokey Smokes loses its case in the state court of appeals, it can attempt to bring the case before the state supreme court. However, there is at least one hurdle that the company must clear before the state supreme court will accept the case: *certiorari.*

Certiorari

certiorari
(Cert) (Latin) "To make sure." An appellate court's authority to decide which cases it will hear on appeal.

State supreme courts have the right to decide which cases they will hear. These courts have an administrative step that all litigants must satisfy before the supreme court will consider the case. This is **certiorari,** or cert. State supreme courts, like the United States Supreme Court, refuse to hear the vast majority of cases that apply to them for appeals. Supreme courts have different standards than courts of appeal. Before a supreme court will consider an appeal, the parties must show that the case has statewide significance or involves an interpretation of the state constitution. Simply showing that the case is important to the individual parties is not enough. The parties must meet the hurdle of certiorari by explaining the significance of the case in the petition for certiorari.

Petition for Certiorari

The appeal to the state court of appeals in the case of Kara v. Smokey Smokes was a relatively simple and straightforward proposition. The cigarette company simply moved for a new trial, and when that request was denied, it filed a notice of appeal in that court. But things are different when the company wishes to appeal to the state supreme court. Before the state supreme court will even consider the merits of the appeal, it must be satisfied that the case warrants a grant of certiorari. The company must show that the issues involved in the case have broader implications for the entire state. One way that it might raise such an argument is set out in Figure 13.10.

FIGURE 13.10
Excerpt from the Petition for Certiorari by Smokey Smokes

. . . Appellant Smokey Smokes, Inc., shows that the issues involved in this case involve an interpretation of the state Consumer Protection Statute and that the trial court's ruling in this case will result in the filing of hundreds of cases by smokers against any cigarette company that has ever conducted business, shipped product, or marketed cigarettes in this state.

FIGURE 13.11   The State Supreme Court's Ruling in *Kara v. Smokey Smokes, Inc.*

"The petition for certiorari filed by appellant Smokey Smokes, Inc., is denied."

The appellee also has the right to file a motion opposing the granting of certiorari in this case. Here, the appellee will argue that the decision in this case has no broader implications than the rights of the parties involved in the case between Kara and the cigarette company. The ultimate decision to grant certiorari and allow the case to be appealed to the state supreme court is in the hands of the state supreme court justices.

Granting Cert

If the state supreme court grants cert, the court has agreed to hear the case. The appeal will now proceed in an almost identical fashion as the procedure followed in the state court of appeals. The parties will submit written briefs that include statements of facts, arguments, and all of the other features that we mentioned in our previous discussion of appellate briefs. Simply because a party has been granted cert does not mean that he or she will ultimately win the appeal. Granting cert simply authorizes the continuation of the appeal. The court is free to rule any way that it sees fit.

Denying Cert

If the state supreme court denies cert, it means that the court has refused to hear the appeal (see Figure 13.11). At this point, the appellate process is essentially over. The party can file a motion for rehearing that asks the court to reconsider its ruling, but the court rarely overturns its own decision. At this point, the only option left to a litigant is to file a petition for cert with the United States Supreme Court. We will discuss the U.S. Supreme Court in the next section.

THE UNITED STATES SUPREME COURT

Our discussion about appeals has thus far centered on the state appellate system. The federal appellate system is organized in almost exactly the same way. However, instead of covering a single state, the federal system covers the entire nation. Because of the size of the United States, the country has been divided up into different circuits, with one circuit often encompassing several states. Appeals from federal trial courts (called federal district courts) are brought to the Federal Circuit Court of Appeals that has jurisdiction over those states. These courts are situated in a major city in one of the states inside the federal circuit. All of these courts are governed by a uniform set of rules governing appeals. The Federal Rules of Appellate Procedure govern everything from when a party is permitted to appeal to the typesetting and formatting that a brief must contain when it is presented to an appellate court for filing.

If you ignore the fact that the federal system covers the entire nation, you will quickly see that the federal court system is also arranged as a pyramid, with federal trial courts at the bottom, Federal Circuit Courts of Appeal in the middle, and the United States Supreme Court at the top.

Like a state supreme court, the United States Supreme Court is the final authority on the interpretation of the United States Constitution. In the United States, there is no court higher than the U.S. Supreme Court. Because litigants in the state court system always have the option of appealing to the U.S. Supreme Court, that court has become the de facto court of final appeals for states as well.

 CYBER TRIP

California Courts of Appeal	http://www.courtinfo.ca.gov/courts/courtsofappeal/
Supreme Court of Texas	http://www.supreme.courts.state.tx.us/historical/recent.asp
Supreme Court of Ohio	http://www.sconet.state.oh.us/default_highres.asp
Florida Court System	http://www.flcourts.org/
Court of Appeals of Georgia	http://www.gaappeals.us/

Evans v. CenterStone Development Co., (35 Cal. Rptr. 3d 745 (2005),
*747–758 (Cal. App. 4 Dist., 2005))
Rylaarsdam, Acting P. J.

After we decided two earlier appeals related to the disputes noted here, plaintiffs Kirk S. Evans (Evans), Kirk S. Evans, Inc., KSE Development, Inc., and the Kirk and Laurie Evans Trust now appeal from a judgment entered after confirmation of an arbitrator's award. They also appeal from orders compelling arbitration, denying a petition to vacate or modify an arbitration award (this is not appealable but can be reviewed from the judgment) (*Mid-Wilshire Associates v. O'Leary* (1992) 7 Cal.App.4th 1450, 1453–1454, 9 Cal.Rptr.2d 862), and denying and striking requests for trial de novo. They contend the arbitrator acted in excess of his powers and committed misconduct and that the order compelling arbitration was improper. We disagree with all of these assertions and affirm the judgment.

Defendants CenterStone Development Company, a California corporation (CenterStone), Ernest V. Castro, Sr., Harold G. Woods, Jr., Harri Keto, CenterStone Carlsbad, LLC, A California Limited Liability Company, CenterStone Cerritos, LLC, and Beaumont Holdings filed a motion for sanctions, arguing that plaintiffs' briefs violated the Rules of Court and their appeal was frivolous. We agree with both contentions and grant the motion. We publish this opinion because this case presents a prime example of a frivolous appeal and of flagrant violations of the rules pertaining to appeals. We also publish this opinion to discourage parties to arbitration agreements from frivolously seeking judicial review of matters not cognizable in our courts.

FACTS

CenterStone, a real estate development company, was owned by Evans, Castro, and Woods, with Evans acting as president. After disputes arose among the principals, Evans was ousted. In August 2000, the parties entered into a written settlement agreement resolving litigation among them.

The agreement contained an arbitration provision that stated disputes would be decided by arbitration conducted by the Judicial Arbitration and Mediation Services (JAMS) using its Streamlined Rules; discovery was to be governed by Code of Civil Procedure section 1283.05 "as determined by the retired Judge hearing the matter." The settlement agreement also contained a confidentiality provision, which stated that the "parties . . . shall not discuss, reveal, or disclose to any third party, other than their lawyers or accountants . . . on a need to know basis, any of the facts, circumstances, [or] disputes leading up to the Litigation and shall keep the terms and conditions of this Agreement strictly confidential, unless otherwise compelled under law, or as may be needed to defend against or prosecute any litigation."

At the time CenterStone terminated Evans, it also discontinued using the services of two brokers, JoAnn Ulvan and William Geller (brokers), who subsequently sued defendants. Defendants contended plaintiffs provided information to the brokers, in violation of the confidentiality provision in the settlement agreement, to support the brokers' lawsuit against defendants. Defendants initiated arbitration proceedings against plaintiffs for breach of the agreement and sought damages that "could exceed $2,000,000."

Thereafter, JAMS sent the lawyers for the parties a letter confirming the commencement of arbitration. It included a copy of its Streamlined Rules and a list of three proposed arbitrators. The parties were advised that if they could not agree on an arbitrator, they should each strike a name from the list and rank the other two in order of preference. Defendants selected Judge Smith as their first preference. Evans himself called, e-mailed, and faxed JAMS advising he wanted Judge Ryan to act as arbitrator. JAMS telephoned plaintiffs' attorney to explain that, since Judge Ryan was not one of the three arbitrators on the list, the parties had to agree to her or plaintiffs had to use the strike list. Plaintiffs' attorney never responded, and in May 2002[,] Judge Smith was assigned as the arbitrator.

When JAMS notified the parties of the selection, it also sent a disclosure statement, revealing it had found no matters where Judge Smith had acted as an arbitrator in any cases involving the parties or their counsel. The notice also gave the parties 15 days to disqualify Judge Smith; neither side did so.

Part of the settlement agreement required defendants to pay certain sums to plaintiffs. In December 2002, alleging defendants had breached the agreement, plaintiffs filed an action in the Superior Court to compel payment or rescind the agreement. Defendants then filed a motion to compel arbitration pursuant to the terms of the settlement agreement, which the court granted. Although defendant Keto was not a party to the settlement agreement, he agreed to have the claims against him also submitted to arbitration.

The arbitration of all the claims occurred during September 2003[,] and written closing briefs were all filed by October 9. The arbitrator issued his preliminary award on November 5, finding that plaintiffs had breached the confidentiality provision and the covenant of good faith and fair dealing in the settlement agreement by disclosing information to the brokers. He awarded defendants almost $1.1 million, which constituted the amount of attorney fees and costs they had spent defending the brokers' action.

The award also found plaintiffs were entitled to an offset of $900,000 for monies defendants had withheld once plaintiffs breached the settlement agreement. It reserved jurisdiction to determine accrued interest on the offset funds owed to plaintiffs, to determine the amount of attorney fees and costs to be awarded to defendants, including time for additional briefing, and to correct clerical errors and issue a final award.

On November 19, plaintiffs filed a motion to reopen or for reconsideration, which the arbitrator denied. In late November, defendants made a motion for attorney fees and costs. On December 17, the last documents regarding this motion were filed.

On February 13, 2004, the arbitrator issued his final award, which set out the amount of attorney fees awarded to defendants but otherwise was essentially identical to the preliminary award. It again reserved jurisdiction for 60 days to determine the amount of interest and to correct clerical errors.

DISCUSSION

Introduction.

Public policy supports minimal judicial participation in arbitration proceedings. (*Moncharsh v. Heily & Blase* (1992) 3 Cal.4th 1, 9, 10 Cal.Rptr.2d 183, 832 P.2d 899 (*Moncharsh*).) Courts do not review arbitration awards for factual or legal errors (*Jones v. Humanscale Corp.* (2005) 130 Cal.App.4th 401, 407, 29 Cal.Rptr.3d 881), including sufficiency of the evidence or reasoning of the arbitrator (*Moncharsh*, supra, 3 Cal.4th at p. 11, 10 Cal.Rptr.2d 183, 832 P.2d 899). When a court does review an award, it draws all reasonable inferences to support the decision and "displays substantial deference towards the arbitrator's determination of his or her contractual authority." (*Jones v. Humanscale Corp.*, supra, 130 Cal. App.4th at p. 408, 29 Cal.Rptr.3d 881.)

Streamlined Rules.

A theme underlying several of plaintiffs' arguments is the applicability of the JAMS Streamlined Rules. Plaintiffs contend the 2000 version of the rules in effect at the time the settlement agreement was signed apply. We disagree.

Preliminarily we note that, despite their heavy reliance on the 2000 version of the rules, plaintiffs never clearly gave a record reference to enable us to review them. All of their direct citations were to the 2002 version, even though they constantly argued those did not apply. The one reference to the 2000 rules they did give was buried in the brief and so oblique as to be meaningless. Although not required to conduct a search (*Del Real v. City of Riverside* (2002) 95 Cal.App.4th 761, 768, 115 Cal.Rptr.2d 705), we were faced with the challenge of sorting through over 6,600 pages of transcripts in 23 volumes to locate the 2000 version in order to be able to address plaintiffs' arguments.

The rules themselves demonstrate the frivolous nature of the plaintiffs' contention. Rule 3 of the 2000 rules states that "JAMS may amend these Rules without notice. The Rules in effect on the date of the commencement of an Arbitration . . . will apply . . . unless the Parties have specified that another version of the Rules will apply." Contrary to plaintiffs' argument, the settlement agreement does not refer to any version of the rules. Thus, even assuming plaintiffs were relying on the 2000 version, those rules themselves plainly advised them that different rules could be in effect when and if an arbitration took place. The arbitrator did not exceed his powers by using the later rules.

Timely Award.

Nor are we persuaded by plaintiffs' argument the arbitrator's final award was not timely and he thus lost jurisdiction. Plaintiffs rely on the Streamlined Rules that state the final award should be served within 30 days after the hearing closes. The hearing closed on October 9 and the arbitrator rendered a preliminary award on November 5, 2003. In that award he reserved jurisdiction to determine interest and attorney fees and correct clerical errors.

The record reveals that even if the award was late, which we do not decide, plaintiffs waived any objection to the timing. JAMS rule 22(a) states that when a party believes the rules have been violated, he or she must "promptly . . . object in writing [or] the objection will be deemed waived." In addition, section 1283.8 provides that a party waives a timeliness objection "unless he gives the arbitrators written notice of his objection prior to the service of a signed copy of the award on him."

Plaintiffs' objection was made after service of the final award and only a few days before service of the corrected final award. Plaintiffs did not object within the 30-day period after the interim

award or 30 days after the final award, both of which reserved jurisdiction to amend the award. In fact, plaintiffs impliedly, if not explicitly, accepted the award, treating it as timely, by filing motions to correct the award, an opposition to defendants' motion, a motion to reopen, and a motion for reconsideration.

Although rule 19(a) of the Streamlined Rules provides for an award to be issued within 30 days after the hearing closes, it also allows for a longer period for good cause. Plaintiffs' conduct and the issues requiring further decision support a finding there was good cause for delay. The arbitrator had the right to reserve jurisdiction to determine attorney fees and interest. (*Hightower v. Superior Court* (2001) 86 Cal.App.4th 1415, 1433–1434, 104 Cal.Rptr.2d 209.) He also had the power to amend the award any time before it was confirmed so long as it was "consistent with other findings on the merits of the controversy" and did not prejudice a party. (*Delaney v. Dahl* (2002) 99 Cal.App.4th 647, 658-659, 121 Cal. Rptr.2d 663.) Here, inserting the amount of attorney fees and interest was appropriate.

We also reject plaintiffs' complaint that the final award was improper because it was faxed and not served by mail. Section 1283.6 states that service may be personal, by mail, or as provided in the agreement. The 2002 Streamlined Rules provide service "may be made by U.S. mail"; they do not require it.

Litigation Privilege.

Plaintiffs contend the arbitrator did not rule on their defense that Evans' testimony in a deposition in the brokers' case against defendants was protected by the litigation privilege (Civil Code section 47, subdivision (b)) and thus could not be the basis for a finding that he breached the confidentiality provisions or the covenant of good faith and fair dealing in the settlement agreement. In the first place, even if the arbitrator did fail to address this issue, it is entirely within his powers under the arbitration agreement and not reviewable on appeal. (*Moncharsh*, supra, 3 Cal.4th at p. 28, 10 Cal.Rptr.2d 183, 832 P.2d 899.)

Furthermore, plaintiffs raise this issue in a two-page footnote in the introduction to the opening brief. This is a violation of court rules that require arguments to be contained in discrete sections with headings summarizing the point. (Cal. Rules of Court, rule 14(a)(1)(B).) We do not have to consider issues discussed only in a footnote. (*Roberts v. Lomanto* (2003) 112 Cal. App.4th 1553, 1562, 5 Cal.Rptr.3d 866.)

Moreover, as defendants point out, plaintiffs waived this issue by failing to raise it in the trial court. Even after this specific warning about the deficiency of their argument contained in their brief, plaintiffs were unable to show they had brought up the issue in the trial court. The best they could do was point to a single page in their petition to vacate the award, which they inaccurately characterize as "more precise[ ], among other places." They did not direct us to any other "place," if there was any, and we refuse to search through 170 pages of transcripts to determine whether we can improve on plaintiffs' argument. (*Del Real v. City of Riverside*, supra, 95 Cal.App.4th at p. 768, 115 Cal.Rptr.2d 705.)

And the cited page is inadequate. Plaintiffs have not shown they made any argument in the petition to vacate or any other motion or petition filed in the trial court where they raised this issue for consideration. Their record reference is to an argument contained in a footnote in an arbitration brief attached as an exhibit to the petition to vacate. This was not sufficient to request a ruling from the trial court or to preserve the issue for appeal. (*Britz, Inc. v. Alfa-Laval Food & Dairy Co.*, supra, 34 Cal.App.4th at p. 1102, 40 Cal.Rptr.2d 700 [trial court must review de novo any claim of arbitrator misconduct if issue "properly raised"]; *Robinson v. Grossman* (1997) 57 Cal.App.4th 634, 648, 67 Cal. Rptr.2d 380 [issues not raised at trial not reviewable on appeal].)

Answer to Complaint.

Plaintiffs fault defendants' failure to file an answer to their complaint, in violation of the Streamlined Rules. They claim that since there was no written waiver of the rules, the arbitrator had no authority to consider defendants' defenses. Plaintiffs fail to point to anything in the record showing they objected to the lack of an answer (JAMS rules 22(a)) or that they were in any way surprised or prejudiced by defendants' evidence or legal theories offered in opposition to the complaint. They waived any claim on this ground.

The Arbitrator Was Not Biased and Did Not Commit Any Misconduct.

Another ground for vacating an arbitration award is where a party's rights "were substantially prejudiced by misconduct of a neutral arbitrator." (§ 1286.2, subd. *753 (a)(3).) None of the several claims plaintiffs make on this basis has merit.

Disclosure and Disqualification.

Plaintiffs maintain the arbitrator failed to make required disclosures under section 1281.9. Specifically, they complain that, although he made initial disclosures that he had no relationships with parties to the arbitration and their attorneys, the disclosures were not complete. Plaintiffs fail to apprise us what conflict there was that required the arbitrator to make a disclosure, and therefore they have waived this claim. (*People v. Stanley* (1995) 10 Cal.4th 764, 793, 42 Cal.Rptr.2d 543, 897 P.2d 481.) We again decline the opportunity to search the record to determine if they advised the trial court in this regard.

In addition, plaintiffs contend that once their complaint was ordered to arbitration, the arbitrator did not make disclosures as to defendant Keto and other additional parties named as defendants, and defendants' new lawyers. Section 1281.9, subdivision (a) requires an arbitrator to disclose anything that would cause a reasonable person with knowledge of those facts to believe the arbitrator would not be impartial. Contrary to plaintiffs' claim, there is no requirement in either the Code of Civil Procedure or the Ethics Standards for Neutral Arbitrators in Contractual Arbitration (Cal. Rules of Court, appen., div. VI) to disclose the lack of any such information, what plaintiffs call "nondisclosures."

Under section 1281.91, subdivision (a), if an arbitrator fails to make required disclosures under section 1281.9, he must be disqualified if a party serves a notice of disqualification within 15 days after any disclosure was due. Here, plaintiffs did not serve a notice of disqualification. Pursuant to section 1281.91, subdivision (c), plaintiffs' failure to timely serve the notice waives disqualification unless the arbitrator makes a material omission or misrepresentation in his disclosure.

Plaintiffs complain that because the arbitrator did not disclose the lack of any conflicts, they had no way of knowing whether there were any. But "[w]hether an award is tainted by bias because an arbitrator failed to disclose a particular relationship is a factual determination made by the court reviewing the award. [Citation.] The party claiming bias bears the burden of establishing facts supporting its position. [Citation.] The test is objective, i.e., whether the relationship would create an impression of bias in the mind of a reasonable person. [Citation.]" (*Reed v. Mutual Service* Corp. (2003) 106 Cal.App.4th 1359, 1370-1371, 131 Cal.Rptr.2d 524.)

Plaintiffs fail to point to anything in the record to show any bias based on failure to disclose. They rely merely on lack of disclosure

without telling us what the arbitrator should have disclosed other than a disclosure that there was nothing to disclose. *Azteca Construction, Inc. v. ADR Consulting,* Inc. (2004) 121 Cal.App.4th 1156, 18 Cal.Rptr.3d 142, which plaintiffs cite, is inapt. There, the proposed arbitrator disclosed several relationships that potentially affected his neutrality. One of the parties timely filed a notice of disqualification on that basis. The arbitrator should have disqualified himself under section 1281.91, subdivision (b)(1), which provides for disqualification under those circumstances, but failed to do so. Such was not the case here.

The same is true for plaintiffs' related claim about Karla Adams, a JAMS employee. Adams was "temporarily assigned" to act as the arbitrator's case manager. When JAMS learned Adams's former husband had previously worked for *754 "one of the parties," it assigned a different case manager and notified the parties. Based on the JAMS administrative notes for the arbitration, it appears Adams was assigned to the matter for less than one month and made only one entry during a nonactive period at the time the parties were waiting for the trial court's ruling on the motion to compel arbitration of plaintiffs' complaint.

Within a week after JAMS sent the notice, plaintiffs' lawyer sent a letter to JAMS containing a request to appoint another arbitrator. Less than one week later, JAMS reconfirmed that Judge Smith would act as the arbitrator.

Rule 12(j) of the JAMS Streamlined Rules provides that "[a]t any time during the Arbitration process, a Party may challenge the continued service of an Arbitrator for cause . . . based upon information that was not available to the Parties at the time the Arbitrator was selected. . . . JAMS shall make the final determination on such challenge, and that decision shall be final." Here, JAMS made its decision to keep Judge Smith as the arbitrator. The burden is on plaintiffs to show bias, and nothing in the record supports it. Adams was only briefly assigned to the matter, and there is not a shred of evidence she had any influence on the arbitration proceedings at all.

In connection with these arguments, plaintiffs also attack the initial selection of Judge Smith as the arbitrator. However, their unilateral request for Judge Ryan and their failure to strike a name from the three-name list of potential arbitrators were not in accordance with the procedure set out by the JAMS rules. And after JAMS notified plaintiffs' counsel of the deficiency, he did not respond.

Plaintiffs' claim, without benefit of record references, that they were not represented by counsel at the time they received the original strike list from JAMS is irrelevant and not borne out by the record. Moreover, although plaintiffs assert defendants agreed to Judge Ryan by failing to object to their request, nothing in the record shows a copy was sent to defendants. Finally, once Judge Smith was appointed, plaintiffs did not object. There is no basis for vacating the award based on the selection of the arbitrator or the disclosure and disqualification process.

Rulings and Conduct of the Arbitration.

Plaintiffs challenge the arbitrator's rulings on discovery and admission of evidence during the proceedings. Although not clearly stated, we presume plaintiffs contend this is some kind of misconduct on the part of the arbitrator. (§ 1286.2, subd. (a)(3), (4).) They complain, again without record references, that the arbitrator quashed subpoenas duces tecum whereby they were seeking financial records related to funds withheld by defendants and the accrued interest on those funds. In quashing the subpoenas, the arbitrator ruled the documents sought were not relevant because there was no issue as to the amount of funds.

Here, the settlement agreement provided for discovery pursuant to section 1283.05. Under that section, arbitrators have great latitude and discretion when ruling on discovery matters. (§ 1283.05, subd. (b); *Alexander v. Blue Cross of California* (2001) 88 Cal. App.4th 1082, 1089, 106 Cal.Rptr.2d 431 [where discovery allowed by arbitration agreement, arbitrator does not exceed power even if discovery rulings incorrect].) Even had the arbitrator's ruling been incorrect, which we do not and cannot decide (*Moncharsh,* supra, 3 Cal.4th at p. 11, 10 Cal.Rptr.2d 183, 832 P.2d 899), it certainly was not because he exceeded his power. Nor did he do so, as *755 contended by plaintiffs, by admitting a declaration as to the amount of interest.

Likewise, the arbitrator's admission of documents that allegedly had not been produced by defendants in discovery was not misconduct. The arbitrator has broad discretion in conducting the hearing and ruling on admission of evidence. (§ 1282.2, subd. (c); see also § 1283.05, subd. (b).) And he is not required to follow the rules of evidence and procedure. (§ 1282.2, subd. (d).) The rulings about which plaintiffs complain do not constitute misconduct.

Comprehensive Rules.
Plaintiffs contend the arbitrator improperly rewrote the arbitration agreement by using the JAMS Comprehensive Rules instead of the Streamlined Rules. Plaintiffs do not direct us to a copy of the Comprehensive Rules, but claim they do not limit awards to $250,000. However, the Streamlined Rules in effect at the time of the arbitration did not have such a limit either.

Even if the arbitrator used the Comprehensive Rules, he did not rewrite the contract. Again without benefit of record references, plaintiffs purport to recite particulars of a telephone conference with the lawyers and the arbitrator wherein they discussed use of the Comprehensive Rules and the arbitrator's reference to a notation in his file showing the parties' agreement to use those rules. The arbitrator sent the parties a copy of his written memo to the case manager documenting that agreement. He provided this not just to defendants' attorney, as plaintiffs represent, but to both sides. The parties were free to orally agree to use the Comprehensive Rules, and plaintiffs have provided no authority to the contrary. There was no misconduct.

Order Compelling Arbitration.
Plaintiffs challenge the order of the superior court sending their complaint against defendants to arbitration. The only reason they advance in support of their argument appears to be that defendant Keto, a lawyer who helped negotiate the settlement agreement, was not a party to that agreement. However, plaintiffs failed to mention that Keto agreed to submit to arbitration pursuant to the settlement agreement. (*Izzi v. Mesquite Country Club* (1986) 186 Cal.App.3d 1309, 1319, 231 Cal.Rptr. 315 ["Plaintiffs' attempt to avoid arbitration by arguing the arbitration clause cannot be applied to named defendants who were not signatory to the . . . agreement requires only cursory discussion"].) In addition, the claims against Keto arose out of the settlement agreement and were essentially the same as those against the other defendants. (*Metalclad Corp. v. Ventana Environmental Organizational Partnership* (2003) 109 Cal.App.4th 1705, 1717–1718, 1 Cal. Rptr.3d 328 [nonsigner may enforce arbitration provision where claims against him are "'intimately founded in and intertwined with'" contract at issue].)

Plaintiffs rely on a statement in the arbitrator's opinion that, because Keto did not sign the settlement agreement, he was not a necessary party to the arbitration. This statement was made in an entirely different context, and, in any event, is irrelevant since Keto agreed to the arbitration. Because the contractual arbitration was binding, by consenting to arbitration Keto perforce was agreeing it would be binding. And he has not challenged the award.

Miscellaneous.
Because of the lack of organization and the improper format of plaintiffs' briefs, arguments in addition to those we have discussed may have been alluded to or raised in other than the discussion section. To that extent or to the extent plaintiffs mentioned other issues without fully or properly briefing them, they are waived. (*Alameida v. State Personnel Bd.* (2004) 120 Cal. App.4th 46, 59, 15 Cal.Rptr.3d 383; *Roberts v. Lomanto,* supra, 112 Cal.App.4th at p. 1562, 5 Cal.Rptr.3d 866.)

Sanctions.
Defendants seek sanctions for plaintiffs' filing of a frivolous appeal and for violation of appellate rules. Although sanctions could be awarded on either ground, the record supports a granting of the motion on both bases.

Rules Violations.
Sanctions are warranted for a party's unreasonable violations of the rules of appellate procedure. (Cal. Rules of Court, rule 27(e)(1)(C); *Pierotti v. Torian* (2000) 81 Cal.App.4th 17, 29, 96 Cal.Rptr.2d 553.) Plaintiffs' briefs are cornucopias of such violations, as detailed in defendants' motion and noted several times in this opinion.

California Rules of Court, rule 14(a)(1)(B) requires each argument raised to be in a separate section with a heading summarizing the point. Plaintiffs' issues are haphazardly splashed throughout the brief, beginning in a two and one-half page footnote in the introduction, continuing through the section purporting to be a statement of facts, and finally ending in the discussion section. As defendants noted, plaintiffs' opening brief is "repetitive, tangled and, at times, utterly incoherent. . . ." Defendants assert this required them to devote far too many hours to be able to craft a reply. We believe them; we were required to spend an inordinate amount of time deciphering the claims ourselves. "[A]n opening brief is not an appropriate vehicle for an attorney to 'vent his spleen' after losing at an arbitration hearing." (*Pierotti v. Torian,* supra, 81 Cal.App.4th at p. 32, 96 Cal.Rptr.2d 553, fn. omitted.)

Similarly, plaintiffs failed to "provide a summary of the significant facts limited to matters in the record." (Cal. Rules of Court, rule 14(a)(2)(C).) The recitation was not in summary style, was overly lengthy, and included irrelevant information and argument. Plaintiffs presented "facts" not supported by or contrary to the record and failed to include other relevant facts. For example, several times they emphasize their claim that the arbitrator was biased because he sent a copy of his internal memorandum to defendants only. But the record is quite clear that it was sent to both parties. Moreover, plaintiffs repeatedly cite to 170 pages of their motion to vacate without directing us to specific pages and fail to advise us that most of the statements in the declarations were stricken by the trial judge and cannot support their claims.

These violations continued in the reply brief even after defendants had highlighted them in the motion for sanctions. "'We consider the failure to comply with these rules in [appellants'] opening brief to be compounded and unreasonable when, after the respondents pointed out these errors, counsel for [appellants] violated the same rules in the reply brief.'[ ]" (*Pierotti v. Torian,* supra, 81 Cal.App.4th at p. 31, 96 Cal.Rptr.2d 553.)

Plaintiffs also egregiously violated the rule requiring specific page citations. (Cal. Rules of Court, rule 14(a)(1)(C); *Byars v. SCME Mortgage Bankers, Inc.* (2003) 109 Cal.App.4th 1134, 1140–1141, 135 Cal.Rptr.2d 796 [facts and arguments must be supported by required record references, including "providing exact page *757 citation"].) Often they failed to make any reference to the record. To the extent they did provide citations, too many times it was to hundreds of pages in the transcript, referring to an entire document rather than a specific page. It was not until their opposition to the motion for sanctions, where they argued they had provided page point references, that plaintiffs actually did so. And most of those references were to statements in declarations that had been stricken. Moreover, even had they been correct, citation at this point was too little, too late. Although we are not required to plow through mounds of appendices, at times we did, and we have no doubt defendants had to expend substantial additional and unnecessary time because of this violation.

Further, the appellants' appendix did not conform to the rules. California Rules of Court, rule 5.1(b)(2) provides the "appendix must not contain documents . . . that are unnecessary for proper consideration of the issues." Despite their claim to the contrary, many of the documents in the 23 volumes were never referenced by plaintiffs and were not necessary to our determination of the issues. Plaintiffs assert "[t]his is a complex appeal documented with volumes of paper" and that they "wanted to provide the Court with 'complete' documentation. . . ." However, the appeal was complex only because plaintiffs caused it to be so by raising issues not properly before us. Nor did the appendix contain an alphabetical index or list the volume where a document first appeared, making an already unnecessarily unwieldy appendix even more difficult to navigate. (Cal. Rules of Court, rules 5.1(d)(1), 9(b)(1).)

Plaintiffs' passing apologies for "non-substantive 'infractions' of this Court's rule[s]" are really a failure to recognize the overall scheme of the Rules of Court and the extent of their violations. Especially in light of their continuing disobedience, this disingenuous contriteness does not relieve them from an award of sanctions.

Frivolous Appeal.

In addition to these rules violations, the substance of the appeal was frivolous. In an arbitration, "the parties do not get to appeal an adverse decision." (*Saika v. Gold* (1996) 49 Cal.App.4th 1074, 1076, 56 Cal.Rptr.2d 922.) That is just what plaintiffs have tried to do here. Courts have repeatedly instructed litigants that challenges to the arbitrator's rulings on discovery, admission of evidence, reasoning, and conduct of the proceedings do not lie. (*Moncharsh,* supra, 3 Cal.4th at p. 28, 10 Cal. Rptr.2d 183, 832 P.2d 899; *Harris v. Sandro* (2002) 96 Cal. App.4th 1310, 1313, 1314-1315, 117 Cal.Rptr.2d 910; *Pierotti v. Torian,* supra, 81 Cal.App.4th at p. 25, 96 Cal.Rptr.2d 553.) Plaintiffs' crude attempt to characterize their claims so they would fall within acceptable bases for an appeal is an artifice we condemn.

Further, most of plaintiffs' claims are patently disingenuous. Arguments regarding use of the Streamlined Rules, failure to find the arbitration was binding, the selection of the arbitrator and his subsequent disclosures or lack thereof, and the order compelling arbitration distort the law, the facts, and logic. Sanctions may be awarded when an appeal "indisputably has no merit—when any reasonable attorney would agree that the appeal is totally and completely without merit." (*In re Marriage of Flaherty* (1982) 31 Cal.3d 637, 650, 183 Cal.Rptr. 508, 646 P.2d 179.) Using an objective standard, this appeal is frivolous.

Sanctions Award.

Because of the many violations of the Rules of Court and the patently frivolous nature of the appeal, and to discourage *758 similar conduct in the future, sanctions must be substantial. (*Pierotti v. Torian,* supra, 81 Cal.App.4th at p. 34, 96 Cal. Rptr.2d 553 [sanctions higher when "two separate (yet interrelated) wrongs" and due to degree of frivolousness]; *Alicia T. v. County of Los Angeles* (1990) 222 Cal.App.3d 869, 885-886, 271 Cal.Rptr. 513 [substantial sanctions to deter similar violation of Rules of Court violations].) Under the arbitration agreement defendants are entitled to attorney fees and we remand to the trial court to determine the amount of attorney fees defendants reasonably incurred in defending this appeal and the attorney fees reasonably incurred in making the motion for sanctions. (See *Otworth v. Southern Pac. Transportation Co.* (1985) 166 Cal.App.3d 452, 461-462, 212 Cal.Rptr. 743.) Using the amount thus determined as a lodestar, the court shall award an equal amount to defendants as sanctions. A mere award of attorney fees, to which defendants are entitled under the contract, would fail to compensate defendants for the burdens imposed on them as a result of this unnecessary and unnecessarily burdensome appeal. Sanctions are awarded jointly and severally against plaintiffs and their lawyer.

DISPOSITION

The judgment is affirmed. Respondents are entitled to sanctions for the conduct of appellants and their counsel for bringing this frivolous appeal and for violating California Rules of Court, rules 5.1(b)(2) and 14(a)(1)(B) & (C) and (2)(C). The matter is remanded to the trial court to determine the amount of sanctions to be awarded in accordance with the formula described in this opinion. Sanctions are awarded against appellants and their counsel, jointly and severally. All sanctions are to be paid within 30 days after the order of the superior court fixing the amount of the award. Randall S. Waier and the clerk of this court are each ordered to send a copy of this opinion to the State Bar of California upon issuance of the remittitur. (Bus. & Prof.Code, §§ 6086.7, subd. (a)(3) & 6068, subd. (o)(3); *Caro v. Smith* (1997) 59 Cal. App.4th 725, 740, 69 Cal.Rptr.2d 306.) Respondents shall recover their costs on appeal.

Source: From Westlaw. Used with permission of Thomson/West.

Case Questions:

1. What were the underlying issues in this case?

2. How did the arbitration agreement factor into the contested issues?

3. According to the court, what is the public policy with regard to court participation in arbitration agreements?

4. What does the court have to say about the plaintiffs' references to the arbitration rules in their brief?

5. How do the plaintiffs violate the court's rules about presenting arguments in their brief?

6. What does the court have to say about the poor organization and presentation of the plaintiffs' brief?

7. According to the court, are sanctions proper against the plaintiffs for the manner in which they have brought their appeal?

Eye on Ethics

UNFAVORABLE CASE LAW

You might have a natural tendency to downplay or even ignore adverse case law as you research issues on appeal The situation can arise in several contexts, but the most common is that as you research a particular issue, you find cases that both support your client's position and clearly go against your client's position. The tendency is to focus on the cases that are helpful to the appeal and to put aside those cases that are not. But that is a mistake. Most courts have rules that require the parties to submit both cases that support a position and those that do not. In addition, ignoring cases that go against your own position can only end up hurting the client.

The opposition will certainly find those cases and play them up in their own brief. Better that you discuss them in yours and show how they do not apply, or that they should be overruled, than to simply ignore them and hope they go away.

As you research cases in preparing any document, especially a brief, you should always be careful to point out any cases that run counter to your argument. Make sure that the attorney knows about these cases and has fashioned an argument to deal with them. In the long run, it is not only the ethical thing to do but also the most practical. If there are numerous cases going against your client's position, perhaps it is time to reconsider the appeal or perhaps even settle the case before it goes to appeal.

Real Paralegal Life: Building a Skill Set

JANICE JOHNSON

For Janice Johnson, who spends a lot of her time working on personal injury and Social Security cases, computer programs are her lifeblood: "We use Abacus as a database and tracking system here in our office. I don't know how we survived as well as we did before we went to this system. Today, not to have some type of product program for client information and management along with a deadline system is living in the dark ages and asking for a malpractice situation to occur. I don't know how many work hours we've saved over the years since we began using Abacus merely in looking at the computer file rather than hunting down the physical file when a client or contact called me, but I dare say over the past 5+ years since we got Abacus, we've probably saved a number of days if not a few weeks in man hours spent looking for files alone. Unless something was logged onto the system incorrectly, nothing is ever filed incorrectly on Abacus. I wish I could say that for our physical files.

"I encourage all my clients who have email addresses to please contact me in that manner. I get the contacts in an extremely timely manner without having an interruption while a client is in my office. I can also respond back without getting caught on a call that ends up going entirely too long because a client can't stop him- or herself from going on and on and on with questions that I've already answered or which really aren't that pertinent to the handling of the case anyway. Also, I have a word-for-word record of what information was given to the client through the email contacts."

A Day in the Life: Janice Johnson

The office where Janice Johnson works emphasizes the team approach to working on cases: "When certain events occur in cases, we may have two or more persons working on different aspects of one case simultaneously. This is much more effectively done when each person can access the file via technology at his or her desk rather than trying to split up the physical file between us.

"We still use the old 'client list' file on our word processing system along with other forms files that we've developed over the years. I highly suggest that an office go with Microsoft, as we have had some problems when we needed to transfer data electronically, and we find almost everyone in the world uses Microsoft but us.

"I use the Internet on a nearly daily basis. Due to my narrow area of practice I don't generally use traditional legal research but tend to look for medical dictionaries online and drug listings. I track down obscure medical providers out of my normal area of operations, and used it last summer after the death of a client to track down in minutes where and what was required to obtain the death certificate and autopsy reports in a 'crossroads' metropolitan area which had 3 different offices which could have been my correct source depending on the exact location of the death within the city. I research medical conditions online extensively."

Real Paralegal Life: Building a Skill Set

RESEARCHING THE RULES TO APPEAL A CASE

Locate your state's rules of appellate procedure and copy the provisions related to the appearance of appellate briefs. What do the courts require in terms of formatting, paper selection, and font size? How many copies of the brief must be served on the court? Does the court allow for electronic filing of briefs?

Career Prep

Use an Internet search engine to locate appellant and appellee briefs from various sites. What do these briefs have in common? What conclusions can you draw about the presentations, formatting, and argument you should use in creating your own briefs?

Summary

When a party loses at trial, he or she has the right to appeal the decision to an appellate court. The appeals process begins when the losing party files a motion for new trial. When that motion is denied, the party then has the right to file a notice of appeal and have the case transferred to the jurisdiction of the appellate court. In most states and at the federal level, the first level of appellate court is called the court of appeals. The appellant files a brief in this court requesting that the court of appeals reverse the trial court's decision. The appellee also files a brief requesting that the court leave the trial court's finding intact. Appellate briefs have a standard format, with specific sections for the statement of facts, enumeration of errors, argument, and conclusion. Most cases that are heard on appeal employ written briefs, but there are provisions that allow parties to request an oral argument before the appellate court.

Appellate courts have limited jurisdiction and can only take four different actions in a case on appeal. When the appellate court affirms the lower court's decision, it agrees with that decision and allows it to stand. However, when a court reverses the lower court's decision, it disagrees with the trial court and overturns that court's decision. Appellate courts can also modify lower court decisions or send the case back to the trial court for additional hearings on a remand.

Appellate courts are organized in a hierarchy, with the most powerful court at the top and the trial courts at the bottom. On the state level, the most powerful court is usually called the state supreme court, and it has the final say about interpretations of state law. The United States Supreme Court is the highest court in the country. It is the court of last resort for all types of appeals.

Key Terms

Motion for new trial, 288
Jurisdiction, 288
Notice of appeal, 288
Appellant, 289
Appellee, 289
Record, 290

Stare decisis, 292
Affirm, 294
Reverse, 294
Remand, 294
Certiorari, 295

Review Questions

1. What is a motion for new trial?
2. Explain the basis of appellate jurisdiction.
3. What is a notice of appeal?
4. What is the appellate record?

5. What is an appeal?

6. What is a brief?

7. List the basic components that an appellate brief contains.

8. What is the purpose of a statement of facts in an appellate brief?

9. What is an enumeration of error?

10. What is oral argument?

11. The chapter suggests that appellate courts have limited powers. Explain.

12. What is the difference between affirming and reversing an appeal?

13. What is the purpose of a remand?

14. Explain the organization of state courts.

15. What is certiorari?

16. What is the basis for granting or denying certiorari?

17. What types of cases do not have certiorari requirements?

18. What is the name of the highest court in the United States?

19. What is the purpose of federal circuit courts?

20. What is a brief bank?

Discussion Questions

1. If you were going to organize a system for appealing cases, which aspects of the current system would you keep and which aspects would you eliminate? Explain your answer.

2. What are some reasons for and against certiorari?

3. Are there some types of cases in which appeals should not be allowed? Why or why not?

Exercises: Skill Builders

Based on the jury verdict form provided in the Baker case (Appendix B), prepare a motion for a new trial on the defendant's behalf.

Portfolio Assignment

Portfolio Assignment 13-1: Create a brief bank. If your firm does not already have a brief bank, perhaps you should create one. A brief bank is an archive of the appellate briefs filed in previous cases that can be quickly and easily retrieved. There are many issues in appeals that recur over and over again. Why reinvent the wheel each time, when you can rely on previous research and writing to minimize the time it takes to create a new brief? In the old days, paralegals would make hard copies of appellate briefs and then file them according to subject or put appellate subjects on index cards to help retrieve the brief later. These days, most paralegals keep brief banks on a computer. After all, the briefs are almost always created using a word processing program like Word® or WordPerfect®. Why not use this same system to create a brief bank?

Each argument section of old briefs can be pulled out and indexed separately. The subjects could be saved on the computer hard drive (and on a back-up floppy or CD) as follows:

- Appeal: Waiver of issue by failure to object at trial.
- Appeal: Failure to conform to appellate rules.
- Cert: Petition for cert to state supreme court.
- Cert: Petition for cert to U.S. Supreme Court.
- Evidence: Hearsay exceptions.
- Evidence: Demonstrative.
- Witnesses: Unavailable for trial.
- Witnesses: Expert witness in auto reconstruction.
- Witnesses: Expert witness in medical standard of care.

Prepare the basic formulation of a brief bank by reviewing recent decisions from your state's highest appellate court. Choose topics related to civil litigation, including evidence law, expert witnesses, pleadings, and motions, to name a few.

Portfolio Assignment 13-2: Explain the possible rulings that an appellate court can make in a case.

Vocabulary Builders

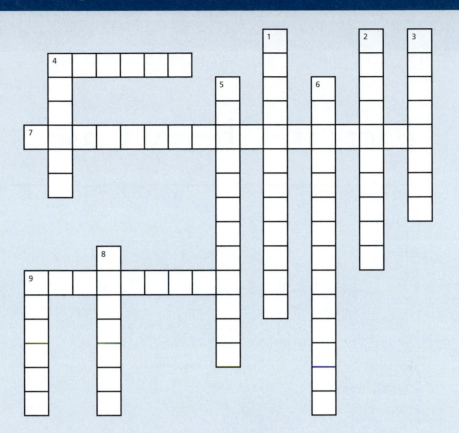

ACROSS

4 The appellate court requires additional information or an evidentiary hearing because it cannot conduct such a hearing itself. The case is temporarily transferred to the trial court for a hearing and then resent to the appellate court.

7 A motion made by the party who lost at the trial court level; this motion requests a new trial on specific grounds; if denied, it triggers the appellate process.

9 Person bringing the current appeal from an adverse ruling in the court below.

DOWN

1 (Lat.) "stand by the decision"; the principle that appellate courts will follow clearly established precedents in their decisions.

2 The power of an appellate court to decide which cases it will hear.

3 The person who won in the lower court.

4 The entire body of evidence, witness transcripts, pleadings, motions, discovery materials, and any other material admitted during the trial.

5 The power of a court to make rulings.

6 A request to an appellate court that it assume jurisdiction in the case and docket the case for an appeal.

8 To _____ a lower court's decision is to set it aside.

9 The appellate court's final decision supports the decision made by the lower court.

Appendix A

Facts in Cherry Case

MEMORANDUM

TO: Paralegal
From: Al Alvin
Re: Mr. Cherry
Date: November 14, 2006

   I met with Jack Cherry today. Please see the attached notes of our conversation. I'm still evaluating whether or not to take his case. I'd like you to take a look at the information that he has provided us so that you can be up to speed when we meet on Friday to discuss this and several other new cases.

MEMORANDUM

TO: File
From: Al Alvin
Re: Notes of meeting with Mr. Cherry
Date: November 14, 2006

   I met with Mr. Jack Cherry today and he relayed the following facts to me.

   Mr. Cherry works for the National Park Service and maintains their mobile equipment. He has worked for the NPS for 27 years and does plan on retiring when he reaches 30 years. Before that, he was in the military and did 20 years of service. He reached the rank of Master Sergeant. He was honorably discharged. He has no criminal record and has only had two speeding tickets in the last 20 years. His wife, Maria, works at the Federal Correctional Institute downtown. She has worked there for almost 30 years.

   Last month, Sarge, as he likes to be called, was shopping at Big Buys. He was looking for a digital music player. He'd been told by a friend that Big Buys has a nice selection. He went into the electronics section and saw several models but wasn't sure how to choose between them. He couldn't seem to get anyone's attention in the digital section, so he picked up an iPod Nano and walked into another section. He doesn't remember what section it was, but the associate there said that he didn't know anything about music players and advised him to seek advice in that section. Sarge explained that he couldn't get anyone's attention, and the associate just repeated that he should go back there. Sarge went back to the music section, still couldn't get anyone to talk with him, and took the iPod up to the front counter. He was going to buy it anyway but then said that he got disgusted with the whole place, stuffed the iPod into a magazine rack by the register, and walked out. He said that the alarm did not sound as he went through the door. He was almost at his car when three big men in blue shirts ran up to him, knocked him to the ground, and accused him of being a shoplifter. They dragged Sarge back inside and put him in the security room. He said that he repeatedly told the men that he hadn't stolen anything. One man reached into the front of his pants to look for the iPod and Sarge admits that he called the man a name. When they didn't find the iPod they kept him for a while, insisting that he sign some kind of waiver. He refused, and they finally let him go.

He hadn't realized it while he was in the office, but his nose had been bleeding and when he got home that night, he had two black eyes. He'd seen enough action in the military to know that his nose was broken. He thinks that it was broken when the men tackled him to the ground and pushed his face into the asphalt. He says that his nose "hurt a little" but didn't seek medical treatment for two more days. By the time that he did see his doctor, his nose had set, and the doctor said that, short of re-breaking his nose, there wasn't anything he could do. Mr. Cherry presented the following materials for our review:

One incident report from Big Buys—he says he obtained it from a "friend" but refuses to identify the person.

One letter from Big Buys's corporate headquarters advising him not to come to any Big Buys stores again.

One photograph of Sarge with his two black eyes.

One summary medical narrative from his doctor.

A series of medical bills that have been sub-totaled.

Incident Report—Big Buys, Inc.
Person making report: Bert Bertson, Store Manager
Date of report: September 1, 2006
Date of incident described in report: August 27, 2006
Describe incident:

Security Officer Briggs notified assistant manager Steve Austin that customer had taken an iPod from the digital music department and concealed it about his person. Customer then left through the front entrance. Security Officer Briggs notified S.O.'s Stratton and Pullstart, and they apprehended the man in the parking lot. The man was combative and verbally abusive. They asked him to return into the store, and the man attacked them. They were forced to defend themselves and, after using reasonable force to subdue him, brought him within the store. The man refused to tell the officers where the iPod was and offered to allow them to search his shirt and pants. Security refused. They were about to call the police when the man admitted that he had thought about taking the iPod but had dropped it by the merchandise detectors before going out. He refused to sign a confession and was advised to never return to any Big Buys store.

America Buys Big Buys
Big Buys, Inc., a wholly owned subsidiary of
Big and Better Buyers, Inc.
21 Corporate Ave.
Placid City, Placid 66556

October 14, 2006

Jack Cherry
21 Robin Hood Terrace
Placid City, PL 66554

Mr. Cherry:

Be advised that because of your actions on August 27 at Store #121 in Placid City, PL, you are barred from entering any Big Buys or Big and Better Buyers, Inc., store facility. If you do return, you will be cited for trespass, and the police will be summoned to remove you from the premises. Big Buys will prosecute you for any and all applicable criminal charges.

Please govern yourself accordingly.

Sincerely,

Cal Calvin
Corporate Counsel for Big Buys, Inc.

Medical Narrative
August 29, 2006
Dictated by Mary Medico, M.D.
Transcribed by N.B.

Patient came into today, complaining of sino-facial discomfort. X-rays revealed a small fracture of the nasal process. Patient advised that he had been in scuffle with men in a parking lot and had been pushed to the ground. Injury is consistent with this report. Patient given Darvocet for pain and advised to avoid any contact or further lacerations to face. Patient also advised that bone has already begun to heal and no further medical treatment warranted at this time.

Medico and Sturgeon, PLLC
A Medical Corporation

Summary of charges:

August 29, 2006
 Examination, etc. $457.25

Harm and Caring Pharmacy

One Rx for Darvocet, 20 mg: $142.32

Appendix B

Facts in Baker Case

IN THE GENERAL COURT OF JUSTICE
COUNTY OF LONDON
STATE OF PLACID
CIVIL ACTION FILE NO: 07-x-8974-6

Mary Alice Baker,	) **COMPLAINT CONTAINING**
Plaintiff	) **JURY TRIAL DEMAND**
	)
v.	)
	)
Great Goody Grocery Store, Inc.	)
& Steve Doe	)
Defendants	)

Plaintiff, by and through his attorneys, complains of the defendants as follows:

1. Plaintiff is, and all times hereafter was, a citizen and resident of the Town of PLACID CITY, County of LONDON, State of Placid.

2. Plaintiff alleges upon information and belief that the defendant Great Goody Grocery Store, Inc., is, and at all times hereafter was, a corporation organized and existing under the laws of the State of Placid, licensed to do business, and in fact doing business, in the State of Placid and having a registered agent for the service of process by the name of Paula Purple, located at 2156 Alder Circle, Suite 12 B, Placid City, Placid, 27562.

3. Plaintiff alleges upon information and belief that the defendant Steve W. DOE is a citizen and resident of the County of London, State of Placid.

4. Defendant Great Goody Grocery Store, Inc. (hereafter referred to as "Defendant Goody"), did, at the time of the incident complained of, own, maintain, and manage a retail establishment ("store") within the city limits of Placid City, Placid, and located at 123 Greengrocer's Lane, Placid City.

5. On May 12, 2005, plaintiff was a customer at the store located at 123 Greengrocer's Lane.

6. After making her purchases inside the store, plaintiff exited the premises and proceeded to her automobile, parked in the customer parking area in front of the store.

7. As plaintiff was loading her groceries into her car, she was attacked by defendant Steve W. Doe.

8. Plaintiff was dragged from her car, in full view of security cameras set atop light poles in the parking lot by Defendant Goody.

9. Security agents, employed by Defendant Goody, noted the abduction and contacted police after witnessing the assault on the plaintiff.

10. Plaintiff was dragged into an area of shrubs and undergrowth adjacent to the parking lot and was beaten and sexually assaulted by Defendant Steve W. Doe.

11. Defendant Goody had a duty to plaintiff because plaintiff was a customer at its establishment and Defendant Goody breached this duty of due care by the following acts of negligence:

   a. Employees, agents, and supervisors at the store failed to follow their own safety procedures.

   b. Employees, agents, and supervisors at the store failed to intercede in the assault on the plaintiff, even though they were aware that it was proceeding.

   c. Defendant Goody failed to provide safe conditions for the plaintiff and other customers.

   d. Defendant Goody failed to act to protect the plaintiff.

   e. Defendant Goody failed to put customers on notice that Defendant Doe was dangerous and that he had attempted to assault other customers.

   f. Defendant Goody breached its duty to plaintiff by failing to notify plaintiff that Defendant Doe had a history of violence toward women.

   g. Defendant Goody did not prevent Defendant Doe from repeatedly returning to its premises and harassing its customers.

12. The negligence of Defendant Goody was a proximate cause of the injuries sustained by plaintiff and joined and concurred in the intentional acts of Defendant Doe bringing about the plaintiff's serious, painful, and permanent injuries and damages, all of which exceed the sum of Ten Thousand Dollars ($10,000.00), and which include, without limitation, the following:

   1) bodily injury and resulting pain and suffering;

   2) medical expenses, including the costs of therapy;

   3) loss of earnings and earning capacity;

   4) punitive damages as a result of the defendants' reckless and wanton conduct.

WHEREFORE, the plaintiff prays the Court as follows:

   1. That the plaintiff have and recover from the defendants, jointly and severally, a sum in excess of Ten Thousand Dollars ($10,000.00) for compensatory and punitive damages as alleged above.

   2. That the plaintiff have and recover the costs of this action.

   3. For a trial by jury.

   4. For such other and further relief as the Court may deem just and proper.

This the 6th day of April, 2006.

Rhonda Roe
Attorney for Plaintiff
2121 Elm Lane
Placid City, PL 06254

IN THE GENERAL COURT OF JUSTICE
COUNTY OF LONDON
STATE OF PLACID
CIVIL ACTION FILE NO: 07-x-8974-6

Mary Alice Baker, Plaintiff	) **ANSWER OF DEFENDANT**) **GREAT GOODY GROCERY**) **STORE, INC.**)
v.	))
Great Goody Grocery Store, Inc. & Steve Doe Defendants	)))

Now comes the defendant Great Goody Grocery Store, Inc., hereafter referred to as "Defendant Goody," by and through counsel, responding to the allegations contained in the complaint of the plaintiff, and allege and say:

FIRST DEFENSE

Defendant Goody responds to the individual allegations of the plaintiff's complaint as follows:

1. The allegations contained in paragraph number one are admitted based upon information and belief.

2. The allegations contained in paragraph number two are admitted.

3. The allegations contained in paragraph number three are admitted.

4. The allegations contained in paragraph number four are admitted.

5. The allegations contained in paragraph number five are admitted.

6. The allegations contained in paragraph number six are admitted.

7. The allegations contained in paragraph number seven are admitted.

8. The allegations contained in paragraph number eight are denied.

9. The allegations contained in paragraph number nine are denied to the extent that Defendant Goody's employees and supervisors were not aware of the assault on the plaintiff until sometime after it had begun.

10. The allegations contained in paragraph number ten are admitted.

11. The allegations contained in paragraph number eleven and all of its subparts are denied.

12. The allegations contained in paragraph number twelve and all of its subparts are denied.

SECOND DEFENSE

13. Defendant Goody reiterates and reaffirms its responses to paragraphs one through 12 of the complaint and further says that the allegations contained in the complaint should be dismissed for failure to state an action upon which relief can be granted.

THIRD DEFENSE

14. Defendant Goody reiterates and reaffirms its responses to paragraphs one through 13 of the complaint and further says that plaintiff should have and recover nothing from the defendant because plaintiff was contributory negligent.

FOURTH DEFENSE

15. Defendant Goody reiterates and reaffirms its responses to paragraphs one through 14 of the complaint and further says that the plaintiff should have and recover nothing from the defendant because the action is barred by the statute of limitations.

Bartholomew Simpson
Attorney for Defendant Great Goody Grocery Store, Inc.
133 Montford Ave.
Placid City, PL 06254

IN THE GENERAL COURT OF JUSTICE
COUNTY OF LONDON
STATE OF PLACID
CIVIL ACTION FILE NO: 07-x-8974-6

Mary Alice Baker,)	**PLAINTIFF'S FIRST**
Plaintiff)	**INTERROGATORIES TO**
)	**DEFENDANT**
v.)	
)	
Great Goody Grocery Store, Inc.)	
& Steve Doe)	
Defendants)	

To: Defendant Great Goody Grocery Store, Inc.

I herewith serve upon you the following written interrogatories under the provisions of Rule 33 of the Rules of Civil Procedure.

You are required to answer these interrogatories separately and fully in writing under oath and to serve a copy of your answers on the undersigned within 30 days after service hereof.

These interrogatories shall be continuing in nature until the date of trial, and you are required to serve supplemental answers as additional information may become available to you.

1.

Identify any individual that you are aware has personal knowledge of the facts and circumstances of this case, including eyewitnesses and any individuals who arrived on the scene within two hours after the occurrence.
Answer:

2.

If anyone investigated this matter for you, including but not limited to employees, agents, supervisors, corporate personnel, private investigators, or insurance adjusters, state their name(s) and address(es), and state whether such investigation was reduced to writing. If said investigator obtained any signed statements or recorded statements, identify the person who gave the statement and attach to your Answers a copy of any said statement.
Answer:

3.

If you know of the existence of any pictures, photographs, charts, diagrams, recorded images, videotapes, digital media, or objects relative to the attack on the Plaintiff on the day and time alleged in the Complaint, the Plaintiff's physical condition, or the scene of the occurrence, identify the substance of such recording and the present custodian of each such item.
Answer:

4.

Please list all insurance agreements you have regarding the store location, the corporation or other policy that may, in any way, have any bearing on the occurrence, including the name of the insurance company, the name of the policy owner, the policy number, the type of coverage, the amount of coverage (specifying its upper and lower limits), and the effective dates of said policy for the past five (5) years.
  (a) In answering this interrogatory, take into consideration all policies possibly affording coverage, including any excess or umbrella policies which might afford coverage to you;
  (b) if there is any questionable liability insurance coverage, state the basis for denying or questioning the coverage that might otherwise be afforded.
Answer:

5.

State all store and/or corporate policies regarding premises liability, injuries to customers, investigation of accidents or injuries to customers, whether ruled accidental, negligence, or intentional actions by third parties.
Answer:

6.

State the name and address of each person whom you expect to call as an expert witness at trial, and state the subject matter on which the expert is expected to testify, and for each such expert identified, state the following:

    (a) The substance of the facts and opinions to which the expert is expected to testify, and a summary of the grounds for each opinion;

    (b) The identity of any and all documents submitted or supplied to the expert in connection with his or her opinions and testimony; and

    (c) The qualifications of each such expert, listing the schools attended, years of attendance, degrees received, experience in any particular field of specialization or expertise, and all publications authored, including the title of work and the book or journal in which it was published and the date of publication.

Answer:

7.

Identify each person answering or assisting in the answering of these interrogatories, and if more than one person is involved, state which answers were made by or assisted in by each person so identified.
Answer:

8.

Please state whether or not you have agreed to indemnify or hold harmless the other defendant from any judgment that might be obtained against him or to pay some portion of said judgment or pay the costs of defense or some portion of the costs of the other defendant for defense of this action.
Answer:

9.

Identify any employee, agent, supervisor, corporate officer, board member, or anyone else affiliated with the store location or the Great Goody Grocery Store, Inc., who was disciplined, reprimanded, or sanctioned for any action or inaction on the date of the occurrence.
Answer:

This the 6th day of April, 2006.

_____

Rhonda Roe
Attorney for Plaintiff
2121 Elm Lane

Placid City, PL 06254

REQUEST TO PRODUCE

1. Pursuant to Rule 34, please produce at the offices of the undersigned at 10:00 a.m. on June 1, 2006:

    (a) a copy of any video, surveillance tape, digital media, still photograph, diagram, chart, or visual description showing any portion of the occurrence;

    (b) a copy of all exhibits you plan to introduce in this case in chief or which you intend to use to cross-examine any witnesses who are testifying on behalf of the Plaintiff;

    (c) a copy of any document referred to in the answer to these interrogatories.

This the 6th day of April, 2006.

_____

Rhonda Roe
Attorney for Plaintiff
2121 Elm Lane
Placid City, PL 06254

IN THE GENERAL COURT OF JUSTICE
COUNTY OF LONDON
STATE OF PLACID
CIVIL ACTION FILE NO: 07-x-8974-6

Mary Alice Baker,)	**NOTICE OF DEPOSITION**
Plaintiff)	
)	
v.)	
)	
Great Goody Grocery Store, Inc.)	
& Steve Doe)	
Defendants)	

TO: Ernie Orange

You are hereby notified that on the 9th day of July, 2006, at 9:00 a.m. at the offices of Brenda Barrister, Placid City, PL, and continuing from that period until completed, the plaintiff will take the deposition of Ernie Orange upon oral examination pursuant to Rules 26 and 30 of the Rules of Civil Procedure. The deposition will be taken before a Notary Public or some other officer duly authorized by law to take the deposition.

This the 8th day of June, 2006.

_____

Rhonda Roe
Attorney for Plaintiff
2121 Elm Lane
Placid City, PL 06254

CERTIFICATE OF SERVICE

This is to certify that the undersigned has this date served the forgoing upon all other parties to this cause in the following manner:

(   ) By delivering a copy thereof to the attorneys of record for said parties or to partners or employees at the office of such attorneys.

(   ) By depositing a copy thereof in a postpaid wrapper in a post office or official depository under the exclusive care and custody of the United States Post Office Department properly addressed to the attorneys of record for said parties.

This the 8th day of June, 2006.

_____

Rhonda Roe
Attorney for Plaintiff
Elm Lane
Placid City, PL 06254

IN THE GENERAL COURT OF JUSTICE
COUNTY OF LONDON
STATE OF PLACID
CIVIL ACTION FILE NO: 07-x-8974-6

Mary Alice Baker,	)	**DEPOSITION OF ERNIE W.**
Plaintiff	)	**ORANGE**
	)	
v.	)	
	)	
Great Goody Grocery Store, Inc.	)	
& Steve Doe	)	
Defendants	)	

PURSUANT TO NOTICE To Take Deposition, the within deposition of Ernie W. Orange was taken by me, Calvin Courtreporter, a Notary Public and Court Reporter for the State of Placid, on Tuesday, July 9, 2006, beginning at 8:59 a.m., in the offices of Rhonda Roe at 2121 Elm Lane, Placid City, PL, as required in Rules 26 and 30 of the Placid Rules of Civil Procedure.

STIPULATIONS:

IT WAS STIPULATED AND AGREED by and between counsel for the Plaintiff and counsel for the Defendants that each question is deemed to be followed by an objection and that each answer or portion thereof is deemed to be followed by a motion to strike, except as to the form of the question; said objections and motions to strike to be ruled upon by the presiding judge at any hearing or trial of this cause.

SIGNATURE: The Deponent, by and through counsel, did expressly waive his right to read and sign this deposition.

Ernie W. Orange, being first duly sworn to tell the truth, the whole truth, and nothing but the truth of his own knowledge concerning the within matter, testified as follows:

Q: (by Ms. Roe) Mr. Orange, can you describe your job duties at Great Goody Grocery Store?
A: I am the manager. I hire and fire employees; I enforce store policies and I also control daily orders, inventory management, things like that.

Q: Were you present on May 12, 2005, at the store at 123 Greengrocer's Lane?
A: Yes.

Q: When did you first become aware of the attack on Ms. Baker?
A: One of my department managers came to me and said that the security officer had seen something on one of the monitors.

Q: Who was this department manager?
A: Dave Smith.

Q: What, precisely, did Mr. Smith tell you?
A: Well, I don't remember precisely what he said. That was over a year ago. But he said something about a woman getting jumped in the parking lot.

Q: He used the phrase, "getting jumped"?
A: Something like that.

Q: And what did you do after Mr. Smith told you this?
A: I went to the security office.

Q: What did you do there?
A: I looked at the monitors, and by that time, there wasn't anything.

Q: What do you mean, "by that time"?
A: I mean, Smith had come to me and said that the lady was getting attacked, and by the time I got to the security office, there wasn't anything going on. I didn't see anything on the monitors.

Q: Were the monitors working?

A: Yes, I don't mean that they were broken. They just showed the parking lot, cars, white stripes, people. No attack. Nobody getting beaten up or anything.

Q: Did you ask Mr. Smith what he'd seen?

A: Yes.

Q: What did he say?

A: He said that the security officers had come to him and said that some lady was getting attacked in the parking lot.

Q: Who was the security officer?

A: Ray Able.

Q: Did you question Mr. Able?

A: Yes, I did. He said that he saw a man in a black shirt hit some lady and then drag her off.

Q: He said that he saw the woman get hit?

A: Uh, yes. That's what he said.

Q: Did he do anything other than call Mr. Smith?

A: I don't know.

Q: Did you do anything when you heard that one of your customers had been dragged out of the parking lot screaming?

A: Look, I didn't know that she was a customer, or had been a customer. I didn't know that she'd been screaming either. There isn't any sound, no microphones, on the security poles.

Q: Let me ask you again: Did you do anything to help the woman?

A: I called the police.

Q: Did you go into the parking lot?

A: I did later.

Q: No, I'm talking about right then, right when the woman was being attacked, did you go into the parking lot and try to stop it?

A: No.

Q: Why not?

A: We have a policy to call the police. We're supposed to call 911 and then wait for the police.

Q: You have a policy that says you aren't supposed to help customers who are being attacked?

A: Well, we have a policy that says that the police are supposed to handle violent attacks.

Q: Did you feel any compunction to go out there yourself?

A: Compunction?

Q: Did you feel that it was morally wrong for you to stay inside your store, safe and sound, while that lady was being beaten up?

A: It isn't my place to say what's moral or not.

Appendix C

Facts in Apple Case

<table>
<tr><td colspan="2">TRAFFIC ACCIDENT REPORT

PLACID COUNTY POLICE DEPARTMENT

Date: November 18, 2006
Time (reported to dispatch): 11:25 a.m.

Occurred in BURKE County, Town of Placid City, PL.
On Burke St. at Burnett St. (Intersection).</td></tr>
<tr><td>Vehicle 1</td><td>Vehicle 2</td></tr>
<tr><td>Owner: Billie S. Apple
Driver: same</td><td>Owner: Mary Ann Doe
Driver: John M. Doe</td></tr>
<tr><td>Address: 1001 Burkemont Ave.
Placid City, PL 00550</td><td>Address: 201 Maple Drive
Placid City, PL 00550</td></tr>
<tr><td>Same address as D/L?
Yes</td><td>Same address as D/L?
Yes</td></tr>
<tr><td>Driver's Phone: 555-1212</td><td>Driver's Phone: 554-1213</td></tr>
<tr><td>Race/Sex: B/F</td><td>Race/Sex: W/M</td></tr>
<tr><td>D/L No. 23654</td><td>D/L No. 52687</td></tr>
<tr><td>D.O.B. 5-12-71</td><td>D.O.B. 8-12-58</td></tr>
<tr><td>Veh Year 88
Make: Buick
Type: Sedan</td><td>Veh Year 02
Make: Ford
Type: Pickup</td></tr>
<tr><td>License Plate: MPH 3210</td><td>License Plate: PXH 2564</td></tr>
<tr><td>VIN: 2G4W65233123J</td><td>VIN: PT235645132K</td></tr>
<tr><td>Damage to vehicle: Yes
Description: Damage to right front passenger side, extensive, 1st quarter panel, passenger door.
Estimate: Excess $5,000</td><td>Damage to vehicle: Yes
Description: Damage to left front driver's, extensive.
Estimate: Excess $5,000</td></tr>
<tr><td>Removed to: Presley's Body Shop
111 Oak St.
Placid City, PL 05503</td><td>Removed to: Presley's Body Shop
111 Oak St.
Placid City, PL 05503</td></tr>
<tr><td>Other property damaged: None</td><td>Other property damaged: None</td></tr>
</table>

Witnesses:
A. C. Doyle
221 B Baker St.
Placid City, PL 05503
Phone: 212-555-1818

Ellery Queen
100 Elm St.
Placid City, PL 05503
Phone: 212-555-5236

Ray Chandler
234 Pine St.
Placid City, PL 05503
Phone: 212-555-1234

Narrative:

Received call from dispatch at 11:22 a.m. of MVA at intersection of Burnett and Burke St. Arrived 11:25 a.m. Vehicle #1 resting against telephone pole across intersection. Vehicle #2, inbound lane of Burke. (See diagram.) Driver Apple still behind wheel of car, complaining of chest and neck pain. EMT advised. Driver Doe standing beside own car. Doe advised that he was driving through green light on Burke, went through intersection of Burke and Burnett, and Driver #1 (Apple) ran red light and pulled out in front. Says accident unavoidable.

Witness Doyle heading north on Burnett, behind Vehicle #1. Says that light turned green and that Vehicle #1 proceeded into intersection and was struck by Vehicle #2. Says that Vehicle #2 driver was clearly at fault, must have run red light.

Witness E. Queen heading south on Burnett. Wasn't paying attention to light, but saw Vehicle #1 pull into intersection and saw Vehicle #2 coming from left. Knew that there was going to be a collision. Saw Vehicle #1 pushed across intersection and into telephone pole. Heard Vehicle #2 skid just before collision.

Witness Ray Chandler was heading east on Burke. Says that light had just turned red and that driver of Vehicle #2 was trying to beat the light through intersection. Says that when #2 hit #1, pushed #1 across intersection and almost hit his car before coming to rest against telephone pole.

Based on statements, Driver John Doe charged with failure to yield and failure to obey traffic device.

Physical measurements:

Skid marks for Vehicle #2 were 32 feet. Glass from Vehicle #1 right front headlights found as marked on diagram. Based on skid marks, glass, and other debris, Vehicle #1 going approximately 5 mph at time of impact. Vehicle #2 going approximately 45 mph at time of impact.

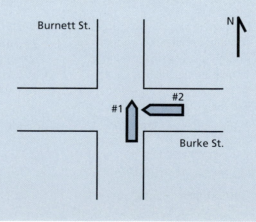

STATE OF PLACID   IN THE SUPERIOR COURT
COUNTY OF BURKE   FILE NUMBER: _____

BILLIE S. APPLE,)	
Plaintiff,)	
vs.)	**COMPLAINT**
)	**JURY TRIAL DEMANDED**
JOHN M. DOE)	
)	
Defendant.)	

Complaint and Demand for Jury Trial

Plaintiff complaining of the defendant says:

1. Plaintiff BILLIE S. APPLE, hereinafter referred to as "Plaintiff," is a citizen and resident of BURKE County, State of Placid.

2. The defendant, JOHN M. DOE, hereinafter referred to as "Defendant," is a citizen and resident of BURKE County, State of Placid.

3. On November 18, 2006, at 11:15 a.m., plaintiff was operating her vehicle in a northerly direction on Burnett Street, and was required to and did stop for a red light at the intersection of Burnett and Burke Streets, Placid City, State of Placid.

4. The traffic light on Burnett Street changed to green, and the plaintiff did then proceed, at a normal rate of speed, into the intersection.

5. The defendant, driving in a westerly direction on Burke Street, failed to stop for a red light at the intersection of Burke and Burnett Streets.

6. As a result of the defendant's failure to stop for a clearly indicated red light in his lane of traffic, defendant did strike the plaintiff's automobile as the plaintiff was proceeding through the intersection.

7. Plaintiff's automobile was struck by defendant's automobile, causing extensive damages in excess of $10,000.

8. As a result of defendant's negligence, plaintiff was injured in the collision.

9. Plaintiff's physical injuries included a severe facial laceration, broken ribs, internal injuries, neck trauma, and nerve damage to her right arm.

10. As a result of this collision, plaintiff received serious, painful, disfiguring, and permanent bodily and psychological injuries, causing medical and other expenses and decreased her earning capacity.

First Claim against Defendant Alleging Negligence

11. Defendant was negligent in that he:
    a. Failed to keep a proper lookout and keep his or her vehicle under proper control;
    b. Ignored traffic signals directing him to stop his car at the intersection of Burke and Burnett Streets;
    c. Ignored the presence of vehicles proceeding through the intersection in a lawful manner;
    d. Drove in a careless and reckless manner;
    e. Struck the plaintiff's car on the left front passenger side;
    f. Drove at an excessive speed; and
    g. Failed to reduce his speed or take any other steps to avoid a collision.

12. The alleged negligence of defendant herein was a proximate cause of the injuries to plaintiff.

Plaintiff demands a trial by jury.

Plaintiff hereby prays that she have and recover of the defendant all compensatory damages incurred or to be incurred in excess of $10,000 and punitive damages in an amount to be determined by the jury with interest from the date the suit is instituted, costs, and such other relief as may be just and proper.

This the 1st day of May, 2007.

_____

Brenda Barrister
Attorney for Plaintiff
State Bar No. 004567
1001 Burkemont Ave.
Placid City, PL 00552

_____

IN THE SUPERIOR COURT
STATE OF PLACID
COUNTY OF BURKE

BILLIE S. APPLE,	)	
	)	
Plaintiff,	)	
	)	
vs.	)	**ANSWER**
	)	**OF DEFENDANT**
JOHN M. DOE	)	
	)	
	)	
Defendant.	)	

ANSWER

COMES NOW, John M. Doe, defendant in the above-styled action and hereby files this, his Answer to Complaint, File Number CV 07-1245 alleges and says:

1. The allegations contained in Paragraph No. 1 of the Complaint are admitted, upon defendant's information and belief.

2. The allegations contained in Paragraph No. 2 are admitted.

3. The allegations contained in Paragraph No. 3 are admitted to the extent that upon defendant's information and belief, the plaintiff was traveling in a northerly direction on Burnett Street; the remaining allegations are denied.

4. The allegations contained in Paragraph No. 4 are denied.

5. The allegations contained in Paragraph No. 5 are admitted to the extent that the defendant was traveling in a westerly direction on Burke Street; the remaining allegations are denied.

6. The allegations contained in Paragraph No. 6 are denied.

7. The allegations contained in Paragraph No. 7 are admitted to the extent that there was a collision between defendant's automobile and plaintiff's automobile; the defendant is without sufficient information to respond to the remaining allegations in this paragraph.

8. The allegations contained in Paragraph No. 8 are denied.

9. The defendant is without sufficient information to respond to the allegations contained in Paragraph No. 9.

10. The defendant is without sufficient information to respond to the allegations contained in Paragraph No. 10.

11. The allegations contained in Paragraph No. 11, including all sub-parts, are denied.

Defendant's First Counterclaim against the Plaintiff

Defendant hereby incorporates all previous paragraphs of his Answer, numbered 1–10 and further alleges this Counterclaim against the Plaintiff:

12. That the plaintiff failed to obey the traffic signal at the intersection of Burke and Burnett Streets on November 18, 2006.

13. That the plaintiff failed to keep a proper lookout and to keep her vehicle under proper control.

14. That the plaintiff failed to obey the rules of the road by proceeding through the intersection before the light had changed to green.

15. That as a direct and proximate cause of plaintiff's negligence, the defendant received physical, emotional, and psychological injuries when his automobile impacted the plaintiff's automobile.

16. That as a direct and proximate cause of the plaintiff's negligence, defendant did incur property damages in excess of $10,000.

WHEREFOR, defendant prays that the plaintiff receive nothing from him; that the defendant have and receive of the plaintiff compensatory damages in excess of $10,000 and any and all other awards that the court deems just and proper.

This the 15th day of June, 2007.

_____

Sally Solicitor
Attorney for Defendant John M. Doe
State Bar No. 897465
1040 Easy Street
Placid City, PL 05562

IN THE SUPERIOR COURT
STATE OF PLACID
COUNTY OF BURKE

BILLIE S. APPLE,	)
	)
Plaintiff,	)
	)
vs.	)
	) **PLAINTIFF'S FIRST INTERROGATORIES**
	) **TO DEFENDANT**
JOHN M. DOE	)
	)
	)
Defendant.	)

To: Defendant John M. Doe

I herewith serve upon you the following written interrogatories under the provisions of Rule 33 of the Rules of Civil Procedure.

You are required to answer these interrogatories separately and fully in writing under oath and to serve a copy of your answers on the undersigned within 30 days after service hereof.

These interrogatories shall be continuing in nature until the date of trial and you are required to serve supplemental answers as additional information may become available to you.

1. State your full name, current address, date of birth, social security number, and work address or if you are the representative of a company answering these Interrogatories state your title, your affiliation with the Defendant, and the length of time you have been employed by the Defendant, and list all the positions you held in the past and your current position.

   Identify any individual that you are aware has personal knowledge of the facts and circumstances of this case, including eyewitnesses and any individuals who arrived on the scene within two hours after the occurrence.

   If anyone investigated this matter for you, including medical experts, private investigators, or insurance adjusters, state their name(s) and address(es), and state whether such investigation was reduced to writing. If said investigator obtained any signed statements or recorded statements, identify the person who gave the statement and attach to your Answers a copy of any said statement.

   If you know of the existence of any pictures, photographs, plats, visual recorded images, diagrams, or objects relative to the occurrence, the Plaintiff's physical condition, or the scene of the occurrence, identify the substance of such recording and the present custodian of each such item.

   Please identify the owner and the driver of the vehicle involved in the accident with the Plaintiff and under what specific circumstances the driver of the vehicle was permitted to operate the owner's vehicle on the date of the accident.

   Please state the relationship of the driver to the owner of the vehicle which was involved in the accident with the Plaintiff.

   Please state where Defendant John Doe was heading to at the time of the accident and where Defendant John Doe was coming from and his expected time of arrival.

   Please list all accidents involving Defendant John Doe within the past five (5) years. For each such accident, please include the name and address of any driver of vehicles involved, the name and address of any other driver involved, the court and case number of any action that resulted, and the result of each such action.

   Please list all insurance agreements you have regarding the vehicle operated by Defendant John Doe at the time of the collision with the Plaintiff, including the name of the insurance company, the name of the policy owner, the policy number, the type of coverage, the amount of coverage (specifying its upper and lower limits). and the effective dates of said policy for the past five (5) years.

   Identify the property damage done to each vehicle as a result of the accident and which parts of those vehicles were damaged in the occurrence complained of, the name and address of the person or entity who repaired each vehicle, and the date and cost of repairs. If the vehicles have not been repaired, state the present location of said vehicles, the days of the week, the time of day, and the places they may currently be seen and identify any photographs of the vehicles involved in the collision.

   Please state with specificity exactly how this accident took place and include in your answer the date of the accident, the time of the accident, the location of the accident, where your vehicle was just prior to the accident, where the Plaintiff's vehicle was just prior to the accident, how far away the Plaintiff's vehicle was just prior to the impact, the speed of your vehicle just before the accident, the speed of the Plaintiff's vehicle just before the accident, the speed of the vehicles upon impact, and the exact locations in relation to the roadway upon impact; if this was a chain reaction accident, identify the sequence of the impacts between the vehicles.

   State what investigation, if any, you did to ensure that the driver of your vehicle was a safe driver.

   State the name and address of each person whom you expect to call as an expert witness at trial, and state the subject matter on which the expert is expected to testify, and for each such expert identified, state the following:

   (a) The substance of the facts and opinions to which the expert is expected to testify, and a summary of the grounds for each opinion;

   (b) The identity of any and all documents submitted or supplied to the expert in connection with his or her opinions and testimony; and

(c) The qualifications of each such expert, listing the schools attended, years of attendance, degrees received, experience in any particular field of specialization or expertise, and all publications authored, including the title of work and the book or journal in which it was published and the date of publication.

2. Please state if you or any expert who will be testifying on your behalf have ever been the defendant in any other action, and if so, please state:
   (a) the state and county in which said action was filed and the file number;
   (b) the name of the plaintiff in said action;
   (c) a brief synopsis of the substance of said action;
   (d) the outcome of said action.

3. Please state whether any of the expert witnesses who will testify on your behalf have previously testified in any medical malpractice trial or deposition. If so, please list each time the witness testified, including the name of the court, whether the witness testified for the plaintiff or defendant, and whether the witness in any prior testimony in a medical malpractice case was paid compensation for testimony. If so, for each act of testimony, state the amount of compensation so paid and by whom.

4. Please state whether any of the expert witnesses who will testify on your behalf have ever served as an expert witness or testified in any medical malpractice case for defendant's attorney or any other member of defendant's firm. If so, state the name and the action in which the testimony was given, the time and place, and amount of compensation paid the witness, indicating the source of compensation paid the witness.

5. Identify each person answering or assisting in the answering of these interrogatories, and if more than one person is involved, state which answers were made by or assisted in by each person so identified.

6. Please state whether or not there is any agreement, formal or informal, written or otherwise, wherein you or your attorneys have agreed to present a common defense with one or more of the other defendants with regard to the trial of this case. If your answer is yes, please state (a) whether the agreement was in writing; and (b) if it was not in writing, the substance of the agreement.

7. Please state whether or not you have agreed to indemnify or hold harmless one or more of the other defendants from any judgment that might be obtained against them or to pay some portion of said judgment or pay the costs of defense or some portion of the costs of one or more of the other defendants for defense of this action.

8. State the name and address of any medical malpractice liability carrier and the named insured (if different from you) and the policy number and policy limits of any medical malpractice liability policy that affords coverage to you for the occasions which are the subject of this lawsuit.
   (a) in answering this interrogatory, take into consideration all policies possibly affording coverage, including any excess or umbrella policies which might afford coverage to you;
   (b) if there is any questionable liability insurance coverage, state the basis for denying or questioning the coverage that might otherwise be afforded.

9. Please state for yourself and for any experts who will testify on your behalf the following:
   (a) whether you or they have ever had a medical license revoked, suspended, or terminated in any state or country, or a staff privilege revoked or curtailed in any hospital, and if so, please indicate:
      (i) whether it was suspended, revoked, terminated, or otherwise restricted, at what hospital, and by whom and the date it occurred;
      (ii) the reason for any such limitation, curtailment, or revocation, and whether your license was ever reinstated.

10. Please state the following for yourself and for any experts who will testify on your behalf the following:
   (a) in what area of medicine you specialize, and the exclusive dates you have practiced in such specialty;

 (b) any training you have had in any medical specialty, including but not limited to the name and address of each institution where you trained, inclusive of dates you trained, description of training program, and the length of time you spent in the diagnosis, treatment, operative, and post-operative care of problems in this specialty;

 (c) whether you are now or have ever been a member or diplomat of any specialty board; if so, state:

  (i) the name of the specialty board;

  (ii) the inclusive dates of your membership;

  (iii) if you are no longer a member, the reason for termination;

  (iv) the qualifications required in order to take the membership examination;

  (v) the number of times you took the examination and the dates thereof.

11. State the name and address of all hospitals to which you are associated and your position with such hospital.

12. Have you or any expert who will testify on your behalf ever taught in a medical institution? If so, state:

 (a) the name and address of each such institution;

 (b) your position at each such institution;

 (c) the dates you taught at each such institution;

 (d) the names of the subjects you taught.

13. Have you or any of the experts who will testify on your behalf ever written or contributed to any medical textbook, paper, or article? If so, state:

 (a) the title of each subject matter;

 (b) the date of publication;

 (c) the title of publication, edition, and pages on which each article appears;

 (d) the name and address of any other persons who contributed to each such article.

14. State all awards and honors you or any of the experts who will testify on your behalf have received concerning your medical profession.

REQUEST TO PRODUCE

1. Pursuant to Rule 34, please produce at the offices of the undersigned at 10:00 a.m. on _____, 20__ :

 (a) a copy of any article contributed by you or by each expert expected to testify on your behalf to any medical textbook, paper or article;

 (b) a copy of all learned treatises relied upon by you and any expert expected to testify on your behalf;

 (c) a copy of all exhibits you plan to introduce in this case <u>in chief or which you intend to use to cross-examine any witnesses who are testifying on behalf of the Plaintiff;</u>

 (d) a copy of any document referred to in the answer to these interrogatories.

This the ____ day of _____, 20__.

Glossary

A

12(b)(6) motion A motion under the provisions of Rule 12 of the Rules of Civil Procedure that challenges the basis of the complaint for failure to state a claim upon which relief can be granted.

admissibility A ruling on whether the jury will be allowed to view proffered evidence.

admit To agree or stipulate to the allegations presented in a complaint.

affidavit A sworn statement.

affirm Disposition in which the appellate court agrees with the trial court.

affirmative defense An "excuse" by the opposing party that does not just simply negate the allegation, but puts forth a legal reason to avoid enforcement. These defenses are waived if not pleaded.

answer The defendant's response to the plaintiff's complaint.

appellant The party filing the appeal; that is, bringing the case to the appeals court.

appellee The prevailing party in the lower court, who will respond to the appellant's argument.

appraisal The evaluation by an expert of the cash value of a contested item.

arbitration Alternative dispute resolution method mediated or supervised by a neutral third party who imposes a recommendation for resolution, after hearing evidence from both parties and the parties participated in reaching, that is fully enforceable and treated in the courts the same as a judicial order.

associate attorney An attorney who is an employee of an attorney partnership.

attorney–client privilege The legal relationship established between attorney and client allowing for free exchange of information without fear of disclosure.

authentication Proof by an officer, witness, or certifying document that evidence is what it is claimed to be.

B

bad faith Intentional misrepresentation, wanton disregard for truth, fraudulent activity that can be the basis for an additional award of damages to the party that can establish such activity occurred.

bar examination A test administered to graduates from approved law schools that determines the applicant's knowledge of the law and suitability to practice in the state.

beyond a reasonable doubt The requirement for the level of proof in a criminal matter in order to convict or find the defendant guilty. It is a substantially higher and more-difficult-to-prove criminal matter standard.

burden of proof Standard for assessing the weight of the evidence.

C

calendar call A mandatory court hearing in which the judge inquires about the readiness of the parties to go to trial; also known as a docket call.

caption The full name of the case, together with the docket number, court, and date of the decision.

case evaluation The process of investigating the facts, issues, and legal implications of a proposed lawsuit before it is ever filed.

case law Published court opinions of federal and state appellate courts; judge-created law in deciding cases, set forth in court opinions.

cause of action A personal, financial or other injury for which the law gives a person the right to receive compensation.

certificate of service Verification by attorney that pleadings or court documents were sent to the opposing counsel in a case.

certification The recognition of the attainment of a degree of academic and practical knowledge by a professional.

certiorari (Cert) (Latin) "To make sure." An appellate court's authority to decide which cases it will hear on appeal.

challenge An attorney's objection, during voir dire, to the inclusion of a specific person on the jury.

circumstantial evidence Evidence that suggests a conclusion.

class action A lawsuit involving a large group of plaintiffs who have been certified by a court as having mutual interests, common claims, and a representative plaintiff who will pursue the action on the basis of the entire group.

clear and convincing evidence Having a high probability of truthfulness, a higher standard being preponderance of the evidence.

clerk A government official responsible for maintaining public records.

collateral source rule A rule of evidence that prohibits the jury from being informed about the plaintiff's other sources of compensation, such as insurance, worker's compensation, and so forth.

commingling A term for mixing a client's funds with the attorney's personal funds without permission; an ethical violation.

common law Judge-made law, the ruling in a judicial opinion.

compensatory damages A payment to make up for a wrong committed and return the nonbreaching party to a position where the effect or the breach has been neutralized.

complaint Document that states the allegations and the legal basis of the plaintiff's claims.

compulsory counterclaim A counterclaim that is required to be pleaded because the facts relate to the same transaction as that set forth in the original complaint.

concurrent jurisdiction Jurisdiction over the subject matter exists in both state and federal court, unless statutorily prohibited.

conflict letter A letter sent by an attorney to the judge explaining that the attorney has several different appearances scheduled for the same date and detailing which courts the attorney will go to first.

contingency fee The attorney's fee calculated as a percentage of the final award in a civil case.

counterclaim A claim made by the defendant against the plaintiff—not a defense, but a new claim for damages, as if the defendant were the plaintiff in a separate suit; a countersuit brought by the defendant against the plaintiff.

court reporter Individual who transcribes the court proceedings and certifies their authenticity.

cross-claim lawsuit A lawsuit against a party of the same side; plaintiffs or defendants suing each other (defendant versus defendant or plaintiff versus plaintiff).

cross-examination Occurs when the opposing attorney asks the witness questions.

D

damages Money paid to compensate for loss or injury.

declaratory judgment The court's determination of the rights and responsibilities of a party with respect to the subject matter of the controversy.

default judgment A judgment entered by the court against the defendant for failure to respond to the plaintiff's complaint.

defendant The party against whom a lawsuit is brought.

demonstrative evidence Any object, visual aid, model, scale drawing, or other exhibit designed to help clarify points in the trial.

deny To disagree with or contest the allegations presented in a complaint.

deponent The party or witness who is questioned during a deposition.

deposition A discovery tool in a question-and-answer format in which the attorney verbally questions a party or a witness under oath.

deposition digest A summary of deposition testimony of a witness.

dispositive motion A motion that terminates some or all of the pending issues in a case.

direct evidence Evidence that establishes a particular fact without resort to other testimony or evidence.

direct examination Occurs when the attorney questions his or her own witness.

disbarment Temporary suspension or permanent revocation of an individual's license to practice law.

discovery The pretrial investigation process authorized and governed by the Rules of Civil Procedure; the process of investigation and collection of evidence by litigants; process in which the opposing parties obtain information about the case from each other; the process of investigation and collection of evidence by litigants.

domicile The place where a person maintains a physical residence with the intent to permanently remain in that place; citizenship; the permanent home of the party.

E

equity The doctrine of fairness and justice; the process of making things balance or be equal between parties.

evidence Any fact, testimony, or physical object that tends to prove or disprove allegations raised in a case; must be reasonably calculated to lead to the discovery of admissible evidence.

exclusive jurisdiction Only one court has the authority to hear the specific case; for example, only a federal court can decide a bankruptcy case.

excited utterance An exception to the hearsay rule that allows a statement made spontaneously after a shocking event to be admissible at trial.

exhibit A document attached to a pleading that is incorporated by reference into the body of the pleading.

F

fair market value The amount that a willing buyer would pay for an item that a willing seller would accept.

forum The proper legal site or location.

G

general damages Those that normally would be anticipated in a similar action.

general jurisdiction The court is empowered to hear any civil or criminal case.

guilty A verdict only available in criminal cases in which the jury determines that the defendant is responsible for committing a crime.

H

hearsay An out-of-court statement offered to prove a matter in contention in the lawsuit.

I

impasse The declaration by the mediator that the parties are unable to reach an agreement.

impleader The involuntary addition of a new party to the litigation; a party without whom all issues raised in the case could not be resolved.

in rem jurisdiction A court's authority over claims affecting property.

initial client meeting The first meeting with a prospective client in which information will be gathered, additional information requested, and the attorney–client relationship formed.

injunction A court order that requires a party to refrain from acting in a certain way to prevent harm to the requesting party.

interpleader The deposit of contested funds with the court, followed by the removal of the filing party from other action in the suit.

interrogatory A discovery tool in the form of a series of written questions that are answered by the party in writing, to be answered under oath.

intervention The voluntary insertion of a third party into a pending civil action, often to resolve issues directly related to the third party's interests.

J

JNOV (judgment notwithstanding the verdict) Asks the judge to reverse the jury verdict based on the inadequacy of the evidence presented to support the law and the verdict.

judge Trier of law.

judgment The court's final decision regarding the rights and claims of the parties.

judgment on the pleadings A motion that alleges that if all of the allegations raised in the pleadings are true and correct, the movant would still be entitled to a ruling in his favor and a dismissal of the opposition's pleadings.

judicial notice A request that a court accept evidence as fact without the necessity of further proof.

jurisdiction The power or authority of the court to hear a particular classification of case.

jurors Those people who have been selected to sit on a jury; they will consider the evidence and reach a verdict in the case.

jury charge Directions for the jury regarding what law applies and how it applies to the facts of a case; also known as *points of charge*.

jury strike The removal of a jury panel member, also known as a jury challenge.

L

lay the foundation The presentation of sufficient background material to establish the relevancy and competency of a particular piece of evidence.

legal document assistant A specialized type of paralegal, legally able to provide assistance to clients in preparing forms.

legal secretary A secretary trained to perform specialized tasks directly related to the practice of law.

liability A jury's determination that one party is responsible for injuries to another party; the basis for an award of damages.

licensure The requirement of governmental approval before a person can practice a specific profession.

limited jurisdiction The court is empowered to hear only specified types of cases.

loss of consortium A claim filed by the plaintiff's spouse for the loss of companionship in the marriage caused by the injuries.

M

material fact A fact that is essential to the case and its holding; a fact that, if different, might alter the entire outcome of the case.

marital privilege An evidentiary protection that permits married individuals to refuse to testify against one another.

mediation The process of submitting a claim to a neutral third party who then makes a determination about the ultimate liability and award in a civil case.

medical authorization A form, signed by the client, that allows the legal team to review and obtain copies of the client's medical records.

mitigation of damages The obligation to offset or otherwise engage in curative measures to stop accrual of unreasonable economic damages; that is, to minimize the damage incurred through affirmative actions.

motion A procedural request or application presented by the attorney in court.

motion for directed verdict A request by a party for a judgment because the other side has not met its burden of proof.

motion for more definite statement A request by a defendant for additional specificity of plaintiff's complaint.

motion for new trial Post-trial relief that requests a new trial on the same issues for specific reasons that must be clearly explained and argued in the motion.

motion for summary judgment A motion by either party for judgment based on all court documents.

motion in limine A request that certain evidence not be raised at trial, as it is arguably prejudicial, irrelevant, or legally inadmissible evidence.

N

notice of appeal Puts the trial court, the appeals court, and the opposing party on notice that the judgment entered is challenged.

O

ordinance A law passed by a local government, such as a town council or city government.

overrule A judge's ruling in disagreement with the party who raised the objection.

P

panel A group of people who have been called for jury duty; the final jury will be selected from this group; also known as venire.

paralegal A person qualified to assist an attorney, under direct supervision, in all substantive legal matters with the exception of appearing in court and rendering legal advice.

partners Attorneys who own the law firm and split the profits and losses.

partnership Business enterprise owned by more than one person, entered into for profit.

partnership agreement The contract between the partners that creates duties, establishes responsibilities, and details benefits of the attorneys involved in the partnership.

per diem (Latin) "by the day" or daily.

peremptory jury strike An attorney's elimination of a prospective juror without giving a reason; limited to a specific number of strikes.

permissive counterclaim A counterclaim that is not required to be filed with a complaint because the facts do not arise out of the same set of circumstances as the complaint.

personal jurisdiction A court's power over the individuals involved in the case; when a court has personal jurisdiction, it can compel attendance at court hearings and enter judgments against the parties.

plaintiff The party initiating legal action.

preponderance of the evidence The weight or level of persuasion of evidence needed to find the defendant liable as alleged by the plaintiff in a civil matter.

pretrial conference The meeting between the parties and the judge to identify legal issues, stipulate to uncontested matters, and encourage settlement.

pretrial order An order, prepared by the trial judge with the input of the parties, that summarizes key issues in the case, including witness order, evidence, and other critical concerns.

prima facie (Latin) "At first sight." A case with the required proof of elements in a tort cause of action; the elements of the plaintiff's (or prosecutor's) cause of action; what the plaintiff must prove; accepted on its face, but not indisputable.

private reprimand The minimum censure for an attorney who commits an ethical violation; the attorney is informed privately about a potential violation, but no official entry is made.

privilege Reasonable expectation of privacy and confidentiality for communications in furtherance of the relationship such as attorney–client, doctor–patient, husband–wife, psychotherapist–patient, and priest–penitent.

probate court The court empowered to settle estates for those individuals who have died with or without a will.

process server A person statutorily authorized to serve legal documents such as complaints.

professional corporation Business form organized as a closely held group of professional intellectual employees such as doctors.

province of the jury An issue that is exclusively the responsibility of the jury to determine.

public reprimand A published censure of an attorney for an ethical violation.

punitive damages An amount of money awarded to a non-breaching party that is not based on the actual losses incurred by that party, but as a punishment to the breaching party for the commission of an intentional wrong.

R

record Documentation of the trial court, including pleadings, physical evidence, transcript, and decision of the trial court.

release A discharge from the parties' performance obligations that acknowledges the dispute but forgoes contractual remedies.

relevance Reasonably related or associated with the ultimate facts and legal theories.

remand Disposition in which the appellate court sends the case back to the lower court for further action.

removal Moving a case from the state court to the federal court system.

reply The responsive pleading provided in Rule 7 to a counterclaim.

request to admit A document that provides the drafter with the opportunity to conclusively establish selected facts prior to trial.

request to produce A discovery device that requests the production of certain items, such as photographs, papers, reports, and physical evidence; must specify the document sought.

res judicata (Latin) "The thing has been adjudicated." The principle that a court's decision on a particular matter is binding on future litigation between the parties; sometimes referred to as "res adjudicata."

reverse Disposition in which the appellate court disagrees with the trial court.

Rule 11 One of the major rules under the Rules of Civil Procedure; it requires an attorney to investigate an action before bringing it.

S

self-authenticating document A document that is authorized by statute and that can be used without additional offer of proof.

settlement A negotiated termination of a case prior to a trial or jury verdict.

skip tracing A general term for tracking a person who has absconded or is attempting to avoid legal process.

special appearance A term describing a defendant's contest of jurisdiction; the defendant enters the court for the limited purpose of contesting the case, but does not submit to the court's jurisdiction for other purposes.

special damages Those damages incurred beyond and in addition to the general damages suffered and expected in similar cases.

standing Legally sufficient reason and right to object.

stare decisis (Latin) "Stand by the decision." Decisions from a court with substantially the same set of facts should be followed by that court and all lower courts under it; the judicial process of adhering to prior case decisions; the doctrine of precedent whereby once a court has decided a specific issue one way in the past, it and other courts in the same jurisdiction are obligated to follow that earlier decision in deciding cases with similar issues in the future.

state bar The organization that licenses and oversees the practice of law and the conduct of attorneys in the state. An attorney must be a member of the state bar before he or she will be allowed to practice in that state.

statute Written law enacted by the legislative branches of both federal and state governments.

statute of limitations Establishes the applicable time limits for filing and responding to certain claims or legal actions.

stipulation An agreement between attorneys and parties in a case about a procedural or factual issue.

style Also known as caption; the heading or title used in all legal pleadings.

subject matter jurisdiction A court's authority over the res, the subject of the case.

submission The agreement to arbitrate a specific matter or issue raised between the parties.

subpoena duces tecum A type of subpoena that requests a witness to produce documents.

subrogation The right to sue in the name of another.

sustain A judge's ruling in agreement with the party who raised the objection.

T

tendering The process of admitting evidence in a trial by asking the court to rule on relevance.

temporary restraining order A court order barring a person from harassing or harming another.

temporary suspension A punishment for an ethical violation; an attorney is temporarily prohibited from practicing law or representing clients.

testimonial evidence Oral statements made by a witness under oath.

U

umpire A person with greater authority than an arbitrator; this person has the authority to make a final and binding decision when an arbitrator has been unable to do so.

unauthorized practice of law Practicing law without proper authorization to do so.

unlimited liability A finding that a business owner's personal assets may be used to satisfy a judgment against the business.

V

verification Acknowledgment by a party of the truthfulness of the information contained within a document.

voir dire The process of selecting a jury for trial.

W

witness locator service A company that provides information about a witness's former addresses, telephone numbers, employment, and current location.

work product An attorney's written notes, impressions, charts, diagrams, and other material used by him or her to prepare strategy and tactics for trial.

Case Index

Subject Index